TRUFFAUT

TRUFFAUT

ANTOINE DE BAECQUE AND SERGE TOUBIANA

TRANSLATED FROM THE FRENCH BY CATHERINE TEMERSON

ALFRED A. KNOPF • NEW YORK • 1999

. . . carrying his concentrated burden, his perpetual suspense,
ever so quietly . . .
—Henry James, "The Beast in the Jungle"

CONTENTS

CONTENTS

CONTENTS

5. THE SLOW YEARS: 1962–1968

6. PARALLEL LIVES: 1968–1971

CONTENTS

CONTENTS

Illustrations follow pages 48 and 208

THE FILMS OF FRANÇOIS TRUFFAUT

TRUFFAUT

1.
A CLANDESTINE CHILDHOOD: 1932–1946

At six o'clock in the morning on Saturday, February 6, 1932, Janine de Monferrand gave birth to a son, whom she named François Roland. Not even twenty, she had her baby in secret, at a good distance from her family's apartment on rue Henri Monnier, where she still lived. Her parents, Jean and Geneviève de Monferrand, had known of her pregnancy for only the last three months. Catholic families frowned upon unwed mothers, and this was particularly so among the Monferrands' neighbors and acquaintances in the ninth arrondissement, a quiet, insular, almost provincial neighborhood in the north of Paris. Janine had found sanctuary with a midwife, over half an hour's walk from home, on rue Léon Cogniet, near the Parc Monceau. Two days later, the child's birth was registered at the town hall of the seventeenth arrondissement.[1]

THE SECRET CHILD

The infant was immediately placed with a wet nurse—first in Montmorency, then in Boissy-Saint-Léger—and would only rarely see his mother before the age of three. But after twenty months in obscurity, he at least gained an adoptive father. On October 24, 1933, two weeks before marrying Janine de Monferrand, Roland Truffaut legally recognized the boy, who had been

3

listed as "born of an unknown father."[2] Yet the young couple's wedding, on November 9, did not put an end to the secrecy regarding the infant's existence. Indeed, while "the great injustice had been redressed by a man with a noble heart" and the couple was now accepted at the family dinner table, young François remained in the care of the wet nurse. In the spring of 1934, Roland and Janine had another son, whom they named René, but the baby died before he was two months old. One wonders how, had this brother lived, the shared childhood might have affected François's creative outlook and his path in life. But François Truffaut remained an only child, and an unwanted one.

Deeply shaken by the death of their little René, the young couple decided to leave the family enclave and move into a modest two-room apartment on rue du Marché-Popincourt, in the Folie-Méricourt neighborhood. It was now, more than ever, out of the question for them to take in François. The child reminded his young mother of a gloomy period in her life: "René's death was a tragedy," recalls Monique, Janine's younger sister.[3] "For, suddenly, what everyone in the family had until then been hiding became obvious: that François existed, that he would be an embarrassment, the victim of a rigid society and an unloved child." With François in distant banishment, they continued to pretend he didn't exist. Between increasingly rarer visits, the boy was wasting away, eating very little, and growing sickly, with a sallow complexion. Sensing he might die, his grandmother, Geneviève de Monferrand, decided to take him in, when François was nearly three years old. Legitimate in the eyes of the law, forgiven in the name of Christian charity, adopted by his grandmother, he found a home in the small Monferrand apartment at 21 rue Henri Monnier. Jean and Geneviève occupied the bedroom; Bernard, their fourteen-year-old son, slept in the vestibule; Monique (their youngest child, aged ten) and François slept in the living room. Geneviève de Monferrand, "Damère Viève," had accepted François into her care, under the strict gaze of her "straitlaced" husband, who would never forget "Janine's follies with workers in the neighborhood or disreputable types, sometimes even with foreigners."[4]

MY GRANDFATHER, A PRIM DISCIPLINARIAN

The Monferrands, originally from Berry, belonged to the minor nobility. After a strict Jesuit education, Jean de Monferrand followed his parents to Paris in 1902. He met his wife, Geneviève de Saint-Martin, through the personal ads. She was from the Oc region, between Auch and Brugnac in the Lot-et-Garonne, where part of her family—also from minor nobility—still lived. After graduating from the lycée in Agen, she went to Paris to complete her literary studies. The young couple married in 1907 and settled in Aubervilliers. Following the births of their first two children, Suzanne and Janine, Jean was drafted into the army. Like all men of his generation, he would remain profoundly shaken by the Great War. The experience tempered his conservative ethos, and introduced a certain humanism into a cultural background marked by nationalism, Catholicism, and legitimism. He and Geneviève had two other children—Bernard in 1921 and Monique in 1925. Very much satisfied with the rectitude and discipline of their own good upbringing, they raised their four children in a strict but generous way. At the end of his life, François Truffaut tried to describe the ambiance of his early childhood: "There had been titles in the family. My grandfather, a prim disciplinarian who was always impeccably dressed, was frightening to us, particularly at mealtime. He was really a pain in the neck. For example, at the dinner table, my aunt Monique, who was very mischievous, would take a fistful of salt and throw it behind her, just like that, and I would roar with laughter. He would immediately grab me by the collar and say, 'Take your plate to the kitchen!' I would finish almost all my meals in the kitchen. That's what the Monferrand atmosphere was like."[5]

The family had moved into the apartment on rue Henri Monnier after the war. Jean de Monferrand worked very close by, overseeing the letters to the editor at *L'Illustration,* one of the most important periodicals of the time, which had its offices on rue Saint-Georges. Though the position was a modest one, he was proud of being the editor of a column. Although the Monferrand family always lived quite frugally, the atmosphere at home was a literary and musical one. Geneviève, a former schoolteacher, was a music lover and very well read. An occasional writer, she had penned a novel entitled *Apôtres* (*Apostles*),[6] written in a very mannered style and permeated with mystical fervor. Geneviève shared her passion for reading with François, taking him, at the age of five or six, on long walks through the Drouot neighborhood, from bookstore to bookstore, and to the public library in the ninth arrondissement. All four Monferrand children inherited their mother's interest in literature and music, though they took quite different career paths. Bernard, the third-born, chose the military, first attending Navale and then, at the end of the thirties, entering Saint-Cyr military academy. Monique, the youngest child, studied the violin and graduated from the Paris Conservatoire during the Nazi Occupation. Janine, the second child, was more dissolute and fickle; she was impeded in her studies by her love affairs and, above all, by her status as a single mother. Nevertheless, she kept up with the theatrical and literary events of the prewar period. But she had to go to work. In 1934, her father got her a job as a shorthand typist at the weekly magazine *L'Illustration,* where she earned eleven hundred francs a month.

For the Monferrands, physical exercise, especially mountain climbing, was as important as intellectual activity. The whole family belonged to the Club Alpin français (French Alpine Club, a prestigious mountaineering society), and in the early thirties, Jean was vice president of the Paris chapter. It was there at the club that Janine, who had a certain standing as the vice president's daughter, met Roland Truffaut, a mountaineering enthusiast. He was not much older than she; of medium height and somewhat scrawny, he often wore a beret and tended to lean his head forward. But he was amusing, attentive, dexterous, and, above all, very well versed in matters concerning snap hooks, ropes, and ice axes.

The different branches of the Truffaut family had lived for several generations west and south of Paris, between the Vexin Normand and the Orge region, with some members moving close to the center of France, to Valigny, in the Allier, where Roland was born in May 1911. These were agricultural areas, populated with prosperous farming families and rural artisans—a completely different milieu from the Monferrands', which was more closed, more cultured, but less affluent. In the 1920s, Roland's parents, Mr. and Mrs. Ferdinand Truffaut, had settled in the Essonne, about sixty miles south of Paris, in Juvisy-sur-Orge, a large market town that was still rural, though the farmland was already giving way to industrial development and a network of roads. The couple lived in a modest but pleasant house, with a courtyard, a garden, and, in the back, a workshop giving out on the countryside. Ferdinand Truffaut was a stonemason, working primarily with marble. He had a good reputation—for his carving skill as well as for his modest prices, which hadn't gone up, it seemed, since the early twenties. He worked on commission, making bowls, ashtrays, marble legs for stone tables, and especially tombstones for the nearby cemetery. Life in Juvisy was quiet in the beginning of the thirties, at the time when the couple's three children, Roland, Robert, and Mathilde, were finishing their studies.

Roland Truffaut moved to Paris in 1929 to get a diploma in architecture. He found work at eighteen as an architectural draftsman—in other words, as the most junior member in an architectural firm—drawing map layouts and blueprints for current projects. He earned just enough money to rent a room in the Lorettes district and pursue his passion for mountaineering. He could even buy the latest equipment and take advantage of the Club Alpin's outings to Savoie, Switzerland, the Vercors, or, better yet, the rocky inlets near Marseilles and the Italian Dolomites. At the end of the thirties, his profession and his passion converged when he found work as the architect and decorator for the French Scouts, les Éclaireurs de France, on rue de la Chaussée d'Antin.

By then, he had met Janine de Monferrand at the Paris headquarters of the Club Alpin, where she was one of the organizers. A small woman, about five foot one, she was lively and dark-haired, slightly plump, and quite seductive. The engagement was short, and the marriage quick. The couple earned a modest living[7] and pursued their Sunday mountaineering activities. On the eve of the war, Roland Truffaut became a member of the Club Alpin's board of directors, and later he was elected vice president of the Paris-Chamonix chapter; he was actively involved with the magazine *La Montagne* and in managing mountain refuges. Janine de Monferrand did not always follow dutifully in his tracks. Independent and cultivated, she often preferred evenings at the theater or at the Gaumont-Palace movie theater to the Club Alpin's meetings at rue de la Boétie. She read a great deal, especially the trendy writers of the period, such as Maxence Van der Meersch and Charles Morgan, or "modern writers" like André Gide, Jean Giraudoux, and Paul Valéry. She cared about her appearance and spent whatever money she could spirit away from her husband's mountaineering passion on making herself elegant. She also had a few love affairs, and never really bothered to hide the fact, since Roland Truffaut was so wrapped up in his club and his expeditions. There was a "Monsieur Robert," for example— Robert Vincendon, a quasi-official lover, who joined the family dinner table every Thursday evening and never failed to bring a gift—a bottle of wine for Roland or a book for his mistress. In the midst of all these activities, they lived like a childless couple; François was merely a shadow.

Geneviève de Monferrand devoted a great deal of time to raising her "last three children"—Bernard, who was filled with dreams of the army; Monique, whose life revolved around music; and her grandchild, François, who had been snatched from death's door. It was she who had "wanted" François and saved him twice—first when she dissuaded her daughter Janine from having an illegal abortion in 1931, and later when she went to fetch him at Boissy-Saint-Léger, where he was visibly wasting away. By all accounts, the boy—who was nicknamed "Papillon" ("Butterfly") and "Farfadet" ("Elf"), and had very fine blond hair worn in a pageboy—was "extremely alert" and cheerful, though "skinny and of delicate health."[8] At seven, his hair turned brown; he was still "a bit pale and olive-skinned" and "alternated between vivaciousness and melancholy," "long silences" and "frenzied chatter."[9] By the end of the thirties, François was already extremely attached to his neighborhood; he knew its every nook and cranny, having tramped through it often on lengthy walks with his grandmother. If you head up the rue Henri Monnier toward the hill of Montmartre, you find a tangle of little streets leading to the steamiest boulevards in Paris, in the area of Clichy, Place Blanche, and Pigalle. Parallel to the rue Henri Monnier, walking uphill and downhill from west to east, you find the rue Blanche, rue de La Rochefoucauld, rue des Martyrs, rue Rodier, and rue de Rochechouart, and a great many little side streets—rue de Douai, rue Condorcet, rue Chaptal, rue de la Tour d'Auvergne, rue de Navarin, rue Choron. These form a tight urban web, one of the most densely populated areas in the capital. It is the heart of a nineteenth-century neighborhood, the "quartier des Lorettes," also called the "New Athens," traditionally a neighborhood of artists and demi-mondaines, artisans and prostitutes, shopkeepers and junior civil servants. The atmosphere is quiet, despite the noise and cries of the market on rue des Martyrs. Aside from a few private mansions built around the end of the nine-teenth century by wealthy men for their mistresses, the apartments are mod-est, with small rooms.

Truffaut was enrolled at the nursery school on rue Clauzel, and here he learned the alphabet. Reading with his grandmother was a favorite pastime. In first grade, at the primary school of the Lycée Rollin on avenue Trudaine, his report cards throughout 1938–39 were very good. He was an honor stu-dent, among the top five in his class. His teacher, Monsieur Dubuc, wrote, "François is a good student with a lively mind and a keen intelligence. His pleasant disposition and even temper have won him the sympathy of all."[10]

In the summer, Geneviève de Monferrand rented a large house in north-ern Brittany, near Saint-Brieuc, in a small village called Binic—the Ty Rose villa, rue de l'Yc, a two-story house with a garden, close to the sea. François, who hated bathing and swimming,[11] spent his time running around or play-ing in the sand with a group of turbulent older cousins. In September 1939, when France entered the war, Geneviève decided to extend their vacation and spend the year in Brittany. Her son Bernard and her husband, Jean, were drafted, as was her son-in-law Roland Truffaut; all three were sta-tioned in Satory, near Paris. Life in Brittany seemed easier to cope with than an extended waiting period in Paris. After François recovered from a worri-some case of jaundice, he and the Monferrand children attended the village school, at the top of the cliff. François was probably more unruly here than in Paris, for, on February 15, 1940, his grandmother sought help for the first time: "François looks much healthier than he has in a long time and has a good appetite, but he has broken out with such bad pimples that some of them look like little boils. Because of this, I can partly forgive his unruly, inattentive, contentious mood. He is learning a lot in class, good things from his teacher but distressingly bad ones from his classmates, who are really naughty. Roland should write to him in a firm tone and tell him he has to obey without talking back and bear criticism patiently (he sometimes goes so far as to shrug his shoulders). None of this is serious, but it must be nipped in the bud. If not, I'll soon become a frantic little old woman."[12]

After spending a second summer in Binic, Geneviève returned to Paris with all the children at the beginning of the school year, September 1940. François entered third grade at the same Lycée Rollin. He kept up the reading and work habits his grandmother had instilled in him and remained a gifted student, but bad behavior had rubbed off on him from his cousins and classmates at the small school on the cliff, and he had become difficult. The comments of his teachers reveal as much: "An extremely intelligent child, who is very good in oral exercises, but so absorbed in play, so absentminded and talkative that his excellent qualities are wasted. Good in French. If he showed a bit more care and were more attentive, he would do extremely well."[13] This did not prevent him from being an honor student and entering the next grade. The following year, after another happy summer in Binic, a similar statement was made on his report card: "He has no trouble understanding anything, except discipline. . . ."[14]

Under his grandmother's wing, François's life consisted of reading, walks, neighborhood errands, school, and summers spent in Brittany; occasionally, there were unwelcome interruptions, including his parents' visits. They rarely went to Binic, usually spending the summer at the other end of France, in the mountains, but every so often they visited the apartment on rue Henri Monnier. François Truffaut retained bitter memories of these visits: "With my father everything went well, but with my mother not at all. Subsequently I came to understand this phenomenon, from reading about it in books. My mother, whom I rarely used to see—mainly on those weekends when I would stay with them—my mother would suddenly want to act the part and would take it into her head—at my grandmother's, for instance—that I should finish eating some dish I couldn't stand, like lentils, until I'd get nauseous and vomit in my plate. Then she'd get angry and lock me in the back room; she'd yell and scream at her own mother and accuse her of being lax in my upbringing; and then she'd break down in tears when she realized she was also to blame. Each time there were scenes and head-on clashes, so much so that I could predict it all and I'd come to dread the times when my mother would come to visit us. My father used to just laugh it all off, while my grandfather—whom I disliked because he acted curt with me and never talked to me, about books, theater, or even the army, which he adored—my grandfather refused to see or understand what was happening, he'd just go into his study and read his newspaper."[15]

Also interrupting life's quiet flow on rue Henri Monnier were François's visits to his paternal grandparents' home in Juvisy. He spent some of his vacations there at Easter or on All Saints' Day. When he stayed for longer periods of time, he would accompany his grandfather to the workshop, or to the cemetery where he did his marble work. At the Truffauts', there was no talk of literature or recent shows, but much discussion of the family, which would cause François, as an adolescent, to suspect his grandmother of reporting all his remarks to his parents. Otherwise, these stays were remarkable for their inactivity: "It was funny, vacations at Juvisy were usually spent at the edge of the road, watching the cars leave for the weekend. There was no highway at the time, and people left on Saturday. They all headed down the road; and on Sunday night the cars headed back up. My grandfather, my grandmother, the dog Scout and I, we would sit on our chairs and watch the cars."[16] François loved the big bowls of cream his grandmother made with Heudebert flour—the only thing he really enjoyed eating in his entire life.

MY MOTHER

In August 1942, Geneviève de Monferrand died of pleurisy, with tubercular complications. François was in Juvisy, at his paternal grandparents', when the news came to them—news they had been dreading for several weeks. There was a family meeting, from which the ten-year-old was excluded, only to be told of his grandmother's death several hours later. His paternal grandparents were perfectly willing to keep him in Juvisy, but Roland, in spite of Janine's reluctance, now insisted on having François come to live with them full-time. This is how the couple, now in their early thirties, suddenly found themselves caring for a child whom they had rarely seen—a cyclothymic, irritable, clever, hypersensitive, somewhat sickly boy. François was aware of being an encumbrance, particularly to his mother, to whom the child represented the errors of her wayward youth. After the happy years living with his grandmother, François was now left to his own devices in a more indifferent, not to say hostile, world.

Shortly before his death, Truffaut described his adolescence as "an unhappy period, but it was intertwined with a happy side, though I didn't quite realize it."[17] He clearly remembered the mixture of fascination and hatred that bound him to the woman whom he was only then coming to know. "*My* Mother"—the possessive could be construed as ironical—was the title he planned to give the introduction to his projected autobiography.[18]

> What I went through with my mother is difficult to explain. It could probably be better explained in a novel—though Léautaud describes things like this very well in his diary. Bossiness mixed with a touch of contempt, a certain way of calling me "my child" or "silly little fool," or "little idiot," and of ordering me around, treating me like a servant, seeing how much I would put up with without complaining, though she didn't go so far as to hit me, not often at any rate. . . . True, my birth had really burdened this woman, and then she had been unburdened when my grandmother took care of me for her. How fantastic! Then suddenly, after the summer of 1942, she had to take me in, or

thought she had to. It was when I understood this that I began to hate my mother, when I felt I was a nuisance to her. There were signs of this, admittedly small little things, but which hurt me terribly. For example, at every medical checkup, the doctors always said I had to have my tonsils operated on, and my parents were always putting off the operation; then there was the sentence that recurred every Spring, with the vacation approaching—"What are we going to do with the kid?" The underlying thought, which they didn't even bother to hide from me, was always—"How can we get rid of him?" And then the other thing that was hard to swallow was two or three Christmases all by myself, while my parents were in the mountains with friends. At first, this was presented to me as something good: I could do whatever I wanted in Paris, without any interference, I'd have a bit of money, I could go to the movies or the theater with my cousins. . . . I know each time I was terribly depressed.[19]

"In spite of everything that had gone on between them, the hatred and the lack of understanding," his childhood friend, Robert Lachenay, wrote, "he very much admired his mother, quite simply because she was a beautiful woman, an independent woman."[20] François tried to please her by behaving like a model child, like a man almost; for example, when he was left alone, he tried to repaint the walls, the ceiling and the doors, so his parents would "find the house improved when they returned," or he tried to upgrade the old electrical wiring, placing new sockets and redoing the splices and connections. In spite of his good intentions, these efforts sometimes ended catastrophically. "It wasn't a problem with my father, he always laughed things off, but with my mother it was harder. Her reaction was unpredictable, and sometimes very negative: 'Stupid little idiot, silly fool, no one asked you to do this. . . .' "[21]

In his recollections, Truffaut frequently remarks upon Roland Truffaut's laughter and jokes. He took everything in good humor: the outbursts between mother and son, the boy's stories from school, particularly if off-color or anticlerical, their financial problems, even Janine's suitors—"Madame's gentlemen." A pleasant evening at the theater or the local cinema, and the trials of the day were completely forgotten. This often exasperated his wife—and led to frequent arguments—but delighted François, who always encouraged Roland's joking temperament. But there was one thing that was hardly ever a joking matter—mountaineering; if the itinerary for a big hike was mislaid, ropes tangled, or a set of snap hooks lost, Roland Truffaut's angry fits were like high-altitude storms.

Roland Truffaut never told François he was his adoptive father. But as he approached adolescence, François surmised as much from telltale signs.

First, he noticed his parents' unease when he asked questions about his childhood and his separation from them; then there was his grandmother's and mother's obsession that others think of him as two years younger than his real age. He never found their explanations for this convincing—particularly the one about keeping him eligible for the "children's rate" on the train to Fontainebleau. These suspicions were encouraged by his reading of the great novels of the nineteenth century: "Unfortunately, I gradually felt something was wrong and it stemmed from . . . Charles Dickens. Like all big readers in such cases, I invented a complicated story for myself about the mystery surrounding my birth. . . ."[22] It seems that as an adolescent he was especially struck by one of the first sentences of *David Copperfield*—a most memorable novel for him, along with *Great Expectations:* "I was a posthumous child. My father's eyes had closed upon the light of this world six months when mine opened on it. . . ." Truffaut later wrote, "I tried to work things out on my own with this book and this sentence, which was really very intriguing."[23]

At the beginning of 1944, shortly after turning twelve, François was rummaging in a closet while his parents were out, and he discovered a small 1932 Hachette almanac that belonged to Roland Truffaut. In it were recorded different events—hiking itineraries, birthdays to remember, and evenings at the theater. François found no special mention of anything on February 6, the day of his birth. His suspicions were confirmed once and for all several weeks later, when he came upon the *livret de famille,* the family record book. Roland Truffaut was not his father, and from then on, he felt a pang of sadness when he laughed at the man's jokes.

TRUANCY AND LIES

François had begun living with his parents at the start of the school year, in September 1942, when he was ten and a half. For a couple with a child, all the apartments they lived in—rue Clignancourt in 1942, rue Saint-Georges in 1943, and rue de Navarin, which they moved into in January 1944—were cramped. "Still, at 33 rue de Navarin, second floor left, I lived for nearly five years," Truffaut recalled. "It was very difficult living under the same roof in such a tiny apartment. There was a room that served as a dining room and there was my parents' bedroom, and a little entrance adjoining the kitchen, which was also a bathroom. The toilets were on the landing, half a floor down. Everything was so precarious that my father had built a structure as my bed, in the entrance, that was a kind of bunk which folded up during the day and unfolded at night thanks to a pivoting mechanism. He joked about it being like a mountain refuge. For me, it was my bed every single night and not much of a joke."[24] This structure, which is now famous from scenes in *The 400 Blows,* inevitably reinforced the child's feeling of being unwanted and of interfering with his parents' privacy.

Roland and Janine regularly left their adolescent son all alone in the apartment on weekends when they went hiking and rock-climbing in Fontainebleau. They would set off on Saturday morning and return Sunday afternoon. He would read, tinker, and get bored, confining himself to his room and the kitchen, where precooked meals had been left for him, but he still preferred this kind of idling to rock-climbing, for which he rapidly developed a loathing. When he was older, he would take advantage of his parents' absence to go out with his friends, sometimes staying with one of them for the night.

Janine and Roland did not always understand François's attitude; they considered him lazy and attributed his recalcitrance to an adolescent phase that he would grow out of. They looked down on him as a boy who had been overly spoiled by his grandmother, and for preferring the closed-in atmosphere of the Lorettes district to the great outdoors. Roland Truffaut described this lack of communication in his book, *Du Kenya au Kilimandjaro,* published by Julliard in 1953: "My son François will never understand anything about mountaineering. Feeling both convinced and hopeless about this, I have long stopped trying to influence him. . . . He prefers his scooter and the movies, and feels there is no way of eating that is more unpleasant than gobbling food crouched in front of a tent, even if the landscape is gorgeous. His tastes differ from mine. . . ."[25]

François did, however, agree to accompany his parents to Fontainebleau on the weekend when they decided to make a film. *Les Visiteurs du samedi soir* was a parodic remake of a recently released Marcel Carné film, *Les Visiteurs du soir,* known in English as *The Devil's Envoys.* They used some fifty yards of airplane cloth that had been found in the forest and a 16-mm camera borrowed from a friend; Roland Truffaut wrote the script and, with his long nose, played the part of the elderly duenna; Janine played the young female lead; Monique de Monferrand was in charge of the music; the extras were members of the Club Alpin. Everyone participated, including François, who was recruited to play the midget. "This provided a little adventure,"[26] he said later. But most of the time, he preferred to withdraw and stay quietly uninvolved, pretending to be unaware of the couple's marital problems, avoiding conflict, and keeping his opinions and adventures to himself. He never asked for anything, but stole regularly from the family till to achieve a measure of independence. François would also make up stories, lying compulsively as a way of settling his score with reality. None of this went unnoticed, and his parents openly complained to relatives and close friends: "François is turning into more and more of a thief and a liar. He shows no respect for us anymore, for he steals from us and has started lying for no reason."[27] The misunderstanding deepened, and with it, alienation on both sides.

His first year with his parents was also his last at the primary school of the Lycée Rollin, where the effects of his deteriorating family life soon became apparent. Madame Mollier's first trimester assessment—"a good little student, though occasionally a bit talkative"—gave way to a much harsher comment in the final trimester—"I was very disappointed by this student at the end of the year. He was increasingly disruptive in class and learned his lessons less and less well. In spite of his bad performance, he would derive no benefit from repeating the year."[28] François was required to take an exam to determine his fate: If he did well, he would be admitted into sixth grade at the Lycée Rollin; if he failed, he would be placed into a "graduating class" for the worst students and given a certificate. The exam was scheduled for September 1943, but François did not take it.[29] Over the next three years, from September 1943 to June 1946, he would attend three different neighborhood schools, two on rue Milton and one on rue Choron, barely earning his diploma in June 1946.

Truffaut appraised this period of his adolescence at the end of his life:

These were good schools, a bit dirty, grimier than the Lycée Rollin, but you got used to them. What was more difficult, for me, was going from one teacher to many teachers. This may have had something to do with my grandmother, who had accustomed me to certain educational methods, but I suddenly had the feeling of being abandoned, like a lost object of no interest. Sometimes it was funny, with all those new teachers, who had often just taught primary school, we'd get some weird characters. One of them kept saying, "Things are gonna get rough, Truffaut, watch out!" I liked it, because his voice had a real peasant twang.[30]

These scenes and characters remained permanently engraved in the future filmmaker's mind and he drew inspiration from them for *The 400 Blows:* Ducornet, the dry and authoritarian literature instructor on rue Milton, who punished Truffaut for lifting entire passages from Balzac in his composition; Petit, the mathematics teacher on rue Choron, a former Resistance fighter in the FFI (Forces françaises de l'intérieur) who sold his students photos of himself in full uniform; the gym teacher who was so lenient that he lost practically all his students between the school yard and the stadium, they having been swallowed, as it were, by the portes cocheres along the way.

Nothing contributed to the school troubles of François—nicknamed "the meteor"[31] by the priest at catechism—as much as his truancy and absences. The most foolhardy episode took place in April 1944:

> I had taken volume one of *The Three Musketeers* out of the library and on a Tuesday I cut classes in order to read volumes one and two. I was determined to get all three volumes and read them in a square I knew near Montmartre, far enough away from school that no one would see me. So, on Wednesday I cut class again and spent my day reading. Then, at nightfall, a magnificent sight took place, a bomb attack on La Chapelle. I was a bit worried but delighted. A few minutes later, I see people rushing into a subway entrance, for shelter. I immediately run down to the Marcadet métro entrance, for the Boulevard Barbès is already being pelted with bombs. Inside the station, I joined a crowd of people and waited. Finally I slept there all night, with Alexandre Dumas tucked under my arm, and never even thought of my parents. In the morning, I went to school, thrilled that I could tell my chums about it. But my mother, who had been worried to death, came to get me in the middle of class. I felt awful.[32]

For Truffaut, school, instead of being educational, was an environment for fabricating lies, for creative falsifications; if classes had to be cut in order to read Balzac or Dumas, if playing hooky was required in order to experience real life, then the thing to do was to defy authority and lie, as one does with one's parents. Hence the well-known reply he came up with in the fall of 1944 when he had to justify a recent absence, a reply that as a filmmaker he would put in the mouth of his screen hero Antoine Doinel fifteen years later: "It's my mother, sir. . . . She died. . . ."[33]

LACHENAY, THE FRIENDFRIENDFRIEND

If school had any value to François, it was as a place to make friends. Friendship provided him refuge and made it possible for him to forget his family's indifference and his teachers' oppression. "At the beginning of the academic year of 1943, at the school on rue Milton, when the recess bell went off, a boy spoke to me as I was going down the stairs, 'I'm sure you pinch money from your parents,' he said. I looked at him but refused to answer. An hour later, he came into class, in the middle of our French course, with a proctor. The teacher, who seemed to know him, said to him: 'Go sit next to Truffaut, the two of you will make quite a pair.' It was Robert Lachenay, who became my closest friend."[34]

The two boys were very different. Robert was older; always the worst student in class, he had just been moved back into sixth grade when he came to sit by François, under Monsieur Ducornet's stern gaze. He was also tougher, more self-confident and mature, knowledgeable on politics and history, and in coping with the school bureaucracy; he was the driving force of the mischievous duo, already adept at playing hooky, as well as forging excuse notes and signatures on report cards. Lachenay's outspokenness was what first attracted François to him. Robert also knew how to lie, of course, and always did so with impressive aplomb. Above all, he minced no words in describing people, whether classmates or teachers, parents or neighborhood shopkeepers. This candor was completely foreign to François, who was accustomed to leaving things unsaid.

Their families were alike, as Lachenay points out: "He felt his father and mother were a bit casual, mine were of the same ilk, though very different. We were really all alone, the two of us, making up for a family and giving each other support in our loneliness. Being a child is very hard, you're forever either hounded or neglected—by your parents at home and by your teachers at school, and in those days teachers really gave you rough treatment—it was a reign of terror. We had joined forces to resist this."[35]

The two boys used to walk to school together; François waited for Robert every morning at the corner of rue Henri Monnier and rue de Navarin. The Lachenays lived at 10 rue de Douai, just beyond rue Pigalle, south of Place Pigalle, in a very large eight-room apartment that fascinated François. Robert enjoyed relative freedom at home. His mother worked in the theater sporadically but otherwise spent most of her days cloistered in one section of the apartment. She was an alcoholic and when she did go out, she would sometimes be brought home staggering. His father, an elegant, rather lordly man, was secretary of the Jockey Club; his mind was preoccupied by horses and bets, and in this period of shortages he benefited from certain material advantages.[36] (The children had access to a refrigerator which, during the Nazi Occupation, was almost always full, and occasionally dined at Trémolo, a restaurant on rue de Biot where Monsieur Lachenay had an account.) The races were his sole passion and cost him dearly; it was not unusual for bailiffs to show up at the house. The apartment was gradually emptied of its furniture; only the most useless keepsakes and trinkets were left, giving the place an antiquated, slightly eerie charm that the two boys adored. They occupied a special space—Robert's room was at the end of a long corridor and isolated from the rest of the apartment; it was sheltered from prying eyes and off limits to the bailiffs. And—the ultimate amenity of freedom—it had its own service stairway. François spent many long hours there in the spring of 1944, and throughout 1945; sometimes, during periods of truancy, he would sleep over several nights in a row. It was the perfect refuge from parents and school: a place where the two friends talked and read and could indulge in the occasional smoke or drink.

I SÉVIGNE, YOU SÉVIGNE

The summer of 1945 marked the beginning of a long correspondence between these friends. "I can't do without writing you every day, do likewise," François advised from Binic, where he was spending his vacation. "I sévigne, you sévigne, we sévigne," he would quip, playing on the name of Madame de Sévigné, famous for her correspondence. "I go kayaking and write five letters a day. Write me! Write me!"[37] Truffaut's precocious passion for letter-writing would become a lasting and vitally important outlet for him. His letters show his growing friendship with Robert Lachenay—the "old pal," the "old chap," the "friendfriendfriend," or, more generally, "dear Robert"—in whom "Francesco," "Phronssouat," "your chum," "your buddy," "the truffle," or, more often, "your friend François" confides.

Whenever one of the two had to leave a school, the other managed to follow. So Robert and François were together in grade after grade, and they hardly associated with the other children their age, with the sole exception of Claude Thibaudat—later an impersonator and variety show entertainer known as Claude Vega—who was the same age as François and shared a passion for movies, reading, songs, and especially the music hall. The son of a concierge on rue des Martyrs, Claude walked to school with them every day. "As kids," Claude Vega recalls, "we formed groups according to our affinities. 'Let's go there, how much money do you have?' 'This is what I have left, okay I'll round things off,' somehow we managed. We used to swap photos. François would say to me, 'Do you really like that still from the film?' Our tastes weren't always the same, but we respected each other's tastes, we were discreet and didn't say anything. I wanted a photo of Yvonne Printemps and Pierre Fresnay and he said to me, 'Don't worry, I'll find you one.' I was deliriously happy when he gave me a photo he had succeeded in pinching."[38]

They considered school a transitional period in their lives and sought a way of establishing their independence.

As Truffaut explained, Robert Lachenay, Claude Vega and I had in common that we lived projected into the future, the near future, a future that had to be close at hand. We were always discussing what we would do in two or three years. For example, we came up with the same idea, in the fall of 1945, a little venture that brought in a bit of money. It was a very simple idea, the idea of creating a *Pariscope* [arts and entertainment listing] before the time. In those days, because of paper shortages, film, theater and cabaret announcements were listed in the papers in very tiny, close print. We were all three nuts about film and theater. I used to fetch wine for my parents near Barbès, and I'd stop at every movie theater, on the boulevards, to look at the stills of the films that were playing and check the programs for the following week. So, since each of us was doing the same thing in our own separate comings and goings, we were able to make little information-filled booklets.[39]

The three teenagers recopied their findings on loose sheets, which they then stapled together; the dates and show times of *Three Waltzes,* with Pierre Fresnay and Yvonne Printemps, at the Gaieté-Rochechouart might appear next to a portrait of Fresnay drawn by Claude Thibaudat. Truffaut wrote one-sentence plot summaries and Lachenay checked the spelling of all the proper names. They produced twenty, and eventually thirty, copies which they sold door-to-door on rue des Martyrs. They made a good team, and even put together shows: "There was a maid's room on the seventh floor at my friend Vega's house and we staged five or six shows, essentially 'poetry evenings.' Claude was the star and recited verses from Racine, I must have given a rendition of [Baudelaire's] 'Albatross,' and Robert told anecdotes. Most of the time, we would restrict ourselves to building scenery for Claude's appearances. But in this too, we made a bit of money by charging a small admission fee for people in the building, our parents and classmates."[40]

When they were not holed up in Robert's room, the three boys roamed around the neighborhood. On boulevards Pigalle and Rochechouart, the street entertainers and vendors offered their attractions from December to March; there was fun to be had in the numerous churches in the Lorettes district—poor boxes to pry open, candles to light, and priests to imitate; the shopkeepers were jokers and complainers—the charcuterie saleswoman on rue des Martyrs or "Jo," the greengrocer on rue Lepic. Every so often they rushed over to Lachenay's grandmother, Madame Bigey, who generously loaned them money. In the squares surrounding the "New Athens," they could read and recover from their sleepless nights. And then there was the whorehouse on rue de Navarin, very close to the Truffaut apartment.

For Pigalle is also the neighborhood of the Moulin Rouge and of all the most daring Paris sex shows. There are streetwalkers on the boulevards, and brothels tucked away on the adjacent streets. "Near where we lived," Truffaut recounted, "there was a house which I called 'the Gothic house'

18

because it had two or three niches and a somewhat elaborate facade. It was a former mansion for nineteenth-century grisettes, and there was really nothing Gothic about it. The place fascinated us. . . . We were perfectly aware that it was a whorehouse. Sometimes we even played pranks—for example, if a straitlaced guy with a briefcase and umbrella on rue des Martyrs happened to asked us for directions to rue Navarin, we'd say 'It's the first street on the left and you'll find number 9 right there.' We knew we were behaving like wise guys, and it sort of aroused us."[41] Prostitution was a mysterious world close by, a possible refuge—still prohibited, but not for long—and a necessary passage to adult life.

THE STORY OF A CHEAT

The performing arts, in all shapes and forms, played an essential role in François Truffaut's youthful years. But reading was what allowed him to dream of another life. Although his grandmother had initiated him into this pleasure, he also owed his taste for books to Janine and Roland.

> My parents were between twenty-five and thirty-five years old, and since they had just recently been students, they talked about everything at home, not just about mountaineering, but also about plays, movies, and books. That's lucky for a child, lucky if he's interested. When I was researching *The Last Métro,* I realized that I knew about all the things that were talked about at the time, like the book *Bodies and Souls* by Maxence Van der Meersch, the Baroque Spanish play *La Celestina,* which had just been staged, or *The Master Builder,* or the plays produced at the Théâtre de la Ville with Charles Dullin—these were topics of conversation for my parents and their friends, and I absorbed it all by listening to them. Also, I used to always go down to buy the newspaper in the morning, and I loved reading it in the street on my way back. So that by the time I got home, I knew what my parents were going to comment on, even if I couldn't predict what they would say.[42]

Reading was also the best way of forgetting a mother who "could stand me only if I was silent," a remark Truffaut would later use in *The Man Who Loved Women.* So as an adolescent he spent hours sitting on a stool engrossed in a book, carefully turning pages as unobtrusively as possible, not daring to make the slightest noise or rustle. Robert Lachenay, his first confidant, was also his first friend to share his passion for literature: "We could spend our afternoons discussing, for example, whether George Sand had slept with Doctor Pagello while Musset was dying. . . . Then François discovered Balzac and in the course of our lengthy conversations—in class, in my room, in squares—he succeeded in convincing me that Balzac was a better writer than Paul de Kock, because though I used to read, I was much less discriminating than he was. François was much more methodical; he would tell me about *Le Lys dans la vallée* [*The Lily in the Valley*], and the kiss on Madame de Mortsauf's shoulder which had deeply moved him. I sort of followed in his footsteps, so I started reading Balzac."[43]

Voracious reading habits turned Truffaut into a bookstore habitué at an early age. He used his pocket money, whether he managed to earn it by working or could pilfer it from the family till, to build up an entire library. In a letter to Robert Lachenay on September 18, 1945, after returning from vacation, he described his latest acquisitions in detail:

> Oh! Oh yes! The Eiffel Tower is still here. . . . I've been Parisian now for five days. My first errand was for my "Fayards" [a series of small books with woodcut illustrations]. . . . The shopkeeper on rue des Martyrs opposite the Médrano has a huge number of them. I'm going there tomorrow. This afternoon in the rue Mansard I bought 36 classics; out of these the only ones you're missing are *Candide* [Alfred de Vigny's], *Stello* (2 volumes), *War and Peace* (8 volumes), [Alfred de Musset's] *Histoire d'un merle blanc* [*Story of a White Blackbird*], [Alphonse de Lamartine's] *Premières Méditations poétiques* [*First Poetic Meditation*], [Alphonse Daudet's] *Tartarin de Tarascon 2*, [Marc Allégret's] *Fromont jeune* [*Young Fromont*], that's 4, there are only 18 volumes that you don't have out of what I bought and you'll find them at home when you return. I now have 295 books; I'm missing 90 for the complete collection.[44]

He would eventually acquire those ninety missing books. When he worked for a few weeks in the book and stationery store at the Palais-Royal, he managed to buy the complete set of Fayard classics, from A to Z, for 3,500 francs. Truffaut remained a great reader all his life, but he gave up on comprehensiveness, concentrating more and more on his own personal tastes. According to the screenwriter Jean Gruault, "François remained willfully ignorant of Rabelais, Dante, Homer, Melville, Faulkner and Joyce, but had a thorough knowledge of Balzac, Proust, Cocteau, Louis Hémon, Roché, Audiberti, Léautaud, and he liked Thomas Raucat, Jouhandeau, Céline, Calet, Albert Cohen. . . . He also had a weak spot for unrecognized writers like Raymond Guérin. He would read and re-read his books, and they were filled with notes and underlined passages, which showed he applied the same sustained, meticulous attention to the works he read as to the films he watched over and over again."[45]

Absorbed though he was in his library, Truffaut's main escape, even in those early days, was the screen and the darkness of movie theaters. His line "Life was the screen"[46] summarizes his adolescent passion. His first impressions as a moviegoer—precocious, furtive, and vivid—were linked to a magical spot: a theater with continuous showings on Place de l'Europe, a five-minute walk from his parents' apartment. He had gone there for the first time before the war with his aunt Monique; on the screen, the two youngsters had seen a church, then a marriage—"I watched in amazement, but before I knew it, it was over!"[47]—François Truffaut's primal movie scene. His first real film experience took place in the autumn of 1940, when he was eight and a half; he saw Abel Gance's *Paradis perdu* (*Four Flights to Love*) at the Palais-Rochechouart. One of the big hits of the Occupation, this melodrama was made famous by its title song. A very youthful Micheline Presle has two parts in the film; she plays Janine, the wife of a painter who becomes famous by designing dresses for a couturier (Fernand Gravey), and she plays their daughter Jeannette. This film had a church scene as well, at the end of the film, when Jeannette marries her fiancé as her father looks on and then dies in the course of the ceremony. The rustling of silky dresses, love that inspires life and death, mysterious births, religion, and melodrama—these are the recurrent themes in most of the films seen in those days by the youthful Truffaut. For instance, another indelible memory was *Mademoiselle ma mère*, a 1937 film by Henri Decoin, with Danielle Darrieux and Pierre Brasseur, in which a man marries a woman young enough to be his son's sister—"a film that I liked for its shocking, you might say incestuous, subject matter."[48] Truffaut had no criteria yet for selecting films; he saw everything (just as he read everything), certainly over half the two hundred French films made during the Occupation. "I didn't exactly know what my tastes were. I liked great music in films, I also liked a certain religiosity, and stories of doomed love. . . . For my taste, after *Paradis perdu*, came Clouzot's *Le Corbeau* [*The Raven*], because it was *noir* and hard-hitting, and then Bresson's *Les Anges du péché* [*The Angels of Sin*]."[49]

He had begun to see two or three films a week, starting at age twelve—a passion centered at first exclusively on French films, since American ones were banned and filmgoers were not much interested in German films. This is hardly surprising: French movies made during the Occupation left a deep impression on the minds of people at that time.[50] And in spite of a production reduced by half, the war years, paradoxically, could surely be considered a golden age. It seems that being cut off from the world allowed the

"French school" to express itself at its best. The industry was freed from competition with American films, and the anarchy and producer rivalries of the thirties had come to an end; it was now able to develop with the same aesthetic biases, conforming to classical cinema "in the French style," with the same filmmakers—with a few exceptions, such as Jean Renoir, René Clair, Julien Duvivier, who had left for Hollywood—and the same actors— except for Jean Gabin and Michèle Morgan, who were also expatriates. Most of the recognized filmmakers remained: Marcel Carné, Jean Gré- millon, Abel Gance, Henri Decoin, Christian-Jaque. Some new ones emerged: Henri-Georges Clouzot, Claude Autant-Lara, Jacques Becker, Robert Bresson, and it was at this time that the most emblematic film of the French school was shot: Marcel Carné's *Les Enfants du Paradis* (*Children of Paradise*).

The young Truffaut's pocket diaries in the mid-forties show he went to see *The Raven* thirteen times, *Children of Paradise* nine times, and Autant-Lara's *Douce* (*Love Story*) seven times. But this love of French film would soon turn to aversion when a large number of American films began to arrive in France in the summer of 1946, and he discovered a whole new realm of auteurs and actors.

François Truffaut scoured all the movie theaters in his neighborhood, first, at the beginning of the war, with his aunt Monique and later with his buddies Robert Lachenay and Claude Thibaudat. There were over twenty movie houses between the Place Clichy and the rue de Rochechouart— including the Clichy, the Artistic, the Trianon, the Gaieté-Rochechouart, the Palais-Rochechouart, the Roxy, the Pigalle, the Cinéac-Italiens, and the fabulous Gaumont-Palace with its six thousand seats. These dream palaces exuded a special atmosphere during the war; the constraints and hardships of the Nazi Occupation could be forgotten. For young film buffs, this clan- destine other life was richer, more exciting, and more challenging than school, family, and society. At night, parents went to the same movie the- aters to which their children had escaped earlier in the day, having plotted, cut school, or avoided the family meal. "I saw my first two hundred films on the sly," Truffaut wrote, "playing hooky and slipping into the movie house without paying. . . . I paid for these great pleasures with stomachaches, cramps, nervous headaches and guilty feelings, which only heightened the emotions evoked by the films. . . . I felt a tremendous need to enter *into* the films. I sat closer and closer to the screen so I could shut out the theater."[51] At age twelve, when his parents went to the theater, he would make believe he was asleep, then rush out for the start of a film at one of the neighbor- hood theaters; he often ran out before the end of the film to get home before his parents. This explains why he often saw the same film twice;

when he accompanied his family the second time around, he had to take care not to reveal the plot. At thirteen, he was often trailed by men as he came out of the movie theaters near Pigalle: "I had the feeling of these guys on the lookout for kids at nightfall and pursuing them for no apparent reason. It was rather sinister. We were frightened, but we enjoyed the fear."[52] These early experiences of watching films on the sly, as a clandestine activity, became, for Truffaut, a defining condition of cinema. From then on, love of cinema represented a pocket of resistance in the culture of the period—a parallel society, forming a countercultural network, cultivating a taste for secrecy and contraband, and gradually taking the shape of an intimate diary, shared with faithful initiates.

SUMMER CAMPS

In adolescence, Truffaut also discovered a "new life" in the summer camps he attended after the Liberation. Roland and Janine Truffaut used to spend their summers in the mountains, and camp was the ideal answer to the eternal question "What are we going to do with the kid?" "The turning point," Truffaut explained years later, "was summer camp the year of the Liberation. That year, in the spring, my mother brought home a miraculous address, a camp reserved for the children of the employees of the Félix-Potin grocery chain. My parents had nothing to do with the food industry, but they must have had connections. So, I responded with a key question, 'Is it co-ed?' "[53] Between July 10 and August 29, 1944, he found himself near Montereau, housed in a castle that was coveted by two different armies: First, another wing and a section of the park were occupied by German soldiers; then, in the course of the summer, they were succeeded by the Americans. The relations between the soldiers and the children remained the same in both cases, a mixture of mistrust and attraction, petty theft and exchanges: "We would go into the military trucks and pinch iron cigarette boxes and cans of rationed meat packed in paraffin wax. Sometimes the soldiers would catch us and give us a beating, at other times they would joke around and let us take what we wanted."[54]

In mid-August 1944, the camp director, Monsieur Corneville, was arrested in the presence of the teenagers by Resistance fighters, and taken to the city for interrogation. The counselors had fueled a rumor that he had sold the Germans part of the food supplies left by the French army in 1940. "The director was arrested and returned several days later, but it created a scandal. This gave us a feeling of great freedom because since authority had been overthrown we had the right to do anything. We slept in the park, we woke up whenever we wanted, we split up into small autonomous groups and built huts. We lived like adults but in our own way—in other words, very childishly so. We talked with the American soldiers, explored the cellars of the castle, and stole valuable books, with beautiful bindings, from the library. . . . It was wartime but without any feeling of danger. And relations with girls were easier."[55]

Not only did the young Truffaut confront history in this summer camp; he also had his first encounters with love—the subject matter of his future adult narratives: "I met lots of people there—the boy who later opened the restaurant Le Tourtour; the actor Jean-Claude Arnaud, who played valets in Molière and acted in that Saroyan play I'm so fond of, *My Heart's in the Highlands*. I met him and his brother, Chouchon, and his two cousins, Monique and Nicole, whom I immediately fell in love with. It was very colorful and also very important, that camp."[56]

He returned to the summer camp two years later, after a difficult school year. It was still the same Félix-Potin connection, but the camp this time was located at Les Sables-d'Olonne, in Vendée (Brittany). The group from Montereau was more or less restored. They enjoyed the same freedom, and were sometimes just as unaware of danger: "I remember distinctly that on the beach, at Les Sables-d'Olonne, our little group of five or six teenagers found a grenade in the sand. We spent two hours trying to make it explode. It was incredibly foolish. Fortunately, we were lucky and nothing happened, but I can still see it very vividly, this gang of kids playing with death, with grown-up weapons; we had an enormous freedom which we didn't really know what to do with."[57]

That year, movies were shown once a week, a whole series of adventure films that François wasn't particularly enthusiastic about, except for the ones with Tyrone Power. But more important, he met his first youthful love. Liliane Romano was new to the little group in the camp, but she had impressed the others with her storytelling talent. She was marvelous at recounting films, and they would all sit in a circle around her, listening and visualizing the scenes she described. François, at fourteen, was completely infatuated, to the point where he was bold enough to slip a note into Liliane's shorts, and she slipped him a note in reply. "Then what happened was exactly like the last scenes of *Small Change*, when the friends shout, 'Liliane went out to kiss you,' the confusion of the two dormitories, the meeting in the stairway and the first kiss. . . ."[58] He would recapture this very kiss thirty years later, reproducing its childish ceremonial aspect, but at the time it had opened a new world for him, the world of feelings and physical love, and from then on he threw himself into this world with passion and clumsy stubbornness.

François had hopes, from this first real kiss, that he could continue to see Liliane in Paris once summer camp let out. He sent her a little note at 12 rue Traversière, where she lived, and asked her to meet him under the big clock at the Gare de Lyon. He waited there half a day. Several days later, the Truffauts received a registered letter; it was addressed to Roland, who wasn't at home. Janine put the letter on the mantelpiece and then went out on errands. François looked at the letter in his usual way, and went pale when he saw the sender's name: Monsieur Romano. He decided to open it: "Your son waits around the Gare de Lyon every day for my daughter Liliane. I feel this is inappropriate behavior at their age and that you should tell your son to stay home. I'm making sure my daughter stays home. Best regards."[59] Determined to destroy this "time bomb," he went down to the toilets half a floor down, tore up the letter, and flushed the toilet several times to destroy the evidence. When his mother returned, he decided that the best way of defending himself was to initiate the attack, so he improvised a strange lie— a lady had come to pick up the registered letter, which was not meant for Roland Truffaut but for someone else. Years later, Truffaut recalled his mother's reaction: "You stupid fool, you silly little idiot! Why did you give her the letter? It was for your father. And then who was this lady? It's inconceivable to give a letter to a woman you don't know, there's something fishy about this, this woman had to come from somewhere, didn't she?" To extricate himself from this trap of his own making, François lied again and described a redhead in a blue smock, a "hairdresser," which was what the Truffauts called the prostitutes from the whorehouse on rue de Navarin. Janine at once grabbed her son by the arm and dragged him down the stairs. "What was your hairdresser like? I'm sure you'll have no trouble recognizing her. Let's go look." At rue de Navarin, an unfriendly lady opened the door and Janine asked her, "I'd like to know if you have a boarder who is a redhead and wears a blue smock?"[60] Furious, the "head hairdresser" slammed the door in their faces. François had never before confronted such intense anger from his mother.

There were other tragicomic ordeals, with François invariably playing the part of the bashful lover whom Liliane avoided and ran away from. Once, for example, he went to pick her up outside the Cours Pigier and she jumped onto a bus platform to get away from him. From this first experience of unrequited love, which caused him much unhappiness, we can already glean the plot of François Truffaut's screen love stories, where everything stubbornly resists the hero's will and his desire to seduce. Truffaut would not see Liliane Romano again until 1958, twelve years later; then, as a reader of *Arts,* she wanted to meet the critic who had courted her so assiduously.

WAR IS A THEATER

Though he lived through the war as a child and adolescent, Truffaut rarely dealt with it in his films, transposing *The 400 Blows* to the fifties and *Small Change* to the seventies. Only in *The Last Métro* would he make use of specific memories from that period. "During the war, the Lycée Rollin acquired a prestigious image. It had a little chapel that had been closed for a long time and which was reopened in 1943 by a cardinal who had the reputation of collaborating with the Germans—Suhard, the archbishop of Paris. He came to bless the chapel. A children's choir sang, and I received communion for the first time. So a friend asked me: 'Did you have breakfast before?' I answered: 'Yes.' He responded: '*Oh, là, là!* You're in bad trouble!' That was typical of the mood during the Occupation."[61] In the film, after the sequence where the children's choir sings, "Dear Lord, dear Lord, save France in the name of the Sacred Heart," Truffaut implanted another recollection from the Occupation:

> My uncle, Bernard de Monferrand, set up a Resistance network; he was in the Vercors region. He and my grandfather were caught one day at the Gare de Lyon, when they were passing messages. I put this physical detail into *The Last Métro*[62]—or at least, for me, that's what I transposed. All hell broke loose at home that evening when we found out. My grandfather was released that night because of his age, but my uncle was held prisoner. . . . Afterward, during the entire war, there was a map on the mantelpiece with little French flags to locate where Bernard was. This mixture of fear and pride with regard to the Resistance was a bit ridiculous; for it had a much flimsier reality than the contraband of beans and sausages which everyone partook of when they came back from the mountains, the Alps, with 25 kilos of grub in their bags. I had a distinct feeling that the mountains served primarily for sneaking food back to Paris, and in some sense, I thought of the Resistance as something like a mountain hike, only longer. As for my Uncle Bernard, he survived. We all went to wait for him, three days running, at the Gare de l'Est; it was quite a scene, but it still resembled a country outing, like when I would come back from summer camp.[63]

Many years before *The Last Métro*, occupied France, the France of the Resistance, seemed like theater to Truffaut's adolescent eyes. Onstage, ceremonies were acted out which, viewed from afar, seemed slightly ridiculous but which included moving and picturesque details. Mass in the collaborationist church and Resistance plots were staged on the same set—hence, there were no good guys or bad guys; it was like the park, at Montereau castle, where the American soldiers, though more attractive, resembled the Germans in an uncanny way. And Cardinal Suhard was acting a part, just like Truffaut's grandfather Jean de Monferrand—one a collaborator before God, the other a novice Resistance fighter.

In its refusal to choose, in its aloofness with regard to political commitment—which it sees as theatrical performance—*The Last Métro* reaches far back and is a far more personal film than is generally thought. It also contains a moral insight into the period: "It is hard to tell if that period was theatrical because of the adolescent way I perceived things," Truffaut said, "or because the French at the time didn't want to take a close look at the reality of things. For had they faced the truth squarely, they would have seen France as a country of resigned people, faced with the effortlessness of collaborating and the dangers of Resistance."[64] Such was the ethical principle that the adolescent Truffaut derived from his first experience of politics and history. "What right have you to judge me?" was a justified retort to parents, teachers, and strangers who cast a disapproving eye on his truancy, his petty thefts, and his enormous lies, while they themselves were passive spectators watching the theatrical entertainment of collaboration and Resistance.

One particular image struck him at the time and reinforced his convictions. A newsreel at the Cinéac-Italiens in September 1945 showed the liberation of the concentration camps, with the living dead leaving their barracks. It made the theater of occupied France appear even more ridiculous and petty, and the resigned spectators even more passive and grotesque.

Truffaut's mistrust of all forms of proper, decent, righteous, official discourse, and of politicians and cultural institutions in general, was best expressed in a school paper he wrote in eighth grade, on December 11, 1945. This paper, which can be considered his very first essay of film criticism, discusses the "Why We Fight" series produced by Frank Capra and other propaganda films made by French directors, like Jean Renoir, who had emigrated to Hollywood. The reader can sense the young Truffaut's deep skepticism of Liberation rhetoric.[65] He is far from duped: "The film explains how France naïvely declared war on Germany in order to save Poland. But voluntary generosity is no longer of this world, since it has been expediently replaced by individualism and self-interested help." Nor does he believe in the legend of a unified French Resistance: "If France were not America's shortest path to Europe, if Syria were without oil, Nazi boots would still be treading the French pavements, for our Resistance was pathetically weak and unable to do anything without help from the Allies." The paper's disabused tone earned its thirteen-year-old writer a mark of 4 out of 20, and the comment "Cynicism offensive to our History." Yet, with its good vocabulary (and good spelling), the essay expresses a precept and state of mind that Truffaut would abide by all his life: Don't believe what you are told by those in power—or by adults in general.

Lapsing into acute mythomania, in an attempt to impress his friend Lachenay, François Truffaut pretended that he had attended the Pétain trial in the summer of 1945: "For reasons I can't disclose in this letter, I had to go to Paris for a week. Believe it or not, I was present when the Pétain verdict was announced, at 1:05 in the morning at the Palais de Justice [law court]. A riot almost broke out, for 11 people were distributing tracts inciting people (for I was not alone!) to break down the police barricades. The problem was, some people wanted to kill him and others wanted to free him. Nine persons were arrested and 7 had loaded firearms. . . ."[66] From attentively reading a newspaper account, Truffaut cast himself on the scene. Verdict, atmosphere, police, the pitched battle between pro- and anti-Pétainists—he described it all with a precocious journalistic talent and a gift for hoaxes. But it is easy to guess where his youthful sympathies lie—with Pétain, the insulted elderly man who has been divested of all power. His feelings of rebellion are stirred up against the victors, the all-too-powerful actors in the political arena—and this defined his attitude to life, as well. François Truffaut wanted to make his entrance into life by the "wrong door"—the door he was never shown, in family or school. His rebellion, he said, consisted of three contradictory impulses, "staying out of trouble," "spitting on their graves," and "becoming a respected somebody."

2.
FOUR HUNDRED BLOWS:
1946–1952

Life in postwar France was difficult, and everything needed to be rebuilt. The point, therefore, was to hurry, find work, and enter adulthood. François Truffaut, at fourteen, was a perfect example of such eagerness, as illustrated by his burning impatience to leave school and family and start living on his own. His father registered him at the school of commerce on avenue Trudaine, which had a good reputation, but after a few weeks of erratic attendance, he dropped out. Then it took him only a few days to get expelled from a similar school on rue de la Victoire. From that time on, he embraced his chosen fate as an autodidact. The model for his thoughts and actions was the hero of Sacha Guitry's *Le Roman d'un tricheur* (*The Story of a Cheat*), played by Guitry himself. Guitry was not looked upon with much favor after the Liberation, for, to put it mildly, he had not exactly been a Resistance fighter during the Nazi Occupation— though, for François, this fact undoubtedly added to the film's provocative power. The film was not recent, having been made in 1936, but Truffaut regarded it as *the* film of the Liberation period and went to see it twelve times between 1945 and 1946.[1] As a teenager of the Lorettes district, François found it exhilarating to identify with the adolescent hero of the film: the sole survivor of a detestable family, all of whom are poisoned by a dish of mushrooms, he becomes a bellhop in the Grand Hotel of Saint-Raphael and then a croupier in the Monte Carlo Casino. Many years later, in his preface to Guitry's book, *Le Cinéma et moi,* Truffaut wrote: "Expect nothing from others; when you need something take it, for it won't be given to you; get ahead without recourse to violence; don't get attached to people; learn to be self-reliant; set up a free and easy schedule—such is the moral of *The Story of a Cheat,* a moral that makes no claim to being moral but consists only in protecting oneself from the moral code of others."[2] He was especially impressed by Guitry's style, his highly personal elegance, his casual way of denouncing a society's injustice and moral blindness in a few sentences and a few scenes. "Citizen Sacha"—to use the nickname Truffaut gave him when he died in 1957—embodied the ideal figure of the free man, above convention, indifferent to the judgment of contemptuous intellectuals and the condemnations of political conscience.

SMALL JOBS

In the autumn of 1946, François Truffaut began roaming through the best bistros and big hotels in the neighborhood around the Opéra, trying to make contact with elevator men and bellhops, whose occupations had, for him, a mythical dimension. But he found his first job through the want ads. At the end of September 1946, he was hired by the firm Albert Simpère et Compagnie on avenue de l'Opéra, an important grain merchant on the Paris market. Truffaut was in charge of sorting the sacks shipped from the Ile-de-France countryside and then allocating them to the proper warehouse. He was essentially the company's "jack-of-all-trades"—secretary, deliveryman, receptionist, warehouseman, and errand boy—or "pen pusher and messenger,"[3] as he put it in his journal—going from one warehouse to another, to all parts of Paris, on foot and on bicycle, which he preferred. He remained at this full-time job from October 1946 to June 1948. "I used to give my entire salary to my parents and they gave me back a third. They wanted to be fair."[4] He could therefore rely on thirteen hundred francs a month for his books, films, and other pleasures—a sum that allowed him to try to live like an adult.

Robert Lachenay had moved out of his parents' apartment and into a maid's room nearby, which now became the two friends' new headquarters. They led a difficult life, for they no longer benefited from Monsieur Lachenay's wartime privileges. The food vouchers he had received through the Jockey Club were still valid at the time of the Liberation, but he was now divorced from Robert's mother and implicated in shady black-market activities. He hardly ever saw his son, and then in 1947, he died quite suddenly, in the military hospital where he was being held. Daily life in Robert's room—where François began to stay more and more often—was very unpre-

dictable. On payday, there would be some pleasant surprises on the menu—
"cooked potatoes to eat with bread, a slice of good ham, two slices of salami,
a few walnuts, an orange, and—surprise, surprise—a chocolate éclair."[5] But
their resources gradually dwindled and by the end of the month, unwilling
to call upon their parents, they would reach such a state of poverty that they
were forced to fast: "I can't tell you how often it used to happen to us, we
would go without eating for three days, or have no fire, fuel or electricity in
the room, and swap clothes so we could take turns being presentable for
work,"[6] Lachenay recalled.

Robert and François tried to supplement their incomes through their
passion for movies. They continued making listings of neighborhood movie
houses, now broadened to include the theaters between the Etoile and
Clichy, and sold them on rue des Martyrs. They also started a small traffic in
film stills, which they stole at night by dismantling the glass displays on the
facade of movie theaters with a screwdriver (Truffaut would put these night-
time outings on film in *Day for Night,* as part of the director Ferrand's
dream). A note to Robert dated January 17, 1948, attests to their feverish
activity: "Let's meet at the Studio Raspail and try to get stills from *Goodbye
Mr. Chips* and, especially, *The Story of a Cheat.* We can also try to get the
stills at the Abbesses movie house. That's the easiest because there's no one
around. The time to go is around 11 or midnight. . . . This week we have
photos from *Napoléon, Les Inconnus dans la maison, The Story of a Cheat,
Fanny, Scampolo.* I think they'll bring in a good price."[7]

In their struggle, they shared a genuine solidarity. Truffaut brought stuff
from home and Lachenay, whose small jobs paid better, helped support his
young friend. This was true during the summer of 1947, for instance, when
Lachenay worked as a warehouseman in an arms factory. "You're offering to
give me three hundred francs a week," Truffaut wrote him, "that's too much,
150 to 200 is more than adequate. If possible, I'd rather you brought back a
can of condensed milk and some butter because, as you know, I'm a big
eater in the morning."[8] Truffaut never forgot about these accumulated hardships and debts when his material conditions improved. He would always be
sympathetic to friends in need, regularly extending financial help, supporting a large number of close relatives and friends, and often paying off their
bills and back taxes.

Training for adult life also meant chasing after girls. The two friends were
initiated into romance together, even though the younger François was the
more precocious. The adventures they shared involved recopying a great
many quotations from novels and poetry in bookstores. And there remains a
small bawdy library assembled in those days.

The movies played a fundamental role in arousing their senses, sometimes in a trivial and fetishist way, as Truffaut himself related: "A friend

claimed that his mother and her coworkers, who were usherettes at the Gaumont-Palace, used to pick up at least sixty pairs of women's underpants, between the seats, in the boxes and the rows, every Sunday night after the last show. . . . Need I say that this number—we checked every week, it varied by about ten, at most—gave us food for thought in a way that had nothing to do with the art of filmmaking."9

However, literary and cinematic substitutions, though indispensable, were soon no longer enough for François Truffaut. In his romantic life, there seemed to be two types of relationships: those with cultured, proper young women, with whom he was rather ill at ease and whom he hoped to seduce by being patient and stubborn, and passing affairs, in which he gave expression to his precocious Don Juanism. Liliane Romano was his first great love, a long-awaited and unrequited one. But at about the same time, he met his first mistress, Geneviève S., who was older than he and, in the fall of 1946, a secretary at Simpère's. He wrote about it—in yet another instance of literary transposition—to his friend Lachenay on December third: "Concerning you-know-what, it went more or less as you predicted, in other words it wasn't quite right; we'll do better next time. But all in all I'm pleased."10 Starting at age fourteen, Truffaut had discreetly integrated the sexual act as a vital part of his life. But from the start he was possessed of a sense of propriety: He always lowered his eyes when watching overtly sexual scenes in films, including his own.

THE MAGIC BOOKLETS

In adolescence, François Truffaut made it a point of honor to see three films a day and read three books a week—on his own or with a friend, but trusting only his own judgment. To Lachenay, Truffaut made a case for the autodidact's extremist attitude: "I'm wary of our 'culture,' in France, which drives us apart from the people and their tastes; I now prefer judgments of the heart to those of the intellect."11 Aspiring to erudition, he devised a classification method early on—he created a folder for each filmmaker, "starting with the French director Marcel Abouker and ending with the American filmmaker Fred Zinnemann."12 Into these folders, he filed away articles clipped from *L'Ecran français* (The French Screen), *Cinévie, Cinévogue, Ciné-Miroir, Paris-Cinéma, Ciné-Digest,* and *Cinémonde.* The little closet at rue de Navarin where he stored his archives was soon inadequate. Owing to his parents' complaints, he decided in the fall of 1947 to move his archives into Robert's room, where they took up half the available space. The two adolescents lived in the midst of their files and books—a spatial metaphor for their beleaguered state of mind, material proof of their accu-

mulated learning, and foreshadowing as well the erudite cult of lists, classifi-
cations, and filmographies that would characterize the golden age of
cinephilia in the fifties and sixties.

Truffaut had found another resource to fill the gaps in his knowledge—
L'Ecran français, the most comprehensive postwar film weekly. Between
April 13 and December 7, 1948, over fifteen letters signed "F. Truffaut,
Paris, 33, rue de Navarin" appeared in the magazine's letters-to-the-editor
column, which was entitled "Lend Me Your Pen," and whose editor was a
young thirty-three-year-old critic, Jean-Charles Tacchella. "He badgered
me with questions," Tacchella recalls, "constantly demanding new filmographies. His passion delighted me. At the time I myself was spending half my
life on filmographies and the other half inside movie theaters, and now I had
found my best reader. In any case, my most assiduous reader."[13]

This learning method bore fruit, with the teenage Truffaut soon looked
upon as a "living cinematheque," impressing his friends with his many feats
of knowledge and beating other young film buffs in contests. For example,
when Pathé-Cinéma held a contest on Vittorio De Sica's *The Bicycle Thief*
in 1948 Truffaut came in second and the answers on his questionnaire were
brilliant. He won, as might be expected, a marvelous bicycle.[14]

His erudition was primarily the result of dedicated movie attendance at
theaters and film clubs. There were over four hundred movie houses in
postwar Paris, huge picture palaces and small neighborhood theaters, and
nearly two hundred of these were in the area around the Truffaut apartment, between Place Clichy and the Opéra, Pigalle and Barbès, and down
the *grands boulevards* between the Porte Saint-Denis and the Capucines.
And it was truly a golden age of film societies and clubs, with a great many of
them throughout the capital. The young Truffaut trained his eye by attending film-society screenings: "I was fanatic about joining," he said, "I had this
compulsion to join and become part of these places where films were programmed, presented and discussed."[15] The first film society he so diligently
attended, starting in 1945, was the Delta, which presented French films of
the thirties on Tuesday evenings. He was also very fond of the Ciné-Club de
la Chambre Noir (Dark Room), which featured Cocteau films. And there
were also more prestigious film societies, like the Ciné-Club of the *Revue
du cinéma,* the leading film magazine put out by Gallimard between 1946
and 1948, whose contributors included Jean George Auriol, Jacques
Doniol-Valcroze, Pierre Kast, Jacques Bourgeois, and André Bazin—all
members of the "new criticism" which had established itself after the Liberation.[16] This was where, on certain Saturday afternoons, he first attended
important discussions on aesthetics—on Orson Welles, Renoir, and
Rossellini and neorealism. "This film club was very important to me, it
drove me to lie to my parents, and to play 'Boy Scout hooky' because I was

sometimes supposed to go camping with friends on Saturday afternoon."[17] Last but not least, was the most highly regarded film society of the immediate postwar period, the Ciné-Club des Techniciens du Film—in principle, for professionals only. "Their screenings were held on Saturday morning at the Studio des Champs-Elysées, and as I recall I managed to get in on many a Saturday."[18] In the spring of 1948, he saw Alfred Hitchcock's *Rope* there for the first time.

In addition to film societies, there were specialized movie theaters, such as the Studio des Ursulines, the Salle des Agriculteurs, Studio 28, and the Champollion, that showed revivals of important films, making it possible to acquire a sound knowledge of film history. There was also a network of theaters that distributed exclusively American films. For these, you had to use cunning, evoke pity, and in some cases pilfer the booklets of tickets that were printed and distributed by the big Hollywood companies with offices in Paris. "If you succeeded in getting your hands on one of these magic booklets," Truffaut recalled, "you could get to see five American films in one week six months before they opened in Paris."[19] When the ban on American films was lifted in France, in 1946, there were about fifteen Paris movie houses—including the Caméo, the Artistic, the Vendôme, the Studio Raspail, the Broadway, and the Studio Marbeuf—where Parisian film enthusiasts could discover the Hollywood production of the past decade in English with French subtitles—Orson Welles's *Citizen Kane* and *The Magnificent Ambersons;* the films of John Huston, Howard Hawks, Preston Sturges, and William Wyler; Hitchcock's first American films; some of the most important genre films, screwball comedies, *films noirs*, thrillers, and musicals.[20]

The greatest film school of all was Henri Langlois's Cinémathèque, which Langlois resumed operating toward the end of December 1944. He created the Cercle du Cinéma (Film Circle), on rue Troyon, and showed the great American silents to a very young, often overflowing, audience. The faithful followed when the Cercle du Cinéma left rue Troyon for the theater of the Ingénieurs des Arts et Métiers on avenue Iéna; there it presented the first Eisenstein festival to sold-out audiences, on Tuesday and Wednesday evenings at 6:30 and 8:30 p.m. In October 1948, the first Musée du Cinéma opened, another incarnation of Langlois's Cinémathèque, in a mansion on avenue de Messine. The screening room could seat sixty people and squeeze in about a hundred. More often than not, people would be squeezed in. To make sure they got seats, Truffaut and Lachenay once again resorted to cunning. The easiest strategy was to hide in the toilet until the next show. Or better yet, make use of negotiating skills: By donating the most valuable and interesting still photographs in their collection to the

Musée du Cinéma, they obtained free admission, for a period of time, to the Cinémathèque.

RENOIR, WELLES, AND BRESSON

François Truffaut saw a great many films between the ages of fifteen and eighteen. Besides Sacha Guitry's *The Story of a Cheat* and Henri-Georges Clouzot's *The Raven*, which he knew shot by shot and line by line, he was greatly influenced by two other movies—Robert Bresson's *Ladies of the Park* and Jean Renoir's *The Rules of the Game*. When first released, in 1939, *The Rules of the Game* had been a commercial failure, misunderstood by the critics and the public—a severe blow for Renoir. When rereleased in 1945, it gave rise once again to heated polemics; Renoir was accused of having betrayed his art as a result of his stay in Hollywood. Truffaut saw the film twelve times in a period of several weeks; it was the great revelation of his fourteenth year. He saw Renoir as the most important filmmaker, someone who chose to remain free as a man and as an artist in the face of his detractors' conventionality and skepticism. In one of his very first essays, in April 1950, Truffaut wrote: *"The Rules of the Game* can be considered the greatest film in the history of cinema."[21]

Robert Bresson's *Ladies of the Park*, which was released in 1944, was also greeted with skepticism by the French critics; they found fault with the performances of the actors, what they called Bresson's "icy" distance, the film's cruelty, and its literary style. Truffaut led a crusade at school, in film clubs, and at the family dinner table, with varying success; for his own part, he came to believe that a film's merit often lies in an unbending determination to express feelings and passions with sobriety and simplicity, decency and restraint.

Guitry, Renoir, Bresson—at fourteen, François Truffaut had already given direction to his cinematic crusade: defending "auteur films," as he later called them. The last building block in his early education was Orson Welles's *Citizen Kane*. "This film has inspired more vocations to cinema throughout the world than any other," Truffaut wrote in 1967, in an article eloquently entitled "Citizen Kane: The Fragile Giant." "Because Welles was young and romantic, his genius seemed closer to us than the talents of the traditional American directors. . . . We loved this film absolutely because it was so complete. . . ."[22]

The film's Paris release, on July 10, 1946, at the Marbeuf, provoked the first important postwar debate among film lovers. Many critics—influenced by the harsh criticism of Jean-Paul Sartre, who had seen the film in New

York in 1945—had a negative opinion of it, either because of its literary pretensions or on account of its "expressionism." André Bazin defended the film during a stormy showing at the Colisée in the autumn of 1946 and wrote a response to Sartre in *Les Temps modernes.* "Great directors before Welles still had to perfect a technique; with this dazzling young man,"[23] technique was a given and the auteur, a true demiurge, could finally exploit it as he pleased. The days of the pioneers were over, cinema's formative years were in the past, opening a new era where technical skills no longer needed to be learned, but fully mastered to give rise to a personal style.

The plea for *Citizen Kane* represented, above all, the manifesto of a generation—that of postwar film enthusiasts in support of the new American cinema. In the French political context of the late forties, the American film industry was the greatest source of dissension among the critics. To defend Hollywood films was considered by many an unpatriotic provocation, a form of cultural dandyism that challenged the Marxist, and Marxist-oriented, left-wing culture subscribed to in intellectual circles. The young Truffaut witnessed these clashes at a time when he was still unsure where to position himself. He knew very few other film enthusiasts, and the learning process was often solitary. André Bazin was an eminent figure, as were Alexandre Astruc and Roger Leenhardt. But Truffaut was beginning to feel a growing desire to share his love of cinema.

ADVENTURES IN FILM MANIA

In October 1948, in his first public display of film enthusiasm, François Truffaut decided to start a film club—the Cercle Cinémane (the Movie Mania Circle). Robert Lachenay was appointed general secretary and manager—being eighteen, he was fully qualified to handle the finances. Truffaut reserved for himself the title of artistic director. The first step was to find a theater. Truffaut managed to convince Monsieur Marcellin, owner of the Cluny-Palace on Boulevard Saint-Germain, to rent him the theater every Sunday morning for 4,000 francs a showing. Then he solicited films from the French Cinémathèque. Henri Langlois agreed to lend him two shorts, René Clair's *Entr'acte* and Luis Buñuel's *An Andalusian Dog,* for the first showing, set for Sunday, October 31, at 10:15 a.m. Truffaut also tried to borrow a feature film, Jean Cocteau's *Blood of a Poet,* but here he came up against the Fédération française des ciné-clubs (French Federation of Film Societies), which he had refused to join or rent films from. Langlois wanted to help him and other film-loving young people free themselves of the Federation's control—he would have liked to lend out his prints free of charge, and short-circuit the official film-society network—but he could not defy the powerful Communist-influenced Federation. He felt obliged to turn down Truffaut's request for *Blood of a Poet.*

The fate of the Cercle Cinémane's inaugural screening seemed uncertain, and at the last moment, Truffaut postponed it to Sunday, November 14, in the hope of still convincing Henri Langlois. Instead, Langlois sent him a letter of warning dated November 4: "Given your love of films, allow me to inform you that you are wrong to embark in an enterprise like the one you've described to me without outside cooperation. For the disagreement between the Cinémathèque française and the Fédération française des ciné-clubs concerning the lending of films is not a question of persons or politics, but quite simply a legal impossibility that obliges the Cinémathèque, for all its desire to remain a living body, to stand passively by and not interfere in the film-society movement."[24]

Truffaut persisted in his hopes and wrote to Jean Cocteau directly, inviting him to come with his own print and introduce the film. They posted small flyers around the Cluny-Palace and distributed them in film clubs around the Saint-Michel neighborhood, announcing the screening of *Blood of a Poet* "in the director's presence" as their first event. Needless to say, this program caused a sensation, for to hear Cocteau was a great occasion. After the René Clair and Buñuel shorts were shown, the hundred or so spectators awaited Cocteau's arrival impatiently. They soon understood that they'd been tricked, and almost caused a riot. Though Truffaut and Lachenay got off without reimbursing the audience the full price of admission, their Cercle Cinémane lost much of its credibility. However, their receipts covered the price of the theater rental and even brought in a profit of nearly one thousand francs, and Monsieur Marcellin allowed them to continue the venture, audience complaints notwithstanding.

Subsequently, however, the film club's financial stability was threatened by the debts that Truffaut accumulated in paying for the weekly screenings and the rental of films. Indeed, he had reached an agreement with Monsieur Guillard, head of the film division of the French Boy Scouts and one of his father's colleagues, to rent films on credit from MGM, thereby bypassing the Fédération française. The Boy Scouts paid for the rentals on the basis of Truffaut's promise to reimburse them from his Sunday-morning box-office receipts. The same contract was drawn up with Monsieur Marcellin of the Cluny-Palace. But their debts increased—8,000 francs after the second program on Sunday, November 21, of Edmund Goulding's *White Banners* and 7,500 francs after the screening of Fred Niblo's *Ben-Hur* on November 28 . . . Truffaut was having the utmost difficulty paying for everything.

He was not helped by circumstances. Bored with his oppressive, repetitive job, he had quit the Simpère company five months earlier, at the end of June, and had used his twelve thousand francs in earned salary as start-up financing for the film club. He had since found part-time work in a book and stationery store near the theater of the Comédie-Française, a job that paid far less. He had deemed it unnecessary to inform his parents, who still believed he was employed at Simpère's, since François continued to give them part of his salary and showed them pay stubs bearing the company name. Janine and Roland Truffaut were unaware that the money came from loans, and that François had stolen the pay stubs before leaving the firm. As far as they were concerned, aside from his passion for movies, which they considered excessive, he was pursuing a normal career path and not causing too much trouble. This was hardly the case, as became clear when a typewriter mysteriously disappeared from Roland Truffaut's workplace, the offices of the French Boy Scouts on rue de la Chaussée-d'Antin. François stole it one evening in mid-September while Robert kept a lookout for the night watchman. Two days later, they sold it to Jacques Enfer,[25] an older film-buff friend, for four thousand francs, a sum that helped finance the first Cercle Cinémane screenings. But even though he sold some of his books and borrowed money from the owner of the bookstore where he worked and from Robert's grandmother, Madame Bigey, Truffaut couldn't pay off his debts.

Their November 28 screening of *Ben-Hur* was a washout. Truffaut was forced to admit as much to the Cluny's owner, pleading overwhelming competition from other film societies. Indeed, the ciné-club of Travail et Culture (Work and Culture), an association devoted to political and cultural activism, held screenings on the same day and at the same time; these were presented by André Bazin, and people flocked to every screening to hear the brilliant critic and teacher. Full of pluck, Truffaut decided to go see Bazin, determined to convince him to change the dates of his screenings.

On Tuesday, November 30, 1948, arriving at the third-floor offices of Travail et Culture, he was unaware how crucial this encounter would be for him. Bazin, an understanding and spontaneously generous man, felt an immediate sympathy for the ardent young film enthusiast. At the time of this first meeting in his grimy little office, Bazin was thirty years old; thin, slightly stooped, with a lively look in his eye, he was the figure whom young critics rallied around.[26] His articles in *Le Parisien libéré* had earned him a certain celebrity, even beyond film circles, so that this office, where he wrote up his daily notes on the movies he would be presenting at different film societies, was well frequented. For Truffaut, it would become a new film school—the place where, by chance, he would meet Alain Resnais, an active member of the Ciné-Club de la Maison des Lettres; Remo Forlani, the future radio broadcaster; Chris Marker, the young editor in chief of the newsletter *Doc*, published by the association Peuple et Culture; and Alexandre Astruc, whose mind was already on filmmaking, though he had written a noteworthy first novel, *Les Vacances,* which had been published by Gallimard in 1945, and was a regular contributor to *Les Temps modernes.* Janine Kirsch, André Bazin's future wife, worked here as well; she was the assistant to Jeanne Mathieu, head of the association's theater division. As head of Travail et Culture's film division, Bazin supported the opening of film clubs in schools and some of the big factories in Paris and the neighboring suburbs. For him, cinema was the key to educating a people recovering from the misfortunes of the war. In the period after the Liberation, the "right to equal access to culture," one of the statutes of Travail et Culture, and education for the working classes were the prime focus of many projects of political activism; hence the new interest in cinema and the messianism which both friends and detractors saw in André Bazin.

COLLARED

As soon as he emerged from the offices of Travail et Culture, Truffaut had to come back to earth, for his debts had not evaporated. Two days later, Monsieur Guillard of the French Boy Scouts complained to his colleague Roland Truffaut, who was stunned to hear that his son owed Guillard 7,850 francs. On the evening of December 2, Roland waited for François at rue de Navarin to demand a thorough explanation. In the course of an extremely tense exchange, he forced his son to confess everything. Roland agreed to forget the past, provided François gave up his ruinously expensive activities for the Cercle Cinémane and found a stable job; he made him spell out his vagaries and debts in writing: "I swear under oath that the following facts are true. I left my job at Simpère five months ago and brought home forged pay slips for purposes of deception. I sold books at the book-and-stationery store La Paix Chez Soi. I stole a typewriter from the offices of the French Boy Scouts and sold it for 4,000 francs to Jacques Enfer in September 1948. I owe money to: Monsieur Prévost, 855 francs; Madame Bigey, 10,500 francs; Monsieur Marcellin, 2,500 francs; Monsieur Guillard, 7,850 francs; La Paix Chez Soi, 2,500 francs; Chenille, 250 francs; Geneviève, 150 francs."[27] Humiliated and defeated, François signed this pitiful confession, and Roland Truffaut reimbursed each of his creditors one by one—a sum totaling 24,605 francs, the equivalent then of slightly more than a month's salary.

Whether motivated by his prior commitment (the prints had already been ordered and the publicity launched), or by recklessness, defiance, or bravado, François had programmed three other screenings for his Cercle Cinémane at the Cluny-Palace—King Vidor's *The Citadel* on December 5,

John Ford's *The Long Voyage Home* on the 8th, and finally, on the 11th, one of his favorite films, Orson Welles's *The Magnificent Ambersons.* In celebration of this final screening, François even ran an ad in *L'Ecran français,* noting that "journalists and students from the Institut des Hautes Etudes Cinématographiques [IDHEC, the famed French film school] are cordially invited." He and Lachenay went in person to the offices of MGM to pick up the prints of the Vidor and Ford films, promising to return the following day with 5,000 francs, the rental cost of the first film. They needed only about sixty spectators to cover their expenses, but on that Sunday, December 5, only about twenty people showed up. Since MGM had not been paid, on Tuesday they notified Monsieur Guillard, who passed the complaint on to Roland Truffaut. Infuriated, Roland decided to take extreme measures.

On the evening of December 7, François was nowhere in sight. However, Roland knew where to find him the following day at 5:30 p.m.—at the Cluny-Palace, just before the John Ford screening. In the foyer, where he was mingling with several friends, including Lachenay, "Roland Truffaut barged in, grabbed François by the shirt collar and dragged him away, declaring there would be no further mischief from us because we would not be seeing each other again for a long time,"[28] Lachenay wrote, recalling the scene he had tearfully witnessed. The father took his dazed son back to rue de Navarin. Janine left everything up to her husband. She had long since lost interest in her son's future, and now saw him only at mealtimes, when they often quarreled violently. Following a stormy argument, Roland Truffaut took François at the stroke of 9:00 p.m. to the closest police station, on rue Ballu. There, presenting the confession that François had signed several days earlier, Roland requested that he be placed in a center for delinquent minors. The police registered his complaint and perused the incriminating document in which the teenager had confessed to his lies, thefts, and debts. Roland Truffaut thereupon left the station, abandoning his son to police custody.

François spent the night at the station, where, to make room for three prostitutes, he was moved from the main cell to a smaller, individual one. During this transfer, he saw his friend Robert, who was trying, in vain, to plead his case. He then had to wait for the president of the court of the arrondissement to confirm his detention. All day he stayed in his cell, followed by another night on a straw mattress—thirty-two hours in the little police station a few hundred feet away from his parents' apartment.

At dawn on December 10, he and four other prisoners were driven in a van to the police headquarters on the Ile de la Cité. After undergoing the humiliating rituals of detention—registration, photos, fingerprinting, and body search—he spent another two days waiting for a decision to be made concerning his place of assignment. It was already late Saturday afternoon when he was transferred to the Paris Observation Center for Minors, in Villejuif, on avenue de la République, just beyond the Porte d'Italie. There he endured another round of humiliations—depositing his civilian clothes at the clerk's office, the loan of a uniform, dorm assignment, the first blows of a ruler administered by a monitor. Thus was François Truffaut initiated into the "paternocratic" law of the French Civil Code, whose articles 375 and 377 stipulate: "A father having grave cause for discontent with his child's behavior can have recourse to the following means of correction: . . . From sixteen to the age of legal adulthood or emancipation, a father has the right to request his child's detention for a period not exceeding six months."

JUVENILE DELINQUENT

When he arrived in Villejuif, François Truffaut was allowed to write to his parents, fully aware that all incoming and outgoing mail was opened and read by the office of the Clerk of the Court. His first letter ("Dear Daddy and Mommy") was devoid of hatred or emotion, and of a purely practical nature. He asked his parents only for a bit of jam, and his files on Charlie Chaplin and Orson Welles. Roland and Janine couldn't understand this "completely cynical absence of regret and remorse,"[29] and interpreted his coldness as a new act of defiance. As a result, they did not go to visit him in Villejuif for two months.

The Observation Center for Minors was a big building protected from the outside by tall dark walls. A large courtyard, dreary and gray, was used for the adolescents' quasi-military exercises, under the educators' supervision. The classrooms, refectory, and dormitory were all kept under surveillance, and corporal punishment, as well as psychological humiliations, was applied as deemed appropriate. The pathos of Christmas Eve would remain vivid in Truffaut's memory for a long time: "Four or five wafers, a chocolate bar, a tangerine, and no corrective blows that evening,"[30] he wrote his mother. Then, from January to the beginning of March 1949, François spent most of his time in solitary confinement. He celebrated his seventeenth birthday detained in a cell, from February 5 to 8, after attempting escape and "insulting an educator," and he was not even allowed to see his mother on her first visit, February 6. After that, he had to go into the infirmary, since blood tests made several days after his arrival in Villejuif showed he had syphilis—probably from visits to the whorehouse on rue de Navarin or other encounters in his already-active sexual life. In the postwar period, syphilis—with its undermining cankers, which in extreme cases could lead to paralysis and death—was still a relatively common disease. But since the early forties, thanks to penicillin, it had been far easier to cure. Truffaut was admitted into the infirmary on January 11 for his first weeklong stay. The treatment consisted of seven injections a day, every three hours, starting at six o'clock in the morning. This visit was followed by another two stays, one at the end of January and the other from February 28 to March 5. Soon he began to measure time in terms of his injections: "I was injected 38 times in 6 days, and I'd like to receive Jacques Prévert's *Paroles* before the next 38, which are to take place in the near future. With my books, it's more tolerable,"[31] he wrote his mother on March 8.

Over the course of three months François wrote some ten letters to his parents, begging for eyeglasses or complaining of the cold, requesting books, or news of his close friends and relatives, looking for ways to bear the loneliness and the bullying. "I read, I sleep, I eat, I live, in three-hour slices between each shot, on my tummy, for the nurse has turned my august buttocks into a painful sieve,"[32] he wrote his mother on February 28. His spirits were low; he seemed resigned and bitter, as can be seen from this short melancholy note written on the day after his birthday: "I have no choice but to keep living for another four or five months in the Center before being transferred to a farm or professional training school until I am eighteen, or, if you don't take me back at eighteen and I don't want to enlist, until I am twenty-one."[33]

However, thanks to the complicity of Mademoiselle Rikkers, the institution's psychologist, Truffaut wrote more freely to his friend Lachenay, flaring up angrily against repression and lack of understanding. In mid-January of 1949, he wrote Robert a veritable good-bye letter, tragic and romantic, signed "François-Jean Vigo": "I'm reminded of Jean Vigo, whom you used to allude to whenever I coughed too much or lost my breath climbing up your five flights of stairs; though I have one or several points in common with Jean Vigo—or soon will have—I'm sure I'll die before I have time to make a *Zero in Conduct*. I'm also reminded of Raymond Radiguet, though I know I won't have time to live and write *The Devil in the Flesh*." And he concludes with the wrenching comment, "I'm going to die, I'm sure of it."[34] In his moments of deepest despair, Truffaut clung to the books, novels, journals, and magazines he had received from his mother, Lachenay, and his friend Claude Thibaudat, and from Chenille, a former classmate whose parents ran a stationery store on rue de Navarin.

Meanwhile, he stood trial in the beginning of February. This was not a simple matter, for during his cross-examination François confessed to a number of additional thefts and loans. Roland Truffaut had paid off most of his son's debts, with part of the savings he had set aside for his next expedition up Kilimanjaro. He tried in every way possible to dissuade creditors from demanding payment or lodging complaints: "My son is in the hands of the law since December 8 and I know nothing concerning your bills," he wrote, for instance, to *L'Ecran français* when they demanded to be paid for the ads François had placed. "I'm taking the liberty of warning you against this fly-by-night Cercle Cinémane founded without my knowledge, and I would be grateful if you would cancel any orders or requests for service under that name which you might receive. I feel I should also warn you that since my son's arrest, some of his friends might have used the name to place orders." Though Roland's colleague Monsieur Guillard had refrained from lodging a complaint, there was still another problem in François's file, concerning the typewriter theft. A lawyer, Maurice Bertrand, had been assigned, and François had confessed. The court judge for the ninth arrondissement had to rule on all these points—acknowledged debts paid by the father and thefts confessed to by the son. He proved to be rather lenient, sentencing Roland Truffaut to pay a 12,000-franc fine on behalf of his son, and ordering that François be placed in a home after his release from Villejuif, until he reached his majority or age of legal independence, with the possibility of part-time outside employment if he found an employer.

Still, Truffaut did find some small consolations during his detention. Because he was cultivated and engaging when he opened up, several adults in the correctional institution and the judiciary took an interest in his case. Raymond Clarys, director of the Villejuif Observation Center, grew fond of him in spite of his misdemeanors, and brought François a regular supply of newspapers and movie magazines. There was the all-important Mademoiselle Rikkers, the "spychogist," as Antoine Doinel would call her in *The 400 Blows.* She met with him for several long conversations and played a decisive role in improving his legal situation; soon the initial diagnosis—"psychomotor instability with perverse tendencies"—was dropped and replaced by a detailed portrait of a youth "using repeated lies to escape" a family environment and an emotional situation that the psychologist saw as "traumatizing."[35] Her fondness for him was such that she met with his parents and his close friends, such as Lachenay, to help speed up his release. Then, in March 1949, she contacted André Bazin and requested his intercession on her young patient's behalf. Though Bazin hardly knew François at the time, he went to see Mademoiselle Rikkers at her home on rue du Pot-de-Fer. Not only did he agree to vouch for François; he promised to find him a job at Travail et Culture. Mademoiselle Rikkers agreed to continue monitoring François's progress after his release. Thanks to all these guarantees, the judge decided to place François Truffaut in a religious home in Versailles three months before his scheduled release. On March 18, 1949, the seventeen-year-old youth was granted semifreedom.

I DON'T GAZE AT THE SKY FOR LONG

On the morning of March 18, 1949, François Truffaut was taken to the Guynemer home, on rue Sainte-Sophie, in Versailles. A religious boarding school under the authority of the Seine-et-Oise Association familiale et sociale, its regulations were strict, though less restrictive than those of the Villejuif Observation Center. The nuns of the Notre-Dame parish were an improvement over the Villejuif educators, though Truffaut would not have fond memories of the dormitory, the attendance checks, the strict schedules, and the prayers preceding meals.

François still bore the psychological marks of his recent ordeals. This is clear from the essay he wrote for his literature teacher at the boys' day school he attended on boulevard de la Reine in Versailles. The assignment was to "describe the most beautiful or saddest adventure in your life." Truffaut approached the theme existentially, describing his whole life as a "sad adventure." His despair is expressed in simple, logical language, devoid of ornament and as naked as a prison wall: "My life, or rather my slice of life to this day, has been banal to the utmost. I was born on February 6, 1932; today is March 21, 1949, therefore I'm 17 years 1 month and 15 days old. I've eaten almost every day and slept almost every night; I think I've worked too much and haven't had very many satisfactions or joys. My Christmases and birthdays have all been ordinary and disappointing. I had no particular feelings about the war or the morons who took part in it. I like the Arts and particularly the movies; I consider that work is a necessary evil like excreting, and that any person who likes his work doesn't know how to live. I don't like adventures and have avoided them. Three films a day, three books a week and records of great music would be enough to make me happy to the day I die, which will surely occur one day soon and which I egoistically dread. My parents are no more than human beings to me; it is mere chance that they happen to be my father and mother, which is why they mean no more to me than strangers. I don't believe in friendship, and I don't believe in peace either. I try to stay out of trouble, far from anything that causes too much of a stir. For me, politics is merely a flourishing industry and politicians intelligent crooks. This sums up my adventure; it is neither gay nor sad; it is life. I don't gaze at the sky for long, for when I look back down again the world seems horrid to me."[36]

Yet François Truffaut had decided to struggle and pull through. He tried to adapt to the supervised schooling, though eventually his rebellious streak would reassert itself. In the beginning of August he would be punished for "leading a big disorderly outbreak into which he had dragged three of his younger classmates," resulting in broken windowpanes and insulted teachers. On September 13, 1949, the director of the home would write Roland Truffaut that "unfortunately" his son was "a bad influence" and he was obliged to expel him.[37] On September 17, Roland Truffaut would have to sign a check in the amount of 19,860 francs to pay for damages, room and board, and accumulated debts. His expedition to the Kilimanjaro was once again postponed.

François's extremely tense return home hastened his falling-out with his mother. He took everything out on her and blamed her directly, while appealing to Roland for understanding and trust. Yet, though Janine Truffaut had gone to see François infrequently in Villejuif and Versailles, and had stayed only very briefly each time, making him feel she visited him out of pure obligation, Roland had never gone to see him at all. But therein was the family paradox—in the inversion of symbolic roles. The revelation of his adoption, instead of estranging Truffaut from his substitute father, brought him closer to a man whom he considered basically kind, although weak— weak in being too much in love with his wife. It was his mother whom he now hated and resented. He confided his intimate feelings to Roland, on April 2, 1949: "Dear Daddy, the reason I'm divulging my sorrows to you is that, contrary to what you think, you're the one I trust. I did not, as you believe, feel estranged from you by discovering my filiation. Though it estranged me from Mom, it brought me closer to you. Indeed, before knowing the truth, I suspected there was something abnormal in my family situation and I even thought that though you were my real father, Mom wasn't my real mother. I believed this for a long time for your behavior and mother's confirmed this idea. This is why I was shattered to learn that the opposite was true. But psychologically you're still my real daddy and Mom a stepmother. She may not be an evil stepmother but she's not a mother either. . . . In my new life, I want to make you my confidant and tell you all my little problems."[38]

Roland Truffaut felt obliged to show this letter to his wife. François felt betrayed. His divisive strategy further exacerbated Janine's hostility. The April 2 letter had been a result of growing animosity. Janine, aiming for his most sensitive spot, had blamed all his troubles on Robert Lachenay, "the evil genie" who had led his younger friend down the path of truancy, financial irresponsibility, and even debauchery. According to her, not only had Robert taken François to prostitutes but the two boys had had a homosexual relationship at the elder's initiative, "which could be clearly proved through medical analyses and tests on the syphilis strain,"[39] she had written him in stinging terms. Deeply hurt by this accusation, François had defended himself as best he could, pleading complete awareness and maturity, and argued for a second medical assessment: "I will forestall any medical inquiry," he had written his parents on March 27, 1949, "by expressly requesting from Mademoiselle Rikkers a medical exam for Robert Lachenay to dispel all suspicions in that area. By the way, speaking of him, I should tell you that your ideas about him are completely wrong. He is a much more scrupulous boy than I and he never would have done half of what I did. Furthermore, he was an excellent friend since, to help with the film club and my debts, he didn't hesitate to sell a bound set of Buffon's complete works and lots of other books."[40]

These exchanges, filled with suspected betrayals, hatred, and libelous accusations, provoked a quasi-definitive rift between François and his parents. He yearned for his complete independence, which he would obtain a year later, on March 10, 1950, a month after his eighteenth birthday, when Roland Truffaut signed a declaration granting him legal emancipation.[41] François then became free, released from parental guardianship, but his freedom was founded on a family trauma that would forever leave its mark and occasionally show its deep effects in the coming years.

In reform school, in Versailles, his freedom was relative; he was penniless, had no clothes, and wore shoes with holes. But on Thursdays and Sundays, he could borrow the gardener's bicycle and get to Paris in an hour: "It was beautiful weather and I raced like a madman," he wrote to Lachenay in April 1949. "I went to see Madame Duminy and Claude Thibaudat, on rue des Martyrs. As I approached the house, which I had not seen for four months, I pictured a cold welcome and reproaches, which is why, on Place Pigalle, I continued along the same road down the boulevards and decided to go see an assistant director friend who lives at La Chapelle. At his mother's insistence, I ate at their house, and in the afternoon I left the bicycle there and we went to see Bazin at Travail et Culture, on rue des Beaux-Arts. We wrote to Jacques Becker. I've started to look for work. Mademoiselle Rikkers, the psychologist whom I go to every Sunday, is also looking into it."[42] Paris belonged to him once again.

UPSETTING THE APPLECART

François Truffaut again devoted his free moments to cinema. In Versailles, he helped Abbé Yves Renaud—French teacher, film enthusiast, and friend of André Bazin—in programming the day school's film club. As for Bazin, he did not forget his promise to find work for his young protégé. He appointed François as his personal secretary at Travail et Culture, a job that did not pay very much, only about 3,000 francs a month, but which helped convince the judge to allow François to live on his own in Paris. To fully enjoy "his new life," he had to find a room to live in. He had suffered too much in Villejuif and Versailles to want to return to those places; he preferred "to live on 200 francs a day and tighten my belt,"[43] as he wrote to his father. Roland, who had given him a stern warning that if he got the least bit into debt or if Roland heard the least complaint, he would "strike back, without any compunction,"[44] agreed to make a last effort. Starting in September 16, 1949, he rented a room for him on the fifth floor of a building on rue des Martyrs, at 1,500 francs a month.

Thanks to André Bazin, François attended the meetings of the film society Objectif 49, a gathering place of artists, writers, students, and Parisian critics. Founded by the advocates of the new criticism—Bazin, Astruc, Kast, Doniol-Valcroze, Bourgeois, Tacchella, and Claude Mauriac—and benefiting from the sponsorship of such filmmakers and writers as Jean Cocteau, Robert Bresson, René Clément, Jean Grémillon, Raymond Queneau, and Roger Leenhardt, Objectif 49 showed its members only new, unreleased films. An exclusive but highly influential club (those "snobs,"[45] as the Communist filmmaker Louis Daquin called them in *L'Ecran français*), Objectif 49 was launched by the big premiere of Jean Cocteau's *Les Parents terribles* (*The Storm Within*) at the Studio des Champs-Elysées. Cocteau brought his prestigious literary backing to the club and played a crucial role in coordinating plans and initiatives. Truffaut met him for the first time in the offices of Objectif 49.

It was the beginning of the Cold War, with tensions running high in intellectual circles, and film criticism was divided along political lines. The Communists had taken over *L'Ecran français* and thrown out Bazin, who was probably considered a "Catholic leftist." In addition, Jean George Auriol's *La Revue du cinéma*, whose contributors included Bazin, Doniol-Valcroze, Astruc, and Kast, filed for bankruptcy after being dropped by its publisher, Gaston Gallimard. Objectif 49 became the forum of the new criticism. Its screenings were jam-packed, and important filmmakers came to present their work—among them, Roberto Rossellini, Orson Welles, William Wyler, Preston Sturges, Roger Leenhardt, Jean Grémillon, and René Clément. Encouraged by their success, the organizers of Objectif 49 decided to create a festival, which they hoped could rival Cannes: the Festival indépendant du Film Maudit (Independent Festival of the Accursed Film) in Biarritz.

The first festival took place in late July 1949. Naturally, Bazin, a key figure in the movement, insisted that his young personal secretary join him; so Truffaut boarded the night train at the Gare d'Austerlitz on the evening of July 29. Penniless, he could not afford a berth and traveled in discomfort amid the noise and heat. The morning of July 30, he wrote Robert Lachenay a postcard: "Dear old pal, trip dreadful, weather so-so. The festival opens tonight with Marcello Pagliero's *La Nuit porte conseil*. Cocteau has arrived. Photos and more photos, the beach is straight out of Jean Vigo, with framings straight out of Hathaway, a depth of field out of Welles, and perspectives out of Fritz Lang. Will write long letter on Tuesday. I'm almost broke. François Toréador."[46] Put up, like a great number of young festivalgoers, at the dormitory of the Biarritz Lycée, Truffaut was caught up in the slightly mad, eccentric ambiance and the all-night festivities—such as the costume ball on August 2, an "Accursed night" organized by Alexandre Astruc and Marc Doelnitz, near a place called the Lac de la Négresse (Lake of the Negress). To get in, Truffaut had even bought himself a bow tie, but he found the atmosphere too social and fashionable: "The festival is unfolding quietly with no great surprises," he confided to his friend Lachenay. "To my great amazement, Cocteau recognized me because of bow tie and Bazin, but he gains nothing from being approached, in fact no more so than Grémillon or Claude Mauriac. The town is horrible and so are the inhabitants and the tourists, but Bazin is very well liked for his film presentations and discussions."[47]

Fortunately, the four films he saw every day took up most of his time. A group of young film enthusiasts was formed during some of the special screenings (the long version of Vigo's *L'Atalante,* shown for the first time; the preview of Welles's *The Lady from Shanghai;* or the European premiere of Renoir's American film *The Southerner*) and during the nocturnal discussions in the Lycée dormitory—a group that would soon be talked about: Truffaut, of course, as well as Jacques Rivette, Claude Chabrol, Charles Bitsch, Jean Douchet, and several others. Eric Rohmer, who was also in Biarritz and was the eldest in the group, vividly remembers meeting François Truffaut there for the first time, and how he was introduced to him, with a big wink, as Bazin's secretary. These radical and insolent young people made it a point of honor to dissociate themselves from Objectif 49; they spent their time denigrating the way the festival was organized, though those in charge were critic friends who were better established than they were, like Bazin and Doniol-Valcroze. This polemical spirit was what bound the group of film enthusiasts together, as did their common passion for actresses and filmmakers like Gloria Grahame and Ingrid Bergman, Alfred Hitchcock and Fritz Lang.

When he returned to Paris in the late summer of 1949, Truffaut lived through his most intense period as a film enthusiast. His loneliness and troubles were over; he was now part of a group. Others joined the clique from the Biarritz dormitory—Jean-Luc Godard, Suzanne Klochendler (soon Schiffman), Jean Gruault, Paul Gégauff, Alain Jeannel, Louis Marcorelles, Jean-José Richer, and Jean-Marie Straub. They assembled at the weekly screenings of the main Paris film societies. On Tuesdays, they met at the Studio Parnasse, where Jean-Louis Chéray led the discussions with energy and passion, ending with a film quiz that entitled the winner to a free

1. François Truffaut. *I had to read in silence . . .*

2. ABOVE: Roland and Janine Truffaut.
The great injustice has been redressed
by a man with a noble heart . . . (Bernard
de Monferrand).
3. LEFT: François on vacation with his father,
Roland Truffaut.
4. BELOW: François Truffaut and his grandmother, Geneviève de Monferrand, in 1939.

5. RIGHT: François Truffaut with his paternal grandmother in Juvisy. *Vacations were usually spent at the edge of the road watching the cars leave for the weekend.*
6. BELOW: Class portrait at the school on rue Milton in 1944. François Truffaut is seated in the first row, third from left. In the same row, at far right, is his friend Claude Thibaudat (who later made a career as Claude Vega). *Good little student, though occasionally a bit talkative . . .* (report card).

7. TOP: Weekend in Fontainebleau. *From left:*
François, Roland, and Janine Truffaut. *My son
François will never understand anything about
mountaineering . . .* (Roland Truffaut).

8. CENTER: François's film society membership
card.

9. RIGHT: I.O.U., December 8, 1948.

10. OPPOSITE: François Truffaut and Robert
Lachenay on Boulevard Saint-Michel, in 1948.
We had joined forces to resist . . . (Robert
Lachenay).

11. ABOVE: Jean-Pierre Léaud in *The 400 Blows:*
Antoine Doinel as a juvenile delinquent.
12. RIGHT: Notebook containing the first draft of
the screenplay for *The 400 Blows.*

13. ABOVE: Self-portrait by Truffaut, showing him handcuffed between two soldiers.
14. LEFT: François Truffaut in 1951. *A self-hating autodidact.*

15. LEFT: Paris, 1952: François Truffaut, free at last . . .

16. ABOVE: André Bazin, Truffaut's spiritual father. *A man of conscience . . .*

CAHIERS

DU CINÉMA

Nº 1 • REVUE DU CINÉMA ET DE TÉLÉCINÉMA • AVRIL 1951

17. ABOVE: François Truffaut and Jacques Doniol-Valcroze
at *Cahiers du cinéma*.
18. LEFT: *Cahiers du cinéma*, April 1951, number 1.
19. BELOW: First polemical essay: *A Certain Tendency of
the French Cinema* . . .

UNE CERTAINE TENDANCE
DU CINEMA FRANÇAIS

par François Truffaut

Jean Aurenche

« On peut aimer que le sens du mot art soit
tenté de donner conscience à des hommes
de la grandeur qu'ils ignorent en eux. »
André Malraux
(Le Temps du Mépris, préface).

Ces notes n'ont pas d'autre objet qu'essayer de définir une certaine tendance
du cinéma français — tendance dite du réalisme psychologique — et d'en
esquisser les limites.

DIX OU DOUZE FILMS...

Si le cinéma français existe par une centaine de films chaque année, il est
bien entendu que dix ou douze seulement méritent de retenir l'attention des
critiques et des cinéphiles, l'attention donc de ces Cahiers.
Ces dix ou douze films constituent ce que l'on a joliment appelé la *Tradition
de la Qualité*, ils forcent par leur ambition l'admiration de la presse étrangère,
défendent deux fois l'an les couleurs de la France à Cannes et à Venise où, depuis
1946, ils râflent assez régulièrement médailles, lions d'or et grands prix.

★

Au début du parlant, le cinéma français fut l'honnête démarquage du cinéma
américain. Sous l'influence de *Scarface* nous faisions l'amusant *Pépé le Moko*.
Puis le scénario français dut à Prévert le plus clair de son évolution, *Quai des
Brumes* reste le chef-d'œuvre de l'école dite du *réalisme poétique*.
La guerre et l'après-guerre ont renouvelé notre cinéma. Il a évolué sous
l'effet d'une pression interne et au réalisme poétique — dont on peut dire
qu'il mourut en refermant derrière lui *Les Portes de la Nuit* — s'est substitué
le *réalisme psychologique*, illustré par Claude Autant-Lara, Jean Delannoy,
René Clément, Yves Allégret et Marcel Pagliero.

20. LEFT, ABOVE: The critic at work, 1959.
21. RIGHT, ABOVE: François Truffaut and Max Ophuls. *I have the feeling, though I can't explain why, that you will become someone important.* (Max Ophuls).
22. LEFT: Truffaut and Jean Cocteau on the set of *Testament of Orpheus* in 1960.
23. BELOW: François Truffaut and Jean Renoir.

24. TOP: Madeleine and François Truffaut's wedding,
October 29, 1957, in Paris.
25. CENTER, LEFT: Truffaut with his mother, Janine, on the
day of his wedding.
26. CENTER, RIGHT: Madeleine and François Truffaut, with
Rossellini, a witness at their marriage.
27. RIGHT: The family at La Colombe d'or: François,
Madeleine, Éva, and Laura.

28. LEFT: Truffaut with Bernadette Lafont and Gérard Blain, the lead actors in *The Mischief Makers*.
29. BELOW: Summer 1957, shooting *The Mischief Makers* in Nîmes: Truffaut, Claude de Givray, Bernadette Lafont.
30. BOTTOM: The last day of the shoot of *The 400 Blows* on the beach.

31. LEFT: Jean-Pierre Léaud and Madeleine and François Truffaut, May 4, 1959, in Cannes, just before the screening of *The 400 Blows.*
32. BELOW: The front page of *Arts:* Jacques Audiberti's article on *The 400 Blows.*
33. BOTTOM: *Clockwise, from left:* The actress Claire Maurier (Antoine Doinel's mother), Cocteau, Truffaut, Albert Rémy (Doinel's father), the American actor Edward G. Robinson, and Jean-Pierre Léaud.

Samedi 3 sept 1960

mon
François

Ton film
est un
chef d'oeuvre,
une manière de
prodige
et j'
t'embrasse
Jean
*

34. ABOVE: Truffaut, Charles Aznavour, and Marie
Dubois on the set of *Shoot the Piano Player*.
35. RIGHT: A Cocteau drawing with an inscription in
praise of Truffaut.
36. BELOW: Hitchcock's telegram to Truffaut.

F602/WLA252

WEST LOS ANGELES CALIF 107 1/52 11 308P PDT

LT
MR FRANCOIS TRUFFAUT 25 RUE QUENTIN BAUCHART PARIS

CHER MONSIEUR TRUFFAUT VOTRE LETTRE MA FAIT VENIR LES LARMES AUX YEUX
ET COMBIEN JE SUIS RECONNAISSANT DE RECEVOIR UN TEL TRIBUT DE VOTRE
PART STOP JE SUIS TOUJOUR EN TRAIN DE TOURNER THE BIRDS ET CELA CONTINUES
JUSQUAU 15 JUILLET STOP APRES

F602/WLA252 2/55
CELA JE DEVRAI COMMENCER LE MONTAGE CMA CE QUI PRENDPA QUELQUES
SEMAINES STOP JE PENSE QUE JATTENDRAI QUE LE TOURNAGE SUR THE
BIRDS SOIT TERMINE ET JE ME METTRAI ALORSEN CONTACT AVEC VOUS
AVEC LIDEE DE NOUS RENCONTRER VERS LA FIN AOUT STOP MERCI ENCORE
POUR VOTRE CHARMANTE LETTRE SINCERES AMITIES CORDIALEMENT VOTRE
    ALFRED HITCHCOCK

37. François Truffaut, Alfred Hitchcock, and Helen Scott, in August 1962, during their interview sessions.
38. Truffaut and Helen Scott.

39. Hitchcock and Truffaut, 1962.

entrance ticket. Thursdays were reserved for the Ciné-Club du Quartier Latin, where the key figure was Maurice Schérer. Thirty years old in 1950, with a stern appearance, schoolboyish and deadpan, Schérer taught French at the Lycée Lakanal in Sceaux and signed his articles on cinema with the pseudonym Eric Rohmer. He used his Thursday afternoon screenings to teach film aesthetics. He was also editor in chief of the monthly *Bulletin du C.C.Q.L.* (Ciné-Club du Quartier Latin), first issued in January 1950. The young film enthusiasts regarded Rohmer as a kind of older brother and addressed him with the polite *vous* form to show their respect. "He was honest, upright, very professorial. He always lent us a bit of money when we were broke, but in exchange you had to give him a receipt, anything from a used métro ticket to a train ticket, or a grocery-store bill,"[48] his friend Paul Gégauff later wrote.

The other evenings of the week were spent at the Artistic, at the Cinéac-Ternes, at Langlois's Cinémathèque, at the Reflets, or at the Broadway. The screenings were followed by endless discussions and wanderings in the streets of Paris with Jacques Rivette and Charles Bitsch. "As soon as we had walked one of us to his door," Bitsch recalled, "we would start walking the second one to his door, and then we'd resolve to walk the third to his door. And so on and so forth, until fatigue and thirst would drive us into one of the cafés that were still open at that ungodly hour, which inevitably made us go back to our favorite neighborhood, between the Place Clichy and the Place Pigalle. Rested, refreshed, and even giddier from talk, we would resume our rounds until morning."[49]

Jacques Rivette had come to Paris at the beginning of 1949 from Rouen, his native city, to take courses at the Sorbonne. He was barely twenty-one, and he had a distinct preference for film screenings over university lecture halls. Thin, with an emaciated face, lively and passionate, he already lived ascetically and with minimal resources. "He looked like the Cheshire cat in *Alice in Wonderland*," Claude Chabrol recalled. "He was tiny. Hardly visible. He seemed not to eat. When he smiled, he disappeared completely behind his magnificent teeth, which made him no less ferocious."[50] Rivette was the group's conscience and spokesman, and as such, he would leave a deep mark on Truffaut, incarnating an opinion and film judgment for which he would have the highest respect. "Rivette was the great talker," Jean Douchet later remarked. "He was the group's secret soul, the occult thinker, a bit of a censor. In fact we called him 'Father Joseph.' His judgment was always very abrupt, very contradictory, he never hesitated to burn what he had adored."[51] Nicknamed "Carolus" by his young companions, Charles Bitsch had an entirely different personality. He was the faithful follower, someone to confide in, always ready to give a helping hand. His father ran a bistro on Place du Palais-Royal, directly opposite the Comédie-Française, where the group often gathered around a table with some drinks and discussed films.

François Truffaut's entry into this crowded, hectic scene of Paris film enthusiasts[52] upset the applecart. The youngest of the group, he was considered a troublemaker. "In the beginning, for about six months, we couldn't take him seriously, he was too bruised,"[53] Chabrol said, a remark confirmed by Gruault: "Let's admit it, François's aggressiveness, his state of perpetual agitation, like a crazed mosquito, got on our nerves."[54] The first thing that struck everyone was Truffaut's physical appearance. Short, five feet four, he had a lively, thin, almost skinny body. He was excitable and had quick, jerky gestures and a dark, piercing gaze. He exuded intensity and elation, in contrast to the photos of him from that period; in these, he is often striking a pose, so that one sees a presentable young man, sometimes smoking a pipe and smiling behind a pair of obtrusive, heavy glasses—for Truffaut was nearsighted, having only 4/10 vision in each eye.

Younger, more rebellious, and more impecunious than the others, Truffaut had to prove himself before being adopted by the small, closed, demanding circle of film enthusiasts. This required time—time to see more films, subdue his impulsiveness, and gain self-confidence in discussions, as well as time to work and write. One of his outstanding qualities was his great capacity for work. He was surely one of the most faithful members of the audience at the Cinémathèque screenings—along with Rivette, Douchet, Godard, and Suzanne Klochendler—and also one of the most diligent: He had a mania for making files and clipping articles, for devouring the specialized press and taking abundant notes. Though he lacked Rivette's ease in speech and writing, or Godard's intuition, his most important asset at the beginning of his career was this scholarly labor, which was evident in his very first essays. Truffaut began as a typical Eric Rohmer disciple, since his first two film reviews were accepted by the *Bulletin du C.C.Q.L.* and published in the spring of 1950. The first describes René Clair's visit to the film club and is a straightforward account by a habitué. The second, a month later, discusses *The Rules of the Game* at great length. Since he had seen the film twelve times by then, when he saw the uncut version, he was able to spot thirteen new scenes and four new shots—precious pearls that he listed learnedly in a column of the *Bulletin*. "Thanks to these thirteen scenes, thanks to Renoir, it was a wonderful evening,"[55] he wrote in conclusion. Far from making a sensational entrance into the world of criticism, Truffaut entered discreetly, combining precision and modesty, as though he wanted to erase the memory of his first months as an embarrassing troublemaker. An eighteen-year-old autodidact under the friendly patronage of Rohmer—whom he soon felt he could nickname *"le grand Momo,"* taking inspiration from Rohmer's real first name (Maurice)—Truffaut learned to train his eyes and write. Working relentlessly, he would not be long in finding his own personal style.

LOVE AT THE CINÉMATHÈQUE

On his own at last, François Truffaut was living in a room on rue des Martyrs, in the heart of his childhood neighborhood. But he had difficulty adjusting and making ends meet, for his salary from Travail et Culture grew more and more irregular. Bazin was no longer in good graces. The Cold War was raging and the Communists, who controlled the association, looked disapprovingly upon this left-winger who had had the pluck to denounce the "Stalin myth" in the journal *Esprit*. In January 1950, Bazin suffered an acute attack of tuberculosis and had to leave Paris for over a year to take a cure in a sanitarium in the Alps. Truffaut, who hadn't been paid since Christmas 1949, had to resign.

That same January, Robert Lachenay found him a job as an acetylene welder in a factory in Pontault-Combault, in the Seine-et-Marne, a half hour from Paris by bus, "a place which was miles from anywhere, with a church, two hotels, a few farms and a population of around 2,000."[56] There was very little here to delight a young Parisian film enthusiast, except for the prospect of a regular salary. Indeed, the work was exhausting, but well paid—almost twelve thousand francs a month. But then came some bad news—Lachenay was being sent to Germany for his military service. Deprived of his childhood friend and Bazin, Truffaut would once again be alone. On New Year's Day, 1950, they threw a going-away party for the future soldier at the home of a girl Robert was madly in love with. François, too, was in love with his date that night, Mireille G., an ardent film lover, clever and pretty, slightly older than he. The two had been living together for three weeks, in the room on rue de Martyrs, the first lasting relationship in Truffaut's love life.

Work at the Pontault-Combault factory was strenuous—ten hours of welding a day. But then came the first paycheck, on January 18, 1950: 5,748 francs. The very next day, his day off, Truffaut attended the 4:00 p.m. screening at the Cinémathèque. It was on that day, after having watched her and hesitated for a long time, that he first spoke to Liliane Litvin, a young aficionada of the Cinémathèque. As an excuse to speak to her, he used the book by Hervé Bazin that was tucked under her arm; this led to a lively conversation and the promise to meet again at a forthcoming screening on avenue de Messine. This meeting turned François's life upside down. He decided not to return to the factory. His constant wish was to see Liliane, not realizing that he wasn't the only young man courting her. Jean Gruault and Jean-Luc Godard were also captivated by the young girl, whom Gruault later described as "a gang leader with a very lively personality, petite, slightly plump, with a round face, and light brown, very curly hair."[57] Charting her love life with virtuoso skill, the fickle Liliane set up separate dates with each one of her suitors at the Cinémathèque. They also took turns calling at the Litvins' home, which was in the seventeenth arrondissement. Liliane's stepfather was a garage owner, her mother cooked excellent kosher meals, and both parents were sociable and talkative. Jean-Luc, Jean, and François were warmly welcomed for lunch or dinner. Each one paid discreet court to the girl and her parents, and caught the occasional television broadcast at their house—a rare treat in Paris in 1950. They discussed literature to impress both mother and daughter, the latter a great admirer of André Gide. Truffaut knew Gide's work almost as thoroughly as he knew Balzac's, but to no avail: Liliane would give herself to none of them.

Of the three suitors, Truffaut was the one who took this platonic romantic relationship most to heart, alternating between joy and despair, with fits of jealousy and rage, while Liliane considered him only a friend. "Normally I shouldn't be in love with her. Each time we have a serious discussion, she laughs. All the same, I wait for hours in front of her door, freezing my balls off,"[58] he wrote in his journal. Later that June, after four months of ups and downs, Truffaut would take a daring step; he would move into a hotel directly across the street from the Litvins, on rue Dulong, so he could spy on Liliane. Delighted, Liliane would visit his room, even taking her parents there, but she still would resist throwing herself into this love quadrille with Gruault, Godard, and Truffaut. In the meantime, during the spring and summer of 1950, Truffaut had countless liaisons—with Mireille, Madeleine, Janine, Gisèle, Geneviève, Monique, and Charlotte. But Liliane Litvin "still remained as elusive as Proust's Albertine."[59] Truffaut would retain a taste for concurrent relationships, happy and unhappy, for a long time to come. Each woman was not only lovable but essential because different. *The Man Who Loved Women* was probably born in that spring of 1950; Truffaut had just turned eighteen.

Without his salary as an apprentice welder, Truffaut found himself penniless at the end of January 1950. Lachenay, though no longer present, had left him his room, which François had rented to a friend for 1,880 francs a month. And he earned a bit of money helping Rohmer contact film distributors, carry reels, and edit the *Bulletin du C.C.Q.L.*, but not enough to live on. So he borrowed small sums here and there, three hundred francs or so. Then, in the beginning of March, he sold off half of Robert's library to a bookseller for three thousand francs. This infuriated his "dear old soldier," causing the first real quarrel between the two friends.

THE CLUB DU FAUBOURG

Probably to impress Liliane Litvin, Truffaut started going to the prestigious Club du Faubourg. Founded in 1917, this old institution welcomed inquisitive minds, enthusiasts, journalists, and the Paris smart set three times a week (in the late afternoon, Tuesday, Thursday, and Saturday) to meet and discuss recent shows, books, and social issues or to attend debates between writers. Every year, at the end of June, the Faubourg organized an eloquence competition; the qualifying contests held throughout the season were very popular events. Liliane's parents attended on Tuesdays, for the meetings were at the Villiers-Cinéma, not far from their house. During the week of February 27 to March 3, 1950, Truffaut participated in a discussion on gangster films and another on the Festival du Film Maudit. Though at first confining himself to cinema, he soon ventured easily into literature, or subjects he knew from personal experience, such as the competence of juvenile judges. François Truffaut felt at ease, for his talent was recognized. His ardor and competence impressed the club's habitués, among them Aly Khan, the fabulously wealthy playboy; Armand Piéral, a writer and the literary editor at Laffont; and the actor Jean Servais. Léo Poldès, the club's director, was also impressed, as was Marc Rucart, a senator and former minister, one of the many politicians who attended the gatherings there. On December 26, 1950, he wrote to Truffaut:

> Be assured of my esteem since the day I first saw you speak at the Club du Faubourg. This esteem stems from the courage you seemed to have, the clarity of your talks and "objections"; and from the fact that you spoke as if you were twenty years older than you are. Of course, you almost always shocked me, as you shocked nearly the whole audience. . . . Rightly or wrongly, you took pleasure in rising up against those who seemed stronger, more experienced, or older than you; and in the fear that people would think you incapable of further "plunging into the fray," you used the words most likely to offend and to provoke indignation. This was the mark of an inferiority complex that had to be overcome at all costs, a need for preventive attacks, an expression of your youthful rebellion against the less youthful, a manifestation of your ruthless opposition to all forms of conformism and traditionalism. Not being one to judge by results, I suspected the causes for your atti-

tude. I never learned what these were, but my suppositions strengthened my esteem, and gave rise to my sympathy, and even to a tender curiosity.[60]

During the spring of 1950, Truffaut thereby became the Club du Faubourg's mascot, and he attracted a growing list of admirers, many of whom were writers or aristocrats. Hence, Louise de Vilmorin, Aimée Alexandre, and the Countess du Pasthy would be his three benefactresses for a long time to come. The first, a well-known writer, the author of *Madame de . . .* , was a friend of Cocteau and André Malraux, and her salon at Château de Verrières-le-Buisson was renowned. Aimée Alexandre was Russian, a writer and a disciple of Bachelard. Following a brilliant presentation by Truffaut, she sent him the following note, echoing Rucart's impression: "My dear, delightful friend, you've suffered and struggled so much that your mental age is at least double your physical age. And I'm convinced that one day you'll become a marshal without having been a corporal."[61] Aimée Alexandre would remain one of François Truffaut's confidantes until her death, in the early seventies. As for Countess du Pasthy, a great collector of valuable objects, she wrote Léo Poldès a letter filled with affection for "our youngest member, François Truffaut": "This person has unquestionable genius. This genius has not yet manifested itself, for up to now the struggle for daily bread has fully absorbed him, but he knows what he wants, and has willpower. He'll become an artist. He'll produce a life's work. He'll succeed. Furthermore, he's a kind soul and has a treasure trove of tenderness."[62]

The ease and culture of this aristocratic milieu fascinated Truffaut and he felt encouraged to display his brilliance. Later, he would recall Louise de Vilmorin, Aimée Alexandre, and Countess du Pasthy in conceiving Fabienne Tabard, the incarnation of the seductive and refined woman played by Delphine Seyrig in *Stolen Kisses*.

SOCIETY REPORTER

In April 1950, Pierre-Jean Launay, *Elle* magazine's literary editor and a friend of Louise de Vilmorin, Aimée Alexandre, and Léo Poldès, attended an eloquence competition François Truffaut had signed up for. On that day, Truffaut won his set, and Launay immediately made him an offer to work at the well-known women's weekly.

This first experience as a journalist allowed Truffaut a new lifestyle for several months. He "treated his pals," dressed up, took Liliane to the theater, spending everything he earned. He was now thrown into Parisian literary and journalistic life as a society reporter. In addition to *Elle*, he contributed to other publications, *Ciné-Digest, Lettres du monde,* and *France-Dimanche,* sometimes as a photographer: "I took my first 'photo-flash' steps at Le Méphisto cabaret and one of my pictures is going to appear in *France-Dimanche*—the actress Annette Poivre and her daughter at the bar."[63] For six months, from May to October 1950, Truffaut took on a large number of assignments to maintain his new lifestyle, and his metamorphosis. He had never been so prosperous and now he could even support his friend Lachenay in the army, sending him money, clothes, books, and food.

But he soon found himself overworked because of his double career as journalist and photographer. His articles included a report on the fashion shows, the elegant shops near the Opéra, and several portraits of popular actresses—Michèle Morgan, whom he met at the Gare de l'Est on the set of René Clément's *Le Château de verre;* Martine Carol, with whom he lunched at the Billancourt studios, where she was being filmed in *Caroline chérie.* "She's a very decent girl, the victim of stupid publicity, she has a lot of talent,"[64] he wrote to Lachenay at the beginning of August.

The event Truffaut followed most attentively for *Elle* had nothing to do with film; it was the trial of Michel Mourre, a twenty-two-year-old man famous throughout France. A former novice, who had been expelled from a Dominican monastery for atheism, he had managed, a year before, to ascend the pulpit at Notre-Dame on Easter Sunday and proclaim in a loud, clearly audible voice, "God is dead." This scandalous blasphemy almost got him sent to Sainte-Anne psychiatric hospital. The Church of France's trial against him was followed intently at the end of May 1950. Truffaut saw Mourre as a figure he could identify with, the kind of outlaw who was inevitably attacked by the establishment—whether political, academic, institutional, or—as in this case—religious. It was like the compassion that he had felt for Marshal Pétain, not a political sympathy, but one for lost causes generally, whatever they might be, and "a shared emotion with all the maligned of the earth,"[65] he wrote. Mourre was acquitted on June 14, and Truffaut got on well with him when the two men had lunch together the following day. Three days later, Truffaut had written four articles on the affair, which he intended to offer to the various magazines he was writing for.

He went to Hesdin, in the Pas-de-Calais, from June 8 to 13, 1950, to watch Robert Bresson shoot the final scenes of *Diary of a Country Priest,* adapted from the novel by Georges Bernanos. Meeting Bresson "is fantastic," he wrote Lachenay, but five days on the sad and rainy set "is too long and boring."[66] Truffaut extracted five articles from this experience, but he was beginning to tire of his new profession. Though journalism had its good sides—meeting people, living well, the enjoyable frenzy of deadline writing—it also had its shortcomings, particularly its superficiality. "I'm bored . . . and I'd like to give it all up," he confided to Lachenay as early as July 21, 1950.

TWENTY-FIVE RAZOR SLASHES

François Truffaut was weary of journalism, but also drained by his relationship with Liliane Litvin, which was turning into a farce. On the evening of June 13, 1950, just after returning from the set of *Diary of a Country Priest,* he moved into the furnished room on rue Dulong that he had rented a week before, across the street from the Litvins; he wrote a long letter to Lachenay, describing the room in detail, and he even included a sketch of the layout.[67] His dream was for Liliane to move in with him, but she seemed unwilling to do so, for she was very busy preparing for her baccalaureate examination.

Truffaut was preparing for a kind of exam himself, that of the eloquence competition at the Club du Faubourg, to be held on Tuesday, June 27, at the Villiers-Cinéma. He was among the eleven finalists and the great favorite of the habitués. The competition included an assigned topic—"Paris in 1950"—and an improvisation on a theme to be divulged only at the last minute. Truffaut hoped against hope that Liliane would come, but in vain. On the night of the competition, deprived of his desired listener, he sulked: "I disappointed everyone because I had an infinitely bored, tired, monotonous air, implying 'what a stupid subject.' I came out third out of eleven."[68] He was given consolation prizes—a bottle of Ricard, some beauty products, and several lottery tickets, which he gave to Liliane's parents.

The beautiful Liliane flunked her exam as well, and did not get her baccalaureate degree. But this hardly deterred her from celebrating her birthday, on July 4, and inviting all her friends and acquaintances to an empty ground-floor apartment across the street from her parents' house. "There were over 40 people, including Claude Mauriac, Schérer, Alexandre Astruc, Jacques Bourgeois, Ariane Pathé, Michel Mourre, the cream of 16mm and journalistic Paris," Truffaut reported to Private Lachenay, languishing in his German barracks. Godard, Rivette, Chabrol, Gruault, Suzanne Klochendler, and her sisters also attended the party. "The rest of the evening was straight out of *The Rules of the Game.* Intrigues, rows in the street, doors slamming, Liliane played Nora Grégor, she switched 'Saint-Aubains' 4 or 5 times, I was Jurieu, there was bound to be a victim."[69] Who the victim would be was obvious. In the early morning, Truffaut went home, lay down in bed, and administered twenty-five razor slashes to his right arm, drenching the sheets in blood. Then he fainted. At 11:00 a.m., Liliane walked in and found him unconscious. She revived him, nursed him, and bandaged his arm. "Now, with my arm in a sling,

I'm like Frédéric Lemaître in *Children of Paradise* and I tell everyone I suffered a sprain,"[70] wrote Truffaut, ironically transposing the events of his life
into fiction. As for Liliane, she disappeared for two days, whereabouts
unknown, leaving her young neighbor weak and depressed.

By way of recovery, Truffaut stepped up his activities in the summer of
1950, attending the second Festival du Film Maudit in Biarritz from September first to twelfth. Over the course of a year, he had gained status; and
as the special correspondent for *Elle*, he was put up at the Casino-Bellevue
Hotel instead of in the lycée dormitory. But the ambiance on the Basque
coast was morose; indeed, the festival would turn out to be the last project
of a dying Objectif 49. Truffaut then went to spend about ten days in
Antibes, Cannes, Nice, Saint-Tropez, and Cap-Ferrat, seeking scoops and
hanging around the entrances of the villas and luxury hotels of the Riviera,
in the hope of intercepting a film star or a leading Paris personality.

When he returned to Paris at the end of September, Truffaut was joyfully
reunited with his friend Lachenay, who was on leave. They went to the
movies and had long conversations, as in the past. Truffaut was slowly recovering from a bad patch, and once again André Bazin would try to help him.
At the end of August, Truffaut had gone to a sanatorium in the Alps to visit
him. During their meeting, the critic suggested they collaborate on a biography of Jean Renoir, his favorite director. Truffaut would have the task of
establishing a complete filmography. The project had been commissioned by
the English journal *Sight and Sound* and Bazin offered to split the payment
of 26,000 francs. Truffaut had started his research when the deal fell through.

Truffaut then focused on a film project. He hoped that in writing his first
screenplay, *La ceinture de peau d'ange* (The Angel Skin Belt), he would
regain a zest for living. In August, he had written to his friend Lachenay, "I
have 25 reels of film stock, in other words, 1 hour and 40 minutes of screen
time. My film will be about 45 minutes long, so I have some leeway. I have
the 16-mm camera and the cameraman, I have all the actors. I'm only missing some costumes and a large room as the set of a dining room with a
40-amp meter for the lighting."[71] *La ceinture de peau d'ange* is about a communicant, and he had obviously conceived and written the story with the idea
of casting Liliane Litvin in the female lead. On the day of her First Communion, a young girl is raped by her cousin in the family attic. Six years later, she
gets married, and during the wedding dinner she goes up to the attic to look
for her childhood toys, which are locked away in an old trunk. Her husband's
boss, a guest at the wedding, joins her in the attic; under the pretense of con-
soling her for her melancholy, he throws her down on an old couch.

In this fantastical screenplay, with its sexual and blasphemous overtones,
there were parts for Jacques Rivette (the cousin) and Alexandre Astruc, as
well as a part for Truffaut himself, as the communicant's brother. Truffaut

hoped to win support from the Church of Paris, presenting the film, there-fore, as a documentary on First Communions. To win over the religious authorities, he relied on the help of Abbé Gritti, Abbé Ayfre, and Father Yves Renaud of the Versailles film club, all close friends of André Bazin. But the Paris bishopric decided not to support this unorthodox documentary, and in later years, when Truffaut became a filmmaker, he wisely never reconsidered this first youthful screenplay.

ENLISTMENT

In October 1950, Robert Lachenay returned to Germany to finish his mili-tary service. Liliane was still as elusive as ever, and André Bazin's tuberculo-sis kept him far from Paris. Truffaut was alone and still bored with journalism. On an impulse he decided to enlist for military service instead of waiting to be drafted. On October 29, he went around to the Reuilly-Diderot barracks, the Ministry of the Armed Forces on rue Saint-Dominique, and the Palais de Justice to get a certificate of his police record. Then the countdown began: In two weeks he would leave. "Of course, I've requested the occupation troops in Germany,"[72] he wrote Lachenay, who was enthusiastic at first: They would be closer to each other and could spend their leaves together in Coblenz. But two months later, when he heard what Truffaut had really signed up for, Lachenay changed his mind. Instead of leaving for Germany at the beginning of November as planned, Truffaut enlisted for a three-year term in the artillery—motivated by unrequited love, bravado, disgust with his Paris life, and, no doubt, the sizable bonus awarded to enlisted men. He was now due to leave for Indochina six months later. Robert Lachenay could not comprehend his friend's decision: "François, why did you do this? François, now we'll be separated for three years; I can't believe it, it's hard for me to accept the idea that you won't be in Paris when I return. I wonder what I'll do, how I'll live, how I'll get used to not seeing you, you and your briefcase, your papers, your eyeglasses, your humble pants and socks. . . ."[73]

On December 30, 1950, François Truffaut crossed the German frontier to go to Wittlich and join the Eighth Artillery battalion. He would do basic training for six months before leaving for Saigon. He started his military experience enthusiastically: "I have deliberately made a gift to the French army of three years of my life, three years with no films, no books, no running around, no friends, no initiatives," he wrote his father on January 3, 1951. "I consider this noble. The army is very often misunderstood. To say that mili-tary life is devoid of meaning or logic is as childish as kicking Arabs in police stations or laughing at Russian films."[74] But three days later, Truffaut had already recovered from his illusions and was begging for help from Bazin, Rohmer, and Launay—*Elle's* literary editor—urging them to pull strings so he could be posted to Baden-Baden as a journalist for the *Revue d'information des Troupes d'Occupation en Allemagne* (Journal of Information of the Occupation Troops in Germany). In a letter to Rohmer on January 7, he described the Wittlich camp as a hellhole—the exercises, the discipline, the snow and mud, the compulsory marches with a pack of sixty-six pounds. He pleaded, "Don't forget that on the other side of the Rhine a friend is counting on you. If I die in Indochina, it will be your fault! Hurry."[75] Rohmer, Bazin, and Launay all intervened with the military authorities, but to no avail; the enlisted man remained a "prisoner" in Wittlich. He described to Lachenay his inadequacies as a soldier: "When I say, 'Platoon, at my command, forward . . . march!' no one moves, since only the officer cadet can hear me. . . ." He is incapable of holding a gun: "Of the entire barracks (2,000 guys), I'm the one who least knows how to set the weapon on my shoulder. It's staggeringly awkward and earns me a slew of punishments."[76] It is hardly surprising that Truffaut became the whipping boy of the regiment's noncommissioned officers and that they made his life hell.

The end of basic training felt like a relative liberation. On March 10, 1951, he was finally given a somewhat cushy secretarial job taking phone messages, which left him time to read and write. Truffaut made frequent visits to the infirmary during the harsh German winter, owing to recurrent sinus and hearing problems. He would suffer from these ailments contracted in Wittlich for a long time to come; it was only in the early sixties that he would undergo a nasal septum operation, and the hearing deficit in his right ear, caused by the cold and the noise of cannon fire, turned out to be permanent. "Several times a day I feel like my right ear is being torn off with an enormous pair of tongs, so great is the pulling sensation when a detonation rocks the camp,"[77] he had written to Lachenay in February. Later, Truffaut would use this characteristic for Ferrand, the director he plays in *Day for Night,* who wears a hearing aid.

From his cushy job, Truffaut corresponded with all "his women." First with Liliane Litvin, for whom he still carried a torch. She looked after him, forwarded his mail, and sent him packages of books and magazines. Truffaut hoped for much more—a declaration of love, which never came. But, as he told his friend Robert, my "love life is rather complicated," and "the objects of my love are either 16 years old or 40, with a few ambiguous relationships between these two ages—young women from good families, widows, and my Pigalle 'ladies.' "[78] Truffaut corresponded with Louise de Vilmorin, Aimée Alexandre, and the Countess du Pasthy, his Faubourg benefactresses. "I write them worn-out lies. They respond favorably to these letters which are all feverish declarations of love (success no doubt stems from the fact that I'm not sincere)."[79] The young serviceman vacillated between the melancholy of frustrated passion for Liliane and the cynicism of a ladies' man who was already a blasé manipulator. And in between there were the loose women—the prostitutes he visited regularly, and Geneviève, his first mistress from the autumn of 1946, with whom he corresponded from Germany. "She lives alone and her letters are very tempting. My 1946 dream is beginning to materialize, Geneviève, a Balzacian heroine, my lily in the valley whom I'll once again defile!"[80] he wrote to Lachenay on February twelfth. These real women would later serve as models for the women in his films. Liliane Litvin would be the Colette of *Love at Twenty,* played by Marie-France Pisier; the proper young girls would recognize themselves in the Christine Darbon of *Stolen Kisses* and *Bed and Board,* played by Claude Jade; the mature, elegant women would be perfectly incarnated by Fabienne Tabard (unforgettably played by Delphine Seyrig); while prostitutes would appear in all his works.

THE DIARY OF A THIEF

Deprived of films during basic training, François Truffaut read intensively in the Wittlich barracks. He discovered Marcel Proust, whose *Remembrance of Things Past* he read and reread in January 1951: "It's wonderful and decisive for the fate of the novel: Balzac and Proust are the two greatest novelists in the French language,"[81] he wrote Lachenay on January 26. Another revelation was Jean Genet. Truffaut read *The Thief's Journal* just before he enlisted and recopied one specific passage in a datebook on December 19, 1950. "I was born in Paris on 19 December 1910. It was impossible for me, as a ward of Public Welfare, to know anything else about my civil status. When I was twenty-one, I obtained a birth certificate. My mother was named Gabrielle Genet. My father remains unknown. I came into the world at 22, rue d'Assas."[82] Truffaut, the former inmate of the Villejuif Observation Center, was bound to identify with Genet—the child of an unknown father, the delinquent sent from juvenile centers to prisons, the victim of punishments, humiliations, and unbridled animal sexuality, who finally found salvation in writing.

François Truffaut recopied this excerpt because the date was particularly important to him, as well; on December 19, 1950, he wrote to Jean Genet on the occasion of his fortieth birthday. At the time, Genet was living in a small room at the Hotel Terrass in the eighteenth arrondissement, right near the Montmartre cemetery, and was undergoing a deep moral and intellectual crisis, as well as a physical one—he was suffering from gallstones and would require several hospitalizations in 1950 and 1951. He was destitute as well, and survived by relying on friends who were better off. He also seemed dried up in terms of work, after the intense excitement of the "glory years," from 1942 to 1947. "For six years I remained in that miserable state," he later said, "in that imbecility which is the dregs of all life: opening a door, lighting a cigarette. . . . There are only certain bright spots in the life of a man. Everything else is grayness." Genet would also write in 1954: "The thought—not the appeal, but the thought of suicide, appeared clearly in me toward my fortieth year, brought there, it seems, by my weariness with living, after an inner void opened up in me that nothing except the final sliding away, would seem to be able to abolish."[83] One sees here a meeting of two suicidal souls, and this kindred outlook, in spite of differences in background and age, was surely what brought Truffaut and Genet together. However, despite his state of mind, Genet was also becoming one of the most famous French writers of the period. Each of his books and each of his plays—such as *Haute Surveillance*, which had been performed the previous year at the Théâtre des Mathurins—caused a furor. In 1951, Gallimard started publishing his complete works. And in *Saint Genet: Actor and Martyr*, Jean-Paul Sartre saw him as the poet and protagonist of the century.

In his letter, Truffaut enclosed the essay he had written on *The Thief's Journal* and "The Criminal Child," entitled "Jean Genet, mon prochain" ("Jean Genet, My Fellowman"), originally intended for the journal *Lettres du monde* but, unfortunately, now lost. On March 24, 1951, Truffaut mentioned to Robert Lachenay that he had been "surprised to receive an answer": "He wrote me a really nice letter expressing thanks and kind feelings: he tells me to come and see him when I'm in Paris. It's a fine autograph to have."[84] Genet had indeed written a warm letter: "Dear Monsieur, I am very touched by your note. I am also very surprised that anyone should think of writing to me and writing about my work. You might be disappointed, for I have not fallen out with Sartre, whom I like enormously and very sincerely. Besides, his critical work on me hardly concerns me—it's mostly about himself. Of what you write, I don't know what to say, except that it seems to me much too glowing. If you get a few days off from the army to come to Paris, come by and say hello to me. It would be a pleasure to shake your hand. Kind regards."[85]

The meeting took place in Genet's little hotel room in mid-April of 1951, as soon as Truffaut had his first leave. We can measure the full effect it had on Genet by his inscription on the first page of *The Thief's Journal*, which he gave to François a short time later: "My dear François, don't be hurt, but when I saw you come into my room, it was like seeing myself—in an almost uncanny way—when I was 19 years old. I hope you'll retain your grave expression for a long time and your simple, slightly unhappy way of expressing yourself. You can count on me." With his military haircut, frail appearance, short stature, slightly crooked nose, lively, worried gaze, and melancholy air, Truffaut certainly looked like the self-portrait Genet described in April 1951. But this apparition, in the door frame of a hotel room, also illustrates something Sartre wrote about *The Thief's Journal* at that same time: "Genet sees himself everywhere; the dullest surfaces reflect his image; even in others he perceives himself, thereby bringing to light their deepest secrets."[86] Truffaut's secret, of course, was his unknown father, whom he sought to replace with the artists he most admired. Jean Genet and André Bazin were the first to fit into this surrogate role. Truffaut wrote as much to Lachenay on August 15, 1951: "In three weeks Bazin and Genet did for me what my parents never did for me in fifteen years."[87]

Genet responded to all of Truffaut's letters and requests in the spring and summer of 1951. He wrote him in Wittlich "a very brief word to let you know I haven't forgotten you. Send me news of yourself, ask me for anything you desire, and stop by to see me if you come to Paris. Consider me always your very faithful friend." Above all, Genet sent him dozens of books through Gallimard and it was he who first introduced Truffaut to the publisher's *Série Noire* crime thrillers in August 1951. "I arranged to have some detective novels (hospital reading) sent to you and two packs of Gitanes. Did you receive these?" This would turn out to be essential reading for Truffaut, who would later adapt for the screen works by William Irish, David Goodis, Henry Farrell, and Charles Williams, all authors who had been translated and published in the prestigious *Série Noire*.

This important friendship was documented by a total of eleven letters[88] and two book inscriptions on the part of Genet: "I'm amused by your letter," Genet wrote at the beginning of June 1951. "Do what you want, but don't ask me for such inane explanations. It's true, I don't like letters very much. Forgive me if mine are short. The important thing is that they express my friendship." Truffaut's answers, of which there are about fifteen in all, were longer. Though this friendship had very little concrete effect on the physical conditions of Truffaut's military life, it helped him greatly during that difficult time. So he wrote to Lachenay on November 22, 1951, from his prison cell, when he had thoughts of suicide, "I get only short, infrequent letters from Genet, but it's thanks to them I can hold out."[89]

Their relationship would last after Truffaut's return to civilian life; he and Genet would often take long walks together down the boulevard de Clichy. But it would come to an abrupt end in November 1964, when Truffaut arrived very late to an appointment Genet had set up for him to meet his friend Abdallah, who was looking for work. Truffaut received his last note from Genet on the following day: "Yesterday I asked you to do a young Moroccan a favor, a lost soul, and you kept him waiting for an hour and a half. For his mental health, it was good for him to see how people in film behave and the kind of treatment they deserve. I'm deeply sorry, François, that you've learned to play the part, because I liked you. You can let your laughable misplaced pride go to your head but drop the bad manners, François, and keep up the habit of roaming around the Boulevard de Clichy, because sometimes I need dough. . . ."[90]

THE DESERTER

On May 12, 1951, François Truffaut was pronounced fit for duty by the military physician in Wittlich; he could therefore be posted to Saigon. His departure was set for July 14. He was given several leaves during his final two months, and, naturally, he spent those in Paris, where he fell back into his old life—seeing friends again, going constantly to the Cinémathèque, meeting Genet. He saw a great deal of Liliane Litvin; they went to the movies together and she invited him to her country house. She even became jealous and demanded he break up immediately with Geneviève S., who housed and supported Truffaut while he was in Paris.

Truffaut now began to regret he had enlisted for service in Indochina. On June 8, he wrote to Robert Lachenay for advice, weighing things for and against, only to conclude, "I feel like deserting."[91] On June 21, his letter is replete with cinematic references: "I'll soon find myself in the same situation as Jean Gabin at the beginning of the film set in Le Havre [*Port of Shadows*], except I'll have clothes, work, housing, dependable friends. I'll then be in Gabin's shoes at the end of the film that takes place in Algiers [*Pépé le Moko*], when the ship leaves without him! I don't know if you'll approve of my decision, but I'm convinced it's the best. Don't let anything surprise you when we see each other in Paris, and trust me."[92]

Truffaut had made up his mind: It was utter madness to go to Saigon. He turned in his kit in Wittlich on July 13, said farewell, and boarded the 4:00 p.m. train for Strasbourg. "Incredibly depressed," he wrote in his date book during the train trip. The following day, he was supposed to be in Marseilles to start a month of intensive combat training prior to his departure for Indochina on August 20. On the overnight trip from Strasbourg to Paris, he met a "delightful" young German girl named Charlotte who shared his compartment and helped him regain a taste for civilian life. And in Paris, in the early morning, he ran into Genet—miraculously—on the boulevard de Clichy, and spent the rest of his departure allowance with him. By the early afternoon, he had joined Liliane, Robert, Chris Marker, Alexandre Astruc, and Jacques Rivette, who were waiting for him so they could throw a bash in Rivette's apartment on rue de Clignancourt. Truffaut was therefore not in Marseilles on the night of July 14 to 15, which made him a deserter—or at least put him in what was officially called "a state of illegal absence." He didn't hide at first, and his friends saw him proudly resume his Parisian lifestyle. But soon it became dangerous for him to roam the streets at night because of the possibility the police might ask for his papers. So Truffaut looked for a place to hide. He spent one or two nights at Jean Douchet's, then was back on the street. Once again, André Bazin, who had just returned from a long convalescence in Vernet-les-Bains, in the Pyrénées, proved to be the providential friend, offering to put Truffaut up. Bazin, his wife, Janine, and Chris Marker spent a whole day looking for Truffaut, waiting outside his favorite movie houses for the shows to let out. They finally found him on July 21 and took him back to Bry-sur-Marne, where the Bazin couple lived with their two-year-old son, Florent, and their many pets. They had a small, modest apartment, but it was pleasant—three rooms and a kitchen on the second floor of a house, surrounded by a quiet park, in a peaceful Paris suburb. Though it wasn't fixed up, the maid's room in the attic was habitable—and this was where Janine and André put François up. Bazin felt that, first and foremost, Truffaut should legalize his situation, and he convinced him to go and plead his case before the officers in the Paris area, saying this was the only chance he had of really regaining his freedom. On July 28, Liliane was invited for lunch at Bry-sur-Marne; then they all went to see Robert Flaherty's *Elephant Boy* at the Cinémathèque; afterward, Bazin and his protégé, accompanied by Janine and Liliane, went together to the Prévaûté at the Invalides. The plea for conciliation failed; charged with illegal absenteeism, Truffaut was sent forthwith to the prison of the Dupleix barracks and incarcerated. He was detained for seven days. The Bazins came to see him, and so did Liliane, who even sent him a parcel of books. He was then told that he would have to join the Thirty-second Artillery battalion in Coblenz. This seemed like relatively good news, since his departure for Indochina appeared to have been called off.

On the afternoon of August 3, Truffaut was discovered to have a new bout of syphilis and was rushed to the military medical unit at Villemin hospital, near the Gare de l'Est. Under surveillance and knocked out by the treatment, he was in a state of dreadful boredom and depression; he was cheered only by the visits of the Bazins and Abbé Gritti and by a few letters of friends. Jean Genet tried unsuccessfully to see him after returning from a trip to Stockholm, but he lacked the necessary authorization paper from the examining judge. So he sent François a letter and a big package of books. "Actually, everything is now for the best," he wrote. "Your pox made its appearance at the right time. As a moralist, I would be sorry if you were spared Indochina: the sick are the first who should be sent to slaughter. Jean Domarchi will bring you other books, [Sartre's] *Situations*. What should I wish for you? Recovery? Prison? Psychiatric hospital? Freedom? You don't really seem to me to want it. I'm afraid you have the soul of a desperado. If that's the case, you should come to terms with it, submit to your fate and croak holding a grenade. I like you anyhow, with kind regards and love."[93]

François Truffaut stayed at Villemin hospital from August 3 to September 3, 1951, in a state of physical and mental disrepair, from which he emerged only gradually. The Bazins had left for vacation in the Charente; his Paris friends were out of town. Again, he was alone, ill, and in prison. Genet did his utmost to help him. He remembered René Leibowitz, a psychiatrist friend of Sartre, whom he thought might be able to help Truffaut get out of his predicament. But in order to reach him, they had to wait for Sartre to return from his trip to the North Pole. None of the steps taken by Genet would change the situation, but under his influence, Truffaut started keeping a journal on August 21. The cover of this schoolboy's notebook, a montage of photos and drawings, is itself an homage to Genet and also a kind of self-portrait—sketches of faces, women's bodies, a Pierrot, a picture of Genet's face cut out from a magazine, and the manacled hands of a young man. And under the title *Diary* was this epigraph: "May this notebook be for Truffaut what the *Pierres* [*Stones*] were for Hugo."[94] Inside were notes, drawings, comments on filmmakers and writers, as well as daily impressions, punctuated by letters he'd received and his successive transfers from prison to prison, and barracks to hospital. Locked up and ill, he had plenty of time to read the many books sent to him by Genet, Bazin, Lachenay, and Liliane and to write about them at length. In this journal, Truffaut defined the literary tradition he most admired—Balzac, Proust, and Genet—and rejected "moralizers," such as Eugène Sue and Hervé Bazin, and "writers of contempt," such as Flaubert and Gide. He described his revolts and revelations, and discussed cinema, sharply dismissing postwar French movies as "studio filmmaking based on adaptation." Truffaut also worked on his own image in his journal, molding himself into a provocative figure, worthy of both Balzac and Genet, actor and martyr. "We're handcuffed when we go to the showers. The first time around, I was embarrassed because you have to go through the hospital and people stared at us, but later I was ashamed at being ashamed, because doesn't the 'Genet' position dictate pride in deserving handcuffs? So, now, before going to the showers, I light a cigarette and smirk in a kind of satisfied, slightly aggressive way."[95]

On Monday, September 3, 1951, Truffaut was informed of his impending departure for Germany. He requested a day to put his affairs in order and say his farewells; as soon as this was granted and he was set free, he deserted. For three days, he roamed around Paris, looking for less impecunious friends. Bazin was out of town, and so was Genet. Jean Domarchi and Jean Cau, friends of Genet to whom he had been recommended, were nowhere to be found. And none of the friends he ran into at the Cinémathèque—Rivette, Gruault, or Liliane Litvin—had any money to lend him. On September 7, utterly penniless, Truffaut went to see a doctor who worked at the Cité Universitaire, and a military chaplain, to ask for help. They tried to get him admitted into the Val-de-Grâce hospital with a false certification of ill health. But he was missing a necessary document—permission from the military health unit. On September 8 at 4:00 p.m., as he was going to meet a friend of the doctor's who was prepared to give him the precious document, Truffaut was arrested at the entrance of the building by soldiers who asked to see his identity papers. He was taken to the Dupleix barracks and put in the very same cell where he had been held several weeks before.

ME, FRANÇOIS TRUFFAUT, A SELF-HATING AUTODIDACT

He remained locked up for three days. At 6:00 a.m. on September 12, he was transferred to a police van and taken to the Gare de l'Est. "People look at me, particularly because of my handcuffs. Hatred or sympathy? Neither, probably, just a morbid, animal curiosity, nothing more. In the reserved compartment, I have two guards all to myself and those dopes won't even remove my handcuffs. More asses than bastards, and close to retirement, so they don't want trouble. If only they knew that behind the contemptuous, haughty airs I put on, there's a little boy who would break out in tears from just an affectionate squeeze on the shoulder,"[96] he wrote in his journal. In Strasbourg, Truffaut and his two guards got into a car, and after driving across the German frontier, they handed him over to the police in Kiel, a small German village. His handcuffs were removed, and he was even allowed to buy cigarettes while he waited for his departure to Coblenz at 5 a.m. on Thursday, September 13. He arrived at the barracks at noon, and his hair was cropped.

On the following day, Truffaut was brought before the camp's judicial officer, who suspected him of being a Communist. Truffaut described his youth, "including Villejuif and syphilis," so that on September 15, he was transferred to the army hospital in Andernach, nineteen miles from Coblenz. A new treatment was started as soon as he arrived—more than fifty injections over a period of ten days. When he was cured, he was returned to Coblenz and locked up in the disciplinary area, which was completely deserted. Books were scarce and Truffaut was bored to death; his only entertainment was to get drunk every day with his guards. On the morning of September 30, the guards found him with many razor slashes on his face, neck, and chest. This second suicide attempt landed him once again at the Andernach hospital, this time in the neuropsychiatric unit. "I'm with a guy who never talks, a rookie who couldn't get used to the army; there's also a case of delirium tremens who gets over 40 shots a day; a mental retard who never stops stroking his feet; and another retard who put on his shoes in the middle of the night and grabbed his haversack to go home. Another guy, very young, went crazy from a bazooka exploding right next to him. His name is Dany, but his nickname is Tino Rossi, because he sings incomprehensible songs all day. There's also Terasse, a swinging daddy's boy, and Brault, a painter I like a lot. But he has very violent tantrums. His fingers are contorted, twisted, he brings a hand to his throat and tries to strangle himself, uttering little shrieks and cries. And then there's me, François Truffaut, a self-hating autodidact."[97]

Truffaut would spend a month and a half in the company of the madmen, watched over by brutal male nurses, though they were conscripts like himself. He kept his journal but lived in solitude and self-hatred. It was not until November 27 that he was released from the Andernach neuropsychiatric unit and sent back to the Coblenz barracks. Working in the canteen, he found a more convivial, warmer atmosphere; he was the only man among five women, with one of whom—Laura, a young German domestic—he had a passionate affair.

Meanwhile, in Paris, André Bazin tried to rescue Truffaut from his plight. His direct appeals to the military authorities were fruitless; sometimes his efforts even turned against him, for he was seen as an "antimilitary, Communist intellectual,"[98] and against Truffaut, the "guy with connections." Helped by Abbé Gritti, Bazin finally succeeded—through Raymond Clarys, the director of the Villejuif Observation Center for Minors, and Senator Marc Rucart, Truffaut's old admirer at the Club du Faubourg—in contacting the military examining judge, Lieutenant Le Masne de Chermont. He was the person conducting the investigation of the Truffaut case in view of the trial set for November 22, 1951, before the Coblenz military tribunal. Raymond Clarys forwarded to him the psychiatric file that had been drawn up two years earlier by Mademoiselle Rikkers, while Senator Rucart, a former minister, contacted General Noiret, stationed at Baden-Baden. These appeals seemed promising, as indicated by the note the examining judge wrote to Bazin on October 22: "Let things settle down now and stop moving heaven and earth. . . . From my investigation into this case, I can encourage you to hope for a favorable outcome for your protégé."[99] Similarly, General Noiret reassured Senator Rucart concerning the young man's future: "You can rest assured that this young soldier's case will be given favorable consideration as a result of the particular circumstances you brought to my attention."[100] On Friday, December 7, Truffaut learned from his commanding officer, Captain Wittmann, that there was a very good chance that he would be given a "second-class temporary discharge" and sent back home.[101]

Good news came with its share of humiliations. The Coblenz officers had trouble accepting the decision and submitted the malingerer to harsh discipline. Truffaut now spent most of his time in jail, including Christmas, but a telegram from Janine and André Bazin brought him a bit of comfort: "Thinking of you, be patient, with love."[102] On January 3, 1952, Truffaut went before the discharging board and stood at attention, hair shaved and in an oversized uniform. After a two-hour discussion, during which three captains and two majors described the soldier's "unstable character" and his "perverse delinquent tendency," he was finally given a temporary discharge. His military enlistment was annulled, but he still had eighteen days of duty as a legal requirement. He would spend them back in prison again—a way of depressing the "guy with connections" just a little while longer.

He received letters from his friends—Bazin, Aimée Alexandre, Louise de Vilmorin, Marc Rucart, Lachenay. On January 16, Cocteau even sent him the proofs of his new anthology, *Bacchus*, with a warm and cheering inscription. Nor did Genet forget him: "You're really unlucky! Still in prison! The army is beginning to realize the blunder it made in accepting you. In any case, it's good that you're returning to France. But it's unfortunate you'll be leaving the army for Saint-Germain-des-Prés. Personally, I'd rather see you a soldier. Return anyhow and stop by to say hello. I'm well. I see very few people. You're very nice and I like you a lot."[103] Truffaut, for his part, wrote many letters, and kept track of his readings in his diary—Balzac, Raymond Radiguet, Julien Gracq, and a new journal with a yellow cover that Bazin had sent him, *Cahiers du cinéma*. Liliane's silence weighed heavily on him and intensified his feelings of isolation and humiliation. On February 6, 1952, his twentieth birthday, Captain Wittmann subjected him to insults in front of five witnesses. Truffaut noted down the juicy dialogue in his journal; he would later use it for inspiration in *Stolen Kisses*, for the scene where Antoine Doinel is discharged.

> —*Ah, Truffaut! I believe you're leaving us. Do you know where you'll go when you return to Paris?*
> —*Yes, to Bazin's . . .*
> —*Bazin's? Well, tell your Bazin he'd better give you better advice in civilian life than in military life, because if you'd gone before a military tribunal, you wouldn't have gotten off so easy, nor would he in fact; it's expensive to house a deserter, he must be something your Bazin, he and his friends, antimilitarists, Communists, homosexuals, these people, I spit in their faces, you understand, that's French, right, get it, that's French!*

—It's French, but inaccurate. . . .

—Shut your trap, you're just a quitter, a loudmouth, a stinker, that's all; I'd like to come across you at war; while there are guys getting killed over there in Indochina.[104]

Ten days later, the degradation ritual took place before the disciplinary committee, in the officers' presence. "It is customary to present gunners with a record of good conduct at their release, even when they've committed some minor misdeeds, but those you committed voluntarily are of the type that taint your honor,"[105] the colonel said as Truffaut remained dignified and saluted properly, keeping his thoughts to himself. On the afternoon of Wednesday, February 20, 1952, François Truffaut, finally freed, boarded the train at the Coblenz station. The next day, at 7:00 a.m., he arrived at the Gare de l'Est as a civilian and could inscribe page 184 of his journal in capital letters: "IN PARIS."

3.
LIFE WAS THE SCREEN:
1952–1958

wo hours after getting off the train at the Gare de l'Est, François Truffaut went to boulevard Masséna to see Madame Kirsch, Janine Bazin's mother, who fed him a good meal and gave him the keys to the Bazin apartment, since the couple was out of town. He moved back into his attic room, in Bry-sur-Marne, and tried to forget his year in the military. He realized how much he owed the Bazins, and soon he acquired a taste for the kind of family life he had never known before. "You can laugh, but admit that parents like these are rare. I've had enough of loneliness that gives rise to squalor, listlessness, low morale, etc. . . ."[1] he wrote to Robert Lachenay, who was sad that he had not immediately come to join him in Paris after his return from Germany.

AT THE BAZINS'

Truffaut found material comfort in Bry-sur-Marne, and, more important, an atmosphere that was conducive to work. The only thing troubling him was his relationship with Liliane Litvin, which ended before it had ever really started. Liliane told him that she was pregnant and planned to marry the father of her child. This romantic breakup probably marked the final crisis in Truffaut's youth. In his journal, on May 6 and 7, he wrote, "I've now loved

Liliane for two and a half years and loved only her. It's beginning to last too long. I'm fed up with it. I shouldn't have invited her on Saturday and Sunday. I feel it's putting me through the worst suffering. I won't invite her anymore. This whole thing has to come to an end as soon as possible. I'm waiting impatiently for Janine and André to return."[2]

In the first weeks of his new life at Bry-sur-Marne, Truffaut went to a few screenings at the Ciné-Club du Quartier Latin, with Lachenay, Rivette, Godard, and Rohmer. He also resumed his conversations with Jean Genet, in the latter's little studio behind the Sacré-Coeur. But he devoted most of his time to reading the many books in Bazin's library. Often, he went to Paris with Bazin to see a couple of films. He gradually regained his taste for the cinema, but his moviegoing was far less obsessive than in previous years—as though he were searching for something else, or wanted to extend this period of convalescence. He was perfectly content in this family atmosphere, with André, Janine, and their son, Florent, and there developed a reciprocal relationship between François and André: "They both educated each other,"[3] Janine wrote in 1961, referring to the ties between Bazin and Truffaut. It's easy to see what the critic offered his protégé—experience, an attentive ear, a lively intelligence, and great kindness. The disciple responded with his own qualities—lively conversation, laughter, complicity, vitality. Indeed, Truffaut's arrival enlivened the couple's existence, and it was the most joyous period of their life. "It was the only time I saw André laugh and be happy in spite of his illness,"[4] Janine recalled in a letter to Truffaut in February 1965. Or, as she put in 1984, "a two-year state of grace between a mildly insubordinate young man and a 'man of conscience.' "[5]

But this was only an interlude. In the beginning of April 1952, Truffaut had to find employment. He asked all his friends and connections for help, such as Jean Cau, Jean-Paul Sartre's secretary, whom he'd met through Genet, and Senator Marc Rucart, whom he knew from the Club du Faubourg. Several leads opened up but subsequently fell through. Then he wrote to Louise de Vilmorin, who answered immediately, inviting him to come visit her in Verrières: "I know quite a few people in journalism, including some magazine editors. However, I can't talk to them about you unless I know you better,"[6] she wrote him on April seventeenth. There in Verrières, in her blue living room, Louise de Vilmorin gave him an excellent lead. A new magazine, *L'Express,* was being launched and her friend Françoise Giroud was on the editorial staff. Unfortunately, this lead fell through, as well. Depression threatened again; he was broke and at loose ends.

Many months went by without employment, but Truffaut's tastes and intellect continued to be formed by contact with Bazin, who once again stepped in to help his protégé, getting him some freelance assignments at *Cinémonde* and some work in the film department of the Ministry of Agriculture. The latter involved assisting the directors of ministry-financed documentary films and lasted only a few weeks; the *Cinémonde* work, including a piece on the "new sensual bombshells," allowed Truffaut to write an impassioned homage to one of his favorite actresses: "In the fierce sex derby that makes the whole world focus on Hollywood, Marilyn Monroe is in a class of her own. Among fifty others, Gloria Grahame has had the best start and is a very close contender. You don't need a telescope to follow the progress of this new breed of fillies: they're thoroughbreds, unequivocally. No pair of binoculars or scientific lens could resist the sensual radiations that emanate from their utterly desirable beings."[7] Protected by anonymity, Truffaut wrote at length, in a short, lively, rapid style. If nothing else, *Cinémonde* gave him his first opportunity to focus his journalistic writing specifically on cinema.

THE TIME OF CONTEMPT

François Truffaut next set himself a specific objective whose attainment would bring little money but much prestige—to write for *Cahiers du cinéma,* the magazine founded by Jacques Doniol-Valcroze, Joseph-Marie Lo Duca, and André Bazin in April 1951. He worked for several months on a long article which he handed to Bazin at the end of December 1952: "The Time of Contempt: Notes on a Certain Tendency of the French Cinema." It was a harsh indictment, initially conceived in Germany, where, deprived of movies, he had sifted through countless notes, trying to classify and analyze the films he had seen in his youth. These dozens and dozens of films constituted what Jean-Pierre Barrot, in the postwar *L'Écran français,* called, with marked respect, the "tradition of quality."[8] It was this very tradition that Truffaut would take pains to denounce.

In an early version of this essay, Truffaut confessed to his youthful fascination for the dark atmosphere and seamy stories of traditional French films, particularly those written by the most famous screenwriting team of the period, Jean Aurenche and Pierre Bost. Indeed, this fascination was discernible in *Ceinture de peau d'ange,* the story of the First Communion girl which he had wanted to direct in the fall of 1950. "I'm ashamed I was once able to invent a story that is so stupid and nasty, but you could see the influence of the kind of movies I believed in at the time."[9] A taste for blasphemy, a hatred of family, perverse, cynical characters—these were the main themes of the French cinema of the period, and they could be found even in Truffaut's three-page synopsis. No doubt his own "experience of infamy," being locked up in a military prison, marked a decisive and painful stage in his development. He could no longer bear the "infamous stories" of French movies, or the contemptuous superiority directors and screenwriters displayed toward their screen characters. "The director should have the same humility toward his characters that St. Francis of Assisi had toward God. For us to accept infamous characters, the person who creates them must be even more infamous. Anathema, blasphemy, sarcasm are the three passwords of French screenwriters. Griffith, to take a counter-example, is always great because he was even more ingenuous than his screen characters. These 'superior' artists claim to be superior to their creations; this presumption explains, but fails to excuse, the bankruptcy of the arts since the invention of motion pictures."[10]

The other focus of his attack concerned the French tradition of adapting literary works. Truffaut was convinced that French cinema was a screenwriter's cinema which owed its failings to those of the screenwriters. In the military prison in Andernach, Truffaut had reread Radiguet's *Devil in the Flesh,* which was being serialized in *Ici Paris.* And he drew up many instances of "equivalencies-betrayals" between the novel and Claude Autant-Lara's film adaptation from Aurenche and Bost's screenplay. Truffaut decried the mediocrity of a school that liked to think of itself as true-to-life and psychological, formed by the war, and represented by the screenwriters Aurenche and Bost, Charles Spaak, Henri Jeanson, Roland Laudenbach, Robert Scipion, Pierre Laroche, and Jacques Sigurd. "For them, psychological realism inevitably requires that men be base, infamous and vile ... the films they write are even more base, vile and spineless than anything French art has produced to date."[11] Truffaut also inveighed against films like Jean Delannoy's *La Symphonie pastorale* (*The Pastoral Symphony*) and *Le Garçon sauvage* (*Savage Triangle*), Christian-Jaque's *La Chartreuse de Parme* (*The Charterhouse of Parma*) and *D'homme à hommes* (*Man to Men*), Yves Allégret's *Manèges* (*The Cheat*), *Dédée d'Anvers* (*Dedee*) and *Une si jolie petite plage* (*Riptide*), and *Retour à la vie,* a film made up of sketches by André Cayatte, Henri-Georges Clouzot, Jean Dréville, and Georges Lampin.

Truffaut continued to work on his article after moving in with the Bazins in February 1952. In the course of his research, he even approached Bost and, by flattery, succeeded in borrowing four screenplays including an adaptation of Bernanos's *Diary of a Country Priest,* which the novelist had rejected during his lifetime and which Aurenche hoped to direct himself. Truffaut would use these documents, obtained in such an inelegant and opportunistic fashion, against Bost, as damaging firsthand evidence in the campaign he intended to wage.

Truffaut gave Bazin the first version of his article in December 1952.[12] Thirty-one typed pages, it was often awkward and violently polemical in tone. His attack on the "blue chips" of French cinema was sometimes personal. Aurenche is characterized as "a dropout from directing who made one or two commercial shorts," Jeanson is written off as "base and ignoble," and Françoise Giroud is accused of having "boundless bad taste." He denounces the plots of "quality films" with great violence: Autant-Lara's *Le Blé en herbe* (*The Game of Love*) is "a gross lesbian story," and Yves Allégret's *Les Orgueilleux* (*The Proud and the Beautiful*) elicits an outraged witticism: "If Yves Allégret is really honest with himself, within the next three years he should show us Madame Michèle Morgan in Australia without panties surrounded by kangaroos decimated by typhus, transformed for local reasons into a nasal hemorrhage. If my prediction doesn't come true—which is probable—I will have been right in accusing Monsieur Allégret of being the most conformist of film directors."

The essay appealed to André Bazin, but not for a minute did he imagine it in *Cahiers du cinéma* without changes; he asked his protégé for a revision with fewer examples, fewer quotes, and fewer personal attacks, as well as a positive section to offset his denunciations. Truffaut followed this advice and worked on the article for almost a year. In the meantime, Bazin suggested he write a few brief essays on current films in order to practice his critical writing skills, promising to get them published in *Cahiers du cinéma*. In March 1953, Truffaut's first piece appeared in the magazine—a few pages on a small American film that had gone more or less unnoticed, David Miller's *Sudden Fear*, with Jack Palance, Gloria Grahame, and Joan Crawford. "The craftsmanship of Hollywood motion pictures is perfect even in 'Z movies.' This upsets the hierarchy . . . for the only things that count here are an ambitious screenplay and the director's reputed market value. . . . There, in contrast, a clever, beautiful and sober story, directed with professionalism and precision, Gloria Grahame's face and a steep Frisco street—all contribute to the stature of a cinema that proves to us every week that it is the greatest in the world." From month to month, Truffaut extolled American B movies, praising their modesty and production speed, compared to the sluggishness of French films. His admiration for vitality in cinema would have an effect: Samuel Fuller, Nicholas Ray, Edgar G. Ulmer, Allan Dwan, Ernest Schoedsack, Richard Fleischer, Tay Garnett, André de Toth, to name only a few, owe their critical fate in France partly to Truffaut's informed gaze.[13]

In March 1953, Truffaut was publishing so many articles in *Cahiers* that he soon decided he couldn't sign them all with his own name. A certain "François de Monferrand" broke into print and then, in November 1953, one "Robert Lachenay"—his two favorite pseudonyms. The critic could thereby vary the style of his contributions: François de Monferrand used jokes, puns, and spoonerisms, while Robert Lachenay indulged in suggestiveness and fetishism. The latter, for example, started a cult for Marilyn's underwear in a passionate review (November 1953) of *Niagara* entitled

"*Niagara*'s Underpinnings." But on each, the polemical mastery bears the unmistakable mark of their creator.

On November 5, 1953, Truffaut gave Bazin and Doniol-Valcroze the new version of his long article, now entitled "A Certain Tendency of the French Cinema." Two days later, he returned the scripts, which he had borrowed a year earlier, to Pierre Bost with a malicious, rude note: "I didn't expect that reading these screenplays would be so fruitful and revealing. That's my excuse, as well as the desire not to leave anything to chance and to do a comprehensive job. I hope I haven't put these documents to too bad a use. With all my gratitude and respectful good wishes."[14]

Doniol-Valcroze and Bazin hesitated. By attacking the establishment head-on, they felt, the article might puzzle readers with such proclamations as this: "Though the French cinema exists thanks to about a hundred films each year, it is understood that only ten or twelve deserve the attention of critics and film enthusiasts, hence of *Cahiers*. These ten or twelve films constitute what has nicely been called the tradition of quality; because of their literary ambition, these movies compel the admiration of the foreign press, and uphold France's colors twice a year, in Cannes and Venice, garnering medals, gold lions and first prizes quite regularly since 1946."

Fearing "A Certain Tendency . . ." would shock part of the readership, and wishing to mitigate its offense to director friends such as Clément and Clouzot, Doniol-Valcroze felt he had to run a nuanced explanatory editorial in the same January 1954 issue of *Cahiers du cinéma*. He found an elegant way of taking responsibility for publishing the article while declaring that he did not necessarily share all the views expressed: "Clearly, we realize the polemical style of some of the assessments could raise objections, but we hope that beyond the tone—which involves only the author—and regardless of certain specific value judgments—these are always individually questionable and we are far from unanimously agreeing with them—the reader will nevertheless recognize a critical orientation, or better yet, a point of theoretical convergence that is ours." Doniol-Valcroze's preemptive commentary was courageous, but customary precautions were useless and soon the devastating effects of this article written by a twenty-one-year-old unknown became manifest.

On January 28, the main subject of conversation at the professional critics' luncheon was Truffaut's article. The camps were clearly divided. On one side were the indignant defenders of French cinema, led by Denis Marion of *Paris-Cinéma;* on the other were Doniol-Valcroze and Claude Mauriac, who sided with the young critic. A writer and movie reviewer for *Le Figaro*, Claude Mauriac offered staunch support. On February 13, he wrote, "We have long felt there were flaws in the work of those recognized masters of

French motion picture quality, Jean Aurenche and Pierre Bost. . . . We should be thankful to a young critic, Monsieur François Truffaut, for shedding light on this subject for us in a brilliant article just published in *Cahiers du cinéma.*" The following week, Mauriac discussed the article again, and though he reproached the author for "a certain moralizing tone," he added, "We cannot help but agree with Monsieur Truffaut's conclusions."

The counteroffensive was not long in coming. On February 25, a second critics' luncheon was devoted to the "Truffaut affair." This time, the screenwriters came to defend themselves. Doniol-Valcroze gave the following account: "Present are Charles Spaak, Georges Cravenne, Jacqueline Audry, Pierre Laroche, Kast and Astruc . . . and the discussion is far-ranging. Neither Bazin nor I, though we reflected at length before publishing the study, could imagine that it would have such an explosive effect."[15] Feeling singled out by Truffaut, who had denounced "Charlespaak" as "the language that is fluently spoken in French films," the screenwriter Charles Spaak wrote Doniol-Valcroze a bad-tempered note, typifying the indignation, surprise, and also superiority the screenwriters' guild felt toward the "young whippersnapper": "A single thought came to my mind on reading *Les Cahiers du cinéma.* In a note, at the bottom of page 29, your collaborator expresses how impatient he is to see 'Feyder and Spaak fall into permanent oblivion.' On the face of things, I think many of us will find it far more difficult to forget Jacques Feyder's name than to recall François Truffaut's."[16]

Aside from the furor among film professionals, *Cahiers du cinéma* also received quite a few letters from indignant readers. Many of them felt betrayed, and reproached the magazine for abandoning the serene spirit of film studies for the sake of a polemic. Some readers faulted Truffaut's article for its anti-French, pro-American bias; others hated its "reactionary and pious tone."[17] Opinion was split at the magazine itself concerning the article. Pierre Kast, who was close to René Clément and Jean Grémillon, was its fiercest opponent; he denounced the article's imprecatory tone and its moral judgments, which he called "critical dogmatism," or "the colonization of *Cahiers* by the priest party."[18] André Bazin also answered his young protégé. In his critique of Autant-Lara's *Blé en herbe,* published in February 1954, he brought up the subject of fidelity to literary works: "It cannot be doubted that Aurenche and Bost have imposed the notion of fidelity as a positive value. I know that François Truffaut challenges this, but he is wrong, at least to the extent that the liberties taken by the screenwriters of *La Symphonie pastorale* stay within the relatively narrow framework of equivalencies that are seen as necessary. . . . In sum, like hypocrisy to virtue, their very infidelities are yet another homage to fidelity." While he didn't consider them masterpieces, Bazin defended Autant-Lara's films—and he defended them specifically against Truffaut.

"A Certain Tendency . . ." was the subject of much discussion at the time of its publication and the affair turned a large group of French critics against Truffaut. But over time, this essay would determine the new orientation of *Cahiers du cinéma*, because it rallied a great number of film devotees who completely ignored and scorned the French tradition of quality, heaping praise on Hollywood auteurs instead.

THE YOUNG TURKS

Since *Cahiers* had supported Truffaut's polemical stance, he felt he had to involve himself completely in the fight on its front lines. Bazin and Doniol-Valcroze had shown real tolerance in publishing an article whose ideas they didn't completely share. They also worked for other newspapers; Bazin wrote every day for *Le Parisien libéré;* Doniol-Valcroze was the film critic at *France-Observateur.*

In the winter of 1953–54, they welcomed Truffaut onto the *Cahiers* staff.[19] The magazine had its offices on the Champs-Elysées, at number 146. It was a comfortable space, about sixty feet square, with a view on the avenue, loaned by the magazine's financial backer, Léonid Keigel, a film distributor who directed *Cinévogue* and a Paris movie theater called the Broadway. There was also a small, darker room at the end of a hallway, giving out on an inner courtyard; this was reserved for editorial meetings. There were three worktables: one for Doniol-Valcroze, one for the secretary, and a large one for the editorial staff, where discussions took place and the layout was designed. Each editor kept his own hours. The morning was good for quiet discussions with Doniol; 3:00 p.m. on Tuesdays was the time to listen to Bazin; early afternoon was the time to go over a piece with Truffaut; and somewhere around 6:00 p.m., between film showings, was when articles were assigned. In 1954, *Cahiers*'s founders, Bazin and Doniol-Valcroze, had as collaborators former critics from Objectif 49, such as Alexandre Astruc, Pierre Kast, and Jean-José Richer. There was also a group of "Young Turks," followers of Eric Rohmer, who had forced open the door of the prestigious magazine thanks to François Truffaut: Jacques Rivette, Jean-Luc Godard, Claude Chabrol, Charles Bitsch. Being familiar with each person's qualities and faults, his tastes and knowledge, Truffaut decided who got assigned what.

There were occasionally eventful moments, as when Godard was caught "borrowing" from the cash box, or when Michel Dorsday challenged Pierre Kast to a duel. At other times, there was much laughter—when Chabrol stopped by, and starting in 1956 and 1957, when young actor friends like Jean-Claude Brialy and Jean-Paul Belmondo made it a habit to drop in and clown around whenever they were near the Champs-Elysées. The staff members were good listeners, and very soon novice directors Jacques Demy, Pierre Schoendoerffer, and Agnès Varda came by to describe their projects, get advice, and make contacts.

Between March 1953 and November 1959, François Truffaut published 170 articles in *Cahiers,* mostly film reviews of five to six typewritten pages, or interviews with film directors, a genre that he was particularly fond of. Aside from his long January 1954 essay, "A Certain Tendency of the French Cinema," he didn't publish theoretical articles, leaving them to Bazin, Rohmer, Rivette, or Godard. Truffaut didn't claim to be an intellectual; his aim was to meet film directors, attack opponents, and assert his opinion— unconventionally, cunningly, offhandedly, and sometimes with a certain arrogance—on *all* the films showing in Paris. On average, Truffaut saw more than one film a day, thereby living up to his reputation as the critic who "saw four thousand films between 1940 and 1955."

The group of young critics at *Cahiers* whom André Bazin had nicknamed the "hitchcocko-hawksians," in reference to their two favorite film directors, clustered around Truffaut. Each had his role. Jacques Rivette was the best friend and the true movie-loving companion, whose opinions were most authoritative and reliable and whom the younger Truffaut consulted constantly. Eric Rohmer was like an older cousin, somewhat strict and austere, although Truffaut sometimes cajoled him. Truffaut and Rohmer even collaborated on several projects, among them a screenplay written at the end of 1953, *L'Eglise moderne (The Modern Church).*[20]

Some other "cousins," with similar tastes, joined this trio, such as Chabrol and Godard. Chabrol, then a skinny live wire, found time amid studies in pharmacology, literature, and the law to worship Hitchcock. The first to settle down (Chabrol married in 1956 and lived in the middle-class comfort of an apartment, as opposed to a room), he was of great help to the group, thanks to his knowledge of English—an invaluable asset in meetings with Hollywood directors—and his position as press attaché for Fox, which gave him access to previews and reliable information. Jean-Luc Godard was Swiss, from a good family, and had come to Paris to complete his studies, first at the Lycée Buffon, then at the Sorbonne. His love of movies brought him to the Ciné-Club du Quartier Latin, where he met the other Young Turks. Put in contact with Doniol-Valcroze (their mothers were friends), he was first given the opportunity to write for *Cahiers du cinéma* in January 1952 and quickly carved a niche for himself there thanks to his impertinence and taste for paradox. He was the most taciturn of the group, acting most like an artist and dandy, and he fascinated the others, probably because he also kept his private life shrouded in mystery—his trips to Switzerland and throughout the world, his family, and his love life.

Truffaut, a true group leader at *Cahiers du cinéma,* also attracted several very young critics into its fold. Charles Bitsch, a Paris friend; André Martin, the animation specialist; Fereydoun Hoveyda, a young Persian science fiction enthusiast; François Mars, a lover of burlesque; Jacques Siclier from Troyes; André S. Labarthe from Sarlat; and Claude Beylie, Claude de Givray, and Luc Moullet—these were the younger members who would take over the magazine when Truffaut, Godard, Chabrol, Rivette, and Rohmer would go on to direct. Truffaut, for them, was a charismatic figure with whom they could identify. But he was also very demanding, and he didn't hesitate to curb polemical passions when he felt they were unjustified—for example, he refused to publish a piece on the Venice Film Festival by a friend, Jean-Marie Straub, because he found it very violent and radical. Indeed, Truffaut feared overly imitative behavior on the part of his young disciples, as he wrote to Luc Moullet in March 1956: "Your pieces are difficult to publish in their present state. I should have written to you at greater length explaining how things had been for us, how our pieces had been rejected. One article, with which I'm hardly satisfied today, 'A Certain Tendency of the French Cinema,' required several months' work and five or six complete rewrites. Yes, I admit, we were a bit frightened of you. First of all because we once shared your aggressiveness (sincere and fanatical) and it's a shock to see this eternal recurrence at the *Cahiers,* this perennial revival of the same sarcastic attitude. . . ."[21]

Truffaut would often approach writers to solicit articles or excerpts of screenplays. The most decisive meeting was with Jacques Audiberti. Audiberti was known for his plays, but Truffaut was particularly taken with his novels (*Monorail, Le Maître de Milan,* and especially *Marie Dubois*), where he saw a world that reflected some of his own obsessions. "The same question is asked tirelessly in all his books: why don't women desire us the way we desire them, i.e., a priori, systematically, physically and abstractly, and for what they are: the hunchback for her hump, the bourgeoise for her hat, the prostitute for her thighs, the prude for her virtue, the plump girl for her curves and the thin one for her bones?"[22] In the beginning of 1954, Audiberti published a new novel with Gallimard, *Les Jardins et les Fleuves,* which Truffaut read with great eagerness. He was particularly struck by a passage about Charlie Chaplin's Tramp. Truffaut seized the opportunity; on the last Wednesday of May 1954—it became a memorable date for him—he wrote Audiberti: "Would you be willing to write a column which would be entitled 'Le Billet d'Audiberti [Audiberti's Letter]' or a kind of 'Perpetual Column on Woman on Screen,' thoughts on the actresses and heroines in the films you were seeing?"[23] Audiberti accepted immediately, and he wrote a monthly column for *Cahiers* from July 1954 to December 1956. This gave Truffaut the opportunity to meet with him regularly. They were instantly taken with each other, and would always remain so. Later, Audiberti would be the first devotee of Truffaut's films, praising *Les Mistons* (*The Mischief Makers*) and, later, *The 400 Blows* in *Arts*. Truffaut considered him one of his masters, and the only one, except for Cocteau, who knew "how to describe both films and film actresses."[24] In an homage to him, Truffaut wrote, "Jacques Audiberti, with his scarred mug of a vacationing old sea dog, was a colossus of Antibes, as handsome and powerful as his books."[25]

PRESS CAMPAIGNS

The publication of "A Certain Tendency of the French Cinema" in 1954 changed François Truffaut's life.[26] A short time later, he was contacted by Jean Aurel, a journalist just a bit older than he, who was editor of the movie pages in the cultural weekly *Arts-Lettres-Spectacles*. In the late forties, *Arts* was the home of the intellectual right wing, a group nicknamed the "*hussards*" (hussars, for their unsubtle, rough-and-tumble style), which included Jacques Laurent, Michel Déon, Roger Nimier, Marcel Brion, and Antoine Blondin. The weekly was unabashedly polemical and attracted famous contributors. Aside from the "*hussards*," these included Cocteau, Audiberti, Louise de Vilmorin, Claude Roy, Maurice Clavel, Maurice Pons, Claude Roger-Max, Pierre Seghers, Pierre Marcabru, Ferdinand Alquié, and Jean Cathelin. Ruthless and provocative, *Arts* instigated big cultural debates; in the fifties, it was the true rival of the left-wing journals and magazines like *Les Temps modernes*, *Les Lettres françaises*, and *L'Express*.

The magazine belonged to a wealthy art dealer, Daniel Wildenstein, who gave the weekly's managing editor, Jacques Laurent, complete editorial freedom. Laurent put Aurel in charge of the movie pages, with the task of developing an incisive and original tone. Seduced by the verve and style Truffaut exhibited in *Cahiers,* Aurel asked him to write for *Arts*. Truffaut was quick to seize the opportunity, for not only was *Arts* an unhoped-for platform; it also offered substantial freelance pay (seven hundred francs per manuscript page, five times more than *Cahiers du cinéma*), and writing for them would solve his financial problems. Truffaut continued his demolition job on the "tradition of quality" in the columns of *Arts*. Rough, polemical, moralizing, and imprecatory, Truffaut attacked left-wing intellectuals and their "cultural political activism."[27] He showed his worth, publishing 528 articles in five years—in other words, an average of two articles a week, filling almost single-handedly the entire movie page, under his own name or a pseudonym.

Truffaut was in great demand during this period. Between January and September 1954, he published twelve articles under the name François de Monferrand in the Catholic weekly *Radio-Cinéma-Télévison,* the forerunner of today's *Telerama.* Between July and September, at Doniol-Valcroze's request, he suggested several articles to the left-wing weekly *France-Observateur.* Between May and August 1956, he contributed to *La Parisienne,* a literary and socialite magazine with right-wing tendencies. Then in April 1956, when Philippe Boegner launched a new liberal daily, *Le Temps de Paris,* with the ambition of rivaling Hubert Beuve-Méry's *Le Monde,* Truffaut was asked to be editor of the film section. The paper was a commercial failure and folded a month later, but Truffaut wrote about twenty articles for it during its brief existence.

A film a day, an article every other day—this was the pace the young man kept up, working every night, imbibing Maxiton, cigarettes, and coffee. Life and work were one. He confided movingly to Jean Mambrino, a Jesuit priest and fellow film critic, "Actually I'm very limited, very uncultured (I'm not proud of the fact); I'm just lucky to have some understanding of cinema, to like it, and work like a dog. That's all. Beyond that, any deeper reflection on content is above my poor head. As I hate the fact that I'm self-taught, I don't 'teach' myself anything, or hardly. I'll be saved by the fact that I 'specialized' in the cinema very early on and used the position as much as possible, working every night if need be."[28]

Truffaut put all his energy into his work, letting his personality show through in his writing. He established a "Truffaut tone" with his very first articles in *Arts;* a style blending vehemence and humor, it was rich in wordplay, jokes, and hoaxes and was clearly intended to draw in the reader. "He rewrote all the screenplays with his criticisms, recreated the films with passion, both the positive and negative elements, as he thought he had seen them,"[29] said the producer Pierre Braunberger, an avid reader of *Arts.* Truffaut also gave free rein to his erotic fetishism in his descriptions of the gestures and bodies of women on the screen, praising the "practiced eye" who "is learning the angles suited to revealing a brassiere's fabric and color, and consequently the very life of the breasts it supports," who sees "the sharp angles that capture the diagonal patterns and hems of underpants outlined by a woman's gait." For "the face can pretend, modesty can be false, and virtue simulated, but the brassiere never lies."[30]

Criticism, for Truffaut, was like an intimate journal, unveiling the secrets of an ever-alert sensibility. He was plainspoken in his judgment of works and put all his energy into convincing his readers by means of what he called his "press campaigns." He proclaimed on the first page of *Arts,* in one of his most famous and violent tracts,[31] "You are all witnesses to this trial. . . ." On several occasions, Truffaut supported particular causes; he defended Henri Langlois's Cinémathèque when it was threatened with closure in early 1955; he also brought attention to certain films that had been unappreciated or neglected by critics, such as Joseph L. Mankiewicz's *The Barefoot Contessa,* Alexandre Astruc's *Les Mauvaises Rencontres,* and especially Max Ophuls's *Lola Montès.*

Reactions to his spirited temperament differed. In an internal memo written on November 2, 1955, André Parinaud, the editor in chief of *Arts,* requested Truffaut to show a little restraint: "Letters of complaint are piling up lately, and I know that your present mood won't help matters. You're responsible for yourself, but when the paper is implicated, I request that you be cautious and stay polite. There are things you should avoid, and from now on, in your articles for *Arts,* I forbid you to use terms like 'plagiarized' or 'copied,' or to make physically and sexually discriminatory remarks. You're entitled to dislike skinny women or homosexuals, but you must refrain from expressing this in your columns." However, Jacques Laurent, at about the same time, decided to encourage Truffaut's open revolt against all academicism, feeling that his polemical tone fit into the magazine's way of thinking. Indeed, on July 6, 1955, at Jacques Laurent's and Jean Aurel's request, Truffaut published "Criticism's Seven Deadly Sins." "On the margins of the movies, there is an unrewarding, painstaking and little-known profession— that of 'film critic.' What is a critic? What does he eat? What are his habits, tastes and obsessions?" he asks in the beginning of the article, which is illustrated by an acerbic Siné drawing entitled "A Critique of Criticism." Truffaut's answers, stated in seven points, suggest that critics are neither free nor intelligent. Rather, he says, they are ignorant of both the history and technique of motion pictures, and lack imagination. They are professorial and full of prejudices. He even accuses them of being chauvinistic and of selling out to the highest bidder, since "it is impossible to have a successful career as a critic in Paris without eventually meeting Delannoy, Decoin, Cayatte or Le Chanois." The list of sinners includes Jean Dutourd, François Nourissier, Georges Sadoul, Georges Charensol, Louis Chauvet, Jean-Jacques Gautier, André Lang, Roger Régent, Jacques Lemarchand, and André Billy. The elite critics of the daily and weekly press are all implicated. As a counterpoint, Truffaut adduces the "noncritic film enthusiast," actually a self-portrait of someone defined by two characteristics: a radical point of view—"Everyone has his system. Mine leads me to praise or pan unreservedly"—and honest judgments. Hence, in reviewing Mervyn LeRoy's *The Bad Seed* in *Arts* (1956), and describing a promotional press luncheon he attended where the director was present, he had no compunctions about writing, "I remember eating very well, but I guess gastronomic gratitude is not my strong point, and anyway, it's better never to have met Mervyn LeRoy lest one lose any desire to see a film made by him."

Jacques Laurent openly supported Truffaut, making him the leader of what he called "criticism from the catacombs."[32] In an editorial published in *Arts* in February 1955, he wrote:

> There are two brands of film criticism. The first kind could hang a shingle announcing "good plain fare." It doesn't make waves, agrees eagerly with the tastes of the general public and is practiced by people for whom cinema is not a religion but a pleasant pastime. And then there is an intelligentsia that practices criticism in a state of anger. Truffaut is one of the most gifted representatives of this second kind of criticism, a recent development requiring scrutiny. The intelligentsia I am referring to sees itself as being, or wanting to be, in a state of belligerence. All attacks are worthwhile since the god of cinema will recognize its own. Whether approving or disapproving, these critics are always angry because, judging films according to ethics and esthetics evolved at the Cinémathèque, they are perpetually at war with middle-class criticism and frequently in disagreement with box office receipts, in other words with the public.

Truffaut, then, had sired a new form of film criticism—frank, direct, violent, sectarian, founded on value judgments, always detailed but often provocative and scathing, with no qualms about being peremptory and unfair. This new brand of criticism preached by the Young Turks came to dominate *Cahiers du cinéma* and *Arts,* but throughout critical circles at the time, there was great shock. After the publication of "Criticism's Seven Deadly Sins," Jean Néry, president of the French Association of Film and Television Critics, asked Truffaut to resign from the association. "I assume," Néry wrote him on October 27, 1955, "it is painful for you to belong to a group of film critics whose incompetence, stupidity, cowardice and ineptitude you are constantly stressing, and unbearable for you to remain in their company as a member of an association where we seek to develop mutual respect rather than systematic boorishness."[33] Truffaut replied several days later: "Quite frankly, I regard myself as an excellent—if temporary—critic, and as someone who justifies and honors a group that is not so much an association as a union, needing to protect its members from possible (and permanent) political, police, censorship and publicity pressures. But since it is not for me to judge, I thought it might be useful to include with this letter some testimonials from readers, fellow members and film directors."[34] These testimonials are glowing assessments from such critics as Henri Agel,

Claude Mauriac, André Bazin, and Jacques Doniol-Valcroze, and from prominent directors like Max Ophuls, Abel Gance, Fritz Lang, Nicholas Ray, Roger Leenhardt, and Jean Cocteau. This clearly illustrates Truffaut's tactic of working within, and not outside, the system, and of making it implode under the well-organized, carefully staged blows of his own press campaigns. With Jacques Laurent's protection, the "hussar" could appeal to the readers of *Arts* and call them to witness in the trial he was conducting, while benefiting from the refuge and authority provided by *Cahiers du cinéma* and its group of angry young men who supported him with unfailing loyalty.

A HUSSAR WITH HIS SWORD DRAWN

François Truffaut's writing style, press campaigns, and taste for provocation were typical of the literary right. It's no coincidence, since the papers he wrote for—*Arts, La Parisienne, Le Temps de Paris,* and even *Cahiers du cinéma*—his personal contacts, and his pamphleteering style all suggest rebellion against academicism and the culturally dominant left-wing intellectual circles of the postwar period. Polemics raged between the two camps in the fifties, even if the Communist, social-Christian, humanist left vastly outnumbered the right. *Les Temps modernes* denounced the danger of a "resurgence of fascist intellectuals,"[35] *L'Express* published its first feature on "the right-wing writers,"[36] and in a December 1952 article in *Les Temps modernes,* Bernard Frank singled out the "hussars" as "crusaders of the pen" who charge their enemies "with swords drawn." Jacques Laurent was the leading "hussar," but he founded *La Parisienne* and accepted the editorship of *Arts* under the banner of "political noncommitment." He expressed his objective in an editorial in the first issue of *La Parisienne,* dated January 1953: "Literature has become a means to an end. It is disapproved of as soon as it is anything other than a means"; he wished to sever the ties between literature and politics—that is, between literary circles and left-wing activism.

This was a cause François Truffaut could identify with. In *Cahiers,* he fought against supporters of "films with a message," praising form and mise-en-scène over the screenplay. But this cause was considered reactionary; lack of political commitment was associated with individualism, egoism, formal innovation, dandyism—so many attitudes denounced as impeding the values of cultural, political, and moral reconstruction inspired by the Liberation. Truffaut's many opponents went even further—they assimilated him into the extreme right; his sworn enemies at the journal *Positif,* for example, regularly referred to him as the "fascist" in their letters and columns.[37] They saw in Truffaut an "intellectual vigilante" whose "political choices go hand in hand with a distinct taste for authority and the police."[38]

Truffaut himself enjoyed being provocatively right-wing. His moralistic intransigence in attacking the leading lights of French cinema sometimes induced him to take extreme, dubious, contrarian positions, as when he went so far as to praise American censorship in the January 1954 issue of *Cahiers:* "We can thank American screen censorship for the fact that Marlowe is no longer a homosexual and that the characters become clearly either likable or hateful. Hence the need for moral censorship. . . ." His determination to be a redresser of wrongs, while identifying with minority intellectual groups that were decried, and sometimes even banned, occasionally led him to pure political provocation.

Truffaut pulled no punches in writing about Maurice Bardèche and Robert Brasillach's *L'Histoire du cinéma,* the latter having been executed at the Liberation for collaborating with the Nazis: "Brasillach's political views were also those of Drieu La Rochelle; views that earn their advocates the death penalty are bound to be worthy of esteem. . . ."[39] Two months later, in a complimentary review of Sacha Guitry's *Si Versailles m'était conté (Royal Affairs in Versailles),* Truffaut paid tribute to the monarchy of the Ancien Régime, "which contributed to the grandeur of France for several centuries: Christian feeling and a sense of honor, respect for the clergy and the nobility, the keystones of a justly hierarchical society."[40] But more important, in the winter of 1955–56, he was pleased to establish contact with Lucien Rebatet, a thirties film critic of undeniable talent and a scathing style, who had written for *L'Action française* under the pen name of François Vinneuil, and later for *Je suis partout.*[41] During the Nazi Occupation, Rebatet had been a powerful anti-Semitic voice supporting the purges in the motion picture sector; and in a 1941 book, *Les Tribus du cinéma et du théâtre (The Tribes of Film and Theater),* part of a series entitled "The Jews in France," he called for the "regeneration" of the entertainment arts: "Whatever is undertaken or decided regarding French cinema, it should first be cleansed of Jews. Sooner or later we will have to drive out of our country several hundred thousand Jews, starting with those who do not have residency papers, the nonnaturalized Jews, the most recent arrivals, those whose evil political and financial effects are most manifest, in other words all the Jews in cinema." Does the writer's talent and polemical verve justify forgetting these odious books? Did these writing qualities bring Truffaut close to Rebatet, or Rebatet close to Truffaut? One might be led to believe so by a comment Henri Langlois made to his friend Lotte Eisner shortly before his death in 1977: "There were only two great film critics in this century, François Vinneuil and François Truffaut."[42] This opinion was shared by Claude Elsen, a far more dubious character, the author of a 1943 work that was pulped at the Liberation, *Destin du cinéma* (*Cinema's Fate*), himself a collaborator who was condemned to death in absentia in 1944. Having taken refuge in Spain, he wrote Truffaut a long letter of congratulations in early 1956 at the suggestion of "our mutual friend François Vinneuil-Rebatet," which concluded with this nostalgic sentence: "You very much remind me of what I tried to be before the deluge. Bravo."[43]

Lucien Rebatet himself wrote to Truffaut on November 25, 1955, after having read and appreciated one of his most vitriolic articles in *Arts*, ridiculing Jean Delannoy's *Chiens perdus sans collier:* "I have been wanting to meet you for a year, because you remind me of the young Vinneuil of the thirties. My old friend Jacques Becker said wonderful things about you. . . ."[44] Far from refusing any contact, Truffaut replied to Rebatet politely, and kept up a correspondence with him as "from critic to critic," recommending some small American films to him, such as Tay Garnett's *The Naked Dawn*, Edgar G. Ulmer's *Cause for Alarm*, and Samuel Fuller's *House of Bamboo*. Released in 1952 after spending eight years in jail, Rebatet had resumed work as a critic at *Rivarol*. He thanked Truffaut for his valuable advice: "Colleagues my own age couldn't possibly give me the kinds of tips you generously give me. . . ."[45] Curious to meet the former collaborator, Truffaut even accepted his invitation and spent a whole day with him in late 1955, lunching on board a Paris *bateau-mouche*.

Not all his friends approved of this relationship; Doniol-Valcroze, for example, a former Resistance fighter and left-winger, categorically refused to meet Rebatet,[46] and Pierre Kast expressed great indignation at this "acute attack of Maurrassism."[47] Truffaut saw it as echoing one of the major nonconformist traditions in French culture, the one that leads from the *Action française* to the "hussars," from Maurras to Rebatet.

As a film critic at *Arts*, beginning in the spring of 1954, François Truffaut enjoyed an improved financial situation. His regular freelance work brought in from fifteen to twenty thousand francs a month, thus allowing him to live in furnished hotels and to eat proper meals. He was also able to repay his debts to Doniol-Valcroze, Astruc, and Lachenay. Work absorbed him completely; he spent all his time in movie theaters, editorial offices, and seeing film directors. He avoided society events and literary cafés. Eric Rohmer described the relative colorlessness of this "life outside movies": "We didn't have 'happy years' or 'happy times,' and if anything could claim to apply to us, it would be the sentence of Nizan, 'I'll never let anyone tell me that being twenty years old is the best moment of one's life.' Those years were not only unhappy but colorless: . . . To anyone who asked us, 'What do you live on?' we liked to answer, 'We don't live.' Life was the screen, it was movies, it was discussing movies, writing about movies."[48] They had in common this devotion to cinema and, oddly enough, an extreme reserve about their private lives, which remained secret. Rohmer, Rivette, Godard, and Truffaut shared a puritanical streak; there were ties of friendship among them, but no familiarity. There existed a barrier, a sense of dignity and moral inflexibility that favored reciprocal respect rather than emotional out-pourings.

Though movies monopolized François Truffaut's life, he nonetheless reserved a place for women—seeing them daily, in large numbers, and obsessively. Once again, he had to be treated for venereal disease. His rela-tionships with women were in tune with the frenzied life he led—liaisons and conquests matched his insatiable appetite for films and his critical over-activity. In the notes exchanged between Truffaut and Lachenay during this period, there are many recommendations about girls, good addresses, and pickup spots between the Porte Saint-Denis and Pigalle. Most of Truffaut's involvements at that time were still anonymous and unconnected to movie circles. But these ephemeral affairs were an undeniable part of his life, and he often informed Lachenay of his schedule. "After leaving you," he wrote, "I picked up a girl near the Studio Parnasse; I only had 400 francs left; the hotel cost 500; she lent me 100 francs. I was joining the Bazins at 11 o'clock at the Champs-Elysées and didn't have a cent left to get there, or for break-fast. So I stopped by and pinched 1,000 francs from your black wallet, under the mattress."[49]

This frenetic rhythm might have been an aftereffect of the trauma caused by his definitive breakup with Liliane Litvin; Truffaut seems to have wanted both passing liaisons and one woman to whom he could become attached. In February 1954, he met Laura Mauri, a friend of Jean-José Richer, a young critic at *Cahiers* who was a close friend of Doniol-Valcroze. Truffaut and she lived together for a while in a two-room apartment on boulevard des Batignolles. In 1955, when Truffaut stayed at Roberto Rossellini's house in Rome, and then went to cover the Venice Film Festival for the first time, Laura accompanied him. A pretty brunette, she was lighthearted, short and curvy, and wore elegant, flowing dresses; she seemed the female type he was most attracted to.

Two years later, on January 29, 1956, at a point where his affair with Laura Mauri was fizzling out but hadn't quite ended, Truffaut met Joëlle Robin. In the beginning of March, he left the Hôtel de Tunis, near Place Clichy, where he was living at the time, and moved in with Joëlle on rue de Lincoln, near the Champs-Elysées. He would stay there for eight months. A budding actress, Joëlle Robin had already had supporting roles in several French films and had appeared in Vincente Minnelli's *Lust for Life* in 1956. Having noticed her in a film, Truffaut wrote a profile of her in the February 22, 1956, issue of *Arts*. "Well directed, Joëlle Robin can bring a new flavor to certain films—that of a modern Alice in a reconsidered 'wonderland.' " His article must certainly have furthered their relationship.

FIRST FOOTAGE

Though successfully launched on a career in film criticism, Truffaut did not forget his desire to direct films. Indeed, he was always writing short screenplays and jotting down ideas for films, on his own or with his friends from *Cahiers*. But since *La Ceinture de peau d'ange* in 1950, all his filmmaking attempts had failed. Finally, at the end of 1954, he and Jacques Rivette set up a project for a silent ten-minute short entitled *Une Visite*. Truffaut would have the opportunity to "waste his first film stock."[50] Robert Lachenay was both producer and assistant, and Rivette, who could get film stock at a discount and had access to a silent 16-mm camera, was the cameraman. Truffaut had found a set—Jacques and Lydie Doniol-Valcroze's apartment on rue de Douai, in his old neighborhood. He had also chosen three actors—Laura Mauri, and her friends Jean-José Richer and Francis Cognany. Lydie Doniol-Valcroze insisted he cast her two-and-half-year-old daughter, Florence, whom the members of the film crew had to take turns baby-sitting for. Truffaut created a part for the child in his story, structured around amorous play. A young boy is looking in the classified ads for a room to rent; he finds one in an apartment where a young woman is living alone. She welcomes him amicably, gently making fun of his shyness, for he is rather awkward and provincial. The young woman's brother-in-law, played by Jean-José Richer, comes to the apartment to drop off his little girl for the weekend. During his brief visit, he clowns around, blowing puffs of cigarette smoke like a locomotive, and tries in vain to flirt with the young woman, stealing a kiss on her neck. After this episode, the new tenant also tries his luck with her, awkwardly attempting to hold her hand. Rebuffed, he packs up his suitcase and leaves the apartment. Night falls over Paris, near Place Blanche. The young girl puts her niece to bed, draws the curtains, and pensively sits down beside the child.

In spite of the speed of the shoot—five days—this eight-minute film, with its numerous cuts, required many camera movements. But Truffaut wasn't pleased with it and showed it to no one, not even his friends at *Cahiers du cinéma*. The little reel would lie dormant for many years in a closet in the rue de Douai apartment. It was thirty years later, in 1982, that he came across his first cinematic endeavor again. "At the time he wanted to destroy it, since he felt it was of no interest," recalls Lydie Mahias, the former wife of Jacques Doniol-Valcroze. "But he left me a print because it was a souvenir of my daughter at two. In 1982, François and Rivette summoned us to a screening. He had blown up the short to 35 mm. We had a good time, because Rivette was absolutely delighted with his camera work."[51] After this first setback, Truffaut was very depressed, doubting he had the ability to become a director. Disappointed by what he regarded as mere amateur work, he decided to become better acquainted with the secrets of the great masters and return to criticism.

TRUFFETTE AND RIVAUT

A polemicist with a mischievous spirit, but also a sincere film enthusiast, François Truffaut was very intrigued to meet the film directors he admired. For him, criticism, journalism, and interviews went hand in hand; they were all part of a way of viewing cinema that was based on real involvement, stated preferences, and an intimate knowledge of the secrets of the art. Truffaut and Rivette spent the whole morning of January 20, 1954, taping a long conversation with Jacques Becker. While this method seems obvious today, at the time it was deeply innovative and would radically change the approach to films. The twelve-page spread that appeared the following month would be the first such piece to be published by *Cahiers du cinéma*. The form was not new—Truffaut himself had been very impressed by the publication of Paul Léautaud's radio interviews with Robert Mallet[52]—but to date it had been used only in magazines to report the comments of stars, the moods of producers, or anecdotes about film directors. Truffaut and Rivette had a completely different, very specific goal: to become intimately acquainted with a filmmaker by inviting the auteur to talk freely about himself, his work methods, and his career. They had but one rule—the use of a portable tape recorder to all its advantage. This, too, was new. At the time, the Grundig machine, with its heavy reels of magnetic tape, weighed nearly nine pounds, so that this unheard-of practice did not go unnoticed. On May 14, 1954, *Cinémonde* stressed its "exceptional interest": "These articles are transcribed from tape-recorded interviews, and reproduced intact with all the repetitions and hesitations of spoken language, and all the more precious in that these repetitions and hesitations allow the reader to follow the interviewee's thoughts step by step, down to the smallest details and subtlest twists and turns."

It was "Truffette and Rivaut"—as they called themselves, so inseparable in their work that for a long time Becker thought they were a homosexual couple—who created the rules and chose the first interviewees. They described their method clearly for their meeting with Abel Gance which appeared in the January 1955 issue of *Cahiers du cinéma*: "There are two rules governing our 'interviews with . . .' First, we only choose directors we like. Secondly, we let them express themselves freely and never burden them with embarrassing or insidious questions."

The first interview, with Jacques Becker, the director of *Casque d'or*—one of Truffaut's favorite films—was published in February 1954. "The most authentic and flawless director,"[53] according to Truffaut the critic, was the first of the "masters" to hit it off with the young *Cahiers* rebels. Becker talked with great simplicity and detail for nearly three hours, about his work, his films, and his concept of directing. Between the spring of 1954 and the autumn of 1957, *Cahiers* would publish a series of interviews, conducted mostly by Truffaut and Rivette, with Jean Renoir, Luis Buñuel, Roberto Rossellini, Abel Gance, Alfred Hitchcock, Howard Hawks, Robert Aldrich, Joshua Logan, Anthony Mann, Max Ophuls, Vincente Minnelli, Jacques Tati, Orson Welles, Gene Kelly, Nicholas Ray, Richard Brooks, Luchino Visconti, and, finally, Fritz Lang. This constitutes a corpus that is one of the great innovations of *Cahiers du cinéma,* and it still remains a foundation and pillar of modern criticism. François Truffaut expected a great deal from each of these meetings. They no doubt derived from a deep trait in his personality: the need to find masters and learn from them.

I ADMIRE YOU . . .

Truffaut had carefully thought through his idea and planned it out. In the beginning of spring 1954, he drafted a letter he would send to several directors. "I admire you; I would like to meet you; I would like to write about you and give you exposure in the press. . . ."[54] The letter went out at about the same time to Preston Sturges, Jean Renoir, Luis Buñuel, Max Ophuls, Abel Gance, Roberto Rossellini, Fritz Lang, and Nicholas Ray. They almost all replied, including the foreigners, though some respondents were somewhat blasé, such as Preston Sturges, who wrote on September 1, 1954, "Come to see me whenever you want but you should know that I'll be happy to welcome you only because you're a pleasant young man who is sincerely interested in an art that I very much like. The fact of being spoken about in movie magazines, or having my face reproduced—I don't give two hoots about all of that. . . ."[55]

During the same period, Truffaut started to spend time on the sets of the directors he admired. In October 1954, for instance, he spent ten days on the set of Jean Renoir's *French Cancan* at the Studio Francoeur, and he recounted the experience in *Arts* in the form of a shooting journal. Renoir must have approved of his article, for several times he invited Truffaut to his house on avenue Frochot, near Pigalle, and subsequently allowed him to visit the set of *Éléna et les Hommes (Paris Does Strange Things).* In those years,

Truffaut was also a privileged spectator of all of Renoir's theater experiments. That July, he had assisted Renoir when he was directing Grisha and Mitsou Dabat's translation and adaptation of Shakespeare's *Julius Caesar*. This was when Truffaut first met Jean-Claude Brialy, who was completing his military service in Germany at the time, in the army motion picture unit. There, Brialy had become friends with Pierre Lhomme, the future cinematographer, who suggested that during their leave they go to Arles with some other film enthusiast friends to see Renoir's *Julius Caesar*. These friends were Charles Bitsch, Claude Chabrol, Jacques Rivette, and Jean-Luc Godard. During the entire trip from Paris to the south of France in a beautiful Buick, the only subject of conversation was movies. Jean-Claude Brialy, who had had a strict upbringing and whose father was a military man, couldn't believe his ears. "It was like an underground group preparing a revolution," he recalled. In the morning, the gang arrived at the arena. The ambiance was that of a bullfight, with dust and two hundred extras. "In the midst of all this, Jean Renoir, magnificent, and next to him a young man in black with fiery eyes—François Truffaut." During the return trip, Brialy, who was obsessed with becoming an actor, did everything he could to impress the gang and acted out a whole series of roles—"dancer, old man, young man, Carmen. . . ."[56] The *Cahiers du cinéma* team was certainly smitten, and Brialy would later become their mascot actor. He can be seen in their first films—in short subjects like Eric Rohmer's *La Sonate à Kreutzer* (*The Kreutzer Sonata*) and Jacques Rivette's *Le Coup du berger*, both in 1956; in Jean-Luc Godard's *Tous les garçons s'appellent Patrick* in 1957; and, more importantly, in Claude Chabrol's first two features, *Le Beau Serge* (*Bitter Reunion*) and *Les Cousins* (*The Cousins*), in 1958 and 1959, respectively.

From his contact with directors, Truffaut developed an increasing desire to become a director. Strangely enough, it was Julien Duvivier, an old-timer in French cinema, who suggested that they collaborate on the writing of a screenplay. Truffaut had not always been kind to Duvivier, but he had liked his most recent film, *Voici le temps des assassins* (*Deadlier than the Male*). The two men met in Cannes and discussed a project called *Grand Amour*, about an average man's love life. But Duvivier was monopolized by another project, the adaptation, with René Barjavel, of a murder mystery, *L'Homme à l'imperméable* (*The Man in the Raincoat*).

In mid-August, he wrote Truffaut a wonderful letter: "Last night I had a strange dream. You and I were at Le Havre. We were about to embark for America on a huge ocean liner whose name I saw very clearly: *L'Atlantique*. . . . I was inviting you on the trip!!! But when it was time to board, I noticed that I hadn't booked your passage. . . . You flew into a mad rage, and told me a few plain truths. So I went to see the chief purser, who remembered that I had crossed in 1948 and gave me a cabin. Then all of a sudden we were at sea and I was called to the telephone. . . . I'll never know who was calling me because at that point I woke up." A trip to America, a Freudian slip (one ticket for two!), an angry young man telling an experienced director some plain truths—Duvivier's dream reveals the nature of an ambiguous relationship between an experienced director and a critic who still has some way to go before crossing over to the other side. Yet Duvivier's letter ends on a very amicable note: "I would like to have you as a collaborator, if you still desire it as well. Let me know what you've been up to recently and what your plans are. Please see me as a friend who thinks highly of you and likes you."[57]

OPHULS

Max Ophuls was one of Truffaut's great "masters." They first met in 1953, when the director was shooting *Madame de . . . ;* for the release of the film, Truffaut and Rivette interviewed Ophuls at length in his home in Neuilly. Ophuls had asked his son Marcel to be present on that day to help him with the two *Cahiers* journalists, who he suspected might be slightly confused intellectuals. "As soon as they walked in, something clicked between my father and François. There was no need to translate; one could just sit in a corner and listen to them talk,"[58] Marcel Ophuls recalls. With his mixture of timidity and self-confident judgment, Truffaut seduced the great director. The two men understood each other and later developed the habit of meeting at the bar of the Plaza Athénée Hotel, on avenue Montaigne, for long conversations. This was the period when Truffaut organized vigorous press campaigns to gain appreciation for the "Ophuls style." He had to convince a public that was extremely skeptical and saw the German director as a gentle and eccentric dreamer specializing in slightly sugary Viennese pastries. Neither *Le Plaisir (House of Pleasure)* nor *Madame de . . .* had met with any critical success in France.

In the course of their many conversations, Ophuls and Truffaut discussed *Lola Montès,* the film that Ophuls was scheduled to start shooting in February 1955. Truffaut offered to work for him as an assistant. Ophuls encouraged him and, at the end of January, Truffaut signed up with Gamma Films and its head of production, Ralph Baum, as an assistant-trainee for five weeks, at a salary of 12,000 francs a month. But the contract was annulled because of union opposition. With his years of experience in movies, Baum was probably wary of the idea of giving an indiscreet critic a hands-on job on the set of an ambitious and difficult film. Ophuls, sorry about the decision but unwilling to clash with Baum, wrote to Truffaut on February 17 to express his regrets: "Next time, we will have to make use of you earlier, in the directors' camp rather than the assistants'. I hope Monsieur Rossellini will employ you thus. . . . I have the feeling, though I can't explain why, that you will become someone important in the creative end of motion pictures and that your conversion—from criticism to filmmaking—will occur smoothly."[59]

It was, therefore, in his capacity as journalist that Truffaut spent a week in Nice on the set of *Lola Montès* at the beginning of March. His reportage came out in *Arts* a short time later. At the time of its release, in the end of December, *Lola Montès* provoked quite a critical uproar. When it was first shown in Paris, on December 20, 1955, at the Marignan theater on the Champs-Elysées, the distributor ran an announcement informing the public that it was about to see a film that was "out of the ordinary" and that they still had time to get their money back. During the first screenings, part of the audience made such heckling noises that on two or three occasions the police had to be called in. François Truffaut was on the front lines of what he called the "battle of the Marignan": "Just like the heroine of the title, this film courts the danger of provoking a scandal and exacerbating passions. We will fight, if fight we must! We will argue, if argue we must! This is certainly the kind of cinema we must support, today, in 1955—auteur cinema, which is also a cinema of ideas, with a burst of invention at every image, a cinema that doesn't revive the prewar period, a cinema that beats down doors that have been boarded up for too long."[60] After a three-week run, the film's theatrical release was already threatened.

Truffaut resorted to a petition in a grand attempt to save the film. On January 6, 1956, a short statement written by Rossellini and Truffaut and signed by Astruc, Becker, Christian-Jaque, Cocteau, Kast, and Tati appeared on the front pages of *Arts* and the *Figaro*, requesting that the film's run be extended: "*Lola Montès* is, above all, an act of respect toward the public, which is so often mistreated by low-level entertainments that alter its taste and sensibility. To support *Lola Montès* is to support cinema in general since any serious attempt at renewal is in the best interest of cinema and the public." This was probably the first time in the history of motion pictures that a united front of influential filmmakers stood up for one of their own and dared to go against public opinion. Deeply moved and grateful, Ophuls wrote Truffaut a letter the next day to thank him for his help: "Now that I know you very well, I can confess a daydream I had a while ago. I had a lot of money. I had so much money that I could finance a big production house, a sort of 'European United Artists' and during the whole morning, so they could make their own films and express themselves, the following personalities were signing contracts: Jean Cocteau, Roberto Rossellini, Jacques Becker—how I love to write these names—Christian-Jaque, Jacques Tati, Pierre Kast, Alexandre Astruc. Please be so kind and be my emissary to them."[61]

Truffaut made his way in fits and starts down the road leading from journalism to directing, helped by decisive encounters. His talent and charm constituted undeniable assets, as did the polemical verve he applied to the causes he supported. Above all, he had a gift for delighting the film directors he met, whether it was Julien Duvivier or Max Ophuls.

ROSSELLINI

Max Ophuls hoped François Truffaut would be employed by Roberto Rossellini. In 1954, Rossellini was forty-eight and unappreciated by the Italian critics; his latest films, *Stromboli, I Fioretti, Europa '51 (The Greatest Love)*, and *Viaggio in Italia (Strangers)* were all commercial failures and remained misunderstood. He had just returned from Germany, where he had made *La Paura (Fear)*, an adaptation of a Stefan Zweig story; he was discouraged and pondering the idea of giving up filmmaking. He had moved to Paris and taken up residence in a suite at the Hotel Raphaël, on avenue Kléber, with Ingrid Bergman, their oldest son, Robertino, and their three-year-old twins, Isabella and Ingrid. He had been engaged to direct *Jeanne au bûcher (Joan of Arc at the Stake)*, the Paul Claudel oratorio with music by Arthur Honegger, at the Paris Opéra in June, with Bergman in the title role.

This artistic event filled the gossip columns, for Ingrid Bergman and Roberto Rossellini were among the most famous couples at the time. In its April 3, 1954, issue, *Paris-Match* published a front-page color photograph of the actress holding her two little girls in her arms. For the critical establishment, Rossellini was merely a ghost from the Italian neorealist past. But for the young *Cahiers* rebels, he was one of the world's greatest film directors.[62] Neither outdated nor scandalous, he embodied modern cinema, and the cinema of the future. Once again, Truffaut was on the front lines and publicly hailed the arrival in France of Rossellini and Bergman. On April 6, he made the front page of *Arts* for the first time, thanks to his exclusive interview with Ingrid Bergman and the flashy headline I ESCAPED FROM HOLLYWOOD . . . AND FROM SACHA GUITRY. From then on, Truffaut began a press campaign in support of Rossellini, producing about a dozen articles on the great master over a period of sixteen months. On May 12, in *Arts,* a profile entitled "Rossellini's Life in Eleven 'Fioretti' "; on June sixteenth, a first interview: "I am not the father of neorealism," the director declares, "I work in absolute mental solitude. I suffer from being scorned and insulted from all sides. I have to finance my films myself." On July fourth, another profile, this time in *Radio-Cinéma-Télévision:* "A Man Alone, Roberto Rossellini." Again in July, a second interview in *Cahiers,* conducted this time by Eric Rohmer. Finally, on July 19, a kind of preview in *Arts* of the five Rossellini films that were to be shown in Paris that year: *L'Amore* (*Ways of Love*), *Dov'è la Libertà?, Jeanne au bûcher, Viaggio in Italia,* and *La Paura.*

For the passionate film devotees at *Cahiers,* undeniably, it was exposure to Rossellini that put to the test their desire to make films. With *Viaggio in Italia,* Rossellini proved to them that it was possible to make films with great simplicity by telling a love story between two people in a real location. When the film was released in Paris on April 15, 1955, with the title *L'amour est le plus fort,* it was not just a lesson in filmmaking for Truffaut, Godard, and Rivette but a real revelation.[63] At the same time, the producer Henri Deutschmeister—who had just made Renoir's return to France possible by financing *French Cancan*—gave his friend Rossellini carte blanche. He decided to make a series of full-length 16-mm features, each of which would show an aspect of French life in the mid-fifties. These films would be made under his supervision by Rivette, Rohmer, Godard, Truffaut, Rouch, Reichenbach, Chabrol, Aurel—that is, the future New Wave group four years ahead of its time. "Each of us had to write a screenplay," Claude Chabrol recalls. "This is how I started writing the one for *Le Beau Serge* [*Bitter Reunion*]. Our desire to make films crystallized at the same time. François took the plunge first by directing a short, so I said to myself I would do one, too; it's as simple as that."[64] Significant locations were investigated—the Cité Universitaire, by Rivette and Gruault; the milieu of the press, by Truffaut; the construction site of a large dam in the Alps, by Godard. Several synopses were written, then contracts signed. But the project was too far ahead of its time; it didn't come off—not one foot of film was produced, either by Rossellini or by his disciples.

Of all of them, Truffaut was certainly closest to Rossellini, who made him his assistant—or "factotum," as Truffaut preferred to say, at the whim of projects of the moment and their urgency. For Rossellini could commit himself to a subject one day and ditch it just as quickly, depending on his mood. But as soon as he came up with an idea, Truffaut was enlisted. "And, immediately, one had to buy all the books on the subject, collect research material, contact vast numbers of people, begin writing, and start 'moving.' "[65] Truffaut's first collaboration with Rossellini was in February 1955. From Stockholm, where he was sojourning, the Italian director asked François to find a comedy he could film, with a part for Ingrid Bergman. In response, Truffaut wrote *La Décision d'Isa* (*Isa's Decision*), an eighteen-page treatment for a screenplay. It is the story of a woman screenwriter who discovers, launches, and marries a young Hollywood comedian named Jimmy. But she leaves him when her former husband dies in an accident. The project would be ditched, like many others.

Between 1955 and 1956, Truffaut worked on a dozen film ideas, assembling considerable research material each time, summoning actors, scouting locations, writing synopses. Included among these projects were a filmed biography of Georges and Ludmila Pitoëff and the adaptation of Montherlant's *La Reine morte* (*Queen After Death*). In the spring of 1955, the two men went to Lisbon, where Rossellini planned to shoot the Montherlant, to negotiate a contract. After spending a day in Vevey, where he had gone to visit Chaplin, Rossellini met Truffaut in Lyon. Truffaut described the journey thus: "We tear down the road in his Ferrari, speeding all the way to Lisbon; he drives day and night, and I have to tell him stories to keep him awake; each time he thinks I might be getting drowsy, he hands me a mysterious flask to inhale from."[66] The two men worked in Lisbon for a few days, and tried to meet the director Manuel de Oliveira. But Rossellini, who didn't feel comfortable in Portugal, gave up the project. They returned to France through the south of Spain and Castile. Suddenly, the Ferrari's steering wheel went out of control while they were speeding; miraculously they avoided an accident. Some workers in a small Castilian village managed to make the needed part overnight, and they were able to get back on the road. So, as Truffaut explained, "Moved by the talent, courage and conscientiousness of the garage mechanics, Rossellini decides to return to Castile to film *Carmen*."[67] As soon as he returned to Paris, Rossellini started to approach distributors. Skeptical, they demanded a treatment. Truffaut set to work, equipped with three copies of *Carmen,* a pair of scissors, and a big pot of paste; three days later, he handed Rossellini a script. Rossellini dropped the project almost immediately.

The next idea was to make a "Soviet *Paisan,*" an anthology of six or seven stories typical of modern life in the Soviet Union. Over a period of several weeks, Rossellini and Truffaut had *Pravda* translated for them, read books, and started to shape stories, with the confidential advice of a Russian diplomat. The project, which was doomed from the start, fell through because of a story that the diplomat considered too irreverent. A Soviet citizen spots his wife from a distance and suspects she is on her way to a romantic assignation. He follows her jealously, loses sight of her, and then sees her arm in arm with another man. This happens several times in the space of a few hours. But in the end, one discovers that the city's main department store has received about a hundred samples of the same dress, so on that day, a great many Muscovite women are identically attired.

In September 1956, on his return from the Venice Film Festival, Truffaut spent ten days or so at Rossellini's house in Santa Marinella, near Rome. The project this time involved Truffaut directing his first feature, *La Peur de Paris* (Fear of Paris), which Rossellini would produce with the support of Franco-London Films, Deutschmeister's production company. A contract was signed on November 21. Truffaut was paid 100,000 old francs for the forty-page screenplay, and his contract stipulated a total payment of 1 million francs for directing the film and making the final edit. The project was a coming-of-age story[68]: A young man, returning from military service in Germany, learns about life in Paris through his uncle, a wealthy artist who houses him and gives him an introduction into journalism. Soon sickened by this superficial, cynical life, the young man is saved from suicide by his friend Robert who works with him in the editorial offices of the newspaper. He gives up journalism and ekes out a living for a while illicitly selling poetry pamphlets and books on the street. Then he meets two women; with one, he shares a passionate but platonic romance; the other is an older woman who runs a nightclub and supports him in luxury. Finally, a decisive revelation brings the young man back to his true love. In this story the influence of Rossellini's screen characters is blended with Truffaut's own military, journalistic, and romantic experiences. But once again the project came to naught.

His two-year collaboration with Rossellini ended abruptly, after a last project that Truffaut worked on actively—a documentary on India, produced by the RAI (Radio Televisione Italiana) and directed by Rossellini. The filming was supposed to take nearly two years. As on prior occasions, Truffaut assembled considerable research material; he also acted as the intermediary with Jean Renoir, whose Indian experience—from making *The River* near Calcutta in 1950—was invaluable. Finally, since Truffaut couldn't allot more than a year to a trip so far away, Rossellini went off to shoot *India* on his own in 1957, with Jean Herman as his assistant. "I think it is wise for me to stop working with R.R. before he himself tells me that he can't take me to India or something like that,"[69] Truffaut wrote to Lachenay from Venice on September 16, 1956.

His experience with Rossellini, though outwardly fruitless, played a crucial part in Truffaut's life; it taught him resourcefulness, cunning with producers, and, above all, how to go from project to project, as dictated by imagination or financial opportunity. Though Rossellini lost interest in fiction and turned his attention to filmmaking projects with a documentary slant, Truffaut, for his part, was never attracted to the documentary form and even rejected its philosophy. One can understand his distress, between 1954 and 1956, working on stories, narratives, and scripts with a filmmaker who rejected them on principle. Yet from Rossellini, Truffaut learned the most essential thing—the filming of life.

THE AUTEUR THEORY

Meeting directors such as Max Ophuls and Roberto Rossellini provided François Truffaut with important opportunities to support them. He also developed another, more theoretical but just as radical way of promoting them, which was the *"politique des auteurs* [the auteur theory],*"* a decisive concept that Truffaut himself formulated.[70] The expression became famous, but even today it is often ambiguous. To trace its genesis and comprehend it requires understanding François Truffaut's critical persona. As early as January 1954, his article on *The Big Heat,* with the explicit title, "Aimer Fritz Lang [Loving Fritz Lang]" sets out the basis of his theory: "Shouldn't all of this lead us to suspect that Fritz Lang might be a true film auteur, and if his themes and stories come to us cloaked in the banal appearances of a thriller, war film, or western, shouldn't we see this as a sign of great probity on the part of a cinema that feels no compulsion to adorn itself with enticing labels? We should love Fritz Lang."[71]

Deliberate love and the desire to follow a body of work in the making— for Truffaut, these are the essential elements of the *"politique des auteurs."* This implies, first of all, closeness and intimacy with the author, *all* of whose films must be defended, even those that are flawed. Indeed, it is no coincidence that Truffaut's *"politique des auteurs"* developed into a coherent theory with the release of two movies generally scorned by the critics—Jacques Becker's *Ali Baba et les Quarante Voleurs* (*Ali Baba and the Forty Thieves*) and Abel Gance's *La Tour de Nesle.* These films provided Truffaut with the opportunity to make his manifesto more explicit.

On September 1, 1954, Truffaut published in *Arts,* the laudatory "Sir Abel Gance," wherein he considered the paradox that Gance's silent films were admired while his talkies were disparaged. This was the quasi-unanimous opinion of the critical establishment. Truffaut maintained that Gance's talkies were born of the same visionary genius as his silent films, and that it was inevitably contradictory to praise the latter and denounce the former. "Perhaps I should make the following confession. I believe in the *'politique des Auteurs,'* or, you might say, I refuse to accept the theory, which is so valued in motion picture criticism, of great directors 'aging,' or becoming 'senile.' Nor do I believe in the genius of the émigrés—Fritz Lang, Buñuel, Hitchcock, or Renoir—drying up." In setting down his theory, Truffaut attacks two highly ingrained critical prejudices: aging, and the loss of cultural roots. The directors he loves are "sages," "masters," cosmopolitan spirits, filmmakers who transcend boundaries. "The ten greatest directors in the world are over fifty,"[72] he wrote confidently in January 1958, with the New Wave on the horizon.

Truffaut was in fact disappointed by Abel Gance's *La Tour de Nesle* when it was released in March 1955. But virtuoso strategist that he was, he turned this disappointment into his principal argument in subsequent affirmations of his theory. "There is nothing very interesting to say about *La Tour de Nesle.* Everyone knows it is a commissioned film with a ridiculous budget whose best parts have remained in the distributor's drawers. *La Tour de Nesle*, you might say, is Abel Gance's least good film."[73] Judging Gance essentially on the basis of his potential and the one successful scene he notices in *La Tour*, Truffaut defends its author precisely for having botched his film, but botching it with sublime ease: "Since Abel Gance happens to be a genius, *La Tour de Nesle* is a brilliant film. Abel Gance doesn't possess genius: he is possessed by genius. . . . If you can't see Gance's genius, then you and I don't have the same conception of cinema, mine being the right one, of course. The question now is to see if it is possible to be both brilliant and a failure. I tend to believe that failing is a talent. Succeeding is failing. I would ultimately like to defend the thesis, Abel Gance failed auteur of failed films. I'm convinced that there are no great directors who don't sacrifice something. According to the criticism of our elders, a successful film is one in which all the elements partake equally of a whole which then deserves the adjective perfect. But I decree that perfection and success are abject, indecent, immoral and obscene."[74] With his taste for paradox, here at its extreme, Truffaut used the very deficiency in Gance's work to illustrate his auteur theory. Every auteur film becomes the story of a failure, of perfection sacrificed; and only the whole body of his work, retracing a personal, unique journey, can allow us to understand an auteur. The whole theory is based, therefore, on what could be called the "paradox of the minor film."

His defense of *Ali Baba and the Forty Thieves*, a film Jacques Becker was commissioned to make with Fernandel, published in the February 1955 *Cahiers du cinéma*, also seems intended as a manifesto—as suggested by its title, "*Ali Baba et la 'politique des auteurs.'* " The movie was ignored by the critics upon its release and Truffaut himself was embarrassed by its failings. Again, he used the art of paradox to extricate himself from a difficult position, subscribing to Becker's body of work, "with no exception," in the name of coherence in taste. "Even if *Ali Baba* were a failure, I would still defend it by virtue of the auteur theory to which I and my fellow critics subscribe. This theory, based on Giraudoux's statement, 'There are no works, there are only authors,' consists in denying the axiom dear to our elders, which maintains that films are like mayonnaise, you either succeed in making them or fail." What Truffaut is plainly suggesting, in a way, is a theory of taste as intransigent as the one he had used to attack "quality French cinema" a year earlier in "A Certain Tendency of the French Cinema." As for André Bazin, *Cahiers*'s tutelary figure, he was very skeptical about this critical approach, fearing the perverse effects of the systematic and formalistic praise of minor films.[75] But in spite of Bazin, the auteur theory soon won over a large part of the *Cahiers* editorial staff, for it fit in well with the magazine's personal approach (interviews with the chosen directors) and reinforced its polemical orientation.

Though Truffaut had put forward a critical strategy and a polemical line of defense, the notion of "auteur" still needed to be defined. Like Godard, Rivette, and Rohmer, Truffaut advanced a simple argument: An auteur is primarily and exclusively a director. *Mise-en-scène* is the auteur stripped bare; it is what remains when all the subsidiary aspects of film disappear (screenplay, promotion, etc.). The *only* thing that is beautiful in the movies is the *mise-en-scène;* and this alone defines the auteur. Rohmer expressed it with a quip: "No man shall enter the *Cahiers* Olympus who is not a director."[76] Bazin found it at the core of his study of *Cahiers*'s "hitchcock-hawksian" (that is, auteurist) tendency: "They so value *mise-en-scène* because they detect in it a large part of a film's very substance, an organizing of people and things which has a meaning unto itself, both moral and esthetic."[77]

For François Truffaut, the ideal instance of the "auteur-director" was Alfred Hitchcock, about whom Truffaut wrote profusely—twenty-seven articles in the fifties. The "master of suspense" was the object of true worship. "The greatest inventor of forms," the director par excellence, the one who "makes us experience the vertigo felt by his characters, thanks to the fascination which any formal, quasi-geometric figure exercises upon us. And beyond vertigo, [he] makes us discover the depth of a moral idea, a vision of the world."[78]

What the critic sees in the film, thanks to the mise-en-scène, is a (self-) portrait of the director, the auteur himself. An auteur, then, when all is said and done, is a director who allows his intimate self to be seen on the screen, either through a multiplicity of masks, like Hitchcock, or by revealing himself with complete frankness, like Nicholas Ray. So said Truffaut about Ray and *Johnny Guitar,* a film that moved him so deeply that he saw it over ten times in two weeks: "The mark of his talent lies in his absolute sincerity, his hypersensitivity.... Unlike André Bazin, I believe it is important for a director to recognize himself in the way we depict him and his films. Otherwise we have failed."[79] Recognizing the man who has revealed himself emotionally on screen is the ultimate consequence of the auteur theory. In this absolute love, there is a quasi-anthropomorphic conception of cinema; he who sees one of Ray's films and recognizes him, also sees and recognizes cinema as a whole. Ergo, Ray is cinema.

The auteur theory, as conceived by Truffaut, entails a strategy of continually harassing the enemy—and the enemy, in the mid-fifties, is again, or still, "quality French cinema." Truffaut relied principally on *Arts* to launch his attacks, for it had a wide circulation and as a weekly was better suited to polemic than the monthly *Cahiers du cinéma.*

On March 30, 1955, Truffaut published in *Arts* a tract entitled "The French Cinema Short on Ambition," wherein he suggested a precise rating of the "89 French directors of the day," whom he divided into five categories: the "auteurs"—he identifies nine—Astruc, Becker, Bresson, Cocteau, Gance, Leenhardt, Ophuls, Renoir, Tati; the representatives of "quality": Yves Allégret, Autant-Lara, Carné, Cayatte, Christian-Jaque, Clair, Clément, Clouzot, Delannoy, Grémillon; fifteen "semiambitious directors"; twenty-five "honest commercial" directors; and twenty-nine "deliberately commercial" directors. Similarly, on June 8, 1955, he berated the screenwriters, extending his attack on Aurenche and Bost to the whole profession, which "apes the worst literature" and aspires only to a "stillborn quality" with adaptations of best-selling books.

Truffaut regularly summoned the readership of *Arts* to "rise up against French cinema" and the audiences to "smash the seats when faced with these revolting films."[80] But he was at his most skillful and effective in direct combat—for example, in his lively, vitriolic attack on Jean Delannoy's *Chiens perdus sans collier,* adapted by Jean Aurenche and Pierre Bost from a novel by Gilbert Cesbron. In his November 9, 1955, article in *Arts,* Truffaut seemed to seek a confrontation with Delannoy—he insulted him in order to draw him out in the open, then called public opinion to witness. "It is custom-tailored writing for the Gaumont-Palace by two disillusioned and cynical screenwriters, Aurenche and Bost, who have written 'moving' dialogue, put into images by a man who is not intelligent enough to be cynical, too cunning to be sincere, and too pretentious and solemn to be straightforward." The hoped-for answer was not long in coming; on November 13, Delannoy sent him a registered letter: "What you wrote . . . is so low that I have never encountered anything like it in my twenty years in the profession. You've just broken a record. This deserves to be pointed out."[81] Naturally, Truffaut took advantage of this godsend by publishing an excerpt from Delannoy's letter in *Arts,* along with some of the letters of support he, Truffaut, had received. He thereby orchestrated a Manichean battle between the "incorruptible righter of wrongs" and one of the most eminent representatives of official academicism. On November 26, Truffaut triumphed: "Monsieur Jean Delannoy is the most commercial French director; what more does he want? Unanimous praise from the critics? Impossible! In reply to Jean Delannoy's *lettre recommandée* [registered letter], let me contrast three other letters whose signatories *recommend* themselves only to the grace of God. I guarantee I received no letter supporting *Chiens perdus sans collier*—nor has the management of *Arts;* if I had, I would have published it, not out of esteem for Jean Delannoy, but to balance this futile polemic."

After a year of combat, François Truffaut began a new stage in his career. In the spring of 1956, his popularity was such that his articles commanded the front page of *Arts.* In May 1956, there were four consecutive pieces on what he called the "progressive degeneration"[82] of the Cannes Film Festival. Cannes was an institution celebrating its ninth year; though more open than ever to the international film scene, it was also a fortress of the most established French cinema. On May 23, Truffaut launched an assault on the festival and the Ministry of Culture, which supported it, headlining his piece, CANNES, AN UNQUESTIONABLE SUCCESS? NO, MR. MINISTER! His critique staged a dialogue between the "little guy" who is the keeper of truth and the "big guy" blinded by power: "Movies are for the people who make them, who love them, who go to see them, and not for those who profit by them. The jury should be discharged and the diplomats sent back to their compromises." By violently and insolently attacking the festival, Truffaut gained yet further authority. From then on, every year in May, reports of the Cannes Film Festival in *Arts* would be colored by his moods.

VENICE 56

At the beginning of September 1956, François Truffaut attended Venice's Mostra, a prestigious film festival older than Cannes.

During his ten days at the Lido, Truffaut saw two or three films a day, including Robert Bresson's *Un condamné à mort s'est échappé* (*A Man Escaped*), Kenji Mizoguchi's *Street of Shame,* Nicholas Ray's *Bigger than Life,* Joshua Logan's *Bus Stop,* and Robert Aldrich's *Attack!* He very much wanted to meet Aldrich, a director whom he greatly admired. The meeting finally took place, a memorable event for him: "I met the corpulent genius on the beach and we chatted," he wrote in *Arts* on September 19. "I asked him 60 questions. Watch for the results of this delightful, sublime interchange in our next issue."

In Venice, between two screenings and during the lunch hour, French journalists and film professionals congregated on the Lido beach. The crowd included André Bazin, Jean de Baroncelli, Jean Néry, and Claude Mauriac. Here the foremost polemicists in the "paper war" that was raging in French cinema rubbed shoulders. It was a place for countless small humiliations, poses, and displays of contempt. "I sunbathe next to Carlo Rim," Truffaut confided, "but we make believe we don't know each other, which is sometimes comical since people try to introduce us three times a day, and we have to put on a show of not catching the names. . . . It's insane!"[83] Pierre Braunberger also hung around the Lido beach. He was one of the rare producers in Paris who was interested in young directors and willing to finance their films, mainly shorts. Braunberger admired the young Truffaut's critical talent and wanted François to make a short film for his production house, Les Films de la Pléiade. The two men hit it off, and Truffaut discussed several projects with the producer, whom he nicknamed "Batala," a reference to the fascinating swindler played by Jules Berry in Renoir's *The Crime of Monsieur Lange.*

On the Lido beach, Truffaut also met Madeleine Morgenstern, a pretty brunette with short hair. This perceptive, cheerful young woman was the only daughter of an important distributor, Ignace Morgenstern, the director of Cocinor (Comptoir cinématographique du Nord). While Morgenstern and his wife, Elizabeth, were vacationing in Switzerland, their daughter was representing him in Venice and had the task of finding films that could be distributed in France. Madeleine was twenty-five years old; she had studied English and lived in the United States for several months, and she was now working in Cocinor's publicity department. One evening, Pierre Braunberger introduced her formally to François Truffaut at the Hotel Excelsior, the fashionable festival hangout. The two would meet again on subsequent days, sometimes in the front rows at festival screenings. They enjoyed talking to each other, even though Madeleine didn't feel she impressed the hotheaded critic, whom she knew by his reputation and articles. "When we parted, he promised to write me, which he never did,"[84] she recalls. They would only see each other again six weeks later, thanks to a chance meeting on the Champs-Elysées. "Oh, I wrote you, but I tore up the letter!"[85] he told her, as a way of justifying his silence, shrouding himself in mystery and playing the seducer. They started to see each other regularly and go to the movies together, but it was still only a friendship.

When he left Venice on September 10, 1956, Truffaut went to stay at Roberto Rossellini's in Rome. Exhausted by his strenuous journalistic activity, he yearned for some other occupation, and even considered giving up criticism. Though he remained skeptical about his projects with Rossellini, he found it stimulating to be in close contact with the Italian director. Making a film became his top priority. But the contract signed with Rossellini and Deutschmeister for *La Peur de Paris* would remain in the drawer.

HENRI-PIERRE ROCHÉ

At this point, Truffaut was deeply moved by Henri-Pierre Roché's novel *Jules and Jim,* which he discovered by rummaging through the stalls of secondhand books at the Librairie Delamain on Place du Palais-Royal. He had been intrigued by the title of the novel, which had been published two years earlier by Gallimard and had gone more or less unnoticed. Henri-Pierre Roché was completely unknown and seventy-six years old; *Jules and Jim* was his first novel. "From the very first lines, I fell in love with Henri-Pierre Roché's prose," Truffaut would later explain. "At that time, my favorite writer was Cocteau for his brisk sentences, their seemingly dry tone and his precise imagery. Now, with Henri-Pierre Roché, I was discovering a writer whom I thought superior to Cocteau, for he obtained the same kind of poetic prose with a less extensive vocabulary, making very short sentences, and using everyday words. With Roché's writing, emotion is born from the void, from emptiness, from all the rejected words, in short from the ellipsis itself."[86]

Overflowing with enthusiasm, Truffaut mentioned *Jules and Jim* at every opportunity. Thus, in his review of Edgar G. Ulmer's intimist Western, *The Naked Dawn,* he ventured a comparison, clearly far-fetched for anyone but him: "One of the most beautiful modern novels I know is Henri-Pierre Roché's *Jules and Jim,* which shows us the lifelong relationship of two friends and their common female companion, and the tender love they have for each other, with hardly any conflict thanks to a new aesthetic moral code which is constantly reassessed. *The Naked Dawn* is the first film to make me feel that a cinematic *Jules and Jim* is feasible."[87] This declaration of love soon reached its intended beneficiary. Indeed, one month later, Roché wrote Truffaut a card in his tight, shaky handwriting, thanking him warmly: "I was very touched by your comments on *Jules and Jim* in *Arts,* in particular 'thanks to a new aesthetic moral code which is constantly reassessed.' I hope you will find it again, even more clearly, in *Deux anglaises et le continent* [*Two Englishwomen and the Continent*] which you will be receiving shortly."[88] Several days later, Truffaut received the writer's second novel, just published by Gallimard. After reading it, he felt even more strongly convinced of Roché's greatness, and during the summer, Truffaut went to visit him at his pretty little house in Meudon. He found a tall, thin, lively elderly man, who was working on his third novel, *Victor,* which would remain unfinished and whose hero was based on his friend Marcel Duchamp. Roché described his life to Truffaut, a dilettante's life spent among women, similar to Cocteau's, punctuated by trips and many encounters with his painter friends—André Derain, Francis Picabia, Max Ernst, Wols, Georges Braque (whose boxing companion he was), Marie Laurencin (one of his most faithful mistresses), and Picasso (whom he introduced to Gertrude Stein).

The exceptional bond he developed with a man three times older than himself strengthened Truffaut's desire to adapt *Jules and Jim.* In mid-November 1956, he even considered hiring Roché to write the dialogue for Kathe, the woman Jules and Jim both love. Roché responded enthusiastically to the idea and on November 23, he arranged to have five copies of *Jules and Jim* sent to Truffaut. The latter worked uninterruptedly, annotating, cutting, and restructuring, using Roché's sentences to create a simple, linear narrative. Henri-Pierre Roché would not write the dialogue for Kathe—who became Catherine in Truffaut's version—but he did offer much advice. The truth is, Truffaut was not really ready to make his first film on such a literary and sensitive subject, and the project of filming *Jules and Jim* was constantly postponed. But he maintained his correspondence with Roché, whose last letter was dated April 3, 1959. Because of illness, he was unable to accept Truffaut's invitation to one of the first screenings of *The 400 Blows.* "Dear young friend, your kind letter! If I feel better, I'll go see *The 400 Blows* in Paris. You'll let me know where it is showing. I reread *Jules and Jim* as well. I won't try to visualize it on screen until I've discussed it thoroughly with you, and know how you plan to adapt it. Would you like more copies? A heartfexlt thanks for the photos of Jeanne Moreau. I like her. I couldn't go out to see *The Lovers,* of course. I'm glad she likes Kathe! I hope to meet her one day. Yes, when you return, come to see me whenever you want, I look forward to it."[89] Henri-Pierre Roché died on April 9, 1959, without having seen *The 400 Blows* or having read the screenplay for *Jules and Jim.* At least he had seen Jeanne Moreau's face.

MAKING A FILM

Aware that he was not ready or mature enough to handle the subject successfully, François Truffaut put aside his adaptation of *Jules and Jim.* Other projects occupied him in the final months of 1956: ideas for films, some fully worked out, others not. Among these were several lines jotted down after a long conversation with Jean-Luc Godard one December morning on a bench at the Richelieu-Drouot Métro stop. The story was the following: Having missed the last train for Le Havre, Michel steals an American car near the Saint-Lazare station. After shooting a police motorcyclist who was hot on his tail, Michel, now back in Paris, goes to find his fiancée Betty, a young and pretty American journalist. In the streets of Paris on a late summer day, a frenetic chase takes place, from one movie theater to another. When she is arrested by the police, Betty ends up ratting on Michel, who is hiding out in a barge. He then gives himself up, although he claims to have taken a fatal dose of aspirin. No one believes him and he is hauled into the office of the inspector in charge of the case. "But for once Michel was not lying. As soon as he walks into the office, he collapses, arms stretched out on either side Christ-like, backward, in a single heap. They rush to his side, but Michel is already dead."[90] Three years later, in the summer of 1959, Truffaut's four-page synopsis was developed and changed, thus becoming the screenplay for Jean-Luc Godard's first film, *À bout de souffle* (*Breathless*).

Truffaut had suggested his most promising projects to Pierre Braunberger when they saw each other on the Lido beach. On January 10, 1957, they signed their first contract together, for a short film entitled *Autour de la tour Eiffel* (Around the Eiffel Tower). Truffaut received 75,000 francs for his four-page shooting script of the projected twenty-five-minute film scheduled to be shot in ten days, in 35 mm, with an estimated budget of around 2 million old francs. Joëlle Robin, Jean-Claude Brialy, Edith Zedkine, and Raymond Devos were cast in the four parts. Oddly enough, Truffaut wrote two versions of this story about a person obsessed with seeing the Eiffel Tower. In the first version, Juliette, a young provincial girl who is in Paris to settle an inheritance, wants to go up to the top of the Eiffel Tower, which she sees wherever she goes but is never able to get to. She meets people who could help her—a cattle dealer (Devos) on a short Paris trip, who delivers a monologue on the condition of the peasants instead of giving her directions; an attractive, talkative, cheeky young hussy (Joëlle Robin) who is waiting for a client and whose profession the young provincial girl is clearly far from suspecting; and a playboy (Brialy) who easily seduces her and finally drives her to the Eiffel Tower in his sports car. The other version gives Jean-Claude Brialy the leading role. He portrays a "Paris peasant" who first appears "leading an enormous, reluctant cow at the end of a rope" as he heads toward the Vaugirard slaughterhouses. He walks out of the slaughterhouse with a wad of bills in his hand and sets about visiting the capital. The Eiffel Tower is the first monument to attract him. He sees it from afar but seems to get lost every time he tries to approach it. A talkative, absentminded bistro owner (Devos) is of no use to him, nor is a prostitute. However, a young woman, Juliette, notices him sniveling at the edge of the sidewalk. She invites him to get into her convertible and then drives him to the Eiffel Tower. There, she drags him along on a quick tour of the monument. On their elevator ride up the tower, "the peasant changes imperceptibly: his beret, pulled down to his eyebrows, gradually rises until it vanishes in the emptiness." Up at the top, the peasant discovers "a Parisian Paris down to the fingertips." On their ride down, they are clearly in love and make "the most Parisian of couples"—she still smiling and elegant, he unrecognizable, clean-shaven, and witty—"An Adam of 1957 on the arm of an eternal Eve."[91] Truffaut quickly dropped this project, which no longer amused him. But a remnant of it can be seen in the credits of *The 400 Blows,* with the camera scanning the streets in the west of Paris and coming to a standstill at the foot of the Eiffel Tower. Several years later, Truffaut would collect replicas of the Eiffel Tower in all sizes, and they would be displayed on the shelves of his living room on avenue Pierre-Ier-de-Serbie.

He signed a second contract with Braunberger in March 1957 to contribute to a film with children as the theme. Truffaut, Richard Leacock (the British-born documentary filmmaker, disciple of Robert Flaherty), Claude de Givray, the novelist René-Jean Clot, Jacques Doniol-Valcroze, and Pierre Kast were each supposed to direct an episode. Truffaut's contribution was entitled "Le Mensonge de Bernadette [Bernadette's Lie]." It is the story of an adolescent girl accused by her teacher of cheating. The schoolgirl lies to defend herself and the teacher believes her. Several weeks later, before her First Communion, Bernadette stops eating and speaking. Finally, she leaves a letter on the kitchen table confessing her lie to her parents, then drowns herself in the river.[92]

This collective project was also soon abandoned. For a while, Truffaut envisaged making the film on his own, and he continued writing down anecdotes on childhood and classifying them by theme along with "Le Mensonge de Bernadette." Some of these would be reworked much later, in 1975, in *Small Change*, while one heralds a theme of *The 400 Blows:* "François's truancy. Cuts school. Returns. The note. The schoolbag behind the door."[93] In the spring of 1957, Truffaut was absorbed by the thought of making a film on childhood, but the link was still missing that would allow him to make the creative leap simply and naturally.

BERNADETTE'S SKIRT

In the *Arts* offices on rue du Faubourg-Saint-Honoré, François Truffaut met Maurice Pons, a young fellow contributor to the cultural weekly. Pons was also the author of a book of short stories entitled *Virginales,* which had been published by Julliard two years before. Truffaut very much liked one of the stories, "Les Mistons," and wanted to adapt it for the screen. Pons, who felt an immediate fondness for Truffaut, whom he later described as "a nervous young man, always hurried, with wild hair and beautiful dark eyes, like 'Bonaparte at the bridge of Arcole',"[94] was delighted at the thought. As for Truffaut, he was very impressed by the elegant, concise, almost precious style used by Maurice Pons to tell the story of a group of kids, nicknamed *"les mistons,"* and how they spy on the love affair of a student couple, Yvette and Etienne, intruding on their tennis games and movie dates. And then, how on a beautiful May afternoon, in a clearing where they have followed the couple, one of the boys is caught and given a stern hiding by Etienne. After the vacation, the children learn that Etienne died over the summer in a mountain-climbing accident, and they watch Yvette walk by one last time, in mourning clothes and engrossed in melancholy thoughts. Truffaut was moved by this short story and its evocative sensual power—the physical agitation conveyed, for example, in the description of Yvette's bath. "When she went to the baths at the river, she would leave her bicycle padlocked outside the entrance. Since her skirt always fluttered as she biked, and she certainly wore no petticoat, on hot days the saddle of her bicycle would become very humid. As the weeks went by, the outline of pale rings on the saddle became more visible.

Fascinated, we would walk around this flower of curdled leather, an ace of hearts perched high, whose trips we envied. It was not unusual for one us, unable to endure the strain, to walk away from the group and, with no exhibitionism or false shame, go up and press his face momentarily against this saddle—the confidant of what mystery?"[95]

In April 1957, Truffaut was finally in a position to make his first film. Robert Lachenay, who had just come into a small inheritance, had promised to help him, and Truffaut's confidence was buttressed by having found the actor who could play the part of Etienne—Gérard Blain, whom he had noticed in Julien Duvivier's *Voici le temps des assassins* (*Deadlier than the Male*), a brooding, handsome, and robust young man with a rather touchy personality. In his review of Duvivier's film in *Arts*, on April 18, 1956, Truffaut made a point of praising the new actor to his readers: "Gérard Blain, in his first real appearance, is perfect in the most difficult part." Blain responded immediately on the following day: "When I read you yesterday, it brought tears to my eyes and I didn't dare believe it. I've read almost all your articles and being perfectly aware of the reputation you have among us, I'm even more flattered. You're the only one to have understood me." Several days later, the two young men met and got on well; they began seeing each other in a café near the Champs-Elysées and at the actor's house in Boulogne. At dinner at Blain's house, Truffaut made the acquaintance of his young wife, Bernadette Lafont, whom Blain had met at the Nîmes Festival of Dramatic Art in the summer of 1955, when she was only seventeen years old. Captivated by Bernadette's spontaneity and convinced of Gérard Blain's talent, Truffaut suggested the couple play the lovers in *Les Mistons* (*The Mischief Makers*). He decided to shoot the film in Nîmes, Bernadette's hometown.

Bernadette Lafont had never acted in a film and Blain didn't look favorably upon his wife's embracing an acting career. But Truffaut's offer was an opportunity not to be missed. "I was rather shy; I spoke very little and I was ashamed of my accent," she says today, recalling her debut. "When I asked Truffaut why he had chosen me, he answered, 'I felt you wanted to work in films as much as I did.' And it was true."[96] The young woman began preparing for her part immediately and stopped studying for the baccalaureate exam, which she was supposed to take in June 1957. In May, she took up tennis to prepare for her role, and she followed Truffaut's costume instructions scrupulously: "The dressmaker told me she could make me a complete outfit in two days. I have nothing in white. So I could have two skirts made in that color—a very full skirt for the bike scenes and a narrow one with a slit as you mentioned. Will that be good?"[97] she wrote her Pygmalion on July 8. On two long weekends in April and June 1957, Truffaut scouted the region, accompanied by Rivette, Chabrol, and Brialy, as well as by Bernadette

Lafont and Gérard Blain, who served as guides. He decided on his shooting locations—the Nîmes arena, the Tennis Club, the Place de la Fontaine, and the outskirts of Saint-André-de-Valborgne. Now he only needed to find the money. The budget was far from enormous, particularly since Truffaut could benefit from equipment loaned by Jean Malige, the cameraman who had been approached for the film. Malige owned a ministudio near Montpellier, with a lightweight camera, dolly tracks, an editing table, and sound equipment. The actors were prepared to work on a profit-sharing basis and friends—Robert Lachenay, Claude de Givray, and Alain Jeannel—would be enlisted as assistants. However, there were essential expenses that had to be covered during the shooting and editing, which would take forty-five days.

Madeleine Morgenstern, who had become very intimate with François, asked her father to help finance *The Mischief Makers;* he handed the matter over to Marcel Berbert, his collaborator at Cocinor. The latter still remembers his boss's instructions: "Monsieur Morgenstern said to me, 'This young man wants to make a film. He should go ahead, but I'd rather he set up his own company so he'll be on his own. See what you can do.' "[98] Truffaut was thus able to create his own production company, les Films du Carrosse—an explicit homage to Jean Renoir (his 1952 film *Le Carrosse d'or* [*The Golden Coach*])—with the backing of 2 million old francs, the equivalent of the film's budget, from UFIC, an organization that financed movies. A phone call from Marcel Berbert was enough to convince the official at UFIC to grant this loan to a young unknown, though the volume of work in production at Cocinor was such that the risk involved was really minimal. "For a long time, Truffaut believed that he had been loaned this money because of his pretty face! Similarly, we were held financially liable when he brought his film in to be developed. It was only years later that François realized the truth,"[99] says Marcel Berbert. Helped, without his knowing it, by the man who would become his father-in-law, Truffaut got ready to direct his first film.

THE FILM OF TOMORROW WILL BE AN ACT OF LOVE

Before shooting *The Mischief Makers,* François Truffaut, still a star journalist, was careful not to miss the opportunity of a last press campaign. Shortly before the opening of the Cannes Film Festival, he published an article in the April 20, 1957, issue of *Arts* predicting the worst academicism. On May 15, when the festival was almost over, Truffaut drove the point home, once again in *Arts:* "You are all witnesses in this trial: French cinema is dying from its false legends." The following week, he delivered his final blow: "Cannes: a failure dominated by compromises, schemes and faux pas." According to Truffaut, the French film industry was producing "too many mediocre films," too much of that "quality cinema" he had been denouncing for nearly four years, restricted to narrow formulas, manufactured artificially in obsolete studios, with polished screenplays and actors, fossilized and flaunting a haughtiness and scorn for novelty and youth. As always, Truffaut counterbalanced his attack with praise for the directors he admired—in this instance, Renoir, Ophuls, and Rossellini, three auteurs whose "films are as personal as a fingerprint."[100] In analyzing the crisis in French cinema, Truffaut mentioned higgledy-piggledy the bankruptcy of producers, screenwriters, and directors, all of whom were passing the buck among themselves. He saw only one possible remedy: trust vested in the auteur, simultaneously director and screenwriter, who would freely choose his crew, actors, set, music, and story and converse with his producer as an equal. "The film of the future will be shot by adventurers," he concluded in an article that resembles both a critical testament and an anticipation of his own evolution:

> The film of tomorrow appears to me as even more personal than an individual and autobiographical novel, like a confession, or a diary. The young filmmakers will express themselves in the first person and will relate what has happened to them: it may be the story of their first love or their most recent; of their political awakening; the story of a trip, a sickness, their military service, their marriage, their last vacation . . . and it will be enjoyable because it will be true and new. . . . The film of tomorrow will not be directed by civil servants of the camera, but by artists for whom shooting a film constitutes a wonderful and thrilling adventure. The film of tomorrow will resemble the person who made it and the number of spectators will be proportional to the number of friends the director has. The film of tomorrow will be an act of love.[101]

Once again, Truffaut provoked an outcry in the film industry. (The following year, the directors of the Cannes Festival sanctioned Truffaut and refused to give him journalistic accreditation. He attended nonetheless.) Then Claude Autant-Lara got on the front lines. The director, whose adaptations—Stendhal's *The Red and the Black,* Radiguet's *The Devil in the Flesh,* and Colette's *Le Blé en herbe* (*The Game of Love,* based on *The Ripening Seed*)—were representative of "French quality" but who had also directed more personal, *noir* films, such as *Douce* (*Love Story*), *Occupe-toi d'Amélie* (*Oh Amelia!*) and *La Traversée de Paris* (*Four Bags Full*), tried to silence the angry young man of movie journalism. A week after Erich von Stroheim's death, on May 19, 1957, Autant-Lara took advantage of a radio homage to the deceased director to settle his score with Truffaut. "While I was attending the funeral of the jinxed director Erich von Stroheim this morning, I thought of that young thug of journalism who shamelessly claims that censorship doesn't exist, and I felt like grabbing him by the ears and dragging him in front of the grave of the director of *Greed* and showing him the grave of a director who was the preeminent victim of censorship." Truffaut responded on June 19 with a virulent article, certainly the most polemical one of his entire career. He accused Autant-Lara, whom he called a "false martyr," of being a "bourgeois director," of abdicating intellectually, of lacking courage and hiding behind screenplays written by other people, and of working within a system "spoiled rotten by money," which allowed him to "earn a salary of 25 million to direct Brigitte Bardot in *En cas de malheur* [*Love Is My Profession*] without ever taking the risk of personal creative work." The journalist concluded by saying, "The word courage keeps recurring in this article which is devoted to the kind Claude Autant-Lara lacks. He has only the courage to grumble and denigrate."[102]

On July 3, 1957, Truffaut savored his victory in *Arts*. In answer to Autant-Lara's incensed reaction, he published letters from readers who supported his views and were indignant at the contemptuous term "young thug of journalism"; these letters paint a dark, defamatory portrait of a defeated, embittered director "sold out to a system that is in complete decay."

Autant-Lara was not the only established director with whom Truffaut dueled publicly at this time. Yves Allégret, for example, was accused of contemptuously and artificially reconstructing the world of prostitution in *Méfiez-vous fillettes* (*Young Girls Beware*). Truffaut criticized Allégret for being completely cut off from life, for having never set foot in Pigalle, for being, in sum, one of those "French directors who are bourgeois and have no problems, and whose knowledge of life is limited to the hackneyed gossip of the Elysée-Club, the escalator of the Rex and the Kermesse aux Etoiles."[103] Truffaut also denounced Michel Audiard for his vulgar dialogues and his contempt for his characters.[104] In writing about Carlo-Rim, a director known for his clichés, Truffaut assumed a moral stand, asserting that a filmmaker must never "show contempt for the audience by underestimating it," but, rather, treat "the spectator as his equal" and respect the rule of never including anything in a film "that is supposed to make people laugh unless it makes you laugh yourself, or to make people cry unless it moves you yourself," he wrote on November 6, 1957. Truffaut's diatribe against the "money that makes the bourgeois directors rotten," the corrupt system, and the "civil servants"[105] of the French cinema was completely in keeping with the protest language of the final months of the French Fourth Republic, which called into question the decaying French political and parliamentary system. In the late fifties, France needed fresh air, and a complete overhaul. The need was felt in all areas—political, social, and cultural. In film circles, Truffaut embodied this need for renewal.

Henri-Georges Clouzot and René Clément were the only important directors of "quality French films" who had so far been spared by Truffaut. In fact, Truffaut nicknamed them "the Untouchables."[106] Though Doniol-Valcroze and André Bazin were close to both directors, neither had the power to prevent Truffaut from doing a real hatchet job on Clouzot in the December 1957 *Cahiers du cinéma,* in an article entitled "Clouzot at Work, or the Reign of Terror," which is still surprising today for its violence. "With *Les Espions,* Clouzot has made Kafka in his pants, a seven-word statement which perfectly conveys the exact level of the enterprise," he wrote, basing his demonstration on an account of the shoot of the film, and denouncing the reign of terror the director had enforced on the set. Clouzot and Clément were both expelled from the "cinema of the future," whose advent Truffaut was yearning for; he was particularly harsh in his review of *Barrage contre le Pacifique (The Sea Wall):* "For Clément the main thing is that he shoot a film which costs more than the preceding one and less than the next."[107] Clouzot, the terrorist; Clément, the thoroughly corrupt: The hatchet job was complete.

IF GUITRY WERE TOLD TO ME

In the mid-fifties, Sacha Guitry was still regarded primarily as a man of the theater, an author and wit, and was still tainted by the political and moral charges made against him after the Liberation. As a result, he was ignored by film devotees and scorned by left-wing critics. But Truffaut had remained loyal to the director of *The Story of a Cheat,* one of the films that had most influenced him in his youth. Consequently, any film by Sacha Guitry became the occasion for a merciless fight against the "prejudices of French cinema." In March 1956, he led a crusade in defense of *Si Paris nous était conté,* which he regarded as greatly undervalued by the critics. But the rift—or abyss—that had grown between the critics and the director of *Désiré* and *Donne-moi tes yeux* was even more apparent when Guitry's last two films were released, *Assassins et Voleurs (Lovers and Thieves)* and *Les trois font la paire,* made when he was already disabled and gravely ill. Truffaut took up the challenge and embarked on a particularly bellicose rehabilitation campaign, perhaps his most brilliant fight of those years. On February 13, 1957, with provocative humor, Truffaut entitled his article on *Lovers and Thieves* "Sacha in Top Form," maintaining it was one of the best films of the year, an opinion most critics did not share. Truffaut indignantly affirmed that Sacha Guitry's "unbelievably casual shooting style is a wonderful directing idea, for it is perfectly suited to his sense of humor. I love Sacha Guitry because given the choice between suggestiveness and obscenity, he always chooses obscenity, because his sense of humor knows no boundaries and the infirm, the elderly, children and the dead clink their glasses like everyone else." The young critic's only regret was that he never got to meet the man whom he unhesitatingly compared to Renoir. "In 1955, during the filming of *Lovers and Thieves*, I wanted to interview Sacha Guitry; his secretary replied I could do so only if I prepared my questions ahead of time and submitted them to the master first. Foolishly I refused; I was a dope that day,"[108] he admitted in July 1957, in an homage published at the time of the director's death.

VADIM RIGHT ON TIME

The crusade against "quality cinema" and the desire for renewal focused, in the mid-fifties, around two young directors—Alexandre Astruc and Roger Vadim. For Truffaut, these two names were synonymous with a new, intimate cinema, in touch with life. "Vadim will deal only with the things he knows well—today's girls, quick cars, love in 1957 (and not love copied from prewar films). Alexandre Astruc, on the other hand, has a more abstract temperament and will shoot lyrical films which could be very beautiful and very commercial when the characters are in period costume, and very beautiful and noncommercial when the same characters expressing the same thing are in modern dress," he wrote on May 15, 1957 in *Arts*. His point of view, once again, was hardly shared by most of the critics. Astruc's "precious social whirl" was mocked when *Les Mauvaises Rencontres* was released in 1955, and Vadim was upbraided for his effrontery when he undressed Brigitte Bardot in *Et Dieu créa la femme* (*And God Created Woman*) a year later.

The affair even caused quite a stir when Bardot's picture was splashed all over the front page of *Arts*. FILM CRITICS ARE MISOGYNISTS. B.B. IS THE VICTIM OF A CABAL, was the weekly's headline on December 12, 1950, written by Truffaut. Judged harshly by intellectuals and virtuous censors, French cinema's new star was also the object of constant rumors and malicious gossip in the popular press. Once again, Truffaut outspokenly chose sides: "Bardot, who had the bad luck of appearing in three films in one month, has an army of gossips ganging up against her who, being deficient in mental arithmetic, count on their fingers and are amazed to discover that three times thirty million is far beyond anything they will ever earn with their pathetic freelance assignments as undernourished intellectuals."[109] With the emergence of the Bardot myth, Truffaut finally believed he saw a rift within French cinema—the advent of the liberated female body, and a new eroticism that contrasted completely with the soppiness or bawdiness of most films of the period. "I thank Vadim for directing his young wife by making her repeat everyday gestures in front of the camera, insignificant gestures like playing with her sandal, or less insignificant ones like making love in broad daylight—less insignificant but just as real! Instead of imitating other films, Vadim wanted to forget the movies and 'copy life,' true intimacy, and, with the exception of two or three slightly self-indulgent endings in some scenes, he achieved his goal perfectly."[110] Truffaut's statement certainly didn't displease Brigitte Bardot, who sent the young man a timid and grateful note on December 13: "Dear Monsieur Truffaut, I was immensely touched by the article you published in *Arts*, it encouraged me and I thank you with all my heart."[111]

Truffaut found Brigitte Bardot the equal of Marilyn Monroe and James Dean, a screen presence that rendered most other actors archaic, relegating them to the rank of "quaint mannequins." Vadim was the only one to be filming a woman of his time; other directors were twenty years behind the times. Indeed, *Sait-on jamais?* (*No Sun in Venice*), Vadim's second film, was featured as *Cahiers du cinéma*'s cover story in April 1957. Then, in July, in *Cahiers* once again, Jean-Luc Godard recognized the importance of the phenomenon: "Roger Vadim is 'with it.' No question. His fellow directors, for the most part, are still shooting 'on empty.' No question again. Vadim must be admired for the natural way in which he does what should have long ago been the ABCs of French cinema. For what could be more natural than to *breathe the air of the times*? Therefore we shouldn't be congratulating Vadim for being ahead of time, for actually it's just that while all the others are late, he's right on time."

THE MISCHIEF MAKERS

Being "right on time"—for François Truffaut, 1957 was a turning point. In Nîmes, everything was ready for the shoot, except one small detail: The mischief makers were missing. Truffaut's first task, therefore, when he moved into the Hotel Imperator on July 30, 1957, was to choose the boys who would play in his film. To do so, he placed an announcement in *Le Midi libre*: "Film director seeks 5 boys, 11 to 14 years old, to play 'mischief makers.' " On July 31, out of about fifty boys who paraded through the newspaper's premises, five were selected. August 2 was the first day of shooting in the city's arena, an event that was closely followed by the local newspaper. "It is this morning," reported one journalist, "that the critic (become director) François Truffaint [*sic*] started shooting the scenes of his first film."[112]

The technical equipment was truly rather rudimentary: eight-meter dolly tracks, a dolly that did not need to roll silently since there would be no sound recording, a lightweight 35-mm camera, three sun reflectors, and a photoelectric cell. These were in the hands of a very small crew, consisting of Jean Malige, Robert Lachenay, Claude de Givray, and Alain Jeannel. Thrift called for this minimal crew and equipment, recalls Bernadette Lafont: "There was no money. I lived at my parents' house, and they agreed to put up Claude de Givray. François wanted to be at the Imperator. 'When Madeleine calls me, I have to be in a good hotel,' he said to justify himself. But just to be provocative, he would walk into the hotel with his bike, wearing blue shorts, the hotel being elegant and strict at the time."[113]

On August 5 and 6, the cast and crew moved to the Nîmes Tennis Club, where the progress made by Bernadette Lafont and Gérard Blain seemed very relative, even though they had taken intensive courses since the spring. The first litmus test came on the morning of August 7—with the rushes of the four preceding days. Truffaut analyzed his work with great lucidity, finding these first results uneven, pinpointing a "certain static aspect" and wary of "overly meticulous camera work."[114] On August 8, Truffaut shot the lovers' separation scene at the Montpellier train station, on the platform of the train for Palavas. Bernadette Lafont recalls it was a difficult moment: "François wanted me to cry and I was having trouble. So, to stimulate me, he said, 'You know, Brigitte Bardot (whom we adored, he and I) is not a very good actress. I don't think she could cry, but you'll be able to!' I cried and cried, but the shot wasn't kept in the editing."[115] On the next day, the big scene was shot, in the country near Saint-André-de-Valborgne, when Gérard Blain catches a boy and tells him off: "You nasty little mischief maker!"

In the middle of the filming, during a weekend of rest, Truffaut made a first assessment and decided to give Bernadette Lafont's role greater importance, and to focus more on the children, whom he very much enjoyed directing: "There's such a difference between what I obtained from them in the final days and at the beginning of the shoot that I've completely regained my self-confidence,"[116] he wrote his friend Charles Bitsch. The truth of the matter was that his relationship with Gérard Blain was strained. The actor proved to be capricious and jealous of the attention Truffaut was paying to his young wife. Blain was deliberately pushed aside, and he left the shoot before the rest of the actors and crew. After his departure, the atmosphere on the set improved, probably because Truffaut had also acquired greater self-confidence. Bernadette Lafont recalls that they nicknamed him *"le petit caporal"* (the little corporal), because in profile "he resembled Napoléon at the bridge of Arcole, very inspired, impassioned, consumed with ambition. There was something feminine about him, this way of stealing from others, with genius."[117]

When he returned to Paris on September 7, 1957, François Truffaut was relieved, though exhausted from his five weeks of intensive work in Provence. The first screening of *The Mischief Makers* was held on November 17, in the BBC screening room on avenue Hoche, and the second one, ten days later, at the U.G.C. movie theater on the Champs-Elysées. Truffaut was literally sick with anxiety: An X ray showed he had aerophagia, something he would often suffer from before and after his shoots.[118] He dreaded the cold, impersonal social ambiance of this type of screening. Consequently, he mobilized numerous friends, from *Cahiers* and *Arts*, as well as directors he felt close to—Alex Joffé, Roberto Rossellini, Pierre Kast, Norbert Carbonnaux—and also Audiberti and Cocteau, who saw the film for the first time on November 27. "The theater is very large," Truffaut complained to Lachenay on the eve of this screening, "and I hope you'll be able to come and bring whomever you want."[119] Truffaut was well aware that, this being his first creative endeavor, some people were waiting to get back at him. Indeed, his many enemies would be ready to jump upon the smallest flaw. He was cheered by the reactions of his friends, Rivette, Rohmer, Godard, Doniol-Valcroze, and Bazin, but he would only really be quieted after the private screenings for journalists and industry professionals on December 18 and 19, at the Centre national de la cinématographie. Such producers as Pierre Braunberger, Henry Deutschmeister, and Paul Graetz responded favorably to the film. And so did Simone Signoret, regardless of her misgivings toward a critic who hadn't always been kind about her films. On November 23, Truffaut presented *The Mischief Makers* before a packed audience at the Tours Festival of Short Films, though he didn't dare enter the film in competition. The response was enthusiastic, which immediately made him regret his not daring. Truffaut had won his gamble: His enemies were silent—some had already come around—and only his friends took sides publicly.

Yet it would take a year for *The Mischief Makers* to get a commercial release. On November 6, 1958, it began a run at La Pagode movie theater. In the meantime, it was presented at the Festival du film mondial in Brussels in February 1958, where it won the prize for best director. Press coverage was extensive and often full of praise. "They were waiting to catch him out. He survived the test with honor. He doesn't know how to tell a full-blown story yet, but his humorous sketch is bursting with talent. He has a feeling for imagery, he knows how to direct actors, and above all he has a 'tone' that is both poetic and cruel," reported *France-Soir*.[120] His writer friends at the weeklies orchestrated unanimous approval for his first venture. Claude Mauriac in *Le Figaro littéraire*, Jacques Siclier at *Radio-Cinéma-Télévision*, Jacques Doniol-Valcroze in *France-Observateur*,

Jacques Audiberti in *Arts*, and Paul-Louis Thirard in *Les Lettres françaises* were all complimentary, as well as Claude Beylie at *Cahiers du cinéma*.

Jean Delannoy introduced the only jarring note in this chorus of praise. True, he had been targeted directly, since in one scene in the film, the boys have fun ripping up a poster for *Chiens perdus sans collier*. In February 1958, *France-Soir* reported Delannoy's comments: "The story of *The Mischief Makers* acquires special pungency when you realize that François Truffaut only got to direct his first film thanks to the backing of the prominent distributor of whom he has recently become the son-in-law, and who handled my last two films, *Notre-Dame de Paris* and *Chiens perdus sans collier*, among other things. So, I have the satisfaction of having contributed, to some extent, to the debut of my fiercest opponent."[121] Ambitious critic marries daughter of wealthy distributor to further his career—this rumor would fuel the dark side of the François Truffaut legend for a long time to come.

MADELEINE

Over the last several months, François Truffaut and Madeleine Morgenstern had gotten to know each other well. They saw each other with increasing frequency, shared a common passion for books, and often went to the movies together. He liked to watch her drive when they were in a car; it made him think of the women in Hawks or Hitchcock films. The summer had been devoted to the filming of *The Mischief Makers*, but as soon as it was over, there was talk of a fall marriage. An only daughter, Madeleine lived on rue de la Tour, in the prosperous sixteenth arrondissement, with an intractable mother and a father she adored, and with whom she worked. Marriage with an "antisocial, heretical young journalist"[122] may not have been an act of rebellion against her parents, but it was certainly very daring for the period. A young woman whose upbringing was strict but not religious, Madeleine was captivated by François, by the intense look in his eyes, and by his shyness, "which he used like a screen so he could spend time only on the things he liked, and with the people he liked."[123] He also had a loner quality that made him different from all the young people from good families whom she had met up until then. With François, she had the feeling of discovering another world, another way of living: "He never said anything inconsequential or neutral,"[124] she commented. Her tastes in movies evolved under his influence: "I liked what François liked; even if I was grudging about certain films, I could understand his choices."[125] For Truffaut, Madeleine embodied intelligence and humor, and a certain seriousness, as well as the strangeness of another culture, which he found very appealing. She had great gentleness, and a little something about her reminded him of Leslie Caron. Their love was based on an immediate bond, which, nonetheless, concealed a few misunderstandings. They each fulfilled a deep desire in the other: He could settle down and find stability after his long years of adventure; she could finally escape the family stronghold and taste adventure, after years of being extremely sensible.

The wedding took place on October 29, 1957, at the town hall of the sixteenth arrondissement. For family reasons, the two youths wanted a discreet ceremony, as simple as possible. Madeleine was very worried about her father's health, for he was gravely ill. As for François, his relationship with his parents was so strained that he put off introducing his future wife to them until the very last moment. This is clear from a somewhat curt letter he wrote to his mother in the summer of 1957, informing her of the practical details of his wedding: "It is best that you meet Madeleine after the vacation, and her parents only on the day of the wedding so as to simplify interfamily relationships as much as possible. Madeleine and I are going about things so that this marriage won't be a nuisance for anyone. For the time being, let's not talk about it in the family. At the last minute, so no one will be offended, we might have to invoke a bereavement on the 'opposing side' to justify the 'strict intimacy.'[126]

François made a point of explaining that he was getting married "at the town hall only, since the Morgensterns are Hungarian Jews." This sentence could be regarded as simply informative, but he wrote it as a slap at the Monferrands, whose values he was well aware of—straitlaced, basically nationalistic, and attached to a traditional, Catholic France. Truffaut had deliberately done nothing to bring the two families closer. Indeed, Madeleine Morgenstern confirms that "introducing me to the Bazins was more important to François than my meeting his parents";[127] it was as though the future bridegroom was embarrassed, or too aware that any emotional bond between two families of such disparate cultures was impossible. "His parents weren't unfriendly—they were rather enlightened and pleasant, not brutal at all—but there was such hatred and rebellion in François," Madeleine adds.

Madeleine's father, Ignace Morgenstern, born in 1900, had fled Hungary in 1921, in the aftermath of the counterrevolutionary regime's bloody suppression of the Béla Kun movement. On his arrival in Paris after a stay in Germany, he got a job as an unskilled worker at Renault; then he worked as a runner in the accounting department at Paramount-France. He had very good organizational skills, and learned to speak French, though he never lost his Hungarian accent. Gradually, he moved up through the ranks and became head of production for Adolphe Osso when Osso, founder and president of Paramount-France, created his own company, Les Films Osso.

In 1927, Ignace Morgenstern married his cousin Elizabeth, who had come from Hungary to join him in Paris. In July 1931, Madeleine was born. When Osso Films went bankrupt in 1934, Morgenstern found himself without a job. During the period of the Front populaire, he moved to Lille with Elizabeth and Madeleine and set up the local branch of SEDIF, a film distribution company, whose parent company was owned by the producer Joseph Lucachevitch. In 1939, Morgenstern was drafted. The following year, Elizabeth Morgenstern and her daughter joined the exodus and left Lille, squeezing into a taxi headed for Lyon with six other people. Morgenstern had rented a farm in the village of Frontenas, in the Beaujolais area, where he and his family hid during the Occupation, arduously working the land for a living. Here, Madeleine found solace in reading the classics. At the time of the Liberation, Morgenstern reopened the SEDIF. Then, in 1948, he created his own distribution company, Cocinor, buying up SEDIF from Lucachevitch, who had moved to the United States during the war.

In the 1950s, Ignace Morgenstern became one of the major distributors in Paris. "He was a man who didn't regard making money as contemptible," Madeleine says, "but he was not a big-time gambler. He liked playing chess, and for him, doing business was like winning at chess. It so happened that he won more often than he lost."[128] Morgenstern, who distributed mostly popular films, starring actors like Fernandel or Jean Gabin and directed by such commercially successful directors as Henri Verneuil, was extremely respected at the time among French film-industry professionals. He was a man of his word, discreet, shrewd, intelligent, generous.

When he met François Truffaut, Ignace Morgenstern made no comment to his daughter about this young man who bit his nails and had a timid look in his dark eyes. Morgenstern didn't read *Arts*, which he regarded as too right-wing; he preferred *L'Humanité* and *Les Lettres françaises*, out of ideological conviction, and *Le Figaro*, to keep track of the reviews of the films he distributed. An established and respected distributor working within the popular cinema, he found nothing to draw him close to the young "hussar," this "thug of journalism," whom Madeleine was seeing. But out of respect and love for his daughter he accepted him.

Elizabeth Morgenstern, on the other hand, never hid the fact that she would have preferred her daughter to marry a Jewish doctor or lawyer, or, in any case, someone Jewish. Madeleine describes her mother as an engaging person who nevertheless had an explosive temper. "My only act of independence was to marry François. My mother was possessive, while my father respected the other person's freedom."[129] Clearly, this marriage seemed incongruous to Elizabeth Morgenstern, but she wanted her daughter's happiness above all. She could only look on with disquiet, however, as the wedding ceremony took place.

Truffaut had asked André Bazin to be his witness, and he was also glad of Rossellini's friendly presence at the town hall that day. Claude de Givray was the only member of the *Cahiers du cinéma* group to be present. Madeleine wore a white wedding dress—the only traditional note in the quick, simple, somewhat tense civil ceremony. After the wedding ceremony, the young couple went to see Ignace Morgenstern, who had been advised by his physicians not to leave his room. Then Madeleine and François joined their guests at the Pavillon Dauphine near the Bois de Boulogne for their wedding luncheon.

Fortunately, a few congratulatory messages from the friends at *Cahiers* brought a bit of merriment and humor to this melancholic celebration. For instance, Jean-Luc Godard's: "One must be against one's wife. Congratulations." Or Doniol-Valcroze's: "After Schérer married in Paramé, we have Truffaut becoming Mado's hero. *Cahiers* are becoming bourgeois, and it's all to the good, we'll eat better. Bravo."[130] That night, the couple took the train to Monte Carlo for their honeymoon. Boredom and bad weather made it easy for them to shorten their stay in the principality and leave for Nice, where there was at least a greater choice of films playing at the movie theaters!

Star critic, budding director, happy husband—at twenty-five, François Truffaut had settled down; his bohemian existence was over. The couple moved into the apartment that Ignace Morgenstern had bought for his daughter, on rue Saint-Ferdinand in the seventeenth arrondissement, five minutes away from the Place de l'Etoile. The building was unexceptional, modern and impersonal, but the three-room apartment was comfortable, well laid out, and tastefully furnished. Thanks to the large living room and its many bookshelves, Truffaut finally had space for all the books and most of the files he had accumulated since adolescence, for they had followed him from room to room, hotel to hotel, at the mercy of his moods, his finances, and his restless love affairs.

PUTTING AN END TO CRITICISM

After *The Mischief Makers,* François Truffaut regarded himself as a full-fledged director—young, inexperienced, but a director nonetheless. He wanted to give up movie criticism, since from the outset, he considered the two professions incompatible. "Criticizing a film comes down to criticizing a man, and this I no longer want to do."[131] Refusing to play the role of the "wolf in the sheep barn" and no longer wishing to tell a lazy or unworthy fellow director a few plain truths, Truffaut restricted himself, from that time on, to supporting a few director friends by praising them in writing, especially if they were in need. He let others take over his columns. This posed no problem at *Cahiers du cinéma,* where a new editorial staff formed around Eric Rohmer; it included Jean Douchet, Luc Moullet, André Labarthe, Jacques Siclier, Claude Beylie, and Michel Delahaye. But the situation was more complicated at *Arts,* where Truffaut was nearly as much of a star as Jacques Laurent. Yet, since 1956, Truffaut had brought in his friends—first Rohmer, followed by Rivette and Siclier; then Charles Bitsch, Claude de Givray, Jean-Luc Godard, and Jean Douchet the following year. The Young Turks had developed an efficient infiltration strategy. In 1958, then, Truffaut's name appeared more and more infrequently; he seems to have planned his withdrawal from criticism just as easily as he had previously—thanks to the same friends—stormed onto the movie page of the same cultural weekly.

However, sensing the danger of losing a star journalist, André Parinaud, the editor in chief of *Arts,* became more and more insistent. He was even prepared to give Truffaut a raise rather than see him resign from the movie page. On September 7, 1957, Parinaud tried to clarify matters, requesting in passing that Truffaut attend the Tuesday-afternoon editorial meetings: "I'd like to know whether you're serious about your work. Over the last three years you've achieved a certain success in the profession and I think we've played a part in getting your talent recognized. But it so happens that for the last few weeks your sloppiness has become a serious matter. The movie page has lost its punch. Your little friends, like Eric Rohmer, whatever their competence, lack experience, and as far as that's concerned I think it might be good if Monsieur Eric Rohmer were to school himself elsewhere. I request that you tell him so. . . ."[132]

Simultaneously courted and threatened, Truffaut had to make up his mind. So he chose confrontation through escalation of pressure. The tactic was clear: Either the editorial board would reject his demands and the two parties would break off for good or it would accept that he write for the weekly whenever he wanted and that he could freely assign to his friends the regular articles that he now refused to write. Things came to a head on September 18, 1957, when *Arts* published on its front page his interview with Jean Renoir, who was in Paris for rehearsals of *Le Grand Couteau,* adapted from the Robert Aldrich film *The Big Knife,* which was itself based on a Clifford Odets play. The interview was heavily cut and included an unflattering photo of the director; he looked downcast, his features were drawn, he was gesturing grotesquely with both his hands, and a balloon had him saying, "I don't believe in well-structured theater." Furious, Truffaut complained to Parinaud and reissued his demands for real control of the movie page, including the right to have anyone he chose write for it. At the end of his letter, Truffaut called Parinaud a liar, since he had promised to publish the interview in its entirety. The editor in chief reacted sharply to this demand and justified his cuts on technical grounds: "It saddens me to see how far you're driven by the pretensions of your 'inflated ego,' but your tough-guy airs are too amusing for me to be angered. One of these days, with your bullying attitude I'm sure someone will get a big thrill bringing you back to earth with a couple of slaps. As for me, I have too much work."[133]

At that point, Truffaut tried a more subdued approach, aware that he wouldn't obtain anything through anger: "I don't have an inflated ego, but I feel at this point that merit—yes, merit—entitles me to the complete supervisory capacity that Aurel exercised through terror and intimidation when I first started here. I received enough slaps between the age of ten and fifteen so that new ones wouldn't change my behavior in any way. And that's just it, I knock about in circles (journalism and cinema) where no one knows where to give slaps anymore: they prefer to say yes, and betray me as soon as my back is turned." And he concluded with the following admission: "All I ask for is one thing, control on cinema here."[134] He demanded a letter signed by his editor in chief defining his role. It seems that in this power struggle with Parinaud, Truffaut failed to get his way, though he did get much better payment for his freelance work.

Between the autumn of 1957, when he returned to Paris after shooting *The Mischief Makers* and the following spring, Truffaut underwent a severe crisis in confidence; getting to direct a first feature turned out to be far more difficult than he had realized. Several of his projects—with Pierre Braunberger, for instance—had come to nothing, one after the other. "I have to continue writing articles to make a living, particularly since *Arts* now pays me quite well. But how difficult it is to try to get a bit more film exposed this year!"[135] he wrote on May 6, 1958. This disillusioned, indeed pessimistic, state of mind can be seen in his articles at the beginning of 1958. At a time when renewal and youth could be sensed in a large portion of the press— the first waves of the cinema to come—Truffaut, in *Arts*, systematically went against critical fashion. On January 15 he wrote, "It's too early to clean out the dead wood. The ten greatest directors in the world are over 50." For the first time, Truffaut seemed outstripped by the movement he himself had launched—the coming New Wave—and, indeed, some of his readers reproached him for it.

Though his last articles of spring 1958 constitute an interesting, if rather pessimistic, testament, they are hardly representative of Truffaut's journalism, the medium by which he first achieved fame. It is hard to grasp just how much hatred and admiration he summoned in the mid-fifties. Truffaut wrote that Orson Welles was famous before he had shot a single foot of film; this could also be said about Truffaut. One need only note how often he was alluded to in films at the time. In Christian-Jaque's *Nathalie (The Foxiest*

Girl in Paris), the screenwriter Jean Ferry gave the name Truffaut to a crooked cop; in Edouard Molinaro's documentary on the Banque de France, a man picks up the telephone and says, "Get me Truffaut in the risk department"; and in Léo Joannon's *Le Désert de Pigalle*, one can see a shady character in a disreputable café reading a front-page article in *Arts* signed François Truffaut.

For an entire generation, Truffaut played the part of a catalyst for debate and an authority on taste. He became the spokesman for a culture that had been scorned up to then, the culture of film devotees. Witness this emblematic letter, among so many, written to Truffaut on December 12, 1956 by the very young future editor Christian Bourgois:

I know you only as a byline, but it is affixed to such wonderful rages and such just enthusiasms, week after week for months, that you're a friend: I beg you, continue to express all our disgust at the lazy and dull way of writing film criticism or making films. . . . It seems you have bad press and a bad reputation in film circles, but it takes all the impudence and intellectual dishonesty of our so-called critics and directors not to see in your "executions" and your fits of rage an immense love of cinema. . . . Please keep in mind, dear François Truffaut, that there are many of us, all over Paris and in all the cellars of the neighborhood movie houses, that hate this cinema and film criticism, and we will never think you're violent enough in defending our pale and deeply moving Marilyn. We, too, are in love with cinema, we passionate audience members.[136]

4.
NEW WAVE:
1958–1962

A fter *The Mischief Makers,* François Truffaut's goal was to attempt a first feature film. During the spring of 1958, his plans were still rather vague, but as an apprentice director, he was prepared to seize any opportunity.

Paul Graetz, one of the most important postwar French producers, suggested he write and direct a film on childhood in collaboration with Jean Aurenche. There was talk of casting Yves Montand in the lead as the head of a school. The offer appealed to Truffaut, even though he realized he would be forming an unnatural alliance with the advocates of the kind of cinema he had violently fought against. In January 1958, he regularly lunched and dined with Graetz at the Relais-Augustins to discuss the project, and he had a long meeting with Yves Montand on the afternoon of January 14. But since Truffaut and Aurenche had no real desire to work together, the project lagged and was finally abandoned.

DAYS OF HEAT

On January 24, Truffaut accepted the job of first assistant director on a Belgian feature, *Quelqu'un frappe à la porte.* The shoot was scheduled for March and April of 1958, in Brussels; but in the end, Truffaut would not show up. For in the meantime, he had been invited to a party at the producer Pierre Braunberger's house, on January 25, and had been lured by what he had once called, not without malice, *"l'ami Pierrot's* belly dances."[1] Pierre Braunberger had already talked to him a month before about a novel by Jacques Cousseau, *Temps chaud* (Days of Heat), which depicted the summer romances of several young women in a light and lively tone. Braunberger brought up the book again and convinced Truffaut it would make a good first feature film. On March 14, 1958, the two men signed a contract stipulating that Truffaut was to collaborate on the screenplay, direct and edit the film, and receive 6 percent on box-office receipts, with an advance of 1 million francs—200,000 francs on signing the contract and 800,000 on the first day of shooting.

Truffaut was fully aware of his compromise in accepting an assigned project that Braunberger saw as resembling the films of Vadim, which were all the rage at the time. "As you know," he confided to his friend Charles Bitsch, "I'll be shooting *Temps chaud* in ten weeks in the Midi. . . . For Pierrot it will be a super *And God Created Woman in Black and White,* for me a new *Diary of a Chambermaid,* delirious and baroque. Braunberger thinks it will be pretty to look at and tragic. I hope it will be unnerving and farcical. In short, we understand each other very well, as always. . . ."[2] He worked diligently on the adaptation of the novel and presented Braunberger with a screenplay as early as mid-February. He planned to cast Bernadette Lafont in the lead, rehire the technical crew of *The Mischief Makers,* and cast Jean-Claude Brialy instead of Gérard Blain. By the middle of February, everything was ready for the shoot, but at the last moment, Braunberger decided to wait until the first days of summer: "It's a slightly erotic story, with the heat bringing out unusual behavior in people,"[3] he wrote to Truffaut. To keep Truffaut busy, he suggested he spend a few days directing a short film on the subject of his choice. Truffaut decided to take advantage of the floods just south of Paris to quickly shoot a whimsical story about a young couple in a car trying to drive through blocked roads and flooded fields. Godard helped him with the editing and reworked much of the dialogue. *Histoire d'eau,* shot in two days in the outskirts of Montereau, is an eighteen-minute film dedicated to Mack Sennett, in which Jean-Claude Brialy, dubbed by Godard, displays his comic gifts, while Caroline Dim talks about the rain and the bad weather, literature and love.

Knowing that he would be filming *Temps chaud* in June, Truffaut felt unworried and devoted most of the spring to critical writing and settling into domestic life. He presented *The Mischief Makers* at various festivals,[4] and once again he haunted the offices of *Cahiers du cinéma* and *Arts.* He also took driving lessons so he could get his license. He saw a great many films, one or two a day, spent quite a bit of time with Madeleine, and several evenings at André Bazin's home in Nogent-sur-Marne, where he helped celebrate Bazin's fortieth birthday on April 18, 1958. This quiet waiting period came to a sudden end in the last days of April, when Bernadette Lafont suffered a serious injury. The shooting of *Temps chaud,* scheduled to start on June 15, was once again postponed. Therefore, Truffaut decided to turn to a new project.

ANTOINE'S TRUANCY

In May 1958, Truffaut went to the Cannes Film Festival as a critic for the last time. In retaliation for his virulent attacks of the previous year, the festival directors had refused to accredit him as a journalist. Truffaut counterattacked by signing his front-page byline in *Arts* as "François Truffaut, the only French critic not invited to the Cannes Festival."[5] One week later, he proclaimed, "Unless radical changes are made, the next festival is doomed."[6] Yet the festival was instrumental in Truffaut's directing his first feature.

That year, Ignace Morgenstern made one of the best deals in his career as a distributor. On April 21, 1958, he attended a preview screening in Paris of the Soviet entry at Cannes, Mikhail Kalatozov's *The Cranes Are Flying.* With its fast pace and lyricism, its young, romantic heroes and bold cinematography, the film perfectly expressed the political thaw of the Khrushchev period. Morgenstern saw the film again in Paris on the morning of May 3, this time with his son-in-law, François Truffaut, who immediately convinced him to acquire the rights. A deal was made "for next to nothing"[7] before the festival even opened. Within weeks, Kalatozov's film began showing a profit, as it was awarded the prestigious Palme d'or by the festival jury and became a big commercial success when it was released in June. Given this success, Morgenstern had fewer misgivings about coproducing his son-in-law's first feature. "My father trusted him," Madeleine recalls, "but François had no money; he had only his screenplay, which in the beginning wasn't substantial. My father respected François and found him intelligent, but he hadn't particularly liked *The Mischief Makers.* So, of course, he produced *The 400 Blows* to help our marriage, to give his daughter's husband the opportunity to prove he could make films."[8] For Ignace Morgenstern the financial risk was slight; the estimated budget for *The 400 Blows* was around 40 million old francs, a sum (the equivalent of about 2 million present-day francs) markedly below the cost of the standard French film of the period. On June 22, 1958, Truffaut could therefore calmly note in his diary: "Everything is ready to go."[9]

Optimistic once again, he now had to write a screenplay. He decided to rework "La Fugue d'Antoine [Antoine's Flight]," originally conceived as one episode in a film on childhood. It depicted a specific incident from his own adolescence when he was still a student at the school on rue Milton. He had cut class because he had forgotten to do the assignment he had been given as a punishment. His excuse ("My mother died") had not gone unnoticed, and the following day, his father had come for him in the middle of class and given him a good smack in the face. In the beginning of June, Truffaut fleshed out this incident with childhood memories—his truancies with Lachenay, their trips to the movies, the rotor at the fair grounds, scenes at home with his parents, and the scene on Place Clichy when the adolescent sees his mother in her lover's arms. These were the first pages, a few ideas strung together, that he showed his father-in-law in order to convince him to finance the film.

To complete the screenplay, Truffaut again drew material from his own adolescence, including his stay at the Villejuif Observation Center for Minors in December 1948. He put Lachenay to work: "Note down your ideas and memories, for *La Fugue d'Antoine*. Take a look at our letters from Villejuif, etc."[10] Claude de Givray points out how much the character of Antoine owes to Lachenay: "Antoine isn't Truffaut; he's a combination of the two. He stole a bit from his friend Lachenay's youth. Lachenay was more of the driving force at the time. Truffaut was a bit shy; he was pulled along by Lachenay."[11] Though the narrative was autobiographical down to the last detail, Truffaut wanted to present it as a fiction. He therefore compressed five years of his life into a relatively brief period, which he transposed from the Occupation and the immediate postwar years to the present-day fifties. Finally, he avoided some obvious autobiographical giveaways. For example, Truffaut initially gave his runaway adolescent the name of Antoine Loinod, an anagram and pseudonym of Doniol (Valcroze). Robert Lachenay became René Bigey, in memory of his grandmother. And Truffaut changed his father's passion from mountaineering to amateur car racing.

To better define his characters and master his narrative, he contacted Marcel Moussy, a novelist and screenwriter, and the author of a very popular television series, *Si c'était vous.* "I know you work quickly and structure things with a rigor that I completely lack. On the other hand, I'm thoroughly familiar with this world of twelve-year-old kids that I want to capture on film,"[12] Truffaut wrote Moussy. The two started working together on July 9, 1958, and met about ten times in one month. Moussy worked quickly and was very helpful in constructing the narrative. By the end of the summer of 1958, the screenplay was ninety-four pages long and had acquired its definitive title: *Les Quatre Cents Coups* (*The 400 Blows;* in French, this is a double entendre, because *faire les quatre cents coups* means "to be up to no good").

Now that the film's financing was assured and the screenplay completed, Truffaut devoted his attention to practical matters. He decided to film *The*

400 Blows in black-and-white Cinemascope and to recruit one of the best cinematographers, Henri Decaë, who had worked with Jean-Pierre Melville (*Bob le flambeur* had very much impressed Truffaut), Louis Malle, and Claude Chabrol. With his sharply contrasted black and white, his liking for natural lighting, and his great working speed, Decaë was an ideal collaborator for Truffaut, who probably needed to feel confident on the technical level. But hiring Decaë was the greatest investment of the production—he received the highest salary, 1.5 million old francs, while Moussy and Truffaut were paid 1 million francs each, and all the actors' fees together came to about 3 million.

Permission still had to be obtained from the Centre national de la cinématographie (CNC). In those days, you couldn't just become a director. There were requirements: three professional training courses, three jobs as second assistant director, and three jobs as first assistant director. As the director of two short films, the first of which had never been shown commercially, Truffaut couldn't meet these criteria, and was rather worried when he went before the union committee assembled at the CNC in early September 1958. This was why he chose a first assistant who was more experienced than he, Philippe de Broca. At twenty-six, Truffaut was given a special dispensation entitling him to shoot his first feature.

Truffaut had learned from his experience with *The Mischief Makers* that it was not easy to direct children, but the success of *The 400 Blows* would essentially rest on two adolescents. Given the largely autobiographical screenplay, Truffaut feared the danger of a "whiny, self-indulgent confession,"[13] since his aim was the opposite, to transmit the universal aspect of childhood. He gathered a vast amount of material on adolescent psychology, and especially on difficult, unhappy, delinquent childhoods. During the summer of 1958, he consulted two juvenile-court judges, Mademoiselle Lamotte and Monsieur Chazal, several times. He also worked with Joseph Savigny, the director of the division of supervised education at the Ministry of National Education, and read a great deal, for example *Graine de crapule*, *Les Vagabonds*, and Fernand Deligny's book *Adrien Lhomme*, which influenced some of the sequences in the film. Bazin put him in touch with Deligny, whom he had met after the war at Travail et Culture and who was carrying out experiments that Truffaut wanted to know more about. Settled in the heart of the countryside with about ten autistic children "snatched from the gates of psychiatric institutions,"[14] Deligny was trying to make them "live differently." Truffaut sent him his screenplay in early August 1958, asking his advice. Deligny had some harsh criticism for the scene that involved the conversation with the psychologist, which he called "embarrassing and artificial";[15] Truffaut cut the scene during the filming and replaced it with the young Antoine's improvised confession before the camera. In September, Truffaut spent two days at Petit-Bois with Deligny. In a letter written to Deligny on October 29, 1958, a few days before shooting began, Truffaut mentioned these meetings, which were decisive "in preventing me from rushing into all the possible errors."[16]

The last phase of preproduction for *The 400 Blows* consisted in choosing the actors. Truffaut cast Guy Decomble—whom he had seen in many supporting roles, in particular Tati's *Jour de fête*—in the part of the French teacher nicknamed "Petite Feuille" (Small Leaf). After seeing the comedian Pierre Repp and Henri Virlojeux in the same variety-show program, Truffaut chose them, respectively, for the parts of the English teacher and the menacing night watchman who presides over Antoine's arrest after the typewriter theft. Georges Flamant, who had acted in Renoir's *La Chienne* and in Gance's *La Vénus aveugle*, portrays Monsieur Bigey, René's father, a compulsive gambler and horse lover. With his humorist's fantasy and his sauciness, typical of a Parisian joker and grumbler, Albert Rémy, an actor much in demand in the forties and fifties, was perfect for the part of Antoine's stepfather. Antoine's mother would be played by Claire Maurier, a pretty thirty-five-year-old brunette (her hair would be dyed blond for the part), whose prior experience had been mostly onstage, not on the screen.

To cast the two adolescents, Truffaut published an announcement in *France-Soir* and auditioned several hundred children in September and October 1958. Jean Domarchi, a critic at *Cahiers du cinéma*, had earlier recommended the son of an assistant scriptwriter, Pierre Léaud, and the actress Jacqueline Pierreux. Truffaut was immediately captivated by the fourteen-year-old adolescent, who had already appeared the previous year with Jean Marais in Georges Lampin's *La Tour prends garde!* He recognized traits they both shared, "for example a certain suffering with regard to the family. . . . With, however, this fundamental difference: though we were both rebels, we hadn't expressed our rebellion in the same way. I preferred to cover up and lie. Jean-Pierre, on the contrary, seeks to hurt, shock and wants it to be known. . . . Why? Because he's unruly, while I was sly. Because his excitability requires that things happen to him, and when they don't occur quickly enough, he provokes them."[17]

Jean-Pierre Léaud, then in the eighth grade at Verrières, a private school in Pontigny, was far from an ideal student. "I regret to inform you that Jean-Pierre is more and more 'unmanageable,' " the director of the school wrote to Truffaut. "Indifference, arrogance, permanent defiance, lack of discipline in all its forms. He has twice been caught leafing through pornographic pictures in the dorm. He is developing more and more into an emotionally disturbed case."[18] But this unstable boy, who often ran away with the older students on their nights out, could also be brilliant, generous, and affectionate. Extremely cultured for his age, he was already very good at writing, and he even claimed to Truffaut that he had written a "verse tragedy," *Torquatus.*

Jean-Pierre Léaud's screen tests were instantly conclusive, at every stage, his personality and naturalness commanded admiration. This just confirmed Truffaut's intuition and soon became obvious to the rest of the crew. The figure of Antoine was born. "I think in the beginning," the director wrote, "there was a lot of myself in the character of Antoine. But as soon as Jean-Pierre Léaud arrived, his personality, which was very strong, often led me to make changes in the screenplay. So I consider that Antoine is an imaginary character who derives a bit from both of us."[19] In the part of René, Truffaut cast Patrick Auffay, who was slightly older than Jean-Pierre Léaud, taller, with a more bourgeois appearance, less the young Paris hoodlum than the boy from a good family. A few improvisations quickly persuaded Truffaut that he had finally found his duo.

During the night of November 10–11, 1958, André Bazin died of leukemia. That very morning, Truffaut, tense and anxious, had started shooting *The 400 Blows.* In the evening, he went to Nogent-sur-Marne, where the Bazins had been living for three years. He stayed with Janine by the bedside of the man he considered his adoptive father, mentor, and friend. An atmosphere of bereavement would permeate the shoot, most probably heightening the film's bleakness. While a fictional character was being born, the "real" father met death.

Truffaut explained in writing on several occasions what he owed Bazin. Once, he described him as "a sort of saint in a velvet cap living in complete purity in a world that became pure from contact with him."[20] But he probably never said it with as much emotion as in the special issue of *Cahiers du cinéma* published immediately after the critic's death: "Bazin helped me make the leap from film buff to critic, to director. I blushed with pride when, in the midst of a discussion, he agreed with me, but I felt even greater pleasure in being contradicted by him. He was the Just Man by whom one likes to be judged and, for me, a father whose very reprimands were sweet, like the marks of an affectionate interest I had been deprived of in childhood."[21]

As soon he could, Truffaut left the set of *The 400 Blows* to go to Nogent-sur-Marne and be among Bazin's close relatives and friends. On November 16, 1958, the day of the funeral, he wore a black suit while directing his actors, and he would dedicate his film "to the memory of André Bazin." The most important postwar critic passed away as the New Wave was being born, just as Truffaut was filming the first scenes of *The 400 Blows.* The coincidence was not just symbolic: Becoming a director, for Truffaut, was a way of settling his score with a clandestine childhood and a reckless adolescence. *The 400 Blows* bears the marks of those heartbreaking times and of his painful liberation.

François Truffaut chain-smoked and was racked with anxiety as he started shooting *The 400 Blows*.[22] The first week's shoot took place in a small apartment on rue Marcadet, on the hill of Montmartre, in a three-room apartment that was so tiny it couldn't accommodate the twenty-odd members of the cast and crew. The building was so run-down that sudden voltage changes caused power cuts, interrupting the filming several times. Tense, ill at ease, and feeling judged by his crew, Truffaut limited his appearances on the set to a minimum. As for Albert Rémy, he was almost paralyzed by back pains. In the end, Jean-Pierre Léaud was the most relaxed of the lot, even if he nearly choked on the thick smoke that filled the room during the scene when the Balzac photograph in the little niche above Antoine's bed went up in flames. Truffaut, worried sick about bungling things, paced up and down the set. Hence it was a great relief for the whole crew when, on November 19, they finally went outside on Place Clichy to shoot the scene of the kiss between the mother and her lover—a fleeting figure played by the critic Jean Douchet.

The second part of the shoot, from November 20 to 25, was mainly devoted to the sequences of the two adolescents at René's house. For this, Truffaut returned to the heart of his childhood neighborhood, rue Fontaine, where Claude Vermorel, a film critic close to Bazin and Doniol-Valcroze, had loaned him a large apartment. It is one of the key moments in the film, and the complicitous bond among Jean-Pierre Léaud, Patrick Auffay, and Truffaut worked wonders. Thereafter, the filming was much more broken up, with changes of location every day. Friends stopped by, like Audiberti, Jacques Laurent, and Doniol-Valcroze, and some even performed bit parts, like Jacques Demy and Charles Bitsch, disguised as policemen in the scene at the police station on rue Jouffroy. A very young film enthusiast and avid reader of *Arts* by the name of Bertrand Tavernier asked his teacher for permission to watch the filming for a day. A few days later, to save money, Truffaut's cast and crew moved into the offices of SEDIF, the company directed by Ignace Morgenstern, on rue Hamelin to film the sequence where Jean-Pierre Léaud returns the stolen typewriter and is caught by a night watchman. This is the first time in the film when Antoine gets called by his last name, which Truffaut had suddenly changed the previous evening; Antoine Loinod became Antoine Doinel, a discreet homage to Jean Renoir, who had a close collaborator named Ginette Doynel.

During the sequences in a printing shop, which lasted two days, Jean-Pierre Léaud injured his hand rather seriously and the filming fell slightly behind. On the night of December 10, while the crew was shooting the

Doinel family coming out of the Gaumont-Palace—where they had just seen *Paris nous appartient* (*Paris Belongs to Us*) (Truffaut's wink at his friend Rivette, the director of that film)—and returning home in their Dauphine (specially rented for the occasion), the police interrupted the filming, accusing them of disturbing the peace. On Christmas Eve, the filming was interrupted once again, this time by a police van summoned by the owner of the café Le Rendez-vous du Bâtiment; during the sequence with the gym teacher, which required several takes, Jean-Pierre Léaud repeatedly insulted the café owner, while two of his classmates stole cutlery and ashtrays.

Before this, from December 16 to 22, the shoot had moved to Normandy for the film's final sequences, the ones where Antoine is put under observation in a reformatory and runs away to the sea. A big sign saying (in French) OBSERVATION CENTER FOR MINORS had been hastily placed at the entrance of a property that bore no resemblance whatsoever to a prison—the Moulin d'Andé, a very beautiful estate located near Saint-Pierre-du-Vauvray where Suzanne Lipinska, Maurice Pons's friend, welcomed writers and artists. Antoine's long race toward the sea, which closes the film, was shot in the vicinity of Villers-sur-Mer, with a camera Henri Decaë had placed on a camera truck, allowing him to follow Jean-Pierre Léaud as he ran. This sequence ends with Antoine Doinel looking directly into the lens—What right have you to judge me? Léaud seems to be saying to the audience—a rather rare stylistic device at the time, inspired by a shot in Ingmar Bergman's *Monika*.

The many classroom scenes were shot right after Christmas at the Ecole technique de photographie et de cinéma, on rue de Vaugirard, as the school was closed for the vacation. After forty days of work, Truffaut gained self-confidence. The shoot had been carefully planned out. He could now face with greater equanimity the group scenes of adolescents, which were the hardest to direct.

The filming of *The 400 Blows* ended on January 5, 1959. Marie-Josèphe Yoyotte had already started the editing, so that by early February, Truffaut would be able to view a first version. Jean Constantin composed guitar music, simple but insistent, like a ritornello, which was perfectly suited to the mood of the film. Within two months, Truffaut would deliver the answer print of his first feature film.

On January 22, 1959, Madeleine Truffaut gave birth to a little girl at the American Hospital in Neuilly. They named her Laura Véronique Annie Geneviève, after her grandmothers. Although the first day of filming had been marked by mourning, the postproduction period was heralded by a birth.

Doniol-Valcroze, Rivette, Godard, and Rossellini reacted enthusiastically at the first screenings of the film, and on April 2, the press screening at the Marbeuf was equally encouraging. On the 14th, to everyone's surprise, the Cannes Festival committee, influenced no doubt by the movement that was emerging in support of young cinema, suggested to André Malraux, the Minister of Cultural Affairs, that the film be included as one of the official French entries, along with Marcel Camus's *Orfeu Negro* (*Black Orpheus*) and Alain Resnais's *Hiroshima mon amour*. "When I told Monsieur Morgenstern that I had received a phone call from Jacques Flaud, the director of the Center, informing me that the film had been selected, he didn't believe me,"[23] Marcel Berbert recalls. On April 22, in his violent attack on "quality" French directors in the columns of *Arts,* Jean-Luc Godard could exclaim, "Today, as it happens, we have won a victory. It is our films that make it to Cannes to prove that France has a pretty face, cinematographically speaking. And next year it will be the same. Repress all doubts! Fifteen courageous, sincere, lucid, beautiful new films will again block the road for the conventional productions. For though we have won a battle, the war is not yet over."

THE FESTIVAL OF CHILD PRODIGIES

On April 27, 1959, François Truffaut and Jean-Pierre Léaud rented tuxedos in Paris, in anticipation of the official screening of *The 400 Blows* in Cannes. The director arrived on the morning of May 2 with Madeleine, Marcel Berbert, Jean-Pierre Léaud—who was accompanied by his parents—Henri Decaë, Claire Maurier, and Albert Rémy. Everyone stayed at the Carlton Hotel. "We didn't even have a poster for the film, just an enlarged photograph of Jean-Pierre Léaud, which we pasted on the wall. And I had someone come and paint the title of the film and Truffaut's name,"[24] Marcel Berbert recalls. He was far less anxious than Truffaut as he had already accomplished a remarkable feat—selling the film to the Americans before the festival, "for $50,000, which was the exact equivalent of the 47 million francs the film had cost."[25] But the real test was the official screening on the evening of Monday, May 4. In the meantime, Truffaut roamed the streets of Cannes looking for friendly faces. Jean Cocteau, the honorary president of the jury, Roberto Rossellini, and Jacques Audiberti, sent by *Arts* to cover the festival, all brought him a bit of comfort; the three men had already seen the film in Paris and were confident of its success. On the night of the screening at the Palais des Festivals, Truffaut was pale and tense. Jean-Pierre Léaud winked at him when the lights were dimmed. The director was soon reassured on hearing the applause that greeted some scenes even before the end of the screening. And when the lights went up, it was a regular triumph; everyone turned toward the young filmmaker to see his face. Coming out of the Palais, Jean-Pierre Léaud was carried by the crowd, amid an indescribable crush, to be presented to the festivalgoers and photographers who were clustered at the bottom of the steps. Introduced by Cocteau, Truffaut greeted people and shook the many anonymous hands that reached up to him; then he led Cocteau to a Provençal restaurant for supper with the actors and the crew of the film.

On the following day, there were big front-page headlines in all the major newspapers. *France-Soir,* for instance, ran the following caption above a photograph of Truffaut coming down the steps: "A 28-year-old director: François Truffaut. A 14-year-old star: Jean-Pierre Léaud. A triumph in Cannes: *The 400 Blows.*" *Paris-Match* described this triumph over four full pages in its May 9 issue: "The Festival of Child Prodigies." *Elle* magazine stressed this newfound youthfulness: "Never has the festival been so youthful, so happy to live for the glory of an art which youth loves. The twelfth film festival has the honor of announcing to you the rebirth of French cinema."[26] Truffaut's film fully embodied this youthfulness, and Léaud, who became the darling of the festival, even more so. Reports on him, his family, his difficult life, his ambitions, and his personality proliferated in the press and on the radio. His Cannes escapades—in restaurants, bars, and nightclubs—his rash statements, his arguments with his parents, fascinated journalists and paparazzi. The serious press followed suit and in a matter of days Truffaut, too, became an emblematic figure. *Le Monde* ran a flattering profile of the young director, as did *France-Observateur.* On May 7, Jean-Pierre Léaud's picture was on the cover of *L'Express. Arts* was not to be outdone, and Jacques Audiberti wrote the following about the "Truffaut epic": "All those who, with no particular animosity toward Truffaut, condemn what they call his careerism and Machiavellianism gave in, reluctantly and instantly, to the breathtaking attraction of the inevitable, the intensely passive pleasure of imagining, ahead of time and in detail, this triumph which was going to occur and which did indeed occur."[27] In *Cahiers du cinéma,* Jacques Doniol-Valcroze wrote, "*The 400 Blows* would really just be a deeply moving film and the confirmation of our friend François's talent, if it were not also a sudden missile exploding right in the enemy camp and that consecrates its defeat from the inside."[28]

Added to these glowing commentaries were congratulatory telegrams from people all over the world, including Georges Braque, Pierre Brasseur, Jacques Flaud, Abel Gance, Jean Renoir, Robert Aldrich, Nicholas Ray, Louise de Vilmorin, and Georges Simenon. The festival jury awarded *The 400 Blows* the prize for best direction. Within two days, foreign distributors scrambled for the film, negotiating with Marcel Berbert for the rights for Japan, Italy, Switzerland, and Belgium. Sales, including in the United States, had already reached 87 million old francs—twice the budget of the film. In the wake of all this attention, *The 400 Blows* opened on June 3, in two movie theaters on the Champs-Elysées. It was an enormous success—almost 450,000 people went to see the film.

The popular as well as the critical press seized on Antoine Doinel's misadventures to illustrate the social issues of child neglect and education of adolescents. PARENTS, WHAT IF THIS WERE YOU? read the headline of the magazine *Nouveaux Jours*, while its competitor, *Bonheur*, warned adults, PARENTS, BEWARE! DON'T LET YOUR KIDS BECOME HOODS! As Truffaut's film came to be used as a pretext for discussions about the abdication of parental responsibilities, its audience widened considerably. But above all, it benefited from and helped propagate the "New Wave" phenomenon. Rapid filming, contemporary characters played by a new generation of actors, shooting in exterior locations with natural lighting rather than in studios, small technical crews and small budgets—thanks to the success of *The 400 Blows* in Cannes, these new ideas gained unexpected popularity. Truffaut's film really seemed to be kicking off the movement, with French film production focusing on the "youthful film" for some time to come. Over the next three years, nearly 170 directors shot their first feature and the trademark New Wave almost became a kind of (uncontrolled) *appellation contrôlée*. Dozens of producers who had previously been wary of youthful cinema suddenly sought to produce small-budget films with unknown actors in the hope of getting a good return on their investments. This marked an important turning point in the history of French cinema.

In fact, the term *Nouvelle Vague* (New Wave) had appeared a year and a half earlier (in *L'Express*, October 3, 1957) in the headline of an article by Françoise Giroud ("Rapport sur la jeunesse [Report on Youth]"). In June 1958, Giroud published a successful book, *La Nouvelle Vague: Portrait de la jeunesse* (*The New Wave: A Portrait of Youth*); although it did not deal directly with cinema, it expressed a need for change within French society. It was the critic Pierre Billard who first applied the term to the new French cinema in February 1958.[29] In the spring of 1959, the expression was heard around Cannes and was used again in the autumn by the regional press when *Les Cousins* and *Les Quatre Cents Coups* were released. Soon the term was echoed in the international press. From then on, there wasn't a single festival in France or anywhere else in the world that didn't include a roundtable discussion on the New Wave. Even publishing tried to exploit a good thing and analyze the phenomenon—three books on the New Wave were hastily published after the Cannes revelation.[30]

In 1959, though the New Wave was generally well received, a counter-offensive was already being launched by its enemies, mainly the advocates of traditional French cinema and a contingent of left-wing critics. At the Cannes Festival, several recognized directors and screenwriters, such as Jean Delannoy, René Clair, Claude Autant-Lara, Henri Jeanson, Michel Audiard, and Charles Spaak—those whom François Truffaut ironically called the "Old Wave" in *Cahiers*[31] attacked the movement acrimoniously. "Amateurism," "intellectualism," "boredom," "self-promotion," "careerism," were the comments that recurred most often in the interviews and writings of the representatives of the established cinema at the time. Another anti–New Wave center was the magazine *Positif, Cahiers du cinéma*'s rival, which accused the movement of being gratuitous, mannered, Parisian, and, above all, of having right-wing tendencies, and which criticized the films for their lack of political commitment.[32]

Though Truffaut himself mistrusted the idea of being recruited for any cause, he tried to analyze the New Wave phenomenon. Through his many polemical articles in *Arts*, he had been the privileged and active witness to the crisis in traditional French cinema. He had called for a profound renewal in subject matter, actors, production, and shooting methods. Under the influence of Renoir, Rossellini, and Ophuls, he had praised the independent auteur, freed from the pressures of stardom and the dominance of screenwriters. This theoretical position provided a strong link between Truffaut the director and Truffaut the critic. For starting with *The Mischief Makers,* he had implemented a rapid and economical filming method, surrounded by loyal technicians, and had written his own stories and dialogues, opening up opportunities for new actors. But he realized that as it was being described in the large-circulation papers, the New Wave, with its many, very uneven "youth" films, represented a trendy phenomenon, a kind of sociological concept, rather than a definite break in the French cinema's habits and practices. Yet, in spite of his denials, he was definitely considered by both his friends and enemies as the leader of the new cinema, while Resnais and Godard tended to be seen as its theoreticians and experimenters. For better or worse, Truffaut's personal fate was bound up with that of the New Wave. In 1959, the worst was yet to come, and for several years, the young director would invest a good part of his energy in defending the movement.

AN EASY TARGET

Being on the front line of the cinema revolution, François Truffaut was an easy target. Some criticized him for resembling what he had formerly fought against, for duplicating the values of a cinema that he himself had denounced. CRITICISM'S TERRIBLE MISCHIEF MAKER HAS BECOME THE ACADEMICIAN OF THE NEW WAVE[33] was the headline in the monthly *Lui*, while on May 15, 1959, another paper announced TRUFFAUT'S BETRAYAL on its cover: "I liked the tough, uncompromising Truffaut," the anonymous journalist exclaimed in this virulent opinion piece, "I liked his pecking on the skull of the pompous old-fashioned film farts, I liked when he was excommunicated by the Cannes establishment. Now I'm mad at him for going to Cannes. . . . He let himself be dressed in a tuxedo, he let himself be swallowed by the big buttering-up factory. Tossed in granulated sugar, tamed and sweetened, what will be left of the former Truffaut?"[34] Adding to this betrayal syndrome was the ironical assessment made by the old-timers whom the young director had greatly helped to shove out: Perhaps the heralded revolution had given birth to a mouse and the youth cinema would soon fall into line with the most commercial productions, they postulated. This is what Charles Spaak wrote in *France-Soir* in early June 1959: "Once launched, Truffaut is blithely preparing himself to cross over to the other side, among the 'real' directors who make films costing 250 or 500 million francs. . . ."[35]

There were also rumors in the press of Truffaut as an arriviste consumed with ambition, ready to make any compromise for the sake of success, cynical, cunning, crafty, hypocritical, and underhanded. "He married the daughter of his worst enemy in order to get financing,"[36] wrote Claude Brulé bluntly in *Elle*, during the 1959 Cannes festival. This part of the story was reiterated in a great many profiles of the "Rastignac of the New Wave": "And then Truffaut got married," noted one journalist, "as was his right, after all. But his father-in-law, alas!, is one of the shrewdest, most reliable producer-distributors of the old French cinema. I say 'alas!' for the tough, uncompromising Truffaut that used to be. We are told that *The 400 Blows* did not cost much. Yet, thirty to forty million still needed to be found and normally this is not so easy. There are many young people, let alone those no longer so young, who have aged with their talent and their ideas merely because they never inherited from a parent, like Chabrol, or married Mademoiselle Morgenstern, like Truffaut. Between the art of motion pictures and its expression there lies money, and I'm afraid that François Truffaut gave it too much thought."[37] Philippe Labro reports a story told by Jean-Pierre Melville, who was a kind of mentor for the directors of the New Wave in the very early sixties: "I see myself walking down the Champs-Elysées with François Truffaut, who says to me in an undertone, 'Beware of Louis Malle, he's an arriviste!' And I see myself walking up the opposite side of the Champs-Elysées with Louis Malle, who whispers: 'Beware of Truffaut, he's an arriviste!' They each used pejorative terms to describe the other, but this was simply because Malle and Truffaut were both ambitious directors."[38]

"Among the men I have known," confirms Jeanne Moreau, "François was the most ambitious, while remaining true to his youthfulness. This kind of ambition is always needed. What you receive from others is different from what you receive from yourself. François received nothing compared to Louis Malle, whose ambition was more raw."[39]

Though the success of *The 400 Blows* had given him self-confidence, François Truffaut was nevertheless extremely sensitive to the attacks and the rumors circulating about him. In a certain sense, he had expected to be mistreated, but he was hurt at being so often the butt of personal attacks, though he himself, in former times, had not hesitated to use such tactics. In retaliation, he decided to give himself another image through several carefully prepared interviews. This authorized self-portrait consisted of a mixture of goodwill and reticence. He stressed his difficult childhood, dominated by his failure at school; he spared his parents as much as he could, banalizing the portrayal of himself as an adolescent, and deliberately underplayed his influence as a critic. Above all, he stressed his passion for film, maintaining that it allowed him to subdue his most shameful passions and forget his difficult relationship with his parents, the juvenile delinquent centers, his violence as a critic and in his love affairs, his distress at being illegitimate, and his ideological position as a "hussar." The violence imputed to him vanished in this moving portrait of an autodidact who had been integrated into the system, raised by cinema, and made the symbol of a classical French art form, full of halftones and subtleties.

FAMILY WOUND

Truffaut was soon faced with hostility on another front. In reading accounts of their son's youth splashed all over the press, Roland and Janine were astounded by what they considered outrageously blackened portraits of themselves. Their reaction was so violent that there was absolutely no question of their going to see *The 400 Blows*. Dishonored, they found themselves being pointed at in their own neighborhood, now recognized as that of Antoine Doinel in the film. Truffaut had failed to foresee the impact his film would have, or the fact that the press would pry into the private life of a filmmaker as it might into that of a famous actor or actress. But though it was too late to correct matters, the director did everything he could to smooth things over, even claiming that his film was not autobiographical. For their part, Roland and Janine took the offensive and encouraged the family to react, before themselves writing indignant letters to their son.

In fact, from the moment he began to shoot *The 400 Blows*, Truffaut had grown aloof. He had no doubt sensed that the autobiographical nature of

the film and the rather negative portrait of his parents were going to provoke his family. He adopted a clumsy, underhanded strategy of avoidance.
He played dead and gave no more news of himself. Roland and Janine
learned of their granddaughter's birth in the press, two months after the
fact: "We hope little Laura is in excellent health," wrote a surprised Roland
Truffaut. "Have we done anything to you? If there is a misunderstanding,
don't hesitate to tell us. . . . It must be possible to clear it up." Roland also
congratulated him about *The 400 Blows* having been selected for Cannes,
confessing "a certain pride at the thought that [he] will represent French
cinema."[40]

Their disillusionment was all the greater when they read the first articles
about the film. Roland made notes on several loose sheets of paper, which
he angrily labeled "The press gone wild: concerning *The 400 Blows*": "You
probably want to make us believe that we're responsible for the way you
are," Roland wrote. "Love of camping maybe, but you, little shit, how much
did you cost me in movies? . . . And what about IDHEC, which I offered to
pay for, little idiot, and which you turned down. . . . Bazin's death is costing
us a pretty penny." Roland's final comments draw the portrait of an arriviste,
an unscrupulous son, a sly and skillful cynic: "Why come to see us on Thursdays for four years running? Sheer hypocrisy. What self-interested sham. . . .
This film, a masterpiece before anyone has seen it. Well-orchestrated publicity. . . . The Morgenstern millions certainly come in handy. . . ."[41]

On May 20, 1959, Roland Truffaut wrote his son a brief, bitter letter:

Maybe you'll now find time to grant me an interview concerning articles that have appeared in the press, obviously very ill-informed, since
I can't imagine you allowed so many inaccuracies to be published. I
leave the day and time of this rendezvous up to you, but I think we'd
better meet at 33, rue de Navarin. In fact, you'll surely be moved to
see these squalid lodgings again where you were so "mistreated" by
ignorant parents that they later allowed you to become a glorious and
disinterested "child martyr." I'm counting on your usual frankness to
accept this little conversation. See you soon . . . ? Your father (merely
legal). P.S. I wish to make it clear that you'll be physically safe when
you come: the garbage will be emptied and I won't inform the police
stations.[42]

He included with his letter a photo of his son on the set of *The 400 Blows*,
where he is wearing a tie, has a cigar in his mouth, and exudes a conquering
air; Roland had inscribed it on the back with this caption: "Portrait of an
authentic shit." For Roland and Janine, it was probably the suddenness of
such public revelations about their son's childhood that provoked such a

strong reaction: A childhood that everyone seemed to have successfully forgotten had reemerged in a devastating manner. The Truffauts ascribed this dark portrayal of his childhood to their son's hypocrisy and careerism, and saw him as corrupted by an unhealthy, dishonest "cosmopolitan milieu."

To justify himself, Truffaut on May 27 wrote his father a long letter, a deeply moving confession in which he revealed his feelings of helplessness:

I regret, like you, the abuses of this publicity; they questioned people who had known me, they purchased pictures from army chums, they simplified, magnified, deformed things, all of which is common in this type of journalism. However, I'm going to denounce all of this exaggeration in *Arts* and partially deny the "autobiographical" side of the film. I think it might be good for us to have an earnest discussion, but only after you've seen the film. . . . Of what happened to me, I only filmed what happens or could happen in other families. I didn't show a little saint, but an adolescent who plays hooky, forges his parents' handwriting, steals money from them, and constantly lies. . . . Despite the unpleasantness of seeing some silly things published in the papers, I haven't the slightest regret about having made this film. I knew I would hurt you, but I don't care, for since Bazin's death I have no parents. I would have shot a truly horrifying film had I depicted what my life was like on rue de Navarin between 1943 and 1948, and my relationship with Mom and you. During the whole period of rations, I didn't eat a single piece of chocolate; you used to take it to Fontainebleau. You went away on Saturdays and left practically nothing for me. I got by by stealing lumps of sugar (whole rows so it wouldn't be too visible). On Sunday nights, I started to live in falsehood and fear. A child who finds he is the only one in school not to have a "snack" can't help wondering. There were also moments of exceptional tension between Mom and me, as when I was on the ground and she kicked me, on a morning when I had stood on line for two hours but had only brought back a box of biscuits. I swear this is true. I became cowardly and underhanded, I "clammed up" and your friends admired my good behavior at the table: I hated Mother in silence and liked you but felt contempt. During medical checkups, what a tragedy when I had to take off my shoes and reveal the state of my socks. . . . There was also a ridiculous little tragedy that influenced my whole life—the test at the Lycée Rollin, a second chance to get into sixth grade. At that time I was still a good student and my flunking had been accidental. I had every chance of doing well on the October test. I was on vacation in Juvisy, and I wrote asking you to come get me on the Sunday before the exam. You didn't come and I couldn't take the test. So then you registered me at the local elementary school where I started to get into trouble. You told me you never got my letter. An extraordinary coincidence: you had spent that weekend in Fontainebleau—surprise, surprise—as usual. How dreary to give up a weekend in the forest to go to Juvisy and pick up the kid. . . . You sign your letter: 'Your father (merely legal)' and I can imagine your bitterness. It so happens that this revelation was a great shock to me and I think I told you it occurred while I was rummaging in a cupboard and found the 1932 diary and then the family record book. Did I also tell you that the family ambiance was such that I was almost sure of a secret concerning my birth; Mom hated me so much that, for a year, I thought she wasn't my real mother. I could go on for pages and pages. No, I wasn't a "mistreated child," but simply one who wasn't "treated" at all, unloved and feeling completely "unwelcome" from the time you took me in to my emancipation. I'm aware of all the facts involved: I had become a lying, thieving, underhanded, secretive and "difficult" child, but I can assure you that my daughter will not be a difficult child. So she can already have her "own" room, we set up our bed in the dining room and we spoil her as much as possible because I believe it's best to err along those lines than the other. The film, which is infinitely less violent than this letter, will certainly hurt you, and it's not true that I don't care. I thought of you constantly while making it and I improvised a few scenes to avoid being unfair, convince you of my good faith and show you, partially, what I think was the truth. You're ironical in your letter about my returning from Cannes "finally freed of my many complexes." You couldn't have stated it better: for two months I've had the feeling of having dispelled an old nightmare and of having become a man who is fit to bring up a child.[43]

Keeping his promise to his father, the day his film opened, June 3, Truffaut denied in *Arts* that he had made an autobiographical movie: "If the young Antoine Doinel sometimes resembles the turbulent adolescent I was, his parents bear absolutely no resemblance to mine, who were excellent. . . ." Truffaut's rewriting of the family saga began on that day, in a radical break with the interviews granted up to then. He thought he had protected the most important thing, his own parents, whom he had lectured vehemently and sincerely in a private letter but whom he preferred to forget about publicly. As his ultimate gesture, he took on financial responsibility for his Truffaut grandmother and started sending her a monthly money order of 20,000 francs as of the autumn of 1959. He met with his father at the Brasserie du Courcelles in early June, but it was a dialogue of the deaf, concluded several days later with this little note from Roland: "We should be happy and thrilled to read or hear about your success. Alas, it merely reminds us of a son who 'scorns and despises us.' "[44]

These exchanges undermined Truffaut's morale considerably. But if he felt guilty, he also felt liberated. He came to regret having publicly stated that the film was not autobiographical. Faced with what he now saw as artistic success but a great mess in his personal life, he decided to break off permanently with his parents. The estrangement would last three years; the silence would be oppressive. It was Madeleine, his wife, who would decide on her own to get back in touch with her in-laws. In January 1962, she secretly sent them a short conciliatory letter, saying, "Forgive my long delay in writing this letter. I should have done so long ago."[45] The Truffauts appreciated her gesture: "Your courageous letter, dear Madeleine, has softened a great bitterness within us. . . ."[46]

In the meantime, on June 29, 1961, a second daughter, Eva, had been born. Madeleine Morgenstern tells of this family schism: "For a very long time, François didn't want his parents to see our daughters. He did a lot for his grandmother, who had left Juvisy to move into a retirement home. On her ninety-second birthday, in 1976, François took his daughters to see her. She died in February 1979. As for Roland, he only met Laura in 1979, when she was twenty. Roland and Eva only saw each other several years later. But Janine, she never knew her granddaughters."[47]

One event would favor something like a reconciliation—Roland and Janine Truffaut's divorce. François immediately wrote to his father in May 1962:

Hearing of your separation, my first reaction was one of absolute joy, but this satisfaction wasn't directed against either of you. It was strange, and I later analyzed the feeling in great detail. I think I love you more separately than together, that's the explanation. On the one hand there's the father and the mother, on the other the parents, it's a different notion. I've always loved my father and my mother, but I haven't always loved my parents, that's the thing. I hope I'm not shocking you by dissecting this so bluntly. I often think of Mom and you, not as parents or in relation to me, but as a couple. I think I've inherited many of mother's traits, for example, critical judgment, quick mood changes from cheerfulness to sadness, and as a husband, I resemble you a lot; at mealtime and before leaving the house in the morning, I make Madeleine and the children laugh with jokes that I got from you.[48]

From then on, François Truffaut saw his father regularly. In the autumn of 1963, he started having lunch once again every other Thursday at rue de Navarin with his mother; by then, she had married Robert Vincendon, the

former lover who had brought François gifts when he was a boy. The outcome, therefore, was on the happier side, even if it was a bit forced. The
fact remains that this family drama undermined Truffaut for many long
years. The impact of film on his personal life was a painful shock to him,
exposing feelings, hatreds, resentments, and memories that had long been
repressed.[49] He enjoyed quick, immediate success, but paradoxically this
very success bruised him. Hence, the heyday of the New Wave he had
helped to inaugurate was not a happy period in François Truffaut's life. In
fact, he confided as much to his mother: "I have the profession I like, uncon-
ditionally, the only possible one for me, and yet it doesn't make me happy.
I'm sad, Mom, very often so sad."[50]

A NEW LIFE

The success of *The 400 Blows* changed Truffaut's way of life; he adopted the
look of a young man from the Right Bank, conventionally elegant, with all
the external signs of success. "François was established in the world; he
knew how to discuss contracts; he wasn't at all marginal; and yet at the same
time he was still a complete rebel,"[51] says Florence Malraux, who first met
him in the early sixties, when he was among a group of directors on the
brink of success—Resnais, Chabrol, Rivette, Godard, Varda, and Demy. "I
never knew which part of his personality overshadowed the other," she continues, "the two strains coexisted. Especially compared to all of us who
weren't set up as yet. François had an office, but he was more of an anarchist
than we were. I always saw these two sides of him, which was his distinctive
feature and therefore his charm."

On the one hand, there was this attachment to his childhood haunts, the
culture of his youth, the songs, the music hall, the insolent Parisian humor
and extravagance, and his ingrained gestures, the Gitane cigarette between
his fingers, the prostitutes he continued to visit, his odd habits—he couldn't
stand certain fabrics, he always followed certain itineraries, he always ate
the same quick meals in the same places, and he always thoroughly emptied
his pockets when he got home. And on the other hand, he had material comfort and everything it entailed, allowing him to support his family and his
own lifestyle, and to help out his friends as well. Simone Jollivet, who was a
close friend of Sartre and Simone de Beauvoir, and whom Truffaut had considered casting in the part of Madame Bigey in *The 400 Blows*, described
him accurately by comparing him, in a certain way, to Jean Renoir and his
"noble, working-class" bearing: "I think, dear Truffaut, that your outstanding qualities are working-class—passions which are sudden, almost
instinctive, sentimental and melodramatic, a taste for the burlesque, for

melodrama, novels, fantasy—while, on the other hand, your appearance and thought have an aristocratic and subtle orderliness. These two kinds of gifts are more difficult to reconcile than any other (it will happen when you will truly have found the 'form' which is yours) and yet these rare qualities are the ones the good fairy left in your cradle and that you cannot disown without renouncing your own self."[52]

In the mid-fifties, when he was already a star critic, his freelance writing assignments and odd jobs brought in 500,000 francs a year, the equivalent of 45,000 francs today. In 1958, with several film contracts added to his earnings from journalism, Truffaut declared a taxable income of over 3 million francs. In 1959, the year of *The 400 Blows*, he declared earnings of 65 million—that is, twenty times more than the preceding year; his 1960 income was about the same. From that time on, Truffaut was a young man who earned a very good living and whose affluence was visible. He dressed well and, since he hated fittings ("He couldn't stand being touched by a man,"[53] says Madeleine Morgenstern), he would order four or five suits twice a year (and for Jean-Pierre Léaud at the same time), as well as solid-color shirts by the dozen, first from Ted Lapidus in 1959 and 1960, then from Pierre Cardin, whom he met through Jeanne Moreau.

Another external sign of success was the beautiful Facel-Véga Truffaut bought himself in late 1959. "At its wheel I bring James Dean irresistibly to mind, but my wife is none too pleased with the comparison,"[54] Truffaut commented. Indeed, the comparison almost became too real when he had a serious accident on December 17, 1962, while driving the "rolling masterpiece."[55] He escaped unharmed, but the car was completely wrecked. "He was a 'nouveau-riche' for two years," says Claude Chabrol, "up until he wrecked the Facel-Véga. . . . This changed him: afterward, he stopped being nouveau-riche."[56] Cautiously, Truffaut resigned himself to a Jaguar sedan, more comfortable for driving his little family around. Money also allowed him to satisfy his curiosity. While tourism and museums would never interest him, and he confined his travels to those required for the shooting and promotion of his films, he always had a passion for music and especially for reading. He therefore built up a fine collection of records, mostly of French popular music (Trenet, Aznavour, Mistinguett, Béart, Francesca Solleville), but also the work of the Québécois Félix Leclerc and some classical music; he owned very little jazz and no opera at all, since he hated it. He also possessed a wonderful library, which included all the books he had kept from his youth, as well as all the latest novels, especially crime novels, and books on cinema. He was the faithful customer of several bookstores near the Palais-Royal, and of Contacts, on rue du Colisée, reputed to be the best cinema bookstore in Paris. He spent hours there, leafing through new publications, rummaging around the old stock, and conversing with the "beautiful Creole saleswoman," Elaine Micheaux-Vigne. He owned a collection of classical nineteenth- and twentieth-century novels, which he had bought at secondhand bookstores whenever he had come across a bargain or something hard to find. He also bought works on child psychology and history books, particularly on the Occupation, the Belle Epoque, or certain major nineteenth- and twentieth-century law cases; he loved Gordeau's comic-strip versions of these cases in *France-Soir*, which served him well in finding subjects for films. When he wasn't filming, Truffaut allowed himself time to read and write, pleasures he considered essential. He also read the daily press (*France-Soir, Le Monde, Combat*), weeklies (*L'Express, France-Observateur, Le Canard enchaîné, Paris-Match*), and many monthlies—film publications, of course, but also *Critique, Les Temps modernes, Diogène, Le Crapouillot*, and *Détective*, for news items and as inexhaustible sources of ideas and subject matter.

PARALLEL FAMILIES

When he was preoccupied or melancholic, as he often was, François Truffaut found solace with his two families, the one he had started with Madeleine, and his professional one, centered around Les Films du Carrosse. "I'm tired, demoralized, and have more and more doubts about the point of making films. My only joy is playing with my daughter, who is becoming terrific. So, I stay home—and I'll stay home all year, as much as possible, so I can play with her and read, read, read, because I wasn't reading enough,"[57] he wrote to a friend on March 29, 1960.

At the end of March, Madeleine, Laura, and François moved into a five-room apartment in a beautiful building on rue du Conseiller Collignon, in the heart of the sixteenth arrondissement. Truffaut agreed to this move reluctantly. Though his family was beginning to feel cramped in the sixth-floor rue Saint-Ferdinand apartment, which was flooded with light, Truffaut liked it. Still, the new apartment had character and family life that was harmonious. Madeleine was distressed by her father's illness, but she was happy, devoting most of her time to taking care of Laura and preparing for the birth of her second daughter, Eva, due in early summer 1961. In her free moments, Madeleine, fluent in English, helped her husband by reading and translating manuscripts, screenplays, letters, and books that he received from England or the United States. She was in good health and in good spirits— Truffaut described her as gentle, charming, and wonderfully sincere[58]—and the couple got on well, usually surrounded by laughter, good humor, and amorous whimsy. Madeleine and François often spent time away from Paris—in Brittany (near Concarneau) or, beginning in July 1959, in Saint-

Paul-de-Vence, where they stayed at the well-known Colombe d'Or. When Truffaut was not making films, they sometimes traveled abroad; in 1960, they went to London, and in the spring of 1962 to Argentina, Brazil, New York, and Montreal.

Truffaut was a fully committed father. "My way of reacting to my children is the exact opposite of what I have lived through," he wrote in 1963. "But I'm still too much of a joker; I think mostly about entertaining my daughters and sparing them any worry, and I don't have very many serious occupations with them, perhaps because they're girls. It is really their mother who takes on the greater responsibility."[59] According to Madeleine, "François got married so he could start a family. This was one of the misunderstandings between us. I got married so I could have a man in my life, get away from my parents, and be left alone. When we had Laura, François was deliriously happy and he wanted to have another child quickly, because he thought I was a good mother."[60] His daughters gave him moments of true happiness at times when he was not directing; he took pictures of them, or filmed them with a small 8-mm camera. He showed them movies very early on; the first film Laura remembers seeing was Charlie Chaplin's *Shoulder Arms,* which she saw with her father at the Cinémathèque when she was four.

In a way Jean-Pierre Léaud was also a member of the family. Since the filming of *The 400 Blows,* Truffaut had adopted him, so to speak, and he spent quite a lot of time at rue Saint-Ferdinand. At the beginning of 1960, Truffaut secured a place for him at the Institut de la Muette, on rue Cortambert, very close to the couple's new apartment. But Jean-Pierre was expelled a few weeks later, at the headmaster's request: "We could have extended the trial period," he wrote to Truffaut, "but he himself made it impossible because of the accounts he gave to his classmates of his marvelous life and his daily earnings, so much so that the families protested against this contagion spreading in class and dangerously stimulating the lust for money that holds sway among today's youth."[61] Truffaut then placed Léaud with a retired couple in Colombes, but despite their goodwill, Léaud displayed volatile and insolent behavior and regularly ran away to Paris. Truffaut then took matters directly in hand again and made him the offer of living alone, at seventeen, in a maid's room, much as he himself had done after coming out of the Observation Center for Minors. Léaud agreed to attend courses regularly at the Centre psychologique et scolaire, an institution specializing in difficult cases.

François Truffaut "brought up" Jean-Pierre Léaud; being only twelve years Léaud's senior, he was like an older brother as well as a father figure. He was also a Pygmalion, for he was very attached to the fictional character he had created; their relationship was complex but fulfilling. Truffaut drew from it the elements that would later constitute the material for some of his films—not just the "Doinel cycle" films, but also *The Wild Child, Two English Girls, Small Change,* and *Day for Night.* As for Léaud, he was literally kept afloat by his protector.

Though he enjoyed family life, in some ways Truffaut must have felt caught in a trap. Even during periods when the couple enjoyed harmony and deep affection, he wasn't faithful. Or rather, he had a very personal interpretation of fidelity: He lived with Madeleine, but pursued both old and new love affairs, and continued to visit prostitutes, as in his youth. He felt no guilt or shame; this kind of love life seemed almost natural to him, so much so that during those first years of marriage, he kept an intimate diary meticulously detailing his amorous encounters. In 1959, for example, he resumed his liaison with Evelyne D., which dated back to the mid-fifties, and saw her regularly in Paris. At the Cannes Festival the same year, even though he was with Madeleine for the official screening of *The 400 Blows,* he felt free enough to approach a beautiful green-eyed brunette several days later. Liliane David, a young actress, was staying in Saint-Tropez during the Festival. "I passed in front of a bistro, Le Festival, right next to the Palais, and a friend introduced me to two people at a table. One of them, the journalist Pierre Rey, was interviewing a guy whose first name was François. He looked at me with an intense gaze. It was our first meeting; I knew nothing about him, or about *The 400 Blows.*"[62] The following day, the two met again at the terrace of Sénéquier in Saint-Tropez: "We spent a long period of time together, talking; we were both shy. I felt I could trust him. He was delighted to hear that I'd been kicked out of the Centre dramatique de la rue Blanche." After a round trip between Saint-Tropez and the Colombe d'Or, Truffaut returned to pick up Liliane David and drove back to Paris with her. He dropped her off in front of her house in Paris, on rue du Colonel-Moll, a street which is perpendicular to the rue Saint-Ferdinand, where he and Madeleine were living at the time. Liliane was living in a maid's room above her parents' apartment. This was the beginning of an affair that would last four years, a tumultuous, intermittent passion, indulged in on weekends away from Paris, on visits to provincial film societies, and during festivals.

His life with Madeleine was constantly threatened by the possibility of embarrassing revelations. It soon became apparent to Truffaut that though he considered his marriage happy, it was unlikely to last. Furthermore, the articles in the press insinuating that he had married for career advancement created tension between the two. "François may have had the feeling of compromising," says Madeleine Morgenstern, "either in his ideas or with regard to his friends, by becoming someone important. This uneasiness is explicit in *Shoot the Piano Player,* and one had to be as blind as I was at the time not to have seen it, but I couldn't do anything about it."[63] During this time, Truffaut used Les Films du Carrosse as a shield, to give himself the appearance of a settled family man, a hard worker whose thoughts revolved only around cinema—the films he liked to see, and the films he planned to make. Methodical, obsessive, Truffaut did not want to waste time. This was also why he kept his relationships with friends separate from his professional relationships. He used Les Films du Carrosse to start another family, parallel to his real family, which allowed him to establish very strong and faithful ties, most often based on one-to-one relationships.

In May 1959, the Carrosse moved into the offices of SEDIF, which belonged to Ignace Morgenstern, on rue Quentin-Bauchart, very near to the Champs-Elysées. Marcel Berbert soon became the manager of the little production company, whose staff included a secretary, Lucette Deuss, and a receptionist, Christiane. Nine years Truffaut's senior but from a similar petit bourgeois background, Berbert was a discreet and serious man, with a face that was both stern and childish; he was sensible and prudent, not very talkative, and always direct. He had been there to advise Truffaut in 1957, when he was an inexperienced, very young director, and he would be there to the bitter end, in an office adjoining Truffaut's, whose door was never shut.

After the success of *The 400 Blows* and the move to the rue Quentin-Bauchart, Ignace Morgenstern went only rarely to the office. "He was ill and sad, yet he was a big strong guy, like a peasant,"[64] Marcel Berbert recalls. This ailing man had not been told the truth about his medical condition. He had been made to believe he was suffering from the aftereffects of a 1957 heart attack, when in fact he had had a ruptured aortic aneurysm, an extremely serious condition. Madeleine knew her father could die at any moment. The doctors had ordered complete rest.

Truffaut had great esteem for his father-in-law. First of all, he was grateful that Ignace had helped him by producing *The 400 Blows,* and more importantly, he valued his moral rigor and professionalism in managing his business. Truffaut was eager to manage his own Carrosse business wisely, under Marcel Berbert's guidance, so as not to disappoint his father-in-law, much less cause him financial difficulties. Morgenstern was far from enthusiastic about *The 400 Blows* (his tastes in motion pictures ran closer to *Chiens perdus sans collier*); nonetheless, despite this and the fact that he was from another age and of a different character, he instilled in his son-in-law a sense of responsibility in business.

In January 1962, when Ignace Morgenstern died at sixty of a second ruptured aneurysm, Marcel Berbert dedicated himself completely to Les Films du Carrosse. "The company kept forging ahead after *The 400 Blows,* with an uninterrupted series of films. François was solely in charge of the artistic end, and me, of managing production. I was executive producer, and line producer—in those days we did everything. I was also in charge of foreign sales."[65] The company operated in this kind of closed circuit, with the sole aim of ensuring Truffaut's independence. Conflicts between the two men were rare, primarily because they trusted each other, but also because Truffaut was reasonable and never made extravagant demands for his films. Life was quiet at the Carrosse, except in periods just prior to filmings. Then frenzy reigned in the cramped offices. Truffaut shut himself in his. He read the newspaper or a book, and wrote letters, trying to subdue the anxiety that gripped him.

FOREIGN CORRESPONDENTS

Starting with *The 400 Blows,* Truffaut began building up an important network of foreign correspondents for the Carrosse. Many were film critics who already knew Truffaut by reputation from his days as a critic and who had translated his writings. There were also directors of festivals and film libraries, with whom he established long-lasting, dependable ties on his trips abroad. They kept Truffaut well informed about the distribution of his films and those of his New Wave friends in every country and actively promoted his films and his books on cinema. These informants also kept him up-to-date on the emergence of new talent in various places. They played a decisive role in the early sixties, in propagating the international renown of the New Wave.

On October 25, 1959, at the opening of *The 400 Blows* at the Curzon Theater in London, Truffaut met Richard Roud, of the British Film Institute, who subsequently played an important part in getting him and the New Wave recognized by magazines and the daily press—first in England and later in the United States, when he moved to New York to become director of the New York Film Festival, where Truffaut regularly presented his films. *The 400 Blows* also had success in Germany, where Truffaut found an efficient intermediary in the person of Enno Patalas, who was editor in chief of the magazine *FilmKritic* in Munich. In Genoa, Gianno Amico, a close friend of Rossellini, translated and published Truffaut's first writings. Franco's Spain, which would always be more resistant to his films, was approached through Antonio Vega de Seoanne at the Festival of San Sebastian, which Truffaut attended in July 1960, and in Barcelona by José Sagré, who translated and published a good many of Truffaut's pieces.

Truffaut regularly wrote to his many foreign correspondents, informing them of his activities, whether scripts in progress, films he was directing, or book projects that might be translated. He welcomed them when they came to Paris, aware of the stakes involved in his films being internationally recognized. Somewhat unexpectedly, it was in Japan that he found his most fervent and efficient supporters. For example, Shukichi Okada, who translated excerpts of Truffaut's first films for his magazine, *The Art of Cinema,* and wrote an essay on the New Wave. In addition to this devoted critic, to whom Truffaut constantly sent material, there was Hisamitsu Nogushi, painter, graphic artist, and jazz musician; he had designed the Japanese poster for *The 400 Blows,* showing Antoine Doinel with his face half hidden by a black turtleneck pulled up to his nose. Truffaut liked the poster enormously, so much so that he used it as part of the set of Doinel's bedroom in his short 1962 film, *Antoine and Colette* (an episode in the film *Love at Twenty*). It has also adorned one of the walls of Les Films du Carrosse since 1960.

PARIS BELONGS TO US

Boosted by the success of *The 400 Blows,* and by the support of Marcel Berbert, François Truffaut wanted to help his New Wave colleagues. First, Jacques Rivette, who hadn't been able to finish his first film, *Paris nous appartient,* which he had begun to shoot in the summer of 1958. Truffaut rescued this film, provided partial financing, and then fought to ensure its Paris release at the Studio des Ursulines in December 1961. He did so because he felt indebted to Rivette, without whom the daring of the New Wave would not have been possible: "The release of *Paris nous appartient* (*Paris Belongs to Us*) is a score for every member of the [*Cahiers du cinéma*] team—or of our Mafia, if you prefer. . . . For Rivette is the source of many things. The example of *Le Coup du berger,* his short film of 1956, made me decide to shoot *Les Mistons,* and Claude Chabrol to be adventuresome enough to make a full-length film from *Le Beau Serge;* and at the same time it moved the most prestigious short-subject filmmakers, Alain Resnais and Georges Franju, to try their first full-length films. It had begun. And it had begun thanks to Jacques Rivette. Of all of us he was the most fiercely determined to move."[66] In exchange for his help, Truffaut borrowed from Rivette, for his future films, his two most important collaborators—Jean Gruault, the scenario and dialogue writer of *Paris nous appartient,* and Suzanne Schiffman, "the omniskilled assistant."

In 1959, Jean-Luc Godard was the only member of the *"Cahiers* Mafia" who had not directed a feature. When *The 400 Blows* was in the works, Truffaut, who greatly admired Godard, tried to convince some producers to gamble on him. Several projects were discussed—for example, an adaptation of Georges Bernanos's *Mouchette.* In the spring of 1959, Truffaut failed to convince Ignace Morgenstern to coproduce with Pierre Roustang Godard's project *Prénatal,* the first version of what was to become in two years *Une Femme est une femme* (*A Woman Is a Woman*). Several weeks later, still hoping to attract his friend's father-in-law, Godard came to Truffaut with the plan of adapting a Simenon novel, *Quartier nègre,* with Nicole Courcel, but once again Godard's project ran aground. It was only with the triumph of *The 400 Blows* in Cannes that his prospects improved. For producers started to pounce on young directors' projects, provided their films required very small budgets. Godard found in Georges de Beauregard a person who was convinced of his talent, but Beauregard would only commit himself if Godard had a story "that made sense." Having run out of ideas, Godard remembered the synopsis of *Breathless* that Truffaut had given him a few years earlier. He asked his friend to flesh out the story quickly, for he wanted to shoot the film very fast, by the end of the summer of 1959. "If you have the time to round out in three lines the idea for a film started at the Richelieu-Drouot métro station (those were the good old days), though I don't have access to Françoise Sagan, I could whip up the dialogues,"[67] he wrote Truffaut. Truffaut's four-page synopsis was enough to convince Beauregard. Out of friendship, and so as to not to add to the film's budget, Truffaut relinquished all royalties for a modest sum, 1 million old francs. He made a point of telling Georges de Beauregard that he didn't want to appear in the publicity for the film except as the author of the original screenplay, and he offered to give his opinion on the final script. "I'm very grateful to you for being so interested in my film," Beauregard replied on July 20. "I know it's out of friendship for Jean-Luc, but believe me, a producer doesn't often have the opportunity to encounter such disinterestedness. Therefore, thank you."[68] On the eve of his first day's shoot for *Breathless,* August 17, 1959, Godard wrote Truffaut to take stock of the situation:

I'll have you read the continuity in a few days. After all, it's your screenplay. I think you'll be surprised once again. Yesterday, I discussed it with Melville. Thanks to him, and from having seen grand Momo's rushes, my spirits are in fourth gear. There will be a scene where Jean Seberg will interview Rossellini [in the end, the part would be played by Jean-Pierre Melville] for the *New York Herald.* I don't think you'll like this film, though it's dedicated to *Baby Doll,* but via *Rio Bravo.* I'd like to write you a lot longer still, but I'm so lazy that this effort will prevent me from working until tomorrow. And we're shooting on the 17th, come rain or shine. Roughly speaking, the subject will be the story of a boy who thinks of death and of a girl who doesn't. The adventures are those of a car thief (Melville will introduce me to specialists) in love with a girl who sells the *New York Herald* and who takes French civilization courses. What bothers me, is having had to introduce something of my own in a screenplay which was by you. But we've become too difficult. We should get down to filming in large quantities and stop being wise guys. Kind regards from one of your sons.[69]

When it opened in Paris in December 1959, *Breathless* was almost as great a commercial success as *The 400 Blows.* The critics regarded it as the New Wave's aesthetic manifesto, a supplement to Truffaut's film, which had marked its public advent. The mission was accomplished: Youth had risen to power in French cinema. Now considered a full-fledged director, Godard no longer needed help from his friend Truffaut; he was already in preproduction for *Le Petit Soldat,* his second film (released in 1963). Completed at the height of the Algerian war, it would cause much ink to flow and incur Gaullist censorship.

FRIENDS FIRST

Even established directors needed help from Les Films du Carrosse, and Truffaut gladly came to the rescue of some of his masters. One of Jean Cocteau's last dreams, at seventy, was to shoot *The Testament of Orpheus,* the third part of the triptych that included *Blood of a Poet* and *Orpheus.* Truffaut and Cocteau had known each other for about ten years and had been friends since the 1959 Cannes Festival. Their friendship can be gleaned from this surprising letter that the poet wrote to Truffaut when the latter was not yet thirty: "I saw in your eyes as you had in mine a heartfelt sincerity whose light the Cannes Festival ignores. By helping you I was helping myself: I was cleansing my soul of so much filth. My film is beginning to take shape. I've established refundable shares of five million based on the work's chances. If you're the delightful madman who wants to embark on my phantom yacht, just write to Gérard Worms, Edouard Dermit or Jean Thuillier. My film will belong to that logic which reason is spared and I'm happy you're intrigued by it. Write me often. Letters like yours are what allow me to live in this world."[70] In June 1959, Les Films du Carrosse promised to cofinance *The Testament of Orpheus,* despite the skepticism of Ignace Morgenstern and Marcel Berbert. Over the summer, Truffaut collaborated on the script with Cocteau, who began shooting in Les Baux-de-Provence in September. Jean-Pierre Léaud had a cameo role, "like a good-luck charm reminding me what I owe you,"[71] the elderly director wrote to his "producer."

Truffaut wanted to help another one of his masters, Roberto Rossellini, who had returned from his long trip with a magnificent film, *India,* which went unrecognized. At that point, Rossellini was on a fresh course, engaged in making didactic and historical films and planning one on Socrates, but obtaining financial backing proved tricky. Finally, the deal was concluded, with Greek, Italian, and Swedish financiers, in association with Les Films du Carrosse. Truffaut seemed happy to help one of his masters extricate himself from a period of dejection and stagnation. "The more I think about your Socrates, the more I believe this is the film you should make right now and that it will be magnificent,"[72] he wrote the Italian director on July 5, 1962.

In September 1960, Truffaut decided to produce an episode film based on Edgar Allan Poe's *Tales of the Grotesque and Arabesque;* it would be a way for New Wave directors to sponsor young directors of short films. Truffaut explained it in a memo to Marcel Berbert: "It seems to me that this collective film deserves to be attempted, for individual short films are fine but difficult to sell. One possibility would be for each episode to be filmed by a new director—Lachenay, Marcel Ophuls, Varesano, de Givray, Gégauff, Demy—but supervised by an established filmmaker—Godard, Malle, Astruc, Resnais, Franju, Chabrol, me. . . . This would give the enterprise a fraternal and even slightly polemical, anti–old wave, quality that would appeal to me. In short, we must fight and take advantage of the door being left ajar to get our friends in before it's too late."[73] Of this collective project, only *The Gold Bug,* a short film by Robert Lachenay, would see the light of day in 1960.[74]

In his dream of making Les Films du Carrosse into a ministudio and spearhead for the New Wave, Truffaut placed great hope in Marcel Ophuls, the son of the director of *Lola Montès,* and in Claude de Givray, formerly the youngest member of the *Cahiers du cinéma* group. In March 1960, the Carrosse signed a contract with Marcel Ophuls for the screen adaptation of Arthur Schnitzler's *The Return of Casanova.* Though the project never came to fruition, a friendship was born. While he was directing *Peau de banane (Banana Peel)* in 1963, starring Jeanne Moreau and Jean-Paul Belmondo, Marcel Ophuls acknowledged his debt to Truffaut: "For three years, it's been you, François, and Jeanne, who have made my film possible. Your loyal friendship has been the most creative I've ever known. I'll never forget it."[75]

Truffaut regarded Claude de Givray as a promising young director and was enthusiastic about producing his first feature, *Tire-au-flanc (The Army Game).* As soon as the Mouëzy-Eon play had been adapted for the screen, the shooting began, in February and March of 1961, in the area of Nice, with a Carrosse team that included Raoul Coutard, Suzanne Schiffman, Robert Lachenay; in the principal roles were Ricet-Barrier, Christian de Tilière, Jacques Balutin, Serge Davri, Bernadette Lafont, Cabu, Jean-François Adam, and Truffaut, who played a rank-and-file soldier. *Tire-au-flanc* was a commercial flop when it opened in December, but this did not prevent Truffaut from entrusting de Givray with the writing and direction of a second picture several months later, *Une grosse tête* with Eddie Constantine, Georges Poujouly, and Alexandra Stewart. Cowritten in August 1961 by Truffaut and de Givray and shot in the autumn, this film flopped as well. From then on, Truffaut gave up trying to be a producer except for his own films, but he had shown unflinching determination throughout the endeavor.

THE STORY OF A SHY PERSON

François Truffaut was eager to begin work on a second feature. Wishing to remain faithful to his agreement with Pierre Braunberger, his first thought was to reconsider adapting *Temps chaud,* with Bernadette Lafont. He worked on the screenplay with Godard, whom Braunberger hired for 130,000 francs in early April 1959. The shooting was scheduled for July 15 to August 30, in Mougins. But the success of *The 400 Blows* changed matters. Truffaut realized he should dispel the image some film professionals and journalists had of him—of a simple little Parisian who had achieved success through nerve and ambition. Childhood and casual love stories had become fashionable subjects, and he felt he should stay away from these, even if this meant revealing other facets of his personality—those of an often anxious, rather pessimistic, pathologically shy seducer. So his second picture would not be the story of success, but of failure, of inner withdrawal, reflecting a more intimate aspect of himself, which Madeleine Morgenstern describes as follows: "Sometimes, when faced with certain situations, François could no longer speak, especially when more than one person was involved or when he felt he was in foreign territory. He had this slightly childish and disconcerting attitude of remaining silent with people who didn't speak the same way he did."[76]

Truffaut found an ideal surrogate in the person of Charles Aznavour. He was captivated by Aznavour's performance in Georges Franju's *La Tête contre les murs (The Keepers)*. He liked his "fragility, his vulnerability, his humble and graceful figure, which made him resemble Saint Francis of Assisi."[77] The two men even looked alike: Short, with the same bearing and the same expressive face, they were both vivacious, excitable, and anxious, but with an elegance in gesture and deportment, and an iron will. They first met in Cannes, on the morning of May 11, 1959, at the bar of the Carlton Hotel. They felt an immediate bond, so much so that they saw each other often in Paris, and wanted to make a film together. Truffaut put aside *Temps chaud* and decided to adapt a David Goodis novel, *Down There*, which had been published in Gallimard's *Série Noire* under the title *Tirez sur le pianiste*

(*Shoot the Piano Player*). Goodis was one of Truffaut's favorite American writers. What he liked about the novel was its fairy-tale aspect treated in a *noir* manner, the plot twists combining unbridled fantasy with the most sordid tragedy—gangsters conversing about everyday life, crooks discussing love, and lovers turned killers. Truffaut gave Aznavour the novel to read; he was enchanted. Then Pierre Braunberger had to be convinced. He accepted Truffaut's conditions: 6 million old francs for himself and 2 million for Marcel Moussy, who would write the screen adaptation and the dialogue. He also acquired the rights to the novel (2 million) and guaranteed Aznavour's salary (5 million). *Shoot the Piano Player* would cost 75 million francs, almost double the budget of *The 400 Blows*, but a sum that was still moderate compared to the budgets for many French films of the period.

In June 1959, Truffaut asked Marcel Moussy again to write the screenplay. They spent two weeks in Saint-Tropez, at the Ferme d'Augustin, and a week at the Colombe d'Or in Saint-Paul-de-Vence. In Saint-Tropez, Truffaut was accompanied by Liliane David and Jean-Pierre Léaud. The young woman was there incognito in another hotel; she was supposed to be watching the adolescent Léaud while Truffaut worked with Moussy. The situation led to an imbroglio, for Truffaut was very worried about protecting his privacy. "I had to keep an eye on Jean-Pierre, who got into a lot of mischief," David recounts. While Truffaut and Moussy were working on the screenplay, Jean-Pierre Léaud, still basking in the glory of *The 400 Blows*, was the darling of the press. A young photographer in Saint-Tropez wanted to do a shoot for *Elle* of Léaud posing with the Saint-Tropez personalities Françoise Sagan, Jean-Pierre Aumont, and so on. "Jean-Pierre succeeded in borrowing the photographer's car," Liliane David says, "and getting into an accident with it. François was furious, since he had to pay the repair costs."[78]

In July, Madeleine and François Truffaut returned to Saint-Paul-de-Vence with little Laura, who was six months old. Then the couple spent time in Saint-Tropez at the Ferme d'Augustin, where Marcel Moussy's wife also joined them. Work progressed rapidly, and on July 17, the screenplay for *Shoot the Piano Player* was ready. Pierre Braunberger was pleased with it. Charlie Kohler is a short, somber, and mysterious man. A dance-hall pianist at Mammy's Bar, pampered by a prostitute, Clarisse, and secretly loved by Léna, the waitress at the bar, he lives alone with his younger brother, Fido. His past first catches up with him when his other brother Chico turns up at Mammy's Bar, with two gangsters hot on his trail. Charlie is reluctantly swept into this shady story by the two gangsters, Momo and Ernest, even though they turn out to be more eccentric than expected. His past catches up with him a second time when Léna declares her love, seduces him, and lures him home. The young woman knows that Charlie Kohler is the pseudonym of Edouard Saroyan, a young piano virtuoso. Charlie/Edouard then tells her the whole story: his young wife, Thérésa, had sacrificed herself for his career by becoming the mistress of an impresario, Lars Schmeel. When she confessed to the misdeed to which he owed his success, Saroyan could not bear the truth and walked out on Thérésa, who committed suicide by throwing herself from the window. Success and glory having shattered his conjugal happiness, Edouard became Charlie Kohler. After a night of love, Léna and Charlie must track down Fido, who has been kidnapped by the two gangsters. They go to the Saroyan family house, deep in the mountains, where they find Chico and Richard, the two other brothers who are hiding out there. A chase begins between the Saroyans and the gangsters. As the story draws to an end, it is Léna, the innocent one, who is struck by a stray bullet, slides to the snowy, bloodstained ground, and dies in Charlie's arms.

"One day," Claude de Givray recalls, "François said to me, 'That's it, this film with Aznavour will be the story of a shy person.' It's true François was shy, but on the other hand, when he spoke about cinema, even when he was very young, he already spoke like a film director. It was his terrain, he could be as daring as he pleased. He, who sometimes had difficulty speaking, became a bulldozer when speaking about things he had knowledge of. François learned to use his shyness. In *Shoot the Piano Player,* this can be seen in Aznavour's part, when he doesn't dare ring a doorbell. François films the gesture in four shots; he was very pleased with this because he had found a filmic device for transmitting this feeling. François used to bite his nails (he used to say that it was very good to bite one's nails, because there was always a woman who wanted to prevent you from doing it!), but as soon as he spoke about things that concerned him—that is, cinema—he would turn into a true professional."[79]

Truffaut was increasingly excited by this story of a shy man who began to bear a likeness to himself. It was not so much the plot as certain significant details that betrayed his most private obsessions. In their poetic dialogue, the gangsters referred to the "magical" power of women, while the Charlie/Edouard character, a famous pianist who had compromised himself to obtain success and had embraced anonymity out of despair, a man pathologically shy yet just as pathologically a womanizer, was of course Truffaut's double.

GOODIS QUENEAU-STYLE

In this film, Truffaut experimented with a new style, based on constant changes in tempo. *Shoot the Piano Player* continually played on these breaks in rhythm, which recall both Queneau and Trenet. For Truffaut, it was "practically a musical film,"[80] composed like a score, mixing several styles. On Pierre Braunberger's advice, he contacted Georges Delerue, a former student of Darius Milhaud at the Paris Conservatoire who would later be the conductor of the Orchestre de la Radiodiffusion française. Truffaut and Delerue understood each other perfectly, as Truffaut himself recalled: "We were at the painful rough-cut stage. Delerue looked and grasped my intentions immediately. 'Okay! This is a *noir* thriller treated in the style of Raymond Queneau, I see what to do.' "[81] This first job would mark the beginning of a long and intense collaboration.

Boby Lapointe is the other musical revelation in the film. Guided by Audiberti, Truffaut picked him out at the Cheval d'Or, a club of cabaret artists: "the house went into a frenzy of joy when he struck up 'Léon,' then 'Marcelle,' and finally 'Avanie et Framboise.' "[82] With their constant puns and rapid syncopated rhythms, these pieces immediately filled Truffaut with enthusiasm, for they illustrated what he wanted to accomplish in *Shoot the Piano Player.* The director hired Boby Lapointe to play himself and sing "Avanie et framboise" in front of the camera in its entirety and in real time on the stage of Mammy's Bar, where Charlie Kohler plays the piano. Pierre Braunberger, who felt it was impossible to understand the meaning of the words, requested that Truffaut cut the song, or add subtitles to the scene. Truffaut refused to make cuts, but he liked the idea of the "subtitled"[83] singer. Later, Aznavour got Boby Lapointe hired for the first half of his recital at the Alhambra, which led to the singer's making his first record.

Simultaneously detective thriller and intimate journal, *Shoot the Piano Player* is surely François Truffaut's true New Wave film. Indeed, he had hired Raoul Coutard, the movement's preeminent cameraman since *Breathless.* "What attracted me to him," Truffaut wrote, "is the originality of his camerawork but also his extraordinarily crude language. . . . Coutard's rudeness makes visitors run away and particularly female visitors. He has no servility in him, and will address a producer, a technician or the female star in exactly the same way."[84] As for Coutard, who was accustomed to working quickly, the shooting conditions of this modest-budget film appealed to him: "I arrived with the bad manners of a press photographer," Coutard explained. "I like quick, candid work. I find the pretty and the 'polished' sickening. I started by eliminating from my films all the so-called artistic effects, all those things cameramen thrive on, and instead of asking for an army of projectors, I used daylight. . . . The result: we shot fifteen times more quickly for ten times less money, and our casual, lively films had more ambiance."[85]

Suzanne Schiffman was also a new recruit for Truffaut. She was an old-time acquaintance from the days of the Cinémathèque and the Ciné-Club du Quartier Latin, a friend of Rivette, Godard, and Gruault. In 1956, after getting a literature degree at the Sorbonne, she went to Chicago for a year on a fellowship given for her work with Edgar Morin, and then lived in Mexico for a year. On returning to Paris, she collaborated on the shoot of *Paris Belongs to Us* in the summer of 1958; then she was hired as script supervisor on *Shoot the Piano Player.* "Braunberger wasn't displeased," she recalls, "because he could pay me far less than the union wage. I found it so wonderful to be paid that I had no desire to argue."[86] Though she lacked professional experience, Schiffman was interested in all aspects of the shoot and had no preconceived ideas. Very soon, her job resembled that of an assistant director. She eventually became Truffaut's indispensable partner, his closest collaborator.

To work with Charles Aznavour, Truffaut hired several actors whom he had initially planned to use in *Temps chaud.* Hence, Nicole Berger plays Thérésa, Edouard Saroyan's wife, who commits suicide; Serge Davri has the part of Plyne, the limited, strapping bar owner with facial injuries, whose loutish appearance conceals great sensitivity and naïve love attachments; Catherine Lutz plays the role of his wife, Mammy, the melancholic owner of the bar. As for Albert Rémy, Antoine's stepfather in *The 400 Blows,* he becomes Chico, Charlie Kohler's crazy, blundering brother. Truffaut also freely punctuated his film with friends, such as the director Alex Joffé; the writer Daniel Boulanger, in the role of a gangster; and the filmmaker Claude Heymann, playing the impresario Lars Schmeel. Still to be cast were the two other main female parts, Léna, the waitress, and Clarisse, the prostitute. On October 14, 1959, Truffaut put a small announcement in *Paris-Flirt* before proceeding to auditions. He had promised the part of Clarisse to Liliane David, who had just appeared in *Breathless* (the friend Jean-Paul Belmondo comes to pinch money from in the wardrobe of the hotel where she is living). Afraid of mixing his love life with his work, Truffaut decided to give the part to Michèle Mercier, the future "Angélique" and star of the sixties. At a second audition, Truffaut fell head over heels for Claudine Huzé, a twenty-two-year-old actress with a round face, blond curls, and charming eyes and mouth, whom he had noticed in a television drama. After a highly comical screen test in which he asked the rather shy young actress to insult him with swearwords, Truffaut offered her the part of Léna. He thus launched Claudine Huzé's career and gave her her stage name, Marie Dubois, in homage to Audiberti's novel: "Marie Dubois is neither a 'chick' nor a 'doll,' she's neither 'titillating' nor 'impish,' but she's a pure and dignified young girl whom one could conceivably fall in love with and be loved by in return. One might not turn around to look at her in the street, but she's fresh and gracious, a bit boyish and very childlike. She's

vehement and passionate, modest and tender,"[87] Truffaut wrote in presenting his discovery.

The filming of *Shoot the Piano Player* began in the last days of November
1959, mostly at Levallois-Perret, then in a brasserie at the Porte Champer-
ret, and ended in mid-January, in a chalet in Le Sappey, located in the Mas-
sif de la Grande-Chartreuse, not far from Grenoble. This is where the last
scenes of the film take place, in the snow, when Léna is killed by a stray bullet during the shoot-out between the Saroyans and the gangsters. Two
nights before the end of the shoot, Marie Dubois's twenty-third birthday
was celebrated with cakes and champagne. Good humor and conviviality
dominated the filming. Truffaut was satisfied, but he realized the editing
and postsynchronization processes would be essential, for the construction
of the film was peculiar: There was a long flashback in the middle and constant rhythm changes and mixing of genres. It was also a "musical film," so
the sound track was particularly important.

THE AMERICAN FRIEND

On January 6, 1960, while he was completing his shoot in Le Sappey,
François Truffaut received a telegram from Les Films du Carrosse: *The 400
Blows* had just been given the prize for best foreign film by the New York
critics. The good news came with an invitation from Daniel Frankel, head of
Zenith International Film Corporation, the film's New York distributor.
Truffaut agreed to make his first trip to the United States. *The 400 Blows*,
which had opened on November 16, 1959, at the Fine Arts theater, had
received glowing reviews. For instance, the day after it opened, Bosley
Crowther, the influential *New York Times* critic, had written, "Words cannot
state simply how fine is Jean-Pierre Léaud in the role of the boy. . . . He will
live as a delightful, provoking and heartbreaking monument to a boy." As for
the film itself, it is "a small masterpiece" that "encourages an exciting
refreshment of faith in films,"[88] Crowther said. The other important critics
all agreed, such as Paul Beckley in the *New York Herald Tribune:* "A film
everyone with a serious concern for fine films will not want to miss,"[89] or
Archer Winsten in the *New York Post:* "*The 400 Blows* brings us one of those
great timeless French pictures that wring your heart with their beauty, truth
and despair."[90]

The United States was pivotal for Truffaut's reputation and commercial
success. It was also the country of the directors he most admired, American
directors and European exiles—Hitchcock, Hawks, Lang, Aldrich, and
Nicholas Ray. And Truffaut realized that his own critical and popular suc-

cess would compel recognition for the New Wave in the United States. But in his ambition to win over America, he had a serious handicap: He didn't speak English. From then on, learning English would become a lifelong obsession.

On January 20, 1960, Truffaut left Paris for New York. The New York Film Critics award ceremony was scheduled for the evening of January twenty-third. He planned to spend two weeks in the United States—one week in New York, a short stay in Chicago, and then a visit to Los Angeles to meet people and visit the mythical studios in the company of Jeanne Moreau. During the award ceremony, Truffaut was deathly pale, unable to utter a single word in English. By his side was one of the actors he most admired, James Stewart, receiving an award for his performance in Otto Preminger's *Anatomy of a Murder*. Audrey Hepburn and Elizabeth Taylor also received prizes, as did William Wyler's *Ben-Hur*, which was chosen as the best picture that year. They all posed for a group photograph. Truffaut smiled shyly, gazing with slight awe at Jimmy Stewart. Earlier, Daniel Frankel had introduced him to the critics in the *New York Times* reception rooms: "M. Truffaut has made his first trip to this country from Paris to be here tonight. This is his very first picture. He is only 27. He is a former movie critic, and the only one we ever heard of who got busy and made a good picture. For showing the rest of the world, New York Film Critics included, how to make a good picture and a masterpiece, may we give him the warm welcome he deserves."[91]

As soon as he arrived in New York, Truffaut made an acquaintance that would be crucial for his American career. Helen Scott was in charge of public relations at the French Film Office, whose director was Joseph Maternati. In this capacity, she welcomed Truffaut at the airport upon his arrival in New York and served as his guide and interpreter. Cultivated, fluent in French, a great film enthusiast blessed with a good New York Jewish sense of humor, Scott had been active in the American Left, and later would be in the feminist movement. During the McCarthy period, she had been blacklisted for so-called anti-American activities along with many other writers, screenwriters, left-wing film directors, and members of the American Communist party. With her thorough knowledge of the New York cultural scene and the press, Scott was an indispensable ally for Truffaut in the United States. She admired *The 400 Blows* and the other first films of the New Wave and devoted all her energy to promoting them, introducing Truffaut, Godard, and Resnais to the American critics as the foremost representatives of the new French cinema. Truffaut was her favorite. During the trip to Chicago, François Truffaut and Helen Scott became friends; they talked for hours on end about movies, their youth, and politics, with "him proclaiming he was of the 'politically uncommitted' generation and me, on the contrary, an old-time activist, trying to explain to him the conditions of my youth in America and of the war in Africa, which had led me to my left-wing convictions."[92]

A snowstorm in Chicago forced Truffaut to cancel the California leg of his journey. Eager to screen a first rough cut of *Shoot the Piano Player*, he decided to return to Paris, happy, thanks to Helen Scott, that he had met David Goodis, whose novel he had just adapted, as well as Henry Miller,[93] for whom he had the utmost admiration. On January 26, Helen Scott also organized a dinner to introduce him to Elie Wiesel, who suggested that Truffaut make a film on World War II and the concentration camps.

When he returned to Paris, Truffaut stayed in contact with Helen Scott, maintaining a faithful, extremely rich correspondence, in which they kept each other informed about the Paris and New York film scenes. Usually very discreet about his relationships with lovers and friends, Truffaut wrote openly to Helen about his moods and feelings at work and of his difficulties in his private life. Of course, he was secure in the knowledge that the distance between New York and Paris guaranteed him a certain discretion; but his willingness to confide in Helen Scott was also due to her abilities at persuasion, for she very much wanted their relationship to transcend the professional. In a letter dated March 3, 1960, several weeks after their parting in Chicago, she complained to Truffaut: "Without expecting you to be as effusive as me, I had nevertheless hoped to receive some personal news from you—your concerns about the new film, your return to Paris, whatever—in short, a sentence, any kind of sentence through which I could recognize my friend Truffaut. But your letter, all bizness [*sic*], could have been written by Tati or any other producer. The handwritten message? You know my mania against formulas; for me only substance counts. In any case, I began to wonder if the tone of my correspondence wasn't inappropriate. . . ."[94] Cut to the quick, Truffaut immediately apologized: "You were right to scold me, for I let myself take the easy way out, dictating several letters every morning to 'expedite current business' and that way I feel like I'm a *big business man*, a *self-made man*, a *first class quality* man [italicized words indicate English in the original], and what not. In short, thanks to you, I'll improve my behavior, I'll resume my habit of typing a few letters myself at home, and my provincial and foreign friends will wonder why I've become so affectionate without suspecting they owe it to Helen Scott, my dear Helen."[95] Beyond the countless puns ("Truffe," also called "Truffaldin: the valet in Italian comedy, hypocritical, cunning and untruthful"), an obvious tenderness ("Scottie" or "Mascotte"), and all sorts of secrets, this correspondence that Truffaut diligently kept up throughout the sixties offers a veritable intimate journal of the New Wave. "Everything you write me is so important to me. I like you almost as much as I like myself, which, God knows, is not saying little,"[96] he wrote her after his second trip to New York in April 1962.

THE ALGERIAN TRAGEDY

On his return from the United States, François Truffaut started to move toward the Left ideologically, no doubt under Helen Scott's influence. On February 12, 1960, he confided to a screenwriter friend his desire "to shoot a political film in the next two years."[97] The idea was derived from his long conversations with Helen Scott and Elie Wiesel. While he liked Scott's outspokenness, caustic humor, political experience, and practical sense, he rather mistrusted Wiesel's "bruised good conscience": "This guy is more moving than likable; I mean that he must be dreadful to live with, moaning and crying over himself, but I admire him greatly."[98] Nevertheless, the subjects discussed during the New York dinner—the war, the Resistance, deportation, the death camps—fascinated the director. Elie Wiesel had given him the proofs of his novel *Le Jour* (*The Accident*) in the hope that he might adapt it for the screen, but Truffaut did not pursue the project. The two men then considered a film entitled *Le Dernier Déporté,* the story of the last convoy of Jews to leave France for the death camps on July 31, 1944, and the return of one survivor. In December 1960, Wiesel wrote to Truffaut: "Now, if you want, or still want, we could start working on your film subject. *Le Dernier Déporté:* the scores to be settled with the men of the past and the future, the anxieties that overwhelm him, the doubts (did it really happen?), the silences—a subject overflowing with rich possibilities."[99] Truffaut spent two months doing research, reading many works on the "final solution" and "on Hitler, Nuremberg, and particularly the wonderful American book by [William] Shirer on the Third Reich."[100] He met a survivor from the last convoy, Alexandre Chambon, French consul in Rio de Janeiro, who had written his recollections of the Buchenwald concentration camp, a grim eyewitness account, in a book entitled *81.490,* his number as a prisoner. For a while, Truffaut considered adapting the book, but then decided against it, rejecting the idea of "staging the false reality of horror": "I couldn't resolve to have characters weighing 30 kilos played by 60 kilo extras, for here, the physical, visual and bodily reality is too important to be sacrificed."[101] But even if Truffaut quickly shelved the project, his initial interest marks a clear ideological change from his attitude as a critic in the fifties, when he categorically rejected any "politically committed" work, met with the wartime collaborator Lucien Rebatet, and was ironical about all "left-wing films."

If his political convictions, and consequently his public image, had changed, this was in large part due to events connected with the Algerian war. Although no subject outside the movies had led him to take a public stance while writing for *Arts*, now the situation in Algeria sometimes caught his attention. Twice, Truffaut took a skeptical position with regard to the French military involvement there. First, on March 12, 1958, in his review of *Paths of Glory*, Stanley Kubrick's anti-militarist World War I film, banned in France for undermining army morale, Truffaut himself adopted a clearly antimilitarist stance, derived, no doubt, from his own bad memories of military prisons and hospitals. On October 8, 1958, in one of his last reviews, he reaffirmed the same bias in discussing the revival of Jean Renoir's *Grand Illusion*. In a long digression, Truffaut alluded to his conversation with the director Pierre Schoendoerffer, a former news reporter in Indochina, and, breaking a taboo of the French press, he drew a parallel between the anti-colonial struggle of the Vietminh and the NLF in Algeria, clearly enjoining the French army to withdraw. Feeling deep indignation at the torture practiced by French officers in Algeria, he had absolutely no faith in the army's ability to resolve the crisis, and he let this be known in the right-wing *Arts*, thereby creating a controversy.

The Algerian war would affect Truffaut directly on March 9, 1960, when Cécile Decugis, his editor for *Shoot the Piano Player*, was imprisoned for having rented an apartment in her name that was used as a headquarters by NLF activists. In a matter of days, Truffaut raised over 20,000 new francs for Decugis's appeal.[102] During the spring of 1960, he made regular trips to the Roquette prison to assure her of the loyalty and solidarity of the *Piano Player* cast and crew.

It was not so much the Algerian cause itself that moved Truffaut as it was the defense of basic liberties in time of war. He made financial contributions to a good number of independent periodicals—banned and clandestine—that sympathized with the NLF, such as the newspaper *Liberté-Vérité*, edited by Pierre Jean Oswald (he subscribed by sending a check for 4,000 new francs), or *L'Espoir d'Alger*, the "last free newspaper" published in Algeria, whose editor, Guy Teisseire, was a film enthusiast.[103] In June 1960, Truffaut also became passionately interested in the Maurice Audin affair, the case of a twenty-five-year-old scientist and member of the Algerian Communist party who had been arrested three years earlier by French paratroopers and had never been heard from since. The French army's official explanation was that the young academic had been inadvertently shot during an attempted escape. The "Audin committee," made up of Chatenet, dean of the Paris Law School, Pierre Vidal-Naquet, Jacques Panijel, Michel Crouzet, and Luc Montagnier, thought, on the contrary, that he had died under torture and that there had been an attempted cover-up. The Audin affair shed a very harsh light on the military practices that revolted Truffaut. He even considered making a film about Audin, but then reconsidered, writing in *Clarté*, the Communist student monthly:

> The affair is so clear in itself that it needs no comment. Perhaps it could be done by sticking to the facts. But a fiction film entails looking for other people's motives, not just their political motives but their personal motives. In the end, the film would merely consist in showing a victim, a man who had been subjected to an entirely unjust and appalling fate, and, on the other, the mechanism leading up to it. This would be inappropriate, for to show something is to ennoble it. A film of this kind would satisfy neither Madame Audin nor the Audin committee, because other people's motives would have to be investigated. Which would require being interested in the agonies of conscience of—this will make you bristle—General Massu, who allowed torture in Algeria and covered it up.[104]

Freedom of expression, the struggle against censorship and torture, antimilitarism—all these causes reinforced Truffaut's convictions, but he still hesitated to take a public position. He had always hated "the good conscience of the Left," he told Helen Scott, "those who suddenly discover one day that everyone on this earth ought to have enough to eat."[105] He would overcome his reluctance thanks to the damning testimony of his friends Claude de Givray and Claude Gauteur, who served in Algeria for two years and gave him an inside description of the army's despicable conduct. On August 28, 1960, Gauteur wrote Truffaut a distressing letter that thoroughly convinced him:

> I swear to you that when you see kids that are all skin and bones, pustules and rags, creep through the electrified barbed wire to lick an empty sardine can or pick up a few centimes that an irresponsible soldier has purposely thrown in that precise spot, I swear to you that when you realize the extent to which these "full-fledged French people" have been exploited, you switch from feeling to reason, from dilettantism to vigilance, from noncommitment to receptiveness. . . . To this day I have seen only four *fellaghas* [independence fighters], beaten up, "fate unknown" (wonderful euphemism), and they disturb my sleep twice every night. What's in store for me in the next eight months of duty? The reconquest of Morocco under the orders of Comrade Soustelle? Everything's swaying, you feel you're changing; you watch yourself disintegrate, a rather repulsive sight. . . . Yesterday I murdered my first "fellouze." Disgusting. The guy had a bullet that

literally came out of his rear, he was shitting blood. He didn't die on the spot and we evacuated him by helicopter. Fortunately for him, he succumbed to his wound, because with the bundle of coded documents he was carrying, he wasn't about to lead the good life! Lady torture was getting ready for a feast! Dear old boy, I can't tell you how fed up I am; I feel I've aged ten years. It's getting rougher and rougher. I'm no more distressed by the "friendly" losses than by the "enemy" losses, for everything here is pettiness in trying to keep oneself alive, a vegetative, absurd life.[106]

THE MANIFESTO OF THE 121

On September 13, 1960, Truffaut received the "Declaration on the right to insubordination in the Algerian war," which Dionys Mascolo sent to him: "If it meets with your approval, as we all hope, could you please send it back, with your signature, as well as the typewritten text included with it, to D. Mascolo or Marguerite Duras, 5, rue St-Benoît, Paris 6e. It's urgent, of course. Kindest regards."[107] The famous "Manifesto of the 121"—so named because of the 121 artists, writers, and academics who first signed it—had been circulating illegally since early July. It had been initiated by Dionys Mascolo, Marguerite Duras, and Maurice Blanchot, soon joined by Jean-Paul Sartre and Simone de Beauvoir. It appealed for the support of all the French soldiers who had deserted in Algeria or before being sent to fight, and also of all the French who were in some way helping the NLF. As far as the government, the army, and much of public opinion was concerned, this declaration was treasonous; it was denounced as defeatist, anarchist, and left-wing, and legally prosecuted as such. For Truffaut, the manifesto expressed his own indignation—it denounced torture, rejected the army's actions, demanded freedom of expression, and supported deserters. Some of his friends were among the original 121: Florence Malraux and Alain Resnais, Maurice Pons and Claude Sautet. Truffaut signed on September 13, and though the manifesto and the names of the signers were banned from the French press, his gesture did not go unnoticed; his former allies and friends at *Arts* and *La Parisienne* responded en masse to the 121 with their own "Manifesto of French Intellectuals," published in the October 12, 1960, issue of *Carrefour*. They denounced the "professors of treason" and proclaimed their loyalty to the French army, which was "fighting for France in Algeria" and had "been accomplishing a civilizing, social and humane mission for years." This was signed by about three hundred academics, clearly right-wing, as well as by the "hussars" Roger Nimier, Jacques Laurent, Thierry Maulnier, Michel Déon, and Antoine Blondin.

The Algerian problem had become a source of painful conflict among French intellectuals,[108] reshuffling the alliances of the postwar period. Truffaut's own public and spectacular shift from the Right to the Left pleased his friends—particularly Helen Scott and David Goodis, who sent him warm congratulations from New York. Even some erstwhile opponents gave him credit: Robert Benayoun, for example, himself a signer of the Manifesto of the 121, an "anti-Truffaut" critic of the fifties and scourge of the New Wave, wrote him in the beginning of October 1960: "I heard they were making trouble for you and I want to assure you of my complete sympathy. I knew that your outstanding qualities were honesty and sincerity. I now know to add courage."[109] Aside from Truffaut, Jacques Doniol-Valcroze and Pierre Kast were the only ones from the *Cahiers* group to sign the manifesto.

On September 28, 1960, the Council of Ministers retaliated against the signers of the manifesto. Questions were raised in the opposition newspapers: "A WITCH-HUNT WOULD BE DEADLY FOR FRENCH CINEMA" was Georges Sadoul's headline in *Les Lettres françaises* on October 6, while in the Communist weekly *France nouvelle,* Jack Ralite compared the "Gaullist repression" to a "French McCarthyism."[110] In Italy, England, and Germany, journalists raised the possibility of shattered careers for Alain Resnais, Truffaut, Françoise Sagan, Roger Blin, Alain Cuny, Simone Signoret, Laurent Terzieff, and Danièle Delorme, all of whom had signed the manifesto. Truffaut, somewhat panic-stricken, wrote to Helen Scott on October 1, 1960, dramatizing matters:

Events have worsened significantly in the last few days, politically. If you read the French newspapers, you know that the "artists" who have signed the manifesto supporting insubordination are now on an official blacklist: banned from TV and radio appearances, or from performing in subsidized theaters. For movies, it is very complicated (fortunately), for there is talk of depriving us of the automatic subsidy granted to all French films, and the different types of existing quality bonuses and advances on box-office receipts. Malraux is in charge of working out the details of this sanction. In short, it's a terrible mess! All of this has plagued me of course and prevented me from concentrating on my work. If I spoke English, I would seriously consider trying my luck in America, but I have a terrible complex about languages; there would also be possibilities in Italy, where I have lots of friends. I'm simultaneously discouraged—because every day there are new charges and threats and my shady military past as a deserter will no doubt be exploited by the right-wing papers—and stimulated, for it is enough for me to be prevented from making films and all my doubts on the subject are removed. The 121 signatures have grown to 144

over the summer, and to over 400 since, and now the police are carrying out searches to prevent the number from growing; many teachers
who have signed might be dismissed. Strange climate. It will be very
tricky for me to supervise *Tire-au-flanc* officially and I'm afraid they
will eliminate the quality bonuses on the shorts I produced. Will I
have to leave France to shoot my next film?[111]

After "hiding out" at the Colombe d'Or, Truffaut was summoned to
police headquarters, on quai des Orfèvres, to testify as soon as he returned
to Paris, on October 7, 1960. But he chose not to appear and stayed cloistered at home. Several days later, thanks to campaigns in the French and
international press, the sanctions against the signers of the manifesto were
lifted. The blacklist was abolished; de Gaulle would not be another
McCarthy. Truffaut's commitment against the Algerian war was a meaning-
ful step in his life; it gave him legitimacy as a left-winger and reinforced his
reputation as an honest, sincere, and courageous artist. He would always
bear a deep grudge against General de Gaulle and the France of the early
sixties: "A country that can say 'yes' to de Gaulle is a country that doesn't
give a damn whether culture disappears or not, hence that doesn't give a
damn about my films,"[112] he wrote to Helen Scott on the eve of the referen-
dum to elect de Gaulle president through universal suffrage.

THEY SHOOT AT THE PIANO PLAYER

Shoot the Piano Player had been a pleasant film for Truffaut to shoot, but
turned out to be a difficult and tedious one to edit. He admitted to a feeling
of "blind panic about any screenplay structured around flashbacks."[113] The
editing of *Piano Player* had been conceived around one long flashback concerning the tragic love affair between the pianist Edouard Saroyan
(Aznavour) and his wife, Thérésa (Nicole Berger). The sound track was
equally complex, with a proliferation of false leads, changing atmosphere
and songs. Claudine Bouché, the editor of films by Michel Boisrond and
Alexandre Astruc, stood in for Cécile Decugis at the last minute. Truffaut
offered to show her the rushes at the Boulogne studios. "Since François had
used playback on the set, all the rushes were postsynchronized, with no
clear preference on his part. It was a nightmarish screening, endlessly long.
François didn't utter a word. I didn't know what to say to him; I was afraid to
commit a blunder. I hadn't read the screenplay, and the whole thing seemed
strange to me, because I wasn't used to films that were so minimally structured. The sound wasn't always audible. At around one in the morning,
Truffaut asked me if this could make a film. This made me furious: How

could a director like him ask me such a question? By chance, I told him it reminded me of Queneau. I later found out that I hadn't been mistaken."[114]

When the film was shown to the actors and some friends in June 1960, and to a few journalists later on, reactions were mixed, which depressed Truffaut and undermined his confidence. Pierre Braunberger found the film puzzling. It was true that Truffaut had wanted it to stand in stark contrast to *The 400 Blows*. Rather than present another story about children or adolescents and simple emotions, he gave his audience gangsters, prostitutes, and a pianist undermined by melancholy—a pure fantasy picture, constantly alternating between tragedy and comedy, part thriller, part musical. His radical change of genre took the public by surprise.

In addition, there were problems with the censors. Truffaut had cut a sequence that might have proved offensive—of a little cat run over by the gangsters. But another scene, where Michèle Mercier gets into bed with Aznavour and exposes her breasts, was considered too risqué. Truffaut shortened the scene but refused to cut it. The censorship board remained inflexible: *Shoot the Piano Player* was banned to those under eighteen.

Truffaut eventually lost interest in his film, which was badly received when it opened over the summer in several resort towns like Vichy, Deauville, and Biarritz. He turned his thoughts to other projects, including the *Tire-au-flanc* script he was to write with his friend de Givray. Braunberger tried to motivate him: "You're the greatest director, the most intelligent man in movies, a wonderful friend, and I'm very fond of you," he wrote him from Saint-Jean-de-Luz on August 20, 1960. "I'm prepared to start all over again on the same film under the same conditions. . . ."[115] But a week or two later, when it began to look as if *Piano Player* might be a commercial flop, Braunberger's tone changed; he harassed Truffaut with telegrams, enjoining him to promote his film: "Paris is where your career will be decided for the next five years and specifically how your film will fare in the world. This is why I'm in no hurry to release it and am looking for the best way of presenting it. It's not easy: should it be called 'a comic *film noir*,' 'an eccentric *film noir*,' a 'drama of love and humor,' a 'burlesque tragedy,' a 'film where the good guys are sometimes bad and the bad guys are sometimes likable'? You're much more qualified than me for this kind of game. So pull yourself together and help me. I'm really counting on you. . . ."[116]

When all was said and done, *Shoot the Piano Player*, which opened in three Paris theaters on November 25, 1960, did not do particularly well—71,901 ticket sales after a six-week run. Its run ended on January 3, 1961, and Truffaut considered it a dreadful failure, even though this hardly jeopardized Les Films du Carrosse. Earlier that fall, Jean Cocteau had tried to cheer him up. "I can't abide your fears, my darling François," he wrote him.

"Of course it's difficult, but you couldn't do anything badly even if you went out of your way to try."[117] At least Truffaut found out who his true friends were, for far fewer people came to congratulate him than at the release of *The 400 Blows.*

THE GREATEST SWEETHEART

In his disappointment over *Shoot the Piano Player,* François Truffaut found comfort with Jeanne Moreau, an actress he had long admired. In 1957, he had written, "[She is] the greatest sweetheart in French cinema. While gangsters and gangs kill each other, she dances in a tutu in a circus, is tortured by a sadist and makes her way through bursts of submachine-gun fire, with thoughts only of love. With trembling lips, wild hair, she ignores what others call 'morals' and lives by and for love. Messieurs, producers and directors, give her a real part and we will have a great film."[118]

Jeanne Moreau had since become a star and had appeared in several noted films, including Louis Malle's *Ascenseur pour l'échafaud* (*Elevator to the Gallows*) and *Les Amants* (*The Lovers*) and Roger Vadim's *Les Liaisons dangereuses* (*Dangerous Liaisons*). Truffaut had met her for the first time in Cannes in 1957, at the screening of *Elevator to the Gallows.* "François gave me *Jules and Jim* to read and we met regularly to discuss it," Moreau explains. "François wasn't a very talkative person, but this did not prevent a deep bond from developing between us very quickly. Usually, when people first get to know each other, they exchange a lot of memories. For us it was silences—we exchanged a lot of silences. Fortunately, there was the correspondence; we soon talked a lot by letter."[119]

In *Arts,* François Truffaut defended *The Lovers,* which caused a scandal when it was shown at the Venice Film Festival in September 1958: "Louis Malle, with Louise de Vilmorin's admirable support, has pulled off a film which is perfectly familiar and almost banal, absolutely tasteful and morally unassailable."[120] Later the same year, Jeanne Moreau made a cameo appearance in *The 400 Blows,* on Jean-Claude Brialy's arm. She became an important person in Truffaut's life, embodying professional success, the glory and myth of the star, and the free woman in love with life. For the former critic, who had long been smitten with actresses on screen, the meeting with Jeanne Moreau was like a revelation. Florence Malraux recalls, "He was enthralled by her for several years, partly because she was a star, probably the only one he knew. Sometimes François called me at midnight to ask me if I knew where Jeanne was. I was a witness to this fascination, which he didn't hide from me. But I wasn't intimate enough with him to ask questions."[121]

"I was accustomed to fame," confides Moreau, "and my life consisted of enjoying only its pleasant aspects. Moreover, my Anglo-Saxon origin constituted an additional opening to the world, to different lifestyles and cultures. I made François discover Henry James and drink champagne."[122] Generous and convivial, Jeanne Moreau had a lifestyle that was indeed very different from Truffaut's; he always went to the same restaurants and had no interest in sharing the pleasures of good food. His friendship with her would unlock his ambitious strivings. For Truffaut could think of nothing else but making a great film with the woman who had become his friend. And this great film would be *Jules and Jim*.

But the adaptation of Roché's novel wasn't quite ready. In the meantime, Truffaut considered making another film with Jeanne Moreau, *Le Bleu d'outre-tombe*, based on a novel by René-Jean Clot; it is the story of a schoolteacher who is persecuted by an entire town when the parents of her students learn that she had once been put away in a psychiatric hospital. Les Films du Carrosse had already optioned the novel, published by Gallimard, and Clot had been hired to adapt it and write the dialogue.[123] But then tragedy struck. In February 1960, Jeanne Moreau was in Blaye, near Bordeaux, for the shooting of *Moderato Cantabile* (the Peter Brook film based on the novel by Marguerite Duras, in which Moreau plays opposite Jean-Paul Belmondo) when her son Jérôme, aged ten, was seriously injured in a car accident. The child remained in a deep coma, hovering between life and death, for two weeks. To comfort her, Truffaut went to join her for several weekends. *Le Bleu d'outre-tombe* was postponed for a year and then abandoned. After *Moderato Cantabile*, Jeanne Moreau immediately started work on Antonioni's *La Notte*, while Truffaut finished the screenplay of *Jules and Jim* as quickly as possible.

WAVERING WAVE

The failure of *Piano Player*, and the uncertainties threatening this third film, occurred in a climate that had become inimical to the New Wave. In 1960–61, the films of young directors suffered serious commercial setbacks; ticket sales for Godard's *A Woman Is a Woman* were 65,000; for Chabrol's *Les Godelureaux*, 53,000; for Demy's *Lola,* 35,000. Furthermore, Godard's second film, *Le Petit Soldat,* fought a losing battle against censorship—in September 1960, with the Algerian war raging, it was banned in France and French territories overseas. Truffaut painted a very pessimistic picture for his friend Helen Scott: "I'm not a persecuted victim, and I don't want to talk about a plot, but it's clear right now that films by young people, as soon as they stray from the norm, come up against a barrier on the part of exhibitors and the press. Such is the case for Mocky and Queneau's *Un couple,* De Broca's *Farceur (The Joker),* and also *Piano Player.* It's true that this year there are a great number of old-fashioned big French films that will stay in the theaters for a long time. It smacks of the revenge of the Old Wave— Clouzot's *La Vérité (The Truth),* *La Française et l'Amour* (a despicable film), Cayatte's *Le Passage du Rhin (The Crossing of the Rhine),* and even Vadim's *Et mourir de plaisir (Blood and Roses).*"[124]

Many journalists and professionals held the New Wave films responsible for the desertion of the movie theaters during the early sixties. The movement became a scapegoat, its pictures considered too intellectual or boring, and so keeping the crowds away. "The turning point," Truffaut wrote to Scott, "the switch from praise to systematic denigration, occurred with La Patellière and Michel Audiard's film, *Rue des Prairies,* which was presented as an anti–New Wave film in its publicity: 'Jean Gabin settles his accounts with the New Wave.' "[125] In *Arts,* the screenwriter Michel Audiard accused the new directors of being responsible for the public's disgust with movies and hence playing into the hands of television:

Ah! rebellion, how novel! Truffaut went through it. A charming boy. One eye on the little anarchist's manual, the other on the Catholic ratings; one hand clenched at the future and the other hiding his bow tie. Monsieur Truffaut would like to persuade the Fouquet customers that he's a menace, a dangerous individual. This makes the connoisseurs laugh, but it impresses poor Eric Rohmer. Because, while in the old days people who had nothing to say used to get together around a teapot, today they get together in front of a screen. Truffaut applauds Rohmer, who, the previous week, applauded Pollet, who next week will applaud Godard or Chabrol. These men operate like one big family. Such has been the game of French cinema for over a year. The practical result—1960 ends with hits by Delannoy, Grangier, Patellière, Verneuil, those baldies, those hideous professionals. Yuck! This is what they've achieved, or rather what they had achieved. For it wouldn't make sense to still talk about them in the present tense. The *Nouvelle Vague* is dead. And now we know it was really more vague than new.[126]

Jacques Lanzmann wondered in *Arts:* "Does the young French cinema have its future behind it?" In 1960, the magazine *Positif* published an entire issue against the New Wave. And in February 1960, Jean Cau, Sartre's former secretary at *Les Temps modernes,* went to see "some new French films" for *L'Express.* His opinion was harsh: "I'd say that for ten years these 'young people' kept yelling at us something like, 'Oh, if only we were given a camera!' . . . We ended up taking them up on it. We gave them one. What do they have to say? Oh how amazing, nothing! What do they have in their heads? Oh how surprising, a pea! And in their hearts? Oh, how pitiful, water! I admit I'm absolutely speechless with astonishment and sadness. . . . We now know the young directors have virtually nothing to say."[127]

These accusations came at a time when Godard and Truffaut, the leaders of the new cinema, were feeling particularly vulnerable and demoralized. "Me too, I'm feeling completely lost, *caro* Francesco," Godard wrote his friend. "I'm shooting in a strange zone. I feel there's something very beautiful hovering around me. But each time I tell Coutard to pan and capture it, it's gone."[128] The ban on *Le Petit Soldat* increased his distress.

Privately, Truffaut had no hesitation about expressing some harsh criticisms about films that were labeled "New Wave" but that "badly harmed" young French cinema, "stories that group together in a few minutes everything that young directors have been justifiably reproached with for some time—amateurism, snobbishness, and eccentric and incomprehensible characters."[129] But in reply to attacks, some by journalists who had been fervent supporters of the movement two years before, he decided to counterattack. "Before, in interviews, Godard, Resnais, Malle, Chabrol, I and others, we all used to say, 'The New Wave doesn't exist, the term is meaningless.' Then I proclaimed my membership in the movement. One had to be proud of being New Wave just as one had to be proud of having been Jewish during the Occupation,"[130] he said. In spite of *Piano Player*'s lack of success, Truffaut wanted to remind people that there was a "New Wave spirit." He wrote his friend Helen Scott, "Good films are shot in rooms, with one's ass in a chair."[131]

In October 1961, Truffaut granted Louis Marcorelles a long interview in *France-Observateur.* Truffaut spoke as a director, producer, former critic, and, above all, as the leader of the New Wave:

> I recognize that there's a malaise, a bad moment to get through and a need for solutions. I attribute this malaise to the following paradox: the "new cinema's" main concern was to emancipate itself vis-à-vis the motion picture industry. Because of various pressures, films had become impersonal. We believed that everything had to be simplified so we could work freely and make *humble* films on *simple* subjects, hence the quantity of New Wave pictures whose only common feature is a sum of rejections—the rejection of extras, of theatrical intrigue, costly sets, explanatory scenes; these films often have three or four characters and very little action. Unfortunately, the linearity of these films ties in with a literary genre that very much annoys the critics and the first-run public right now, a genre that we might call "Saganism"

[i.e., from the novels by Françoise Sagan]: sports cars, bottles of scotch, short-lived love affairs, etc. The deliberate lightness of these films passes for frivolity—sometimes wrongly, sometimes rightly. The confusion lies in that the qualities of this new cinema—gracefulness, lightness, a sense of propriety, elegance, a quick pace—parallel its faults—frivolity, lack of thought, naïveté. The result? All these films, whether good or bad, work against each other! The paradox is that this praiseworthy effort at lightness has borne fruit three years too late, at a time when audiences are being lured with an offering of the most solemn, most spectacular pictures ever made. In the old days, there used to be one superproduction a year, biblical or otherwise. Today, in the wake of *Ben Hur*, there's one a month. These are antitelevision films; our touching or humorous little films, shot casually and quickly, don't stand a chance against them.[132]

For several months, Truffaut remained on the offensive. He even took up the pen again, to support some "films by friends." In *Arts*, on December 20, 1961, he published a long, favorable article about Rivette's film *Paris nous appartient* (*Paris Belongs to Us*), entitled "The New Wave Is Not at Death's Door." Later, he praised Jacques Rozier's first film, *Adieu Philippine,* and called it an "uninterrupted poem," stating it was "the clearest success of this new cinema, a film where spontaneity is all the more powerful when it is the result of long and careful work. . . . If for no other reason, the new wave had to come in order to portray characters fifteen and twenty years old—a gap of only ten years between them and the directors, just right for the directors to have gained some perspective without losing along the way the accuracy of tone that is an end in itself, as in certain Raymond Queneau novels."[133] Then it was Godard's *Vivre sa vie* (*My Life to Live*) that received Truffaut's enthusiastic support; he even admitted to Helen Scott that he had cried on seeing it, even on seeing it a second time, "and my God I don't often cry at the movies."[134]

In the defense of the New Wave, Truffaut put pressure on *Cahiers du cinéma* to adopt a more committed attitude toward the films that best represented its spirit. Under the editorship of Eric Rohmer, the yellow-covered magazine—which Truffaut was still very attached to—was rather circumspect about new French films and preferred to champion Hollywood films of the early sixties, such as those directed by Vincente Minnelli, Otto Preminger, Alfred Hitchcock, Howard Hawks, Samuel Fuller, and Franck Tashlin, thus resisting any systematic, militant defense of the New Wave. First surprised, Truffaut became indignant. With the support of Doniol-Valcroze and Godard, he saw to it (not without a bad conscience, and later even remorse) that Rivette replaced Rohmer as the editor in chief of

Cahiers. From then on, the magazine would openly defend the films of the New Wave.[135]

Truffaut also strongly supported Janine Bazin's and André S. Labarthe's project for a series of made-for-television portraits called *Cinéastes de notre temps (Directors of Our Day).* In January 1962, Janine Bazin contacted the research services of the RTF [Radio Télévision Française] headed by Pierre Schaeffer, with the idea of giving young New Wave directors the opportunity to tape long interviews with the directors whom they regard as their masters. Janine Bazin included *Cahiers du cinéma* critic André S. Labarthe in her project, as well as François Truffaut. A trial film was shot in February 1962 in Rome, in which Truffaut interviewed Roberto Rossellini at length on his films and his conception of cinema; the trial was enough to convince Pierre Schaeffer to gamble on *Cinéastes de notre temps.* The first portrait was of Luis Buñuel and was shot in Spain over the summer of 1963 by Labarthe and a television crew directed by Robert Valey. The series was launched; fifty-odd portraits followed one after the other throughout the sixties. Truffaut himself would be honored in 1965; his portrait, *François Truffaut: L'esprit critique (François Truffaut: A Critical Mind)* was directed by Jean Chartier and consisted of interviews intercut with excerpts from his first films.

THE WHIRLWIND OF LIFE

Truffaut couldn't afford another flop after *Piano Player.* Les Films du Carrosse's financial situation was not very solid. And since Ignace Morgenstern's death, Truffaut, with the help of Marcel Berbert, was solely responsible for his little production company. "I have the additional responsibility of not squandering his widow's money and that matters," he wrote to Helen Scott. "I'm dreadfully tense right now. This is certainly partly out of pride, vanity, careerism and God knows what other dishonorable but irresistible drives: I desperately want *Jules and Jim* to be an absolute success, not like *Piano Player.*"[136]

In September 1960, Truffaut spent two weeks alone at the Colombe d'Or, in Saint-Paul-de-Vence, reworking the adaptation of *Jules and Jim,* for he was dissatisfied with the version he had presented to Henri-Pierre Roché three years earlier. Taking inspiration from the *Carnets (Notebooks)* which Roché had kept for nearly sixty years, starting in 1901, and the triangular affair of Helen Hessel, Franz Hessel, and Roché, Truffaut refocused the screenplay on Catherine's simultaneous love for two men, two very dissimilar friends—Jim, the cultured, elegant Frenchman and womanizing dandy (Roché's self-portrait), and Jules, the more naïve, generous, gentle German,

whom Catherine would marry and who would become the father of her little girl, Sabine.

For one weekend, Jeanne Moreau joined Truffaut in Saint-Paul-de-
Vence. The film would clearly reflect their relationship, as Truffaut admitted to Helen Scott: "*Jules and Jim* will be a hymn to life and death, a
demonstration through joy and sadness of the impossibility of any love combination apart from the couple."[137] But the screenplay, too faithful to the
novel, was still wobbly. So Truffaut decided to hire Jean Gruault, whose
recent theatrical adaptation of Diderot's *La Religieuse* (*The Nun*) had very
much impressed him. Gruault was instantly attracted to Roché's novel and
accepted Truffaut's offer. In January 1961, the two men set to work structur-
ing a story focused on this pure "*amour à trois,*" a term that they planned to
use as the film's subtitle.[138]

Truffaut chose Henri Serre to portray Jim; he was a young, as-yet-
unknown actor who was performing a comedy duo at the Cheval d'Or
Cabaret. Truffaut was struck by his physical resemblance to the youthful
Roché: Tall and thin, he had a deep, gentle voice, and terse, rapid gestures.
Choosing someone to portray Jules was trickier. Truffaut wanted a foreign
actor, for he was convinced that an accent and hesitant speech would help
make the character moving. At one point, he considered Marcello Mastroianni, which would have facilitated an Italian coproduction. But out of
faithfulness to the book, Truffaut finally opted for a German-speaking actor,
Oskar Werner. A famous stage actor in Germany and Austria, he was the
director of the Vienna Burgtheater and had received much acclaim for his
role as Hamlet in the early fifties. Though he had not had any big screen
parts, Truffaut had been very struck by his appearance in Max Ophuls's *Lola
Montès.* Contacted through Marcel Ophuls, Werner accepted Truffaut's
offer, after an interview in the presence of Jeanne Moreau. She was the real
star of the film, and Truffaut was convinced that he was offering her a part
commensurate with her talent. Jean Moreau was at the height of her fame,
but she had been slightly frustrated by her last two films, particularly *La
Notte,* which she hadn't much liked. Truffaut picked up on this when he
stated his desire for *Jules and Jim* to contrast with *La Notte.* "Antonioni had
exploited the 'Bette Davis' side of Jeanne Moreau—the sullen face; she
never laughed. I wanted to lift her features up; she has a surprising laugh. In
fact there's a scene in the film when she says, 'But I also know how to smile.'
And then you see she can have another face."[139]

For Jeanne Moreau, this first real collaboration with Truffaut partook, as
she puts it, of those "ineluctable harmonies that some call chance." "After
the fulfillment I had experienced with Louis Malle, I was a bit of an orphan
as far as movies were concerned. And sharing such a wonderful debut with
François was something that reconciled me with myself."[140] In the part of

Catherine, Moreau would portray Truffaut's vision of the supreme woman, fragile and *fatale*, intelligent and lively, funny and tragic, free and haughty, a woman who followed the impulses of desire to the bitter end. The fusion between the fictional character and the actress seemed obvious, and Truffaut wanted to be a witness to it.

Before the preproduction and shooting of *Jules and Jim*, Truffaut went to stay with Jeanne Moreau on several occasions, in the house she owned at La Garde-Freinet. "It was a refuge for François, not only because of my presence, but also because of the people I had working for me, including one woman called Anna, who was wonderful and looked after him. This place suited him. Usually, I sensed it was linked to personal and emotional crises, though he didn't spell it out. He could read or write; he felt protected by our friendship."[141] There, Truffaut saw Jean-Louis Richard again, the actress's former husband, whom he had met a few months before at a private screening of *The 400 Blows*. He was very struck by Jean-Louis Richard's qualities—his devastating humor, his rejection of fashion, and especially his playful personality. The two men became friends, and immediately discussed the possibility of several common projects. Above all, they had a lot of fun together. Jeanne Moreau's relationship with her former husband was one of friendship and great tenderness; she admired him and cared about his opinion on everything that concerned her professional life. Richard was friends with Danièle and Serge Rezvani, who also had a house at La Garde-Freinet. Naturally, he introduced them to Truffaut, who then had the idea of including a song by Rezvani in *Jules and Jim* (or rather a song by Cyrus Bassiak, the name he used as a composer, though in the film he acted under the name Boris Bassiak), "Le Tourbillon de la vie (The Whirlwind of Life)," sung by Jeanne Moreau.

At La Garde-Freinet, the group of friends banded together and enjoyed great merriment. With Jeanne Moreau, Truffaut experienced moments of euphoria, the most harmonious, youthful moments of his life, and the most amorous as well. "After dinner, Jeanne would sit under the linden trees and start singing," recalls Florence Malraux, who was an assistant on the film, her only Truffaut film, after which she began her long collaboration with Alain Resnais. "There was already something of *Jules and Jim*."[142] Truffaut was caught up in this ambiance, so that sometimes he joined in the singing. "François and I used to perfect our song numbers together," says Jean-Louis Richard. "We used to sing Trenet's 'Le Soleil a rendez-vous avec la lune,' something he could never have done in public. Sometimes we also disguised ourselves."[143] *Jules and Jim*, one of Truffaut's most solemn films, took shape in these lighthearted and happy surroundings. "It was a time when everything was possible and nothing was solemn," says Jeanne Moreau, "as though François were discovering joie de vivre: Serge's songs, car trips, going to the market. . . . Time was devoted to reading, to making discoveries, rather than foreseeing the future or making ambitious plans. This was due to the house, but it was also a true liberation of the body."[144]

THIS PURE TRIANGULAR LOVE

Once the screenplay was completed, François Truffaut was struck with a case of nerves as the shoot date approached. "We didn't have a distributor yet," Marcel Berbert recalls. "The only financing we had came from SEDIF. Truffaut asked me, 'What should we do? Should we drop it or continue?' I answered, 'Let's continue!' " Berbert was aware of the financial risks, having noticed how hesitant distributors became upon reading about the project. Most of them had no faith in the film. " 'What kind of subject is this? A man stands idly by while his wife is making love to another man?' Some of the reactions we got were incredible; they really annoyed François and me,"[145] Berbert says.

As a result *Jules and Jim* would be made very inexpensively, before the budget had been fully accounted for. Truffaut completed the casting with Marie Dubois and the little Sabine Haudepin. Locations were hastily found and a large number of scenes would be shot in places loaned by friends. Hence on April 10, 1961, the first day of the shoot, they all convened at the Moulin d'Andé in Saint-Pierre-du-Vauvray, in Normandy, where Truffaut had filmed the last scenes of *The 400 Blows*. Truffaut used a minimal crew, about fifteen people, which was what he liked. To set his mind at rest, he first shot a few secondary scenes. He covered himself with multiple takes— seven on average for each scene at the beginning of the filming, as opposed to three during the last weeks. Finally, to create an atmosphere that he felt would be propitious to this story of amorous excitement, Truffaut requested that all the actors be present at all times, even if they weren't in the scenes being filmed. But the early stages of the shoot were difficult because of the many location and set changes (Normandy, followed by Ermenonville, Paris, and Beaumont-sur-Oise for several World War I scenes in the trenches). The days were clouded by a host of problems—Marie Dubois twisted her ankle; Jeanne Moreau had the beginnings of a sore throat; Henri Serre wounded his left heel in a trench, so that he was tense and not very credible in the boxing sequence, which was shot two days later at the Lamotte gymnasium on rue Louis-le-Grand.

Thanks to Jeanne Moreau, Truffaut gradually regained confidence. "There was harmony in our work, the idea of a tandem—riding on the same bike and at the same rhythm." Truffaut himself acknowledged this: "Jeanne Moreau gave me courage each time I had doubts. Her qualities as an actress and as a woman made Catherine real before our very eyes, made her plausible, crazy, possessive, passionate, but above all adorable, i.e. worthy of adoration."[146] Motivated, focused, and happy during the shoot, "full of generosity, ardor, a feeling of collusion, and an understanding for human frailty,"[147] Jeanne Moreau strongly believed in the film and in Catherine, the character she was portraying. Liliane David, who stopped by the set, recalls a very unusual, quasi-passionate ambience: "It was complicated because everyone was in love with Jeanne Moreau—the producer Raoul Lévy, who came by unexpectedly, Henri Serre, François himself. He was literally fascinated by her. The ambiance was euphoric at times and at times painful, almost tragic."[148] Jeanne Moreau realized that shoots are always intense, collaborative moments, and even more intense when the picture depicts amorous passion. The relationship between a director and his actress is almost always altered. "It's an extraordinarily intimate exchange, which can lead to a romantic relationship, and sometimes to a much more complex, subtle relationship which is difficult to imagine and which is akin to artistic creation,"[149] Moreau confides.

Oskar Werner and François Truffaut maintained an excellent relationship during the filming; the Austrian actor turned out to be cheerful, perceptive, focused, and very friendly. The cast and crew had dinner together every evening. "François usually sat at the end of the table, and some evenings he didn't open his mouth," Florence Malraux recalls. "He sort of relied on me, asked me to handle Oskar Werner, to whom I was teaching some French, which he spoke poorly. Werner sang some Mozart in the car. He was wonderful."[150]

In May, the cast and crew moved near Saint-Tropez, and afterward near Saint-Paul-de-Vence, to shoot a few happy *ménage à trois* sequences. Marcel Berbert took this opportunity to go to Cannes, while the festival was in full swing, in the hope of finding a distributor. "In extremis, I was able to sell *Jules and Jim* to Cinédis for 20 million old francs, which wasn't much money for a film that cost seven times that amount."[151] But this money was vitally needed to finance the last weeks of filming. The most important scenes were shot from mid-May to early June in Jules and Catherine's large German-Style chalet in Molkenrein, which is located in the Vosges. Some of the sequences were tricky. A camera crane and a helicopter were required for the train scenes taken at the Landenbach-Vieil Armand station, while Jim and Catherine's lengthy mutual confessions had to be shot in "day for night," with a special filter that would re-create a nocturnal atmosphere.

In mid-June, after the cremation scene of Catherine and Jim had been shot at the crematorium in the Strasbourg cemetery, the entire cast and crew returned to Paris for a few additional sequences. Then everyone separated sadly; Oskar Werner returned to Vienna for an opera; Henri Serre went back to his cabaret comedy duo with Jean-Pierre Suc; Jeanne Moreau got ready to shoot *Eva*, directed by Joseph Losey. The relationship between her and Truffaut gradually changed over the filming, from a tumultuous passion to a tender and affectionate friendship—enduring, strong, and vital. An impossible love had finally found an aesthetic form—this film they had made together, which the director summarized to Helen Scott as follows: "In spite of some scenes that didn't come off that I'll cut or maybe fix up, I think the characters are more alive than in my other films. It's a risqué melodrama yet very moral."[152]

As soon as the filming was over, Truffaut was worried once again, for the first rough cut of *Jules and Jim* was two and a half hours long. The film therefore had to be tightened up in the editing. In contrast to *Shoot the Piano Player*, with its free tone and unbridled rhythm, *Jules and Jim* played on a certain formal classicism, as if to emphasize its daring subject. "What seems acceptable today, a woman in love with two men and the lover of both, was not so unobjectionable thirty years ago," says Claudine Bouché, who edited Truffaut's film. "We recorded part of the narration to measure its duration. Then we recorded it in its entirety, with the voice of the actor Michel Subor, and we edited it with the picture. We got Georges Delerue's music, which was very beautiful. When we listened to the mix of music and voice-over, things got complicated. Sometimes the fortes were too loud and covered the narration. And François wouldn't consider giving up these musical moments, which were so beautiful and lyrical. For the scene where Catherine picks Jim up at the station after the war and takes him back to the chalet, there was very beautiful music. To work in Michel Subor's voice, the narration had to be rerecorded in relation to the music."[153] She also confirms the free and easy style of the filming: "When Jeanne Moreau sings 'Le Tourbillon de la vie,' there's a moment when she makes a gesture because she's made a mistake and switched two verses. This is the take François and I chose. Being very professional, Jeanne didn't ask for the take to be interrupted; she simply made this gesture to indicate she had made a mistake. I knew François would accept this take, because Jeanne's gesture gives her even more charm."[154]

In need of an independent opinion, Truffaut called in Jean Aurel, the former *Arts* journalist turned filmmaker, whom he trusted completely when it came to editing or narrative structure. "I had just made a film, *14-18*, with a narration that Truffaut admired," says Jean Aurel. "He wanted to make sure the voice-over matched the picture, that it corresponded to the image, so the film would be effective. The narration cast the film in a sort of fictional past. This meant a lot to François. The film didn't exist without the narration. We watched it several times, and I made a few suggestions for moving the voice in relation to the picture. It was an interesting experiment, which made it possible to space out a sentence in relation to the picture."[155] "Showing a film to Aurel is like calling in a plumber who would not just repair a leak, but also locate it. He comes in, watches the film, takes notes in the dark, and then we talk"[156]—this is how Truffaut would describe the person whom he would thereafter always turn to at the final-edit stage of his films. As for Aurel, he defines himself as an "adviser" specializing in the "moving around of sequences,"[157] valuable work, requiring both critical judgment and the ability to imagine new solutions. Thanks to Aurel, *Jules and Jim* acquired its definitive shape, particularly the voice-over narration, which takes up nearly fifteen minutes of the sound track.

During the whole four months required for the editing and postsynchronization of *Jules and Jim,* Truffaut was haunted by a relentless, irrational fear of death. Though he was not even thirty, he identified, somehow, with Henri-Pierre Roché: "I tried to make the film as though I were a very old person, and at the end of my life. It was probably the first time I really experienced a fear of death,"[158] he said. In *Jules and Jim* as in *Shoot the Piano Player,* melancholy ultimately takes possession of all the characters. "This is the third time it's happened to me—starting a film with the thought that it's going to be amusing and realizing along the way that it will be saved only by its sadness,"[159] he wrote to Father Jean Mambrino on the eve of *Jules and Jim*'s first sound-mixing session. Exhausted, he realized he had made his most difficult and daring film. But he felt confident, convinced he had given a wonderful part to a great actress—Jeanne Moreau—whose friendship he had won in the process.

THE WOMEN CRY

Truffaut was much encouraged by the first private screenings of *Jules and Jim* before its release. His close friends found the film moving and his writer friends—including Queneau, Audiberti, and Jules Roy—were enthusiastic. "The women cry, many of the men are slightly bored. It's my first deliberately boring film (1 hour and 50 minutes). Frankly, thanks to the three actors, it holds up better than my previous films,"[160] he wrote to Helen Scott.

The response that meant the most to him was that of Jean Renoir, who was very moved by the film. Truffaut kept the letter Renoir had sent him from Hollywood in February 1962 tucked in the inside pocket of his suit jacket for a long time:

> I wanted to tell you that *Jules and Jim* seems to me the most accurate expression of contemporary French society that I've seen on-screen. By situating your film in 1914 you gave your depiction an even more exact tone, for the birth of today's way of thinking and behavior dates back to cars trimmed with gleaming brass. The hint of immorality which apparently crossed the mind of some confreres seems inexplicable to me. The observation of a consequence can't be immoral. Rain wets; fire burns. The resulting wetness and burn have nothing to do with morality. In a few years we've gone from one civilization to another. The leap is more formidable than the one made by our forefathers between the Middle Ages and the Renaissance. For the Knights of the Round Table, sentimental adventures were the subject of great fun, for the Romantics, the pretext for a flood of tears. For the characters in *Jules and Jim* it is something else again, and your film contributes in making us understand what this "something else" might be. It is very important for us men to know where we stand with women, and equally important for women to know where they stand with men. You help dissipate the fog that envelops the essence of this question. For this, and for many other reasons, I thank you with all my heart.[161]

Cocteau saw in *Jules and Jim* the revelation and recognition of a great literary figure hitherto unknown to the public: "He was the most delicate and noble soul,"[162] he wrote concerning Henri-Pierre Roché, who had been one of his friends. Denise Roché's reaction was of course very important to Truffaut: "I wish I could have seen your *Jules and Jim* with a fresh eye," she wrote him. "But in spite of wanting to create a vacuum I watched your film as though I myself were Pierre—and I know he would have felt great joy and a passionate interest. I am quite moved. In any case, I spent an extremely interesting two hours, steeped in freshness, poetry, innocence, impetuous ardor and anxiety. Yes, Pierre would have been very happy."[163] But the most moving and most unexpected response reached Truffaut at the end of January 1962. "I am, at 75, what is left of Kathe, the awesome heroine of Pierre Roché's novel, *Jules and Jim*. You can imagine the curiosity with which I waited to see your film on the screen. On January 24, I ran to the movie theater. Sitting in that dark auditorium, in the dread of veiled resemblances and more or less irritating parallels, I was soon swept along, gripped by the magical power—yours and Jeanne Moreau's—with which you revived what had been lived through blindly. The fact that Pierre Roché was able to tell the story of the three of us and kept it very close to the actual events, has nothing miraculous about it. But what disposition in you, what affinity, could enlighten you to the point of making the essence of our intimate emotions perceptible? As far as this goes, I'm your only authentic judge, since the other two witnesses, Pierre and Franz, are no longer here to express their 'yes' to you. Affectionately yours, dear Monsieur Truffaut."[164] This magnificent letter was signed by Helen Hessel, Roché's real-life heroine.

Nearly all the critics sung the praises of the film. A CELEBRATION OF TENDERNESS AND INTELLIGENCE was the headline of Jean-Louis Bory's review in *Arts*. "The first engaging film of the New Wave," admitted René Cortade in *L'Express*, while Georges Sadoul gave his column in *Lettres françaises* the title "Making Others Feel Good." The large-circulation papers—*Le Monde, Combat,* and *Le Figaro*—all concurred. The only negative article was Bernard Dort's in *France-Observateur;* he panned the films and the personality of François Truffaut: "Instead of an elderly man's account of a dreamily remembered youth, Truffaut's *Jules and Jim* is the film of a young man gambling on old age. A film of a New Wave which, with the help of a star, winks allusively at 'old fogeys.' "[165]

Though the critical response was excellent, Truffaut feared censorship, for he was aware that this *amour à trois* could be considered shocking to those of conventional morals. Unfortunately, his fears were well founded. After screening the film on November 24, 1961, the monitoring committee, whose president was Henri de Segogne, authorized its distribution but restricted it to audiences over eighteen, a severe handicap for the film's commercial prospects. Truffaut immediately appealed to have the restriction lifted. But despite prestigious testimonials by Renoir, Cocteau, Armand Salacrou, Pierre Lazareff, and Alain Resnais, who all vouched for the film's "nonimmoral character," the decision was upheld. *Jules and Jim* started its exclusive Paris engagement on January 24, 1964; it had a run of almost three months and an audience of 210,000 people, meaning it was a relative success. Truffaut then threw his energies into the promotion of the film, traveling all around the provinces to show it to full and attentive houses. The regional press no longer welcomed him as an *enfant terrible* or ambitious youngster, but as a serious, human, timid, polite filmmaker.

Alain Vannier, who had met Marcel Berbert in the days when he worked at Cocinor, was in charge of selling the foreign rights to *Jules and Jim*. "I was instantly enthusiastic, although the screenings were really going rather badly,"[166] he says. Vannier immediately called the boss of the English company Gala Film Distribution, which he represented in Paris. "Buy the picture!" replied Kenneth Rive, who caught a plane from London to sign a contract with Les Films du Carrosse. Later, during his first trip to the United States, Alain Vannier spoke highly of *Jules and Jim* to two Harvard students, Cyrus Harvey and Brian Halliday, who ran a film society and had created a small independent distribution company, Janus Films, in Cambridge, Massachusetts. So on February 20, 1962, SEDIF, acting on behalf of its coproduction with Carrosse, signed a contract with Janus Films for the U.S. distribution of *Jules and Jim*, "excluding Puerto Rico" but including "ships flying U.S. colors," with a guaranteed minimum sum of forty thousand dollars on American box-office receipts. From that time on, Alain Vannier was put in charge of the foreign sales of Truffaut's films, except for his American coproductions (primarily with United Artists). Very close to Gérard Lebovici, the head of Artmédia, Vannier would become an important associate in the production and financing system that Truffaut set up, with Marcel Berbert's help, in the course of his career.

Jules and Jim was banned outright in Italy on June 22, 1962. Truffaut went to Rome to support the public protest orchestrated by Dino de Laurentiis, the distributor of the film; the protest was also supported by such illustrious intellectuals as Alberto Moravia and Roberto Rossellini. On July 2, the ban was lifted, and *Jules and Jim* opened to critical acclaim in Rome, Turin, and Milan on September 3.

Truffaut traveled to many major European cities with his film—Brussels, London, Munich, Berlin, and Stockholm—and later to the Mar del Plata festival in Argentina, to Rio and Puerto Rico, and finally to New York. These efforts bore fruit: The film was a success in Germany, as well as in England, Belgium, and Sweden. But for Truffaut, the New York release was of vital importance. He arrived in New York with Madeleine on April 11, 1962, after attending the Mar del Piata festival. They were welcomed by Helen Scott, who had organized everything according to her friend's wishes; he had expressed a desire to meet such American film directors as Joshua Logan, Sidney Lumet, John Cassavetes, and Arthur Penn. The day after his arrival, the French Film Office in New York threw a reception in his honor. Truffaut mentioned a project that was dear to his heart—establishing a French Cinema Week in New York, with unreleased New Wave films such as *Lola*, *A Woman Is a Woman*, *My Life to Live*, and *Shoot the Piano Player*. The idea was realized several years later by the critic Richard Roud when he made this a part of the New York Film Festival. On April 17, Truffaut was due in Cannes as a member of the festival jury, but *Jules and Jim* opened in New York on April 25, where it enjoyed an exclusive four-week engagement and received glowing reviews. Jo Morgenstern (no relation to Madeleine) hailed the "Return of Movie 'Boy Wonder' " on the front page of the *Herald Tribune*, while Bosley Crowther in the *New York Times*, Andrew Sarris in the *Village Voice*, Archer Winsten in the *New York Post*, and Paul Beckley in the *New York Herald Tribune* all heralded *Jules and Jim* as one of the most original and engaging works in French cinema.

A MUSICAL INFATUATION

In June 1961, François Truffaut accepted a commission to direct a short subject produced by Pierre Roustang, which he promised to deliver at the beginning of the following year. This was the first and last time he would bow to the requirements of a commission. His main motivation was to follow up on the adventures of Antoine Doinel. Roustang wanted five young directors from different countries each to make a short film on the theme of adolescent love as part of an episode film to be entitled *Love at Twenty.* Truffaut recommended Marcel Ophuls and Renzo Rossellini (Roberto's nephew) to Roustang, who had already recruited the Polish film director Andrzej Wajda and the Japanese director Shintaro Ishihara.

Truffaut drew on his youthful memories for the screenplay of *Antoine and Colette,* essentially taking his inspiration from his thwarted love for Liliane Litvin in the very early fifties, but he changed a few details. For instance, Antoine and Colette, his two protagonists, meet at a youth concert, not at the Cinémathèque; and Antoine works in record manufacturing, not as a factory worker. Though he had accepted the commission with enthusiasm, Truffaut was exhausted by the shooting and promotion of *Jules and Jim.* "I'm very bored at the thought of making this short film," he admitted to Helen Scott. "I would have liked to leave *Jules and Jim* with renewed virginity. I haven't prepared anything, I have no script, no notes, no ideas, I'm exhausted, dried up, sterilized."[167]

He placed an announcement in *Cinémonde* to cast the part of Colette: "François Truffaut seeks fiancée for Jean-Pierre Léaud and for *Love at Twenty.* Jean-Pierre's partner must be a real girl, not a Lolita, not a leather-jacket type, not a little young woman. She must be simple and cheerful, and have a good average culture. If too 'sexy' please abstain." He immediately received a note from Mario Brun, a journalist at *Nice-Matin,* who sent along a picture of a young girl from Nice, Marie-France Pisier, whom he had noticed in an amateur theatrical troupe. Truffaut had planned to schedule his auditions in the beginning of January 1962, just before the start of the shoot. In the meantime, he had wanted to stay at the Colombe d'Or for a few days around mid-December in order to rest and finish writing the screenplay. He had lunch in Saint-Paul-de-Vence with Mario Brun, who introduced him to Marie-France Pisier. He made her read for the part that very afternoon. Already under her spell, he asked to see her again the following day.

On returning to Paris, Truffaut continued casting. The two adolescents from *The 400 Blows* had matured. Jean-Pierre Léaud, whom Truffaut had lodged and educated over the last three years, was more disciplined, and also more melancholic. Patrick Auffay was cast as René again, Antoine's friend. In *Antoine and Colette,* they meet, talk, reminisce about an incident in *The 400 Blows,* and evaluate their respective chances as suitors, Antoine with Colette, René with his cousin. After choosing Rosy Varte and François Darbon to play Colette's parents, Truffaut scheduled auditions for the part of the young girl. Two candidates stood out—Marina Bazanov, the granddaughter of Helen Hessel, the real-life Kathe of Roché's novel, and Marie-France Pisier. More joyful, more charming, and also more casual, Pisier fit the character better. During the screen tests, she recalls, "he didn't really look at me, he was only interested in my voice. François always attached great importance to voices and their rhythm. For this he kept urging me, 'Faster, faster, Jeanne used to say it faster.' He liked the fact that I could speak quickly, and I later realized the importance this had for the character in the film: the girl had to be more comfortable with words than Léaud."[168]

The filming of *Antoine and Colette* began on January 15 with a small crew of Carrosse regulars grouped around Raoul Coutard and Suzanne Schiffman. It lasted only a week and took place near Place Clichy and Batignolles, with a few sequences shot in the Pleyel concert hall. "I recall a very important scene, the scene of 'musical infatuation,' Marie-France Pisier remembers, "one of the first we shot. We had to make a series of incredibly specific gestures, which François insisted on, probably because they had a very intimate resonance for him. He said to Jean-Pierre, 'Turn your head to the side, no not too much,' and to me, 'Grasp the chain you're wearing around your neck, lift it up to your mouth, not twice, just once, do it again, cross your legs, not twice, just once, more decisively. . . .' It was really like a musical score."[169]

In the end, the shoot went well. It was well paced, lively, and sometimes improvisational, which suited Léaud's and Pisier's acting. Truffaut ended up liking this picture, which had initially bored him, and even regretted that he hadn't made it into a feature. But the film into which this episode was inserted was not particularly good. Truffaut supervised it, working with Claudine Bouché, whose editing table was at Les Films du Carrosse. "The episodes were all too long," she says, "We had to make cuts and find an order for them."[170] Marcel Ophuls's sketch was the only one that Truffaut liked. Jean Aurel was in charge of finding elements that would link the five episodes. He decided on a song with the recurrent theme of "love at twenty" (sung by Xavier Depraz), and photos by Cartier-Bresson. The film was greeted with indifference and closed after two weeks. Truffaut was quite disappointed, for he had grown to like his surrogate's timid, fruitless loves. The tone for the "Antoine Doinel adventures" had now been set, a lighter, more whimsical and melancholic one than could be anticipated from *The 400 Blows.*

Truffaut had already become enamored of Marie-France Pisier during preproduction on the film—so much so that he wanted to leave Madeleine and the children. He confided in Helen Scott, in an unusually intimate letter: "I'm very tired, very much on edge and sad, because I'm terribly in love with a young girl who is seventeen and a half; just for her, to make myself available for her, I'm going to bring tragedy around me and it's distressing. Not counting the fact that I might be ruining the next two or three years for her too. Dear Helen, I'm up to my neck in tragedy and havoc. You'd like the girl; she's modern, very feminist, left-wing, Sartre-Beauvoir, very hardworking (political economics in order to become a legal adviser) and an actress since I met her when I was looking for a girl to play opposite Jean-Pierre. This girl is very frank, direct, very strong and at the same time very childlike. She'll be very tough with me, that I know . . . ; we'll fight, I'm sure; I admire her enormously and I'm very distraught."[171]

Indeed, on December 25, 1961, Truffaut left the apartment on rue du Conseiller Collignon and moved into a hotel. He would return a month later. But for Madeleine, his unexpected departure was a trauma. At first, he didn't mention Marie-France Pisier, of whose existence Madeleine was completely unaware; instead, he talked about their disagreements, his need for solitude, and "the hypocrisy involved in staying together."[172] *Jules and Jim* (the filming itself as well as the subject of the film) made him come to the painful realization that he found living as a couple at once indispensable and unbearable.

At the beginning of 1962, Truffaut believed his breakup with Madeleine was virtually inevitable. This saddened him immensely, as did the prospect of being separated from his daughters, Laura and Eva. And once he had moved out, he grew fearful of committing himself to Marie-France Pisier, bewildered by this girl of seventeen who was now giving him a hard time. To make matters worse, Jeanne Moreau had fallen in love with someone else and was neglecting him, as he angrily reported in a letter to Helen Scott.[173] As always in his periods of romantic depression, Truffaut immersed himself in his work; the shooting and editing of *Antoine and Colette* occupied him full-time.

After a month-long "truancy," a shamefaced Truffaut decided to return home. His reconciliation with Madeleine was sealed with a journey: She accompanied him on a business trip to the United States in April. The girls were left in the care of their governess, Sylvia, while the couple traveled with Marcel Berbert to the Mar del Plata festival (where *Jules and Jim* was awarded the prize for best direction), and then to Rio and New York. Truffaut was visibly bolstered and relaxed, thinking he had resolved his romantic crisis. Several months later, after spending a quiet summer with Madeleine at the Colombe d'Or, he seemed to have rediscovered the virtues of marriage, even if professional anxieties assailed him once again: "Right now I'm going through a period where my morale is low," he wrote to Helen Scott on October 18, 1962, "for no reason, really, since things are going very well with Madeleine and the two girls are wonderful; like a bureaucrat, I come home every evening at around six and play with them for two hours. I no longer go to the office in the morning for the same reason."[174] The "pure triangular love" had temporarily been dispelled by conjugal happiness regained.

THE TRIAL OF THE NEW WAVE

In early 1962, French cinema was in a new crisis. Not only had attendance at movie houses plummeted since the end of the fifties, but so had the New Wave euphoria. It was once again very difficult for a beginner to set up his own business, and the movement, which had been heterogeneous from the start, had now been fragmented by rivalries. A mentality of "everyone for himself" sometimes developed into outright confrontation; war was declared, a prelude to what the large-circulation papers had been calling the "death of the New Wave" since the beginning of 1962. "I'm therefore depressed for no good reason," Truffaut wrote to Helen Scott later that year. "Business is not going too badly, in spite of the crisis we're facing; I'm among the five or six directors whose forthcoming film people have faith in and *Jules and Jim* is still doing very well in France, Belgium and Italy. You're right, dear Helen, when you say I want it all, but for the time being, I myself don't even know what I'm missing."[175]

This crisis revolved around a specific conflict in which Truffaut was one of the main protagonists. The trouble had started back in 1960, with *La Bride sur le cou*, which was to have been Jean Aurel's first film, starring Brigitte Bardot. On December 4, 1960, only three days after shooting started, the producers brought in Roger Vadim, Bardot's ex-husband, to supervise the filming. On December 12, Aurel understood that this was not mere supervision but outright replacement. He left the set, denouncing the behavior of his star and Vadim. They defended themselves, citing Aurel's inability to direct Bardot.

Truffaut, siding with his friend Aurel, exposed the situation in a vitriolic article in the December 22, 1960, issue of *France-Observateur*. He upheld the "moral code of the film auteur" and denounced Vadim's "unfraternal" attitude. The article was perceived, of course, as an internal family quarrel. Truffaut's conclusion amounted to a strict warning: "The fact is, as far as I'm concerned, Roger Vadim now belongs to that group of film people who are capable of anything and of whom one should be wary." In addition, twenty-seven directors signed a declaration in support of Aurel, upholding the rights of "the film auteur" and the freedom of each person "to improvise at will on the set"—two fundamental principles for the New Wave. Vadim counterattacked by taking Truffaut to court for libel.

The affair led to a sensational trial that opened on January 29, 1962, before the Seventeenth Magistrate's Court in Paris. In the Vadim camp were Louis Malle, Michel Subor, and Brigitte Bardot, who was there in person to certify her good faith and discredit Aurel's "cinematic improvisations." In the Truffaut camp were Resnais, Melville, Godard, Chabrol, Kast, Sautet, and de Broca. After a farcical session, with Bardot pouting in the witness box and Godard banished from the courtroom for "insulting a witness," the judge ruled in favor of Vadim and sentenced Truffaut to pay him one franc in damages.

The sensational atmosphere surrounding the trial, as created by the large-circulation dailies, was revealing of the crisis of confidence at the time—the crisis in French cinema generally and in the New Wave specifically. It marked the end of an era, the (ephemeral) reign of the young directors. For the press, the producers, the public, the new French cinema was dead and buried.

Truffaut escaped the general negative climate; thanks to *Jules and Jim,* he was one of the five or six directors with a future. Paradoxically, this exceptional status was probably the main cause of his depression. The death of the New Wave gave rise to strong feelings of guilt: "I'm in the process of becoming a bastard. But I'm not yet hardened enough and it's very difficult, very painful,"[176] he confessed to Helen Scott. His feelings were exacerbated by the fact that he had to relinquish all coproduction projects and concentrate solely on his own films. It was during this period, for example, that he gave up the idea of producing Rossellini's *Socrates;* his reasons were irrefutable, but he realized he was disappointing a close friend, and he was disappointed in himself. "The truth is," he wrote Rossellini with a heavy heart, "we don't have the same ideas on how to make movies. I find everything you do good, right and logical as long as you're doing it. If I were to meddle, we would be heading for catastrophe."[177]

Family crisis and professional difficulties and rifts combined to make Truffaut feel isolated. He was successful, but the others had failed; the contrast caused quite a number of misunderstandings and accusations. Some protégés, who had been discovered and financed by the director of *The 400 Blows,* reacted with great violence when he withdrew into himself. "You have gone over to the powerful, we remain poor,"[178] wrote Michel Varesano, a director of shorts who had hoped to find a producer in Truffaut. Even Robert

Lachenay, his childhood friend and long-standing confidant, felt forsaken, and he expressed his bitterness in a moving appeal in the spring of 1962:

> I'm sorry to feel a kind of coldness and embarrassment coming between us. You're in large part responsible. I have so much respect and admiration for you that I can no longer behave as your equal and friend, though I would very much like to. My financial dependency makes matters even worse. But though I can't at present reach up to you, nothing prevents you from reaching down to me and treating me the way you treat Jean-Pierre [Léaud], for example. Material help means nothing if you can't give me help from the heart. We must become the complicitous friends and companions of former days again, the complicitous friends and companions of *The Story of a Cheat* and *Pépé le Moko*.[179]

Jean-Luc Godard wrote him a short, melancholic note at this time: "We never see each other anymore, it's silly. Yesterday I went to Claude's [Chabrol] set, it's terrible, we have nothing in common anymore. Like in the song—come the pale morning, there isn't even friendship left. We've each gone off on our own planet, and we can't see each other in close-up anymore, only in full shot. The girls we sleep with separate us each day even more, instead of bringing us closer. It's not normal."[180]

5.
THE SLOW YEARS:
1962–1968

In spite of the favorable reception of *Jules and Jim,* François Truffaut was plagued with what he called the "melancholy of the third film." "I think I've noticed," he admitted in an interview, "that generally speaking, every director has three films to make in his lifetime, the first three that spring from his most secret self. After that, he engages in a career, which is different."[1] For Truffaut, the only way to shatter this inevitability was to undertake an extremely ambitious and personal film.

Fahrenheit 451 would provide such a challenge. He first heard about Ray Bradbury's novel on a Sunday in August 1960, during an evening at Jean-Pierre Melville's. Liliane David, who was with him, remembers this dinner, where the producer Raoul Lévy was also a guest: "Raoul Lévy, who was a wonderful storyteller, started to tell the story of *Fahrenheit.* François was hanging on his every word; then he asked who the author of the novel was."[2] Lévy promised to get Truffaut a copy.

SCIENCE FICTION

Though he was no great lover of science fiction, the story of *Fahrenheit 451,* in which books are of primary importance, was bound to make an impression on François Truffaut. For here was a man who collected all kinds of books, old and recent, from thrillers to art books, and spent hours in book-stores—a passion both intellectual and physical. Bradbury's novel was part science fiction, part philosophical tale, blending political analysis with a defense of literature—all themes that fascinated Truffaut. Montag, *Fahrenheit*'s hero, is a fireman who is regularly sent on book-burning missions to destroy the books discovered in the homes of private individuals—books having been banned by a sanitized society where the audiovisual is king. But books, considered responsible for all evils, take revenge when Montag falls under the influence of a young woman and neighbor and—in defiance of his captain, his wife, and common sense—starts to look at them, preserve them, and read them. Informed on by his wife, pursued by the state police for his immoral attitude, he ends up taking refuge on the other side of the river, in the forest of the "book-men," a dissident minority who have decided to pre-serve the written heritage of the world by each adopting the identity of a book and even taking its title as a last name, thus incarnating the book as a way of rescuing it from the flames.

Truffaut was aware that a screen adaptation of *Fahrenheit 451* would be a costly project, because of the costumes, the many extras, and the futuristic set and atmosphere. At first, he considered a coproduction with Raoul Lévy, out of loyalty to the person who had inspired the project, but then changed his mind because the producer of *And God Created Woman* had a reputa-tion for indecisiveness.[3] He then had the idea of a French-American co-production between Carrosse and Astor Films—the New York distributor of *Shoot the Piano Player*—starring Paul Newman. This was the first time Truffaut contemplated making a film in the United States. In April 1962, he met Paul Newman at the Mar del Plata festival. That February, he had writ-ten to Ray Bradbury, who lived in Los Angeles, and the two met several weeks later in New York, in the offices of Don Congdon, the writer's agent. Helen Scott acted as interpreter in a conversation involving the rights to *Fahrenheit 451*. But Bradbury expressed his preference for a screen adapta-tion of one of the short stories included in his *Martian Chronicles*. Congdon confirmed that Bradbury was not very excited at the prospect of a screen adaptation of *Fahrenheit 451*, which had already been given a theatrical adaptation several years earlier.[4] A possible plan was that Truffaut and Brad-bury first collaborate on an adaptation of *Chronicles*. With this in mind, Bradbury and his family would spend two months in France, at the expense of Les Films du Carrosse, so that the two men could work on a screenplay in French. *Fahrenheit* would be put on the back burner. "If everything goes well with their work on the short stories, we would then be very happy to make arrangements for Monsieur Truffaut to buy and produce the novel *Fahrenheit 451*,"[5] Don Congdon wrote in a memo to Helen Scott on the day following their meeting.

Truffaut left New York having misunderstood the arrangement; he thought he was in a position to acquire the rights to *Fahrenheit,* while Bradbury was actually only offering to first collaborate with him on an adaptation of *Martian Chronicles.* As soon as he returned to Paris, he wrote Bradbury a long letter explaining his motivations:

> To do a good job on a film taken from several of your short stories, a big effort would have to be made, in preproduction, scouting futuristic locations, ultramodern costumes and props, so that later I might be less inspired for *Fahrenheit.* Also, I only shoot one feature film every eighteen months. If I were to first shoot a film based on your *Chronicles,* this would put *Fahrenheit* off till 1964, and I think it would be too late by then, even for the producers of the film—since Gagarin [Soviet cosmonaut, first manned space mission, 1961], the same films can't be made. It's very important for *Fahrenheit* to be the first European science-fiction film. Hence I think we should negotiate the rights to *Fahrenheit* with Mr. Don Congdon immediately and work together this summer, at dates convenient to you, in conceiving a film which we could begin to shoot at the end of the year.[6]

But Bradbury turned down Truffaut's proposal: "I have spent so much time, over the years, on various aspects of FAHRENHEIT 451, both as a novel, and as a stageplay, never produced, that I feel I would be the wrong person to try to adapt it for the screen. I am very tired, very exhausted, on this novel, and would do you a disservice if I accepted the commission to write it for you in screenplay form. Therefore I suggest you arrange to buy the rights from my agent Don Congdon and hire another writer to do the screenplay."[7] Having developed a certain wariness from his first experiences collaborating with writers,[8] Truffaut actually felt relieved. Bradbury and he had become friends and would correspond regularly, with Truffaut keeping the writer informed of his progress.

On July 19, 1962, Les Films du Carrosse bought the rights to *Fahrenheit* for $40,000, a significant sum for a small production company. Truffaut had to seek outside financing to make the film. Since it was clear to him that it would be in French, he gave up the idea of casting Paul Newman in the part of Montag and thought of Jean-Paul Belmondo instead. Truffaut and Belmondo discussed *Fahrenheit* when they met at the Berlin Film Festival at the end of June 1962. But the actor was not free until the spring of 1963 because he was scheduled to act in Jean-Pierre Melville's *Le Doulos,* and his financial requirements were such that collaboration was impossible. The project got mired again.

Fahrenheit got passed around to several screenwriters over a period of several months. Still enthusiastic because of his work on *Jules and Jim,* Gruault took up the project first. Then Marcel Moussy labored on a second version of the screenplay. Dissatisfied, Truffaut started work on a third version, this time with Jean-Louis Richard, Jeanne Moreau's ex-husband, whom he had first met in the days of *The 400 Blows.* Richard, an actor by training, was not a professional screenwriter, but the two men got along extremely well. Richard's sense of humor offset Truffaut's anxieties, and his independent spirit and personality—which, as Madeleine puts it, was "as countertrendy as can be"—appealed to Truffaut. "Our friendship and our conversations were transmuted into work,"[9] says Richard.

In February and March of 1963, Truffaut moved into the apartment of the Résidence Saint-Michel—bought by Madeleine's parents and located in the hills above Cannes—with his wife and two daughters. At the same time, he rented a room for Jean-Louis Richard at the Hotel Martinez. Every day he joined his friend at the hotel and the two men worked in a euphoric spirit. As Truffaut recounted it, "One of us would climb on top of a piece of furniture, the other would lie down on the floor, and we would continue talking and miming a scene. One day, a bellhop walked in. He saw Jean-Louis Richard on an armoire and me lying on the fireplace at the other end of the room. We looked at him casually. He let out a funny scream."[10]

In March 1963, the *Fahrenheit* screenplay was completed. Truffaut thought he had found in Henry Deutschmeister a reliable producer who would provide financing for two-thirds of the budget, estimated at nearly 3 million new francs. With Belmondo out of the running, Truffaut considered Charles Aznavour for the part of Montag. Aznavour read the novel and accepted. "The other firemen will be short and thin like him. They'll be small men,"[11] Truffaut wrote to Bradbury, explaining his casting decision. Then he scouted numerous locations, searching for the ideal set for the film. Since Deutschmeister usually coproduced his films with Dino de Laurentiis, he tried to convince Truffaut to shoot in Italy, but the idea was quickly rejected. The south of France was considered, and then the Paris suburbs. "I'm going to visit the housing blocks in Sarcelles, Meudon, Antony, etc. I think of you a lot while writing the screenplay, the Montag character will be rather strong, I think, and better than in the novel,"[12] Truffaut wrote to Aznavour. Meanwhile, he also mobilized the Carrosse team—Delerue for the music, Coutard for the camera (for the first time, Truffaut planned to make a color film), and Suzanne Schiffman. But just when everything seemed settled, it all fell apart again. Truffaut no longer found Aznavour right for the part of Montag. Then Deutschmeister failed to find financing, in France or abroad; the project didn't seem to convince any of the major distributors. " 'People won't believe in it, it's science fiction, leave that to the Americans,' this is what I hear all day every day whenever the labor strikes give me the opportunity,"[13] the director wrote to Helen Scott.

In the meantime, Truffaut reworked the screenplay. He considered hiring an unknown to help him—Maurice Pialat, whose short film, *Janine*, he had admired. Truffaut proposed a collaboration and Pialet accepted, but in the end, Truffaut preferred to turn to Claude de Givray, his longtime collaborator. The following autumn, a fourth screenplay of *Fahrenheit 451* was ready. Through these successive versions, Truffaut was really seeking to reassure himself and forget the setbacks and delays in the production. From one postponement to another, over two years would go by without his making a film, even as his "writing studio" was working at full capacity. "This left him with very bad memories," Marcel Berbert recalls. "He said he would never again lose two years getting a film into shape."[14] Les Films du Carrosse was in a difficult situation, and the moderate success of *Jules and Jim* was a mere memory: "Most of our liquidity has been absorbed in the relatively expensive rights of *Fahrenheit*, the four successive treatments, and a variety of production costs,"[15] Truffaut himself admitted to his Canadian distributor, André Pépin.

HITCHCOCK

While waiting to direct *Fahrenheit 451*, François Truffaut pursued another project: interviewing Alfred Hitchcock, one of his "filmmaking masters," on his career and work. The idea had occurred to him during a trip to New York in April 1962, in the course of a luncheon with Bosley Crowther, the *New York Times* critic, and Herman Weinberg, the head of the film department at the Museum of Modern Art. Truffaut was astounded by the American critics' deep disregard of Hitchcock's work; for them, he was merely a good technician, a cynical and clever "master of suspense," a "moneymaker." Truffaut and Helen Scott conceived the interview project together and decided to divide up the work. Helen was put in charge of finding a New York publisher, while Truffaut would submit his proposal to Robert Laffont as soon as he returned to Paris. "The goal of this book is to change the idea Americans have of Hitchcock,"[16] he wrote to Don Congdon at the end of April 1962.

Truffaut had already encountered this lack of comprehension of Hitchcock's work in France in the fifties. As far as he and his friends at *Cahiers* were concerned—Rohmer, Chabrol, Rivette, and Godard—the "master of suspense" concealed his genius and intelligence behind a good-natured, humorous veneer, in order to better attract a large audience.[17] Truffaut suggested the following explanation for this dissimulation: Hitchcock was the "biggest liar in the world," for he himself was a Hitchcockian character, haunted by a secret that had to be kept and that he feared having to reveal. "The man who excels at filming fear is himself a very fearful person, and I suspect that this trait of his personality has a direct bearing on his success. Throughout his entire career he has felt the need to protect himself from the actors, producers, and technicians who, insofar as their slightest lapse or whim may jeopardize the integrity of his work, all represent as many hazards to a director. How better to defend oneself than to become the director no actor will question, to become one's own producer, and to know more about technique than the technicians?"[18]

On June 2, 1962, Truffaut wrote Hitchcock a long letter. He reminded him of their first meeting: "A few years ago," Truffaut wrote, "in late 1954, when I was a film journalist, I came with my friend Claude Chabrol to interview you at the Saint-Maurice studio where you were directing the post-synchronization of *To Catch a Thief*. You asked us to go and wait for you in the studio bar, and it was then that, in the excitement of having watched fifteen times in succession a 'loop' showing Brigitte Auber and Cary Grant in a speedboat, Chabrol and I fell into the frozen tank in the studio courtyard. You very kindly agreed to postpone the interview which was conducted that same evening at your hotel. Subsequently, each time you visited Paris, I had the pleasure of meeting you with Odette Ferry, and the following year you even said to me 'Whenever I see ice cubes in a glass of whisky I think of you.' One year after that, you invited me to come to New York for a few days and watch the shooting of *The Wrong Man*, but I had to decline the invitation since, a few months after Claude Chabrol, I turned to film-making myself. I have made three films, the first of which, *The Four Hundred Blows*, had, I believe, a certain success in Hollywood."[19] Then Truffaut got down to the main point, the project of a long tape-recorded interview that would cover Hitchcock's entire career, in view of a book that would be published simultaneously in New York and Paris. He mentioned Helen Scott, who would translate this long conversation. While waiting for Hitchcock to agree, Truffaut planned to research and prepare several hundred questions on each film, covering both the English and American periods of the director. And he ended his letter with the kind of praise that couldn't fail to move the recipient: "The body of the work would be preceded by a text which I would write myself and which might be summarized as follows: if, overnight, the cinema had to do without its soundtrack and become once again a silent art, then many directors would be forced into unemployment, but, among the survivors, there would be Alfred Hitchcock and everyone would realize at last that he is the greatest film director in the world."[20] Flattered, moved, delighted, Hitchcock wasted no time in answering with a long telegram, in French, sent from Los Angeles: "Dear Monsieur Truffaut, your letter brought tears to my eyes and how grateful I am to receive such a tribute from you. Stop. I am still shooting *The Birds* and this will continue until July 15. Stop. Then I will have to begin the editing which will take several weeks. Stop. I think I will wait until the shooting of *The Birds* is finished and then contact you with the idea of getting together around the end of August. Stop. Thank you again for your charming letter sincere regards cordially yours Alfred Hitchcock."[21]

In seclusion at the Colombe d'Or, Truffaut set to work preparing the interviews. He gathered substantial research material, not just books and articles on Hitchcock but also the novels and short stories that the director had adapted for the screen, including those of Boileau and Narcejac and of Daphne du Maurier, the filming of whose novel *The Birds* Hitchcock was just then wrapping up in California. Meanwhile, in New York, Helen Scott was collecting American research material, including the then-unpublished interviews conducted by Peter Bogdanovich, the young American critic and future director who would contribute most to the recognition in the United States of Hitchcock's importance. In mid-July 1962, Truffaut went to Brussels, where Jacques Ledoux, the director of the Royal Cinémathèque of Belgium, organized three days of screenings for him of Hitchcock's British films, with which Truffaut was ill acquainted (and liked only moderately), including all his silent films. Truffaut also took advantage of all the summer revivals in Paris—*North by Northwest, I Confess, Rear Window,* and *Rope.* He then had to attend to the practical details of his first trip to Hollywood. He estimated its cost at $3,500, a sum that was lent to him by Les Films du Carrosse. "Choosing the right tape recorder is important," he wrote to Helen Scott on June 20, 1962, "because it shouldn't be an ordeal for me to carry it, and yet we have to be able to record for a long time without changing tapes. Please find out."[22] Inevitably, the plan was that Hitchcock and Truffaut would each speak in his own language, and Helen Scott would be their interpreter. Truffaut prepared a long questionnaire on each of the films, covering the genesis of each project, the drafting of the screenplay, the direction, and Hitchcock's feelings about the final result. Everything was minutely worked out. The goal was "accurately describing one of the finest and most complete directing careers." Truffaut wanted the book to be "very specific in terms of the intellectual, cerebral, but also manual and material 'crafting' of films," a book that would finally divulge the "secrets" that Truffaut had been trying to unveil for a long time: "This book on Hitchcock is merely a pretext for self-instruction. I would like all the people who make films to learn something from it as well as all those who want to make films."[23]

Helen Scott's role in this project was crucial, and Truffaut willingly acknowledged as much: "Don't let me down, or I'm cooked. If I didn't have you, I never would have considered, or dared to undertake, half of my American activities and especially the Hitchcock book."[24] He used all his influence to stand up for her with publishers who tended to overlook her contribution because they preferred to list only the two film directors as the authors: "If Helen had not been such a brilliant intermediary, the idea for this book would not even have occurred to me,"[25] he wrote to Simon and Schuster, his American publisher. Helen Scott received a first installment of six hundred dollars plus 10 percent of the royalties. Last but not least, Truffaut was convinced that Helen Scott would get along marvelously with Hitchcock: "He'll fall madly in love with you, and having always remained slightly anti-American, he'll be seduced by your European (Continental) liveliness and especially your sense of humor."[26]

Then they had to wait for Hitchcock to reply and set the date for their meetings. On August 9, Truffaut finally received a telegram from Hollywood: "Could you and Miss Helen Scott come to Beverly Hills to start work Monday August 13? If possible can you come by plane to be here Sunday or Monday morning? Reservations will be made for you Beverly Hills Hotel. In that case could work all week."[27] After a brief stop in New York, Helen Scott and the one she called her "hitchcoquin" (*coquin* meaning "little rascal") arrived in Los Angeles on August 13, Hitchcock's sixty-third birthday.

The two friends first dropped off their luggage at the Beverly Hills Hotel; then they went to dinner at the Hitchcocks' house on Bellagio Road in Bel Air. An appointment was made for the following day, in one of the offices of Bungalow 142, at Universal Studios. Hitchcock's chauffeur would come to pick them up in their hotel on Sunset Boulevard. At the appointed time, the master of the house turned on his charm—anecdotes, witticisms, jokes that made Helen laugh heartily, but not Truffaut, who didn't always grasp their full meaning and was eager to get down to serious matters. "Puritanical or not," said Helen Scott, "Hitchcock would occasionally interrupt the taping to give a salacious variant of the Cinderella story or make a nasty remark about an ex-co-worker. To put us at ease, the Master immediately told us to call him 'Hitch,' which I did. But throughout our entire stay, François continued to call him respectfully 'Monsieur Hitchcock,' while the latter answered with 'François, my boy.' "[28]

The interviews between Hitchcock and Truffaut lasted six days. During this time, their lively conversation included anecdotes, bawdy jokes, and discussion of shooting techniques and plot construction. Everything happened as Truffaut and Scott had hoped; Hitchcock was specific, voluble, spirited, and delved willingly into the technical or interpretative details suggested by his interlocutors. He even discussed aspects of his childhood and adolescence, and his ambivalent relationships with actresses—subjects about which he was usually not forthcoming.

After this long series of interviews, Truffaut returned to Paris, where he immediately felt nostalgic about the "week when I fulfilled an old dream—talking with Hitchcock to my heart's content about cinema."[29] This California sojourn greatly contributed in drawing Helen Scott and François Truffaut closer together—not only because they had proved a good team but also because something of a misunderstanding arose, causing a greater complicitous bond between them. For Helen Scott, of course, was in love with Truffaut, while he saw her as a caring "Jewish mother," with a marvelous sense of humor, but not at all as a mistress. The relationship inspired many sexual jokes. "I feel terribly like a bachelor since our painful separation at the Los Angeles airport,"[30] Truffaut wrote her as soon as he arrived in Paris. From that time on, Helen Scott would have but one desire—to work by Truffaut's side. She wanted not only to help him and become his "political mentor" but to feel like and be recognized as a full-fledged collaborator. But for the time being, Truffaut primarily needed Helen posted in New York to watch over the American publication of the Hitchcock interview book.

In September, Truffaut arranged for the interviews to be transcribed, more than forty hours on tape. On Helen Scott's advice, he hired a young American student, Linda, gave her board in Paris, and paid her to type up the English part of the interview. Meanwhile, two secretaries from Les Films du Carrosse, Lucette Desmouceaux—who had recently become Claude de Givray's wife—and Yvonne Goldstein, set to work transcribing the French version. But soon, "due to Helen's strange diction,"[31] the French version started to lag behind. So they adopted another approach; Yvonne and Lucette used Linda's transcribed English text as the starting point, and with the help of Truffaut's old friend Aimée Alexandre, they did their best to translate Hitchcock's words into French. Then, in his free time between the different screen adaptations of *Fahrenheit,* Truffaut made a great many changes and corrections, which had to be made in the English version, as well: a real headache.

In March 1963, Truffaut was already worried about the considerable delay his book had incurred. But in April, when he found the time to reread the first version of the manuscript, he was pleasantly surprised. He shut himself up in his office for ten days and dictated the quasi-definitive French version to Lucette de Givray. Each time he introduced a change in the interviews translated from the English, Truffaut was careful to make note of the fact for Helen Scott. "On the whole," he wrote her, "I try to maintain a conversational tone and avoid academic turns of phrase. I would like you to do your translation work with the same casualness, even if it means keeping some familiarities and possibly even some bad language. The only scruples to have concern the purely technical passages (which in the end are rather few), where you will have to get help from someone in movies, like Arthur Penn, or, better yet, someone bilingual like Sidney Lumet, who would be happy to help us out."[32] By late summer 1963, the double transcription work was completed, which both relieved Truffaut and left him with a big void. "My dream would be for this book never to be published," he wrote to Helen Scott, "and that you and I spend a month bringing it up to date every year, adding new questions and new 'interviews' with the maestro, in short, a yearly Hollywood vacation of a few weeks."[33] The illustrations still needed to be taken care of, for the book required an iconography that would give full meaning to the visual examples described by Hitchcock. Truffaut contacted all the distributors systematically—in France, Italy, and England—to obtain sets of publicity stills, he visited press agencies and Cinémathèque archives in search of precious documents, and borrowed films from the Paris offices of Universal, Paramount, MGM, and Warner Brothers and had individual frames printed at the expense of Les Films du Carrosse. In early March 1964, he spent three days in the British Film Institute's photographic lab, scanning through fourteen old dupes of English films for frames to develop and print. This is how Truffaut came to know by heart each sequence Hitchcock had shot in the course of his long career.

Two long years after recording the interviews, Truffaut set himself the goal of "finishing the book by the end of 1964."[34] The complexity of the task had been underestimated by all concerned; however, it allowed Truffaut to acquire an even more intimate knowledge of Hitchcock's films and gave him the opportunity to fulfill a long-standing desire—of following, from A to Z, religiously and in detail, the making of a book. At a time when Truffaut was involved telling the story of "all books, from Gutenberg to our day"[35] in *Fahrenheit 451*, he was also personally living his daily life with a "book in his head."

TRIP TO TOKYO

In late 1962, with *Fahrenheit 451* and the Hitchcock interview book progressing too slowly, Truffaut sometimes wanted to "close down Carrosse and put the key under the mat."[36] He decided to travel. His aim was to promote his films, but for Truffaut, who felt himself at the time to be in a state of "romantic availability,"[37] each trip was also the occasion for encounters with women. His first destination was Stockholm, in January 1963, where *Jules and Jim* was being highly praised in the press. In the beginning of March, Truffaut was welcomed in Israel by his Tel Aviv distributor, Lucas Steiner.[38]

Jules and Jim also met with success in Israel. In the spring of 1963, he went to Japan for the first time. In the beginning of April, he was received for about ten days in Tokyo by Marcel Giuglaris, the director of Unifrance Japan, and by Kashiko Kawakita, whose company was distributing *Jules and Jim*. Truffaut made the acquaintance of Koichi Yamada, a young French-speaking Tokyo film enthusiast, who would become his official Japanese correspondent and, over the years, one of his closest friends. Truffaut would play host to him regularly at the Carrosse office during his long stays in Paris in 1965 and 1966; he showered him with books and journals, and recommended films to him, introducing him to Langlois's Cinémathèque. He even coproduced Yamada's short film, *La Marchande de poèmes* (The Vendor of Poems), shot in Japan in the summer of 1964. Truffaut made this 1963 trip to Tokyo under the auspices of Unifrance, as part of a delegation that included Alain Delon and Marie Laforêt—in connection with René Clément's film *Plein Soleil (Purple Noon)*—France Roche, Françoise Brion and Alexandra Stewart, the beautiful Canadian-born actress. "François took me under his wing, and it was in Tokyo that I saw *Jules and Jim* for the first time. I shed many a tear. . . . We spent the night talking,"[39] says Stewart. Tokyo became the birthplace of the amorous friendship between Truffaut and Alexandra Stewart, the woman whom he soon called in intimacy "Sandra, my vague star," a tender allusion to Visconti's 1965 film with Claudia Cardinale, *Sandra (Vaghe Stelle dell'Orsa)*. It was a carefree relationship, "nothing serious or passionate, I made him laugh; he could let himself be light and childish,"[40] comments Stewart, reminiscing about a thirty-year friendship. As proof of his attachment, Truffaut would recommend her to Arthur Penn in 1964, when the American director was looking for an actress to play opposite Warren Beatty in *Mickey One*.

Truffaut met two women in Japan who would later appear in his fictional universe, fused in the guise of Kyoko, Doinel-Léaud's pretty mistress in *Bed and Board*. The first was called Kyoko K., a young model and friend of Koichi Yamada. Later she would write him ardent little notes, rather like the messages given to Antoine Doinel by his Japanese mistress: "Come back to Japan, please, please, please . . . François. And promise to give me a day with you. I'd like to spend the day talking, laughing and strolling with you; Kyoko and François only . . . Kyoko loves François. . . ."[41] The second was a charming and very distinguished woman, discreet and passionate, whose name was Shinobu. This first trip to Japan was an intense, lighthearted period in Truffaut's life, which made him forget his Paris worries. "I was melancholic on returning to Paris, for of all the many foreign trips I've made for Unifrance over the last three years, this one, to Tokyo, was the most instructive, most exciting and most pleasant,"[42] he wrote his Japanese distributor immediately upon his return.

THE SOFT SKIN

Since conditions were not yet ideal for filming *Fahrenheit 451*, and the transcription of the Hitchcock interviews left him with time on his hands, Truffaut decided to undertake a new film. "The film will be indecent, completely shameless, rather sad, but very simple. Quick in the writing, quick in the filming, quick to be released and, I hope, quick to pay for itself,"[43] Truffaut announced to Helen Scott. On July 20, 1963, Jean-Louis Richard and he met again at the Hotel Martinez in Cannes. They wrote the script for *La Peau douce* (*The Soft Skin*) in less than a month, holed up, as though the fact of exploring this adulterous story required complete isolation.

The starting point was a double erotic fantasy, as Jean-Louis Richard tells it: "Originally two images had struck François's imagination. A woman and a man kissing in a taxi and the sound of their teeth clinking. And female legs in silk stockings, crossing and uncrossing, and the sound of stockings rubbing against one another. The kiss in the taxi of course is an adulterous kiss. I don't think there are many husbands who kiss their wives making their teeth clink."[44] The screenplay was completed on August 20, 1963. As Truffaut had predicted, *The Soft Skin* is the autopsy of a couple, "an incredibly depressing film, hopeless, with no solution."[45] Pierre Lachenay is a well-known intellectual, a Balzac specialist, and editor of a literary journal, *Ratures*. He is often invited to give lectures in France and abroad. He leads a bourgeois life with his wife, Franca, and their little girl, Sabine. During a trip to Lisbon, for a Balzac conference, he is seduced by a young airline stewardess, Nicole, who is staying in the same hotel. Lies begin to undermine Pierre's hitherto-stable marriage. Lachenay sees Nicole again in Paris, takes her along for a weekend conference in Reims, and wants to live with her. Franca, who has learned of his affair, throws him out after a bitter quarrel. Pierre moves out of the couple's apartment, but Nicole, who values her freedom, refuses to move in with him. Lost, Lachenay decides to go back to his wife. But Franca bursts into the restaurant where he is lunching alone at his usual table and shoots him dead.

When Truffaut sent Helen Scott the script of *The Soft Skin* in September 1963, he explained that he drew his inspiration from true stories. "These ideas about adultery have been running around in my head for such a long time that one might not sense the haste with which I worked,"[46] he pointed out, asking Helen to be as discreet as possible about the project. Truffaut always filed away press clippings on news items he found interesting, with the thought that he might one day use them to write a screenplay. *The Soft Skin* drew inspiration from the famous "Jaccoud affair" in Geneva in the mid-fifties, and from the "Nicole Gérard affair," named after the forty-one-year-old woman who walked into le Petit Chevreau, a restaurant on rue de la Huchette in Paris, on June 26, 1963, and killed her unfaithful husband with two shots from a hunting rifle.

But though the tragic outcome is identical, the characters, situations, feelings, and dialogues in the film are radically different. To better situate *The Soft Skin* in Truffaut's filmography, these news item should be treated as decoys for deflecting the curiosity of journalists and critics. Other details hint at an autobiographical inspiration. At first sight, the character of Pierre Lachenay seems remote from the director. He is older and an academic, probably modeled on the writer Raymond Jean, with whom Truffaut presented *Jules and Jim* to the students at the University of Aix-en-Provence in June 1962, and on Henri Guillemin, a prominent Balzac specialist and one of the best-known literary critics in the sixties. He is also meant as a tribute to his childhood friend Robert Lachenay, with whom Truffaut discovered Balzac. But there is no doubt that the character of Pierre resembles Truffaut himself, with his obsession for detail, his timidity and awkwardness, his need for social recognition and material comfort, and, somewhat paradoxically, his lack of adjustment to bourgeois routine and married life. The fact that Truffaut, for budgetary and practical reasons, used his own apartment on rue du Conseiller Collignon as the Lachenay apartment in the film furthers the autobiographical hypothesis. Was this an immodest desire, or an obsession with realism? The scenes of the Lachenay couple certainly bear a relation to those of the Truffaut couple. *The Soft Skin* is a film on adultery as told by Truffaut; it is studded with intimate details related to his love life, with his expressions and fantasies—for example, the sable-colored Scandale stockings and delicate garters worn by Nicole. *The Soft Skin* condenses Truffaut's romantic adventures into one story, centering on his marital crisis with Madeleine a year before. Nicole, the airline stewardess, brings to mind Truffaut's long affair with Liliane David, who remembers a trip to Le Mans where Truffaut presented *The 400 Blows*. "All I saw was the hotel room and a street giving out on a little square where the film was showing. I couldn't even go see the film because it was sold out."[47] The scene in the hotel, the compulsion to hide Nicole from the conference organizers, the scene in which Lachenay runs out to buy his mistress stockings—*The Soft Skin* literally recaptures several incidents from this affair, which actually came to an end at the time of the filming, when Liliane David married Michel Dreyfus, on October 19, 1963.

But even more than his relationship with David or that with Marie-France Pisier, with whom Truffaut had made a plan, finally aborted, to run away, above all *The Soft Skin* reflects his relationship with Françoise Dorléac. The film was born of their meeting during a trip to Tel Aviv organized by Unifrance Film in March 1963. Twenty-one, a former Christian Dior model, Dorléac was the eldest of the four daughters born to the actors Maurice Dorléac and Renée Simonet. Like her sister Catherine Deneuve, she was beautiful, refined, and graceful. During this trip in Israel, Truffaut and Françoise Dorléac overcame a certain mutual reticence. "I had an inexplicable prejudice against him and he later admitted to me that he had one against me as well," Françoise Dorléac confided at the time. "He thought I was unbearable. And then we got to know each other. I read books voraciously and he lent me some of his. We discussed them and this was the beginning of a mutual discovery."[48] They saw each other again in Paris, just before the actress flew to Brazil to shoot the film that would make her famous, Philippe de Broca's *That Man From Rio,* with Jean-Paul Belmondo.

When she returned from Brazil, Truffaut offered her the part of Nicole in *The Soft Skin.* On reading the script, she didn't like the part, finding the character too harsh. Truffaut would have to exert all his persuasive powers and charm to convince her. "Nicole ended up resembling me, François made her talk like me, tell stories that happened to me with slight changes. This explains why today I'm not so sure about not liking her anymore,"[49] the actress explained when the film opened. Indeed, "Framboise," as Truffaut nicknamed her, alluding to Boby Lapointe's song in *Shoot the Piano Player*—"Avanie et Framboise"—lent her voice, gestures, and rhythm to the woman she played in *The Soft Skin,* making her elegant, lively, reserved, and sensitive, at times violent, and always mysterious.

Truffaut sought an experienced stage actor for the part of Pierre Lachenay, finally selecting Jean Desailly, a member of the Comédie-Française, whose performance had impressed him in December 1961 in a production of René-Jean Clot's *Arc en Enfer,* where he played opposite Silvia Monfort. Truffaut cast Nelly Benedetti, a stage actress whom he had noticed in Claude Autant-Lara's film *Les Régates de San Francisco,* in the part of Franca. She confers upon her character an unquestionable seductiveness, which bears no resemblance to the cliché of the abandoned wife. Truffaut chose Daniel Ceccaldi for the part of Clément, Lachenay's provincial, clinging friend. And he reenlisted Sabine Haudepin, two years after *Jules and Jim,* to play the couple's little girl.

For his fourth film, Truffaut trusted his usual team—Raoul Coutard for the cinematography, Georges Delerue for the music, Claudine Bouché for the editing, and Suzanne Schiffman as script supervisor. He also hired Jean-Pierre Léaud, as well as his friend Jean-André Fieschi from *Cahiers du cinéma,* as apprentice assistant directors. Truffaut's cast and crew worked as an extended family on all his films, but this did not prevent him from being tense and nervous at the beginning of each shoot. Doubtless under the influence of his conversations with Hitchcock, he wanted his film to be intricately edited, with multiple shots and framings. "Up to now, on the first day of a shoot, I've always felt as though I were sending a boat out to sea and that my work thereafter consisted in standing at the helm day after day and avoiding the shipwreck to which I might inevitably be led by my mistakes in calculation at the preproduction stage. Keeping a ship on course in the storm is very tiring, but it's also very thrilling. If you're going to bring a wreck back to port, you might at least hope for a beautiful wreck. Now, I'm weary of this maritime imagery and I'd like my fourth film not to be a ship in distress, but a train crossing through the countryside. I'd like it to be a fine journey, smooth and harmonious, devoid of chaos or switching errors. Instead of hurriedly covering up weaknesses through improvisation, I'd like improvisation to be limited to the oiling of wheels, or the adding of a car without veering off course or slowing down."[50]

On Monday, October 21, 1963, the filming of *The Soft Skin* began at the Auberge des Saisons, in Vironvay, near Louviers in Normandy. For three days, Truffaut shot the most intimate scenes of the film in La Collinière, the ones in which Pierre Lachenay and Nicole spend a weekend together in a bungalow. For several erotic, not to say fetishistic, shots (Pierre removing the sleeping Nicole's stockings and caressing her thighs), Truffaut used a small six-man crew. Unexpectedly, on the second day of filming, the whole crew found itself rushing around in pursuit of a small cat who obstinately refused to lap up the milk from the bowl on the breakfast tray left by the lovers in front of their door. Irritated and amused, Truffaut would reuse this incident ten years later in *Day for Night*.

To minimize expenses, Truffaut had decided to concentrate shooting in the Paris area. There were many scenes that were filmed in the Orly airport over a three-day period, with Nicole as an airline stewardess.[51] The scenes of the Lisbon hotel where Pierre first meets Nicole, and Lachenay's lecture, were actually filmed at the Hotel Lutetia in Paris. The famous elevator sequences, cut and edited in a Hitchcockian rhythm, were taken at the renowned Roux and Combalusier elevator factory in Paris. The shots of the Lisbon street scenes would take only a few hours. A minimal crew accompanied Truffaut, Desailly, and Dorléac; they took the plane on November eighteenth from Orly and returned the following day. The director even managed to ground the plane with several Portuguese extras on an isolated runway of the Lisbon airport and film some additional footage, from 7:00 to 10 a.m., of airline stewardesses at work on board. Back in Paris, the domestic scenes were filmed, first at Nicole's, in Florence Malraux's studio on rue du Télégraphe in the twentieth arrondissement; then, December 2–9, 1963, in Truffaut's own apartment on rue du Conseiller Collignon. "Since no error of taste makes me recoil, the domestic rows will take place in my apartment, if you see what I mean . . ."[52] he had earlier written to Helen Scott. The last three days of filming, just before Christmas, were done at night in the restaurant Le Val d'Isère on rue de Berri, very close to the Champs-Elysées. This is where Franca bursts in and kills Pierre with a hunting rifle.

By the time he had finished this shoot, Truffaut was exhausted, weary, demoralized, and thinner, for his relationship with the actors had not always been ideal. Though Françoise Dorléac had been "charming, excellent, and as well-behaved as Jeanne on the set of *Jules and Jim*," Jean Desailly didn't "like the film, the character, the subject or me,"[53] Truffaut admitted. Truffaut's relations with him—an actor who was used to the quiet tempo and customs of the best Paris theaters—remained "hostile and deceitful"[54] throughout the filming. "Desailly was not happy on the set," says Jean-Louis Richard, who makes a brief appearance in the film.[55] "He was a terrific actor but also François's antithesis on the set. They didn't understand each other at all."[56] Claudine Bouché, who edited *The Soft Skin*, also recalls the tense relationship between Desailly and Truffaut. "François hated Desailly for a silly reason—he disliked physical clumsiness. In one scene, Desailly couldn't close his attaché case at the first try. François's fussiness and tyranny was such that he couldn't bear it when an actor needed a second try for a gesture. Also François didn't like to direct actors who were taller than he. Later he told me he should have chosen Jacques Dutronc for *The Soft Skin*, because he was his height. It was a quip of course, for François had a taste for paradox."[57]

The editing lasted three months. Bouché shortened the film by over forty minutes, cutting entire sequences and speeding up the rhythm. Truffaut was rather pleased: "The Nicole character improved greatly along the way, thanks to Dorléac and my interviews with three air stewardesses prior to the filming. . . . This picture will be more powerful during the marital sequences when 'things are going badly' than when things are 'going well.' Finally, I admit that while I despise Desailly the man, Desailly the actor did a good job playing the part of the bourgeois trapped by events. I've shown him as hypernervous, almost on the edge of madness, to avoid (a) blandness (b) a bourgeois tragedy. I like the film. I have only one reason to be worried: the 'mass audience' might dislike the leading character. Aside from that, I don't think it's possible to feel bored and as a whole it won't be too sordid."[58]

THE THICK SKIN

Truffaut had to get the mix of *The Soft Skin* done by the beginning of April so he could have a print by May, since the film had been selected to compete in the Cannes Film Festival. Five years after *The 400 Blows*, the director once again experienced the ordeal and excitement of an official screening on the Croisette. Claudine Bouché and Jean-Louis Richard supervised the finishing touches, as Truffaut was in New York during most of April working with Helen Scott on the manuscript of the Hitchcock interview book. Prospects seemed excellent since, for the first time in his career, no cuts or restriction had been imposed by the censorship board. Yet Françoise Dorléac's thighs had been closely scrutinized by the censors, since about thirty photos from the La Collinière sequence can still be found today in the board's archives.

Everything went well until the screening in Cannes on May 9. "Everyone wanted to see the film,"[59] recalls Marcel Berbert, who was so harassed that he had to buy tickets, since he didn't have enough invitations to go around. The morning press screening went badly, and so did the subsequent press conferences. Truffaut was tense and on the defensive. The evening screening was, the director admitted, a "complete fiasco."[60] Claudine Bouché, who was by his side, still remembers "the way people shifted in their seats."[61] *The Soft Skin* was very badly received, almost booed. The financial consequences were immediate; the Italian and Spanish distributors withdrew their initial offers. "The day after the screening, no one at the festival knew me anymore; I had become anathema,"[62] Berbert recalls. The contrast with the triumph of *The 400 Blows* in the very same place was striking, and noted by many journalists in their articles the following day. Once the trial was over, however, Truffaut found his good spirits again, as can be seen by the telegram he sent Helen Scott on May 10: "Fortunately I have a thick skin. Stop. In spite of the flop we're having a lot of fun and all is well."[63]

But this slightly ironic, whimsical distance with regard to his own disappointments concealed a very deep malaise. This extremely personal film in which he put so much of himself was being rejected. His clinical view of the couple had been unconvincing, both to those who saw him as the filmmaker of rebellion (*The 400 Blows*) and to those who had become accustomed to his being more feverish in his depiction of feelings (*Jules and Jim*). There was quite a bit of misunderstanding on the part of the critics; (the Communist) *L'Humanité* as well as (the right-wing) *Le Figaro* referred to the director's *"embourgeoisement,"* even though this was certainly Truffaut's most "experimental" film, for even if the subject was bourgeois, it was treated in a very daring way. "Soft-skinned François comes after hard-nosed François," confirmed *Le Parisien libéré*, while for the weekly *Candide*, "The New Wave lions have been tamed." *L'Express* and *Carrefour* hammered the point home, finding the film "boring" and denouncing a "distressing Truffaut." There were only a few articles to comfort the director, who was wounded by all those negative reviews: Michel Mardore's in *Lui* ("a beautiful film, reactionary and moral") and André Téchiné's, in his first essay for *Cahiers du cinéma*. But Godard's comments made him happiest. "I saw your film again on the big screen of the Olympe. It was even bigger than the screen. Warm kisses to Françoise Dorléac. If she hears people say it is acted like [a play by Henri] Bernstein, she can just answer: Why, don't you like Jews?"[64]

The Soft Skin opened in Paris on May 20, 1964. Burned by the Cannes reception, the distributors chose to show it in only three movie houses. The film would nevertheless run for twenty-three weeks, though attracting an audience of only 120,000, which just about covered Carrosse's investment. The company was soon heartened by the film's unexpected success in the Scandinavian countries, and in Germany, England, Canada, and Japan. In December 1964, Truffaut would make a triumphant Scandinavian tour. Three hundred and fifty articles appeared in the Swedish, Norwegian, Danish, and Finnish press, three hours on television, the University of Aarhus's Honored Artist prize—his success was impressive. In 1965, *The Soft Skin* was the number-one box-office hit in Copenhagen and number four in all of Finland.

THE SEPARATION

Truffaut was deeply hurt. "My spirits are low, I'm eager to leave Paris and rest, I'm tired."[65] He received the following note from his friend Claude Jutra, the Québécois director: "I found your characters very sad. As a friend, this vague bitterness that the film exudes frightened me a bit, since I know your films resemble you, point per point, at the time when you make them. I therefore hope the next one will be cheerful."[66] After *The Soft Skin,* the breakup with Madeleine was imminent and, this time around, definitive. "We are separating, Madeleine felt very alone during this filming,"[67] Truffaut wrote Helen Scott, aware that marital hypocrisy was no longer appropriate. It was Madeleine who had taken the initiative to separate. "François was relieved; that was just what he was waiting for," she says today. "I felt it had to be done; he wasn't very pleasant at home, probably because he was very much in love with Françoise Dorléac."[68]

Truffaut left the family home for a three-room apartment he rented on February 18, 1964, at 35 avenue Paul Doumer, a minute away from Madeleine's. The hardest thing, Truffaut admitted, was "not seeing the children every day, but I'm entirely to blame for it all."[69] Laura and Eva, ages five and two and a half, respectively, came regularly to see him. The couple maintained an excellent relationship, affectionate and friendly, so much so that Madeleine seriously contemplated François's return. Yet Truffaut himself, who promised to return to rue du Conseiller Collignon, did not want to rush matters. For nearly a year, their relationship teetered between hope and disappointment, but by the end of 1964, they had to admit to a deadlock: "Our mutual efforts were no more successful than a disarmament conference," he wrote to Helen Scott on November 27, 1964. "I do nothing with my freedom and yet I feel I can't do without it. We will soon have been separated for a year and we have become accustomed to it, each in a different way, and our quirks and habits have only increased."

In early 1965, Madeleine took the initiative in asking for a divorce. The proceedings started on February 8 and the divorce was granted on December 6, with Truffaut promising to pay a monthly alimony of 1,000 francs for each child. "The divorce posed no problems," says Madeleine, "first of all there was no financial problem, no inordinate demand, on either side. Furthermore, the intellectual esteem we had for each other remained unchanged, and his love for his daughters was visible."[70] In the meantime, Truffaut moved once again, on May 15, 1965, into a five-room apartment on rue de Passy, not far from his family. He could have his daughters over and have a live-in governess "to take care of the housework, the cooking and the sewing."[71] From then on, he devoted part of his free time to Laura and Eva, who grew up seeing a father on weekends "who systematically preferred to resort to jokes rather than fatherly authority, but was clearly a father, not a friend, capable of getting mad and punishing us on occasion, when jokes were no longer enough!"[72] Laura now recalls.

Truffaut's romantic adventures were still numerous, but none was really fulfilling to him; he admitted as much to Helen. He did not seem comfortable, and was often "depressed," "feeling awful," and "incapable of loving. . . . I still have nothing serious in my life and my critical attitude, which now reaches beyond obsessiveness to pure madness, prevents me from falling in love. I know that in talking to you about the sex lives of these ladies I'm only talking to you about my own, but too bad."[73]

At the same time, there were mounting problems at Les Films du Carrosse. Aside from *The Soft Skin* and *Mata-Hari,* the film directed by Jean-Louis Richard and starring Jeanne Moreau, the production house really had no immediate projects lined up, and *Fahrenheit* was too costly: "We couldn't find money in France. The film was difficult to make because of the special effects, the fires,"[74] recalls Marcel Berbert. The situation was so precarious that in September 1965, Berbert expressed his desire to work on other productions so as to relieve Carrosse's cash flow. "François thought I wanted to leave Carrosse, which wasn't the case."[75] Though hurt, Truffaut nonetheless convinced him to stay with the company full-time, promising that, after *Fahrenheit,* he would resolve to produce a greater number of movies, more quickly and on limited budgets.

Truffaut's relationship with his mother-in-law, which had never been wonderful, was more and more tense. Now that her daughter was divorced,

1. François Truffaut and Jeanne Moreau during the filming of *Jules and Jim*, 1961. *A story focused on this pure triangular love . . .*

2 and 3. RIGHT & BELOW: Françoise Dorléac and François Truffaut during the filming of *The Soft Skin*, 1963. *The film will be indecent, completely shameless . . .*

4. BOTTOM: Jeanne Moreau and François Truffaut during the filming of *The Bride Wore Black*, 1967. *It is an extremely intimate exchange that can lead to an amorous relationship . . .* (Jeanne Moreau)

5. OPPOSITE, TOP: Jean-Pierre Léaud, Claude Jade, and François Truffaut during the filming of *Stolen Kisses*, 1968. *The new adventures of Antoine Doinel . . .*

6. OPPOSITE, CENTER: Claude Lelouch, Jean-Luc Godard, François Truffaut, Louis Malle, Roman Polanski at the Cannes Festival in May 1968. *The country was paralyzed and it was logical to stop the festivities . . .*

7. OPPOSITE, BOTTOM: François Truffaut and Jean-Pierre Léaud confronting police forces in front of the offices of the Cinémathèque française, rue de Courcelles, on February 20, 1968. *The friends of cinema demonstrate in support of Henri Langlois.*

8. Jean-Paul Belmondo, Catherine Deneuve, François Truffaut during the filming of *Mississippi Mermaid*, 1969.
—*Does love hurt?*
—*Yes, it hurts. It hurts when I look at you.*
—*Yesterday you said it was a joy.*
—*Yes. It's a joy and a misery.*
9. François Truffaut, Jean-Paul Belmondo, Suzanne Schiffman during the filming of *Mississippi Mermaid*, 1969.

10. The end of the shoot of *The Wild Child*, 1969. *First row, left to right:* Jean-François Stévenin, Suzanne Schiffman and Pierre Zucca. *Second row:* François Truffaut, Catherine Deneuve, Jean-Pierre Cargol (fourth from left). *Third row:* Nestor Almendros (seventh from left). *Last row:* Marcel Berbert (far left).

11. François Truffaut and Nestor Almendros during the filming of *Two English Girls*, 1971.
12. François Truffaut, Kika Markham, Jean-Pierre Léaud and Stacey Tendeter during the filming of *Two English Girls*, 1971.

13. Marie-France Pisier and François Truffaut during the filming of *Stolen Kisses*, 1968.
14. Jacqueline Bisset and François Truffaut during the filming of *Day For Night*, 1972.

Jean-Luc. Pour ne pas t'obliger à lire cette lettre désagréable, jusqu'au bout, je commence par l'essentiel : je n'entrerai pas en co-production dans ton film. Deuxièmement, je te retourne ta lettre à Jean-Pierre Léaud : je l'ai lue et je la trouve dégueulasse. C'est à cause d'elle que je sens le moment venu de te dire, longuement, que selon moi tu te conduis comme une merde.

En ce qui concerne Jean-Pierre, si malmené depuis l'histoire de la grande Marie et plus récemment dans son travail, je trouve dégueulasse de hurler avec les loups, dégueulasse d'essayer d'extorquer, par intimidation, du fric à quelqu'un qui a quinze ans de moins que toi et que tu payais moins d'un million lorsqu'il était le centre de tes films qui t'en rapportaient trente fois plus.

Certes, Jean-Pierre a changé depuis les 400 coups mais je peux te dire que c'est

15. Jean-Luc Godard and François Truffaut, 1967. *From solidarity . . .*
16. *. . . to breakup.* First page of Truffaut's letter to Godard breaking relations with him, 1973.

17. Yul Brynner giving François Truffaut the Oscar for best foreign film for *Day For Night*, 1974. *I'm very happy because* Day For Night *is about film people like you; it's your trophy . . .* 18. Steven Spielberg, François Truffaut during the filming of *Close Encounters of the Third Kind,* 1976. *I needed a man who would have the soul of a child . . .* (Steven Spielberg).

19. Éva, François, and Laura Truffaut.
20. Truffaut directing little Gregory during the filming of *Small Change,* 1975.
My films are a critique of the French way of bringing up children . . .

21. *I watch her act, I help her as I can, uttering thirty words when she would like a hundred* . . . François Truffaut, Isabelle Adjani, Madame Baa during the filming of *The Story of Adèle H.*, 1975.

Cette scène n'est pas satisfaisante car confuse.
Il faut qu'on comprenne qu'elle a demandé des renseigne-
-ments sur Pinson mais en demandant à Lenoir de ne [11] pas
parler d'elle ... c'est ce qui doit ressortir du dialogue ...

8 . CABINET DE MAITRE LENOIR . INT. JOUR

il faut
voir plus atté
noire scru-
-puleusement.

L'avocat dit à Miss Lewly, quelques jours plus tard,

qu'il a bien réussi à retrouver le Lieutenant Pinson,

mais que celui-ci ne peut la voir actuellement, étant | vaseux

gravement malade. Il mentionne l'adresse du
casernement mais il a obtenu celle d'une
maison privée où Pinson se rend souvent, chez une
Il ne peut ajouter aucune précision et laisse sans   jeune veuve

réponse les questions inquiètes de sa cliente.

quelles questions

9 : CAMPAGNE   Celle-ci lui règle ses honoraires et sort.

Ici devrait se placer la scène où elle marche
dans la campagne parallèlement au régiment de
Pinson - Longtemps il ne la voit pas puis il croit la
reconnaître et ils
prennent le galop
(Page 84 .)

10. RUES D'HALIFAX . EXT. JOUR

Miss Lewly ~~~ dans les rues, désemparée.

Filature

~~Soudain elle est dépassée par une~~ voiture découverte où
se trouvent Pinson et la femme aux chiens
~~qui~~ s'arrête ~~un peu en avant d'elle~~, devant une librai-

rie militaire "la maison "Gossip"). ~~Une ordonnance se~~

~~précipite pour ouvrir la portière à un officier très élan~~

(Oui, on peut conserver l'ordonnance)

*) faut - ils à cheval ou
à pied ? décisions

22. Excerpt from the script of *The Story of Adèle H.*, annotated by François Truffaut.

23. Catherine Deneuve, François Truffaut, and Suzanne Schiffman during the filming of *The Last Métro*, 1980.

24. Fanny Ardant and François Truffaut during the filming of *The Woman Next Door*, 1981. *Neither with you nor without you* . . .

25. François Truffaut, Fanny Ardant, and Jean-Louis Trintignant during the filming of *Confidentially Yours*, 1983.
26. Gérard Depardieu and François Truffaut during the filming of *The Woman Next Door*, 1981.

27. Jean-Pierre Léaud and François Truffaut, at the time of *Love On the Run,* 1979. *The end of the Doinel cycle . . .*
28. Charles Denner and François Truffaut during the filming of *The Man Who Loved Women,* 1976. *The story of a skirt-chaser . . .*

29. François Truffaut in *The Green Room*, 1978. *I'm faithful to the dead, I live with them . . .*

Elizabeth Morgenstern saw no reason to do her ex-son-in-law any favors. Up until then, Les Films du Carrosse had been renting space at a preferential rate in the offices of SEDIF, the company she and Madeleine had inherited. When a much higher rent was demanded in renewing his lease, Truffaut decided to move out. By chance, Alain Vannier, who handled the foreign sales of Truffaut's films, knew of an available space. Les Films du Carrosse moved into new offices on June 20, 1965, at 5 rue Robert Estienne, a dead-end street off rue Marbeuf. Originally a third-floor apartment, it had been renovated with wood paneling and Japanese wallpaper. In this dream office, surrounded by books and magazines, Truffaut welcomed his friends and collaborators in comfortable leather armchairs.

During this same period, an unpleasant plagiarism case upset life at Carrosse. In the spring of 1963, François Truffaut and Jean-Louis Richard had written a screenplay for Jeanne Moreau based on the life of Mata Hari, the famous German spy who had been active in Paris during World War I. Directed by Jean-Louis Richard and entirely produced by Les Films du Carrosse, *Mata-Hari* opened with some success on January 29, 1965, attracting an audience of 180,000 in two months. The following June, a plagiarism suit was filed against the film. Michel Binder, director of the Société Financière de Production Cinématographique, accused Richard and Truffaut of having lifted ten specific details from a preexisting screenplay by Paul and Cathy de Sainte-Colombe, authors who were under contract to him for a projected film on the same subject, to be directed by the American Edgar G. Ulmer. The Paris Court of Appeals ruled in favor of the plaintiff, and on June 16, the judges ordered the confiscation of all prints of the film and the deduction of 250,000 francs from box-office receipts, the equivalent of the sum Binder had paid his scriptwriters.[76] This put a severe dent in Carrosse's finances. The lawyer defending the company in this affair was Georges Kiejman, and this occasion marked the beginning of a long collaboration and deep friendship between him and Truffaut.

In the autumn of 1965, to rescue his company, Truffaut began assigning projects to his team of scriptwriters. In a letter dated November 27, he enumerated these to Helen Scott: "(1) *The Wild Child* (the story of the wolf-child I told you about); (2) *La Petite Voleuse* (like Bergman's *Monika,* the birth of femininity and flirtatiousness in a delinquent girl, a female *400 Blows*); (3) a story in the style of *Piano Player* or Godard's *Bande à part* (*Band of Outsiders*) for Jean-Pierre Léaud, perhaps an early Goodis novel; (4) a comedy drama about a young couple who separate and make up, possibly for Romy Schneider and Belmondo; (5) and finally, the film I've been talking about for a long time, in which all the action would take place in a school. That makes five projects, of which at least two will be under way next month. All of this is confidential. I'm telling you because I tell you everything, but keep it to yourself."[77] Truffaut inaugurated a regimen he would follow all through the succeeding years with his screenwriters—Jean Gruault, Jean-Louis Richard, Claude de Givray, and Bernard Revon. He would see them separately, for weekly "feverish and fast"[78] work sessions. This spate of projects, initiated simultaneously, would keep him busy for a time, and result in a series of films shot at a rapid pace.

BONNIE AND CLYDE

Offers to work on other projects came to him from abroad. He gave two of them very serious consideration. One involved directing an episode of *Les Trois Faces,* produced by Dino de Laurentiis, with Princess Soraya in the lead. Truffaut was interested in the offer of a 300,000-franc salary, "enough money to buy an apartment,"[79] he admitted to Helen Scott. Intrigued, as well, at the thought of giving Soraya her film debut, he went to Rome in mid-July 1964 and met Franco Brusati, the Italian screenwriter. But soon thereafter, Truffaut changed his mind about directing a commissioned work and apologized to Soraya: "Yesterday, I gulped down a huge glass of tomato juice that was probably too chilled and it made me ill all evening and all night and I realized that Roman life was not for me. I was discouraged, tired and above all in need of a vacation. So I left for France and gave up the idea of shooting the episode. . . ."[80]

The other project was far more exciting. In mid-December 1963, Truffaut received a telegram from Lewis Allen, an independent producer he had met in New York, informing him that he owned the rights to a script being written by two young screenwriters, Robert Benton and David Newman. Friends of Helen Scott, Benton and Newman had selected Truffaut as their first choice for director, for they had admired *Jules and Jim* and *Shoot the Piano Player.* The story they were working on was being serialized at the time as a comic strip in *France-Soir*—which was how Truffaut first learned of Bonnie and Clyde's mad and murderous rampage through prewar Texas. On January 2, 1964, Elinor and Norton Wright, the producers who had taken over the project in New York, sent Truffaut a first version of the *Bonnie and Clyde* screenplay. Claudine Bouché immediately gave him a reading of it in French. It was then passed around the Carrosse office and aroused much enthusiasm. Convinced of the story's cinematic qualities, Truffaut contemplated directing his first American film.

On March 26, 1964, he flew to New York for a monthlong visit. He stayed at the Algonquin Hotel, on Jeanne Moreau's recommendation. Fortunately, in New York, he had Helen Scott, with whom he worked very hard reconciling the two versions of the Hitchcock interview book and solving some final translation problems. This was the first time he was staying for such a long time; "New York seems very provincial to me, and that's a surprise. But the other times, with films to present, journalists to meet and so on, American life seemed less calm to me. On this occasion, I take my time."[81]

During his stay in New York, Truffaut met several times with Robert Benton and David Newman to discuss *Bonnie and Clyde.* "I think the script could really be terrific," he wrote to Berbert; "we could substitute this project for *Fahrenheit.*"[82] But Truffaut still felt a certain apprehension about making a film in the United States—because of his poor knowledge of English, for one, but also because he knew shooting conditions would be significantly different from those he was used to and which he owed to his extremely loyal technical crew and the financial independence of Les Films du Carrosse. The producers at the time had already started scouting locations in Texas, with the aim of shooting the film the following summer in the Dallas area, where small towns had barely changed since the thirties. With an estimated budget of $500,000, the film would be less costly than the average American film, which reassured Truffaut, who was frightened by big-budget Hollywood productions.

At the end of April, Truffaut was hesitating between *Fahrenheit 451,* whose production problems were still unsolved, and *Bonnie and Clyde,* the B film to be directed in haste over the summer of 1965. The American offer appealed to Truffaut; he considered Jane Fonda for the part of Bonnie, particularly since she had said she would be delighted to work with him. The producer Jacques Bar arranged a meeting between Truffaut and Fonda, but nothing came of it. Leslie Caron—a close friend of Warren Beatty, who traveled to Paris in the sole hope of being cast as Montag in *Fahrenheit*—arranged a lunch date with Truffaut at the Berkeley on avenue Matignon. This would also be an opportunity for her to make Truffaut's acquaintance. "Like a military officer on a campaign, Warren wanted everything to be fully planned out. He said to me, 'Listen, I don't speak French; it would be too long for me to spend the whole meal with Truffaut, so I'll join you for coffee.' "[83] At the end of the luncheon, Truffaut brought the conversation around to *Bonnie and Clyde* and praised the script, describing the story of the two youthful gangsters in the America of the thirties. On the following day, Beatty flew to New York and met with Robert Benton. "He phoned me immediately," Leslie Caron recounts, "and told me the screenplay was terrific, though he was a bit worried because Westerns were not doing well at the box office. He sent me the script, and I immediately told him it was wonderful, and not really a Western."[84]

After much thought, Truffaut decided against accepting the offer: "You should know that of all the screenplays I've turned down in the last five years, *Bonnie and Clyde* is by far the best,"[85] he wrote to Elinor Jones. And he added in his letter, "I took the liberty of giving *Bonnie and Clyde* to read to my friend Jean-Luc Godard and he too liked the script a lot." Godard sent Truffaut a telegram from the Venice Film Festival, where he was presenting *Une Femme mariée* (*A Married Woman*): "Am in love with Bonnie and also with Clyde. Stop. Would be happy to speak with authors in New York."[86] The first contacts between Godard and the screenwriters were fruitful, but the deal eventually fell through because of scheduling problems.

Truffaut's decision not to do *Bonnie and Clyde* was founded on new hopes of making *Fahrenheit 451*. It seemed, briefly, like the shoot could take place over the summer of 1965, but then coproduction problems cropped up once again. Hearing that Truffaut was free, Elinor Jones approached him again for *Bonnie and Clyde*. Truffaut, who was very tempted by this new offer, demanded a salary of $80,000, and set two conditions—that Helen Scott be hired as his personal assistant, and that he be allowed to cast Alexandra Stewart in the part of Bonnie Parker. Jones agreed to these conditions. Now all that remained was to find a star for the part of Clyde Barrow in order for shooting to begin in early July. The New York producers sent a telegram suggesting Paul Newman. Truffaut turned the suggestion down, arguing "The film would become too important and disproportionate. Stop. Scooter Teague and Robert Walker seem to me adequate for the two male parts. Stop. I don't see stars in this film, but cable me your suggestions as you go along."[87] The producers gave up the idea of Paul Newman, but they insisted on a star for financial reasons, and suggested Warren Beatty. This time, Truffaut's opposition was forceful and unequivocal. "Actually," he wrote to Elinor Jones, "I have no admiration for Warren Beatty and, moreover, he seems to me an extremely unpleasant person. As far as I'm concerned, he and Marlon Brando, and several others, are on a little list that I've classified in my head as 'Better not to make films at all than to make films with these people.' "[88] In the meantime, though, Warren Beatty, who liked the project, had bought the rights to the screenplay and had decided to hire Arthur Penn as director; he had just worked with Penn on *Mickey One*. Truffaut was thus definitely out of the running. *Bonnie and Clyde* would be filmed over the summer of 1966, starring Beatty and Faye Dunaway, and would become one of the biggest commercial hits of the decade.

DEGREES FAHRENHEIT

Under the impetus of two young independent American producers, Eugene Archer and Lewis Allen, *Fahrenheit 451* was once again moving forward. "The time is ideal for a gifted young French director to make a low-budget film in America," Eugene Archer wrote Truffaut. "More than anything, the industry needs the example of a really brilliant film made in a wholly personal and artistic way for a moderate cost. It could be a decisive factor in starting a new trend, away from the super-spectacles with costs of millions of dollars, toward the kind of personal cinema that you and Jean-Luc and André Bazin—and I, in my own way—have always tried to encourage."[89]

Attracted by this offer, which testified to the New Wave's recognition abroad, Truffaut had the *Fahrenheit* script translated into English and gave it the title *Phoenix*, which seemed more international. Lewis Allen, who took personal charge of the project, proved to be efficient. In 1963, he bought the rights to the Bradbury novel from Les Films du Carrosse ($34,000) as well as the adaptation made by Truffaut and his successive screenwriters ($30,000). "Lewis Allen's involvement was unhoped for," Truffaut wrote enthusiastically to Helen Scott. "Les Films du Carrosse is presently staying afloat thanks to the advance he paid us for the *Fahrenheit* script. Our arrangement stipulates that the film can't be made with any other director but me, which reassures me. I can't lose the script."[90] Truffaut began to believe seriously in an American version of the film. Under Allen's aegis, a number of American movie stars were contacted for the part of Montag. Allen submitted the names of Marlon Brando and Paul Newman, the latter having already been contacted by Truffaut the previous year: "He is very handsome, particularly when he is filmed in color, and I prefer him to all the Hollywood actors who have box-office appeal—Hudson, Peck, Heston, Brando, Lancaster."[91] But Truffaut expressed skepticism, terrified at the prospect of his film being engulfed by the star system. "A costly film, a costly Newman . . . What would become of my independence then?"[92] Truffaut suggested other names: Montgomery Clift, Sterling Hayden—the hero of *Johnny Guitar* (one of Truffaut's cult pictures), but who hadn't appeared on screen for nearly five years—or Terence Stamp, "a sort of English-speaking Oskar Werner,"[93] who had impressed him in Peter Ustinov's *Billy Budd*. Contacted by Lewis Allen, Paul Newman was prepared to commit himself to the venture, either immediately, or in a year, in the summer of 1964. Truffaut and his producer opted for more time: The filming of *Fahrenheit*, starring Paul Newman, was scheduled for July 1964.

In September and October 1963, while Truffaut was shooting *The Soft Skin*, preproduction proceeded on *Fahrenheit*. The American producers scouted locations for futuristic scenery—Toronto, Seattle, for its elevated subway, Philadelphia. Allen favored Toronto, whose "advantages are now more and more considerable,"[94] but also expected to shoot several sequences in the Seattle elevated train. The next task was to complete the casting for Linda, Montag's wife; Clarisse, his young girlfriend; and the captain of the fire brigade. Truffaut and Allen agreed on Jean Seberg for the first and Jane Fonda for the second, and they sent the script to Albert

Finney, Max von Sydow, Peter O'Toole, and Sterling Hayden for the part of the captain. Then a few technical points had to be settled, particularly the question of color. Shooting in color was a commercial imperative, of course, but Truffaut had no experience with color. Allen suggested hiring the photographer Richard Avedon as an adviser, but Truffaut categorically refused: "I don't like the idea of cinema being a plastic art; I prefer to think of it as a dynamic art. And color is dynamic, thus naturally filmable."[95] To facilitate his relations with the American producers, Truffaut needed an intermediary, someone he completely trusted who was familiar with his work methods. He succeeded in getting Helen Scott hired, who dreamed of assisting him on a set.

Bad news: Paul Newman had decided not to accept the part of Montag. Lewis Allen explained. "Mainly, Paul visualizes the picture as something quite different from the way you and I see it. He thinks it is a sociological document and he is very interested that these political and sociological aspects be emphasized."[96] Allen then suggested Kirk Douglas, but Truffaut preferred Terence Stamp, of whom he had said a month before: "I'm convinced this actor will someday become very important in American cinema."[97] Allen, though wary, sent the screenplay to Stamp.

Truffaut had by then completed the shoot of *The Soft Skin.* Though he was still skeptical about the financial backing of *Fahrenheit 451*, his real concern was linguistic. How would he manage to communicate with non-French-speaking actors and technicians? With Helen, he twisted the problem around: "As for English, don't worry, I won't learn a word until the first day of filming. Don't tell me I should know English to make this film, since I'm making the film so I can learn English!"[98] But the problem still remained. He made a great effort and in January and February of 1965 took an intensive six-week course of daily private lessons. By the end of the six weeks, he could read letters, articles, and even novels, but his conversational skills remained limited, and his ability to express himself in public even more so.

In the spring of 1964, good news arrived: Terence Stamp liked the script and accepted the part of Montag. His financial requirements were reasonable, but he was unavailable for the next year because of a previous commitment to make *The Collector,* directed by William Wyler. Truffaut had finally found the ideal lead actor for the film, and Lewis Allen still had a year to complete the budget requirements, which were estimated at around $900,000. The American producer was in negotiation with MCA, a European subsidiary of Universal Studios, headed in London by the director Tony Richardson and Oscar Lewenstein. This meant filming in a studio in suburban London.

In the meantime, Truffaut contacted Oskar Werner and offered him the part of the captain of the fire brigade. The Austrian actor replied two days later: "Enthusiastic to work on *Fahrenheit* with you. Stop. Love."[99] As far as the two female parts were concerned, Clarisse (the young woman who intrigues Montag, seduces him, and incites him to clandestine reading) and Linda (his lawful wife, who ends up denouncing him to the chief of the fire brigade), Truffaut and Allen had contacted Jane Fonda and Julie Christie, the latter replacing Jean Seberg, who had dropped out. Fonda and Christie both accepted. Finally, Welles's and Hitchcock's composer, Bernard Herrmann, whom Truffaut admired and whose every record he owned, agreed to compose the musical score for the film. The two men met in London and enjoyed hours of conversation about *Citizen Kane* and *The Birds*. In that late autumn of 1964, everyone fully expected to meet again in Toronto or London in the spring, when the camera would begin to roll on the set of *Fahrenheit 451*, now the title preferred over *The Phoenix*.

Then Sam Spiegel entered the picture. Considered one of Hollywood's most important independent producers, he had just had an enormous commercial hit with David Lean's *Lawrence of Arabia*. In his negotiations with Lewis Allen, he threw everything into question. The names of Robert Redford, Richard Burton, and Elizabeth Taylor were bandied about, so that the projected budget now reached the $3 million range. Truffaut, who was kept out of the negotiations, became very worried. Fortunately, in mid-June 1965, Spiegel abandoned the project because of casting disagreements. Lewis Allen then signed with MCA, and granted Universal worldwide distribution rights. *Fahrenheit* was to be the first of MCA's independent coproductions in London; the second was *The Countess from Hong Kong*, which Charlie Chaplin was to shoot almost simultaneously, with Sophia Loren and Marlon Brando. The negotiations with Spiegel had again delayed matters; Truffaut's filming, now to be held at Pinewood Studios in suburban London, was postponed to January 1966.

In June and July 1965, Truffaut went regularly to London to meet with Terence Stamp and get ready for the shoot. The two men got on instantly, particularly since Stamp was of French descent on his mother's side and absolutely bilingual. Stamp, who was sometimes difficult and temperamental, was clearly enthusiastic about working with Truffaut and, at twenty-five, had just earned the award for best actor at Cannes for his performance in *The Collector*. In the beginning of August, Lewis Allen came up with an idea that appealed to Truffaut, namely to cast Julie Christie in both female roles—as the cold and elegant Linda and, wearing a wig of very short hair, as the playful, mischievous, slightly boyish Clarisse. Putting his producer in charge of explaining this sudden casting change to Jane Fonda, Truffaut wanted to tell Julie Christie the news in person. In early September, he flew to Madrid, where the actress had been shooting *Doctor Zhivago* for over six months. She was delighted at the prospect of playing both female parts. She and Truffaut were immediately drawn to each other; it was love at first sight. The young Englishwoman, who spoke French well, was impressed by Truffaut's imagination and enthusiasm, while he was seduced by her liveliness and wit. "Julie's was the first miniskirt I laid eyes on. It wasn't common at the time: I thought she was a bit crazy. . . . In fact, she was merely ahead of the times. There was also her voice, which somewhat contradicted her looks. As though she had drunk 1,800 whiskies, which wasn't true. She doesn't smoke, she doesn't drink, but she bites her nails badly. Like me. We hit it off immediately."[100] This close, amorous liaison would last for the entire period of the *Fahrenheit* filming.

Things did not go so smoothly when Truffaut told Terence Stamp that he had decided to give Julie Christie two parts. Convinced that Truffaut and she were stealing his show and shrinking his part, Stamp threatened to resign. Truffaut pleaded with him: "My dear Terry, you possess extraordinary talent and doubtless a marvelous career awaits you. You're a very great actor, the sort of poetical actor who is so needed in today's cinema, now that Hollywood is incapable of recruiting anything but playboys or G-men. . . . Using Julie Christie to play both Linda and Clarisse finally allows me to solve the eternal problem of the thankless part versus the glamorous part, show two aspects of the same woman, and also prove visually that for most men, wife and mistress are the same."[101] Truffaut used countless arguments, reminding him that *Fahrenheit* was "first and foremost the story of Montag the fireman," and how they had remained loyal to him when Sam Spiegel, in the course of negotiations, had demanded another actor for the part of Montag. But Truffaut's efforts were to no avail. Stamp was jealous and hurt; he felt betrayed. His decision was final.

Truffaut and Allen came up with a hasty compromise solution. They offered the part of Montag to Oskar Werner, who accepted, though the change made him ill at ease. He began the filming in a tense state, and suddenly required more money. For the part of the captain, Allen and Truffaut considered Sterling Hayden again, but he hesitated, having just completed a strenuous shoot, Stanley Kubrick's *Dr. Strangelove*. Then British Actor's Equity demanded a British actor, since Terence Stamp had dropped out. Faced with union pressure, Truffaut preferred to wait until the beginning of the filming rather than hire the first British actor to walk in the door: "In any case they all have a crooked face and a theatrical accent."[102]

Fahrenheit had exhausted Truffaut even before he had gotten around to making the film. He had been nurturing the project for four years, through four different versions of the script with four different screenwriters. At least a half dozen producers had shown interest in it, and about twenty actors had been considered. Now that he would finally be making the film, he seemed indifferent, nearly passive, as though inwardly drained, and crushed by the excessive weight of the production. Truffaut liked to say, and liked to have his screen characters say, that love stories have a beginning, a middle, and an end. In many ways, the same could be said of films: *Fahrenheit 451* seemed to have outlived its life span before being made.

THE FOREST OF BOOK-MEN

In late 1965, François Truffaut made frequent trips from Paris to London to work with the actors and the crew of his film. He stayed in a suite at the Hilton from January 1966 until mid-June. Typically, Truffaut was not distracted by the swinging London of the sixties, with its effervescent musical scene and its innovative fashions, the most dynamic metropolis of the day. He didn't even see his friends, such as Roman Polanski and Françoise Dorléac. All he knew were the streets along a few taxi routes—the road to Pinewood Studios, and to the screening rooms of the British Film Institute or the National Film Theatre.

On the eve of his first day of filming, Godard came to see him; Truffaut took him around the sets and showed him the footage of his color tests. Then the two men buried themselves in a screening room at the British Film Institute to watch von Sternberg's *The Scarlet Empress,* with Marlene Dietrich, a film Truffaut called "the best, the craziest, the best performed."[103] Obsessed by his work, he saw himself as a director in exile, a state that suited him. He was accompanied throughout his London stay by his two personal assistants—Helen Scott and Suzanne Schiffman. "During the *Fahrenheit* shoot," the latter remembers, "there was an English script supervisor, of course, and I discovered the joy of not having to do production reports or log sheets every night. I spoke English, which François refused to do, and I was completely available: we worked together continuously."[104] Nicknamed "Suzanna the perverse," an allusion to Luis Buñuel's *Suzana la Perverse,* Suzanne Schiffman was completely integrated into Truffaut's creative process—there wasn't a single idea, a single new line of dialogue, a single detail, that wasn't discussed with her before he tried it out on film.

On January 11, 1966, two days before the shoot was to begin, Truffaut had to find, in extremis, an actor for the part of the captain of the fire brigade. On seeing Martin Ritt's *The Spy Who Came In from the Cold,* in which Oskar Werner had a role, he noticed an actor of Irish descent with an inimitable accent, Cyril Cusack, who he felt would be good for the part. Now that the cast was complete, the shooting could begin on Thursday, January 13, at Pinewood, stage 106.[105] These large studios, forty-five minutes away from the center of London, constituted a regulated world, Truffaut discovered, with very strict standards and numerous highly competent technicians. Indeed, Nicholas Roeg, *Fahrenheit*'s director of photography, had a team of nearly fifty people working for him. For the first time, Truffaut had two makeup girls and four wardrobe girls. Often these constraints irritated him: "Union rules are very strict, since, for example, if we're using two cameras, Nick Roeg doesn't have the right to be the cameraman on one of the two."[106] But there are also advantages: "Pinewood is a real studio, comfortable and wonderfully well equipped. At an hour's notice, I can ask for one or two additional cameras, and they come with camera operators and focus pullers recruited on the spot, who are available at all times."[107] His overall feelings were mixed. "For or against my will—more likely against—*Fahrenheit* will be slightly too English for my taste," Truffaut confided to Marcel Berbert. "I'm snowed under with work by this insufficiently prepared film. Every weekend I must write memos for the sets, the costumes, the props, etc., to avoid bad surprises. The quality of the work is improving a bit, but it's so slow!"[108] For this shoot, Truffaut adapted and changed his style, shooting a maximum of three takes and developing only one. Only the action scenes were filmed with three cameras.

Philippe Labro, who was then a star reporter for *France-Soir*, spent several days in London on the set of *Fahrenheit 451*. "I was taken over by a woman, a sort of domineering whale, likable in a syrupy way, but also metallically protective: She was Helen Scott."[109] She was both François Truffaut's interpreter and personal assistant; she could tell him if the actors' performances were convincing or not, since Truffaut, with his inadequate knowledge of English, was sometimes unable to judge. "It was the first time I saw Truffaut on a set," Labro explains, "he looked puzzled, wondering if he was right to make this film. He seemed like a stranger on the set, as though the film were at the mercy of some other, completely undefined entity, which was the foreign language."

Truffaut recalled only a few good days in a shoot that lasted three and a half months. One such was that of the firemen's book-burning scenes. Truffaut had personally chosen the books in a flea market and in a couple of London bookstores. A whole intimate library went up in flames—Proust, Klossowski's *Roberte de soir*, Audiberti's *Marie Dubois*, Genet's *The Thief's Journal*, Miller's *Sexus*, Paul Gégauff's *Rébus*, Queneau's *Zazie*, and a pleiad of Anglo-Saxon writers he admired, such as Twain, Dickens, Melville, Salinger, Defoe, Lewis Carroll, and Thackeray. There were also books on cinema, such as Chaplin's *My Autobiography*, and issues of *Cahiers du cinéma*, one with a still from *Breathless* on the cover, the other with a picture of Anna Karina as a nun—Truffaut's way of showing his solidarity with

Rivette at a time when *The Nun* had been banned in France by the Gaullist censors.[110]

There was another happy period as the filming drew to a close in April 1966, when the cast and crew met at Black Park, a forest near Pinewood, for exterior shots. This was the spot Truffaut had selected for the kingdom of the "book-men"—those victims of the authoritarian regime who had learned certain works by heart, such as Plato's *Republic, Wuthering Heights, Ulysses, Waiting for Godot, Henri Brulard,* Saint-Simon's *Memoirs, Martian Chronicles,* and *David Copperfield,* as a way of rescuing the literary heritage of past centuries from the flames. The weather was dreadful—cold, rainy, and windy. The first takes were catastrophic, and Truffaut had to reshoot all the sequences. Yet, with the passing days, the director gradually found his hallmark style. The last scenes of the film, in the snow, were the only improvised moments in sixty-seven days of shooting.

On the advice of Jean-Louis Comolli, editor in chief of *Cahiers du cinéma,* Truffaut kept a diary describing in minute detail the various stages of the "saddest and most difficult"[111] moviemaking experience he had had to date. *Cahiers* published the diary from March to June 1966. In it, Truffaut tells of his tense relationship with Oskar Werner. Their reunion, four years after *Jules and Jim,* was initially warm and friendly. But by the end of the first week, their relations began to deteriorate. Increasingly haughty, Werner demanded star billing and constantly challenged the director's decisions, insisting on explanations that Truffaut refused to give him. On February 1, the director recounted their first conflict in his journal: "Because of a flamethrower dangerously handled near his back by Cyril Cusack, Oskar Werner becomes nervous, and the two of us break out into a violent quarrel for five minutes."[112] Truffaut resented Werner's starlike capriciousness, his timorousness in the face of difficulties, his heavy-handed acting, and, above all, his lack of humor and imagination. The two men had very different conceptions of the Montag part. Werner wanted to portray a hero, while Truffaut detested heroism. "I soon rediscover my antiheroic bias. I'll never be able to film courage, probably because it doesn't interest me. Courage seems to me an overrated virtue, compared to tact, for example. I'm sure that General Oufkir, the 'bad guy' in the Ben Barka affair, is a courageous man, but in terms of tact, he's got a long way to go."[113]

The constant power struggle between the director and his lead actor dominated the filming of *Fahrenheit.* On February 18, Werner refused to act a scene with his flamethrower, and Truffaut had to use his stand-in. On the 22nd, Werner took the liberty of giving Julie Christie and Cyril Cusack acting instructions. "We must put up with each other until the end of April," the director told his actor. "It isn't the film you envisioned and it isn't the film I envisioned, it's somewhere in between, and that's the way things are.

Now, if you don't like the scene the way I'm filming it, you can just stay in your dressing room and I'll shoot without you or use your stand-in."[114] Werner finally yielded, but he sabotaged the last line in the sequence, which Truffaut sacrificed in the editing. The actor refused to give in completely, and he showed up on the set after Easter weekend with his hair cut very short at the nape of the neck and the back of the head, claiming he had fallen asleep at the hairdresser's. Furious, Truffaut could only shoot him facing the camera or wearing a cap, and he had to use his stand-in for scenes where Montag would be seen from the back. After a thirteen-week shoot, completed on April 15, 1966, Truffaut could finally write: "This is the end of my collaboration with Oskar Werner, whom I won't see again before his departure for Hollywood tomorrow, nor, I hope, in the near future."[115]

In early May, the director worked at Pinewood Studios with his English editor, Thom Noble, on a first rough cut of almost two hours. Truffaut wasn't pleased with it. In the beginning of June, he summoned Jean Aurel to London for advice. Aurel felt the film was slow in taking off, and that the female characters should be introduced in reverse order. Truffaut also relied on Bernard Herrmann, who composed almost an hour of music to match the mood of Nicholas Roeg's cinematography, essentially the aggressive red inspired from Hitchcock. Thanks to Herrmann's sharp, strident score, *Fahrenheit* sometimes takes on the tense rhythm of a suspense film.

Fahrenheit 451 was finally completed on July 20, 1966. Though Truffaut was pleased with some of the scenes because of their color or music, or because of Julie Christie's gesture, expression, or the intonation in her voice, he didn't like the film as a whole. Was his poor English at fault? "Unfortunately," he wrote Thom Noble, "we won't have the opportunity to work together on my next films, for, after seeing *Fahrenheit* over and over again, I realize I should give up the idea of making films in English until I really know the language."[116] On June 10, Luigi Chiarini, the director of the Venice Film Festival, came to London to screen the film and decided to present it as an official selection. For Truffaut, this was a first, and also an encouragement. In August, there was another piece of good news from California. Ray Bradbury had seen *Fahrenheit 451* at a Universal screening and liked it: "How rare it is for a writer to walk into a motion picture theater and see his own novel faithfully and excitingly told on the screen. Stop. Truffaut has given me back a gift of my own book done in a new medium by preserving the soul of the original. I am deeply grateful."[117] Even if Truffaut didn't share the writer's enthusiastic reaction, he was touched by it.

In Paris the critical response was cool, polite at best. Michel Cournot, in *Le Nouvel Observateur,* was frankly hostile and rebuked Truffaut for having tried to imitate American movies. *Cahiers du cinéma's* attitude was emblematic of the press's embarrassment about *Fahrenheit 451. Cahiers* was proud of printing Truffaut's journal of the shoot, but Jean-Louis Comolli's positive review of *Fahrenheit* read like a personal favor. In *Cahiers'* list of best films of 1966, *Fahrenheit* would be ranked as number fourteen.

Fahrenheit was well received in Venice, at the September 7 screening, though it was not among the prizewinners three days later. On September 15, on the eve of its commercial release, a gala was held at the Marigny theater in Paris. Among those attending was a radiant Julie Christie, who was wearing a dressy miniskirt. Truffaut had arranged for everyone in the audience to receive a copy of the Bradbury novel, and among the guests, there were about fifteen members of the Académie française who had been invited to "celebrate books." This tie-in with established writers made Truffaut's cinema seem slightly stilted and outmoded, poles apart from the new cinema emerging at that time everywhere in Europe, under the influence of the French New Wave, whose standard-bearer he had been just a few years earlier.

Fahrenheit 451 could not be considered a box-office success, selling only 186,000 tickets during its eighteen-week run. This was not a good return, given the cost of the film. It fared no better in New York, where it opened on November 2, 1966. When all was said and done, Truffaut felt only relief at being rid of a project that had occupied him for six years. "I can tell you quite frankly that I can breathe more easily now that our long, common adventure of *Fahrenheit 451* has come to an end," he wrote to Ray Bradbury. "Even if it was an exciting adventure, I must admit I often felt crushed by the scope of the project. Perhaps I was too ambitious, and I constantly feared my efforts wouldn't be equal to your work."[118]

THE HITCHBOOK

In the summer of 1965, at the same time as he was starting the preproduction work for *Fahrenheit 451*, François Truffaut was finishing his book of Hitchcock interviews, exasperated at being behind schedule. He had to write the preface, which was "terribly difficult to do,"[119] he wrote Helen Scott, for it had to be addressed to critics and film enthusiasts as well as to a wider American and French readership. Truffaut completed the first version in mid-May, twenty-odd pages, which he sent to Scott for translation.

In mid-August 1965, Hitchcock received a copy of the interviews in English, just when he was immersed in the preproduction of *Torn Curtain*. Truffaut felt impatient and worried; with no news from Hitchcock, he no longer had control of the project. Then, in October, he received a long letter, in which Hitchcock poured out all his feelings about his new film, its structure and the choice of actors, and concluded with just two quick sentences on the interviews: "You have done a wonderful job. Two or three small changes will have to be made so as not to offend anyone. All is well."[120] Included with this letter was a carefully annotated copy of the interviews. Truffaut and Helen Scott were relieved. It was only later, when the book was in galleys, that Truffaut learned that Hitchcock was not quite satisfied with the English text, which he felt wasn't "sufficiently colloquial,"[121] and that this was delaying American publication. On July 27, 28, and 29, 1966, the three collaborators met at Claridges in London for a final interview devoted to *Marnie* and *Torn Curtain,* bringing the entire undertaking to a close. In August 1966, Truffaut had the huge manuscript of *Le Cinéma selon Alfred Hitchcock* delivered to his publisher, Robert Laffont—over 750 pages and 300 photos. "If I were to produce the book according to your specifications," the publisher wrote Truffaut, "it would be 416 pages long in a large 15.5 × 24 cm. format and carry a minimum price tag of 57 francs. I feel this price would be prohibitive for a certain kind of customer."[122] He raised the possibility of a paperback edition, which would require substantial cuts in the manuscript. Truffaut refused and managed to persuade Laffont that the book had chances of attracting a wide readership—not just film enthusiasts.

The following summer Laffont produced a large, almost square edition of 260 pages, including nearly 350 photos. It looked splendid—and Truffaut was very proud of it. It came out in October 1966. The American edition, *Hitchcock* by François Truffaut, was published by Simon and Schuster in November 1967 and looked even more elegant than the French book. Though sales in France stagnated at around 5,000 copies, in the United States the book was a commercial success—it sold 15,000 copies in hardcover and 21,000 in paperback. Between 1967 and 1973, Truffaut earned $23,000 in royalties. He set the money aside for Helen Scott, without whom he could never have successfully completed the book. Loyal in friendship, discreet in his way of helping friends, Truffaut would make several deposits in her bank account to "feed the brat,"[123] as he put it.

Critics in France hailed this new type of book: "a revolution in film criticism,"[124] wrote *Les Nouvelles littéraires.* Just as Truffaut got news of the first foreign publications, in Germany, Italy, Spain, Denmark, and England, he also received the compliment that moved him most, from Hitchcock: "I think the book has turned out wonderfully well, and I must congratulate you. I think the illustrations make a big difference to it. *Bravo et milliers de mercis.*"[125] The two men had become friends and would write to each other regularly—short, affectionate notes, long letters, and mutual words of advice on scripts in progress. Up until Hitchcock's death in 1980, Truffaut would never fail to visit the "master of suspense" whenever he was in California; he wrote articles and prefaces about him, and took part in tributes to this man who, largely thanks to Truffaut himself, was finally recognized in the United States as a full-fledged auteur and true creative genius.

DEATHLY PALE THRILLER

To live up to his promise to Marcel Berbert, who was worried about Les Films du Carrosse's financial situation, François Truffaut planned to get back to work very quickly and direct what he called a "B picture." He had in mind a small film with a budget of $400,000 for the spring of 1967. *La Mariée était en noir (The Bride Wore Black)* was a project that actually dated back to the summer of 1964; it had been conceived as a tribute to Jeanne Moreau, a woman he loved and one who had become an intimate friend.

At that time, Jeanne Moreau had just broken up with Pierre Cardin. She had left the Paris designer's apartment and moved in with Micheline Rozan, her agent, before going to stay in her own house in the Var. Feeling extremely despondent, she had called Truffaut, who, having just broken up with Madeleine six months before, was also undergoing a crisis in his personal life. They picked up the thread of a love affair that had started during the pre-production of *Jules and Jim*. "In the Midi, we were perfectly happy together. As always, I am confronted with the same problem—whether to fight it or not fight it, whether to wait for things to happen or make things happen, pessimism or optimism, whether to live for the future or the present, whether to want or not want, etc."[126] Their liaison lasted all summer and into the filming of *Mata-Hari* in the fall. "We're not too easy on each other, but we treat each other with great gentleness and tenderness, we're a bit fearful of each other but not too much. . . ."[127] Truffaut wrote to Helen Scott. The desire for a second shared project was born from this brief new love affair.

Truffaut started looking for a really good part for Moreau. In August 1964, he asked Helen Scott to help him acquire the rights to a detective novel by William Irish, *The Bride Wore Black*, which he had read as an adolescent. Irish, whose real name was Cornell Woolrich, was a literary celebrity in the early thirties. Later, he lived as a recluse with his mother in a New York hotel room. A diabetic and an alcoholic, he had found it difficult to recover from his mother's death in 1957, but he had lived on for eleven years in desperate solitude. Affected with gangrene, he had had to have a leg amputated. At his death, he left Columbia University a trust fund of a million dollars. He was the bard of *noir*, of black gloom and darkness, words that recur obsessively in almost all his titles: *The Bride Wore Black, The Black Angel, The Black Path of Fear, Rendez-vous in Black, Waltz into Darkness*. Truffaut was fascinated by his work and would end up adapting two of his novels—*The Bride Wore Black* and *Mississippi Mermaid (La*

Sirène du Mississippi was the French title of *Waltz into Darkness*). He also wrote two very appreciative articles about him. "I see Irish . . . as the artist of fear, terror and sleepless nights. There are very few gangsters in his books. When there are, they are in the background. The plot usually centers around an ordinary man or woman with whom the reader can easily identify. But Irish's heroes never do things by halves and no unforeseen event can stop their march toward love and death. His world frequently also includes amnesia and mental problems, and his hypervulnerable, hypersensitive fictional characters are at the opposite extreme from the usual American hero. Just as there is a touch of Queneau in David Goodis, there is a touch of Cocteau in Irish, and it is this combination of American violence and poetic French prose that I find moving."[128]

Through Helen Scott, Truffaut learned that William Irish lived at the Sheraton-Russell Hotel on Park Avenue. He assigned Don Congdon, who had become his American agent, the task of negotiating with the writer for the movie rights to *The Bride Wore Black*. "I suggested to William Irish that we meet for lunch or a drink," Don Congdon recalls, "and he answered that this wouldn't be possible because he wrote in the afternoon. So we agreed to meet at breakfast. When I saw him approaching, I was taken aback; he looked like he had risen from the grave: He was pale, with grayish skin. He was a very secretive, solitary person."[129] Truffaut made a point of telling Don Congdon that he wanted to sign "a simpler, more advantageous contract than the one for *Fahrenheit 451*.[130] On September 17, 1964, Congdon informed Truffaut that Irish's asking price was fifty thousand dollars. Finding the amount excessive, Truffaut limited himself to an option, while Les Films du Carrosse tried to find cofinancing for the film. Oscar Lewenstein, coproducer at MCA of *Fahrenheit 451*, was the first to come to his rescue. Negotiations lasted until the autumn of 1965, with Lewenstein eventually buying the rights to *The Bride Wore Black* for forty thousand dollars. Given this partnership with Lewenstein, Truffaut briefly considered making another film in English at Pinewood Studios in the spring of 1967, but the lukewarm response to *Fahrenheit 451* led him to reconsider. His next film would be made in France and, if possible, co-produced by Carrosse and United Artists, the company with which Lewenstein had reached an agreement.

United Artists delayed in answering, so Truffaut began to consider other projects for Jeanne Moreau. In early 1967, Ray Bradbury suggested that Truffaut direct a short feature adapted from one of his short stories, *The Picasso Summer*. It had a wonderful plot: On a beach in Biarritz, a rich American tourist, George Smith, suddenly sees a small, lean, suntanned man emerge from the water. Using his finger, the man begins to draw on the moist sand with such skill that George Smith is enthralled. Then the little man goes back into the water as suddenly as he had appeared. This man was none other than Picasso. The tide rises and soon his drawings are washed away by the sea. Picasso himself had been contacted by Bradbury and had agreed to take part in the film; Truffaut wrote back to Bradbury immediately to accept his offer. But when he read the screenplay Bradbury sent him, Truffaut was far less tempted: "To be completely frank, since we've always been frank with each other, I must tell you that for me this detailed treatment fails to capture the inventive originality of your short story."[131] In the end, *The Picasso Summer* would be directed by Serge Bourguignon, "but the film was so bad," Bradbury confessed, "it never had a theatrical release."[132]

French offers abounded, as well, but none would retain Truffaut's attention. Certainly not the one made by Nicole Stéphane, the actress who had played in *Le Silence de la mer* and *Les Enfants terribles* (*The Strange Ones*) and who was now a producer. "On rereading *Swann's Way*," Truffaut wrote her, "it became patently obvious to me that I shouldn't touch it and that it just shouldn't be touched. . . . There was no doubt in my mind that you'd have to be a butcher to accept to film the Verdurin Salon and I learned that, far from being at all worried by my silence, you recently contacted just such a butcher, René Clément, who once again demonstrated his shameless vulgarity and instantly jumped on the opportunity."[133]

In December 1966, Oscar Lewenstein finally persuaded United Artists to let Truffaut shoot *The Bride Wore Black* in France and in French. A coproduction arrangement was reached between Les Films du Carrosse and UA that would last about ten years and allow Truffaut to make his films with greater financial peace of mind. Also, in early 1967, Helen Scott decided to move to Paris to be closer to Truffaut, with whom she hoped to work regularly. "François had tried to warn Helen about moving to Paris, feeling she might be under illusions,"[134] says Madeleine Morgenstern. Indeed, Truffaut kept a certain distance from Helen, as was sometimes his way with his best friends, out of self-protection and to avoid causing disappointment. This often gave rise to misunderstandings and a coolness in his friendships, for Truffaut was guided by a strict work ethic that was not to be weakened by personal ties. In Paris, Helen Scott first worked as an agent for Universal Studios, then as a translator, writing the English subtitles for French films. She rented an apartment on rue de la Pompe, very close to rue de Passy, where Truffaut lived. He looked after her, of course, and introduced her to his best friends, eager to increase Helen's chances of finding work. "When Helen came to France, we became good friends," Claudine Bouché recounts. "She used to tell me about her life with François on a daily basis, their quarrels. She wasn't past making nasty cracks. She had a complex about her physical appearance and in her professional capacities had a constant need for some kind of recognition. François advised her to write and do translations in her free time."[135]

In February 1967, Truffaut published an article in *Le Nouvel Observateur* praising Claude Berri's first feature, *Le Veil Homme et l'Enfant* (*The Two of Us*), an autobiographical story of a Jewish child who is taken in during the German Occupation by a retired worker (marvelously played by Michel Simon) "who is fiercely and adamantly anti-Semitic."[136] "He believed in me; he helped me a lot; he encouraged me enormously,"[137] says Claude Berri. A true friendship would develop between the two directors; Truffaut would even be Claude Berri's witness at his marriage to Anne-Marie Rassam in October 1967. A bachelor again, since his divorce from Madeleine, Truffaut found a real family in the Berris—a warm, enthusiastic, rather eccentric family, in whose midst Helen Scott was also welcomed. Claude Berri's brother-in-law, Jean-Pierre Rassam, the most imaginative young French producer of the late sixties and early seventies, became one of Helen's best friends, the person who rivaled Truffaut in her heart.

Several months earlier, during the 1966 Christmas vacation, François Truffaut had moved into the Hotel Martinez in Cannes with Jean-Louis Richard to adapt *The Bride Wore Black* for the screen. The writing of the script progressed rapidly. The plot centered around serial killings, the murderess being Julie Kohler, a young widow in pursuit of her victims. The task facing Richard and Truffaut was to make these murderous acts of revenge seem credible without blackening the part played by Jeanne Moreau. The heroine couldn't be either crazy or hysterical, but obsessive, determined to execute her plan methodically.

In February, Truffaut had a 237-page script; it was rather faithful to Irish's novel, though the names of the characters had been Frenchified. *The Bride Wore Black* is a film with a logical construction and studied effects, carefully calculated to create tension and suspense. Truffaut was particularly mindful not to reveal the plot before the film's release. For this, he pledged the entire cast and crew to secrecy and even distributed a misleading synopsis to the press describing the story as "a woman investigating her husband's disappearance. . . ."[138]

The early days of spring 1967 were devoted to casting, location scouting, and resolving technical details. Six male actors were needed to play opposite Jeanne Moreau, and Truffaut was happy for the opportunity to direct actors whom he had long admired. Among them, his friend Jean-Claude Brialy, "the only dawn to dusk actor," whom he cast in the part of Corey, the only man to escape Julie Kohler's murderous revenge because he had no part in her husband's murder. As Julie Kohler's five victims, Truffaut cast Claude

Rich, Michel Bouquet, Michael Lonsdale, Charles Denner, and Daniel Boulanger.

THE COLORS OF THE BRIDE

On May 16, 1967, Carrosse's usual crew, gathered around Raoul Coutard and Suzanne Schiffman, met in Cannes to begin shooting in a rented apartment at the Résidence Saint-Michel. The fourteen outfits worn by Jeanne Moreau in the film, all in black and white, were designed for her by Pierre Cardin. But *The Bride Wore Black* was a color film and this soon became a subject of dissension between Truffaut and Coutard, his cinematographer. From the very first day of the shoot, Truffaut found the scenes underlit. He quarreled with Coutard for the first time, and interrupted the filming for two days. *The Bride* would turn out to be their last collaboration. "Coutard had always had a bad temper," says Claudine Bouché, the editor of the film, "and François didn't like Coutard's intransigence, particularly since he loved to fiddle with an image and reframe it when he so desired. Coutard called this 'mistreating the film stock.' "[139] As a result of this discord, the filming was tense, with Truffaut expending a great deal of energy on trying to convince Coutard, so that part of the job of directing the actors fell to Jeanne Moreau and Jean-Louis Richard. "It was a difficult shoot," Jeanne Moreau recalls. "There were tensions between François and Coutard because the light was supposed to change radically every week to suggest different locations, while in fact our shooting locations were geographically close. François was very mysterious, very secretive. He never spoke on the set. In *Jules and Jim*, there had been a lot of improvisation, in *The Bride*, none at all. The mood was very different."[140] Aside from the disagreement between Truffaut and Coutard, another difficulty was that the male actors had small parts, which gave them very little time to get into the atmosphere of the film. Truffaut, absorbed in sticking to the logic of his shooting script and more secretive than usual, put Jeanne Moreau in charge of explaining to each actor his part. "François would say to me: 'Listen, you take care of it. . . .' So each time, I had to take over and reassure my next murder victim."[141] The only moment when the cast and crew felt comfortable was when they shot the scenes between Charles Denner and Jeanne Moreau in the painter Fergus's studio. Truffaut had rented Victor Herbert's Paris studio, on rue du Val-de-Grâce, and commissioned Charles Matton to make some paintings, including several portraits of Jeanne Moreau. Truffaut got along well with Denner and put into his mouth many of his own personal expressions and fantasies. Fergus's entire speech on women, which foreshadows *The Man Who Loved Women,* could be likened to the "intimate journal of a womanizer," which Truffaut could have kept on a daily basis. Truffaut spent August through October 1967 editing his film with Claudine Bouché, assisted by Yann Dedet. He commissioned Bernard Herrmann for the music, but this time he was a bit disappointed with the result.

Truffaut had hoped this film would help Jeanne Moreau during a difficult period in her life. But the opposite occurred: Throughout the entire filming, it was Jeanne Moreau who came to his aid. Truffaut extolled her good humor and sense of solidarity to Hitchcock:

> On the set, she is ready to perform quickly or slowly, be funny or sad, serious or nutty, do anything that the director asks. And when misfortune strikes, she sticks by the captain of the ship: with no fuss or to-do, without singing "Nearer, my God, to Thee . . . ,' she will just go down by his side. The danger for her in *The Bride* is that her part is simply too extraordinary; the heroine, a woman who dominates men and then kills them, is too "prestigious." To counterbalance this, I asked Jeanne to play the part with simplicity, in a manner that is familiar and would make her actions unexpected, plausible and human. As I see it, Julie is a virgin, since her husband was killed at the church on the day of their wedding. But this revelation doesn't come out in the film and will have to remain a secret between Jeanne Moreau, you and me.[142]

Truffaut blamed himself and felt guilty for not rendering Jeanne Moreau's beauty on the screen. She looked tired, her face reflecting the trials she had been through in the mid-sixties. Furthermore, Truffaut disliked Cardin's costumes. Of all his films, *The Bride Wore Black* would be the one he liked least, except for the Charles Denner episode and the sequence with Michael Lonsdale.

Released on April 17, 1968, *The Bride Wore Black* sold 300,000 tickets during its fourteen-week exclusive run in Paris and the Paris area; it was therefore an unquestionable success. Furthermore, contrary to Truffaut's expectations, the reviews were not bad. But only one comment on the film really touched Truffaut, and that was Hitchcock's: "I especially liked the scene of Moreau watching the man who had taken poison Arak dying slowly. I think my particular sense of humour might have taken them a little further so that Moreau could have picked up a cushion and put it under his head so that he could die with more comfort."[143] Truffaut wrote two long letters in reply, with lengthy comments on the scripts of *Frenzy* and *Topaz*, which Hitchcock had sent him. However, the French director's "Hitchcockian" period—which started with *The Soft Skin,* included *Fahrenheit 451,* and ended with *The Bride Wore Black*—had not been a resounding success, as Truffaut himself was the first to realize.

FRAMBOISE

"Françoise, Framboise, death in the summer. I knew it was painful. What is solitude? It is the intolerable,"[144] Truffaut wrote ten days after his friend's death. On June 27, 1967, Françoise Dorléac was killed on the road to the Nice airport, burned alive in a car accident. Truffaut was shattered by this tragedy; it left him distressed during the filming of *The Bride*, which took place not far from the scene of the actress's death. Françoise Dorléac and François Truffaut had shared the same literary and cinematic tastes, and they had seen each other very often after their brief romance in the days of *The Soft Skin*. They had remained very close, sharing a tender and solid friendship, almost like Truffaut's friendship with Jeanne Moreau. A month prior to the accident, he had written to her London agent, stressing his intention of working with the twenty-five-year-old actress far into the future: "The problem, for many young actresses, is to make a successful transition from young girl to woman, to switch from juvenile parts to adult ones. Françoise Dorléac, who will always be Framboise Dorléac for me, won't have these difficulties, for she is a precocious, premature woman, with a constructed face and body, constructed firmly, to last. She is the only young actress who might very conceivably have greater and greater appeal. She has nothing to fear from added years, for time works in her favor. I'm delighted to think that I'll be collaborating with her again in 1970, 1976, 1982, 1988, etc., etc. See you soon, Framboise!"[145]

This life cut short intensified François Truffaut's deep melancholy, in a decade of collective vigor and enthusiasm. For him, those years were punctuated by separations, professional and emotional disappointments, hesitations, and bereavements. This was not immediately apparent in the two films he had just directed, *Fahrenheit 451* and *The Bride;* they seem well mastered and clear, indeed almost academic, as many critics pointed out at the time. However, there is a detectable vulnerability in them, a shadow, as suggested by Jean-Louis Comolli in the profile he wrote of Truffaut in *Cahiers du cinéma* in May 1967: "Behind these more or less obvious virtues—an air of such mastery, calm and seriousness that it is sometimes irritating—there is one virtue that is so concealed and secret that it is generally overlooked; it could be antagonistic to all the others except that it is precisely the mainspring of them all—anxiety."[146]

Truffaut remained whimsical and imaginative, but these setbacks and difficulties affected him deeply. Jean-Pierre Melville, in whom Truffaut had confided far into the night of March 20, 1963, when plans for the French production of *Fahrenheit* had fallen through, saw these successive trials as a painful but vital way for him to assert himself: "The failure of *The Soft Skin* and especially of *Fahrenheit*," Melville said at the time to Raoul Lévy, "will allow him to become an adult who will finally know life, thanks to the truly negative experiences of moviemaking, those that enrich even more than they impoverish. This will allow him to change the direction of his work and set it on the right course—not with peace of mind but with true freedom in relation to himself—toward expressing what *one has to say* and no longer what *one would like to say*."[147]

6.
PARALLEL LIVES:
1968–1971

DETECTIVE DOINEL

In 1968, Truffaut thought of a new project involving Antoine Doinel, his creation and alter ego. At first, he had wanted Doinel to be a journalist, in a film with the tentative title *Un jeune homme à Paris* (A Young Man in Paris). But finally he gave up the idea of journalism, as conventional and too literary and instead decided to make Doinel a private detective. The idea came to him from reading the back of a telephone directory: "Dubly Agency: Research, surveillance, investigations." He gave Claude de Givray and Bernard Revon the task of conducting a preliminary investigation into a detective agency, stressing that they be discreet and not mention his name. "Say it's a series for television!"[1] he told them. De Givray and Revon spent the entire spring of 1967 on preproduction work at Dubly Détective, a private agency on rue Saint-Lazare, run by a passionate cinema lover, Albert Duchenne. Claude de Givray recalls these work sessions with Duchenne, who ended up being a genuine collaborator on the script. "Albert Duchenne told us how to draw up a fake adultery report. A detective need only catch a wife in a hotel room with her lover; he requests that the husband be present, but the husband's testimony is insufficient, since he is both judge and litigant. The detective advises the husband to break everything in the room, until the night watchman calls the police. That way, the night watchman is a witness to disturbance of the peace. And it will be on record that the person who caused the disturbance is a jealous husband who had caught his wife in bed with her lover."[2] In the screenplay Doinel, who has just left the army, first gets a job as a night watchman in a Paris hotel and then as a private eye. To complete their research, de Givray and Revon questioned the personnel at the Terrass Hotel overlooking Montmartre cemetery—the very hotel where Truffaut had met Jean Genet sixteen years earlier.

In June, they gave Truffaut a first screenplay while he was completing *The Bride Wore Black*. It was entitled *Baisers volés (Stolen Kisses)*, a title chosen as a tribute to the singer Charles Trenet.[3] Ilya Lopert, head of the French branch of United Artists, was not entirely convinced by the screenplay, but he wanted to continue collaborating with Truffaut. United Artists reached an agreement with Carrosse, whereby they would invest up to $250,000 in the film and the profits would be split between the two companies. This was a smaller financial contribution on the part of United Artists than had been expected, which obliged Truffaut to keep his costs down in making the film.

In December 1967, helped by Revon and de Givray, Truffaut wrote a second version of the script of *Stolen Kisses,* for he wanted it to be a flexible chronicle "so improvisation can have the last word."[4] After the highly structured screenplays of *Fahrenheit 451* and *The Bride Wore Black*, Truffaut returned to moviemaking that renders the small events of life, leaves room for the imagination and the mood of the moment, and draws its inspiration from Renoir and Lubitsch rather than Hitchcock. A few months before the radical student uprisings of May 1968, Truffaut created a hero who seemed anachronistic, from another era, a romantic incapable of adapting to life or finding a stable job. The director's inspiration was entirely culled from the past, from his own youthful memories—the army, the visits to brothels, his desire to be accepted into a family.

Nine years after *The 400 Blows* and six years after *Antoine and Colette*, Truffaut was about to engage in a new collaboration with Jean-Pierre Léaud for the third Antoine Doinel adventure. Now twenty-three, the actor had become one of Godard's emblematic figures; between 1965 and 1967, he had appeared in *Pierrot le fou, Masculin-Féminin, Made in USA, La Chinoise, Weekend,* and the director's episode in *Le Plus Vieux Métier du monde.* He had acquired sufficient presence and strength of character so that Antoine Doinel began to resemble him more and more. In fact, beginning with *Stolen Kisses*, Doinel is part Truffaut, part Léaud. Increasingly, the character's gestures, attitudes, anecdotes, and even memories belong to Léaud himself. Truffaut was fully aware of this and encouraged it, never curbing Léaud's inspiration and improvisations. Léaud still lived in the bosom of the Carrosse family. He was lodged, most of the time, two flights above the company's offices, on rue Robert-Estienne, in an apartment rented by Truffaut on the fifth floor of the building. Except for periods when they were filming separately, Truffaut and Léaud would see each other regularly. There wasn't a single screenplay, a single film, television, or theater project offered to Léaud that wasn't first examined by Truffaut, whose opinion the actor always sought.

In January 1968, with advice from Gérard Lebovici and Serge Rousseau, his friends at the Artmédia agency, Truffaut began casting *Stolen Kisses*. The two women over whom Antoine Doinel is torn, Christine Darbon and Fabienne Tabard, must endow the film with romantic credibility. In the part of Fabienne—a "beautiful woman with a very vague, very gentle air"[5]—Truffaut had always visualized Delphine Seyrig, an actress he had admired in her two Alain Resnais films, *Last Year at Marienbad* and *Muriel*. On December 10, 1964, Truffaut saw Seyrig perform in Harold Pinter's *The Lover* at the Hébertot theater and was very impressed. She invited him to dinner that evening at her house on Place des Vosges. She reminded him of Louise de Vilmorin, the author of *Madame de . . .* , who had captivated him in 1950 when he was a young man; he found a similarity in her delicate traits and, to use Doinel's words, her "very pure oval" face, her pale complexion, "luminous, as though lit from the inside," and her very distinctive phrasing, "an admirable, deep tone." The actress was touched that she was selected for the part: "For me, I told you, the film will be like you and that is what counts. As for Fabienne 'de Mortsauf' I *adore* her. Though I have questions I'd like to ask you about her, and about Félix Antoine Léaud de Vandemesse. In any case, I'm having a lot of fun thinking about them."[6] Truffaut based the plot and atmosphere of the Antoine Doinel–Fabienne Tabard encounter on Balzac's *The Lily in the Valley*, which Jean-Pierre Léaud is reading at the beginning of the film. The analogy suited Delphine Seyrig perfectly; she was the ideal reincarnation of Madame de Mortsauf, the heroine of the Balzac novel.

Though the filming of *Stolen Kisses* was only several weeks away, the part of Christine Darbon, the pretty girl whom Antoine Doinel marries at the end of the picture, was still not cast. In late November 1967, Truffaut had attended the dress rehearsal of Pirandello's *Enrico IV*, directed by the well-known actor-director Sacha Pitoëff at the Théâtre Moderne, and saw a young nineteen-year-old actress, Claude Jade, perform onstage. He returned several times to see her perform, and a month later, he offered her the part of Christine Darbon. Thus did Claude Jade enter the life of Antoine Doinel—and of François Truffaut. From a good Protestant family of university teachers, she had a baccalaureate degree in philosophy and had came to Paris from Dijon, where she had studied dramatic art at the conservatory. Truffaut "was completely taken by her beauty, her manners, her kindness and her joie de vivre."[7] Claude Jade says, "I must have fit the image of the pure young girl. I was the right age and he felt Jean-Pierre Léaud, alias Antoine Doinel, and I could make a plausible couple. The first time I met him, François told me I looked like I belonged in a salon; he had been very amused because I used to answer politely, 'Yes, Monsieur, fine, Monsieur.' He stole little details from everyone—from me, my good upbringing, in my character's nickname, 'Peggy Proper'—Peggy because of her slight British air and because François knew I was the daughter of an English professor, and it amused him."[8]

Daniel Ceccaldi and Claire Duhamel were cast as the likable and friendly Darbon parents: "François said he liked girls who had nice parents,"[9] Claude Jade adds. Michael Lonsdale plays the unforgettable Monsieur Tabard, owner of the shoe shop, nicknamed "the Dinosaur" by his employees. Others in the cast include Jacques Robiolles, who was a friend of Truffaut; André Falcon as the owner of the detective agency; and Harry Max and Jacques Rispal. Truffaut felt very strongly about these supporting roles, for they were to instill life into the milieu in which the film was set. Marie-France Pisier replays Colette in a brief appearance, while Serge Rousseau plays the strange man in the trench coat who trails Christine Darbon and declares his "definitive" love at the end of the film.

In early February 1968, Truffaut was ready to film Stolen Kisses, with a crew that was almost entirely new. Clearly, this was a minor revolution. Suzanne Schiffman, acting as script supervisor and assistant, was one of the few people he kept from his previous team. He hired Denys Clerval as director of photography, Agnès Guillemot as editor, Antoine Duhamel to compose a tune "à la Charles Trenet," Jean-José Richer, formerly at Cahiers, as first assistant, and Roland Thénot, who had already worked on The Bride, as unit manager. All the preproduction work for the film had been accomplished in a mere two months; the success of a project is "10 percent inspiration and 90 percent perspiration,"[10] as the owner of the Blady detective agency observes in Stolen Kisses.

On February 5, 1968, on the eve of his thirty-sixth birthday, Truffaut was back in his childhood neighborhood—Villiers and Montmartre, Notre-Dame-de-Lorette and Place Clichy. The filming of his seventh feature took place at a swift, lively pace over the course of seven weeks. The actors remained true to their ways—Léaud read his lines only at the very last minute, while Claude Jade memorized them as soon as she could. But the ensemble worked harmoniously. The only sequence to present problems was the one in which Fabienne Tabard offers herself to Antoine Doinel in his furnished room; it was filmed on March 1 and 2 at the Avenir Hotel on boulevard de Rochechouart. Delphine Seyrig felt nervous, dissatisfied with her acting. "I very quickly realized how little I contributed to Stolen

Kisses,"[11] she later wrote to Truffaut, though he was sincerely captivated by her elegance and presence. "I'm in despair that I'm so lacking in inventiveness; Jean-Pierre Léaud impressed me—and everyone, I think—with his charm and freedom of movement and speech in front of the camera. You see, he has exactly the qualities I wanted to have. His freedom with words, his ease in improvising, this is what I would most like to acquire. And he has this naturally. I wish I had been more equal to the task."[12] Truffaut, however, felt that all his actors had performed at their best. He thought of *Stolen Kisses*—a light project, hastily written and shot—as one of those movies "saved in the filming,"[13] the kind he generally liked, dear to him because of the good memories they evoked.

SCANDAL AT THE CINÉMATHÈQUE

The filming of *Stolen Kisses* would always remain associated in Truffaut's mind with one of the most exciting periods in his life—the mobilization to save Henri Langlois's Cinémathèque. One of Truffaut's last shots was filmed on March 29, 1968, in front of the locked gates of the Cinémathèque at the Palais de Chaillot. "This film is dedicated to Henri Langlois's Cinémathèque française," it says at the beginning of *Stolen Kisses.* And then we see a sign (in French) that reads CLOSED. THE DATE OF REOPENING WILL BE ANNOUNCED IN THE PRESS.

On February 7, 1968, two days into the filming, Jean-Louis Comolli, editor in chief of *Cahiers du cinéma,* tried to reach François Truffaut on the set. Rumors were circulating about the Cinémathèque's board of directors meeting in two days. It seemed Henri Langlois, the founder and director, was being seriously threatened with removal.[14] A visionary with insatiable energy, though he thrived in constant chaos, Langlois was a veritable symbol, for Truffaut as well as for scores of film lovers. Dismissing him would be a crime of "lèse-cinema." Truffaut, a member of the Cinémathèque's board of directors since the beginning of 1968, had not always agreed with Langlois's conception of his duties as film collector and programmer,[15] but he would be on the front line of the struggle to keep him in his position. Absorbed by his shoot, Truffaut had not planned to attend the board of directors meeting and had sent his proxy vote to Langlois. But Comolli's phone call had made him change his filming schedule for the day; he was at the Cinémathèque headquarters on rue de Courcelles on Friday morning, February 9.

Logically, the board of directors should have extended Langlois's mandate as director of the institution which he had created in 1936. But after paying him a glowing tribute, Pierre Moinot, an official from the Ministry of

Cultural Affairs and also the new president of the Cinémathèque, suggested, oddly enough, that Langlois be replaced by Pierre Barbin, director of the Tours and Annecy festivals. Several members of the board requested a week to make up their minds, but their request was denied. A vote was taken. The minority of independents, among whom were Jean Riboud, Ambroise Roux, Yvonne Dornès, François Truffaut, and several others, walked out of the meeting without voting. Barbin was elected to succeed Langlois. Quite obviously, everything had been arranged beforehand. One month before, rumors had already been circulating in the corridors of the Centre national de la cinématographie (CNC), an organization directed by André Holleaux. Langlois's friends had been wrong not to take these rumors seriously, so untouchable did Langlois seem to them. Two weeks before, during the Tours festival, a secret meeting had taken place among Barbin, Holleaux, Moinot, and Chevasson, an attaché in the cabinet of Minister of Culture André Malraux, to iron out the final details of a scheme that had originated at the highest levels. The maneuver seemed like an attempt to put the CNC, a supervisory government body, in control of the Cinémathèque, an independent nonprofit association with almost 780 members. Only the government subsidies the Cinémathèque received placed it in a dependent position vis-à-vis the Ministry of Cultural Affairs. There lay the great argument of the anti-Langlois faction: He was not a good administrator and put a serious strain on the institution with his odd habits and expenses.

The former *Cahiers* collaborators—Truffaut, Godard, Rivette, Chabrol, as well as Doniol-Valcroze, Kast, Astruc, and Renoir—defended Langlois. And now the protagonists of the fifties rebellion against "official" cinema were famous and had the support of the new generation—Marcel Ophuls, Claude Berri, Luc Moullet, Jean Eustache, Philippe Garrel, and the entire *Cahiers* editorial staff. A Defense Committee was led with ardor by Truffaut; its headquarters were at the offices of *Cahiers du cinéma*.

Undoubtedly thinking the matter was settled, André Holleaux left for a two-week vacation. On February 9 Pierre Barbin, accompanied by a small group of faithful supporters, moved into Langlois's office, making sure to change the locks. Several days later, Langlois's colleagues were fired— Marie Epstein, Lotte Eisner, and Mary Meerson.

On the morning of February 10, Langlois's friends began working shifts to gather the signatures of French and foreign directors. A hundred telegrams were sent from the post office on rue Clément Marot, near the *Cahiers* offices. The magazine's staff and the Carrosse secretaries were glued to the phone. They went through lists of personalities, letting their New Wave elders—excited by this renewed rebellious spirit—do the talking when appropriate. By early afternoon, a motion invited "all friends of cinema to show solidarity with any action that might reverse the arbitrary decision made against Henri Langlois."[16] On February 11, Renoir, Pagnol, and Tati responded, banning the screening of their films at the Cinémathèque if Langlois was not reinstated. Others followed suit—Gance, Resnais, Franju, Godard, Marker, Astruc, Chabrol, Bresson, Mocky, Robert Florey, Richard Lester, Lindsay Anderson, Henri Cartier-Bresson, Michel Simon, Busby Berkeley. They received signed petitions—from members of the association of Danish directors, headed by Carl Dreyer, and from the association of American critics, led by Andrew Sarris—and a manifesto of Japanese film-makers, drafted by Kurosawa, Oshima, Naruse, Yoshida, and sixteen others. There were also impressive telegrams from such well-known personalities as Josef von Sternberg, Jerry Lewis, Gloria Swanson, Chaplin, Rossellini, and Fritz Lang, all of whom banned further screenings of their films at the Cinémathèque pending Langlois's reinstatement.

On February 10, the press joined in. Henry Chapier in *Combat* and Jean de Baroncelli in *Le Monde* both carried the headline SCANDAL AT THE CINÉMATHÈQUE. "France is in no way short of good accountants or good administrators. But there was only one Henri Langlois. Will we accept his being snatched away from us?" wrote Baroncelli. On the 12th, Truffaut, Chabrol, Philippe Tesson, and Henry Chapier (with the famous headline THE MALRAUX MYTH HAS LASTED LONG ENOUGH) all published articles in *Combat*. Truffaut attacked Malraux violently: "Since taking office, all of André Malraux's decisions concerning cinema have been disastrous. A small frenetic figure, isolated in his dream factory which the striking filmmakers have evacuated, André Malraux should be aware that we don't have a short-term antimemory and that we won't forget he 'dropped' Henri Langlois just as he previously 'dropped' Jacques Flaud, Pierre Boulez, Jean Genet, Gaë-tan Picon, Rivette and his friend Diderot."[17]

On February 12, at 10:00 p.m., in response to an appeal launched by Michel Simon and Claude Berri, two to three hundred directors, critics, film enthusiasts, and actors, including many from the cast and crew of *Stolen Kisses* led by Truffaut, Léaud, and Claude Jade, blocked the entrance to the Cinémathèque screening room on rue d'Ulm. The CNC timidly counterattacked—an unsigned article in *France-Soir* criticized "the confusion into which French cinema and the Cinémathèque have been sinking for years."[18] Claude Autant-Lara was the only one to agree; he attacked Langlois and the New Wave rally around the Cinémathèque on the France Inter radio station. At the same time, the closing of the two Cinémathèque screening rooms for "inventory and reorganization" seemed like the first sign of weakness on the part of the new administration. The mobilization culminated on February 14, a day that marked a milestone—never before had policemen been seen charging into a demonstration of directors and actors. In response to an appeal from the "Children of the Cinémathèque," three thousand people reassembled on the esplanade of the Trocadéro. At 3:00 p.m., about thirty vanloads of police and security forces surrounded the neighborhood, barring access to the Cinémathèque. Television cameras were present; the government-owned French stations avoided reporting the events, but they were reported, briefly, on the foreign stations. A tract was distributed and read publicly by the actor Jean-Pierre Kalfon. Then the crowd headed toward the Palais de Chaillot, chanting, "Holleaux resign!" and "No to the Barbinthèque!" The first police cordon and the first clashes occurred in the gardens of the Trocadéro. Godard succeeded in crossing the barriers but found himself alone, surrounded by police, who let him retreat. The demonstrators bypassed the police cordons, headed back up the esplanade, and marched down the avenue du Président Wilson, blocking traffic. At the corner of the avenue Albert de Mun, where most of the security forces were parked, there was a new, more aggressive police barricade. Several ranks of police charged into the demonstrators. Some people were wounded and required help; Truffaut, severely shaken, was cared for in the entranceway to a building. Godard, stunned, looked for his lost sunglasses; Tavernier had blood dripping down his face; Yves Boisset's wife had been thrown to the ground. The crowd surged back to the Trocadéro and Godard, who was now directing operations, shouted orders to disperse. The troops had been driven back by the police assault, but their fighting spirit lived on. Above all, thanks to this demonstration, public opinion took up the cause of Langlois's defenders. It seems unlikely that the police prefect was congratulated by Malraux, or President Charles de Gaulle, that evening.

Taking advantage of this moral victory, on February 16 Langlois's supporters held a press conference at the Studio Action attended by three hundred journalists and five foreign television stations. By then, a new communiqué had come down from the ministry, retreating from the CNC's initial positions and suggesting that Langlois should be appointed to "new artistic duties." The text also announced the shelving of the plan dear to Pierre Barbin, of copyrighting films at the Cinémathèque, along the lines of the Bibliothèque Nationale. That plan would have placed Langlois's museum (shaped by his own personal view of the history of cinema) under permanent government control. Langlois's supporters could therefore adopt a confident, victorious tone at the press conference. Godard and Truffaut were still the main speakers, but Rivette, Chabrol, Kast, Doniol-Valcroze, Astruc, Resnais, and Rouch also had their say, advised by the lawyer Georges Kiejman. The journalists left the conference convinced that it was only a matter of days before Langlois would be reinstated, but no one let up the pressure. On February 20, at about 6:00 p.m., following an appeal by Françoise Rosay, Jean Marais, and René Allio, four hundred demonstrators surrounded the Cinémathèque offices on rue de Courcelles. On the

26th, a "committee for the defense of the Cinémathèque française," made up of about twenty film personalities, was created on Truffaut's initiative, with him as treasurer. This committee was in charge of coordinating the actions that were multiplying in France and around the world in support of Langlois. Renoir was the committee's honorary president and Resnais its acting president. On this occasion, Renoir offered a vibrant tribute to Langlois in the press, calling him "the creator of our very own Louvre" and "the only man who can bring together all filmmakers of goodwill."[19]

VIVE LANGLOIS!

André Malraux understood that he had to back down. On March 5, at a meeting of the Cinémathèque's board of directors, Jean Riboud—head of the Schlumberger oil drilling company and a friend of Langlois and his long-time companion, Mary Meerson—suggested an "advisory committee" be set up with the task of finding a compromise. An independent figure, Georges Vedel, former dean of the Faculté de droit et de sciences économiques de Paris, was appointed director. As another proof of goodwill, Rivette was included among the five "wise men" on the committee. The members decided to schedule an extraordinary general meeting of the Cinémathèque membership on April 22, 1968, the only authority that could officially reverse the February 9 decision.

In the meantime, there were ongoing power struggles. Pierre Moinot, the president of the Cinémathèque, tried to eclipse Pierre Barbin, who clung to his prestigious position of artistic director. Lotte Eisner and Mary Meerson were still undesirables at rue de Courcelles. The defense committee began to worry about management's tergiversations and thought the latter might try to take advantage of a deteriorating situation to set up the new Cinémathèque. Truffaut decided to come out once again in the press and denounce the ministry's compromise solutions. He wrote in *Combat* on March 11, 1968:

> If the Moinot-Barbin duo were just dolts eager to have their blunder forgotten, the fight would indeed be almost won and we could believe that the administration was preparing Barbin's departure and Langlois's return within a proper lapse of time so as not to lose face. In my opinion the opposite is true. For we are facing ill-intentioned people who on some days are afraid, but on others are carried away by the disproportionate promotions they gained through political connections. . . . Formerly, the government used to get rid of blunderers, tactless fools and boors by sending them to Algeria or New Caledonia. In the France of

1968, the Moinots and Barbins cling to Paris, they want to eat at Lipp's, bring festivals to a close, hand out little medals to visiting foreigners and bouquets of flowers to female stars; they dig in their heels, take root, irritate, and they aggravate their cases.

The Langlois affair took a political turn. On March 21, Grenoble rallied to the cause, at the initiative of the two city's film clubs and the local section of the PSU (Socialist party). Le Rex movie theater was too small to accommodate the audience that came to listen to the eminent speaker defending Langlois—Pierre Mendès-France, elected several months earlier as deputy of the city. Truffaut organized this meeting personally, with the help of Jean-Louis Comolli and Georges Kiejman, who was close to Mendès-France. "Grenoble is the biggest punch we could throw at present," Truffaut wrote Comolli on March 8. "Also, I think we should let it be known. . . . Let's try to see each other tonight after the shoot, possibly at my screening of dailies (8:00 p.m., Ponthieu theater), to look into the situation."[20] Several days earlier, during questions addressed to the government at the National Assembly, François Mitterrand had tried to destabilize Malraux on the Langlois issue. The conflict had thus turned overtly political, a development that the committee for the defense of the Cinémathèque wanted to take advantage of. Indeed, on March 26, Truffaut sent Mitterrand a letter and a packet of information on the subject, for use on April 8, when the opposition leader was to appear on the television program *Face à Face*: "We hope that on April 8 you will take advantage of the opportunity to break the silence that the ORTF [French government radio and television] has maintained on this affair since the beginning,"[21] Truffaut wrote to Mitterrand.

On Monday, April 22, 1968, several hundred members of the Cinémathèque française assembled at the auditorium of Arts et Métiers on avenue d'Iéna for the special general meeting on Langlois's fate. Dean Georges Vedel read out the advisory committee's conclusions: "The Cinémathèque, a nonprofit association, will be organized and managed like a private group without state interference into its internal affairs. . . ."[22] Langlois was unanimously reelected to his duties as artistic and technical director. Pierre Moinot and Pierre Barbin were removed, as was the board of directors. On May 2, the theater on rue d'Ulm reopened its doors. Moved and beaming, Langlois encouraged lengthy applause for Truffaut and ended his welcoming speech with a resounding "Make way for the movies!"

For the public present that day, the event was essentially political. Directors and film enthusiasts had had their first taste of territorial struggles waged against the administration and the Gaullist government—street demonstrations, militancy, and defense committees. Every Langlois supporter had lived through his own May '68 two months early. Pierre Kast showed foresight in pointing this out in April, in the two-hundredth issue of *Cahiers du cinéma,* which was dedicated to Langlois: "I realize that though it's impossible to shout 'Long live Castro' without shouting 'Long live Langlois,' it's perfectly possible to shout 'Long live Langlois' without thinking 'Long live Castro.' But still, these scuffles, these tracts, these committee rooms, these discussions reach way beyond the Cinémathèque affair. . . . Cinema has become much more than a commodity retailed in specialized places. And defending the existence of the Cinémathèque française is a political act, oddly enough."

In April 1968, though he willingly shouted "Long live Langlois!" Truffaut had no desire to shout "Long live Castro!" Yet his political commitment against the Gaullist government definitely left a deep mark. From the Manifesto of the 121 in the fall of 1960 to the committee for the defense of the Cinémathèque in the spring of 1968, he showed consistency in thought and action. He always rallied to the cause of freedom of expression against a government that he saw as clumsy, interventionist, censorial, and tactless. However, though Truffaut had rubbed shoulders with people on the Left, and considered them more upright and more attentive to creative freedom, he was not ready to commit himself politically, for he deeply distrusted political discourse and people in politics. "There's the blockheadedness of an impossible régime," he wrote to Louis Marcorelles to explain Langlois's eviction, "but also the fact that, from De Gaulle to Mitterrand and Deferre, except for the modest Mendès-France, too many so-called 'elites' don't understand a thing about cinema and never will."[23]

CURTAINS IN CANNES

After his difficult *Fahrenheit* years, François Truffaut's support of Langlois was a marvelous, "rejuvenating experience." The spring of 1968 infused him with unexpected, renewed enthusiasm. He lived through the period in a feverish, intoxicated state, on very few hours' sleep, his energies divided between a lively, quick shoot and the time-consuming demands of activism. "I can still see him on the avenue Albert de Mun," his friend Georges Kiejman says, "running like a rabbit and jumping over a row of cars to reach the front ranks and join those who were about to get beat up by the police. When I saw him bolting in front of me, he seemed the adolescent from *The 400 Blows* and I remember thinking at the time that no matter what age he would live to, he would remain an eternal adolescent."[24]

Undoubtedly, Truffaut was also happy in the spring of 1968, because he was in love with Claude Jade. The feelings were mutual; and for Claude Jade, who had just turned twenty, Truffaut was her first love. Sacha Pitoëff's wife had even gone and told Claude Jade's parents about their daughter's June marriage plans. Before leaving for England to spend time with her sister, Claude had chosen a wedding dress. The decision to get married had apparently been made on an impulse; Truffaut hadn't warned anyone, outside of his family. He had asked Berbert in passing, "Are you free on such and such a day? . . . Fine! You'll be my witness."[25]

In early May, France was shaken by the great student uprisings in the section of the city near the Sorbonne and the erection of barricades on rue Gay-Lussac. On the 13th, a million demonstrators marched down the streets of Paris, from the République to Denfert-Rochereau, and the whole country was paralyzed by the first day of general strikes involving the electrical company (EDF), public transportation (RAPT), railroads (SNCF), post office, and telephones (all government-owned)—strikes that immediately spread to the private sector. Meanwhile, in Cannes, at the start of the twenty-first film festival, all activity was suspended for twenty-four hours, at the request of the majority of film critics present; the screenings of Carlos Saura's *Peppermint frappé* and Frank Perry's *Trilogy*, based on stories by Truman Capote, which had been scheduled for that day, were postponed to May 18. Truffaut happened to be in Cannes between the 11th and 13th, preparing for two events he felt very strongly about. On Saturday, May 18, he was to join Claude Berri, Roger Vadim, Jacques Robert, and Claude Lelouch, for a press conference, presided over by Alain Resnais, explaining the initiative of the committee for the defense of the Cinémathèque; in the afternoon, he and Henri Langlois were to preside over a tribute to Georges Sadoul, the Communist critic who had died the previous fall. On May 13, given the scope of the general strikes and the first factory sit-ins, Truffaut advised the festival director, Robert Favre Le Bret, simply to interrupt the festival proceedings. He refused. That evening, Truffaut was back in Paris, supervising the editing of *Stolen Kisses* with Agnès Guillemot. The student movement was gaining momentum, and so were the factory strikes; Truffaut followed the events closely on the radio. But not even for a minute did he consider joining the street demonstrations; he remained an attentive witness.

On May 17, in the late morning, he drove back down to Cannes, making good time on deserted roads. At noon on the same day in Paris, a meeting of the technicians' union had been joined by a delegation of striking directors, and it was decided to call for a meeting of all industry professionals, that very night, at the Ecole de Photographie et de Cinéma on rue de Vaugirard, which was occupied by its students. At 9:00 p.m., the entire profession was gathered shoulder-to-shoulder on rue de Vaugirard. The meetings and demonstrations surrounding the Langlois affair had mushroomed into the "Etats généraux du cinéma français" (Estates General of French Cinema), an open call for greater freedom in film and television. Over twelve hundred professionals and students held regular meetings for over two weeks; they took part in endless debates, worked on committees, and presented plans for changing and renewing the film industry. This was tantamount to a small revolution in French cinema, which up to then had customarily been compartmentalized, torn with dissension, and under the supervision of the CNC. Two decisions were made in the course of this first meeting of the Etats généraux: first, a vote in favor of a film workers' strike, effective the next day—thereby interrupting the filming of Gérard Oury's *The Brain* at the Saint-Maurice Studio and the editing of *Stolen Kisses;* second, a motion requesting the shutdown of the Cannes festival, as a show of solidarity for the striking workers and students.

That night, Jacques Rivette, who was present at the first meeting of the Etats généraux, contacted Truffaut at the Hotel Martinez and informed him of these developments. Truffaut in turn notified the other directors attending the festival (Godard, Malle, Lelouch, the Czech filmmakers Jan Němec and Miloš Forman, Resnais, Richard Lester, Roman Polanski, Carlos Saura), suggesting they take action as quickly as possible. Those whose films were in competition—Forman (*The Firemen's Ball*), Resnais (*Je t'aime, je t'aime*), Lelouch (*Grenoble*), Němec (*A Report on the Party and the Guests*), Lester (*Petulia*), and Saura (*Peppermint frappé*)—were advised to withdraw their films, while Malle and Polanski promised to resign from the jury. On the morning of May 18, Truffaut, speaking on behalf of the Etats généraux, called on the many critics and directors attending the press conference on the Langlois affair to shut down the festival. One hour later, Godard suggested occupying the large auditorium of the Palais where the films were to be shown. As the hall filled up with spectators for Saura's film, a delegation made up of Truffaut, Malle, Godard, Gabriel Albicocco, Berri, and Lelouch walked onstage and announced the festival shutdown. The "conspirators" were joined by other directors and friends, such as Jean-Louis Richard and Jean-Pierre Léaud. In an unbelievable brouhaha, everyone awaited the decision of the jury as it deliberated on whether to resign, and that of the competing filmmakers while they discussed whether to withdraw their films. Stormy discussions took place during this waiting period; the majority "reformists" suggested a festival overhaul (more unofficial selections, possible retrospectives and discussions, repeal of the prize giving) while the "radicals" demanded an immediate shutdown. The news they received reinforced the latter's stance: Four members of the jury had resigned (Roman Polanski, Monica Vitti, Terence Young, and Louis Malle), and an ever-growing number of directors were withdrawing their films. Robert Favre Le Bret then proclaimed the festival noncompetitive but still on. Most of the public attending the festival was satisfied and loudly requested the showing of Saura's *Peppermint frappé*, starring Geraldine

Chaplin. Onstage, the "radicals" stuck to their position and tried to prevent the screening. Shoulder-to-shoulder, they faced a turbulent, enraged audience. Cheers rose from the public as the lights came down and the screening began. But the curtain was held firmly closed by the rebels, including Saura and Geraldine Chaplin, who were soon roughed up by police forces. Godard was slapped in the face and once again lost his glasses; Truffaut was tackled at the waist and thrown to the floor by an angry audience member. Several minutes later, the lights went on and Favre Le Bret made a second statement, announcing the cancellation of the afternoon and evening screenings. Interminable discussions continued far into the night in the large auditorium of the Palais. The "radicals" succeeded in their bid for power: At noon the following day, Favre Le Bret, feeling unable to pursue his mission, brought the festival to a close.

The "saboteurs," the "luxury fanatics" were violently attacked by the Gaullist press and the Cannes audience, for having "torpedoed" the festival "for good."[26] Truffaut justified himself in an interview: "No one seemed to want to understand that the country was paralyzed and that it was logical to stop the festivities. We had to get the festival to shut down and we did. This could have been done more elegantly, but in such circumstances you leave elegance in the cloakroom and even mislay the key. I know that a lot of people will reproach us for our attitude in Cannes for a long time to come, but I also know that two days later, when there were no more planes, no more trains, no cigarettes, no telephone service and no fuel, the festival would have been held up to incredible ridicule if it had continued to function."[27]

Meanwhile, in Paris, the Etats généraux tried to organize a mobilization. On May 19, the technicians union joined the directors from the government-owned radio and television stations (ORTF), the students from the Institut des Hautes Etudes Cinématographiques (IDHEC) and the Etats généraux in proclaiming an unlimited strike with sit-ins in the workplaces: "We film professionals (directors, technicians, workers, students and critics) are on strike for an unlimited period of time to denounce and destroy the reactionary structures of a cinema which has become a commercial commodity. We will give up our fight only when we have become the administrators and managers of our own profession."[28] The determination to do away with the existing state-controlled structures was affirmed on May 21. On that day, the Etats généraux voted on a motion declaring the abolition of the "CNC's privileges": "The Etats généraux of French cinema consider the CNC's reactionary structures abolished. It follows that its existence, representativeness and rules are no longer recognized by the profession. The new structures of our profession will have to grow out of the Etats généraux."[29] The motion of May 21 would be a milestone in cinema's utopian May landscape, even if nothing came of it. Three other general assemblies met on May 26 and 28 at the Centre culturel de l'Ouest parisien, in Suresnes, and presented nineteen plans for restructuring French cinema; June 5 was devoted to a tricky synthesizing project, which would quickly fall into oblivion—particularly since the legislative elections (June 23 and 30) gave General de Gaulle an overwhelming majority at the National Assembly. Abolishing the CNC was now out of the question.

When he returned from Cannes on May 19, Truffaut refused to become involved in the Etats généraux. On the 21st, he became disenchanted when attending a session where he found the idealism, lack of realism, and lack of preparation profoundly irritating: "There were workers there who wanted to shoot 140 films a year instead of 80," he said, "which is impossible; there were creative people who wanted greater freedom, hence fewer union constraints with all the same acquired benefits; and budding directors whose chances of entering the profession were so slight that they hoped for a revolution so that everything could start again from scratch. These meetings were bound to fail, and I should add bound to fail even if a left-wing government had come to power, because cinema will always be at the bottom of any government's list of concerns."[30] Similarly, Truffaut refused to join the Société des réalisateurs de films (Society of Filmmakers), which was being created then at the initiative of some of his friends, among whom were Kast and Doniol-Valcroze. In justification, he explained, "I feel solidarity for Rivette, Godard and Rohmer because I like them and admire their work, but I don't want to have anything to do with Jacqueline Audry, Serge Bourguignon, Jean Delannoy or Jacques Poitrenaud. The fact of having the same profession is meaningless to me if admiration and friendship don't come into play."[31]

On the other hand, Truffaut felt close to the student movement, especially at the end of May and the beginning of June, when it began to flag under political pressure and police repression. "I admire the students and I approve of their fight," he wrote in *Les Nouvelles littéraires*. "I didn't have the luck to be a student, only a schoolboy who had to earn a living at fourteen. Some people pursue their studies, me, I've been pursued by studies. Because of that, my knowledge is full of holes and I'm slower than others at understanding what has to be understood."[32] As a show of support for the student cause, on May 8, at the request of Marguerite Duras, he had signed a manifesto on their behalf. On the 15th, he had donated one thousand francs to the Committee on Direct Action and Creativity. Though he refused to visit the occupied Sorbonne—"I didn't want to act like a tourist, a member of the Paris 'smart set' "[33]—he often dropped by the Théâtre de l'Odéon, which was occupied and the scene of permanent discussions until it was "cleaned out" by the police on June 14: "I went there often, almost every evening at one point. One felt the need for a place where anyone could say anything they liked, as you can in the streets of London."[34]

Moreover, in a spirit of solidarity and for the first time in his life, Truffaut took part in the last big student demonstration in the Latin Quarter on June 1, 1968; he had refused to do so on May 24, when the Etats généraux du cinéma had marched for the day of social action organized by the CGT (union). "I've always been an individualist. I've always considered the people in the political contest as opponents. This may be for personal reasons: the cops beat me up when I was a kid, and I've always felt that political parties never concerned themselves with the one thing that touched me in life, antisocial people. . . . So what moved me about the students was that they were returning the blows they'd received from the police. I followed their entire movement; I even marched, though I had never marched before. I feel an enormous admiration for young people who are capable of chanting 'We're all German Jews!' I never thought we'd ever see intelligence, humor, strength and justice in the street at the same time. This is what stirred me."[35]

THE FAMILY SAGA

After these weeks of political unrest and excitement, Truffaut backed down, in a somewhat cowardly fashion, from marrying Claude Jade, pleading he didn't feel ready for the commitment. The May events—the disorderly spectacle, which he had witnessed with delight—probably played a part. Truffaut became aware of the generation gap between the young actress and himself, but also of their different views of life. Helen Scott, in whom he had confided, had had no compunctions about dissuading him: "You'll just gobble her up!"[36] she had said about Claude Jade. His close friends, such as Helen and Claude de Givray, saw him as a bit of a Bluebeard. And suddenly, at thirty-six, the ghosts of his childhood revisited him.

Several months earlier, when he was finishing *Stolen Kisses,* Truffaut, like the clients in the film, met with Albert Duchenne, the owner of the Dubly detective agency. His purpose was to request a confidential search for his biological father—the man who had seduced his mother, Janine de Monferrand, made her pregnant in the spring of 1931, and then mysteriously disappeared.

Albert Duchenne took personal charge of the case and after several weeks of investigation handed Truffaut a confidential report.[37] According to his findings, Truffaut's father was Roland Lévy, born in Bayonne in 1910, son of Gaston Lévy and Berthe Kahn. After attending secondary school on the Basque coast and obtaining his baccalaureate degree, he moved to Paris in the late twenties and attended dentistry school in the Lorettes neighborhood. This was where he met Janine de Monferrand. He saw her in the early thirties but then left her before François's birth. After his studies, Roland Lévy settled in the Opéra neighborhood and began practicing dental surgery in 1938. Being Jewish, the man presumed to be François Truffaut's father had had to leave German-occupied Paris and take refuge in the provinces. The detectives tracked him down in Belfort, where he had settled in 1946. There he became engaged to a fellow dental surgeon, Andrée Blum, almost ten years younger than he, whom he married in July 1949. They lived in a building on boulevard Carnot, in the center of town, and had their dental practice on the third floor. The couple had two children, but they separated in 1959 after ten years of marriage.

François Truffaut was simultaneously distressed and relieved by this revelation. So he didn't completely belong to *her* family. He was deeply troubled to discover that the person who was probably his father was Jewish —the discovery gave the May students' chant "We're all German Jews" a truly stirring overtone. In a long, unpublished conversation with Claude de Givray at the end of his life, Truffaut confided that "he had always felt Jewish."[38] He connected this feeling with his penchant for outlaws, martyrs, social outcasts, marginal people, and his affirmation of the "other," which he claimed he himself had been all through his youth. He had already discovered his Jewishness in September 1945 at the Cinéac-Italiens when he saw the films of the liberation of the concentration camps. As he sat in the dark theater all alone, the young François—ignored by his mother, beaten by police, and sent away to a reformatory—felt like the "Jew" of the Truffaut-Monferrand family. Later, cinema contributed to his feelings of identification: There in the movies, which he saw over and over again, was a free space, separate from the world, a smuggled "other world" where the "Jew" could finally live a full life, with no constraints. Subsequently, in a certain sense, he created a double for himself,[39] which was the inverted portrait of the "Jew"—the young "hussar," the brilliant journalist fascinated by Rebatet, the ambitious director, the bourgeois, the politically uncommitted artist. At every opportunity, however, the "Jew" would resurface and peer through the overly smooth portrait presented to the press, and then his true personality would be revealed—that of the adult still affected by his battered childhood, the man who had constant feelings of guilt (in both his romantic disappointments and his professional setbacks), the loner fleeing society. This wild side always prevailed over his civilized alter ego, and it drove him to live like an outlaw in the midst of his success, and on the fringe of society in spite of the recognition he had gained. This conflicting impulse had nothing to do with the lifestyle of an "accursed artist"; it had a deeper origin, in a fate he had accepted since childhood—being the "Jew" of others, especially of an intolerant family.

In the spring of 1968, Truffaut kept his Jewish origins secret. He told only Madeleine and Helen Scott, and two film producers, Pierre Braunberger and Ilya Lopert. But it was reflected in some of his actions. For example, at a time when many of his friends leaned toward an anti-Zionist leftism, a year after the Six-Day War, he became, at Ilya Lopert's request, a member of the Fonds de solidarité avec Israël, and thereafter regularly contributed several thousand francs in annual dues.

On August 22, 1968, Janine de Monferrand died of cirrhosis of the liver. His mother's death abruptly thrust François Truffaut back to the wounds of his childhood. "Helen Scott had to push him to get him to go to the funeral,"[40] Madeleine Morgenstern recalls. For Truffaut was far from reconciled with his mother, for whom he felt a deep-seated resentment. The funeral ceremony on August 28 at the Church of Saint-Vincent-de-Paul, near the rue La Fayette, was particularly painful for him, since the Monferrand family was hostile to him. It was only after his mother's death that Truffaut's anger would gradually be dispelled. He even felt touched when he emptied her apartment on rue de Navarin and found documents that she had lovingly kept—"press clippings about him, with deletions and markings, which proved that she had been interested in him and not indifferent,"[41] says Madeleine.

All these events occurring in rapid succession in a period of months—Françoise Dorléac's death, the discovery of his real father, his mother's death, his hasty retreat from marriage—led François Truffaut to reexamine his life in detail. At the end of the summer of 1968, he immersed himself in the papers he found in the family apartment, his school and personal notebooks, his letters as an adolescent, the traces of his early life—his arrest and detention, his passion for films, and his military detention in 1951. He also worked on the various intimate journals he had kept in his youth, made rewrites, and gave them shape and focus. Moreover, he set down on paper various parts of his life: "My Childhood," "My Military Life," "My Articles," "My Films," "My Women," "My Friends." He contemplated using these meticulously kept documents—in which dates and facts were amassed in a precise, almost compulsive way—to write his autobiography, a project he abandoned in order to put together a collection of his main articles on cinema, *Les Films de ma vie*. During this same period, he came up with the idea for several more intimate and autobiographical films, including *L'Homme qui aimait les femmes* (*The Man Who Loved Women*), *La Chambre verte* (*The Green Room*), and *L'Amour en fuite* (*Love on the Run*). In sum, Truffaut tried to "explain his life" and come to terms with his own history; looking backward, he reworked the different strands of his life, from film to film, woman to woman, death to death,[42] recording everything in writing and putting it away in his most secret files.[43]

Yet one vital part of his life remained unknown: Why had his real father left Janine de Monferrand? Why wasn't his name François Lévy? Had the young dentist rejected a woman he considered too different from him, given his ambitions and his religion? Or had the Monferrand family interfered in the romance and wrecked it forever? Truffaut wrote to his family requesting information concerning his birth and his real father. The only person to reply to his letter was Suzanne de Saint-Martin, his maternal grandmother's sister-in-law: "I want to assure you on the subject of your birth (not that I know the exact name of your father), but I was in Paris at that time for my final teaching exams. I used to spend Sundays at your grandmother Viève's house. Your grandfather, Jean, very much the snob and very devout, was furious about Janine's follies with the workers in the neighborhood, people of common birth; but he never mentioned Jews, and he certainly would have with even greater wrath. . . . No, you're a real Frenchman from the Languedoc, from Brugnac, where your grandmother was born. . . ."[44] This letter, by its very denial, strengthened Truffaut's conviction that Roland Lévy had been banished from Janine de Monferrand's life because of anti-Semitism.[45] As practicing Catholics, titled nobles, and former anti-Dreyfusards, the men in the Monferrand family couldn't accept a Jew among them.

Though Truffaut tried to reconstruct the family saga, the story of his origins, certain doubts remained. One day in September 1968, he went to Belfort. He kept in his archives a map of the city with the route from the station to the boulevard Carnot neatly mapped out in pen.[46] Starting at seven in the evening, he posted himself at the foot of a six-story building dating from the early postwar period. According to the detective's report, Roland Lévy went out every night after dinner for a short walk in the neighborhood. He lived alone and followed a strict daily routine. At 8:30, a man in his sixties, stout and of medium height, muffled up in a gray coat, a scarf tied around his neck, opened the door to the building. But just then Truffaut turned away; he felt he couldn't disrupt a man's habits with the sudden revelation that he was his son. That night, he took a room in town and isolated himself in a movie house where they were showing Chaplin's *Gold Rush*.

WHAT IS LEFT OF OUR LOVES?

This succession of events in spring and summer 1968 sheds light on François Truffaut's many separate, compartmentalized lives—interconnected by secret pathways. A hardworking, active movie director; a militant film devotee when championing Langlois; a "saboteur" at the Cannes festival, determined that cinema be in sync with a country on strike; a "student" in May; a "Jew" who discovered himself as such at the death of his mother; a womanizer—Truffaut succeeded in being all these personalities simultaneously; he showed no loss of composure with close friends and family, though, within himself, these many interconnections troubled him deeply.

Unexpectedly, thanks to *Stolen Kisses,* Les Films du Carrosse was financially sound once again. This film, which Truffaut had shot in a carefree spirit, with the Langlois affair absorbing his energies almost every evening, had been, as he himself put it, "sacrificed."[47] Simultaneously whimsical and rather nostalgic, it also seemed completely out-of-date in the atmosphere of May '68. Paradoxically, what might have seemed a handicap turned into an asset. The carefree spirit of the shoot gave the film rhythm, freedom, and melancholy, and its slightly outmoded ambiance proved perfectly attuned to audience expectations; after a spring of feverish political activism, the autumn mood was light and frivolous. The revolution had failed and, with it, the documentary and the political film. The audience returned to fiction, dreams, nostalgia, and smiles. This turn of events doesn't detract at all from Truffaut's personal merit, but it explains the unusual commercial fate of this small film.

Stolen Kisses was shown in preview on the closing night of the Avignon Festival, August 14, 1968. In 1968, the festival itself was an event, rocked by the "spirit of May." There were violent protests against Jean Vilar, the director of the festival; the Living Theatre imposed its conception of happenings; and the CRS (National Guard) was deployed in the streets. *Stolen Kisses* seemed completely out of step with this atmosphere. But the thirty thousand viewers present made the film into a triumphant success. The paradox was immediately apparent: The film captivated audiences but was perceived as anachronistic, almost reactionary. Released on September 4, 1968, in three Paris movie theaters, *Stolen Kisses* was favorably received by the press, which kept alluding to the "timeless" theme of the film. *Freshness, spontaneity, intensity, humor, freedom, emotion, tenderness, modesty,* and *comedy* were words used constantly with reference to it. In *Paris-Soir,* Michel Aubriant painted a revealing portrait of a mellowed Truffaut, "all sugar and spice": "It is incredible how much he has changed in ten years, the insolent young man who used to fight tooth and nail against a certain kind of old fogy cinema. Only imbeciles don't change. And grand principles are meant to be transgressed. Yes, Truffaut has evolved. One can't forever be breaking windows and throwing cobblestones."[48] Truffaut's reputation was now based on this rejection of trendiness and modernity: For the popular press, he incarnated the cinema of bygone days. These critics were all unaware of the fact that, deep down, this "acceptable" and "mellowed" Truffaut concealed secrets and facets of his personality that were far more somber and morbid. This gloomier side is revealed in his film in the disquieting character played by Serge Rousseau (one of Truffaut's best friends and Marie Dubois's husband), the man in the trench coat, who suddenly materializes at the end of *Stolen Kisses* to declare his "definitive love" to Claude Jade, a love stronger than death.

After a four-month run in Paris, the success of the picture was clear: 335,000 tickets had been sold. Awarded the Louis-Delluc Prize, on January 9, 1969, it attracted almost fifty thousand new viewers. *Stolen Kisses*, which had been made for a modest sum, brought in three times its investment. It was very well received in New York, by the press and by the public. "Everything Truffaut touches seems to be spontaneously invested with the lyricism that marks his greatest films. It is one of Truffaut's best,"[49] wrote Vincent Canby in the *New York Times*. It did very well at the Fine Arts Theater, where it opened on March 3, 1969. Not since *The 400 Blows* had any Truffaut film "brought as much money into the till."[50] Les Films du Carrosse thereby recovered from its troubled period of the late sixties and got a new start. *Stolen Kisses*, a "sacrificed," modest, outmoded film, set Truffaut back on the path to success.

BELLE DE NUIT

The unexpected popularity of *Stolen Kisses* allowed Truffaut to finally take on a more ambitious film, *La Sirène du Mississippi* (*Mississippi Mermaid*), which he had nurtured for a long time. He had read William Irish's novel *Waltz into Darkness* about ten years earlier, when Madeleine Morgenstern had given it to him while visiting him in Nîmes on the set of *The Mischief Makers* in August 1957. But the idea of adapting it to the screen dated to the summer of 1966. He was completing *Fahrenheit 451* when the brothers Robert and Raymond Hakim offered to finance his next film, provided he cast Catherine Deneuve in it. The actress was working with Luis Buñuel at the time, on *Belle de jour*, a Hakim production. Truffaut was invited to view some rushes and have lunch with her. He was completely won over. A very short time later, he went to the Hakim brothers with the idea of adapting *Waltz into Darkness* with her in the lead female role and Jean-Paul Belmondo playing opposite her. During the autumn of 1966, negotiations took place between the Hakim brothers and Gérard Lebovici, the owner of Artmédia and the agent of the two stars, but they broke off abruptly when the "Brothers Zaquime," as Truffaut nicknamed them, demanded the right to approve the final cut.[51]

The *Mississippi Mermaid* project then made the rounds. A German producer offered to buy back the rights from the Hakims and cast Brigitte Bardot and Jean-Paul Belmondo as the couple. Truffaut refused; he would have no one but Catherine Deneuve for the film and she would have no other director. Then in autumn 1967, Truffaut was notified by Don Congdon, his New York literary agent, that the Hakims didn't actually own the rights to the Irish novel and that he had been "completely hoodwinked."[52] The rights belonged to Twentieth Century–Fox, which was asking fifty thousand dollars for them. Though Les Films du Carrosse couldn't afford to pay this amount of money, Truffaut could fortunately count on the help of three friends, Jeanne Moreau, Claude Lelouch, and Claude Berri, who put up the required amount. At that point, Truffaut and Marcel Berbert started working out the financing of the film with United Artists. It was budgeted at 8 million francs, which made it the director's costliest production. The shoot, which was to take place in Corsica and last twelve weeks, starting in December 1968, was the only "folly" Truffaut ever allowed himself: Each scene would be filmed in the exact order of the screenplay, "in order to respect the dramatic progression needed for the acting couple's performance."[53]

Truffaut worked alone on adapting the Irish novel, for none of his usual screenwriters were available. He wished to remain faithful to the novel but decided to transpose the action from the New Orleans of 1830 to present-day Corsica. Louis Mahé, the rich owner of a wine-producing estate, marries Julie Roussel, a young woman from the Continent, whom he meets through the personal ads. When the *Mississippi* arrives in the port of Calvi, Louis is surprised by Julie's youth and beauty and falls madly in love with her. They marry, but shortly thereafter the young woman robs him of all the money in their joint bank account and disappears. She had actually been manipulated by her gangster boyfriend, Richard, into impersonating the real Julie Roussel, who had been thrown overboard. Depressed and bitter, Mahé moves to the Riviera, runs into Julie Roussel by accident, and wants to kill her. She then explains her behavior in a long confession: Her real name is Marion Bergamo; she had been a ward of public welfare, shuttling from orphan homes to reformatories, before prostituting herself in the bars of Antibes and Nice. This is where she had met Richard, her lover and procurer, recently arrested. Marion begs Louis's forgiveness, saying she wants to reform her ways. Louis is still in love with her. The couple get back together and live happily in a large house near Aix-en-Provence—until Detective Comolli comes on the scene, the detective hired by Mahé and Julie Roussel's sister to track down Marion. To protect her, Louis kills Comolli. The couple then has to go on the run, fleeing first to Lyon, then to the Alps, in the hope of crossing the frontier. There, in a snowbound chalet,

Louis realizes that Marion is killing him with rat poison so she can get rid of him and escape. Out of love, he accepts his fate. When Marion becomes aware of this sacrifice, "love opens her eyes" and the two lovers wander off together in the snow.

Truffaut's screenplay is not so much a detective story as a *noir* love story, about a passion that can lead only to death. *Mississippi Mermaid* was to be an intimate account of a tragic romance. Everything hinged on the couple and the verisimilitude of their amorous relationship. This was why Truffaut was so eager to work with Jean-Paul Belmondo and Catherine Deneuve, France's two biggest stars and also, in his opinion, her two best actors. On the surface, Louis Mahé, the character Belmondo was to play, is a well-connected, rich, attractive, and amusing man. But he is also shy, awkward, betrayed, swindled, constantly made a fool of by Marion, and pathologically in love. Truffaut's secret twist consisted in reversing the roles: "Catherine Deneuve is the tough guy, the hood who has been through hard times; Jean-Paul Belmondo is the frightened young girl who expects everything from marriage. He finds a wife through the personal ads. I was tempted to have him say, during the credits, 'Young male, twenty-nine, virgin, seeks marriage, etc., etc.' Though he doesn't say it, for me Belmondo is actually a virgin!"[54] At the height of stardom, Belmondo had to accept this ambiguity and risk disappointing his public by going against his virile image as an actor. He would have to convey both strength and fragility. Hesitant, Belmondo finally let himself be convinced by Gérard Lebovici and accepted the part. But deep down, he had certain misgivings about the character; he realized he might "look like an ass,"[55] he admitted to Suzanne Schiffman.

Catherine Deneuve also accepted a part that did not match her image and was fraught with paradoxes. "What I like about her," Truffaut wrote, "is her mysterious quality. She is wonderfully suited to parts involving a secret, or a double life. Catherine Deneuve adds ambiguity to any situation and any screenplay, for she seems to be concealing a great many secret thoughts, we sense there are things lurking behind the surface. . . ."[56] Catherine Deneuve formally accepted the part at the beginning of February 1968, then left to spend most of the summer and fall in Hollywood for the filming of an American film, Stuart Rosenberg's *The April Fools*, costarring Jack Lemmon. Every so often, she wrote Truffaut long letters, expressing her expectations and doubts and requesting information about the screenplay. On September 2, Truffaut clarified his intentions and explained his belief in the intrinsic value of what he called "films with couples": "American films were never better than when James Stewart played opposite Katharine Hepburn, Cary Grant opposite Grace Kelly, Bogart opposite Bacall. With *Mermaid*, I very much want to show a new glamorous and striking pair: Jean-Paul, alive and fragile like a Stendhal hero, and you the blond siren whose chant would have inspired Giraudoux."[57] The success of the film therefore depended on this harmony, provided the sensitivities of each could be overcome. Truffaut asked Catherine Deneuve to be the "stronger half of the couple" in the film and during the shoot, "including being slightly bitchy," which would be bound to hurt or perturb her male alter ego. He described to her a "film of mad love," which assumes a great "familiarity" between the two characters in the drama: "Concentration and perfect harmony among the three of us will restore intimacy to this love life. I won't ask you play any sexually explicit scene, but an underlying sexuality must be felt at all times."[58] In *Mississippi Mermaid,* Catherine Deneuve's costumes are by Yves Saint-Laurent, her favorite designer, whom she introduced to Truffaut. "They met once, they didn't need to talk much, there was such an understanding," she later told Laurence Benaïm, Saint-Laurent's biographer. "Truffaut's ideas about clothes were very close to those of Saint-Laurent, even though he didn't like pants. He always spoke about women's legs. He only liked skirts with movement, he never liked anything straight, tight, stiff. . . ."[59]

During the fall of 1968, Truffaut asked Michel Bouquet to play detective Comolli, a secondary role but important in conveying the threat of the police hanging over this passionate love story. The part of Jardine, Louis Mahé's trusted right-hand man, quite naturally went to Marcel Berbert, since this was very much the part he played in daily life at Les Films du Carrosse: "It was to save money,"[60] Marcel Berbert admits. They had decided to cancel the shoot in Corsica, though Truffaut had stayed there for a week in the spring of 1968, scouting for locations. It lacked mystery. Above all, it was impossible to imagine, for the coherence of the plot, that Louis Mahé could live in Corsica and be so completely out of step with Continental France. Marcel Berbert recalls that on a Sunday morning, he received a call from Truffaut: "I've thought about it; we'll shoot in New Caledonia. Could you tell me how much more it will cost?" Berbert says, "I had a planisphere on my desk. I looked: New Caledonia, twenty thousand kilometers away. Then I saw Réunion Island, ten thousand . . . A cost-saver in the same amount!"[61] A mere four weeks before the start of the shoot, everything had to be rearranged, but the idea of shooting on Réunion Island appealed to Truffaut. A French overseas department, Réunion Island had a deeply colonial economy and society. It is a little island with a hilly, tortuous landscape, situated east of Africa's southernmost tip; here, Louis Mahé would become a believable character; a descendant of one of the oldest families of French settlers, living in a beautiful, large, inherited house, it was just possible that he might have kept his virginity and innocence while managing one of the island's biggest tobacco plantations.

THE *MISSISSIPPI* CREW

On November 15, 1968, barely two weeks before the beginning of the film-ing, François Truffaut flew to Réunion Island. No plans had been made there yet. Jean-José Richer, Roland Thénot, Marcel Berbert, and Truffaut had two weeks to scout for locations, reserve hotels, find a house and a ciga-rette factory for Louis Mahé, a steamship for Julie Roussel's arrival, and a small church in the bush for their marriage. In a letter, Truffaut described his first impressions of the island: "On arrival, dismay, distress and disap-pointment. Then, after a few days, its charm begins to take effect. . . . The landscapes were often beautiful (not always) and the human types gorgeous, especially as far as the women and children are concerned. For the film, that's a definite advantage over Corsica. . . ."[62]

Indeed, the location scouting was fruitful—the Sainte-Anne chapel for the marriage, about thirty miles from Saint-Denis, in the heart of a magnifi-cent volcanic landscape; for Louis Mahé, the Bel-Air villa, a stately white mansion owned by a big family of settlers in Tampon, a property above Saint-Denis; and the Law Son cigarette factory, right in the center of town. As for Truffaut, he stayed at the Relais Aériens Français, a residence over-looking Saint-Denis, with a magnificent view on the Indian Ocean. The rest of the crew and the two stars arrived at the end of November. Jean-Paul Bel-mondo took up residence at the Hotel Saint-Gilles, in the heart of Saint-Denis, while Catherine Deneuve moved into the Relais Aériens. "I strut around self-confidently, but as you might suspect, I'm petrified three days before the shooting, and plagued with the usual escapist fantasies: 'What if Catherine Deneuve were to break a leg . . . or Jean-Paul were to come down with tonsillitis . . .' In other words, once again they'll have to literally drag me to work, la Schife [Suzanne Schiffman] will have to kick me in the ass to get me going,"[63] Truffaut wrote to Helen Scott, forecasting a difficult shoot because of the distance from Paris, as well as the demands and whims of his actors.

"The filming is ideal and everything is going for the best,"[64] Truffaut wrote to Lucette Desmouceaux, his secretary at Les Films du Carrosse. The director was happy, reassured by his harmonious relationship with Cather-ine Deneuve. During the first few days, communication on the set had been rather tense, and strong gusts of wind had prevented them from filming a series of helicopter shots. But very soon, everything went smoothly. Cather-ine Deneuve dispelled all her director's apprehensions. "I had a certain pre-conception of Catherine Deneuve before filming *Mississippi Mermaid*. I thought she had an exaggerated sense of her interests as an actress and that this would go before the interests of the film. I suspected she was a perfectionist, hence always disappointed. I didn't think she was wholeheartedly behind the film, so I was slightly wary of her; I thought she would be too concerned with details and would often request explanations and justifications. In sum, in spite of my desire to work with her, I started the film with certain prejudices that she immediately guessed. While she was in America working on *April Fools,* I wrote to her in Hollywood and sent her some sly little warnings, like: 'When working on my films everyone is in a good mood,' or 'We must not think we'll make a masterpiece. We'll try to make a lively film.' Because of this, during the first days of the shoot, we were on our guard, then I discovered very fast that we thought the same way and agreed on everything."[65]

Truffaut's portrait of Catherine Deneuve in his long text, soberly entitled "Working with Catherine Deneuve," is not just an encomium of the actress he had just directed. No doubt Truffaut wrote the essay in part to promote his film and to justify the choice of Catherine Deneuve as its star alongside Jean-Paul Belmondo. However, it is also possible to read between the lines and see it as a discreet and modest declaration of love to the woman herself—her ambiguity, her personality, her beauty. "Indeed, Catherine Deneuve is so beautiful that any film she stars in could almost dispense with telling a story. I am convinced that the spectator will find happiness in just looking at Catherine and that this contemplation is worth the price of admission!" When he praises Catherine Deneuve, Truffaut describes the actress's physical appearance—her gentle face enhancing the occasional severity of her gaze—as well as her character, her way of moving, talking, dressing, wearing makeup; he is under the spell of her voice and mysterious quality.

During the filming of *Mississippi Mermaid,* Truffaut was not unlike the above-mentioned spectator watching his favorite screen heroine. Not only did the shoot take place under ideal conditions, but it was over those eighteen days on Réunion Island that their love story began. "Usually François was incredibly naive and thought no one noticed his affairs during filmings. In this instance, there was no attempt at secrecy. For her and for him, it was serious, not just a filming fling,"[66] recalls Marcel Berbert.

Though he remained tactful and in good spirits, Jean-Paul Belmondo felt slightly jealous of the favored treatment his partner received from the director. Witnesses remember that he and his girlfriend, Ursula Andress, who had joined him on Réunion Island, preferred not to take meals with the others on the set and isolated themselves in their villa. On December 23, before leaving the island, the producers threw a cocktail party for the actors and crew and also invited the island officials who had facilitated the making of the film. "Belmondo dropped by for only fifteen minutes; he smiled the whole time but didn't linger,"[67] Marcel Berbert recalls.

The shoot resumed on December 30 in Nice, following the screenplay in sequence. First came the scenes in the clinic where Louis Mahé, in a state of severe depression, is undergoing a sleeping cure to recover from Julie Roussel's departure and betrayal. This required three days of filming in the gardens of the Musée Masséna and in an adjoining clinic on the Promenade des Anglais. Then came the principal scenes between Louis Mahé and Marion, a "very spoken and very spontaneous dialogue which I draft from day to day a few hours before shooting the scenes."[68] This intimate ceremonial begins with Marion's long confession to Louis Mahé. For this monologue, Truffaut reworked, word for word, excerpts of a tape he had made in October 1965 of Mireille G., the first woman with whom he had ever lived, back in 1949, and whom he saw again in the south of France[69]—her reminiscences included receiving public welfare, acquiring her first pair of high heels at fourteen, stealing money from wallets, having kleptomania, and going to reform school.[70]

As an homage to his friend Jacques Audiberti, who had died in 1965, Truffaut had the idea of filming this sequence in a hotel that was situated on a square named after the writer in his native city of Antibes. He also rebaptized the hotel "Monorail," which is the title of an Audiberti novel. A night scene had to be filmed in which Belmondo, as usual refusing a stuntman, was to climb up the facade of the hotel and make his way into Marion's room. During the climb, he slipped, smashing a neon light, and was left suspended in space. Two hours later, the scene was reshot, after the crew had repaired the set.

The filming proceeded near Aix-en-Provence, where Louis Mahé and Marion renew their romance: declarations, love games, caresses; the transition from the formal *vous* to the informal *tu;* the double confession in front of the fireplace; the scene of Catherine Deneuve undressing by the side of the road;[71] the purely fetishistic sequences where the woman wears the "clothes of sexual fantasies" (sable-colored stockings, a pink silk slip, a scant little dress with eight buttons that the man unfastens one by one); the embraces that follow the dramatic events (the murder of detective Comolli and Louis returning with the money). It is a very intimate world that is depicted in *Mississippi Mermaid,* as Catherine Deneuve very insightfully points out: "François made love stories in which sexuality was always present. Usually the sexuality is ethereal, with modesty prevailing. But if his films are looked at attentively from that specific angle, for example *Mermaid,* you can see just how sexually violent and explicit they are."[72]

Late January and mid-February 1969 found the cast and crew in Lyon, then in Le Sappey, north of Grenoble, in the Chartreuse mountain range, where Truffaut had filmed the last scenes of *Shoot the Piano Player.* In fact, he used the same chalet for the last scenes of *Mississippi Mermaid,* when Deneuve poisons Belmondo with rat poison. This is where the last lines of the picture are exchanged: "Does love hurt?" asks Marion. "Yes, it hurts," Louis replies. "It hurts to look at you, you're so beautiful." And Marion says, "Yesterday you said it was a joy." In conclusion, Louis responds, "Yes. It's a joy and a misery." On the evening of February 15, the entire cast and crew partied together and belatedly celebrated Truffaut's thirty-seventh birthday: "The *Mississippi* crew requests the pleasure of your company at the Mermaid Party in honor of François Truffaut beginning at 10:00 p.m. at the Hotel des Skieurs (evening dress not required . . .)."[73]

Between March and May 1969, François Truffaut edited his film with Agnès Guillemot, assisted by Yann Dedet. For the opening credits, he used a montage of personal ads read in a voice-over and an excerpt from Jean Renoir's *La Marseillaise,* of which he had just seen a restored print.[74] "It's a great source of happiness for me to be associated with this picture,"[75] Renoir wrote, touched by this gesture. In the beginning of June, as was his habit, Truffaut scheduled a screening of *Mermaid* for his friend Jean Aurel, who suggested a few editing changes. "The film isn't fantastic, but it isn't a failure; the two lovers are very good,"[76] Truffaut confided to Helen Scott.

When the film opened on June 18, 1969, the critics all expressed disappointment. Jean-Louis Bory set the tone in *Le Nouvel Observateur:* "The 'Truffaut' touch makes for a gorgeous film which leaves me cold. Because of all the sauce? Is the bride too beautiful? Too haute couture? It's the metamorphosis of *Shoot the Piano Player* into an ultraposh boutique product. Ideal colors and international stars. I miss the old film, the poor one, in black and white. For these stars, in point of fact, are an encumbrance. . . ."[77] The intimate, passionate love story went unnoticed, overshadowed by the reputation of the stars and the "mass audience" look of the film. *Mississippi Mermaid* was then and still is misunderstood. In spite of its two big stars, audiences didn't flock to see it; it barely sold 100,000 tickets by the end of July 1969, when it was pulled from the theaters. It was a severe letdown. Les Films du Carrosse pulled through relatively well, but United Artists was very disappointed.

Paradoxically, Truffaut was little concerned by this flop. Spring 1969 was the happiest period of his life. Overlooking his usual extreme discretion, he couldn't resist confiding in two or three friends. To François Weyergans: "I'm the happiest man on earth. . . ."[78] To Helen Scott: "My personal life is very good. . . ."[79] And he wrote to Aimée Alexandre, his old friend of Russian descent, then aged seventy-seven years old, "My personal life is once again organized around the happiness of an amorous relationship."[80] This happy "amorous relationship" bore the delicate, regular features of

"Kathe de Neuve," as Truffaut sometimes called her with tenderness and irony.

The filming of *Mermaid* brought them together. The very theme of the movie, the story of a passionate love in which there is no other woman or man, probably had something to do with it. "It's the first time I've really dealt with a couple," said Truffaut to a reporter from *Télérama*. "In *Jules and Jim* or *The Soft Skin*, the scenes with couples always refer to a third person—the one who isn't there. Here the man and woman are happy together, or when they hurt each other, it comes only from themselves."[81] While he was shooting *Mermaid* in sequence—which allowed him to "construct" his couple on screen in precise fashion from one location to the next, charting a progression that was both physical and emotional—Truffaut was having a romance with the star of his movie. The bond that united them brought a perceptible, sensual joy to the filming, such as Truffaut had not felt on a set since *Jules and Jim*; it also gave the film the appearance of a real declaration of love. During the entire shoot, no one knew of their liaison outside of the cast and crew, even though there was a hint in the fact that Catherine Deneuve gave the first dance to François Truffaut at a soirée at the Hotel des Skieurs in Sappey. Several days later, *Paris-Match* published a photograph of the couple, "Catherine and Truffaut beneath the same umbrella,"[82] arm in arm in the snow.

"We agree on everything," said Truffaut gladly, alluding ambiguously to his professional relationship with the actress. "Catherine is not much of an actress in life," he added. "In fact, she is uncalculating and prefers to take things as they come, very comfortable in some situations and very unhappy in others. But she doesn't show it and has a propriety that I greatly appreciate. She has none of the vanity of her talent. For her, happiness is the only important thing. The rest is derisory. Catherine is like that."[83]

For Truffaut, this relationship was at once a consecration and the source of a deep upheaval in his life. Generally quite reticent, he confided movingly to his friend Claude de Givray: "My life is like a Hollywood comedy!"[84] To Helen Scott he wrote: "My private life is much more exclusive than before."[85] And to Aimée Alexandre: "We hardly ever go out to dinners, because of all the plays to see, the movies, and the evenings we spend watching television."[86] The couple indulged in no offbeat behavior, and led a very discreet life shared with only a few select friends. Very infrequently, photos of them at movie premieres appeared in the press, but they were both careful to protect their private life from the social gossip columns and the rumor mill.

In October and November 1969, Truffaut spent several weeks in Toledo, Spain, where Catherine Deneuve was filming one of her best roles, *Tristana,* directed by Luis Buñuel. Truffaut stayed at the El Marron Hotel, taking advantage of his vacation to work on the script for *Bed and Board*. His co-scenarist, Claude de Givray, who came for a short stay to discuss the screenplay, remembers that Truffaut had absolutely no interest in tourism. "He never set foot in the old quarter of town. He had a theory that cities were not meant for sight-seeing, like Cocteau's old saying: 'He dies, struck by the picturesque.' For him, it was really obscene to visit a city where people lived."[87]

THE WILD CHILD

By the end of June 1969, it was clear to Truffaut that *Mississippi Mermaid* was his biggest box-office failure. Fortunately, by then he was already completely immersed in the preproduction of *L'Enfant sauvage* (*The Wild Child*), which he was to begin shooting on July 2. Ever since *The 400 Blows*, Truffaut had been interested in educational experiments with difficult—autistic or delinquent—children. During the spring of 1964, his curiosity had been aroused by the review in *Le Monde* of a book by Lucien Malson, *Les Enfants sauvages: Mythe et réalité* (*Wild Children: Myth and Reality*). The author, better known as a jazz specialist, was a professor of social psychology at the Centre national de pédagogie, where he studied "children who had been deprived of all human contact and had grown up, for one reason or other, in complete isolation."[88] The most instructive of the fifty-two cases analyzed by Malson was that of Victor of Aveyron, a child who in 1798 had been discovered in the forest by hunters.

Truffaut immediately bought about ten copies of Malson's book, as he customarily did when he was interested in a book for his work. Jean Itard, a brilliant physician who specialized in the study of auditory processes, had conducted an experiment that fascinated Truffaut. In December 1800, at twenty-nine, Itard was appointed director of the Institut national des sourds-muets (National Institute for Deaf-Mutes) in Paris, where he had been working for some time—specifically on the ten-year-old wild child found in Aveyron, who had become an object of public curiosity. Two opposing theories prevailed in medical circles at the time. For some, the child was a mental defective or idiot whose parents had tried to kill him—he had a deep scar on his throat—and who had been left for dead in the forest. Given this hypothesis, he was at best a fun-fair curiosity, who really should have been locked up in Bicêtre hospital with madmen and other incurables. For others, including Jean Itard, the child had indeed escaped his parents' knife but was not retarded. Isolation, absence of human communication, and want of affection had made him "wild." Itard obtained permission to place the child under his care, on condition he demonstrate the results of his instruction. He undertook the task of educating the child, whom he baptized Victor. Little by little, the child learned to use his senses and intelligence, to walk erect, behave properly at the table, and dress on his own; after a time, he could understand simple speech and pronounce some words. Eventually, Victor went on to live to age forty, under the care of a governess, Madame Guérin, in a little house on rue des Feuillantines, near the Institut; he worked at small tasks and lived very frugally.

François Truffaut first considered making a film based on this story in the autumn of 1964 and assigned it to Jean Gruault. By mid-January 1965, the latter suggested a possible theme for the story but his idea didn't completely satisfy Truffaut, so the scriptwriter did further research. He consulted educational treatises on deaf-mutes, read Condillac's *Treatise on the Sensations* (1754), and delved into articles in medicine and psychology that dealt with autistic children. By mid-November 1965, Truffaut had annotated Gruault's 243-page typewritten manuscript and returned it to him for a rewrite. A year later, after more "Ping-Pong work"[89] as Gruault called it, the script had grown to almost four hundred pages, meaning over three hours of film time by Truffaut's calculations. It had to be shortened by half. Finally, with some advice from Jacques Rivette, Truffaut and Gruault pared it down to 151 pages in the summer of 1968. The screenplay was dense, tense; Truffaut used the words *rigorous, logical, scientific,* and *poetic,* to describe it.[90]

To make this film, Truffaut met with an ear, nose, and throat specialist who was experimenting with the use of tuning forks on deaf-mute children. He involved Roger Monnin, the father of one of his friends, a deaf-mute who was in charge of several associations for the handicapped. Lastly, he again consulted Fernand Deligny (as he had for *The 400 Blows*), who now ran an experimental clinic for autistic children in Monoblet, a small hamlet in a remote section of the Cévennes.[91] In the autumn of 1968 Truffaut asked Suzanne Schiffman to go to Monoblet to observe a young boy whose behavior, according to Deligny, was surprisingly similar to Victor's. "Your description of his behavior is so similar to what Itard described in his writings and to what we want to achieve in the film that I find it extremely disconcerting," Truffaut wrote to Deligny. "In any case, I think your boy should serve as our model in selecting the boy who will actually play the part and should inspire us for his style of bodily comportment."[92]

With *The Wild Child,* Truffaut wanted to take a strong position regarding a cause for which he had fought with consistent determination and energy—the welfare of unhappy children. Along with freedom of the press and military insubordination, it was the only cause Truffaut was ready to take up at any time. Children, he felt, lack any protection and are helplessly trapped when those around them become violent and abusive. Truffaut took a radical position and accused politicians of indifference to this serious social problem:

> There can be no doubt that the number of abused and merely unhappy children will increase considerably in the years to come. Naturally the same is true for juvenile delinquents. Anyone can point to the reasons for this: too many unwanted children, housing crises, overcrowded schools, teacher shortages, derisory social assistance. The only solutions to such social problems are concrete—hence financial—hence political—and we know that elected officials only think about children when they reach voting age. Greater severity toward physically abusive parents is also a solution to be considered. Unfortunately, this solution will not be adopted by the administration because it is unpopular. Which is why we have every reason to be pessimistic, completely and unequivocally pessimistic.[93]

Given his deep concern, Truffaut collected press clippings on cases that appalled him—child suicides, health-care establishments found guilty of mistreating retarded children, physical cruelties inflicted by parents. In March 1964, he had become a member of the sponsorship committee of the Secours populaire français and in the spring of 1967, he had been made president of the benefactors' committee for SOS Villages d'enfants, an association that had centers for taking in battered children. Finally, in April 1968, he accepted the radio station France-Culture's offer to devote a daylong program to him, provided the broadcast focus exclusively on the cause of abused children. The program was aired on April 2, from 2:00 p.m. to midnight, and the station's switchboard was flooded with calls and testimonies. The broadcast was covered extensively in the press and Truffaut received almost two hundred letters from listeners. Some of these were from former abused children, or from watchdog committees, attesting to the accuracy of Truffaut's views. Truffaut had stood up against the rule of silence and the misuse of parental authority with the aim of initiating a real public debate. Likewise, the film about Victor of Aveyron, the abused and abandoned wild child, was an attempt to use cinema for educational purposes. Truffaut's pedagogical vocation was never better expressed than in *The Wild Child*, a film that is both optimistic and despairing—optimistic, because of its great confidence in the acquisition of culture; despairing, because this education brings with it the realization that society is a den of torturers and cowards.

Truffaut went to United Artists for financing, but Ilya Lopert was reluctant to commit himself; he found the screenplay "too documentarylike," as he told Jean-Louis Livi. Furthermore, Truffaut specifically wanted the film to be in black and white. Things looked bleak, so much so that, in September 1968, for the first and only time in his career, he applied for an advance on box-office receipts from the CNC. Gérard Lebovici then played a decisive role in convincing Lopert to rescind his decision and invest 2 million francs in *The Wild Child*. Jean-Louis Livi, Lebovici's right-hand man but also Ilya Lopert's son-in-law, remembers these negotiations between Truffaut and Lopert, the European production head of United Artists. "Imagine offering a big American company a black-and-white film with no stars when Truffaut was getting ready to make a film with Deneuve and Belmondo!" Still skeptical, Lopert agreed, on one condition—combining the box-office receipts of *The Wild Child* and *Mississippi Mermaid,* a film he was certain would bring in profits. "The Americans were counting on the success of *Mermaid* to absorb the losses of *The Wild Child;* the exact opposite occurred,"[94] recalls Marcel Berbert. "Ilya was smart to accept both films, for he didn't want to risk losing Truffaut,"[95] Jean-Louis Livi concludes.

On the advice of his location manager, Roland Thénot, Truffaut decided to shoot *The Wild Child* in Aubiat, in Auvergne, where the Thénot family owned a nineteenth-century manor house that could be made into Dr. Itard's house. For the black-and-white cinematography, Truffaut hired Nestor Almendros, Eric Rohmer's director of photography on *My Night at Maud's,* whose very refined, original, and simple lighting he had very much admired. This was the start of a long collaboration, a close artistic and professional bond, and an enduring friendship: Almendros and Truffaut would make nine films together, including Truffaut's last, *Vivement Dimanche!* (*Confidentially Yours!*)

During the preproduction of *The Wild Child,* Truffaut and Almendros viewed several films: Arthur Penn's *The Miracle Worker,* about the childhood education of Helen Keller, Bresson's *Diary of a Country Priest,* Bergman's *Monika,* and several silent films by Griffith and Dreyer. With its grainy black-and-white quality, the opening and shutting of an iris, used here by Truffaut as a recurrent punctuating device, *The Wild Child* is also an homage to the classical age of cinema. "Truffaut wanted me to create a certain archaic tone," Almendros later explained, "he likes the transitions and fades of the silent cinema. I had to study the problem: how to produce fades outside the laboratory (the dupe negative lowers the quality of the shots). I came up with the iris that was used in silent filmmaking. . . . J. C. Rivière, my assistant, set out to find an old iris, one of those used in the early days of the cinema. He found one. . . . The outline of the iris was . . . precise, and we got a perfect effect of a dark ring slowly closing until it isolated the essence of the image and then ended in total darkness."[96] At the same time, Suzanne Schiffman made the rounds of the schools around Nîmes,

Arles, Marseilles, and Montpellier, looking for a boy who could be cast as Victor. Schiffman interviewed and photographed nearly 2,500 children, five of whom were selected as finalists and summoned to Paris for screen tests. On June 6, Truffaut wrote to Helen Scott that he "had found the little boy."[97] He was Jean-Pierre Cargol, a twelve-year-old gypsy with a dark complexion, a "very animallike" profile, a lively and nimble body. The boy was the nephew of the guitarist Manitas de Plata. "He's a very handsome child, but I think he really looks like he came out of the woods," Truffaut wrote to Helen Scott.[98]

Truffaut cast stage actors in the other parts: Françoise Seigner of the Comédie-Française as Madame Guérin, and as Pinel, Jean Dasté, director of the Saint-Etienne theater and an actor in films by Jean Vigo (*Zéro de conduite* and *L'Atalante*) and Renoir (*Boudu Saved from Drowning, The Crime of Monsieur Lange, Grand Illusion*). Finally, he cast his collaborators in the small parts—Claude Miller, his wife, Annie, and their baby, Nathan, play the Lémeri family, whom Jean Itard occasionally goes to see with Victor, while Jean Gruault appears as a visitor in the sequences shot at the Institut national des sourds-muets.

Truffaut would vacillate for a long time over the part of Dr. Itard. He first considered television actors, then the journalist Philippe Labro to emphasize the educational tie between Itard and the wild child. Then he looked for someone unknown, who would make the character more believable. In fact, though he didn't dare admit it, Truffaut saw himself in the part. Suzanne Schiffman was the only person he let in on the secret, days before the beginning of the shoot. Even Berbert didn't know. "It's true, he didn't have the nerve to tell me. As in many instances, he told Suzanne and she went by my desk one day and said, 'You know who's going to be Dr. Itard? François!' I said, 'Oh, really? No kidding!' "[99] Truffaut thought he would feel more comfortable "inside the frame," directing a child who never talks. "Casting someone else in the part of Dr. Itard would have put an intermediary between Jean-Pierre Cargol and me, and I'd have had a lot of trouble directing him."[100] Gruault fully agreed: "Itard is seen almost exclusively in his professional capacity, which is very close to that of director."[101]

The filming of *The Wild Child* began on July 2, 1969, deep in the forest, with takes of the child hurriedly climbing up a tree to escape the dogs pursuing him, then finding shelter in a burrow. Thanks to small, specially made invisible sandals, Jean-Pierre Cargol could run around in the undergrowth without difficulty. The ambiance on set was studious; Truffaut stuck to his screenplay, which he found "well constructed," and harmony reigned. "Here in this manor, lost in the gentle rolling hills of la Limagne—to quote the guidebooks—far from the telephone, the traffic jams, the news, and even vacationers, work is going very well."[102] Catherine Deneuve joined him on location for much of the summer, which made Truffaut happy.

The Wild Child presented Truffaut with a new challenge—directing a child while being both in front of and behind the camera. To instruct Jean-Pierre Cargol, he used comparisons: "For the expression in his eyes, I would say, 'like a dog'; for his head movements, 'like a horse.' I mimed Harpo Marx when wide-eyed wonder had to be conveyed. But nervous laughter and rage were difficult for him, because Jean-Pierre is a very gentle, happy, well-balanced child who could only do quiet things."[103] While Truffaut was acting his part, Suzanne Schiffman took on the duties of assistant director; she was in charge of shouting "Roll" and "Cut" and stood in for Truffaut during rehearsals. Truffaut found this first experience as an actor extremely enriching: "On a movie set, the look in an actor's eye is very surprising; it reflects both pleasure and frustration. Pleasure because the feminine side in every man (and to a greater extent in every actor) feels fulfilled in being an object. Frustration, because there is also always some greater or lesser degree of virility that wants to rebel against this same condition."[104] With *The Wild Child,* he would learn in concrete, physical terms all that the directing of actors implies.

At the end of August, the cast and crew were back in Paris, for a last week of filming at the Institut national des sourds-muets. Then, after a shoot that had lasted fifty days, everyone separated. As a parting gift, Jean-Pierre Cargol was given a small 8-mm camera and he vowed to become "the first gypsy film director."[105]

THE CARROSSE KEEPS ROLLING

Before *The Wild Child* was even released, François Truffaut was in the streets of Paris filming *Domicile conjugal (Bed and Board),* the third installment in the adventures of Antoine Doinel. This would be his fourth movie in two years. Cinema came first in his life. But Truffaut also worked constantly because of an obsessive need for a busy schedule; he never allowed room for the unexpected. He planned things compulsively, months, even years, ahead of time, and compartmentalized his various projects so his screenwriters would remain separate. This sometimes frightened his friends, such as Jean-Louis Richard, who recalls how Truffaut sometimes scheduled work sessions twelve to eighteen months into the future.

Leaving nothing to chance and putting filmmaking before his personal life were two of Truffaut's basic character traits. There was a madness in this dizzying immersion in work as the only salvation and escape from the melancholy of life. Shooting film after film kept him in a state of elation, and it was also the best way of retaining a group of trusted collaborators, including scriptwriters and technical crew. Constant work also allowed him to suppress his deep anxieties as the head of a company. ("The Carrosse keeps rolling [*carrosse* means "horse-drawn coach"],"[106] he wrote.) "I am a director-producer in charge of my own filmmaking projects. . . . Since I have been working with American companies for several years, I have lost contact with French producers. For these same years, I must say I've been lucky to work in complete freedom and I have carte blanche to the extent that my films require only medium-sized budgets."[107]

His full acceptance of the status of boss-cum-artist was rather unusual in the post-1968 context, a time when many intellectuals and artists chose ideological commitment on the extreme Left or a life on the margins of society. Some regarded his choice as the ultimate in bad taste. Jean-Luc Godard, for one, in his complete commitment to militant cinema, denigrated Truffaut as "a businessman in the morning and a poet in the afternoon."[108] To those who classified him as a bourgeois director, Truffaut quite frankly didn't know how to respond. "Almost everyone feels insulted when they're called bourgeois, but I don't feel insulted. In fact, I don't feel concerned, probably because, in general, I scarcely take part in life. . . . The designation 'bourgeois' attacks a way of life. I don't have a way of life (I don't live, outside cinema), I don't feel it applies to me and if it's a misunderstanding, I'm in no rush to clear it up."[109]

This insistence on remaining outside society was, of course, the primary characteristic of his protagonist Antoine Doinel, to whom he returned in the seventies with *Bed and Board,* on the advice given him by Henri Langlois after the screening of *Stolen Kisses:* "I want to see this little [Doinel-Darbon] couple again, in the first few months of their married life."[110] In April 1969, in a few work sessions with Claude de Givray and Bernard Revon, the main outline of a new screenplay was worked out. The idea was to give Antoine Doinel work, then a son, then a mistress, and in the end plunge him deep into marital conflict. Of course, Truffaut's personal recollections form the framework of the narrative, mixed together with the real life of Jean-Pierre Léaud. However, as with *Stolen Kisses,* de Givray and Revon added elements from their investigations in the field. Antoine Doinel has a most unusual job—dyeing bouquets of flowers for a florist. This was one of Truffaut's childhood memories: "At 10 rue de Douai, in my neighborhood, there was a florist who dyed flowers in the yard." Even if no one did so anymore, the idea appealed to him, and he decided to keep it as part of the film's antiquated charm. Similarly, Christine's profession—violin teacher— is a clear reference to Monique de Monferrand, Truffaut's young aunt, who became a violin teacher after graduating from the Conservatoire. Using specific recollections as starting points, Truffaut practiced what he called "verification through life,"[111] which involved concealing the autobiographical elements with real details and anecdotes collected by his screenwriters. He thereby made the autobiographical more concrete, but also more universal. For his guiding principle was always the same—avoid trends and clichés, and don't try to be up-to-date.

He was perfectly aware of the disparity between his Doinel of the early seventies and French youth so heavily influenced by the deep upheaval in intellectual fashions and mores effected by the events of May '68. But he fully accepted this, just as he accepted not being a revolutionary director. When he described Doinel, Truffaut was clearly describing himself: "Doinel is certainly asocial, but he isn't revolutionary the way people are today. Given this statement, I can see my films being condemned politically. Doinel isn't out to change society; he's leery of it and protects himself from it, but he's full of good will and wants to be 'accepted.' "[112] In this sense, Truffaut's films were poles apart from Godard's, which were always attuned to the language and forms of the present. Both directors used Jean-Pierre Léaud as an actor, but in opposite ways. Truffaut was often appalled or wounded by Léaud's personal choices and his commitment to left-wing militancy. The actor for his part surely felt closer to Godard, even though, on a human level, he remained extremely attached to Doinel's creator. But Léaud often considered the Doinel persona a burden, and his involvement and work with Godard was a necessary emancipation, even if it meant hurting Truffaut's feelings.

In *Bed and Board,* the Doinel couple's life is depicted in a light comic mode, with a touch of the burlesque. While Christine gives violin lessons, Antoine dyes flowers in the courtyard of their building; there, people come and go—clients from the nearby bistro, a waitress who is in love with him, the occupants of the building, including an old recluse who misses Pétain, and a mysterious stranger nicknamed "the strangler." Failing to achieve "absolute red" for his carnations, Antoine changes jobs; he is hired by the Paris branch of an American hydraulics company to operate ship models. The Doinel couple is expecting a child—Alphonse. But Antoine meets a young and beautiful Japanese woman, Kyoko, who becomes his mistress. Christine finds out about his affair when she comes upon the love notes Kyoko has sent Antoine in a bouquet of flowers; this provokes a crisis in their marriage. She banishes Antoine from their home. He then decides to write a novel about his life. But they miss each other, and Antoine interrupts a tête-à-tête dinner with Kyoko to declare his love to Christine over the telephone. In an epilogue, one year later, we see the young couple back together again, in a reconciliation that is probably illusory.

SCENES FROM A MARRIAGE

An overtly amusing film, *Bed and Board* was also, Truffaut said, a "settling of scores."[113] For the director wanted to put Antoine Doinel to rest. He decided to do so in order to "liberate" Léaud from Doinel, "because it would get in the way of his career,"[114] and also because Truffaut felt he had fully exhausted the character's possibilities. He had made him into a married man, a father and head-of-family, and had given him a job, even though Doinel still oscillated between adolescence and adulthood. "Doinel isn't antisocial, but simply out of step with society. He doesn't reject society; it is society that takes issue with his spirit and style of life. Antoine Doinel, who is bound up with youthfulness, cannot be integrated into a normal society. In adulthood he becomes an impossible character."[115] Yet before parting with his double, Truffaut gave him two gifts—a film, *Bed and Board*, and a book, *The Adventures of Antoine Doinel.*[116] The latter is a kind of novel that traces Doinel's development, from runaway adolescent in *The 400 Blows*, to *Antoine and Colette* and *Stolen Kisses,* to the married man of *Bed and Board.* This narrative, consisting of four screenplays, recounts the birth, life, and personal fulfillment of one of the most famous screen characters in the world.

By mid-November 1969, he had a completed screenplay for *Bed and Board.* Marcel Berbert's estimated budget was modest—3.5 million francs. Truffaut had been annoyed by United Artists' procrastination over *The Wild Child* script and now he wanted to show his resentment by boycotting the American company. Furthermore, Ilya Lopert, with whom he had enjoyed a marvelous working relationship, died of a stroke in January 1970. So Truffaut turned to Hercule Mucchielli, an independent producer (Valoria Films), who contributed 40 percent of the budget and brought in a small Rome-based production company, Fida Cinematografica, which contributed an additional 10 percent. Les Films du Carrosse invested the other 50 percent, and the foreign sales were again entrusted to Alain Vannier. An agreement was signed with Columbia Pictures for American distribution.

Besides Jean-Pierre Léaud and Claude Jade, Truffaut used largely the same cast as in *Stolen Kisses,* most notably Daniel Ceccaldi and Claire Duhamel as Christine's parents. Two weeks before the shoot was to begin, Claude Jade came down with jaundice and had to be looked after by her parents in Dijon. This was just the first contretemps in a film that would soon try Truffaut's patience and goodwill. In the secondary roles, Truffaut cast stage and television actors. Jacques Robiolles and Daniel Boulanger made repeat appearances, and there was one newcomer, Philippe Léotard, aged thirty, a member of Ariane Mnouchkine's Théâtre du Soleil. Last but not least were two parts he felt very strongly about: Kyoko, and "the strangler." Truffaut asked Hiroko Berghauer, a former Cardin model and a "magical" woman, refined and elegant, to be Doinel's Japanese mistress. And in the role of "the strangler"—the strange, slightly effeminate, solitary man who sows terror until the day he is seen performing a skit on television—Truffaut cast his childhood friend Claude Thibaudat, alias Claude Vega. The son of the concierge on rue des Martyrs had become a stand-up comic—known, among other things, for his impersonation of actresses, such as Delphine Seyrig.

As of the first day's shoot of *Bed and Board,* on January 21, 1970, in a small courtyard near Sèvres-Babylone, Truffaut insisted that each scene be reperformed at a faster pace, as fast as possible, to emulate the rhythm of American screwball comedies by Howard Hawks, Leo McCarey (he had gone to see *The Awful Truth* again days before the shoot), and Frank Capra. "Very often," said Nestor Almendros, "he used Capra's technique: he would time the take and if it lasted 20 seconds, he would say, 'Now, let's do it in 10 seconds,' so the actors spoke like submachine guns and sometimes that was the take he'd keep."[117]

Shooting at a fast pace with frequent set changes involved some sacrifices. "*Bed and Board* is probably the least aesthetically pleasing of the films I have made for Truffaut," writes Almendros. "Its interest is concentrated in the situations and characters, and visual quality was of secondary importance."[118] Started in the middle of winter, *Bed and Board* was often filmed in subzero temperatures. Yet the screenplay clearly states that the characters' costumes are "in keeping with the spring season." Dressed in light clothes, Jean-Pierre Léaud, Claude Jade, and the other actors were numb with cold, while the members of the crew were bundled up in overcoats. "Filming a comedy in winter is particularly difficult," admitted Almendros.[119] The days were short, and so the crew was rushed, and Almendros was deeply distressed about shooting in congested streets filled with gawkers. Truffaut was made so nervous that he decided he would never again film in the streets of Paris.

Fortunately, the last part of the shoot, between February 23 and March 18, 1970, was inside. First, there were a few sequences at Christine Darbon's parents' house in Patin, the same house as in *Stolen Kisses.* Then the scenes in the Doinel couple's home, which, for budgetary reasons, Truffaut filmed in his fifth-floor rented apartment above the offices of Les Films du Carrosse on rue Robert-Estienne. Almendros and his crew very much disliked working in such a confined space. As for Truffaut, these last days on the set put him in a state of perpetual irritation.

The irritation would last beyond the forty-three days of filming. He wasn't pleased with the editing or the music of *Bed and Board,* finding neither spirited, light, or rapid enough. This would be his last collaboration with the editor Agnès Guillemot and the composer Antoine Duhamel. Usually very loyal to his technical crew and collaborators, Truffaut could be merciless in his judgments. He never replaced people during a shoot, but those who dissatisfied him were not hired again. Marcel Berbert or Suzanne Schiffman, his close guardian-protectors, did the dirty work of informing people of their dismissal. As time went on, Truffaut became increasingly demanding about craftsmanship. On this score, *Bed and Board,* though not as depressing as the shoots of *The Soft Skin, Fahrenheit 451,* or *The Bride Wore Black,* deeply dissatisfied him. His next films would be made under different circumstances, far from Paris and its problems, and with new collaborators.

THE CAUSE OF CHILDREN

When *The Wild Child* opened on February 26, 1970, François Truffaut was still shooting *Bed and Board.* He considered *The Wild Child* austere and too rigorous to attract a large public. However, whether because of his reputation as a director, the appeal of the story, or the interest in childhood, within several weeks *The Wild Child* sold 200,000 tickets. The critics' unanimous praise certainly helped. Even before its foreign release, the film inspired no less than 150 articles—a quite impressive number.

On September 9, 1970, *Bed and Board* started a successful exclusive run in the same Paris movie houses that had shown *The Wild Child.* Ticket sales were good the first week, at 40,000, then tapered off slightly, but the film still attracted 220,000 people. With his last two features totaling ticket sales of over 400,000 in Paris, Truffaut began to be generally regarded as a popular director—this without even counting the success of *Stolen Kisses* and regardless of the box-office failure of *Mississippi Mermaid.* His fame can be gauged by the quantity of letters he received on *The Wild Child,* many from teachers or high school students. Truffaut conscientiously replied to each student, explaining his ideas, autographing a photo, sending a gift of a record or a book based on one of his films.

During this period of intense professional activity, Truffaut had more than his usual number of television and radio appearances and he used them to cultivate his image as an educational director. He also stressed his interest in childhood, at times polemically. "My films are a critique of the

French way of bringing up children. I only realized this gradually, through travel. It struck me that the happiness of children is completely unrelated to the wealth of their parents or their country. In Turkey, a poor country, the child is sacred. In Japan, it is inconceivable that a mother show indifference to her son. Here [in France] adult-child relationships are always ugly and petty."[120] Given these observations, Truffaut suggested adopting a personal moral code, behavior that is neither "politically committed" nor "model behavior," but deeply sincere and human. At a time when Leftism was triumphant in intellectual circles, he was content to reassert a few basic principles founded on self-determination, humanism, and cunning.

I see life as very hard; I believe one should have a very simple, very crude and very strong moral system. One should say "yes, yes," and do exactly as one pleases. This is why there can't be any direct violence in my films. Already in *The 400 Blows*, Antoine is a child who never rebels openly. His moral system is more subtle than that. Like me, Antoine is against violence because it signifies confrontation. Violence is replaced by escape, not escape from what is essential, but escape in order to achieve the essential. I think I illustrated this in *Fahrenheit*. This is the most important aspect of the film, the apology for cunning. "Oh, really, books are banned, are they? Fine, we'll learn them by heart!" This is ultimate cunning.[121]

Eager to assert his convictions, Truffaut agreed to be the radio host on the midday news show on RTL from June 22 to 26, 1970. He conceived each broadcast as briskly covering a wide range of controversial topics, including the military, arms sales, and television censorship (the canceled broadcast of the film *The French Under the Occupation,* or the fact that Marcel Ophuls's *The Sorrow and the Pity* and Jean Aurel's *L'Affaire Dreyfus* were never broadcast). There were lighter moments as well—a daily tribute to Charles Trenet, music from films, and excerpts from Jeanne Moreau's latest record. Truffaut innovated by having the station commercials read by amateurs or children against the background noise of the city. And every day, Jean Servais read excerpts from *Madame Bovary.*

During this series of broadcasts, Truffaut also made public his "Open Letter to Annie Girardot,"[122] which was very polemical in tone. The actress had just agreed to play the lead in André Cayatte's film, *To Die of Love,* about Gabrielle Russier, a schoolteacher in Aix-en-Provence who had committed suicide when her love affair with a seventeen-year-old student had been disclosed. Truffaut first attacked Cayatte: "Some directors look for subjects, others find subjects, André Cayatte picks them up, he's even capable of digging into the pockets of warm corpses, like Thénardier salvaging the watches of dying soldiers at Waterloo." Then he appealed to Annie Girardot, in the hope that she would reconsider her decision to take part in Cayatte's film: "Gabrielle Russier killed herself because she couldn't bear it anymore, she regurgitated what was being done to her. Self-destruction was her way of shattering the mirror reflecting her hated image. The image is destroyed and it is sacrilegious to reconstruct it, even with talent, even with a sense of propriety. . . ."

The position he took on this event, which was rocking French society at the time, triggered a heated controversy. It was covered in the press and Truffaut received several hundred letters. When he chose to enter the fray, Truffaut made able use of his status as a public personality. His public stand on certain issues contributed to the portrait of a "man who makes no concessions, and is therefore solitary and sovereign," as he described himself to the critic Jean Collet after his RTL broadcasts. "I left the heads of the radio on rather cool terms after several last-minute conflicts: management's refusal to air certain reportages viewed as 'explosive.' "[123] Truffaut took advantage of heated debates to provoke embarrassment and to shed light on hidden facets of French society, politics, and culture. His image as the classic kindly, shy director then reversed itself and he was seen as a sensitive, sincere man, uncompromising in his convictions.

THE NEW RENOIR

François Truffaut's image outside France was clearer: For some American critics, he was a "new Renoir." The success was paradoxical, following as it did the flop of *Fahrenheit 451*, his only film in English. As the United Artists New York press representative put it, in America his films were beginning to cross "the popcorn barrier"[124] separating the elitist culture of certain avant-garde artists from a wider, cultivated public that included students and academics.

Truffaut contributed to his success by traveling abroad with each of his films, whenever he was not tied up on set or in preproduction. As usual, he was methodical and rigorous: "He spoke to each interlocutor—whether a small-time correspondent for a provincial paper, a journalist for a big American weekly, or an important critic for a big Paris daily—with the same clear diction: He made you feel you were his best friend,"[125] says Philippe Labro. It is true that Truffaut also followed up with friendly thank-you notes to critics and journalists for their articles, picking up on a detail from a previous exchange. Claude Chabrol remembers attending one of the first screenings of *Jules and Jim:* "[With the critics] François began a fantastic campaign of seduction. Keeping a serious, skeptical air, he was very shrewd and had them eating out of his hand. He had a terrific trick with women critics of about forty, who liked him a lot. . . . He acted like a baby with his mother, and this worked very well with the ones who literally felt a maternal affection for him. From then on, he succeeded in tracing a rather cushy path for himself with the critics. . . . He had very few bad surprises."[126]

During these last ten years, he had devoted a great deal of energy to consolidating an astonishing network of foreign friends and correspondents. With each, he maintained a steady exchange of letters, as he did with Koichi Yamada in Japan. This was an asset no other French director possessed. For Alain Vannier, the difference between Truffaut and the others is obvious: "François knew how to take his time; he would spend a week in the United States, when any other director stayed only two days. He liked to schedule only three interviews a day with American journalists, giving time to each. As a result, they couldn't get over his kindness."[127]

In 1970, he made constant trips to present *The Wild Child* and *Bed and Board:* Barcelona, Stockholm, London, Lausanne, Geneva, and Zurich, Vienna and Milan, and even Tehran, where *The Wild Child* was awarded the special prize of the jury at the sixth international film festival. This suggests the breadth of the audience for Truffaut's films; his popularity also extended to Japan and Israel. But apart from Paris, the gauge of a reputation was New York, and here in the early 1970s Truffaut's was unquestionably on the rise. Eighty thousand dollars in box-office receipts for *Stolen Kisses* was hardly trivial for auteur cinema. Similarly, *Bed and Board* was a success in January 1971, bringing in $21,657 in box-office receipts during its first four days. Thanks to Vincent Canby in the *New York Times,* Pauline Kael in *The New Yorker,* and Andrew Sarris in the *Village Voice, Bed and Board* was above all a critical triumph. *"Bed and Board* will turn out to be one of the loveliest, most intelligent movies we'll see in all of 1971,"[128] Canby wrote. In September 1970, *The Wild Child* spread from the movie pages to the columns of magazines, becoming a controversial social and sociological subject in the major American papers. It was programmed on campuses with lecture series on education and child abuse. The film was shown at the eighth New York Film Festival. This was the first time Truffaut presented one of his films at the festival. Two years earlier, the festival's selection committee had rejected *Stolen Kisses*, deeming it too casual for New York critics and audiences. But now they were pleased to schedule Truffaut's film for the festival's opening night, September 10, 1970, in the presence of François Truffaut, Catherine Deneuve, and Jean-Pierre Léaud, to whom *The Wild Child* is dedicated. Honored by the mayor himself, Truffaut was unquestionably the star of the festival.

When the film opened on September 27 at the Fine Arts Theater on East 58th Street, the *New York Times* ran a two-page spread on Truffaut. The article delved into his acting performance in *The Wild Child* and painted a very laudatory portrait of him as a man—his life, his opinions, his relationships with American directors such as Arthur Penn, Mike Nichols, and Stanley Kubrick; even his relationship with Catherine Deneuve was mentioned, a taboo subject in Paris and an indication of Truffaut's relaxed, trusting mood during his stay at the Sherry-Netherland Hotel on Fifth Avenue. As for the film, its box-office performance was quite respectable; it brought in nearly $210,000 in the United States and garnered numerous prizes from associations of critics, writers, and clergymen. Three books by Truffaut were published in the United States during that period, which also contributed to his fame. In May 1969, Grove Press issued the translation of *The 400 Blows;* in 1971, Simon and Schuster published *The Adventures of Antoine Doinel;* then in 1973 Washington Square Press brought out the screenplay of *The Wild Child.*

The many letters sent to Les Films du Carrosse attest to Truffaut's celebrity in the United States. Like Bergman and Fellini, he had become a favorite European director on campus and among American intellectuals. Filmmakers like Stanley Kubrick, screenwriters like Robert Benton and David Newman, actors like Gene Wilder, producers like Daniel Selznick, and editors like Michael Korda all heaped praise and kind regards on him. The director of *Vertigo* sent Truffaut a wonderful tribute, written in awkward French: "I screened your wild child which I find wonderful. Please send me an autograph of the actor who plays the doctor. He is terrific. I desire this autograph for Alma Hitchcock. This film flooded her eyes with tears."[129]

SARTRE'S CAUSE

As a public personality, François Truffaut was often asked to take a position regarding important issues in the political life of his country. But though he was passionately interested in politics and read the papers assiduously, he never ceased being wary of political commitment. In 1967, he turned down membership in the Legion of Honor from Minister of Cultural Affairs André Malraux. "I gladly accept rewards for any of my films, but it is not the same where the duty of the citizen is concerned, which I've never known how to fulfill, since I don't even have a voting card. I think you will understand, therefore, that since I have no civic sense, it would be dishonest of me to solicit any national honor."[130] What most bothered him about any political commitment was the simplification of reality, the Manichaeism implied in any militant discourse, for, as he put it, "life is neither Nazi, Communist, nor Gaullist, it is anarchistic."[131]

Given the political and ideological effervescence of France in the beginning of the seventies, inevitably some of Truffaut's friends urged him to commit himself to the Left—Helen Scott, for example, who was now living in Paris and still passionately interested in politics. Or Marie-France Pisier, who had made her acting debut with him in *Antoine and Colette* in the early sixties and had become a militant left-wing feminist. Truffaut maintained a friendly but stormy relationship with her. "François often feigned not to be interested in politics, to the point where sometimes he would tell me that things were going in the right direction in France after May '68 and that it was pointless to always take issue. In fact, François loathed watching people cast themselves self-importantly in political roles, or as moral spokesmen,"[132] says Pisier. As he himself said, he felt no "affection" for society, but he didn't wish to build another one which he would have no great faith in, either. "I would like to be wrong, but when I hear people say, 'We'll build a different society,' I don't believe it. When they say, 'In the future society the factories will belong to the workers,' I don't believe it. The factories might belong to the state, they'll be managed by government employees, but they'll never belong to the workers. I feel there's a huge amount of hoodwinking going on here."[133] As Truffaut swam against the fashionable tide of left-wing ideas and utopianism, there was no trace of cynicism in his remarks, just a spontaneous mistrust, dating back to his adolescence, of grand, generalizing, and (seemingly) generous concepts. For him, the artist—a term he rarely used and never with reference to himself—must defend his own cause before any other, the cause of artistic freedom, a position he discussed at length in a 1967 interview in *Cahiers du cinéma*:

I'm well aware that in troubled periods, the artist feels himself wavering and is tempted to abandon his art and place himself at the service of a specific, immediate ideal. It's the discrepancy between the frivolousness of his task and the seriousness of history's events that haunts the artist; he wishes he were a philosopher. When these kinds of thoughts come to my mind, I think of Matisse. He lived through three wars and served in none; he was too young in 1870, too old in 1914, a patriarch in 1940. He died in 1954, between the war in Indochina and the Algerian war, and had completed his life's work: fish, women, flowers, landscapes, with sections of windows. The wars were the frivolous events in his life, the thousands of paintings he left were the serious events. Art for art's sake? No. Art for beauty's sake, art for the sake of others. Matisse began by comforting himself, then he comforted others.[134]

Truffaut remained impervious to the revolutionary enthusiasm that was sweeping over a great many of his friends in those days. His reaction to a statement supporting Régis Debray, presented to him by his friend Francesca Solleville, is highly revealing. In November 1969, Régis Debray, a young French supporter of Che Guevara, was facing possible execution after two years' military detention in Bolivia. Many Paris intellectuals rallied to demand that he be pardoned by the Bolivian president. Truffaut refused to add his name to a list that already included Jacques Monod, François Jacob, Laurent Schwartz, and Jean-Paul Sartre. This refusal, for which he gave no reason, seemed natural to him, for he lacked the romantic streak that might have led him to join the international revolutionary movement. He was just as skeptical concerning something much more clear-cut, the war in Vietnam, and refused to come out against the American imperialist intervention. This drove Helen Scott to despair, particularly when he told her he could understand the reasons for the American presence in Vietnam: "For me, Johnson, who is trying to withdraw without losing face, is no more responsible for this war than Ho Chi Minh, who declares, 'We will fight until the last man!' Who knows whether the Vietnamese won't become tyrants in turn?"[135]

Truffaut was just as distrustful of the ideological discussions raging in the movie profession. "As you know, I'm completely unfamiliar with 'protest' cinema and my contribution to such a discussion would really be too slight,"[136] he replied, for example, to the director of the Venice Film Festival, who had invited him to take part in a conference entitled "Cinema and Politics" in September 1968. Truffaut also distrusted the Société des réalisateurs de films (Society of Filmmakers), which was born out of the events of May '68, even though its board of directors included several of his friends, such as Jacques Doniol-Valcroze, Pierre Kast, Claude Lelouch, Louis Malle, Edouard Molinaro, and Claude Sautet. Though he replied to its survey on censorship, he stayed away from its press conferences and refused to give the SRF clips from his censored films (*Shoot the Piano Player* and *Jules and Jim*) to use in a montage aimed at popularizing its struggle against censorship. "I cannot agree to join my filmmaker friends in signing a statement against censorship," he wrote in a private letter to Doniol-Valcroze, "because I feel there are countless ways of outwitting censorship and triumphing over it. I won't fight for principles, but for practical solutions."[137] Truffaut rejected grand abstract concepts and mobilizations on general themes. He suggested to Doniol-Valcroze another strategy: "My idea would be to create an anticensorship committee that would include filmmakers, journalists and public figures. These committee members would give maximum publicity to all the outrageous decisions of the censorship board. They would arrange to publish the dialogue or stills of censored scenes in weekly or monthly magazines, and circulate the material to foreign newspapers, radio and television stations. If this were done diligently, the members of the censorship board would eventually be made to feel that, as the saying goes, 'the game isn't worth the candle.' "[138]

Amid all the post-1968 effervescence of ideas, Truffaut preferred to remain a spectator. He favored gradual reform while admitting that "true reforms have been obtained or rather extracted for the last two years thanks to 'revolutionary actions.' Pompidou promises us Sweden with 'more sunshine.' For the moment, he gives us Sweden with more child abuse, more prison suicides, more unemployed, more needy elderly, more censorship, etc."[139] He hadn't liked Pompidou's predecessor, General de Gaulle, either. The only politician Truffaut admired was Pierre Mendès-France, the former president of the Council under the Fourth Republic and General de Gaulle's political opponent, a man of the Left who was upright, rigorous, and competent. Truffaut's reformism was based on confidence in honest, skilled politicians. The ground he trod was rather unusual in the French political landscape of the time; it was a path with no future, but original, wary of leftism and of the more reliable route that led to the founding and eventual success of François Mitterrand's Socialist party.

On occasion, however, issues that were dear to his heart—such as childhood, opposition to the army, freedom of expression, or women's struggle for legalized abortion—brought Truffaut temporarily closer to the Left. On May 22, 1969, for example, he signed a petition supporting Eric Losfeld, the editor of a small anarchist publishing house, Terrain Vague, who was ordered to submit his books to the Ministry of Justice prior to publication. Similarly, in January 1970, he publicly supported the three young conscripts who were sentenced to military detention for being in possession of left-wing antimilitary news publications.

On June 20, 1970, Truffaut joined Jean-Paul Sartre, Simone de Beauvoir, and many other personalities, including Marie-France Pisier, Alexandre Astruc, and Patrice Chéreau, in selling the leftist newspaper *La Cause du peuple* at the open-air market on rue Daguerre and on the avenue du Général Leclerc, in the fourteenth arrondissement. *La Cause du peuple* was the organ of the Proletarian Left, the foremost Maoist movement to emerge out of the events of May '68; the group had been disbanded by the Interior Ministry in spring 1970, and its paper banned; selling it meant arrest, followed by referral to the Cour de sûreté de l'Etat (high court). Sartre had agreed to become the paper's managing director and, in a show of militancy and solidarity, decided to sell it personally in the streets of Paris. Would the police be so bold as to arrest a Nobel Prizewinner? Asked by Liliane Siegel, an intimate friend of Sartre's, to join the protest, Truffaut enthusiastically agreed. "Sartre had drawn up a list of well-known people to contact to sell *La Cause du peuple*," Liliane Siegel recalls.[140]

Marie-France Pisier remembers Truffaut walking in the street, timidly selling *La Cause du peuple:* "He didn't give a darn about the content of the paper, but the idea that a paper could be banned seemed to him utterly objectionable. As soon as it was a matter of fighting for greater freedom, he was there, capable of proving as much by demonstrating."[141] The demonstration went well, even if one policeman, who had recognized Truffaut but not Sartre, briefly tried to arrest the philosopher and haul him into a police van!

On September 8, 1970, during the trial of the militants of *La Cause du peuple,* Truffaut justified his actions before the president of the high court: "I have never engaged in political activity and am no more a Maoist than a Pompidou supporter, as I am incapable of having feelings for any head of state. But I happen to love books and newspapers, and I cherish freedom of the press and the independence of the judicial system. I also happen to have made a film entitled *Fahrenheit 451,* which depicted and denounced an imaginary society in which the government systematically burned every book; I therefore wanted my ideas as a director to be consistent with my ideas as a French citizen."[142]

The year before, Truffaut had taken part in rescuing *Cahiers du cinéma,* which had become, after May '68, a spearhead of militant extreme-Left ideology. The press magnate Daniel Filipacchi, its majority owner since 1964, felt uncomfortable with the theoretical and political commitment of *Cahiers,* whose monthly pages, he felt, neglected cinema news in favor of analyses influenced by structuralism, psychoanalysis, and Marxism. In October 1969, Filipacchi decided to disassociate himself from these views, and on the 21st of that month the two editors in chief, Jean-Louis Comolli and Jean Narboni, were locked out of their offices on rue Marbeuf. Filipacchi and his associates extended the lockout. The publication of *Cahiers* was therefore interrupted, the majority shareholders formulating "specific demands concerning the liberalization of the magazine, which, according to them, had become obscure and dense and was completely devoid of objectivity in the hands of an uncompromisingly totalitarian editorial staff."[143] In ordering the magazine's suspension, Filipacchi demanded that the journal "be solely devoted to defending and illustrating the seventh art."

A meeting was scheduled for October 23 to try to find a compromise. In the presence of Georges Kiejman, the lawyer for *Cahiers,* and the minority partners, Truffaut and Doniol-Valcroze, Filipacchi demanded the replacement of the current editorial staff by a heterogeneous group of known critics, a spectrum that would include Samuel Lachize from *L'Humanité* and Louis Chauvet from *Le Figaro.* When this proposal was rejected, he gave the staff the opportunity to buy its independence—at a high price: 280,000 francs. Truffaut and Doniol-Valcroze each put up 30,000 francs. They then solicited help from all their friends—Nicole Stéphane, Jean Riboud, Pierre

Cardin, Gérard Lebovici, Michel Piccoli, Claude Berri, Pierre Braunberger, Constantin Costa-Gavras. Three members of the editorial staff, Jean Narboni, Jean-Louis Comolli, and Sylvie Pierre, brought the fund-raising to a close. A first agreement was signed on December 30, 1969, between Filipacchi and Doniol and Truffaut, and the purchase was concluded.

Truffaut thus helped to rescue *Cahiers* even though he no longer recognized himself at all in the magazine's tone, as he confided to Sylvie Pierre on November 20, 1970: "I fear things will go from bad to worse with regard to advertisement, cover choices, punctuality of subscriptions, dates of publication, etc., etc. All of this saddens me, even if it no longer concerns me. So much the better if I'm exaggerating and if reality is less bleak."[144] Since he disagreed with the staff and couldn't attend editorial meetings, Truffaut soon requested that his name be removed from the editorial committee. And so it was, in October 1970. The break between Truffaut and *Cahiers* was then complete; it would last six years, a bitter memory for the filmmaker.

BREAKUPS ARE NECESSARY

After directing four films in two years, François Truffaut was exhausted and felt the need to take a break. He confided to Helen Scott that he had no film project scheduled until 1972: "I'll be able to get down to work on several books devoted to cinema and this will take all my time."[145] It was during this period that he collected his reviews in an anthology, *The Films of My Life,* and wrote the prefaces to the books by his "masters," Bazin, Guitry, and Audiberti.

Just as he was hoping to profit from his time off to pull together his book projects and live his new love life to the fullest, François Truffaut would go through one of the most acute emotional crises of his life. After a few months of living with Catherine Deneuve, a breakup seemed inevitable in the fall of 1970. For Truffaut, love of cinema, his desire to make films and his obsession with work were absolute priorities—to which his love life had to yield place. He probably secretly believed that harmonious love relationships were more likely to exist on screen than in real life. At the end of 1970, during the Christmas vacation, while his companion was off skiing, François Truffaut left the apartment and moved into a hotel. Perhaps it was all a complete misunderstanding. Truffaut confided to Madeleine, "I thought she wanted me to leave!"[146] In the belief that he was resolving a crisis, he brought on a break that threw him into a much deeper crisis. "The *Mermaid* is primarily the story of a degradation by love, the story of a passion. I think that most of my films are built around a chain of events in which the protagonist—who is always weaker than his partner—gets caught," he said about his film.[147] These words could not be more appropriate: *Mississippi Mermaid* allowed Truffaut to live a great love story, with a beginning, a middle, and an end. The end, unfortunately, was more like a tragedy than a Hollywood comedy.

This breakup left Truffaut devastated. To his old friend and confidante Aimée Alexandre, he mentioned "a distressing end of year, in morale and love life."[148] She tried to comfort her "dearly beloved little François" in a beautiful letter written on December 31, 1970: "I feel terribly sad about your sadness. Today, I can't prevent myself from telling you what my white hair knows and what you must be aware of from your perceptiveness: there are no accidental breakups. Breakups are always necessary. But we never realize it when they occur, and we suffer as though we had lost the essential, and we blame ourselves for not having known how to overcome circumstances. This suffering is useless, inadequate, yet it is bitter for it absorbs all actions and all thoughts. You've had all the opportunities, too many opportunities, you say. It is true. And you deserved them. But you will still have the one of encountering the essential."[149]

Truffaut had the feeling of a missed opportunity. Undoubtedly, at the time, he even had a deep sense of failure in part of his life, for once again a serious relationship, *la vie de couple,* had eluded him. As his depression worsened, he couldn't sleep, no matter how exhausted; sometimes he spent entire days without leaving the suite he had rented in mid-December in the Hotel George V. Later, he moved temporarily to the fifth-floor apartment in the building of Les Films du Carrosse, where he stayed alone with his dark thoughts. Jeanne Moreau advised him to consult Dr. René Held. This elderly man of seventy-eight, a psychoanalyst and specialist in psychosomatic medicine, completely charmed Truffaut, who found him "colorful and unbelievably full of vitality . . . very talkative and rabidly anti-American."[150] He recommended an anti-asthenia treatment, prescribed sedatives and sleeping pills, and advised Truffaut to take a ten-day sleeping cure. This was the same radical but effective treatment that had brought the Jean-Paul Belmondo character back to normal life in *Mississippi Mermaid.* On January 27, 1971, Marcel Berbert drove Truffaut to the Villa-des-Pages clinic in Le Vésinet, near Versailles, where he remained for a week. Using pep pills and sedatives, Truffaut tried to overcome his depression. As he wrote Aimée Alexandre, with a touch of irony, "the colors of my pills have become my only landscape." Yet, he added, he only felt he had returned to the world of humans when he opened "his window to throw them all out like multicolored confetti."[151]

7.
CINEMA MAN:
1971–1979

"I hope you'll soon see me as I used to be, more cheerful,"[1] François Truffaut wrote to the screenwriter Jean-Loup Dabadie in the beginning of 1971. After his sleeping cure he remained under medical supervision for several months. Subject to sudden attacks of depression, his mood was melancholic. "I am probably in less danger than I was a few weeks ago," he confided to Liliane Siegel. "But the little nightly nightmare, eight times out of ten about Catherine, of course, reminds me of the black hole. In adversity—the word is too strong—one feels one can easily sink into bitterness, denigrating everything and everyone, and this I really don't want."[2] Until spring, Truffaut, under sedatives, lived at a slower pace, conscious of "returning from afar."[3] During this entire period, Marcel Berbert handled the company's business, for which Truffaut was thankful to him: "At the beginning of the year, the Carrosse really had one wheel over the edge; you helped me, quietly but very energetically, to get things back on track. I hope everything will go smoothly from now on."[4]

Madeleine Morgenstern remembers this depressive period as "very violent; it stemmed from his distress at being rejected by Catherine Deneuve. François thought he was in control of the situation—he thought things would evolve slowly, that Catherine would change her mind—but he was brought up short when she did break up with him. He fell apart then; I had never seen François like that."[5] Truffaut lived waiting for Catherine

Deneuve's phone calls, was thrown into a panic at the slightest delay, looked anxiously and incessantly at his watch, and chain-smoked. "I would have done anything to put an end to it," Madeleine added.

During this whole period, Truffaut avoided Paris. Whenever he was obliged to visit at least briefly, he took refuge in a hotel or in his office, and spent much of his time rereading the childhood papers and documents he had recovered in 1968, at the time of his mother's death. This aroused a feeling of guilt which only increased his melancholy. His mourning, two and a half years late, for a mother whom he had never understood, added to the depression caused by his love life and reinforced his feelings of solitude and abandonment. Thanks to the support of his loved ones, he tried to get back on his feet. Madeleine, though she had remarried (a marriage that would last only a few months), was by his side as often as possible. She accompanied him to Nice, where he stayed for a few weeks at the Négresco Hotel, until Jean-Louis Richard joined him to work on a new screenplay (*Day for Night*). Then he went to Jeanne Moreau's for a rest in her house at La Garde-Freinet.

TWO ENGLISH GIRLS

During this dark period of his life, Truffaut found a veritable lifeline in Henri-Pierre Roché's novel *Les deux Anglaises et le Continent* (*The Two English Girls and the Continent*), which he had already read and thought of adapting several years earlier.[6] He read it over and over again, to the point where he knew every single line by heart. Giving up all thought of a sabbatical year, he decided, as a matter of urgency, to make this his next film. Jean-Claude Brialy, his confidant during his depression, fully understood the stakes involved in *Two English Girls* when he wrote to Truffaut: "My thoughts are very much with you right now as you start work on the film which you suddenly called forth to chase the bad clouds from your mind. I hope the work and joy of shooting prevent your being sad."[7] Filming to live, shooting to heal—rarely would cinema have such a vital function.

Ten years after *Jules and Jim*, Truffaut reimmersed himself in Roché's world—though, actually, he had never really cut himself off, since after the writer's death he had remained in touch with Denise, Roché's wife, and their son, Jean-Claude. He had arranged for his secretaries to type up Roché's numerous intimate notebooks, which would certainly have been lost or dispersed if not for Truffaut's stubborn determination to get them published. But his submissions to publishers—Robert Laffont, Flammarion, Hachette, and Gallimard—were rejected.[8] Truffaut would use some passages from these notebooks for the screenplays of *Two English Girls* and, several years later, *The Man Who Loved Women*.

Truffaut had started negotiating with Gallimard for the screen rights to *Two English Girls* in 1968. The publisher had requested 150,000 francs, a sum Truffaut found exorbitant. He had reminded Gallimard that his film *Jules and Jim* had greatly contributed to reviving the sales of Roché's novel. Fifteen thousand copies were sold during the sixties, and translations were published in Italy, England, Germany, and Holland. Truffaut also used as part of his argument Claude Gallimard's refusal to publish Roché's notebooks: "I know that I shouldn't necessarily see a connection between your financial demand for the rights to *Two English Girls* which seems excessive to me, and the minimal interest the Gallimard house shows for Roché's posthumous works, but nevertheless I feel your offer was made without your realizing everything I have done to champion one of your writers and make him known."[9] Gallimard responded by halving their asking price for the screen rights to *Two English Girls*.

Gruault started working on the adaptation, using Truffaut's annotated copy of the novel. He also read Roché's notebooks. It was an arduous task, for Truffaut wished to use extensive material (the novel and the notebooks) to draft a simple and linear screenplay. One year later, in March 1969, Gruault dropped off four large manuscript notebooks at Les Films du Carrosse; these amounted to the first version of the screenplay of *Two English Girls*. Typed, the script, divided into ninety-five sequences, came to 552 pages.

The story is set at the beginning of the century, over a long stretch of time punctuated by separations, trips, reunions, and deaths; it tells of several intertwining lives in a novelistic manner. Two young sisters from Wales, Muriel and Anne Brown, are in love with a Frenchman, Claude Roc, whom they call "the Continent." Claude, a young Parisian (in reality, Henri-Pierre Roché in his youth), plans to make a literary career for himself and gradually becomes an art lover. He was brought up by his widowed mother. In Paris, Claude first meets Anne, who secretly sees him as a good match for her sister, Muriel, whom she fervently admires. Claude then goes to spend the summer in Wales with the Brown family. At first, he hardly notices Muriel, but then he has a sudden revelation of his love for her, so much so that he wants to marry her. But Claude's mother is strongly opposed to their marriage and requests that the two young people separate for a year. When he returns to Paris, Claude has other affairs and sends Muriel a breakup letter that deeply hurts her. Anne, who has settled in Paris to study sculpture, becomes Claude's mistress. When Muriel comes to Paris and her sister tells her of their liaison, she feels completely shattered. She returns to England immediately. Claude sinks into depression, then recovers by telling the story in a novel, *Jérome and Julien*. Several years later, after Anne's death, he sees Muriel again in Calais and they make love for the first time, with Muriel demanding as a condition their immediate and definitive separation.

Discouraged by the scope of the project and the thick script, Truffaut had put it aside for two years. It wasn't until March 1971 that he began to work again on Jean Gruault's enormous opus. Armed with a pair of scissors and Scotch tape, he reduced it to two hundred pages, then asked Gruault to work on it again. While refocusing their attention on *Two English Girls*, they read all the biographies of Charlotte and Emily Brontë, "who were also English, puritanical, novelistic and impassioned,"[10] as well as Marcel Proust's recollections of his youth. "The hero of *Two English Girls* is a bit like a young Proust who might have fallen in love with Charlotte and Emily Brontë, and loved both of them for over ten years without being able to choose one or the other."[11] Anne's dying words—"My mouth is full of earth"—are taken from Emily Brontë. In the final screenplay, *Two English Girls* has shed much of its initial Belle Epoque setting and focuses solely on the feelings that bind Claude, Anne, and Muriel. "This isn't a film about physical love, but a physical film about love," Truffaut pointed out. "It is a romantic story that I wanted to make novelistic. I think that with this work, I wanted to squeeze love dry like a lemon."[12]

But it is a painful love story, and because the film shows this suffering, it can be read as the intimate journal of its convalescing director. Therein lies the true key to this work: the feverishness that binds human beings in passionate intimacy; the impulses that overpower the body and from which no one can free himself—such as Muriel's onanism, the ailing expression in Muriel's eyes when she loses her virginity, Claude's broken leg and his premature aging, Anne's thirst for life and her fatal tuberculosis. Physical and spiritual pain are the raw material of this film, the pain of human beings subjected to the ordeals of intense affections. These sufferings shed a harsh light on the distress of the director, who had himself loved two sisters, one of whom had deserted him in death, and the other in life.

Roché's writing burns like a smoldering inner flame in Truffaut's film. Rarely has the very substance of a book been filmed more forthrightly. Indeed, during the credits, one is shown the pages of Roché's book annotated by Truffaut, his deletions, his hesitations, and the words he circled in ink. The writing is also embodied in the voice-over, read by Truffaut himself with a haste and concentration that shows how deeply he identified with the characters' feelings.

After the success of *The Wild Child* and *Bed and Board*, Truffaut had no trouble finding financing for the film. Berbert and he maintained their collaboration with the independent producer-distributor Hercule Mucchielli.

The estimated budget was 3,850,000 francs, which was modest for a period film requiring several sets and a twelve-week shoot. Columbia Pictures contributed a $400,000 advance for the American distribution rights.

Preproduction, between March and April 1971, was rapid and intense. The Carrosse crew rallied around Suzanne Schiffman. Roland Thénot (location manager), Jean-Pierre Kohut-Svelko (assistant set designer), and Jean-François Stévenin found landscapes in the Norman Cotentin peninsula, which closely resembles Wales, where much of the film is supposed to take place. This choice suited Truffaut, since it made shooting conditions simpler. Stévenin also found a beautiful location in the Jura, near a beautiful lake, and an antiquated railroad surrounded by a forest in the Ardèche.

Truffaut didn't hesitate for a moment in casting Jean-Pierre Léaud as Claude Roc, the attractive, indecisive, fragile young dandy. Truffaut also hoped to dissociate the actor from the Antoine Doinel character. "It's as though you were playing the part of Jim," Truffaut wrote when sending him the screenplay. "This will be the most difficult part for you because you'll have to act as though you were born rich and powerful."[13] To cast the parts of the two English girls, Truffaut turned to Oscar Lewenstein, his friend in London who had produced *Fahrenheit 451* and *The Bride Wore Black*. Almost as soon as Truffaut came out of the clinic, he asked him to set up a casting call for about one hundred young actresses. "They should be between eighteen and twenty-four years old, not too tall to play opposite Jean-Pierre Léaud, and speak French as well as possible."[14] In mid-March, Suzanne Schiffman traveled to London for a first selection. Truffaut traveled himself for final auditions in early April and chose Kika Markham and Stacey Tendeter—the first for the part of Anne, the second for the part of Muriel. The brunette and redhead were unacquainted with each other, nor did they resemble each other, but they would get along perfectly during the filming. While in London, Truffaut also hired Sylvia Marriott, a known British stage actress, for the part of Mrs. Brown, the girls' mother.

Truffaut completed the casting with Philippe Léotard, Irène Tunc, and Marie Mansart, and as was his custom, assigned some of the secondary parts to his collaborators. Georges Delerue appears as Madame Roc's businessman, and Marcel Berbert as the owner of an art gallery. Laura and Eva, his daughters, are in the opening shot of the film, playing by the swing with Mathieu and Guillaume, Suzanne Schiffman's children.

On April 28, 1971, barely three months after leaving the clinic, Truffaut welcomed the cast and crew of the film at the Hague-Dick Hotel, a pension in Auderville in the Cotentin area. The shoot of the *Two English Girls* began nearby, on a beautiful estate rented from the Anquetil family, the ideal set for Mrs. Brown's "Welsh" house. Truffaut had some trees cut down in the garden to clear the view to the sea, but in every other respect the spot was perfect for his project, particularly the wild moor on the edge of the cliff where Claude, Anne, and Muriel pour out their feelings. When it rained, as it occasionally did there in the spring, the cast and crew remained cloistered inside the Anquetil house for the many interior scenes. When the rain stopped, they shot exterior scenes on the cliff. On May 8, Truffaut shot the big reunion scene between Claude and Muriel that occurs at the end of the story; it was shot in Cherbourg, though it is supposed to be set in Calais. Claude is on the quay waiting for Muriel, who disembarks from the boat; they meet again after a separation of several years and will have their sole night of lovemaking. "The sun was reflecting off the water in such a way," said Almendros, "that it was shedding waves of light on the hull of the ship. I said to François, 'Look how beautiful it would be if we could have them meet in front of this shimmering light.' He said, 'Let's go, quickly, we must do it.' We shot the scene and then in the editing he eliminated the dialogue. He put in Delerue's music and said to me, 'When you have an image with light like that, it is the equivalent of a line of dialogue.' It was as though the passion, the inner vibration, were projected in the image. When he saw a strong idea, he was eager to adopt it."[15]

In the beginning of June, one part of the cast and crew went to Lamastre, in the Vivarais, to shoot the station and antique railroad in Cheylard. Then they filmed in Paris and its environs, in various interiors and in the Musée Rodin for the last scene in the film, where, ten years later, Claude thinks he recognizes Muriel's daughter among the visiting English schoolgirls looking at the sculptor's works. The filming ended in July in the Jura, near the Lac de la Motte.

All in all, Truffaut was very satisfied with the shoot and felt he had made his masterpiece. Thanks to the steady support of his friends on the set, he had regained his self-confidence. "I was not alone in digging this first tunnel under the Channel, which, I hope, *Two English Girls* is."[16] Filmmaking turned out to be the most effective way for him to chase away his "dark thoughts" and finally sleep "without sleeping pills."[17] The idea of living alone in Paris became less frightening to him. Truffaut knew that work was his only remedy, the only thing that mobilized him completely and engaged his strongest emotions. "When I am working, I become attractive," he wrote to Liliane Dreyfus during the filming, "I feel it and at the same time this work, which is the best in the world, puts me in an emotional state that is propitious for the beginning of a *love story* [in English]. Before me, there is usually a young girl or woman, agitated, fearful and obedient, trusting and ready to surrender herself. What happens next is always the same. Sometimes the *love story* is synchronized with the filming and ends with it; at other times it continues afterward, by the will of one or both. . . ."[18] His affair with Kika

Markham, which started during the filming of *Two English Girls,* lasted for several months thereafter.

Truffaut gave himself a few weeks' vacation, from July 20, 1971 to the end of August, in a rented house in Antibes, the Villa Mirasol, on boulevard du Cap. It was only a part-time vacation, for he supervised Yann Dedet's editing of his film in the Victorine Studios in Nice. But he could also see Madeleine, Laura, and Eva, who were spending the summer at the Résidence Saint-Michel in Cannes, and entertain a succession of friends— Bernadette Lafont, Liliane Dreyfus, Suzanne Schiffman, Jean Aurel, Jean-Loup Dabadie, Jean-Louis Richard, and Jean Gruault. The last three were each working, separately, on Truffaut's next films—*Such a Gorgeous Kid Like Me, Day for Night,* and *The Story of Adèle H.* Truffaut recovered his good spirits by playing with his daughters, whose "cheerfulness and health" were of great help to him; they recounted the "funny, salacious stories told to them by older girls and which they only half-understand. We laugh a lot. They are thriving, and are far less jealous of one another. . . ."[19]

After a first screening of *Two English Girls* at the Victorine Studios, in the presence of Aurel (his "personal consultant,"[20] as Truffaut called him), Dabadie, and Jean-Louis Richard, the director was confident. "They think it's the most beautiful of my films, thanks to the photography,"[21] he wrote a short time later to Nestor Almendros. At the beginning of September, Truffaut was back in Paris for another screening, on rue de Ponthieu, attended by Léaud, Delerue, Gruault, Gérard Lebovici, Serge Rousseau, and the technical crew. "Everyone is very pleased,"[22] he wrote euphorically to Almendros on September 11. For those close to him, *Two English Girls* is unquestionably his most moving, most formally successful, and most novelistic film. The critic Louis Marcorelles wrote to him: "I felt very close to you in this film which seems to concern you so intimately, not because of any immodesty, but because your sensitivity, your passion show through constantly."[23] Before the film was released, Truffaut received about fifty letters, all laudatory, from friends who had had the privilege of seeing the film at a private screening. "Not only is this your most beautiful film, but the beginning of a new oeuvre, ripened by time and pain,"[24] the director Paul Vecchiali wrote to him, for example. "François, in spite of my enthusiasms at the time, I never believed that the New Wave meant anything else than the desire to take the place of others. Now, thanks to you, a work provides a deep justification for this change,"[25] wrote Jean Eustache. And Denise Roché: "This film is so important that the audience will have the patience and humility to understand it. I watched it—throughout—as though Pierre had been by my side."[26]

After a warm preview screening at the Cinémathèque française, the film came out in seven Paris movie theaters on November 24, 1971. The first two weeks were disastrous—barely thirty thousand tickets were sold. Curiously, the press was clearly divided into partisans and detractors. Many would criticize the film for being cold, gratuitous, even vulgar: "Truffaut dwells on things and even indulges in bad taste by drenching the sheets of a bridal bed with blood,"[27] wrote Robert Chazal about the sequence where Muriel loses her virginity. Truffaut, who had read, annotated, and underlined these remarks, was deeply affected by them. Faced with a double failure, commercial and critical, he reacted violently and decided to pull the film from the Paris theaters and cut it by fourteen minutes. With the running time of *Two English Girls* reduced to one hour and fifty-eight minutes, exhibitors could schedule one additional showing a day. In so doing, Truffaut tried to avert disaster and minimize the loss of money to Hercule Mucchielli, his financial partner, who had already complained about the "length of the film, the occasional unnecessary narration, and especially the bloodstain."[28] "I don't scorn money," Truffaut tried to justify what some saw as self-censorship, "I have no consuming love for it, but the idea of making someone else lose money is unbearable to me. I like my work enough to believe it is interesting, but not enough to believe it is indispensable or irreproachable."[29] Truffaut trimmed his voice-over narration but refused to cut the shot of Muriel's bloodstain, certainly the most intimate shot he ever filmed. He was very attached to Roché's sentence about this: "There was red on her gold." For Truffaut, this moment represented the imprint of unleashed passions. Furthermore, if he chose to shoot *Two English Girls* at a difficult period of his life, it was because he felt that the return to life entailed an excess of lovesickness. Truffaut had recovered perhaps, but *Two English Girls* still preserved the indelible trace of fevered anguish.

Abroad, the reception was better than in Paris. Truffaut traveled to various places with his film, primarily to escape depression. In places other than Paris, he felt more confident, far from the escalating failures that seemed once again to have taken hold of his life. This is clear from the interview he gave to Canadian television in December 1971, where he spoke openly and at length about his childhood and adolescence, his army desertion, the setbacks in his career—all subjects that he was reluctant to broach with French journalists. Truffaut sojourned in Montreal with Madeleine from December 13 to 17. It was then that he recorded the three-hour televised interview with Aline Desjardins, as part of the program *Femme d'aujourd'hui (Today's Woman)*, directed by Gilles Derome: "What I said on that day, I'd never said elsewhere, and I'll never say again."[30] Then Truffaut spent the Christmas and New Year holidays in Athens, with his family—Madeleine, Laura (who was beginning to study Greek and would thereby be encouraged), and Eva. Family harmony, "a very happy moment in a time of distress,"[31] he wrote to Liliane Siegel on December 30, 1971.

THE FEMALE HOODLUM

"When I've just shot a sad film, I have only one desire: to make a cheerful film."[32] To quickly forget the *Two English Girls* disaster, Truffaut started work on a new film three months later. If romantic passion was not understood, perhaps farce would help put him back on the road to success and deliver him from this difficult period. Deliberately funny and nutty, *Une belle fille comme moi* (*Such a Gorgeous Kid Like Me*) rests entirely on Bernadette Lafont's talent. Launched by Truffaut and Chabrol in the early years of the New Wave, the actress had married the sculptor Diourka Medveczki and had had three children. In the late sixties, she made her screen comeback and worked at a frenetic pace, appearing in films by Louis Malle, Philippe Garrel, Jean-Daniel Pollet, and Nadine Trintignant. But her career was truly relaunched in 1969 by *A Very Curious Girl*, directed by Nelly Kaplan. "Bernadette Lafont," as Jacques Audiberti put it, "performs as though her life depended on it." And Truffaut, it could be said, filmed "as though his life depended on it."[33] This shared energy brought the filmmaker and actress close at a time when both needed to immerse themselves in cinema in order to forget life's misfortunes.

In November 1969, Truffaut had read the novel *Such a Gorgeous Kid Like Me* by the American writer Henry Farrell; it had been published the year before in Gallimard's Série Noire under the French title *Le Chant de la sirène*. "One day I happened to start reading this novel on a Paris–Madrid flight," Truffaut explained, "a stewardess who heard me roar with laughter at every page went to warn the head pilot that a passenger had gone crazy and perhaps the control tower should be alerted."[34] The story is about a sociologist (Stanislas Prévine, in the French version) who is investigating female criminals. Through his work, he becomes particularly interested in the case of Camille Bliss, a petulant prisoner whose slang is irresistible and who is suspected of having killed her father and one of her many lovers. Truffaut was attracted to Camille because she was a "female hoodlum,"[35] like Deneuve's character in *Mississippi Mermaid*. A reserved man brimming with contradictions, Truffaut was always attracted by these kinds of women, who reminded him of certain women in his youth.

He learned from Gallimard that the screen rights to the novel were owned by Columbia Pictures. On March 15, 1971, he wrote to Columbia producers Stanley Schneider and Jack Wiener, offering to direct the film for the American company. Columbia temporized, for the project had already been offered to Blake Edwards. But in August, when Edwards turned it down, the way was open for Truffaut. It was then only a matter of specifying the terms of the coproduction deal between Les Films du Carrosse and the Hollywood studio; the latter agreed to finance a film with a budget of about 3 million francs.

While he was in Antibes in the summer of 1971, Truffaut invited Bernadette Lafont to come stay with him and discuss the film with him and Jean-Loup Dabadie. A young screenwriter, Dabadie had just made a name for himself with two Claude Sautet films, *Les Choses de la vie* and *Max et les Ferrailleurs,* and two Philippe de Broca comedies, *La Poudre d'escampette* and *Chère Louise.* "The screenplay of *Louise* is what made me want to work with you, because for the first time I felt I was reading a French script that could be shot as is,"[36] Truffaut wrote to Dabadie in January 1971. Paradoxically, Truffaut's dream was to have a script that was "ready to go," that he wouldn't have to constantly "fill in" and "patch up."[37] "This is what I want and what I need," he emphasized to Dabadie, momentarily preferring a degree of professional comfort in the writing of the screenplay to the "amateurism of his usual collaborators." Dabadie and he hit it off well, with Truffaut finding his "new acolyte funny, friendly and stimulating."[38] The two men worked together for three weeks in Antibes, sketching out the outline of the screenplay, which Dabadie would write the following autumn.

In *Such a Gorgeous Kid Like Me* the sociologist Stanislas Prévine finds out the details of Camille Bliss's past. After causing the death of her alcoholic father as a child, she had been sent to a center for juvenile delinquents. She ran away and married the first man she met, Clovis Bliss, whose mother was hiding a tidy sum. After searching for it in vain, Camille, who dreams of a nightclub singing career, deceives her husband with a singer, Sam Golden. Mad with rage, Clovis gets run over by a car and ends up paralyzed in a wheelchair. Camille then takes up with Arthur, a mystical rat exterminator who loses his virginity with her, but she ends up the victim of a shady lawyer, Murène, who makes her sign compromising papers. Cornered, Camille tries to kill off Clovis and Murène with Arthur's rat-exterminating machine. Arthur saves them but wants to draw Camille into a double suicide by jumping from church towers. Arthur jumps alone. Camille is charged with murder and finds herself in jail. Stanislas Prévine is secretly in love with the woman who is becoming his thesis subject. He succeeds in getting his hands on an amateur film shot at Arthur's death which proves Camille's innocence. Freed, she becomes a famous singer. But Clovis tracks her down and threatens her; she kills him and manages to pin the murder on Stanislas. The sociologist ends up in jail.

The first screenplay didn't satisfy Truffaut. He felt that the character of Stanislas, the investigating sociologist, had been sacrificed in favor of

Camille, the female criminal. Because of this imbalance, Camille Bliss's slang dwarfed Stanislas Prévine's scientific interpretations. "My dear Jean-Loup, I'm not the least bit worried about the way you make Bernadette talk. All will go well. We must rework the 'report' side of the narrative, which will allow us to shoot a film that won't be presented as a comedy, but will be 100 percent deadpan."[39] Dabadie reworked the screenplay, but when Truffaut started the shoot, he was still not satisfied.

He started casting the film in the middle of winter, 1971–1972, with Philippe Léotard in the part of Clovis, Camille Bliss's young alcoholic husband; Guy Marchand in the part of Sam Golden, the star of the Colt Saloon, a slightly vulgar singer with charm; and Claude Brasseur as the shady lawyer who goes by the gentle name of Murène. Arthur, the rat exterminator, is played by Charles Denner, who is different from the other characters, "in his more mystical, more pompous, more puritanical style."[40] Truffaut considered playing the part of Stanislas Prévine himself. He had enjoyed acting in *The Wild Child* and felt ready to renew the experience, for "I'm sure I would be impassive and that a contrast would be created between Bernadette and me,"[41] he wrote to Dabadie. Once the script was completed, however, Truffaut gave up the idea, since he didn't feel prepared to take on comedy. Instead, he chose André Dussollier for the part, a twenty-six-year-old first-prize graduate in comedy from the Conservatoire and a new member of the Comédie-Française. This would be Dussollier's first screen role, and his sober and elegant appearance conferred a suitable air of bourgeois respectability on the part.

Nestor Almendros, who was in great demand with other directors, was unavailable on Truffaut's shooting dates. So the director hired Pierre-William Glenn as director of photography for this comic film, in which speed of execution and pacing were more important than aesthetic qualities. Glenn was to be assisted by his cameraman Walter Bal, and Jean-Pierre Kohut-Svelko was hired as set designer. Aged twenty-six, a graduate of the Ecole des Beaux-Arts in Paris, Kohut-Svelko had already been assistant set designer for *Mississippi Mermaid* and *Two English Girls*. His collaboration with Truffaut was to be long-lasting.

In early February, Truffaut went to live in Béziers for the filming, in a large apartment he had rented in the center of town. He appeared relaxed, and the mild Languedoc winter seemed to agree with him; he took advantage of his housekeeper Marie's presence to invite his actors to dinner as they showed up on location for the shoot. "François loved jokes, and Denner and Brasseur certainly didn't abstain. Twice I saw François laugh so hard that he had to leave the table to go throw up,"[42] Bernadette Lafont recalls. The shooting, which started on February 14, unfolded in a very pleasant atmosphere. "Bernadette, really funny, is always laughing and easy to work with, Claude Brasseur is excellent, Charles Denner sublime,"[43] Truffaut wrote to Liliane Siegel. The film was mostly shot in Béziers, at the B.G.M. Brasserie, on Place d'Espagne, where a set had been created for the Bliss home. The courtyard of the prison where Camille is detained was erected in the former Béziers slaughterhouse; the visiting-room scenes were shot in the courthouse on Place de la Révolution. The cast and crew later moved to the outskirts of the city, then to Sète, and finally to Lunel, where Suzanne Schiffman had found a bar and dance hall with a western ambience, Le Rodéo, which was perfect for Sam Golden's singing act.

Bernadette Lafont's part fit her like a glove, and she was happy to work again with the person who had launched her acting career. "François was very attached to the character of Camille Bliss," she recalls. "He even said that if he had been a woman, he would have been like her, for this woman wasn't rehabilitated by society. She predated original sin."[44] Everything went smoothly until the day following the last day of the shoot. On that day, Truffaut, who was staying at the Hotel Imperator in Nîmes, "forgot" to stop by to pick up Bernadette Lafont, who was living in Lunel with the rest of the cast and crew. "He had said to me, 'Do you want me to give you a ride back to Paris? We're leaving very early tomorrow morning. Be in front of your hotel at nine o'clock.' I was there waiting with my suitcases. I waited until eleven o'clock, but he never showed up! In the evening, I phoned him, hurt, and François burst out laughing: 'My dear Bettine, listen, I forgot about you!' He didn't need me anymore!"[45] After a forty-six-day shoot, Truffaut was exhausted. He had just made two films right after recovering from a depression, and his mind was already on the problems of the next one. Very shortly after returning to Paris, he decided to give himself a few days' rest in Normandy, in the beautiful house Liliane Dreyfus and her husband had acquired in 1968. From then on, the Ranconnière manor near Deauville would become one of Truffaut's favorite spots. "He came often," says Liliane Dreyfus. "He did a lot of work there."[46]

In the meantime, Georges Delerue composed a rhythmical orchestral score and Guy Marchand set to music the two songs written by Jean-Loup Dabadie—Sam Golden's song and the song sung to great acclaim by Camille Bliss at the end of the film. Before it opened, on September 13, 1972, *Such a Gorgeous Kid Like Me* was shown in preview in Lyon, in the presence of François Truffaut and Bernadette Lafont, to inaugurate the renovated Belle-cour movie theater. Bernadette Lafont also presented the film in Béziers on the eve of its Paris release, to an audience of local officials and most of the extras who lived in the city. The actress already felt she was shouldering this film on her own, a film in which she doesn't stop running, and which rests entirely on her energy. "When François saw the audience reactions, he said to me, 'This film belongs to you, this character is you, so you handle it!' He had sensed that the response was unexceptional for him, while things would go well for me."[47]

Indeed, the reviews of the film focused on Bernadette Lafont's performance. After a seven-week exclusive run, ticket sales for the film fell just short of 100,000. It did better in Italy, where it was shown in the spring of 1973 under the title *Mica Scema la Ragazza!* and was helped by catchy slogans such as *"Supercomico, Supersexy, Super-film."* In the United States, *Such a Gorgeous Kid Like Me* was released simultaneously in eight large cities (an exceptional event for a Truffaut film), and it was a reasonable success in spite of a lukewarm, disappointed response from the press. But the director's mind was elsewhere; his thoughts were already on his next film.

DAY FOR NIGHT

During the editing of *Two English Girls* at the Victorine Studios, François Truffaut had become intrigued by the remains of a huge exterior set that had been erected several years earlier for an American production of *The Madwoman of Chaillot*. Though it was slightly damaged, the set consisted of several building facades, a subway entrance, and a Paris sidewalk café. He started to explore the Victorine Studios thoroughly, with a mind to "shooting a film about cinema."[48]

It would be *La Nuit américaine* (*Day for Night*), which he wanted to write with Jean-Louis Richard, with whom he hadn't collaborated since *The Bride Wore Black*. The two men set to work in a rented house in Antibes; using a roll of blank white paper, they set down the main events of the script. "When we had an idea, our problem was to integrate it at a chosen moment in the film and we would inscribe it at a specific place on the big roll. That way we had an almost graphic overview of the film, a story line from which we could deviate, but which allowed us to maintain a pacing,"[49] Jean-Louis Richard explains. The fleshing out of the film progressed rapidly and by mid-August 1971, Truffaut already had the first draft of a screenplay telling the story of a film shoot.

Day for Night was then held in abeyance while Truffaut filmed *Such a Gorgeous Kid Like Me*. In January 1971, he met with Jean-Louis Richard again at Le Martinez, his hotel in Cannes. This was when they came up with the story for *Je vous présente Pamela* (*Meet Pamela*), the film within the film. A young man introduces his fiancée to his father, who falls in love and runs off with her. Suzanne Schiffman, with her thorough knowledge of the technical and human aspects of life on a film set, helped them with the final version of the screenplay. This would be the first time she would be listed as co-scenarist, as well as assistant director, in the credits of a Truffaut film.

Day for Night takes place during a film shoot and mixes the actors' private lives with the plot of the film in which they are acting, thereby showing the ties that bind all the members of a cast and crew. The shooting of *Je vous présente Pamela*, under the direction of Ferrand, is about to begin in the Victorine Studios. The extras are milling in front of a big set. The technicians bombard the director with questions, while the actors gradually arrive on set, each with his or her problems and private concerns. The film's female lead, Julie Baker, a psychologically fragile American star, is expected any minute with her husband, Dr. Nelson. Alphonse, the male lead playing opposite her, has arrived with his girlfriend, Liliane, whom he has succeeded in getting hired as an apprentice script girl. Alexandre, an elderly French actor and veteran of eighty-four films, plays Alphonse's father. In *Je vous présente Pamela*, he has to play opposite a long-lost former mistress, Séverine, an ex-Hollywood star who has been cast as his wife. All the members of the cast and crew are lodged in a hotel, where Ferrand prepares the following day's scenes and dialogues with his assistant, Joëlle. The filming progresses but seems at times to escape Ferrand's control because of the actors' and technicians' personal lives. Thus, when Liliane walks off the set with an English stuntman, Alphonse threatens to bring the entire movie to a halt. Ferrand tries to convince him to continue, while trying to protect Julie Baker, who has just spent the night with Alphonse. The following morning, Alphonse tells Dr. Nelson that he has slept with his wife. Julie is in despair. Her husband forgives her and reassures her. The shooting can now resume. However, the production manager then arrives on the set with dreadful news: Alexandre has just had a fatal car accident on the road to the airport.[50] Thanks to the efforts of the entire cast and crew, the shoot is completed in five days, with a stand-in and some script changes.

LIKE A TRAIN GOING ALONG IN THE NIGHT

With this picture, Truffaut was fulfilling a longtime dream, that of showing the inside workings of a shoot. "I won't reveal the whole truth about filming, but just some real things that happened in my past movies or in other movies."[51] *Day for Night* was meant as a profession of faith in cinema—cinema, the thing he loved best in the world and which often came before his personal life, indeed before life in general. Through fiction, he was able to reveal the things that he was generally loath to bring up in interviews with journalists, or which he saw no point in describing in documentaries about his shoots. *Day for Night* mixes documentary and fiction: It would be a true and sincere film on an artificial world, the world of cinema, where "we do a lot of kissing because we must show our love,"[52] as one of the characters in the picture puts it. A facade of unanimity, a world of pretense, which the production manager's wife, alone in a corner of the set, is the sole person to demythologize: "What is this movie world?" she cries out. "What is this profession where everyone sleeps with everyone else? Everyone is chummy and everyone lies. What's it all about? Do you find it normal? Well I think it stinks. I despise it."[53] In the part of Ferrand, Truffaut—who rarely addressed his collaborators with the informal *"tu"*—did his utmost to give a neutral, professional image of the working film director, and he quite clearly avoided portraying him as an artist. But he was very eager to show the hidden side of moviemaking, the excitement of a shoot and a successful endeavor, with its bonds of friendship and its occasional love stories. Moments of depression, inspirational burnout, quarrels—nothing, not even death, will stop the film, which is like "a train going along in the night."[54]

Yet the film within the film that they are shooting at the Victorine Studios has nothing particularly exciting about it. It is obviously not an "auteur film," but a "bad film," as Jean-Louis Richard says. But the banality of the screenplay of *Je vous présente Pamela* doesn't in the least hamper the crescendo of the shoot, nor does it interfere with the fellowship felt by the cast and crew, or dampen the actors' enthusiasm. For Truffaut, *Day for Night* was a love story, a film devoted to the love of cinema *regardless of everything*. "Foremost in my mind was the Charles Trenet song 'Moi, j'aime le music-hall' where he enumerates with kindness and humor all the popular singers of the day, though they're his competitors. I shot *Day for Night* in the same spirit, my intent was to make the audience happy on seeing a film in the making, to infuse joy and lightheartedness from all the sprocket holes of the film. 'Moi, j'aime le cinéma.' "[55] Many would reproach Truffaut for his kindliness in describing the small world of the most banal kind of cinema—Jean-Luc Godard, for example, who felt Truffaut had sold out with this film.

Once the screenplay was completed, Marcel Berbert drew up a reasonable estimated budget of 3.5 million francs. Yet United Artists refused to finance *Day for Night* because they felt the script was too risky, "too intellectual," and they feared that an uninitiated audience might find the plot of a film within a film disconcerting. Berbert then approached Robert Solo, Warner's London representative, who was a Truffaut admirer. He agreed with alacrity after a first meeting in November 1971. The contract was signed in May 1972.

In the meantime, Truffaut began thinking about the casting with Jean-Louis Richard. Truffaut eventually cast Jean-Pierre Aumont as Alexandre and Valentina Cortese as Séverine.[56] Jean Champion was cast as the producer of *Je vous présente Pamela,* Marcel Berbert's double. Truffaut did not hesitate to cast himself in the part of Ferrand, giving the character his own childlike personality and love for his profession. Jean-Pierre Léaud was to play Alphonse—romantic, often capricious and unstable, to the point of interrupting the shoot. He resembles in every detail the Léaud of the early seventies, whom Truffaut had encouraged to pursue a "real acting career."[57] After *Two English Girls,* Léaud had worked with the directors Glauber Rocha (*The Lion Has Seven Heads*), Luc Moullet (*Une aventure de Billy le Kid*), Bernardo Bertolucci (*Last Tango in Paris*), and notably Jean Eustache, with whom he had just shot *La Maman et la Putain* (*The Mother and the Whore*).[58] Nonetheless, the actor had difficulty ridding himself of the Antoine Doinel persona and his image as "the son of Truffaut." His life consisted of a series of depressions, euphorias, about-faces, money problems, romantic setbacks, so that his fellow professionals found him unsettling. On the set of *A Sentimental Education,* which Marcel Cravenne made for television in 1972, the screenwriter François-Régis Bastide complained to Truffaut: "Everyone in the cast and crew hated him during those three months, and Cravenne didn't utter a single impatient word even though Jean-Pierre called everybody and anybody 'fascist.' . . ."[59] In *Day for Night,* Alphonse is as fragile as the real-life Jean-Pierre Léaud, and his relationship with Ferrand seems modeled on Léaud's relationship to Truffaut. In the scene where Ferrand lectures Alphonse in order to rekindle his self-confidence, Truffaut is clearly addressing Léaud: "Movies are more harmonious than life. There are no traffic jams in movies, no dead spots. Movies go along like trains, you understand, like trains in the night. People like you and me, as you know, should seek happiness in our work, in our movie work. I'm counting on you. . . ."[60]

Truffaut felt Jacqueline Bisset would be ideal for the part of Julie Baker. Of Scottish descent on her father's side and French on her mother's, she began her career as a model and made her first screen appearances in England (Richard Lester's *The Knack* and Roman Polanski's *Cul-de-Sac*), before moving to Hollywood in 1968. Her appearances in Peter Yates's *Bullitt* (with Steve McQueen), Gordon Douglas's *The Detective* (with Frank Sinatra), George Seaton's *Airport* (with Dean Martin and Burt Lancaster), and John Huston's *The Life and Times of Judge Roy Bean* (with Paul Newman) had catapulted her to Hollywood stardom. Her introduction to Truffaut, whom she had admired for a long time, occurred in an odd way. While she was staying for a few days in Paris, Bisset received a phone call at her hotel from Gérard Lebovici: "I'm François Truffaut's agent and I'd like to know what you thought of the script." At first, she thought it was a hoax, and told him she had no knowledge of any script. The misunderstanding was cleared up and Bisset requested that a copy of the script be dropped off at her hotel. "I thought the part wasn't very big, but I'd have taken it even if I'd had only one line to deliver." Later, she had a conversation over the phone with Truffaut: "He told me he didn't have much money to make the film, so he couldn't pay me very much, that it wasn't a particularly big part, that the film had several leading characters. He said all this with great courtesy and humility."[61] Usually, Jacqueline Bisset commanded a salary that was the equivalent of *Day for Night's* entire budget. But the contract she signed with Carrosse in March 1972 stipulated that beyond her salary of 200,000 francs, she was to receive a 20 percent royalty on the profits. This was clear proof of her desire to work with Truffaut, one of the directors she most admired, along with Ingmar Bergman.

For the supporting roles, Truffaut met two young actresses with whom he would work again in the future: Dani, whom he cast in the part of Liliane, Alphonse's girlfriend, and Nathalie Baye, just out of the Conservatoire, whom he cast in the part of Joëlle, the script girl of *Je vous présente Pamela,* whose duties were those held in real life by Suzanne Schiffman from film to film. Baye recounts that one day, as she was coming out of a restaurant on rue Marbeuf with Serge Rousseau, her agent at Artmédia, they ran into Suzanne Schiffman across the street, who was probably on her way to the Carrosse offices. A short time later, Rousseau received a call from Suzanne: "Who was the young girl I saw you with on rue Marbeuf?" Several days later, Nathalie Baye was summoned to the Carrosse. "As soon as he saw me, Truffaut said, 'No, she's not right at all!' We continued our conversation and after a while he said to me, 'Come back tomorrow; we'll do a reading.' The next day we read a scene together from *Such a Gorgeous Kid Like Me.* I had stage fright; I was as red as a beet. At the end, he said to me, 'I'll take you, but you'll wear glasses!' "[62]

To complete his cast, Truffaut hired Bernard Menez, a comic actor, who would give piquancy to the role of Bernard, the propman on the set. Nike Arrighi would play Odile, the makeup girl, and David Markham, the father of Kika Markham, who had played in *Two English Girls,* was cast as Dr. Nelson, Julie Baker's husband. Truffaut gave his friend Alexandra Stewart the part of Stacey, the actress who gets hired in *Je vous présente Pamela* and conceals that she is pregnant. Finally, to give the film within a film greater verisimilitude, Truffaut asked his technicians to play themselves on-screen—Jean-François Stévenin as assistant, Pierre Zucca as unit photographer, Yann Dedet and Martine Barraqué in the cutting room, Georges Delerue as musician, and Walter Bal as cameraman.

On September 26, 1972, the actors and technicians assembled at the Victorine Studios in Nice for a shoot that would last only forty-two days. The lead actors lived in rented villas in the area, near Antibes. Jacqueline Bisset shared her house with Nathalie Baye. *Day for Night* was far from a quiet, restful shoot. Jacqueline Bisset didn't really feel at ease, at least for the first few days: "My French wasn't very good at the time, until François reassured me, 'Don't worry, you're not playing a Frenchwoman; you're an American actress performing in France.' This greatly relieved me,"[63] she says. Alexandra Stewart remembers a preoccupied, unavailable Truffaut: "François was anguished because he was doing everything—he had an acting part, Léaud was causing problems," she recalls. "Walter Bal, the cameraman, had a motorcycle accident; that's why he appears in the film with his arm in a sling. For reasons I couldn't fathom, François had a grudge against me; he blamed me for being late, which was just an excuse, for I've always been punctual. But it's true there were only two makeup girls for several actresses."[64] On Christmas Eve, right after the last days of the shoot, Alexandra Stewart, to her astonishment, even received a very harsh letter from Truffaut accusing her "of having messed up his film."[65] After a falling-out lasting several months, Truffaut apologized. Alexandra Stewart isn't the only close friend to have received this kind of letter from Truffaut, particularly during this period when his life was still unstable and when his character and feelings were subject to sudden swings, from euphoria to melancholy to anger.

Yann Dedet, assisted by Martine Barraqué, started editing *Day for Night* while the film was still being shot. In mid-November, Truffaut could already screen a first version, which he found too disjointed. Three months later, after Jean Aurel had given him some useful advice—for example, to rebalance the film around Ferrand by using a voice-over as much as possible—the film found its true, spirited tone, punctuated by lovely, stirring music. Truffaut was satisfied with the first screenings in March 1973. "I know that the film is touching—and deeply touching—to people in the profession,"[66] he said to Helen Scott. The actors in the film were enthusiastic: Jean-Pierre Aumont said he was "very moved" and "proud to have taken part"[67]; Nathalie Baye hoped to have been "worthy of what you gave me and hoping you'll always be pleased with your former script girl!"[68] Confident, Truffaut agreed to show his film outside competition at the Cannes Film Festival. The official screening took place on the evening of May fourteenth. There, joined by Jacqueline Bisset, Valentina Cortese, Nathalie Baye, Dani, Jean-Pierre Aumont, and Jean-Pierre Léaud, he presented himself to the public as an actor, which would have been unthinkable two years earlier, while he was in the depths of depression.

The following day, *Le Parisien* wrote of a "memorable night,"[69] and Louis Chauvet in *Le Figaro* maintained that the film would certainly have won the Palme d'or if it had been entered in the competition.[70] But Truffaut had wanted to be "outside the Cannes dealings," for "everything in Cannes is really unpredictable, everything is tactical, everything is strategic."[71] *Day for*

Night opened in eight Paris theaters on May 24. The reviews were full of praise. Jean-Louis Bory called it a "perfect film," from "François Truffaut's golden Carrosse," and "a little marvel of comedy, charm and emotion."[72] Jean de Baroncelli saw it as "one of his best films,"[73] and Chauvet hailed it as "the most accomplished work of its kind."[74] But Truffaut's primary concern was the audience's verdict; he hoped to erase his two recent commercial disappointments. Box-office results in Paris were good (nearly 300,000 tickets sold) but mediocre in the provinces. Truffaut thought he knew why: A large segment of the public was under the misapprehension that it was a documentary on cinema, an "overly intellectual" film. He decided that any mention of a "film within a film" in the publicity should be avoided. This is what he wrote to Simon Benzakein, his coproducer: "We should use another slant for the film: 'a movie of love and adventure.' The publicity department should refrain from explaining the title *Day for Night* as the trick effect 'day for night' but stress the double meaning—'a French-Hollywood night of love between Jean-Pierre Léaud and Jacqueline Bisset.' "[75] Truffaut had no qualms about misleading the public if this could benefit a film that was close to his heart.

THE CONFRONTATION

Godard and Truffaut had lost sight of each other since 1968. For quite a while, they had each been engaged in a totally different kind of cinema. While Truffaut openly admired all of Godard's first films (up to *La Chinoise* in 1967), Godard, for his part, didn't conceal his indifference to Truffaut's films, except for *Shoot the Piano Player*. Even today, Godard admires Truffaut the critic, "who knew how to point out what was in a film, or compare two films."[76]

Up until the breakup of the New Wave in the mid-sixties, Truffaut and Godard stood by each other as true and loyal friends. Subsequently, however, while Truffaut carved out a niche for himself and protected his independence as best he could with the help of the American majors, Godard advocated a militant, revolutionary cinema directly connected with reality; he and two allies, Jean-Pierre Gorin and Jean-Henri Roger, were the driving forces behind the Dziga-Vertov Group. "He is engaged in another kind of cinema," Truffaut said of Godard. "He feels that since May '68 it's impossible to make the same kinds of movies and he resents people who still do. I've made a choice, my thoughts are perfectly clear, I want to make normal films, it's my life."[77] The two men kept up an intermittent correspondence. When Godard had a serious motorcycle accident in the fall of 1971 and was hospitalized for a long time, Truffaut contacted him. But they were no longer kindred spirits when it came to cinema or politics, or, consequently, when it came to feelings.

Godard initiated hostilities at the end of May 1973, right after the Cannes Film Festival. He came out of *Day for Night* exasperated and couldn't resist letting Truffaut know immediately. He wrote Truffaut a rather contemptuous letter, whose informal tone is consistent with their long-standing friendship as well as with the left-wing language of the period. "Probably no one else will call you a liar, but I will. It's no more of an insult than 'fascist,' it's a critique, and it's the absence of a critical view such films leave us with—those of Chabrol, Ferreri, Verneuil, Delannoy, Renoir, etc.—that I object to. You say: films are big trains that go along in the night, but who is taking the train, in what class, and who is the conductor with the management's 'stool pigeon' by his side? Such people make film-trains as well. And if you don't mean the Trans-Europ, then maybe it's the train to the suburbs, or the Dachau–Munich train, a station that you can be sure you won't see in Lelouch's film-train. Liar, because the shot of you and Jacqueline Bisset the other night at [the restaurant] Chez Francis isn't in your film, and one wonders why the director is the only one who isn't screwing around in *Day for Night.*" Then Godard gets to the point. Using the tone of a formal request, he asks Truffaut to finance his next project, *Un simple film,* with an investment of 10 or 5 million francs. "After *Day for Night,* you ought to help me, so that audiences don't think that the only kind of movies being made are your kind." He writes in conclusion, "If you want to discuss it, fine,"[78] words that sound more like a challenge than an invitation to dialogue.

Truffaut could hardly have been pleased by Godard's tone or attitude. He felt that Godard had overstepped his bounds and didn't refrain from telling him so. His answer,[79] which runs to about twenty pages in the original, is unrestrained in its violence. He goes over everything point by point. First, their respective relationships with Jean-Pierre Léaud, whom they had both directed over the last several years. Truffaut resented Godard for insulting Léaud in a letter where he reproached him for acting in *Day for Night* and for working with other "*capitulard*" (sell-out) directors, and then demanded money from him. "I'm sending you back your letter to Jean-Pierre," Truffaut says in his answer, "I've read it and I find it disgusting. Because of that letter I feel it's finally time to tell you, at length, that in my opinion you've been behaving like a shit." Truffaut denounces Godard's lies, his superior tone, his "knack for passing himself off as a victim . . . whereas in fact you've always managed to do exactly what you wanted, when you wanted, as you wanted, and have always managed, above all, to maintain the pure, hard-line image you've cultivated, even at the expense of defenseless people. . . ." The image of the subversive artist, the poseur (a shit on a pedestal) annoys Truffaut, who has always had a preference for humble artisans: "The more you love the masses, the more I love Jean-Pierre Léaud, Janine Bazin,[80] Helen Scott, whom you snubbed when you ran into her in an airport. . . ." "The behavior of a shit," Truffaut reiterates in his letter, turning Godard's own political moral system against him, a system whose ostensible leftism fails to conceal a deep elitism. Truffaut also reminds him of his cowardice when they were selling *La Cause du peuple*: "I felt nothing but contempt for you when I saw the scene in *Vent d'est* on how to make a Molotov cocktail, and yet a year later you chickened out when we were first asked to distribute *La Cause du peuple* in the street with Sartre. The idea that all men are equal is theoretical with you, not sincerely felt." Finally, Truffaut calls Godard an impostor and a pathological egoist: "You need to play a role and the role has to be prestigious. I've always felt that true militants are like cleaning women, performing a thankless, daily, necessary task. But you, you're like Ursula Andress, you make a four-minute appearance, just enough time for the cameras to flash, for you to make two or three startling pronounce-ments, and then you disappear, shrouded in appealing mystery. In the oppo-site camp are the small men, ranging from Bazin to Edmond Maire and including Sartre, Buñuel, Queneau, Mendès-France, Rohmer, Audiberti, who ask others how they're doing, help them fill out their social security forms, and reply to letters. They have in common that they can forget their own egos and above all are more interested in what they do than in what they are or what they appear to be." He concludes like Godard: "If you want to discuss it, fine." They never would discuss it. The breakup between them was complete and irrevocable. The time of the "friends in the New Wave"[81] was gone forever.

Though he had unhesitatingly poured it all out and freed himself of the countless misunderstandings that had made his relationship with Godard increasingly awkward and insincere, Truffaut was nonetheless upset. It was a severe shock, a painful falling-out. Janine Bazin, in whom Truffaut had confided, wrote him a long, warm letter: "Your telephone call distressed me and I can't stop thinking about it. You had such a sad voice, just as hurt by Jean-Luc's letter as by the one you had to write him. And I don't know whether you were right to answer him because I don't know if Jean-Luc can quite understand it; I mean I don't know if he can understand that your insults are commensurate with your sadness and friendship for him. I don't mean that Jean-Luc is so lacking in feeling, but still I think his insults are insults that come from the head, whereas yours come from the heart, from your morality of the heart."[82]

In those days, Truffaut's obsession with ideological neutrality appeared to many as faint-hearted opportunism. Some did not hesitate to offer reproachful reminders of his youthful ideals. This attack from the Left disturbed Truffaut, particularly since the criticism came just as he was pulling out of his depression. "Truffaut the traitor" was the refrain, publicly and in several personal letters. Those who judged him with such severity were clearly fueled by a negative view of *Day for Night*, whose moral, they felt, was overly optimistic and conciliatory, vaunting the "magic" of classical cinema and compromise among the members of the profession's one big family. Godard had set the example. Jean-Louis Bory soon followed suit; after an initially favorable reaction to the film, several months later the critic denounced its "consensual and *capitularde*"[83] philosophy. He published an attention-grabbing article in *Le Nouvel Observateur*, "Should We Burn Down the Champs-Elysées?" Truffaut was particularly appalled by one sentence: "Truffaut, Chabrol, Demy, Rohmer have sold out to the system." Truffaut wrote Bory a long letter to justify himself. He went over his entire career, film by film, and explained how each one stemmed from a vital need and had a strictly personal character. "I haven't sold out to the system, I have my own way of working within the system."

My dear Jean-Louis Bory, we have something in common—we both enjoyed our biggest success right at the start. You had the good fortune of immediately being published and recognized, and I did too. Since then, you've published many books with different publishers, and none of your manuscripts was ever rejected, since you had demonstrated your abilities from the beginning. Suppose one day you were to read in the paper: "The manuscripts rejected by publishers, mimeographed booklets, and books published at authors' expense are what constitute the true literature of our time: Genet fell silent in 1968; as for Sartre, Bory, Cayrol, Rezvani, they have sold out to the system." Wouldn't you think, "Here's someone who's completely mixed up and mistakes the container for the thing contained"? You're not a "marginal" author, you're a professional writer; your books are published because they're good, because you have a following, and because the projected printing can be expected to earn back the initial investment. True or false? Though they may not be hot sellers in train stations like Simenon or Guy des Cars, your books can be bought in drugstores and that doesn't make them any worse. True or false? I may be wrong, but as a film director I feel I work in the same spirit as you do as a writer: we choose our subjects freely, we handle them as we see fit and we put them on the market. . . . Good or bad, my films are the films I wanted to make and none other. . . .[84]

Refusing to play the martyr (he left that to Godard), Truffaut pleaded his cause, that of an independent director whose career was punctuated with both success and failure. "I take complete responsibility for the films I make, their qualities and faults, and I never blame the system."[85] Paradoxically, Truffaut's truthfulness sounded false to many of his contemporaries. This exchange with Bory is emblematic of his estrangement from some of the figures from his past during that period.[86] He considered these breakups necessary, though each was painful.

PRIVATE LIVES

The success of *Day for Night* allowed François Truffaut to slow down. Having just directed three films in rapid succession, he decided to take a two-year breather to do other things and travel. This intense activity had exhausted him, though it had helped him climb out of the "abyss" into which he had sunk at the beginning of 1971. Truffaut had spent most of his time away from Paris, making films; hence, he had practically never been alone.

At the time when he decided to give himself a rest, he had no less than four screenplays in progress—*The Story of Adele H.* and *L'Autel des morts* (*The Altar of the Dead*) with Gruault; *Small Change* with Suzanne Schiffman; *Le Cavaleur* (The Skirt-Chaser) with Michel Fermaud—as well as several book projects. Truffaut also spent time completing the "chronologies" of his life, noting down childhood memories and recollections about people he had met. He even promised the publisher Robert Laffont an autobiographical book, which could only be ready in "about ten years, primarily for family reasons."[87] For in describing his youth and his background, his first concern was not to hurt his father, Roland Truffaut.

Having recently turned forty, Truffaut felt the need to put his life in order. But he still had to protect himself, because he knew he was vulnerable. For a while, he continued to live in a suite at the Hotel George V: "He didn't want to leave the hotel," Liliane Siegel recalls, "except perhaps to go to the movies when the theater was already dark. When I came to dinner, he would have the meal sent up to his suite. Since he wanted to determine himself what kind of ties he would have with others, the fact of living in a hotel protected him. It was a way of preventing any woman from moving in with him."[88] Then for several months, he lived in the apartment above the offices of the Films du Carrosse. Finally, he decided to rent a large, sun-lit six-room apartment on avenue Pierre 1er de Serbie, which had two big advantages: It was close to his office and it had a view of the Eiffel Tower. The view from his living room was "his best source of inspiration."[89] Truffaut lived alone, with his housekeeper, Marie; her death in January 1973 would deeply affect him, for this energetic, discreet woman in her sixties had been completely devoted to him. She was succeeded by Emilienne briefly, and then by Carmen Sardà-Canovas, a perpetually sunny and cheerful woman, and a great admirer of the comic actor Fernandel (Truffaut recorded the actor's films for her when they were shown on television). Carmen wasn't a particularly good cook and "if she had been, this was not a quality that would have meant anything to my father,"[90] Laura points out. This is confirmed by Jean Gruault, who was used to seeing his friend Truffaut eat "his eternal overcooked steak smothered in mustard."[91]

Laura and Eva each had a room in the newly rented apartment and would usually spend the weekends with him. In the spring of 1973, Laura was fourteen and Eva twelve. When he was not busy with filmmaking, Truffaut would spend a great deal of time with them, sharing books and movies and deliberately nurturing their different personalities. Laura, the elder, was a daydreamer with a literary bent; Eva was more active and less romantic. "For me, we always chose the more fast-paced, dry, violent films," Eva recalls. "Lang, Sturges, Aldrich, Kubrick. This was the kind of film he couldn't see with Laura. With her, he revealed another side of his personality, other tastes and feelings, more romantic and colorful, like Cukor, Fellini, Hitchcock, musical comedies with Fred Astaire, W. C. Fields comedies, or films like *Pandora* and all the great Chaplin classics, which were rereleased during the seventies. We all three converged on some Mankiewicz films, *A Letter to Three Wives, All About Eve* . . . some Polanski films, and on Dalton Trumbo's *Johnny Got His Gun.*[92] Apart from a love of books and the pleasure of movies, Truffaut also shared with his daughters a love of song; Trenet was their favorite, and some singers from the new generation, like Julien Clerc and Alain Souchon. They also liked humorists, particularly Raymond Devos, for whom Truffaut had immense admiration and whose performances he often attended in Paris and the provinces. And they liked Pierre Dac and Francis Blanche, whose sketches all three found very funny.

When he didn't go to his office, Truffaut received friends and collaborators at home. In the evening, when he wasn't watching television—his favorite pastime—he would share his apartment only with women. "I wouldn't consider having dinner with a man," he wrote in *Paris-Match.* "I have this in common with Hitler and Sartre: I can't stand male companionship after seven in the evening. For me, the evening means private life, in a private place; it's the time for whispered words, shared secrets, sincere exchanges. The only moment which can rival the joy of filming."[93] These were special moments, which he safeguarded and wouldn't sacrifice for any social occasion. Those women closest to him were Madeleine Morgenstern and Helen Scott, and also Liliane Dreyfus, Leslie Caron, Alexandra Stewart, and Liliane Siegel. "Very soon we started talking about ourselves," says Liliane Siegel. "We saw each other often, just the two of us, and spent long evenings sharing a mutual trust and confiding in each other."[94] He often talked about Jean-Paul Sartre with her, for she knew him intimately and Truffaut was fascinated by him. "We spoke a great deal, very freely, it was good," Truffaut wrote her on April 20, 1971, the day after their first dinner. "We did a year's worth of confiding in one evening, which allows me to switch from 'fondly' to 'affectionately.' "[95] With his female friends and former mistresses, Truffaut felt good, providing they each respected what he considered certain essential rules. Discretion was vital and foremost. Whoever infringed the pact of secrecy exposed herself to a violent breakup, usually in writing. Truffaut partitioned his relationships to avoid any short circuits and "complications that bore me."[96] There again, he was capable of great anger when a woman—for example, Helen Scott, whom he sometimes reproached for her lack of discretion—proved unable to keep a secret. Truffaut's relationships with his female friends took various forms. He set the limits between intimacy and friendship. "I'm afraid of ties, I'm afraid of making promises and not keeping them," he wrote to Liliane Siegel. "You shouldn't scare me, when I'm with you I'm happy, very quickly and durably, but it's abnormal that on the following days I'm tortured with the thought that I should be phoning you, as though I were in the wrong, as though I owed you an explanation, as though I were going to be bawled out."[97] With some of his women friends, Truffaut shared the pleasure of going to a film or spending an evening at the theater, activities that he valued infinitely more than a good dinner.

This partitioned, complex life was actually based on simple principles. First among these was the exclusive pleasure of a relationship *à deux,* for Truffaut disliked society life, a waste of time as far as he was concerned. When he couldn't avoid a social event, he didn't seek to impress or be clever; he preferred to listen, laugh, and be a good audience, particularly when he had accepted a dinner invitation because he had been curious to meet someone he admired or whose books he had read. When trapped in a conversation that didn't interest him, he remained silent, allowing long pauses to set in, which eventually embarrassed those around him. "François acted as though he hadn't heard anything, an angel was passing. A person had to be very brave to try to say anything again," Madeleine Morgenstern says. Truffaut found it difficult to bring romantic relationships to a close, so he pursued several simultaneous affairs, which he sought to keep compartmentalized, as discreetly and hermetically as possible. "Once there had been an extended emotional tie, François could not imagine that a woman would no longer be part of his landscape," Madeleine confirms. The relationship between her and Truffaut had never ceased to exist; it was close and intimate, romantic and friendly, with occasional periods when they differed immensely. "The fact that I was a kind of ever-present family reference was not very pleasant for the other women in his life,"[98] Madeleine admits, quite perceptively. When he wanted to break off a liaison, he could be harsh, but usually his love affairs would turn into strong and durable friendships.

After his yearlong depression, François Truffaut resumed a restless love life. He saw Kika Markham again, one of the stars of *Two English Girls,* when the film was being promoted in France, and during several of her Paris trips. Then he had a number of affairs, sometimes with former lovers, sometimes with new ones. And he still had a distinct penchant for visiting prostitutes. On the other hand, since his last romantic breakup, he refused to live as a couple with anyone. "I can only love now through casual meetings,"[99] he wrote to a woman friend. "He had acquired a phobia for conjugal life which he had trouble reconciling with the tender affection he felt for his close relatives and friends," Gruault points out. "He once told me that as he walked up to his landing he always fleetingly felt the same pang of anguish from the recollection of several periods in his life where he knew he would be welcomed by a spouse or female companion whose conversation and possible recriminations he would have to endure, and who would criticize his eating habits, etc. And what a relief it was for him now to know that he would turn the doorknob and walk into an empty apartment where he would be alone with all his books and his television. Yet he wasn't spared the anguish of loneliness. One morning I found him very worried: he had slept very badly, he had had a discharge from his ear and traces of pus on his pillow, he feared a recurrence of the chronic ear infections that had plagued him in his childhood. He admitted to me that he had experienced that night a painful feeling of abandonment."[100]

During *Day for Night,* Jacqueline Bisset was the only woman who really succeeded in sharing his solitude. Their relationship, which started timidly during the filming in Nice, lasted for some time thereafter. Jacqueline Bisset remained in France after *Day for Night,* where she immediately started working on Philippe de Broca's *Le Magnifique* with Jean-Paul Belmondo. She and Truffaut met regularly over the spring of 1973, in Nice, Paris, and Cannes, where they presented *Day for Night* at the festival. Then Truffaut spent the entire summer in Los Angeles, which gave him the opportunity to visit Jean Renoir and to spend time with Jacqueline Bisset again, in her beautiful white house in Benedict Canyon. "Thanks to her, I regained my confidence,"[101] he admitted to Jean-Claude Brialy.

Truffaut was perpetually unfaithful, more out of a need to seduce and be loved than out of Don Juanism. These "other women" were strangers, collaborators, or foreign journalists. First and foremost, they were the actresses in his films. "Women, for him, were always part icon part woman. That's why he loved his actresses: It made his life easier—loving cinema more than anything else, his activity as a director, and the beautiful actresses he cast in his films. Above all, it was a way of perpetuating childhood: woman as mother, woman as doll, woman as fiancée,"[102] says Alexandra Stewart, providing a perfect description of Truffaut's dual obsessions and how they were secretly intertwined—love of cinema and love of women.

Truffaut was not free of remorse vis-à-vis Madeleine and his daughters. Hence the guilt feelings, which partially explain his periods of depression and the more serious crises that affected him in his adult life. When he was not out of town filming, Truffaut spent all his weekends at rue du Conseiller Collignon, to be with his daughters, but also to be with Madeleine, for maintaining a relationship with her surely soothed him. "Those strange moments resembled a true family life," Madeleine explains, "it provided him with a kind of peace. I accepted this situation, for myself and the children, because you can't expect to live for several years with someone as interesting as François and not want something to remain, somehow or other, later."[103]

In Truffaut's life, there was an odd need for stability, even for a certain routine, which coexisted with the need for amorous adventures. Whether alone or with a woman, he needed established markers and rituals to maintain an atmosphere conducive to work (hence his habit of rehiring the same crew from film to film).

THE CALIFORNIA SUMMER

During this two-year respite, François Truffaut spent as much time as possible abroad. He lived in Los Angeles in the summer of 1973, from June to August. "I'm leading a very luxurious life, a bungalow with a patio, a big red car with an automatic shift! For the time being, great solitude,"[104] he wrote to Liliane Siegel. Very soon, some producers interpreted his presence in Hollywood as an indication that he wanted to make a film there. Simon Benzakein, for example, who was working for Warner Brothers, made him the offer of directing a remake of *Casablanca*. Truffaut refused of course:

> It's not my favorite Humphrey Bogart film, and I rate it much lower than *The Big Sleep* or *To Have and Have Not*. So, the thought of directing a new version should logically scare me less and I realize the film would take place in a French ambiance. However, I know American students adore this film, especially the dialogue, and they know every line by heart. I would be equally intimidated by the actors; I can't imagine Jean-Paul Belmondo and Catherine Deneuve succeeding Humphrey Bogart and Ingrid Bergman. I know that people see these things differently in America. The idea of directing a remake doesn't shock me, provided it's a very good, bold story which could be treated with greater candor today, and a title that doesn't carry too

much weight in the history of American cinema. If Warner Brothers really wants me to direct a film, I suggest you send me a list of titles I could select from.[105]

Though being solicited by Hollywood amused him, Truffaut nevertheless turned down all the offers, explaining his reasons at length, courteously and with great professionalism. He never closed the door on the possibility, for the idea of someday making a film in the United States was a rejuvenating prospect. As soon as his situation in France seemed too precarious, as soon as he felt any ideological or professional pressure, he found solace in the thought that Hollywood was prepared to welcome him. It was a way of asserting privilege or special status in the French film industry. It was also Truffaut's discreet way of divorcing himself from the auteur cinema, which he liked (the films of Jean Eustache, Jacques Rivette, or Philippe Garrel) but which he deemed hard to export. A show-business professional and a great admirer of Lubitsch and Hitchcock, Truffaut felt competent to make films in Hollywood, the movie mecca, "provided the story not be too specific in setting or Americanness."[106]

The discrepancy between Truffaut's position as an independent auteur-producer and the rest of the French movie industry was a constant source of misunderstandings—with journalists and critics, but also with his best friends. There is a definite resemblance between the Truffaut of the early seventies and Ferrand, the director in *Day for Night,* a conscientious, budget-conscious craftsman who creates an old-fashioned movie family with his actors and collaborators. During this entire period when French auteur cinema was perpetually confronted by its own fringe status, Truffaut reserved judgment. "I've had too much luck to attack those who have been less lucky than me, it's as simple as that," he said with great honesty to the journalist Guy Teisseire.[107]

Truffaut loved California, first of all for its lifestyle, and secondly because this was where all the directors he admired lived—Renoir, Hitchcock, Hawks, Capra. He felt at ease there, considerably freer in his movements than in Paris. When Leslie Caron asked him one day why he was so fond of California, Truffaut replied jokingly, "Because you can always find a parking space!"[108] To take full advantage of America, he made it a point of honor to lick "the great problem of his life," his difficulty in speaking English. Such was his motive for this long Californian sojourn—taking lessons "with a teacher who has obtained results with morons." So he settled at the Beverly Hills Hotel and took daily six-hour lessons with Professor Michel Thomas, who literally fascinated him. An exceptional teacher and founder of a language school, Thomas was a Frenchman and former Resistance fighter who had been living in the United States since 1947. He had been head of an underground network near Grenoble, and had been tortured by Klaus Bar- bie in Lyon; after the Liberation, he had become an American counterespi- onage agent. The student had every reason to be attentive, the more so since his teacher had successfully taught French to Grace Kelly and Otto Preminger in a matter of months, and had made Yves Montand proficient in the language of Shakespeare and Marilyn. Yet, in spite of painstaking efforts, Truffaut made very little progress, as he himself admitted to Helen Scott: "My teacher says that he finds it more difficult to get me out of the habit of my mistakes than to teach me the correct forms. He never blames me, he behaves a bit like a psychoanalyst, and he has the patience of an angel, but I can sense he is astonished by the extent of my mental block. The truth is that there is in me a refusal to learn that is as powerful as my desire to know."[109]

During that summer of 1973, he, like the rest of America, was completely enthralled by the Watergate affair. American investigative journalism impressed him enormously, compared with the "great amateurishness of French journalism, its fraudulence."[110] He mixed work with pleasure as he watched the live broadcasts every morning and followed the latest develop- ments in the political scandal implicating a large part of the Nixon adminis- tration. The public spectacle of government confronted with its own lies and manipulations fascinated him, and he tried to take advantage of the daily reportage to improve his English. But despite all his efforts, his knowledge of English remained stagnant—though, in its issue of September 2, 1973, the *Los Angeles Herald Examiner* devoted a whole page to an enthusiastic article entitled "Three Hours of Watergate a Day Helped Truffaut Master English." However, Truffaut did acquire a good reading knowledge of English, which allowed him to immerse himself in film literature and histor- ical studies. The first English-language book he bought for himself was Selznick's *Memo*,[111] which he read attentively by the pool of his luxurious California hotel in early July 1973.

In Hollywood as in Paris, François Truffaut's life followed a detailed, immutable ritual. But his outward appearance differed. While dressing aus- terely, in a dark suit and tie, on the Right Bank of the Seine, around Passy, and on the Champs-Elysées, Truffaut used to undergo a radical metamor- phosis as soon as he arrived in California. "He looked fifteen years younger," says Claudine Bouché, the editor of his early days, who had moved to the United States in 1967; she remembers his "elegant, informal outfits."[112] Leslie Caron describes a relaxed, easygoing person, at the wheel of a beauti- ful American convertible. Indeed, Truffaut liked the style and rhythm of California life. Furthermore, since there was no equivalent in Paris, he would often spend hours browsing at Larry Edmunds', the famous cinema bookstore on Hollywood Boulevard. Truffaut adored American biographies of actors and directors, for they were a gold mine of fascinating behind-the-scenes details on the history of cinema, the making of films, and the romances of the stars.

Todd McCarthy, the *Variety* critic and journalist, one of the main people Truffaut associated with when he was in the States, remembers his friend "sitting in a deck chair, a bit isolated, at the edge of the pool at the Beverly Hills, the posh hotel where he stayed whenever he came to Los Angeles. When you know he'd been afraid of water all his life, his presence amidst tanned Californians, sun worshippers and athletic swimmers, seemed all the more incongruous. Even stranger was the fact that it was his favorite place in the world for reading American books on film, for which he had an insatiable appetite. . . . Beautiful women would stroll back and forth wondering who that man was—was it really François Truffaut?—and from time to time, one of them would muster up the courage to go up to him and try to start a conversation. Indifferent to their beauty, which he almost overlooked, François would usually assume a polite but resolutely closed air, with that pregnant silence that reigned around him when he wanted to keep someone at a distance. . . . Finally, slightly embarrassed and at a loss what to say, the gorgeous creatures would withdraw and François would go back to his book."[113]

Truffaut's main purpose in being there was to rest. The only exception was on Saturday nights, when he enjoyed "acting the Frenchman" at parties in beautiful Hollywood villas. Sometimes he became a scathing chronicler of the Hollywood smart set in his correspondence with friends. He wrote to Helen Scott:

> I went to two parties recently. The first was at a charming woman painter's, Barbara Poe, the ex-wife of the *script-writer* [in English] James Poe. When the conversation revolved around food pollution, a woman asked me: "*Et en France, est-ce que vous mettez des préservatifs autour des légumes?*" [And in France, do you put condoms (*préservatifs*) around your vegetables?] It was a *nice party* [in English], everyone was left-wing, great supporters of the town's new black mayor. . . . Last night, another party, much more typical of Hollywood, thrown by the young Peter Guber, head of production at Columbia, the spitting image of the character in *What Makes Sammy Run?* Billiards in a room where the ceiling is decorated with the Company's illuminated posters, barbecue on the lawn, followed by a screening of an unreleased comedy which I didn't watch because I was flirting with Buck Henry, who is really adorable.[114]

Truffaut's favorite ritual was to pay a visit to the Renoirs every Saturday afternoon. Jean and Dido Renoir lived in a redbrick building at the top of

Leona Drive. Renoir had drawn the plans of the house himself, in 1950, before going to India to shoot *The River*. Some twenty olive trees were planted around the house, like those at Colettes, the family house in Cagnes-sur-Mer. In July 1973, Truffaut found Renoir "very old and very tired"; he refused to walk, but regained "his liveliness every afternoon when he dictates his memoirs to his secretary."[115] To his Paris friends, Truffaut stressed Renoir's vitality regardless of his advanced age. "Every morning, Dido Renoir wakes up at seven and waits for the deliveryman to throw the *Los Angeles Times* in front of the house; when her husband wakes up, Dido reads him the most interesting news. At around nine, Greg arrives, a young actor who was a nurse in Vietnam; he comes to massage Jean Renoir's wounded leg, a 1916 war wound that never healed and which caused Octave's famous bearlike gait [referring to the character Renoir played in *The Rules of the Game*]. Renoir then answers his mail, declining all invitations to speak at universities, all offers to preside on juries, and all requests to authenticate his father's paintings—all with the utmost kindness. His politeness is legendary."[116]

The Renoirs considered Leslie Caron, who had been living in Hollywood since the early seventies and was married to an American producer, like their daughter. "I was 'little Leslie'; I never grew up in their eyes,"[117] remembers Caron. A faithful among faithfuls, she met Truffaut at Leona Drive on countless occasions. "Jean had complete confidence in François, who was like a second son. And François venerated him, tried to cheer him up by talking to him about France. Jean used to regain his liveliness when François was around."[118] There was a screen that could be unrolled in the Renoir living room. By removing a painting on the wall opposite, you could aim the beam of a 16-mm army projector, which was permanently installed inside a closet in the hall, at the screen. Jean, Dido, and their guests occasionally watched films, old or new, brought to them by Peter Bogdanovich, Todd McCarthy, or some other faithful friend. "He is sometimes tormented by the thought that he will probably never make another film," Truffaut said, "because he feels he could have done better and more, but we who see his films and love them so, know that he has done the most and done the best."[119]

Truffaut recorded his meetings and experiences in his letters to Madeleine, a tender and light little travel diary.

My little bunny,
   Veronica Lake died, so did Betty Grable, and Robert Ryan, yesterday; this afternoon Nixon went into the hospital and I myself don't feel very well. . . . I've always been told that the great step forward would be to dream in English, actually I wake up at night screaming, "*I am going to buy some for you. . . . I want to buy any,* [in English] etc." In

fact, I'm starting to read the newspapers rather well, but speaking is another matter and as far as understanding is concerned, it won't be this year. I should tell you, my bunny, that if my teacher doesn't leave Los Angeles, I'll stay here longer, until around August 18 or 20 because I don't want to return with the feeling of having failed; if I can do another forty or fifty hours, I must do them. . . . I almost forgot your birthday since I have no reason to look at dates here but, fortunately, one of my nightmares was about you (!) and the alarm went off in my head.* [*"*Gift postponned to sept (sic)."* (Footnote, in English, in the original letter)] . . .

Collective kisses to all 3, I think of you a lot, not just when I write or call (rarely, the telephone *is very expensive* [in English]), tenderly, François.[120]

After his summer in California, Truffaut spent time in New York. At the end of September, three years after the success of *The Wild Child,* he came to attend the screening of *Day for Night* at the New York Film Festival at Lincoln Center. The picture triumphed on the evening of October 1, 1973. Truffaut entered the large hall to enthusiastic applause; at his side was a radiant Jacqueline Bisset, wearing a white dress with a plunging neckline; New York mayor John Lindsay; Jean-Pierre Léaud, and Lillian Gish, to whom, with her sister, Dorothy, Truffaut had dedicated the film. Six days later, *Day for Night* opened to rave reviews at the Fine Arts Theater. All the most important movie critics—Vincent Canby in the *New York Times,* Pauline Kael in *The New Yorker,* Rex Reed in the *New York Daily News,* Judith Crist in *New York* magazine, and Archer Winsten in the *New York Post*—had nothing but praise, and Jacqueline Bisset made the cover of *Newsweek:* A BEAUTY NAMED BISSET. *Day for Night* received several prestigious prizes: It was named best picture by the National Society of Film Critics and was awarded Best Motion Picture and Best Direction by the New York Film Critics. After twenty-three weeks in the theaters, it earned over a million dollars in box-office receipts, as much as all the other Truffaut films distributed in the United States to that date.

Encouraged by this success, during October Truffaut traveled to all the major American cities with *Day for Night.* Four days in Boston, a detour to Montreal, then the San Francisco Festival, where the film was shown on October twenty-fourth prior to the Los Angeles preview scheduled for November third. In the reception room of the Directors Guild, Vincente Minnelli, flanked by William Wilder and George Cukor, extended Truffaut a warm welcome, ending his speech by saying, "And now this film should be listed among the five Oscar nominees for best foreign film." Prestigious supporters such as these were an undeniable asset for Truffaut, who certainly had a chance of winning the famous trophy. He had almost won an Oscar twice before. In 1959, *The 400 Blows* had been nominated for Best Original Screenplay, and in 1968, *Stolen Kisses* had lost the award for Best Foreign-Language Film to Sergei Bondarchuk's *War and Peace*. This time, not only was *Day for Night* nominated, but so was Valentina Cortese as Best Supporting Actress.

Several months later, on April 3, 1974, Truffaut attended the nationally broadcast Academy Awards ceremony at the Los Angeles Music Center. George Roy Hill's *The Sting* was the big winner of the evening, garnering seven awards. But French cinema was honored when an Oscar for Lifetime Achievement was given to Henri Langlois, the director of the Cinémathèque française. Later in the evening, the proceedings were disrupted by a naked man who climbed onstage and interrupted Jack Lemmon's acceptance of the Best Actor award for his role in *Save the Tiger*. It was Yul Brynner who unsealed the envelope to announce the winner in the Best Foreign-Language Film category. Truffaut, seated in the audience in a black tuxedo, betrayed a slight momentary tension when his name was read. Then, onstage, he thanked the audience in English: "I'm very happy because *Day for Night* is about film people like you; it's your trophy. But if you'll agree, I'll keep it for you."[121]

The Oscar added to Truffaut's fame in the United States; like Fellini, Bergman, and Kurosawa, he now belonged to the select group of foreign directors considered dependable box-office draws there. As a result, he received even more film offers from Hollywood, including one for a film on the lives of Ernest Hemingway and F. Scott Fitzgerald, *One Last Glimpse*, based on a novel by James Aldridge. But Truffaut still didn't feel ready for the challenge; he preferred to take advantage of his fame to negotiate better American distribution for his independently made films.

It was then that he decided to use Roger Corman as his distributor. Six years his senior, Corman had directed almost seventy films in England and Hollywood, including six screen adaptations of Edgar Allan Poe, between 1960 and 1964, starring Vincent Price. Since the mid-sixties, Corman had also become a producer and distributor, and the head of his own company, New World Pictures. In Hollywood, he also established a reputation as the most prolific discoverer of new talent: Francis Ford Coppola, Monte Hellman, Peter Bogdanovich, Martin Scorsese, and Joe Dante all made their debut films for him, some featuring the future star Jack Nicholson. As a distributor, Corman specialized in European films, with success, as in the cases of Bergman's *Cries and Whispers* and Fellini's *Amarcord*. This was what persuaded Truffaut to sign up with him for his next four films. "I think that with him I've finally found the ideal distributor. He's Hollywood-based. He feels close to the films he takes on, watches them attentively, has a network of well-established theaters and a very competent staff that includes Jim McBride and Todd McCarthy."[122]

For Truffaut, it was most important to be recognized by his peers—Alfred Hitchcock, Robert Aldrich, Nicholas Ray, Tay Garnett, Samuel Fuller, among the older generation; Miloš Forman, Robert Benton, Arthur Penn, Sydney Pollack, among the younger—these directors were his main champions on the other side of the Atlantic. He was without a doubt the only French director of his generation to have been so respected and honored in Hollywood. In this, he may even have surpassed the other greats of world cinema, Bergman, Fellini, Buñuel, and Kurosawa, who put less energy into following the fate of their films in the United States.

Truffaut also became one of the best-liked directors on American campuses and universities. In the seventies, there were numerous retrospectives and university courses and seminars devoted to his work—Paul Michaud's at Harvard; James Monaco's and Donald Spoto's at the New School for Social Research; Dudley Andrew's at the University of Iowa; Annette Insdorf's at Yale. Truffaut often met young American film enthusiasts in his travels—for example, Leo Moldaver of Cleveland, who organized a tribute to him and wrote him enthusiastic fan letters, or the young Alfred Dolder, who wrote him from Los Angeles on July 12, 1974: "It is thanks to you that I'm in movies, your films are my inspiration, and your love affair with cinema my dream. This letter is a homage to you, the greatest movie director of our time."[123]

POLITICAL COLUMNS

During the whole summer of 1973, François Truffaut was fascinated by Watergate: "I don't understand it at all, but it's fascinating,"[124] he admitted to Liliane Siegel. Richard Nixon, who had "the lead part," interested him less than Nixon's secretary, who had to lie in order to cover up for her boss. Here was politics as suspense, with all the twists and turns and mysteries of an action film, politics that had nothing in common with the politics that grew out of ideological clashes. When politics put society on show like this, Truffaut felt concerned; he even felt stimulated to express his point of view—like a demanding viewer, or film critic.

Hence, when Georges Pompidou died at the beginning of April 1974, Truffaut agreed to write a weekly column in *Le Monde* on the presidential campaign until the election of a successor. He drafted five articles but finally decided against publishing them, doubtless afraid of exposing himself on a terrain that was not his own. Written during the election campaign, these pieces are those of an attentive but sarcastic spectator, voicing his opinion on the performance of the play he is watching. Indeed, the first column is entitled "At the Show":

> Being listened to, being looked at, appearing interesting, that's what matters. The way something is said is more important than substance, this must be acknowledged even though it's shocking. The presidential campaign is show business, and subject to its laws. Experience counts, but not much: there are some good supporting roles—Royer, Krivine, Le Pen, Laguiller, Dumont; there are those who have chosen the wrong vocation and shouldn't be appearing on-screen for lack of talent; there is the fallen star, Chaban-Delmas, foundering in his performance of an outdated play; there is the uninspired but reliable actor, François Mitterrand, who has become a star through hard work; and there is the great actor, the star, Giscard d'Estaing, the one whose quality performance makes one forget the work that went into it, who would triple the number of votes of the other candidates if he were to substitute for them. Giscard d'Estaing with his masterful act of sobriety. You find the term "act" shocking, excessive? Asserting that one will look "deep into the eyes of France," or that the best reforms are those that cost nothing, quoting Napoleon in Corsica and Marcel Pagnol in Marseilles—isn't this performing an act? The French like great men and they have one—Giscard d'Estaing. Thanks to his acting talent, which is immense, he suggests as efficiently as De Gaulle but more subtly, more indirectly, that he is one of those great men, a man who is more than just a president of the Republic, and that he would therefore be making us a gift in accepting to look after us.[125]

Truffaut felt that the opposition press in France was not doing its work, that it "shouldn't let lies and unkempt promises go unnoticed." He was still very influenced and impressed by the role played by the *Washington Post* reporters in uncovering the Watergate scandal. "These people should be called liars when they deserve it, we should tirelessly stress the political world's inadmissible lies and preferential treatments. The serious, opposition press must resolve to inform and oppose; they should take a look at the *Washington Post, Newsweek, Time.* . . ." It was because of this need for vigilance, for a permanent countergovernment, that Truffaut—though politically so moderate—paradoxically praised the French left-wing movement, the only organized force that could make up for the failure of opposition journalism: "Leftism is useful, it has harassing value and can force yesterday's U.D.R. State, tomorrow's Giscardian or Socialist State, to keep their promises."

Given this show, how did Truffaut see the ideal politician? He was extremely wary of the "great man," the "providential savior," and sought to demystify political life. "There are no great men, there are only men, and as far as politics are concerned I tend to prefer those who behave like cleaning women: punctuality, modesty, liveliness, equilibrium, the fight against dust, for cleanliness is daily, carries no prestige, is indispensable and unremitting. I don't necessarily want a little man, but a man who has the disposition of Mendès-France, a man whose commitment is as daily and calm as Sartre's."

In his last column, written on the eve of the presidential election's first round of votes, Truffaut finally justified his own choice. Why did he support François Mitterrand, even though he disliked both the "political actor" and the "man"? Indeed, he had joined the Mitterrand support committee and made a contribution of five thousand francs on May 10, 1974. Even though his convictions were closer to those of Michel Rocard, whose candidacy he had wished for in these presidential elections. For Truffaut, Rocard was among those politicians who displayed a certain skepticism and great lucidity concerning political power, like Pierre Mendès-France, Pierre Cot, and Edmond Maire. Nevertheless, and still without having registered to vote, Truffaut officially backed Mitterrand. "Mitterrand should be supported, not to be 'with it,' to look like good guys, or seem youthful, but simply because it seems to me just."

Sartre occupied a major place for Truffaut in the realm of political and moral ideas and was his main point of reference. He was constantly reading and rereading the philosopher's works. Upon rereading *The Words*, he wrote to Liliane Siegel, "Of course, we have a greater or lesser need for a given book depending on the period of life we are going through, and right now, this book hits the bull's-eye in terms of my fears. I feel that other books by Sartre can give me courage at the present time."[126]

As always with Truffaut, the friendly relationship he maintained with Liliane Siegel was very ritualized. He would go to pick her up at her house, on boulevard Raspail, at around eight o'clock, then take her to dinner in Montparnasse, often at the Palette, one of Sartre's favorite restaurants, and their conversation often revolved around Sartre. Siegel even finds similarities between the two men, "the same way of living a life as regular as clockwork, with mental compartments. . . ."[127] A similar pleasure in the company of women and a similar desire to seduce them. "These kinds of men always wonder if they are loved for what they really are or for what they represent socially," Siegel adds.

During the fall of 1974 came an opportunity for a real rapprochement between Truffaut and Sartre. Marcel Jullian, who had been appointed head of Antenne 2, wanted to undertake a bold television project with Sartre: a series of ten broadcasts of one hour and a half that would present the history of France in the twentieth century. Sartre was very eager for Truffaut to be the director for the broadcasts. Truffaut was very touched and considered the project worthwhile, but he turned the offer down, since his own films claimed too much of his time. Furthermore, he couldn't see himself working for television, which he regarded as "unfair competition" for cinema. And he feared that his public and professional fame might get in the way of Sartre's team, or that, somehow, he might become a pawn for Antenne 2's managers. Though "he stood by cinema," Truffaut nevertheless devoted some time to Sartre's television project. He discussed it regularly with Liliane Siegel, at dinner or in his letters, and she relayed his opinions to Sartre. "So I'm in the background helping you, out of admiration, friendship and a feeling of kinship for Sartre,"[128] he wrote her. For example, he went to the trouble of drawing up a list of potential directors, which included Roger Louis, a journalist and television director whom he admired, and his friend Claude de Givray. But in the meantime, the Sartre project was beginning to fall apart because of internal dissension among the collaborators,[129] violent hostility on the part of the political and television authorities toward a project that they considered left-wing and subversive, Sartre's mistrust, his demand for freedom in his work, and, as a result, his rejection of Jullian's request for a pilot broadcast. In September 1975, the affair broke out publicly; state television, despite its new veneer of advanced liberalism, missed its opportunity with an intellectual of Sartre's stature and censored his project. People say that Jacques Chirac, the then prime minister, had something to do with it.

ISABELLE'S FACE

Truffaut made no films in 1973 and 1974, which put Les Films du Carrosse in financial difficulty. He urgently needed to knock at the door of American financial backers with some new projects. In 1974, the one that was furthest along and which Truffaut was most enthusiastic about was Jean Gruault's, based on the *Journal of Adèle Hugo,* which had been published in the late sixties by Editions Minard and edited by an American university professor in Ohio, Frances Vernor Guille. Captivated by the book, Truffaut had lost no time in giving it to Gruault—not to adapt, but with the idea of fleshing out one episode in the life of Victor Hugo's second daughter, a linear story of mad, unrequited love, with no hope of a happy ending.

In 1863, Adèle Hugo goes to live in Halifax, Nova Scotia, under the borrowed name of Miss Lewly. She has come to join a British army lieutenant,

Pinson, with whom she is madly in love. She takes lodgings with a solitary elderly woman and keeps her real identity secret. But the lieutenant rejects her and asks her to leave. Adèle persists obstinately, redoubling her stratagems and declarations of love to Pinson. She tells her father, Victor Hugo, who is living in exile on the Channel Island of Guernsey, that she has married, and thereby obtains a living allowance from him. Madness gradually takes possession of her soul. Feverish and distracted, she writes diary entries every night, in which she talks about her love and her writing ambitions, and repudiates her father and his name. Then Lieutenant Pinson's regiment is sent to Barbados, in the West Indies. Adèle Hugo follows him. She is found in Bridgetown, distraught and in rags, a madwoman whom children cruelly pursue with their taunts. The last time she runs into Lieutenant Pinson in the street, she doesn't even recognize him. A West Indian woman, Madame Baa, finally takes her in and then accompanies her to France with financial help from Victor Hugo. Adèle is then locked up in an asylum in Paris, where she dies in 1915, still believing in her eternal love.

While Gruault was working on the screenplay—it took him two long years—relations with Frances Vernor Guille became complicated; she demanded a considerable sum for the screen rights (30,000 francs) and the status of coscenarist (with payment of 200,000 francs). Truffaut considered these demands unacceptable. While expressing his "deep disappointment" to her, he contemplated giving up the project "all the more sadly and bitterly as we have never encountered such a situation in our fifteen years of filmmaking."[130]

In fact, Truffaut was playing a tricky game, pretending to be discouraged and on the point of giving up the project, with the sole aim of getting Guille to back down. For he very much wanted to make the film. Indeed, he put all his energy into overcoming the reluctance of Jean Hugo, a writer and painter living in Lunel, who was Adèle's grand-nephew and Victor Hugo's great-grandson, and hence the direct heir and owner of the rights to this adaptation. Jean Hugo hesitated for a long time: "I wonder if this sad story, which was always a jealously guarded family secret, won't be shocking on the screen. Doesn't mental disease, whose signs were very soon apparent in Adèle Hugo, give a pathological overtone to this love story and take away all its human value?"[131] he wrote, somewhat fearfully, to Truffaut. It was only after reading Gruault's first treatment that Victor Hugo's descendant gave his consent, on the sole condition that the writer not appear as a protagonist on-screen. In the meantime, Truffaut had to settle his dispute with Frances Vernor Guille. A compromise was reached involving payment of fifty thousand francs for the "historical supervision" of the screenplay, a nonbinding honorary status.

Marcel Berbert's estimated budget for *L'Histoire d'Adèle H.* (*The Story of Adèle H.*), a period film shot outside, was slightly over 5 million francs. This was too expensive a film for Carrosse to produce on its own. Berbert quite naturally turned to Robert Solo, in the belief that after the success of *Day for Night* and the Oscar for Best Foreign-Language Film, he would encounter no difficulty in putting together a coproduction deal with Warner Brothers. But the company's representative in France turned down the *Adèle H.* screenplay on the grounds that it was too literary. Several weeks later, Truffaut and Berbert, who were used to such unexpected reversals, found a better reception with Jean Nachbaur, the French representative for United Artists, Carrosse's erstwhile partner for *The Wild Child.* But Nachbaur thought the budget too big, which necessitated a revision of the screenplay. Though he had set out to write a novelistic film "à la *Gone With the Wind*,"[132] Gruault condensed his scenes and pruned the story as much as possible. The screenplay he handed to Truffaut in November 1973 was shortened considerably, from 373 to 116 pages. With Suzanne Schiffman's help, Truffaut eliminated most of the costly historical scenes and decided to center the film around Adèle, her madness, her psychotic behavior, and her persecution mania. This was where the whole strength of the film would lie, focused on obsessive love, a theme that was dear to Truffaut.

Now Truffaut had to find the ideal actress. Several years earlier, he had promised the part to Catherine Deneuve.[133] A short time later, he made screen tests with Stacey Tendeter—the actress who had played Muriel in *Two English Girls* and whose physical appearance was right for the part. But he now wanted the heroine to be younger and he began to look for an ingenue. Very soon, he noticed Isabelle Adjani, first in the television broadcast of the Comédie-Française production of Molière's *School for Wives,* and then in Claude Pinoteau's film *La Gifle,* a big hit when it opened in September 1974. Though he didn't know her, he wrote her an impassioned letter to convince her to accept the part of Adèle Hugo, which meant she would have to break her contract with the Comédie-Française: "You're a fabulous actress and, with the exception of Jeanne Moreau, I've never felt such a pressing desire to capture a face on celluloid, immediately, and without further delay. I accept the idea that theater is a noble cause, but my particular area is cinema and I came out of *La Gifle* with the conviction that you should be filmed every day, even on Sunday."[134]

Isabelle Adjani demurred. She was attracted by the part (even though she admitted she thought she was too young for it) and by the director's prestige, but she felt that breaking with the Comédie-Française would be an "act of betrayal, of disloyal severance."[135] Truffaut pleaded even more energetically to persuade her. Not only did he predict a "magnificent career" for her but he confessed his infatuation: "Your face tells a screen story unto itself, the expression in your eyes creates dramatic situations, you could even act in a film with no story line, it would be a documentary on you and would be as good as any fiction."[136] Truffaut wrote to Pierre Dux, the head of the Comédie-Française, on October 23, 1974, asking him to grant Adjani a fourteen-week leave, starting in January 1975. Dux categorically refused. Unwilling to give up on Adjani, Truffaut continued to exercise pressure. When the Comédie-Française threatened the actress with a breach-of-contract suit, Truffaut gave the case to his lawyer, Pierre Hebey, asking him to negotiate a compromise. Isabelle Adjani passively let the adults decide things for her. But by giving up the two parts she was to perform onstage, she was deserting the theater. "After my last performance, some people came to see me to tell me that what I was doing was very bad, that I would always regret it, that things would not go well in the movies. . . . That night I was really stigmatized. . . ."[137]

Now that he had almost kidnapped the nineteen-year-old actress, François Truffaut could get down to the preproduction work on the film. Suzanne Schiffman scouted locations: the filming was to take place in Guernsey, except for the Barbados scenes, which were to be shot on the island of Gorée off the coast of Senegal. *The Story of Adéle H.* would be filmed entirely on islands, in isolated conditions that would be hard on the entire cast and crew. To complete his casting, Truffaut went to London on December ninth, to audition English actors whom he wanted for the supporting roles. He hired Bruce Robinson for the part of Lieutenant Pinson, Joseph Blatchley for the bookseller Whistler, and Sylvia Marriott, the mother of Anne and Muriel Brown in *Two English Girls,* for the part of Mrs. Saunders, Adèle's landlady. Lastly, he had the idea of casting Ivry Gitlis, the famous violinist, in the part of a magician and hypnotist.

On January 3, 1975, Truffaut arrived in Guernsey. He stayed at the Duke of Richmond Hotel, which faced Cambridge Park in the heart of Saint Peter Port. This is the main town on this small island, with its very puritanical atmosphere; its main claim to fame is the fact that it extended hospitality to the exiled Victor Hugo for over fifteen years. The cast and crew had to spend two months there. Truffaut was delighted to work with Nestor Almendros again, four years after their last collaboration. He persuaded him to take on Florent Bazin—Janine and André's son—as assistant cameraman. From then on, Florent Bazin would be assistant cameraman or cameraman on all of Truffaut's films.

Because of the isolation, Truffaut organized a film society in a room of the Duke of Richmond Hotel. Two evenings a week, Claude Miller, the production manager, was in charge of showing films in 16 mm: Welles's *The Magnificent Ambersons,* Chaplin's *The Gold Rush,* Hitchcock's *Psycho,*

Richard Fleischer's *The Vikings,* Murnau's *The Last Laugh,* and Keaton's *The Navigator.* It was a way of relieving tension—"we were stuck,"[138] Isabelle Adjani said. But this austere life also had its advantages: The cast and crew concentrated on their work and the shooting atmosphere was quasi-religious. "Everything is fraught with tension and passion, but internally and with no outward show," Truffaut confided to Liliane Siegel. "For that reason it is rather hard on the nerves, but the rushes are really good. I'm on good behavior and strictly professional, if you see what I mean, and usually I'm thinking of my daughters as I lead Isabelle A. in the direction of children's books for young girls."[139]

Besides the isolation, there were reasons why the *Adèle H.* shoot was very tense and difficult. The film had to be made in two versions, in French and in English, so multiple takes were necessary in order to shoot each scene in both languages. Then, most important, the relationship between the actress and the director was sensitive, not to say passionate. "For Truffaut, *Adèle* is primarily a story about isolation," Isabelle Adjani said. "He knew how to create a claustrophobic atmosphere."[140] As on each of his shoots, Truffaut was in love with his female lead. "I spent my time warding him off as a woman and as an actress,"[141] Adjani later admitted. Truffaut's passion took the form of enthrallment. He seemed hypnotized, more than he had ever been on any of his films. "I watch her act, I help her as I can, uttering thirty words when she would like a hundred, or fifty when only one, but the right one, is needed, for everything is a matter of vocabulary in our strange association. I don't know Isabelle Adjani. Yet, in the evening, my eyes and ears are tired from having looked at her too hard and listened to her all day."[142]

As for Isabelle Adjani, she gave herself entirely to her part; she seemed possessed by Adèle Hugo, a young woman rejected by an older man, Lieutenant Pinson, who was supposed to be the same age as Truffaut. "Adèle was not in love with the young man but in love with her love for him, with her imagined idea of love,"[143] says Adjani. *The Story of Adèle H.,* then, is a film about love as an obsession, with the script reproducing—but with genders reversed—the relationship between the director and his actress. Truffaut was motivated to film extreme close-ups of the face and body of the young actress. "He needed me to be there so he could focus on me, and record this idée fixe he had of me, this rigidity he demanded of my body,"[144] Adjani adds.

"It is not unusual to see the little makeup girls and hair stylists crying behind the set as they hear our young Adèle performing,"[145] Truffaut wrote to Helen Scott. It was Adjani's practice not to rehearse so she could give herself completely during the takes; in this way, she created a climate that often left the director and his team in an overwrought emotional state. So he wrote to Liliane Siegel from Guernsey, asking her to keep her lips sealed for "fear of misunderstandings": "You mention the pleasure I must have directing Isabelle A. It's the opposite of pleasure, it's daily suffering for me, and almost an agony for her. For her profession is her religion, and because of that our shoot is a trial for everyone. It would be too easy to say she is difficult, she is not. She is different from all the women in this profession and since she isn't even twenty, add to all this (to her genius, let's not be afraid of words), an unawareness of others and their vulnerability which creates an unbelievable tension."[146]

After a two-month shoot on the island, one of the longest in his entire career, Truffaut, on the point of exhaustion, left Guernsey with his cast and crew on March 8, 1975. There still remained another week of work in Senegal, involving only part of the cast and crew. They left Paris on March twelfth for Dakar, where Truffaut granted himself a week's rest before tackling the editing of his film. He still had to confront what he called "the trial of the Moritone":[147] seeing Isabelle Adjani's face over and over again on the editing flatbed and wondering whether he had succeeded in obtaining what he had hoped for from her. *The Story of Adèle H.*, Truffaut realized very soon, was a film that had been abducted by his actress's face. Would this, which seemed a strength to him, seem so to others? The initial response of some of his close friends was stern. Gilles Jacob wrote him that "he had felt unmoved";[148] Marcel Ophuls said he was disappointed by the coldness of a film that was "frozen from within by the pallor of Adèle's face."[149] Even Gruault was not convinced by the film, the principal problem being that "Adèle does not go mad because she is in love; on the contrary, she seems mad from the beginning, on the wharf, as soon as she steps off the boat."[150] For Truffaut, this blow struck home, but he would need some distance to comprehend it. In two years, "he would be able to see the film again as though it had been filmed by someone else."[151] For the time being, however, he sensed that there was "something strange and unbalanced"[152] about this film that had sometimes made him shed tears while he was making it.

The Story of Adèle H. opened in Paris on October eighth. Attendance was good during the first week, with 55,000 tickets sold, but soon dwindled because word of mouth was poor. The film fared better in Japan and Italy. It opened in New York on December 22 and was well received by the press. A tragic coincidence: One week after seeing the film, to which she responded enthusiastically and with great emotion, "in tears from beginning to end,"[153] Frances V. Guille, Adèle's biographer, died of a heart attack.

SMALL CHANGE

Even before the release of *The Story of Adèle H.*, François Truffaut was planning a new film—the best remedy for forgetting the tensions and passions of Guernsey. After depicting a young woman's obsessive love and madness, he started work on a film about children. He scheduled the filming of *L'Argent de poche* (*Small Change*) for July 1975, during the summer vacation, a mere four months after his return from Senegal. The screenplay would be built around several little anecdotes he had recorded. Some dated back to the period when he was working on *The Mischief Makers* and *The 400 Blows*—for example, the one of the little girl who had been left home alone by her parents and who yelled from the window "I'm hungry," a true story told to him by Madeleine. Some of the other incidents were autobiographical, like the one of his first kiss, at summer camp in August 1945. Others were taken from news items, or simply invented.

At the end of 1972, the project was still only at the synopsis stage—he had written about ten pages with Suzanne Schiffman. At that point, Truffaut had contemplated an "episode film illustrating different aspects of childhood," with each part a variation on the theme of "children's great powers of resistance and survival."[154] He even considered giving his film the ironic title *The Tough Skin*. In early summer 1974, Truffaut decided to resume work on the project with Suzanne Schiffman. He didn't intend to write a real screenplay, for he wanted to be free to improvise with the children who would act in the film and write the dialogue as he went along, using preestablished situations and including some of his ideas about childhood.[155] It is Truffaut himself—his words, ideas, and intonations—who is echoed in the teacher's long monologue to his young pupils, delivered by Jean-François Stévenin:

> I wanted to tell you that it is because of my own bad memories of my youth and because I don't like the way children are treated that I chose to become a schoolteacher. Life's not easy, it's hard and it's important you learn to steel yourself against it. Note, I said steel yourself, not become hard-boiled. Things balance out in an odd way, so people who have had a difficult youth are often better equipped to confront adult life than people who have been overprotected, or very loved. It's a sort of law of compensation. In time you will have children and I hope you will love them and they will love you. To tell the truth, they will love you if you love them. Otherwise they will transfer their love, affection, or tenderness to other people or other things. Because life is such that it is impossible not to feel love and be loved.[156]

In April 1975, after scouting locations in the center of France, Truffaut decided to shoot his film in Thiers, in the Puy-de-Dôme. At the end of May, he started auditioning and giving screen tests to children every Saturday at Les Films du Carrosse. Among the three hundred who auditioned, fifteen would ultimately be cast in the main parts of *Small Change*. Some children of friends were among the chosen, such as Georges Desmouceaux, the son of Lucette and Claude de Givray, or Philippe Goldmann, the son of the philosopher Lucien Goldmann. Truffaut's daughters also made their real screen debut—Laura as the young wife by the name of Madeleine Doinel, the mother of a baby, Oscar, who refuses to talk and only expresses himself by whistling; Eva in the part of Patricia, the teenager whose little boyfriends take her to the movies in the hope of kissing her.

In June, Truffaut settled in Thiers and hired some local schoolchildren as extras. The wife of the schoolteacher (Jean-François Stévenin) is played by Virginie Thévenet. Marcel Berbert, Roland Thénot, Monique Dury (the costumer) and Thi Loan N'Guyen (the makeup girl) also make appearances in the film, and so does the mayor of Thiers, René Barnérias, in a small part. The shooting of *Small Change* began on July 17, 1975, and lasted two months. Truffaut had rehired Pierre-William Glenn, the director of photography of *Day for Night,* because he wanted the new picture to be filmed at a similarly rapid pace. Truffaut wrote his dialogue hurriedly, every once in a while noting down expressions used by his "actors."

Rather cheerful, but physically exhausting because of the constant attention required by the children, the shoot of *Small Change* left him once again in a state of great fatigue. His physician prescribed a month of complete rest, which he decided to spend in Cannes, then in Los Angeles, at the Beverly Hills Hotel. When he returned to Paris at the end of October 1975, an arduous editing task awaited him—a three-hour rough cut that had to be brought down to an acceptable running time of around one hour and forty minutes.

Six months after the failure of *The Story of Adèle H.,* Truffaut found success again. *Small Change* was a big hit when it opened in ten Paris movie houses on March 17, 1976. Once again, the audience flocked to one of Truffaut's "small" films after keeping away from a more ambitious work. *Small Change* reached ticket sales of 470,000 after a six-month run, equaling the success of *The 400 Blows.* The film also did extremely well abroad—including the United States (it earned almost $1.5 million in box-office receipts), Germany, Scandinavia, and Japan. In the United States, Truffaut had two consecutive successes in the same year—*Adèle H.* and *Small Change*—he could now join the club of "million-dollar directors" whose films cost only half that amount to make.

A MAN WHO WOULD HAVE THE SOUL OF A CHILD

François Truffaut had no further film shoots scheduled until the autumn of 1976. He was giving himself six months to rest, write a few prefaces, and tinker with the screenplay of *The Man Who Loved Women.* On March 2, 1976, his plans were changed by a telephone call from Los Angeles. A twenty-nine-year-old American filmmaker was on the other end of the line, offering him a part in his next film. It was Steven Spielberg, who had attracted attention in 1971 with his first television feature, *Duel.* Though the latter became an American cult movie, Spielberg was better known to international audiences for his second feature film, *Jaws,* the greatest box-office hit in the history of cinema at that time. Spielberg had just completed the screenplay for *Close Encounters of the Third Kind* and offered Truffaut the part of the French scientist specializing in UFOs. "I needed a man who would have the soul of a child," Spielberg later said, "someone kindly, warm, who could completely accept the extraordinary, the irrational."[157] A teenage prodigy, born in Ohio in 1947 and who later studied film at California State College, Steven Spielberg had seen *The Wild Child* and *Day for Night,* two films that had made a deep impression on him. He thought he could count on Truffaut's acting talent for the part of the "child-man," to whom he gave a very French name, Claude Lacombe.

The day after Spielberg's phone call, his producer, Julia Phillips,[158] who worked for Columbia Pictures, arranged to have the screenplay delivered to Truffaut, with French translations scrupulously provided for all the scenes in which he was to appear. About ten days later, on March 15, Truffaut sent the following telegram to Spielberg: "I like the script and I like Lacombe. Stop. I would like to be able to play the part, but I need time to think because I'm supposed to shoot a new film in the beginning of September. Stop. Sincerely yours."[159] Truffaut was tempted by the offer. The thought of acting in an $11 million Hollywood production directed by a talented young man was not only a real novelty but also an exciting challenge. He told Julia Phillips he could only accept under one condition: He had to be free in August to work on the screenplay for *The Man Who Loved Women* in Los Angeles. He also requested information concerning the dates and locations of the shoot, as well as payment he would receive. "I wonder if you'll understand my very special English, I hope so!"[160] he wrote. Truffaut contacted his lawyer in Los Angeles, Louis Blau, and his agent, Rupert Allen, to negotiate his contract. Spielberg and Columbia Pictures did everything to facilitate Truffaut's involvement with *Close Encounters.* They assured him that the shoot, scheduled to begin in May 1976, wouldn't exceed fourteen weeks, that he would be free for two weeks in mid-August, and they offered him a payment that was far from insignificant—$85,000. Truffaut accepted the part of Claude Lacombe, UFO specialist. When he arrived in Los Angeles on May 5, 1976, preproduction on the film was already nearly complete and the shoot was to begin a few days later in Gillett, in the mountains of Wyoming, near the local attraction, the strange cylinder-shaped peak called Devil's Tower.

As soon as he arrived in Hollywood, Truffaut was charmed by Steven Spielberg; the two men shared the same love of cinema, in particular an admiration for Howard Hawks.[161] Truffaut found Spielberg unpretentious, even though he was already "the director of the most *successful* [in English] film in the history of cinema,"[162] and fearless about directing such a huge production. He admired Spielberg's serenity and good humor in fulfilling his "childhood dream." Nevertheless, the first two weeks of the shoot in Gillett were trying. Truffaut was uneasy with the language, lost among several dozen technicians, and homesick. "I like America, but Los Angeles more than Wyoming or Alabama and I miss you, as well as our lunches at the *boulangerie*,"[163] he wrote to his friend Serge Rousseau, whom he used to meet often, when he was in Paris, at the bakery-restaurant on the corner of rue Marbeuf and rue Robert-Estienne, a few yards away from his office. Truffaut, who was never enticed by tourism, even declined visiting the famed Mount Rushmore and seeing the heads of the American presidents carved in stone—the location used by Hitchcock for the final sequences of *North by Northwest*. He spent most of his time just waiting. "It's sometimes amusing, but very slow, very long, and I must admit that the acting profession has its wretched side (or rather sides),"[164] he wrote to Nestor Almendros. Though he sometimes took undeniable pleasure in "acting without stage fright" and often succeeded in making the American cast and crew laugh, Truffaut discovered the frustration of actors, forced to wait between takes in complete passivity and idleness. This was completely foreign to his usual experience on the set, where he could control situations and master his schedule. He felt stymied, "almost like in a (gilded) prisoners' camp,"[165] he admitted to Marcel Berbert, saying that he would never again agree to be directed by other filmmakers. On the set of *Close Encounters*, he discovered special effects and technical processes that were all the rage in American moviemaking (that same year, Spielberg's best friend, George Lucas, started work on *Star Wars*). The actors were filmed performing their scenes with a matte on the upper half of the frame for the subsequent compositing of studio-made video and computer-generated special effects. Here, on this part of the image—and of the screen—the famed flying objects that Professor Lacombe was supposed to tame would eventually be seen. Though a highly sophisticated technique, marking an important stage in the history of cinematic special effects, it slowed the pace of the filming considerably, leading Truffaut to say that Spielberg shoots only three or four shots a day.

After a ten-day interlude in Los Angeles, during which they shot at Columbia Studios (and Truffaut had the pleasure of seeing Jean Renoir and staying at the Beverly Hills Hotel), in June 1976, the cast and crew left for Mobile, Alabama, for two months. There, inside a huge warehouse, gigantic state-of-the-art sets had been built. Truffaut wrote to Madeleine on July 13:

I can't describe the shoot in this enormous warehouse representing a secret, electronically equipped underground passage where the spaceship will land, because we're only beginning to shoot there tomorrow, I think. It's a bigger, larger and taller place than any Hollywood studio, which is why it was chosen—except the production people didn't know there were leaks in the roof (a catastrophe for the set), etc. Later. I saw the warehouse, not bad. We aren't shooting today, a giant mess. There are 120 people besides the cast and crew—extras, a hundred people equally divided into little groups: chemists, engineers, physicians, meteorologists, telephone operators. I don't really understand much; in principle, I direct a pseudo-French group called "the society of light." In the end, the little girls will fly off, the spaceship will arrive, we'll all touch each other, etc. all of this before October, I hope. . . . P.S. . . . : I was just told over the phone that I would have my office tomorrow. It's a wonderful life. Les Films du Carrosse will have an outpost in Mobile![166]

Truffaut eventually became accustomed to this world of technology and excess that was so foreign to him: "I'm learning all sorts of things that will never be of any use to me,"[167] he said facetiously to Marcel Berbert, fully appreciating the talent of his right-hand man at managing his modest film budgets. In Mobile, Truffaut used the private office the producers gave him inside the warehouse studio as a place where he could rest, read, and entertain friends—the star of the film, Richard Dreyfuss, or Bob Balaban, who also played in *Close Encounters,* or the director of photography, the Hungarian Vilmos Zsigmond.

Josiane Couëdel, his secretary at Les Films du Carrosse, sent him his mail from Paris regularly, as well as the newspapers and magazines he liked to read—*L'Express, Le Point, Le Nouvel Observateur, Télérama, Le Film français,* the movie page of *Le Monde.* Between takes, he wrote scores of letters to friends and worked on the script of *The Man Who Loved Women:*

The first version . . . is finished, I'm only 50 percent satisfied with it, but I have the feeling of seeing, much more clearly than usual, what has to be done to improve it considerably and I must say I have time to fine-tune it. . . . For the moment, the question that worries me is this: can women be sent out into the streets of Montpellier in November in summer dresses or would it be more reasonable to wait until the spring of '77 . . . ? The script is getting rather amusing. Since I know ahead of time that Denner's puritanism will prevent many things, I try to find indirect solutions so that, in spite of this, things will be charged with tension and eroticism. I only come up with one really good idea a week, but I've been at it for quite awhile already. . . . Good, fine, I know that eventually I'll be bawled out by everyone and when I say everyone, it starts very close to home. . . .[168]

In mid-August, Truffaut was free for two weeks, as planned. He arranged to have Suzanne Schiffman come to Los Angeles. There, in a suite at the Beverly Hills Hotel, they put the finishing touches on the screenplay for *The Man Who Loved Women,* which Truffaut hoped to shoot in October of the same year. In the beginning of September, he returned to Mobile for the last two weeks of filming. Steven Spielberg shot the end of his film in the huge warehouse that served as a set—the arrival of the spaceship and the fraternizing of the humans and the extraterrestrials, under Professor Lacombe's sympathetic gaze. Now, only ten days of filming remained, which was scheduled for the beginning of 1977—in India, this time, not far from Bombay, where Truffaut would go after directing his own film.

All in all, after a difficult period of adjustment, Truffaut was not unhappy with his experience. He was forced to put himself into someone else's shoes and, moreover, the shoes of a foreigner twice over. Spielberg's conception of Professor Lacombe presupposed a linguistic and cultural estrangement. But even if the world of Hollywood megaproductions was poles apart from Truffaut's conception of cinema—modest, craftsmanlike, uniting a small family of actors and technicians—he doubtless recognized in the character of Lacombe Dr. Itard's double—someone who seeks out extraterrestrials like so many wild children who need to be understood. Spielberg and Truffaut were thus united in the themes they explored.

With his neutral acting style, his luminous and passionate gaze, Truffaut is out of place in this typically American film. This was the effect Spielberg had desired; and for him, Truffaut was the "perfect actor,"[169] the kind who never asked questions and was always available to shoot extra scenes or dialogue. Spielberg wrote expressing his gratitude to Truffaut in December 1977, once the film was completed: "*Close Encounters* is doing beautifully—as I've indicated time and time again, your performance was superb!"[170] He even asked Truffaut to write the introduction to the book about the making of the film.

Released in the United States on February 6, 1978 (Truffaut's forty-sixth birthday), Spielberg's film was greeted with enthusiasm by the critics and the public. One month later, the two filmmakers met in London for a special screening of *Close Encounters* in the presence of Queen Elizabeth. In the meantime, the film had opened in Paris, where it had been preceded by a televised program devoted to Truffaut and hosted by Michel Drucker. The character of Claude Lacombe revealed François Truffaut to countless viewers all over the world who hadn't necessarily seen his films. In some sense, he became more than a director; he became "a humanist,"[171] as Steven Spielberg said of him.

A SOLITARY HUNTER

For a long time, the film that was to become *L'Homme qui aimait les femmes* (*The Man Who Loved Women*) was entitled *Le Cavaleur* (The Skirt-Chaser). François Truffaut had as an epigraph to the screenplay a sentence from a book by Bruno Bettelheim: "It seemed that Joey simply never got through to his mother,"[172] proof, once again, of the autobiographical nature of the story. Truffaut intended to draw the portrait of a womanizer, a man who values the love of women above everything else in his life, as a way of simultaneously repressing and exalting a disappointed first love for his mother. Truffaut was always fascinated by these kinds of men, "who loved women." Not skirt-chasers or Don Juans, for whom seduction is a game, but men for whom seduction is a passion, an idée fixe, a serious, perpetual occupation—as though with every prospective conquest their lives were at stake. Truffaut had known men like this—Henri-Pierre Roché or Jacques Audiberti, for instance—and he himself, though he was shy and had a great sense of propriety, was a ladies' man. Diffidence was part of his charm, and he used it as an asset in seducing women, or in letting women seduce him. Liliane Dreyfus says, for example, "François had a female sensibility; he knew how to read expressions in people's eyes."[173] He sometimes could seem timid with a woman, in the periods of his life when he lacked self-confidence or was reluctant to commit himself. But he could be bold and was capable of badgering women who resisted him or considered him a friend or a pleasant companion rather than a lover. He was "very loyal, but possessive,"[174] by several accounts. "There was always a beginning, rarely an end," Liliane Dreyfus says. "He protected me, like a father, husband, and brother all at once, at every point in my life. Which didn't prevent him from sometimes being cruel, even with the people he loved."[175] "Deeply unfaithful, more out of an appetite for seduction, or a need to be loved, than out of an all-consuming need,"[176] is how Madeleine Morgenstern describes it. Love then changed into friendship, or continued in a more lasting, explicitly sexual way. Jeanne Moreau referred to "inescapable harmonies." The men who knew Truffaut well also have something to say about his charm and his obsessive desire to seduce. Claude Chabrol unhesitatingly says that Truffaut's great theme, in his life and work, was "the search for harmonious relationships," this constant, sometimes desperate quest, for a just equilibrium and happiness. "François was an absolutely charming man, in the literal meaning of the word: He charmed. But I've often asked myself whether he had been happy in his life. . . ."[177] Philippe Labro also describes "this drive, this thirst, this voracious need to seduce. However, François was not a hollow Don Juan. Because what counted most was his work, the idea of imposing his own style and his own world, the desire to exhibit all his talent."[178]

The idea for *Le Cavaleur* owed a great deal to Michel Fermaud. An old acquaintance, Fermaud had met Truffaut in the late fifties in the *Cahiers du cinéma* entourage. The two were about the same age, and they addressed each other with the informal *"tu,"* a privilege Truffaut accorded sparingly. "I often saw Truffaut at the *Cahiers*—saw, I can't say we knew each other then," Fermaud recalls. At about the same time, in 1958, Fermaud wrote a play, *Les Portes claquent* (The Doors Slam), starring Jean-Claude Brialy and Michael Lonsdale, which was a huge hit. "François came to see it. We met; we had long conversations. He knew that I loved women,"[179] Fermaud adds. Out of this shared passion for women, there arose a certain complicity between the two men. Thereafter, however, they lost sight of each other for about fifteen years.

In December 1974, Truffaut got back in touch with Fermaud and invited him to lunch in a restaurant on the Champs-Elysées. He requested that Fermaud help him in shaping his screenplay. As he always did with scriptwriters, Truffaut asked Fermaud to record as many anecdotes about his female conquests as possible. His regular appointments with an usherette in a movie theater, a pickup in a fitting room, a scene in the washroom of a restaurant or department store—all these romantic and sexual stories offer a wonderful gallery of female characters, including the "easy woman" who resists the skirt-chaser, the woman who "seems like an impregnable citadel" yet "pounces on him,"[180] and the married woman who uses all manner of cunning to meet with her lover.

On February 18, 1975, Michel Fermaud gave Truffaut a first set of notes, with a commentary in the form of a self-portrait. "If I understand correctly, the hero is neither a sex maniac nor a skirt-chaser. He just goes to great lengths to conquer members of the opposite sex, satisfy them and get rid of them, as though his life depended on it. Is he motivated by a fear of solitude? You must have had the experience, as I have, of bringing someone home at night not because you desired her all that much, but because you felt a certain anguish. Is he driven by the need to please, affirm himself, or conquer? Is he trying to appease a raging sexual appetite? What social milieu does he belong to?"[181] Truffaut sent his friend's sheets back to him with notes and comments. "François would say to me, 'More like this, more like that.' I would sometimes go against my instincts because I didn't always feel things the same way he did." Indeed, Fermaud was a carefree seducer, a hedonist, but Truffaut wasn't: "He saw me as blessed by the gods, a kind of freak," Fermaud adds. "François was very discreet about his romantic relationships with actresses; I realized this when I worked with him on avenue Pierre 1er de Serbie. I overheard many phone conversations, his imbroglios with women were incredible. There was always an unspoken, hidden undertone."[182] Fermaud furnished Truffaut with a series of anecdotes, light but detailed short scenes, to help him write his screenplay. The hero of *Le Cavaleur,* Bertrand Morane, is a depressive surrounded by women, a conception derived as much from Fermaud as from Truffaut. The autobiographical dimension is particularly obvious in the flashbacks of the film, made up of the hero's childhood and adolescent memories about his mother. "My mother was in the habit of walking around half-naked in front of me," Bertrand Morane writes in his journal. "Not in order to arouse me of course but rather, I assume, to confirm to herself that I didn't exist. Everything about her behavior with me when I was little implied: 'I'd have been better off breaking a leg on the day I gave birth to this little moron.' "

In the spring of 1976, when he joined Spielberg for several months in California, Truffaut took Fermaud's notes with him. Meanwhile, Suzanne Schiffman began outlining a story line and a narrative structure. As planned, the two met in August in Los Angeles and worked on the screenplay together for two weeks. Oddly, the script begins in a cemetery: A man is being buried and the only people at the grave are women who loved him. In his early forties, Bertrand Morane lived in Montpellier and was an engineer at the Institute for the Study of Fluid Mechanics. His job was to test the effects of atmospheric turbulence on model planes, ships, and helicopters. But his only passion was women. None left him indifferent—whether dark or blond, "tall filly" or "little kitten," each had characteristics that fit into a detailed glossary of femininity. Morane loved redheads for their smell, platinum blondes for their artificiality; he loved young women who believed the world belonged to them, mature women who remained flirtatious; and he loved widows because they were available, married women because they were not. For Bertrand, women's legs "measure the world like a compass, giving it balance and harmony."

The hero, as Truffaut conceived him in his work sessions with Michel Fermaud, is a solitary and anxious hunter, who seeks to conquer women even in the face of the worst difficulties—whether an unknown woman whose legs he spots in a laundry, a baby-sitter whose phone number he copies off a bulletin board in a supermarket, a car-rental employee, or the invisible operator of a telephone wake-up service, a café waitress proficient in karate, a deaf-mute usherette in a movie theater, a woman who comes back into his life after a long separation, or one who can make love only in precarious situations. One evening, a not-so-young woman who owns a boutique of fancy lingerie rejects Bertrand Morane's advances; though she enjoys his company, she confesses that she likes only younger men. This rejection induces Morane to write an autobiographical novel which he entitles *Le Cavaleur.* By recounting his adventures, the hero brings the women he has known back to life. He writes in a feverish state and, as he progresses, gives installments of his manuscript to a secretary to be typed. But after the third chapter she refuses to continue, shocked by the book's salaciousness. From then on, Bertrand Morane has to type his manuscript himself, with two fingers. He sends it to several Paris publishing houses. The manuscript appeals to Geneviève, an editor. The editorial committee at Editions Bétany, where she works, agrees to publish the book but suggests another title: *Le Cavaleur* becomes *L'Homme qui aimait les femmes.* Geneviève follows the stages of the project and goes to the plant where the book will be printed, near Montpellier. On that occasion, she spends the afternoon with Bertrand in a hotel room and becomes one of his lovers. After her departure, unwilling to resign himself to spending Christmas Eve alone, Morane roams the streets of Montpellier hoping to meet a woman. He spots one across the street, tries to catch up to her, and is hit by a car. He is taken to the hospital in serious condition. When he comes to, the first thing he sees is a nurse's pretty legs. Unable to resist, he tries to get up, falls out of bed, and dies, like the miser Grandet trying to grasp the priest's gold crucifix.[183] *The Man Who Loved Women* is certainly one of François Truffaut's finest screenplays.

From the very beginning, he had given his skirt-chaser the face of Charles Denner. "I wanted to hear his voice throughout the film. His seriousness appealed to me. I didn't want my womanizer to be too attractive, I saw him as rather anxious, not at all the stereotype of the smug and irritating playboy."[184] Truffaut liked the odd blend of humor and seriousness that characterized this passionate, unpredictable, sincere actor, who, following in the footsteps of Aznavour and Léaud, became Truffaut's screen double. They shared a similar physical appearance, a similar anguish, and a similar lively and worried intelligence. While he was writing his screenplay, Truffaut had discreetly asked Serge Rousseau, Denner's agent, if the actor would be free in the fall of 1976. It was only at lunch in a restaurant on rue François 1er, in November 1975, that Truffaut told Denner the plot of his film and offered him the lead.

Marcel Berbert, in the meantime, negotiated the film's financing with Jean Nachbaur at United Artists. Gérard Lebovici, whom Truffaut had asked to be his agent and negotiate his personal contracts as author-director as well as those of Les Films du Carrosse, raised the bid: He asked United Artists for 6 million francs, which they refused. Berbert showed himself to be more reasonable and reached a compromise. "François sought security; he had Lebovici and me, which represented two different styles, no doubt complementary in his eyes,"[185] Marcel Berbert now explains. As head of Artmédia, Europe's foremost talent agency, representing France's biggest movie stars, as well as screenwriters and directors, Gérard Lebovici was very much concerned about the evolution of the film industry, which had been deeply affected by the growing power of television. Though television had cut into theatrical film exhibition, it was nevertheless contributing more and more to financing film production. Lebovici's entire strategy consisted in making the stars and filmmakers he represented full-fledged producers in their own right. As such, François Truffaut served as a model, since he had always been auteur, director, and producer. Lebovici was conscious of Truffaut's commercial and symbolic value in France and abroad. "Gérard Lebovici gave Truffaut a global view of the system," says Jean-Louis Livi, who was Lebovici's closest collaborator for many years before becoming a producer himself. "They had a great deal in common. First a love for women, and exceptional literary culture. It was easy for the two men to communicate. But there was a fundamental difference; François was fearful in business matters, while Lebovici was adventuresome. François was impressed by this adventuresome side, and Gérard liked François's humility and wanted to help him achieve great things."[186]

In September 1976, when he returned from the United States, Truffaut set about casting all the female parts in *The Man Who Loved Women.* Brigitte Fossey is Geneviève, Bertand Morane's editor and last lover. Leslie Caron makes an appearance as Véra, the woman who had been Morane's great love and whom he unexpectedly runs into one evening. Caron thought that this scene, which resembles a confession of love, was directly autobiographical: "I thought my part in the film was Madeleine's in François's life. I discussed it with Madeleine, who thinks that Véra is more like Catherine Deneuve."[187] Geneviève Fontanel is Hélène, the lingerie shopkeeper whom Morane is attracted to but who turns him down because she prefers younger men. Faithful to Nathalie Baye, with whom he had remained on good terms since *Day for Night,* Truffaut cast her in a small but sparkling role, and he also asked her to do the voice-over for the wake-up service's operator, with whom Morane has a suggestive daily telephone relationship. Truffaut also wanted to work again with Nelly Bourgeaud, who had had a thankless part in *Mississippi Mermaid;* he cast her as Delphine, a married woman with impulsive desires, who leads Bertrand Morane to the edge of madness. Truffaut decided to find actors for the other secondary roles in Montpellier, the city where he planned to shoot his film, for he remembered it fondly from the time he presented *Small Change* there. "I had been told, and it's true, that it's the French city that has the greatest number of pretty girls per square meter,"[188] he wrote, justifying his choice.

In the beginning of October, Truffaut rented a beautiful old house in the center of town, on rue du Carré-du-Roi. He auditioned a great many actors from the south of France for the smaller parts, and called upon two Langue-doc personalities, the film director Roger Leenhardt, member of an important Protestant family of the region, and the critic Henri Agel, to act in the scene in which the members of the editorial committee give their opinion of Bertrand Morane's manuscript and accept it for publication. The filming, which began on October 19, 1976, lasted over two months. During that period, the cast and crew shot in the city streets and in the offices of the *Midi libre* newspaper, particularly the office of Monsieur Bugeon, the managing director, who kindly made the space available for the scenes in the Bétany publishing house. During the Toussaint [All Saints' Day] school holiday, Laura Truffaut took time off from her intensive literary studies to spend a few days in Montpellier with her father, whom she hadn't seen in several months. The days spent on the set of *The Man Who Loved Women*, where she was an apprentice script girl, were "unforgettable" for her, but also put her in a "real quandary"[189] over whether to pursue filmmaking as a career or to continue her studies. The experience occurred at a decisive moment in her life. Laura would finally choose the latter, but not without regret.

François Truffaut, who thought he was making a comedy, realized in the cutting room, as he often did, that his footage was melancholic—to the point where he now considered changing the title to *The Man Who Was Afraid of Women*. In Montpellier, Laura had a feeling of discomfort, almost of pain, because of "those vague cross-references between the story and life; I was seventeen and I understood that even harmonious divorces were synonymous with a true emotional split."[190] The critics didn't respond to *The Man Who Loved Women* as comedy, but as a picture with "a grave, bitter, possibly despairing element."[191] This didn't prevent the reviews from being generally favorable—and unanimous in their praise of Charles Denner's performance.

When *The Man Who Loved Women* opened in April 1977, feminists attacked it as misogynistic and macho. Claire Clouot, for instance, compared it to "an inventory of spare parts exhibiting broads like veal scallops."[192] Though Truffaut found these attacks inappropriate, they did not come as a surprise. A month before the film's release, he had expressly warned Charles Denner about possible criticism and advised him on how to reply: "What are the ladies from the M.L.F. [Mouvement pour la libération des femmes] going to think? On this point, my reply would be that we didn't seek to play up to the M.L.F., but that the female roles, though numerous and episodic, are strong enough to hold their own against Bertrand Morane."[193] Truffaut here disassociated himself from what he called a "servilely feminist atmosphere."[194] It is true that his female characters fit a traditional concept of women, and that, in their diversity, they illustrate his personal fantasies and fetishes: flowing skirts, stockinged legs, preferably in black high-heeled shoes, silk underwear. But this is not so much a misogynistic objectification as a passé image of femininity and female eroticism, bearing the clear stamp of the fifties, the decade of Truffaut's youth. Wary as he was of fashion, including the fashion of feminism, Truffaut took full responsibility for an admittedly dated—but, to his mind, not negative— vision of woman. Remarking on this, Jean-Louis Bory ended his article in the *Nouvel Observateur* with the following statement: "When Bertrand's amorous body, his flesh, is buried in the ground, his love of women continues to live thanks to his book, but it is a passé love in a world where women now wear pants and wish to establish new relationships with men beyond those of a cat and bowl of cream."[195]

In spite of the controversy, *The Man Who Loved Women* was a success, attracting 325,000 viewers in Paris over a twelve-week period. Truffaut traveled with the film to the provinces and other countries, along with Charles Denner and Brigitte Fossey; the success of the film varied according to the local image of the "seducer." In Latin countries, where ostentatious womanizing is traditional, the film was by and large misunderstood, while in Germany and Scandinavian countries, this skirt-chaser's seriousness and melancholy were well received. In the United States, the response was mixed and box-office earnings mediocre. As for American critics, they seemed to have difficulty relating this film—in spite of its significance to its creator—to Truffaut's work as a whole. Six years later, Blake Edwards directed a remake of *The Man Who Loved Women*,[196] starring Burt Reynolds; his brawny self-assurance and flaunted rakishness have little in common with the kind of womanizer portrayed by Charles Denner.

Several months before the release of *The Man Who Loved Women*, on his forty-fifth birthday, François Truffaut met Marie Jaoul de Poncheville, who was soon to become his girlfriend. This beautiful thirty-year-old brunette was brought by Marie-France Pisier to the small dinner party Truffaut was throwing to mark the occasion at avenue Pierre 1er-de-Serbie. "She is my cousin from the provinces," said Marie-France Pisier as she walked in with her and Georges Kiejman. Truffaut was intrigued and instantly attracted to Marie de Poncheville, an editor at the small publishing house Tchou. She reminded him of the fictional woman played by Brigitte Fossey in his film, and he lost very little time in calling her. Marie de Poncheville lived on Place des Vosges and was raising her little daughter, Alice, on her own. Poncheville now says, "It was out of the question for me to have a romantic relationship with him."[197] Truffaut laid siege: "One evening, François rang my doorbell. I had to go out, and he said, 'It doesn't matter, I'll stay here, read the newspapers, and baby-sit for your daughter.' When I returned, he left and said to me, 'See you next Friday!' " This happened several times, and brings to mind the scene in *The Man Who Loved Women* where Bertrand Morane arranges to have a baby-sitter come to his house, with the aim of seducing her. Then one day, this game Truffaut had initiated changed into a ritualized romance. "We saw each other on specific days, but not on weekends: three days at my house, two days at his. Our relationship was rather chaotic. I was free and independent, raising my daughter. I had a certain vision of life: I was in favor of free love, as they used to say at the time."[198] Poncheville upset Truffaut's habits. Her way of life, her many friends, her outspokenness, and the fact that she didn't belong to the movie world—all these things set her apart from Truffaut's usual women friends. They addressed each other with the informal *"tu,"* enjoyed going out to the movies and theater, and made a few trips to the provinces and abroad. Truffaut, who was usually so unsociable, didn't mind attending her parties. "Life was merry. He went along; he accepted being with me in public," she explains. This relationship, which would last two years, seemed to amuse Truffaut and give him some emotional stability. But ultimately, he was a man who didn't believe couples could live harmoniously—though he also claimed to be seeking tranquillity with the "ideal" woman. "He planned out what he conceived to be happiness, with his book collections, his time for reading, his work. He hoped to be happy, but he lived in great solitude," says Marie de Poncheville. Anxious, unable to conceal his disquiet entirely, he suffered regular headaches that kept him awake at night. Something deeper was troubling him, against his will or not, and undermining any romantic relationship.

LIVING WITH ONE'S DEAD

François Truffaut felt a strong tie with the important people in his life who were now dead. "I'm faithful to the dead, I live with them. I'm forty-five and already beginning to be surrounded by dead people."[199] Since André Bazin, who had died immediately before the first day's shoot of *The 400 Blows*, the list of his departed friends had grown—ranging from women he had loved, like Françoise Dorléac, to men he had admired, like Cocteau, whose voice Truffaut "listened to every morning for several days."[200] In January 1977, he was saddened by the death of Henri Langlois, followed by that of Roberto Rossellini six months later. These two men had been like fathers to him, initiating him into the love of films and giving him the desire and courage to make his own. When Rossellini died in Rome, one month after presiding over the Cannes Film Festival, Truffaut paid tribute, in *Le Matin de Paris*, to "the most intelligent man, with André Bazin,"[201] whom he had ever known.

Cruelly, death and cinema seemed to get on well together, Truffaut observed at the time, after seeing his second film, *Shoot the Piano Player,* again. He noted with sadness that "half the actors in it were gone": Boby Lapointe, Albert Rémy, Nicole Berger, Claude Mansart, Catherine Lutz. He missed these departed ones and refused to forget them. "Why not have the same range of feelings for the dead as for the living, the same aggressive or affectionate relationships?"[202] he asked in *L'Express.* For several years, he had wanted to use this idea, that we can and must live with the dead, as the subject of a film, and he wondered "what it would be like to show on screen a man who refuses to forget the dead."[203]

The project dated back to December 1970 and his breakup with Catherine Deneuve. At that time, Truffaut had immersed himself passionately in the novels of Henry James, a writer whom he worshipped—he had visited his homes when he was in Boston, and he collected French and English editions of his books. He asked his friend Aimée Alexandre to translate "The Altar of the Dead," a James short story written in London in 1894 which hadn't been published in France. He collected biographical data, particularly the notebooks for James's autobiographies, in which the author described his lifelong worship of his dead young fiancée. Aimée Alexandre, who was a specialist in Russian literature,[204] recommended he read some short stories by Chekhov and Tolstoy on the same theme. Also, as she had been a friend of Gaston Bachelard, she suggested he read "La Flamme d'une chandelle [The Flame of a Candle]," a marvelous short essay (published in 1961), which made quite an impression on Truffaut.

Time went by and Truffaut made his films according to plan: *Two English Girls, Such a Gorgeous Kid Like Me, Day for Night.* Then in the beginning of 1974, Henry James's story collection *The Altar of the Dead* was issued by Editions Stock, in Diane de Margerie's French translation. "In Henry James's world, the dead have a specific significance—one might almost say, usefulness. In general, they enhance the life of the living by firing the imagination through memory: the hero chooses reminiscence as opposed to future plans, ritual as opposed to action, the past as opposed to the present, defunct loves as opposed to possible loves,"[205] Diane de Margerie writes in her preface, which Truffaut annotated heavily. This was when he asked Gruault (who had just finished the *Adèle H.* script) to adapt the James short story.

Jean Gruault received his contract for "The Altar of the Dead" adaptation in July 1974. "It's not fabulous," Truffaut admitted, "but this is a trial project and if, as is my hope, the film gets made under normal conditions, we can always renegotiate our agreement."[206] Truffaut had already drawn up the main outlines for his project and envisioned an element of "suspense"[207] around the idea of a worshipped dead fiancée and a "mysterious and charismatic" hero. In passing, he recommended Gruault read two other James short stories, "The Beast in the Jungle" and "The Friends of the Friends." He intended to change the atmosphere by transposing the setting from Victorian England to a small provincial French town in the twenties; the story would be "directly linked to the memory of the First World War."[208]

Gruault spent much of 1974 rereading Henry James and immersing himself in his world. By October, he had drafted a first outline of "five acts and around twenty tableaux." In March 1975, he completed a first screenplay entitled *La Fiancée disparue* (The Vanished Fiancée), three thick notebooks crammed with details, places, and situations. Truffaut deemed it too long and complicated and asked his friend to make cuts. This was done within a month, but Truffaut was still dissatisfied. They became uneasy with each other, in part because at this time Gruault had also voiced his disappointment with *The Story of Adèle H.* On November 21, Truffaut wrote to Gruault to sort things out: "I don't always hate misunderstandings, but I don't feel we should allow our friendship to be spoiled by silences for which I'm originally responsible. First, there was my disappointment on reading your *Altar of the Dead;* secondly, there was your disappointment on seeing *Adèle* on the screen. As far as *The Altar of the Dead* is concerned, I gave you too rigid a framework for you to invent anything and you did your best. In fact I liked your work better on a second reading, I had it typed and I'm getting ready to revise it with Suzanne before submitting the fourth version to you."[209]

During this whole period, Jean Gruault was not entirely free, for he was writing the screenplay of *Mon Oncle d'Amérique* with Alain Resnais. As a result, the project of *La Fiancée disparue* was almost shelved. Truffaut looked elsewhere, reread all the volumes of Proust's *Remembrance of Things Past,*[210] and threw himself into Japanese literature, primarily Tanizaki. He asked Koichi Yamada, his Japanese correspondent, to help him find references to the cult of the dead in Japanese literature. He also consulted Eric Rohmer, and sent him "The Altar of the Dead." But it failed to inspire the director of *Claire's Knee.* Truffaut also requested help for the "religious" scenes from the two film enthusiast friends he had met through Bazin—the Jesuit Jean Mambrino and the Dominican Guy Léger. This research shows Truffaut's attachment to this theme but also his hesitation in using it for a film.

Gruault's script remained in a file at Les Films du Carrosse for almost two years. It was only when he was getting ready to shoot *The Man Who Loved Women* that Truffaut decided to work on it again. Deliberately, he set out to refocus the story around a hopeless romantic relationship between Julien Davenne—the man obsessed by the idea that one must live with the dead—and Cécilia, a young woman who is prepared to join him in his cult of the dead because of her love for him. Truffaut also introduced other characters and places that aren't in the James short stories, the young deaf-mute, who is both confidant and wild child, and the quaint magazine *Le Globe*, for which Davenne writes the obituaries.

In mid-October 1976, Truffaut related his ideas to Gruault, who accepted them and went back to work with enthusiasm. In the meantime, Truffaut filmed *The Man Who Loved Women*. In February 1977, a new version of the script was ready, with a number of possible titles: *The Departed Fiancée, The Unfinished Figure, The Mountain of Fire, Those We Haven't Forgotten, Those We Have Loved, The Last Flame, The Others, Them, The Fête of Memory*. Upon reading this new version, Truffaut sent Gruault a telegram from Bombay, where he was filming additional scenes for *Close Encounters of the Third Kind*. "The screenplay is magnificent and I'm very pleased."[211] After some work with Suzanne Schiffman, the final draft was completed in late May 1977. The title was yet to be found, since no one felt happy with any of those suggested.

Truffaut cast Nathalie Baye as Cécilia, the heroine of the film. After her first screen appearance in *Day for Night* and a small part in *The Man Who Loved Women*, Baye had acted opposite Philippe Léotard in Maurice Pialat's *La Gueule ouverte*. She looks back on *La Chambre verte* (*The Green Room*) as an important film for her. "If François asked me to perform with him, it was because he knew I wasn't the kind of actress who caused problems. He could rely on me, which was very reassuring to him,"[212] she says. She would indeed be playing opposite Truffaut in the film, for he had decided to play the part of Julien Davenne himself, after briefly considering Charles Denner, who was not available. But Truffaut was afraid of appearing too old for the part. This so obsessed him that he consulted his hairdresser, who recommended a wig, which he ultimately didn't use. He hoped that by playing the part himself he would give the film a more intimate, authentic quality. "This film is like a handwritten letter," he said. "If you write by hand, the letter won't be perfect, the handwriting might be a bit shaky, but it will be you, your handwriting."[213] Truffaut feared that Julien Davenne might seem ridiculous, even pathetic—a madman with morbid passions. This was another reason why he decided to play the part himself. "He didn't want anyone to stand between him and Julien Davenne, for this undertaking was too intimate," Nathalie Baye confirms. The actress remembers that Truffaut sometimes had severe doubts: "He would say to me, 'It's madness; it will never work!' And he came close to wanting to stop everything."[214]

In addition to Truffaut and Nathalie Baye, the cast includes Jean Dasté (in the part of the *Globe* editor), Antoine Vitez (as a stern clergyman in a short but intense scene), Jean-Pierre Moulin (a widower whom Davenne comforts at the beginning of the film), and Patrick Maléon (a young deaf-mute actor in the part of Julien Davenne's protégé). Some Carrosse technicians and collaborators also make an appearance: Josiane Couëdel, his secretary, who plays a nurse; Martine Barraqué, his editor, who also plays a nurse; and Annie Miller, who plays a dead woman. Lastly, Marie de Poncheville appears in a scene of the film, as the woman whom Davenne's widower friend, Mazet, takes as his second wife.

The shoot, which was in preproduction during the summer of 1977, was to take place in Honfleur. Truffaut asked Nestor Almendros to exploit the contrast between electric light and a flood of candlelight to give the film a ghostly quality. On October 11, 1977, Truffaut began shooting in the Maison Troublet, a beautiful four-story old residence on rue Eugène Boudin. Since the shoot was to last only thirty-eight days and the film had only a 3-million-franc budget, financed by United Artists, he made the most of the large Honfleur house and used it for several sets. He repeated what he had done for *Adèle H.*, and, with the help of François Porcile and Patrice Mestral, prerecorded music taken from the *Flemish Concert* by Maurice Jaubert, a composer who had died at the front in 1940. Truffaut played the music on the set during the takes to help the actors and technicians get into the ritualized, quasi-religious atmosphere of the film. "It's not surprising to find, in the sudden explosive tension and somber conviction of his acting, a direct echo of Jaubert's style, with its gathering momentum and sudden restraint, its reticence and violence,"[215] wrote François Porcile. Several scenes were shot in exteriors; four days were spent in the Caen cemetery, three in the Honfleur auction room, and five inside the Carbec chapel, a small marvel of religious architecture discovered in Saint-Pierre-du-Val, near Pont-Audemer. Inside the chapel, in a set designed by Jean-Pierre Kohut-Svelko and among scores of candles set up by Nestor Almendros, Truffaut placed his personal photos, the faces of departed friends whose memory he was thereby perpetuating. Hence, the figures in Julien Davenne's life are the people in Truffaut's: Audiberti, Cocteau, Queneau, Jeanne Moreau and her sister, Louise de Vilmorin, Aimée Alexandre, Oskar Werner, and Oscar Lewenstein (the producer of *The Bride Wore Black*); there are also portraits of admired writers and musicians, such as Proust, Oscar Wilde, Henry James, Guillaume Apollinaire, Prokofiev, and Maurice Jaubert and his orchestra.

The making of *The Green Room* was in no way gloomy. In fact, it was festive, one of Truffaut's most joyful shoots. "We laughed a lot; we often had irrepressible laughing fits before takes," recalls Nathalie Baye, "so much so that Suzanne Schiffman sometimes had to reprimand us."[216] Marie de Poncheville, who used to join Truffaut in Honfleur on weekends, confirms that "Nathalie had a contagious laugh, like bells ringing!"[217] Truffaut played his part in an expressionless, nearly mechanical way, which inevitably put constraints on Nathalie Baye, who had to adjust her own acting and intonations accordingly. Simultaneously in front of and behind the camera, Truffaut was of no great help to her. Though she has a very happy memory of the shoot, she admits that she sometimes felt alone and missed the presence of a "real" director, more alert to her needs.

By March 1978, Truffaut was ready to show *The Green Room* to his friends. Not since *Two English Girls* was he so showered with praise. "Of all your films it is the one that most moved me and spoke to me, along with *Two English Girls,*" Isabelle Adjani wrote. "I felt good crying in your presence."[218] "*The Green Room,* along with Clément, Visconti and very few others, is part of my secret garden,"[219] Alain Delon wrote him with sincerity. "I found your film deeply moving. I found you deeply moving in your film,"[220] said Eric Rohmer. "I haven't yet told you the emotion I felt on seeing *The Green Room,*" Antoine Vitez wrote him. "What I see in it, deep down, is kindness, and that's what touches me most. Thank you for having included me in it."[221]

Except for François Chalais in *Le Figaro,* the critics were all in agreement. "In its simple and pure line, it resembles a cinematic testament. There will be other Truffaut films, but none that will ever be more intimate, more personal, more wrenching that this *Green Room,* altar of the dead,"[222] wrote Jean-Louis Bory in *Le Nouvel Observateur.* This reception marked a period of accomplishment and fulfillment.

THE EMPTY ROOM

The release of *The Green Room,* on April 5, 1978, brought this state of grace to an abrupt end. It was a dismal failure commercially and Truffaut felt deeply hurt and disappointed. Though he was under no illusions about the odds of a hit, he had hoped the film would at least draw an audience of film lovers. "I don't want admiration, that doesn't interest me. But I want the audience to be really drawn in by the film for an hour and a half. Because I think this kind of theme can touch a deep chord in many people. Everyone has their dead,"[223] he wrote several weeks before the film's release. Truffaut was mistaken. Anticipating the difficulties, he put all his energies—even more than usual—into promoting the film. He wrote the press kit himself, saw to the poster and trailer, planned interviews with journalists and trips around the country. He even attended many of the press screenings prior to the film's release to try to convince reticent critics. He hired the best press agent, Simon Misrahi, a die-hard movie lover who had the reputation of being able to win over the most stubborn journalists. With the help of Misrahi and his collaborator, Martine Marignac, Truffaut attempted the impossible—to convince the public to go see a film on the cult of the dead.

Sensing failure, he decided to change strategies several days before the premiere and deliberately conceal the subject matter of the film, stressing instead his own reputation, the presence of Nathalie Baye, and the film's novel-like atmosphere. Hence he asked Michel Drucker, who was preparing a television broadcast in which *The Green Room* would be promoted, to include only two clips from the film, "which had the advantage of not mentioning death or the dead and presenting four of the film's protagonists."[224] Nonetheless, the public stayed away, refusing to associate François Truffaut's image with what they considered a morbid work. With slightly over thirty thousand tickets sold, the film was a commercial flop comparable to *Two English Girls*. It was more like *"The Empty Room!"*[225] Truffaut wrote to his musical adviser, François Porcile.

Deeply distressed, Truffaut accepted full responsibility for this failure, and even regretted that he had played the part of Julien Davenne: "Charles Denner would have been better than I,"[226] he said in *Paris-Match,* announcing his intention of never acting again for other directors, and of not playing in his own films for the next ten years. On May 10, 1978, he confessed to Annette Insdorf, a young American scholar who was writing a study of his work, that his morale was extremely low. As always, when everything was going badly, he found his only solace in the United States, where he felt he was best understood and best appreciated. In France, the reviews were good, he said to Annette, but "they mentioned DEATH so often that they've made the film as troublesome as *Johnny Got His Gun.* Keep all this to yourself, of course, since the film still has chances in N.Y. (after the next festival), in Scandinavia and Japan."[227]

Truffaut had great expectations for *The Green Room* in Japan, believing a country so attached to funeral rites was bound to respond to the film. He also relied on the New York Film Festival in September, where he would present the film to the American public. He arrived at the festival with Marie de Poncheville, Nathalie Baye, and Helen Scott. The New York premiere was morose, but the mood picked up considerably later in the evening, at a party thrown in Truffaut's honor in a New York apartment. Miloš Forman, the Czech director who had come to live in the United States, had an apartment in the same building. Truffaut and his women friends went to join him to finish off the evening. It was a cheerful evening and, having had a joint, "François didn't have a clue what was going on,"[228] recalls Nathalie Baye.

Truffaut made no secret of a certain weariness when he confided to his New York friend Annette Insdorf that he had "made too many films in the last five years, too many, too quickly. Les Films du Carrosse gives me undeniable freedom, but at great personal cost and above all it prevents me from stopping and thinking. Every month, I turn down offers from Hollywood . . . but one day I'll let myself be tempted before becoming a *has been* [in English]."²²⁹ Was Truffaut already a has-been at forty-six? He imparted his anxiety to a *France-Soir* journalist: "I must hurry. I'm forty-six, I'm enjoying my last years of good health. I want to make as many films as possible so I won't have any regrets later on."²³⁰ Marie de Poncheville confirms his unease: "François was not happy with the life he was leading. He was aware that life was in perpetual flux, which drove him crazy. He hoped to be happy, but he often said he was living like a dog, inflicting things he hated on himself."²³¹ During that same period, on hearing that Jean-Louis Bory was suffering from severe depression, Truffaut wrote him a letter to try to comfort and help him: "Pains of anguish that are like death, the feeling of a black hole, of no longer existing, the unreality of faces in the street—I have experienced all of that, as well as the conviction that it is impossible to make others understand what one is going through, the material world slipping away, this numb emptiness. I have experienced all of that and it took me a year and a half to get over it, before finding the inner strength to bounce back; and it was three more years before I could live normally and love without mistrust."²³² And he encouraged Bory to fight the uphill struggle, to show "valor, gaiety and vitality": "I know, when the time comes, you will find the strength to fight your way back to the surface again, among us." Nine months later, on June 12, 1979, the sixty-year-old novelist and film critic would commit suicide.

During this period, Truffaut first received warnings about his health, which hardly improved his morale. Except for a recurrent ear infection and an operation on his nasal septum in 1960, he had never really worried about his health. In the last days of 1977 and the first months of 1978, Truffaut consulted Dr. Lévy at the Saint-Antoine Hospital, where he underwent colon X rays. He also suffered from sciatica and was treated by Dr. Bénichou at the Saint-Cloud Hospital. On January 20, 1978, Dr. Alexanian prescribed ten days' rest after the filming of *The Green Room*. Several months later, he consulted a cardiologist, Dr. Pauly-Laubry at the Saint-Joseph Hospital; after a complete and satisfactory checkup, the physician put him on a diet and recommended that he exercise, walk, lose a few pounds, and follow a special regimen to reduce flatulence. Truffaut suddenly felt he was aging.

His dark mood and health problems were directly linked to the failure of *The Green Room*. His relationship with Jean Nachbaur deteriorated as well; Truffaut blamed United Artists for not having faith in the film and for not promoting it enough. The studio already had its eye on Truffaut's next film, preferring to forget the commercial failure of *The Green Room*. The director was making the same calculation: *L'Amour en fuite* (*Love on the Run*), a new Doinel film, a surefire success, would compensate for *The Green Room*'s financial loss. But on the advice of Gérard Lebovici, Berbert and he decided to do without United Artists and produce *Love on the Run*—which required a very small budget—on their own. Les Films du Carrosse would thereby get all profits. Jean Nachbaur was rather bitter and found the "maneuver rather questionable,"[233] and his reaction would only widen the rift between the two men.

The United Artists coproduction arrangement dated back to 1967 and *The Bride Wore Black*. It had allowed Truffaut to make eleven films, all financed by French or European subsidiaries of the Hollywood majors, United Artists, Columbia, or Warner, and benefit from virtually complete artistic freedom. From then on, Carrosse had to find other ways of financing Truffaut's films, relying primarily on French television and, to a certain extent, on advance foreign sales. The visionary Gérard Lebovici played a decisive role in working out this new strategy; he convinced Truffaut and Berbert to do without the American studios. Lebovici was on the point of becoming a producer and distributor himself; he had left Artmédia (whose management he had entrusted to Jean-Louis Livi) and created his own company, A.A.A. (standing for "*Auteurs Artistes Associés*"). Lebovici and the many companies he controlled (in production, distribution, sale of video rights, and foreign film export through Roissy Films, the company managed by Alain Vannier) were consolidating a strong empire covering the entire spectrum of the French film industry. A loyal friend of Lebovici, Truffaut was at the heart of this new structure, even if it was out of the question for him to give up his independence.[234]

LOVE ON THE RUN

The commercial failure of *The Green Room* forced Truffaut to put off temporarily projects that were dear to his heart. He decided to postpone the filming of *L'Agence Magic*, though the screenplay, written by Claude de Givray and Bernard Revon, was at a very advanced stage. After *Day for Night*, his film about cinema, he wanted to make one about the milieu of variety theater, as part two of a triptych that would later include a film about theater. *L'Agence Magic* is about a small troupe of variety artists who go on an adventurous tour to Senegal in order to solve their financial difficulties. "François's idea was that the troupe had to be endangered,"[235] Claude de Givray says in summary. The film would follow several characters, young and not so young; show their family ties and romantic relationships, their petty jealousies within the troupe and their personal secrets; a love story between Leslie, a young girl, and an older man, Charles-Henri, nicknamed "the Dauphin"; the troupe's difficulty in finding a theater and their life in a shabby Dakar hotel. Leslie shoots and kills Charles-Henri because he no longer loves her. To avoid cliché, Truffaut had asked his screenwriters to draw inspiration from a news item describing how a man who had just been stabbed got up in normal fashion, walked to the refrigerator, opened it, drank some milk out of the bottle, walked back, and collapsed on his bed. At the end of the story, Leslie's mother, Viviane, turns herself in to the police as the murderess: "Since she was older, she would be entitled to greater leniency and less of a punishment. In any case, she was to blame for Leslie committing this act, for she should have brought her up differently,"[236] is the comment at the end of the seventy-page script. "We had taken inspiration from Michael Curtiz's *Mildred Pierce*, in which a mother, played by Joan Crawford, takes the blame for the murder committed by her daughter, played by Ann Blyth,"[237] Givray adds. But in the end, Truffaut didn't feel like going to Africa, which would have entailed an exhausting shoot. He preferred to put off the project, requesting that his two screenwriters rework the script, since the same story could take place during the Occupation in the unoccupied south of France.

In desperation, and eager to shoot a film quickly, Truffaut decided to go back to his mascot, Antoine Doinel. In his mind, *Love on the Run* was merely an "occasional" film, the opportunity to erase the failure of *The Green Room* and pull himself out of his depression. The film is deliberately structured as the last episode in the adventures of Antoine Doinel; all the stages in a man's life (youth, marriage, first adulterous affair, and divorce) are recapitulated, using many clips from the first four Doinel films. The idea of a film as "a kind of mosaic, the story of a life,"[238] seemed amusing and exciting to Truffaut, who didn't realize at first that it would turn out to be more complex—and even, at times, more agonizing—than anticipated.

At first, to justify the flashback structure, Truffaut considered using psychoanalysis as a narrative mainspring. Stretched out on the couch, Antoine Doinel would recount his life to a psychoanalyst, while scenes from *The 400 Blows, Love at Twenty, Stolen Kisses,* and *Bed and Board* would file by, like someone's memories. Marie-France Pisier would be cast as the psychoanalyst and Léaud as her depressed patient. But finally Truffaut rejected psychoanalysis as a conceit. Even though he had read Bruno Bettelheim for *The Wild Child* and had paid occasional visits to René Held during a difficult period of his life, the discipline was mysterious to him, and he didn't feel competent to use it as subject matter. He was afraid using a psychoanalyst might seem artificial, a concession to one of the fashions of the day. Marie-France Pisier, who collaborated on the screenplay with Suzanne Schiffman, then suggested making Colette a lawyer, with the story revolving around Colette and Antoine's amorous reunion, fifteen years after their flirtation at the youth concert. Antoine recounts his life to Colette during a train trip; she is on her way to another city to defend a client when he runs into her. They fall into each other's arms and the Doinel cycle has a happy ending: Antoine's first great love finally finds fulfillment fifteen years later. Suzanne Schiffman even suggested going one step further and revealing Doinel as a screen character. "This scene is the last scene in the film," she wrote at the end of the synopsis intended for Truffaut. "Antoine pursues Colette down the hallways, runs down the stairs after her and catches up with her, of course. At first, he has trouble calming her down, but since he loves her and she loves him, it will all end well with a final kiss. This is when F.T. enters the shot: he isn't convinced by this end, he shot it because Jean-Pierre and Marie-France wanted it, but he would like to think about it until the next day and try an alternate ending. The assistant comes up to François, who confirms that they will be shooting again the next day. While he goes around convening the crew for the next day, Jean-Pierre and François walk away gesticulating in heated conversation, their silhouettes etched against the light of the hallway leading to the street. THE END."[239] For Truffaut, this conceit was too similar to the one used at the end of *Day for Night*. Marie-France Pisier and Suzanne Schiffman set to work again, helped by Jean Aurel, the "structure specialist." The fact was, Truffaut didn't know how to part with Antoine Doinel. "The more I know him, the less I can make him do anything surprising,"[240] he said. He was willing to keep the reunion with Colette, but not her love story with Antoine. He thus invented a new female character, Sabine, a twenty-year-old woman attracted by Doinel's romanticism. This would be the romantic focus of the film, to avoid having *Love on the Run* find all its energy in the past. Truffaut thought of a new, modern female figure, "a young woman of her time,"[241] and in the part he cast Dorothée, the hostess of a Wednesday-afternoon children's television program, *Récré A2*. In fact, he found Dorothée by watching television. He contacted her on May 8, 1978, scarcely three weeks before the beginning of the filming. The young woman accepted his offer enthusiastically. The gamble of *Love on the Run* rested, in part, on this surprising choice.

A proofreader in a printing house, Antoine Doinel has an affair with Sabine, a saleswoman in a record store. He divorces Christine "by mutual consent"; their son, Alphonse, has grown since *Bed and Board*. In taking Alphonse to the station, Antoine runs into Colette, who has become a lawyer and is on her way to Aix-en-Provence, where she is to defend a case in court. Unexpectedly, at the last moment, Antoine boards the train to be with Colette, who just happens to be reading *Les Salades de l'amour* (*Love and Other Troubles*), the autobiographical novel Doinel was writing at the end of *Bed and Board*. She has bought it from Xavier, the bookseller with whom she is in love. Antoine recounts his life to Colette and tries to seduce her once again. Of course, Colette refuses.

Truffaut found the entire story rather implausible; he considered his script "flimsy, and very hard to improve upon,"[242] though he was about to shoot it. "François hated this project very early on," confirms Marie-France Pisier. "This film was certainly not a happy experience for him. He knew it would be the last Doinel film; but at the same time, he very much wanted Jean-Pierre to work again. He also felt that, with age, Antoine Doinel was becoming less credible because of his unidentifiable social status, and yet to give him a status would be a betrayal of the character's spirit."[243] Truffaut was perfectly aware of the fact that he was giving Jean-Pierre Léaud a poisoned gift, and this made him feel guilty and distressed. For it was risky for the actor to be playing a thirty-five-year-old whom the public was bound to see as antisocial—a person who doesn't drive, doesn't keep fit, and has no real profession. Doinel is "always on the run, always late, a young man in a rush. . . . Antoine should stop . . . running away . . . he should take advantage of the present . . . should stop settling a score with his mother through every girl he meets. . . ."[244] Truffaut wrote to Alain Souchon, requesting that the singer compose a song for the film.

When Truffaut did some final work on the dialogue with Suzanne Schiffman in April 1978, he was in a sullen mood. His relations with Suzanne were tense; and she remembers "ghastly arguments."[245] Feeling trapped, Truffaut wanted to give up or postpone the shoot, which was impossible because of the commitments of the actors and technicians. Marie-France Pisier was free only in June, since she was to start work on André Téchiné's *The Brontë Sisters* immediately afterward. Aside from the family of characters from the Doinel films—Jean-Pierre Léaud, Claude Jade, Dani, Marie-France Pisier, and Rosy Varte—to which he had added Dorothée and Daniel Mesguich (the bookseller Colette is in love with), Truffaut developed a character that had only been glimpsed at in one of the scenes of *The 400 Blows*—Monsieur Lucien, the lover of Antoine Doinel's mother, whom he surprises on Place Clichy. In Truffaut's first film, Jean Douchet, a *Cahiers du cinéma* critic, made a furtive appearance in the part. This time, the character has greater substance, thanks to the actor Julien Bertheau, who has an unforgettable scene, sitting opposite Antoine at a table in a café, not far from the cemetery where Madame Doinel has been laid to rest. Monsieur Lucien admits to Antoine that his mother "was a little bird," a passionate woman and an anarchist. Doinel becomes reconciled with his mother, at least with his memory of her, thereby giving a more poetic, or at least positive, image to the unworthy mother of *The 400 Blows*. This reconciliation, of course, owes a great deal to Truffaut's discovery, right after his mother's death, of the many documents among her belongings that proved her genuine attachment to him.

Beginning on May 29, 1978, the filming of *Love on the Run* lasted only twenty-eight days, for the most part in Paris. The editing, on the other hand, required time, given the complexity of the story, which is interwoven with flashback clips. Alain Souchon and Laurent Voulzy composed the lyrics and music of the film's title song, "L'amour en fuite." "I'm very, very pleased with your song," Truffaut wrote Souchon. "The film is a letter, your song is the envelope for the letter; it frames it. Doinel was always seeking a family, he is happy to play sponger at Souchon's."[246] The answer print was ready just after Christmas, after five months of editing and mixing. The commercial release was scheduled for January 24, 1979. Truffaut remained unconvinced by his film, certain he was "heading straight into a wall."[247] Fortunately, he was relieved by the first reviews. François Chalais, in *Le Figaro*, described a "romantic patchwork" and commented gently, "How time flies. . . ."[248] Jacques Siclier hailed "the collected Antoine Doinel" in an article in *Le Monde* that greatly moved the director.[249] "If I didn't know you, I wouldn't be writing this letter," Truffaut replied. "I'd be happy to just be happy! But we first met, when? About twenty, twenty-five years ago and I associate you with Teisseire, Gauteur, Claude de Givray, all of Doinel's cousins. And why not tell you the truth? After having had so many doubts during five months of editing, it's a real pleasure to feel I've been understood, yes, simply understood."[250]

He also felt reassured by the commercial fate of the film, since *Love on the Run* attracted 250,000 viewers during a three-month Paris run. For the Carrosse, this meant an excellent return on their investment. But Truffaut still felt that *Love on the Run* was a mistake. It would be one of the films that he would always hate to see again, along with *The Bride Wore Black* and *Fahrenheit 451*. His permanent emancipation from Antoine Doinel, a screen persona he had created and lived with for twenty years and who had been seen the world over, made Truffaut feel lonelier, almost like an orphan. For the first time in his life, he said he was a bit weary of making films. On February 12, 1979, when he was invited to be the editor of "Journal inattendu" on radio station RTL, Truffaut declared, unperturbed, "I have no project for the time being. And I'm not looking for one. I've decided to take a bit of a rest, after much strain and worry."[251]

8.
THE UNFINISHED FIGURE:
1979–1984

After *The Green Room*, a box-office flop, and *Love on the Run*, which Truffaut wasn't pleased with, Carrosse needed a project that would be large and ambitious enough to reenergize it. Truffaut wasn't ready to shoot *L'Agence Magic*, for he felt the screenplay needed further development, and his friend Claude de Givray was still working on the script for *La Petite Voleuse* (The Little Thief). This was a long-standing project, since Truffaut had already referred to it in a letter to Helen Scott in November 1964: "*La Petite Voleuse*, a bit like Ingmar Bergman's *Monika*, the onset of femininity and flirtatiousness in a delinquent girl, a female version of *400 Blows*,"[1] loosely inspired by the story told him by one of his first mistresses, whom he had seen again in October 1965. "She has become a bit ugly, like me," he wrote a year later to Helen Scott, and she's done time in prison, has three kids . . . and a bit of everything."[2] The story of *La Petite Voleuse* takes place in postwar Paris, around 1950. The heroine, Janine, a delinquent, could be a younger sister to Antoine Doinel. First she steals cigarettes from American soldiers; then she filches a music box, spends time in a reformatory, and has a love affair.[3]

Jean Gruault was also put to work to find a subject. First they considered adapting *Julien et Marguerite*, a story of incest during the reign of Henry IV. Then the two friends contemplated working on another project, *Petit Roi*, which had been turned down by Jean-Loup Dabadie and Milan Kundera.

But neither of these two ideas led anywhere. Truffaut then suggested to Pierre Kast—whose last film, *Le Soleil en face,* he had liked—that he write a "story for four hands."[4] Kast suggested using two episodes drawn, respectively, from Stendhal's life and Joseph Conrad's life. The first was Stendhal's love affair with Clémentine Curial. He teaches her freedom, love, passion," Kast wrote. "She lets herself be seduced, then turns against him or carries on without him, using everything he gave her and taught her. In sum, he himself will have induced her to free herself of him."[5] The second project was taken from a Conrad novel, *The Arrow of Gold,* "an incredibly beautiful subject and novel,"[6] said Kast. But Truffaut admitted that he had trouble "visualizing"[7] either of these stories and conceded that he was unfamiliar with Conrad's world. During the same period, he also considered collaborating with Francis Veber, the writer of successful comedies directed by Georges Lautner (*The Girl in the Trunk*), Yves Robert (*The Tall Blond Man* series), Philippe de Broca (*Le Magnifique*), and Edouard Molinaro (*A Pain in the A——*). In 1976, Veber directed his own first feature, *The Toy,* with Pierre Richard. Contacted by Truffaut in March 1979, Francis Veber suggested an original screenplay, *Le Garde du corps (The Bodyguard),* but once again, this project never got off the ground.[8]

THEATER DURING THE NAZI OCCUPATION

On April 29, 1979, François Truffaut burst into Suzanne Schiffman's office. "Here, I've got a file on theater and a file on the Occupation. We'll do a film with both."[9] He had had the idea of working on something set during this period for around ten years. "For me, who was an adolescent at the time, the image of France cut in two, divided into Germans and Resistance fighters, is false. I see a much calmer France. One day I'll make a film about it."[10] The idea was still vague, and it involved showing the everyday life of Parisians during the Occupation. By ruling out any ideological consideration and heroic vision, Truffaut wanted to show that the French "were never so free as under the German Occupation," as Sartre had put it. Truffaut had been impressed in 1969 by a film directed by his friend Marcel Ophuls, *The Sorrow and the Pity,* and had played a part in getting it released in a Paris movie theater.[11] Truffaut considered *The Sorrow and the Pity* the first film to show this period in French history as a "nonlegendary story." In an unpublished interview, he said, "It's a film that makes one very critical of films that claim to restore the climate of the Occupation. After Ophuls's work, you can't have clowns play Vichy people or militiamen anymore. Well, maybe I'll return to this someday."[12]

In 1975, when he was writing the preface for an anthology of articles by

André Bazin, *Le Cinéma de l'Occupation et de la Résistance,* Truffaut again felt "a pressing desire to make a film on that period."[13] This is when he first conceived of combining the subjects of theater and the Occupation as the third part of a trilogy on show business: After *Day for Night,* on the cinema, there would be *L'Agence Magic,* on the music hall, and a film on the theater, which he was determined to make someday. He delved into source material, and in October 1976, he asked Jean-Loup Dabadie to read a novel that had a character he found interesting: "In a city, possibly Paris, during the Occupation, a beautiful actress continues to practice her profession, regardless of the possible presence of German officers in the audience. Her husband, a Jew who is supposed to have died or escaped, is actually hidden in the basement of the theater. Such is the basis of the story that we can see oscillating between *The Diary of Anne Frank* and *To Be or Not to Be.*"[14] He also derived inspiration from a Renoir play, *Carola,* filmed for American television by Norman Lloyd. Leslie Caron, who had a part in the film, says, "François arranged to have the play published in *L'Avant-Scène.* And then he made *The Last Métro,* whose subject is very similar to the Renoir play. They have so many points in common that Ginette Doynel and I were very surprised; we thought he could at least have given credit to Jean Renoir. When he came to see me the first time after *The Last Métro,* I told him very frankly that I thought there were resemblances with *Carola.* He was very indignant, and took my comment as a reproach. And we didn't see each other again for a year and a half."[15]

During the Christmas season of 1978, Truffaut and Suzanne Schiffman started working on the "Theater Under the Occupation" file. They gave themselves two weeks to study the press and documents from the period, the books that had been published in those years, old posters, and the memoirs of actors and directors who had worked under the Occupation.[16] Truffaut had always enjoyed reading the recollections of actors and theater people because they were teeming with details about the profession and backstage life—for example, the recollections of Alice Cocéa who was a theater director, or those of Jean Marais, *Histoires de ma vie,* which contained the episode Truffaut would use in the film where the actor chastised Alain Laubreaux,[17] the anti-Semitic critic of *Je suis partout,* who had insulted Jean Cocteau in 1941. Truffaut also had his own specific recollections of the period. He had a daily acquaintance with fear and the need for resourcefulness; he had seen many films made during the Occupation and remembered his parents' conversations about the most talked-about shows and plays. He also went to specialized bookstores—L'Envers du Miroir on rue de Seine, and Les Arcades on rue de Castiglione—and saw certain relevant films again—Lubitsch's *To Be or Not to Be* and Mankiewicz's *All About Eve.* Finally, he gathered personal recollections from his women friends—Nelly

Benedetti, for example, an actress in *The Soft Skin,* who had started her career at the Conservatoire and at the Théâtre de l'Atelier during the war. Simone Berriau, at the end of her life, confided in him, as well; a powerful personality, she had been director of the Théâtre Antoine since 1943, and Truffaut greatly admired her.

Between May and August 1979, Truffaut and Schiffman worked on the script relentlessly. A synopsis was ready by the end of May, and three weeks later, a first detailed treatment of 150 pages. In the summer, Truffaut left Paris for Villedieu, near Vaison-la-Romaine, to take up residence with Marie de Poncheville in a beautiful rental, not far from Suzanne Schiffman's vacation home. They continued working, the result being a second treatment, with dialogue, entitled *Le Dernier Métro (The Last Métro).*

The story takes place in Paris in 1942. Bernard Granger, a young actor from the Grand Guignol, comes to the Théâtre Montmartre, where a new play is being produced, *La Disparue (The Disappearance),* directed by Jean-Louis Cottins. He is hired by Marion Steiner, who is now managing the theater, as her husband, the Jewish director Lucas Steiner, has presumably fled to South America. In fact, unbeknownst to anyone, Marion is hiding Lucas in the basement of the theater. The rehearsals begin. We see Bernard's repeated rejection by Arlette, the costumer; Marion's secret attraction to Bernard, who pursues all women, except the one he dares not approach; the entrance, in the midst of rehearsal, of Daxiat—the critic from the virulently anti-Semitic paper *Je suis partout,* on whom the consent of the censors and the fate of the play depend; the ham brought by a woman dealing in the black market and which Raymond, the stage manager, hides inside a cello case. After the premiere, which is a success, events gather momentum. Daxiat attacks the show mercilessly in *Je suis partout;* Bernard insists that he present his apologies to Marion Steiner and chastises the critic publicly—which angers Marion, whose primary concern is protecting her theater. Bernard, who has witnessed the arrest of one of his friends inside a church, announces to Marion his intention of leaving the theater and joining the Resistance. On the day of his departure, they make love in Marion's office. At the Liberation, Lucas Steiner finally comes out of hiding. Marion goes to visit Bernard, who is wounded, in the hospital. Then the curtain comes down, revealing that this was the last scene in a new play directed by Steiner.

Truffaut knew he was getting ready to shoot his costliest film. Indeed, Marcel Berbert estimated the budget at around 11 million francs. Without the usual backing of an American studio, Carrosse had difficulty financing the project. Over the summer of 1979, Marcel Berbert began by demanding all the money due from creditors for the exhibition of Truffaut's previous films. This was supplemented by a sum from the Fonds d'aide (Assistance

Funds), made available to Les Films du Carrosse by the C.N.C. At the same time, Gérard Lebovici entered into negotiations with the television network TF1, for both *The Last Métro* and Alain Resnais's next film, *Mon Oncle d'Amérique*. The network decided to invest in the Truffaut film, partly for production and partly as payment for the first television screening rights. This was still insufficient financing; a big distributor had to be convinced. Marcel Berbert offered the film to the A.M.L.F. distribution company, which turned it down. Lebovici approached Gaumont, which accepted the distribution of the film in extremis and convinced the Société Française de Production, a television company, to come into the deal, as well. Even though, as Marcel Berbert put it, he felt "he had expended a lot of energy" in these negotiations, Truffaut was relieved to know he could start filming at the beginning of 1980.

In the meantime, he and Marie de Poncheville had broken up after their summer vacation in Villedieu. Very soon after returning to Paris at the end of August, Marie de Poncheville, without warning Truffaut, left for Los Angeles to join an American, whom she would later marry. "That vacation was our last attempt at establishing a close relationship," she says. "It was becoming impossible for me to live according to François's preestablished plan, in which my position was more and more limited."[18]

ANOTHER DOUBLE

Truffaut started casting of *The Last Métro* in September 1979. He had written the part of Marion Steiner with Catherine Deneuve in mind, for he considered her ideally suited to play this vital, energetic, but distant woman on whom the whole film rested. The actress had already agreed to this cinematic reunion with Truffaut at the beginning of the summer. Ten years had gone by since *Mississippi Mermaid*. Once again, Deneuve was to play a woman named Marion. And in the last scene of *La Disparue*—the play being performed on the stage of the Théâtre Montmartre—the lines Catherine Deneuve delivers to Gérard Depardieu are almost word for word the same lines she delivers to Jean-Paul Belmondo at the end of *Mississippi Mermaid:*

> *I come to love and it hurts. Does love hurt?*
> *Yes, love hurts. It hovers over us like big birds of prey, stops and threatens us. But this threat can also be a promise of happiness. You are lovely, Eléna, so lovely that it's painful to look at you.*
> *Yesterday, you said it was a joy!*
> *It's a joy and a misery.*

At the beginning of 1979, Truffaut greeted Jean-Louis Richard at Les Films du Carrosse with the following words: "You've been my scriptwriter, I've been your producer, now I want you to be my actor."[19] He then offered him the part of Daxiat. Richard accepted, on condition that he be allowed to "give the part as much prestige as possible."[20] He would endow Daxiat with a perverse, unsettling personality, a soft voice, a physical appearance that is both childish and imposing, with flashes of near madness in his eyes.

Truffaut contacted the little Sabine of *Jules and Jim* and *The Soft Skin*, who had now become—fifteen years later—a very gifted young actress. He cast Sabine Haudepin in the part of Nadine Marsac, an ambitious young actress determined to succeed, who acts onstage at night and on film sets in the afternoon. At the end of October, Gérard Depardieu was approached to play Bernard Granger, the male lead. Depardieu was in the Vercors at the time, on the set of Bertrand Blier's *Buffet froid*. Truffaut and he got in touch through their agents, Gérard Lebovici and Jean-Louis Livi, who were very favorably disposed to this first meeting, since they were both aware that Truffaut had written the script with Depardieu in mind. Initially, Depardieu was not very enthusiastic; for him, Truffaut had a somewhat passé image. "When Gérard Lebovici and Jean-Louis Livi told me that Truffaut had me in mind, I wasn't at all thrilled. I had loved *The 400 Blows* and *The Wild Child*, but his other films less, including the Doinel films, for I thought they lacked something, perhaps a mean edge."[21] During their first meeting, the actor made no secret of his qualms to Truffaut, who rather liked his frankness. Very rapidly, the two men hit it off; they discovered true affinities. "It was even love at first sight,"[22] says Jean-Louis Livi. More than sympathy, it was the feeling of coming from the same milieu that brought them close. "I was so afraid that he wouldn't be a little hood,"[23] Depardieu said of Truffaut. Won over by the man, he accepted with alacrity the part of Bernard Granger in *The Last Métro*.

For the part of Jean-Louis Cottins, the director who replaces Lucas Steiner and rehearses the actors in *La Disparue*, Truffaut first thought of Jean-Claude Brialy, but the actor had a previous commitment to Francis Girod's film *La Banquière*. He then contacted Jean Poiret, whom he had long admired.[24] The discreet, dandyish, and fashionable homosexual was a complex part to interpret, so different from the comic roles the actor usually excelled at. Truffaut was counting on a surprise effect, bolstered by the fact that Poiret had done very little film work over the previous ten years, appearing almost exclusively on the stage. Choosing an actor for the part of Lucas Steiner was difficult for Truffaut; he felt uneasy about this type of passive, reserved person and he agonized over what was meant by "looking Jewish." He thought of Heinz Bennent, a German actor whose French was excellent, and whom he had liked in two Volker Schlöndorff films, *The Lost Honor of Katharina Blum* and *The Tin Drum*, and in Ingmar Bergman's *The*

Serpent's Egg. But he continued to hesitate until Suzanne Schiffman finally convinced him to cast this non-Jewish actor in the part of a Jew.

He then completed casting the parts of all the individuals who contribute to the life of a theater, the technicians and administrators working in the wings. Paulette Dubost, Lisette in *The Rules of the Game,* was to play Germaine, the dresser. Maurice Risch was cast as the stage manager. Laszlo Szabo, the mascot actor of the New Wave, who had become a director, was to play the part of Lieutenant Bergen, a German officer who is a passionate admirer of Marion Steiner. Andréa Ferréol, who made her début in Marco Ferreri's *La Grande Bouffe,* was cast as Arlette Guillaume, the costume designer, who is wooed by Bernard Granger. Marcel Berbert would make a brief screen appearance as the manager of the Théâtre Montmartre, a part resembling his role in real life. ("He handles the finances,"[25] says one of the characters in *The Last Métro.*) Finally, Richard Bohringer, who was not yet a star, was cast as a Gestapo agent.

THE BEST NOVEL OF THE YEAR

Before starting the shoot, François Truffaut was even more nervous than usual. *The Last Métro* was an ambitious and costly film, and after a bad flop (*The Green Room*) and a moderate hit (*Love on the Run*), he very much needed a career boost. In addition, he had no other script in the works, which was unusual for him. But he was also perfectly aware that the odds were on his side—he had a star duo for the first time since *Mississippi Mermaid.* The preproduction was trying nonetheless. Suzanne Schiffman had trouble finding a theater where Truffaut could shoot the rehearsal scenes. The producers finally resolved to use the Théâtre Saint-Georges a mere two weeks before the cameras were to begin rolling. Just before Christmas, Catherine Deneuve's father, Maurice Dorléac, died, which deeply affected her. And then Truffaut felt dissatisfied with all the scenes in the screenplay involving Marion and Lucas Steiner in the basement of the Théâtre Montmartre; he found the dialogue too literary or too programmatically about "Jews under the Occupation." For a while, he considered sacrificing the character of Lucas Steiner by never showing him on screen. However, two weeks before the beginning of the shoot, he saw a play by Jean-Claude Grumberg, *L'Atelier,* at the Théâtre du Gymnase. He was impressed by the authenticity of the characters, particularly of Léon, the small-time Jewish boss of the ready-to-wear garment workshop where the play is set. Four days later, with the encouragement of Serge Rousseau, he wrote to the author: "Your Léon is sublime, he has everything that my Lucas lacks. Would you accept to kollaborate [the *k* is supposed to look German]? Lucas Steiner will be played by Heinz Bennent, a very good

German actor (*The Tin Drum*) who speaks French well, without a thick accent. The problem is, I have not known how to make him speak, or come alive. There is no doubt in my mind: the solution will flow from the tip of your pen, which is a hell of a lot better than mine."[26] Jean-Claude Grumberg accepted and, several days later, gave Truffaut rewrites of the scenes between Catherine Deneuve and Heinz Bennent, and the scenes with Daxiat. Truffaut was relieved. "I might only keep 30 or 50 percent of your dialogue," he wrote to Grumberg, "either because I prefer my own wording or because I consider it more appropriate to the two actors, but there is no doubt, for me, that the character of Lucas will be enhanced thanks to you."[27]

But other worries claimed his attention. Some rumors in the press concerning *The Last Métro*—Pierre Montaigne in *Le Figaro* alluding to a "remake of *To Be or Not to Be*"—enraged Truffaut and led him to ban journalists from his set. To prevent any leaks, he sent an internal memo to all his coworkers: "We are going to work with the aim of telling an interesting and intriguing story. I suggest that we keep this story secret and avoid talking about it to journalists. Let us even avoid describing the characters. What happens in the Théâtre Montmartre, from the basement to the attic, concerns only us . . . and the public with whom we have an appointment, but not for another nine months (inevitably). . . ."[28]

The Last Métro shoot, which began on January 28, 1980, was therefore shrouded in secrecy. Nestor Almendros's crew spent ten days filming the rehearsals and staging of *La Disparue*. Though available and precise in his instructions to the actors, Truffaut was tense, enduring neither quarrels nor outbursts on the set. There was a muffled atmosphere, with everyone speaking in a low voice and using the polite "*vous*" form. In his letter to Janine Bazin, Truffaut mentioned a series "of catastrophes,"[29] that had upset his work schedule and led to a serious delay. "I hope that the seven remaining weeks of filming will be calmer." Indeed, Catherine Deneuve suffered a sprain from a fall, and Suzanne Schiffman was hospitalized for several days with a serious intestinal obstruction.

Thereafter most of the filming was in a large abandoned factory, the Moreuil chocolate factory, on rue du Landy in Clichy. The space was transformed into a real studio, the cast and crew moved within four different sets designed by Jean-Pierre Kohut-Svelko—Lucas Steiner's basement, Marion Steiner's dressing room and office, the courtyard and street in front of the Théâtre Montmartre, and the exterior and interior of a Paris restaurant during the Occupation. Truffaut took full advantage of this unique site, and the filming finally picked up speed. Nestor Almendros was particularly attentive to the lighting and the colors, using a chromatic palette restricted to browns, ochers, and reds, inspired by the German films of the war period, such as

Josef von Baky's *Münchausen* and Veit Harlan's *Die goldene Stadt* (a poster for the latter can be seen in the film). This precision work on color gives the film an artificial and gentle atmosphere—making all of French life under the Occupation seem like a theatrical stage. Truffaut's progress toward studio pictures, which had started with *Adèle H.* and *The Green Room,* was now complete.

In mid-March, the cast and crew shot a few exterior scenes, first the escape of the collaborator Daxiat, in front of a house in ruins on rue Massenet in Paris, then scenes where the critic goes to the offices of his newspaper, *Je suis partout,* filmed on the premises of *Rivarol,* a right-wing satirical newspaper located in the Passage des Marais in the tenth arrondissement. Then came the sequences in Marion Steiner's hotel room, shot at the Hotel Crillon on Place de la Concorde, followed by the long scene of the actors' dinner after the successful opening night of *La Disparue,* shot in a club near Place Pigalle. Finally, the church scene where Bernard sees the arrest of a Resistance fighter by the Gestapo was shot inside Notre-Dame-des-Victoires. From March 27 until mid-April, the crew moved back into the Moreuil chocolate factory for the basement scenes. The filming of *The Last Métro,* which had lasted fifty-nine days, ended on April 21, 1980. Two days later, Truffaut flew to Beverly Hills, leaving this memo for his helpmate Jean Aurel: "I'm going to sleep in Los Angeles, I'll be back in Paris around May 12. It would be wonderful for me if you were in Paris then, free for lunch, to talk and to look at *The Last Métro,* so ramshackle in its present state."[30]

Almost as soon as he arrived in Los Angeles, Truffaut received the news of Alfred Hitchcock's death, on April 29, 1980. Immediately, "his telephone wouldn't stop ringing,"[31] says Laura, who had been living and studying in Berkeley for several months and had come to spend a few days with her father. On May second, Truffaut and Laura went to the little church on Santa Monica Boulevard, in Beverly Hills, where a Mass was held in honor of Hitchcock. This was the same church where one year earlier, "a farewell to Jean Renoir had taken place," Truffaut wrote, comparing the two ceremonies. "Jean Renoir's coffin had been placed in front of the altar. Family, friends, neighbors, film lovers and people off the street attended the ceremony. For Hitchcock it was different. There was no coffin—it had been removed to an unknown destination. The guests, who had been invited by telegram, were checked in at the door by Universal's security men. The police dispersed the crowd outside. It was the burial of a timid man who had become intimidating and who, for the first time, was avoiding publicity, since it wouldn't help his work—a man who, since his adolescence, had trained himself to be in control of the situation."[32] With the deaths of the two directors he probably most admired in the world coming so close together, Truffaut knew he would no longer have the same pleasure visiting Hollywood, as he had been doing once or twice a year for some time.

The editing of *The Last Métro* lasted four months, and throughout the entire period Truffaut was worried and doubtful about the film's success. Jean Aurel came up with the idea of changing the beginning: "In its previous version, the film started differently. Depardieu went to the theater but didn't meet the woman played by Andréa Ferréol. After discussing the matter, we placed this meeting at the very beginning of the film, which changes an unimaginable number of things. Always following the efficiency principle. The beginning became better, thanks to that scene where Depardieu makes a play for Ferréol, unaware that she's not interested in men. It's a principle of indirect narration inspired by Lubitsch."[33]

Truffaut derived great pleasure from his musical collaboration with Georges Delerue. The two men used several songs from the period, tunes that the young Truffaut had known by heart during the Occupation, one of the great periods for French street songs, such as "Mon Amant de Saint-Jean" or "La Prière à Zumba." Reactions to the first screenings in early September, for friends and later the press, were good. "I'm almost completely reassured concerning the reception the film will get in France,"[34] he wrote to Richard Roud, the director of the New York Film Festival. Indeed, rarely had he received so many positive opinions from such very different quarters—Jean-Paul Belmondo, Federico Fellini, Samuel Fuller, Jean Marais, among others. Nicolas Seydoux, the head of Gaumont, was extremely pleased as well, and he insisted on organizing a glamorous preview screening. Attended by the director and his entire cast, the screening was held in one of the most beautiful picture palaces on the Champs-Elysées, the Paris, a large theater owned by Marcel Dassault. Truffaut used the opportunity to bring together two generations of actors—those who had lived through the Occupation, such as Jean Poiret, Paulette Dubost, Yves Montand, Jeanne Moreau, Jean-Marc Thibault, Julien Bertheau, Simone Berriau, Nelly Benedetti, or Marcel Dalio, who had fled France, and the younger generation, friends of Gérard Depardieu, such as Julien Clerc, Alain Souchon, Miou-Miou, and Nathalie Baye. In the midst of it all was a radiant Catherine Deneuve in an elegant red suit. The atmosphere was warm and confident, yet Truffaut remained tense throughout the entire screening, until the lights went back on. "I went up to François, he was green: 'We're done for,' he said to me, 'they didn't like the film,' " recalled Suzanne Schiffman. "He was never pleased with a film and managed to draw you into his anxieties."[35] But the audience stood and applauded; it was a triumph. The irony was that the following day, Marcel Dassault called Truffaut to tell him that now that he had seen the film, he had changed his mind. He considered the film interesting, but he didn't feel the subject matter, Jews during the Occupation and collaboration, was appropriate for *his* theater and *his* public. He therefore wanted to cancel the run at the Paris, the principal first-run theater for the film on the Champs-Elysées. Truffaut would have to use all his diplomatic skills to dissuade him.

Almost all the reviews were favorable. But Bernard Pivot's article in *Lire* was the piece that most pleased Truffaut. Under the title "The Best Novel of the Year," the host of the television program *Apostrophes* wrote: "Soon to come out, we are told, is a novel by Tournier, a new Sagan, and the latest Rinaldi. Well no, I won't wait to have read them to let you benefit from my discovery, to tell you, indeed to shout from the rooftops, the first and last name of the magnificent novelist whose work has deeply moved, enchanted and enthralled me—to the point where I'm about to commit a crime against this magazine entirely devoted to reading, a crime against its nature and spirit. For this novelist is a movie director—François Truffaut, and his novel is a film, *The Last Métro*."[36] On the very day of the film's opening, Truffaut wrote to Laura to tell her that everything was going well, but that "what counts above all is the paying public." A decisive moment that he called, humorously, "the opening of the mine."[37]

The Last Métro was a smash hit. The Gaumont officials were betting on 10,000 ticket sales a day and 120,000 in the first week. "The Carrosse is keeping the calculators clicking,"[38] Truffaut wrote to Laura. The forecasts turned out to be correct: *The Last Métro* pulled in 126,000 viewers in a week, a record number for a Truffaut film. The following week brought confirmation of the audience's infatuation—so much so that the media was forced to ponder the phenomenon. An overtly classical film, dealing with a period that had not had a good reputation up until then, drew a large public, ordinary people and youth, far exceeding the audience for Truffaut's previous films. By 1980, the French were beginning to show a lively interest in the Occupation and seeking a more accurate view of their own history.[39]

TEN CÉSARS

On January 31, 1981, *The Last Métro* triumphed at the sixth César ceremony that was held at the Palais des Congrès. Nominated in twelve categories, Truffaut's film won ten César awards, France's equivalent of the Oscar, including the most important ones—best film, best director, best actress (Catherine Deneuve), best actor (Gérard Depardieu). But it also received the prize for best screenplay (Suzanne Schiffman), best cinematography (Nestor Almendros), best sound (Michel Laurent), best editing

(Martine Barraqué), best set (Jean-Pierre Kohut-Svelko). An unqualified success in the face of no small competition—Alain Resnais with *Mon Oncle d'Amérique,* Claude Sautet with *Un mauvais fils,* Maurice Pialat with *Loulou,* and Jean-Luc Godard's return to the screen with *Sauve qui peut (la vie). The Last Métro,* even more than *Day for Night,* attracted the honors of the guild that recognized itself in this film, and thereby, in a way, paid homage to itself. At the end of the ceremony, Truffaut, embarrassed by so many awards, expressed his gratitude by repeating almost word for word what he had said in English seven years earlier upon receiving the Oscar for *Day for Night:* "*The Last Métro* was inspired by the life of theater people, I attribute my success to them. I will keep this César for best director at home . . . but for them."

A few days later, Catherine Deneuve and Gérard Depardieu made the cover of *Paris-Match,* "a new film couple who succeeded in touching the public's heart." With its ten Césars, *The Last Métro* was given another boost and attracted an additional 200,000 filmgoers in Paris in the five weeks following the ceremony. Truffaut certainly had no complaint, and he even thanked Georges Cravenne for creating these Oscar-inspired prizes in 1975. "Between now and the end of the month, *The Last Métro* will clear a million in tickets sales in Paris and this is due to the Césars of course. In Montreal, New York, Los Angeles and Boston, we have beaten previous records in each movie house, and the publicity, every time, was based on the ten Césars. In sum, I'm surely not the first to tell you, you were darned inspired on the day you came up with the idea of creating the Césars—and then when you had the courage to carry out your idea. I wanted to express not just my enthusiasm, but also my gratitude, and tell you that you can count on me,"[40] he wrote Cravenne.

The success of *The Last Métro* was a momentous event for Les Films du Carrosse—particularly since no one, least of all Truffaut, had suspected it would do so well. "Today people think *The Last Métro* was bound to be a 'hit' even before it was made: not true, if that had been the case, it would not have been rejected by UGC and AMLF or German coproducers . . .,"[41] he would say later, recalling the many financing difficulties he had had. The euphoria was such that "no one noticed the swastika on the poster was reversed!"[42] Marcel Berbert remembered with irony.

Eager to protect his independence as best he could, Truffaut was tough in his negotiations with TF1, in an effort to postpone the network's first broadcast of the film to as late a date as possible.[43] He even got Gaumont to agree to a second nationwide release sixteen months after the first exclusive run. On March 9, 1983, *The Last Métro* was rereleased with an extra six-minute sequence and attracted close to another 100,000 viewers.

The Last Métro was a smash hit abroad as well. In the United States, box-office receipts were good, with earnings of over $1 million in a nineteen-week run. The film was also nominated for both a Golden Globe and an Oscar for best foreign film. Truffaut's oeuvre was being honored worldwide, with retrospectives in Chicago, London, and Lausanne, and subsequently in San Sebastian and Tokyo. In Florence, Truffaut received the Visconti prize for lifetime achievement, given to him during the David of Donatello cere-mony—the Italian equivalent of the Oscars and Césars.

The Last Métro's triumph in France did provoke a backlash in the press and in the profession. Two days after the César ceremony, Dominique Jamet wrote a scathing editorial on the first page of *Le Quotidien de Paris.* "On seeing Truffaut and his friends stagger under the weight of the ugly lit-tle objects with which we honor great success in the seventh art and wander off under the slightly bitter gazes of Jean-Luc, Claude, Alain, and the others, we couldn't help feeling uneasy. This was giving Truffaut the sole monopoly on talent, elevating him to the status of Commander of French cinema, Boss of the industry, indeed Godfather of the guild. If this were the case, we would have grounds for deploring the extreme poverty of French cinema. Just as one swallow doesn't make a summer, one man doesn't popu-late a desert."[44] Several months later, Alain Rémond in *Les Nouvelles lit-téraires* accused Truffaut of having joined the ranks of the "quality cinema" which he himself used to denounce. "It rolls along smoothly, it works, it takes not the slightest risk. This change in Truffaut does not date from today. The auteur has been left behind. It's a bit sad."[45]

Truffaut was not impervious to these attacks. Of course, he was a man who liked success, a necessary condition to his independence as a director and producer. He also made it a rule to accept only prizes related to his pro-fession. Hence, based on this principle, he had turned down the Légion d'honneur and other awards. Truffaut had accepted the ten Césars because they had been awarded by his peers, but he had been embarrassed by the landslide, especially vis-à-vis directors he admired like Resnais, Sautet, and Pialat. And he was most embarrassed at being made into the "boss of French cinema." Though he refused to be on the fringes like Godard, his greatest wish was to remain an independent craftsman.

More than a director, Truffaut had primarily become a symbol, linking French cinema's different, indeed conflicting, families, tendencies, and clans. The number of screenplays he received at Les Films du Carrosse after the success of *The Last Métro* attests to this fact. In 1980 and 1981, over two hundred projects were dropped off at rue Robert-Etienne, a large number of them originating on the other side of the Atlantic. Many were written by eager young people seeking a godfather and a mentor.

SAUVE QUI PEUT (L'AMITIÉ) . . .
OR SALVAGING A FRIENDSHIP

It was also around this time that Jean-Luc Godard tried to reestablish a relationship with François Truffaut. After their falling out in 1973, the former friends saw each other only once, when they accidentally met in the same hotel in New York. "François refused to shake my hand," Godard recalls. "We ended up waiting for a taxi on the same sidewalk and he pretended not to see me."[46] At the end of the seventies, they kept up a dialogue only via the press. "I don't think François knows how to make films at all. He made one film that truly expressed him, *The 400 Blows,* and that was it: afterward, he merely told stories," Godard inveighed in a *Télérama* interview in July 1978. "Truffaut is a usurper. . . . If he could get into the Académie française, I'm sure he would. . . ."[47] Truffaut didn't react at the time. Then on August 19, 1980, Godard sent a letter to his old companions Truffaut, Jacques Rivette, and Claude Chabrol, suggesting that the three New Wave veterans get together with him in Rolle, Switzerland, where he was residing. He had just completed *Sauve qui peut (la vie)*, with Isabelle Huppert, Nathalie Baye, and Jacques Dutronc, his return to film after several years of political activism and experimentation with video. Chabrol was then finishing *Le Cheval d'orgueil,* based on the book by Pierre-Jakez Hélias, and Rivette, *Le Pont du nord,* starring Pascale Ogier. The only thing these films had in common was their release at around the same time as *The Last Métro.* "Couldn't we stage a 'conversation'?" Godard wrote to his old cohorts. "Whatever our differences, I would be interested in finding out viva voce what's become of our cinema. We could surely find a 'moderator' whom we would all approve of. We could make it into a book for Gallimard or some other house. Personally, I'm all set to invite you to Geneva for a day or two. If feasible, I'd love to show you my 'location.' While a reunion of just two of us might be felt as too explosive; with four of us there should be a way of underplaying the differences in potential so some connections could get through. Best regards anyhow."[48]

This time, Truffaut decided to break his silence:

Your invitation to Switzerland is extraordinarily flattering knowing how precious your time is. So now that you've put the Czechs, Vietnamese, Cubans, Palestinians and Mozambicans back on the right track, you will turn solicitously to reeducating the last outpost of the New Wave. I hope this plan of unloading a hasty book on Gallimard isn't a sign you now don't give two hoots about the Third World. Your letter is terrific and your pastiche of political style very convincing.

The finale of your letter is sure to remain one of your best touches, "Best regards anyhow." So you don't hold against us the fact that you called us crooks, dregs and scum. . . . As far as I'm concerned, I agree to come see your location—what a pretty expression . . . when I think of all the hypocrites who would just say my house—but it's a privilege I'd like to share with others, let's say four or five people who could receive your word and then spread it around everywhere. I therefore request that you invite Jean-Paul Belmondo at the same time as me. You said he was afraid of you and it may be time to reassure him. I'd also very much like Vera Chytilova to be present, whom you denounced as "revisionist" in her own country just at the time of the Soviet occupation. Her presence at our colloquium seems to me necessary, for I'm certain you would help her to obtain an exit visa. Why neglect Loleh Bellon, whom you called a real bitch in *Télérama*. Finally, don't forget Boumboum, our old friend Braunberger, who wrote me the day after your phone call: " 'Dirty Jew' is the only insult I can't tolerate." I'm not excessively impatient as I wait for your reply, for if you're becoming a Coppola groupie, you might be short on time and you should by no means hastily throw together the preproduction work on your next autobiographical film, whose title I think I know: *Once a Shit Always a Shit.*[49]

Truffaut also took advantage of a long interview in *Cahiers du cinéma* to set the record straight. It was an opportunity for him to seal his reunion with *Cahiers* after a long period of estrangement.[50] He assessed his career, discussed his relations with the public, with other directors, with people from the past, with actors, and with the United States. He also stated what he now found difficult to endure: solitude, nonconformism, and . . . Godard, who "belongs to a group of convulsively envious people." This time, the attack was not only private but also public, and it was radical. "Even at the time of the New Wave, friendship was a one-way thing for him. Since he was very talented and already clever at attracting pity, we used to forgive his pettiness, but, everyone will tell you, he already had his slippery side, which he now can't conceal. He had to be helped all the time, you had to do him favors and could expect an underhanded blow in return."

Aside from settling the score with Godard, Truffaut defined his ethics as a director, discussed his love and angst in making films, his abiding by rules of conduct he had set for himself since the beginning of his career—his not wanting other people to lose money, his refusal to pose as an artist, or to criticize those who had had less luck than he in their work. He situated himself at the center of French cinema, or rather "at the extreme center,"[51] independent though working within the system: This was the place Truffaut jealously wished to keep; he constantly dreaded appearing the head of a clique, or, worse still, the cornerstone of the French film industry.[52] He refused, for example, to preside over the Société des réalisateurs de films (Society of Filmmakers), when asked by Marcel Ophuls and Luc Moullet, who were then secretaries general of that organization. He reasserted his independence in a letter to Claude Autant-Lara, who accused him of having "all the powers in French film," stressed his voluntary isolation, and justified himself in these terms: "Anyone could give you confirmation of this—I'm not power-hungry. I have refused to accept the directorship of the *Avance sur recettes* [government subsidy—advance on box-office receipts], the presidencies of the Cinémathèque française and the Société des réalisateurs de films, or to sit on any jury since 1962, or to make the fate of a project depend on my personal taste, or to let my freedom be compromised. I have never made the slightest attempt to seize power in any institution whatsoever, for, as Serge de Gainsbourg would put it, *'J'en ai rien à cirer* [I couldn't give a flying fart].' "[53]

"My only tactic is alternating, shooting a very low-budget film after each costly film, so that I won't be drawn into an escalation that leads to serious concessions, megalomania and unemployment,"[54] said Truffaut to his *Cahiers* interviewers when they quizzed him about his projects after *The Last Métro.* His next film would therefore be in stark contrast to his latest hit. After a period film, he would direct a contemporary film; after one of his longest and costliest shoots, the next one would be among his quickest, and its budget among the most modest. He would abandon historical fresco and classical narrative and return to the intimate journal style to tell a story bordering on madness.

NEITHER WITH YOU NOR WITHOUT YOU

In December of 1979, Truffaut, like a million of his countrymen, had been captivated by a series of five televised episodes on Antenne 2, *Les Dames de la côte* (The Ladies of the Coast), produced by Mag Bodard and directed by Nina Companeez. This historical saga covered a good part of the twentieth century through the fortunes and misfortunes of a French family. It had an illustrious cast—Edwige Feuillère, Françoise Fabian, Martine Chevalier, Evelyne Buyle, and Francis Huster. The female lead was played by Fanny Ardant, a thirty-year-old stage actress who had had very few prior screen appearances. Laura Truffaut, who was vacationing in Paris at the time, recalls being with her father at Avenue Pierre 1er-de-Serbie when they saw the first episode of *Les Dames de la côte.* "I saw my father charmed the first time he saw Fanny Ardant on television; he was really bowled over."[55] Confessing to "television love at first sight,"[56] Truffaut wrote to Ardant at the end of December, suggesting they meet at Les Films du Carrosse.

Their first meeting took place when Truffaut was getting ready to shoot *The Last Métro*. "The next film will be for you," he promised Ardant. They saw each other regularly thereafter, eating lunch together at the *boulangerie* on the corner of rue Marbeuf and rue Robert-Etienne, one of the director's favorite spots. They discussed his next film, which was already being written, and got to know each other. The daughter of a colonel in the cavalry, born in Saumur, Fanny Ardant first followed her father in his various missions around Europe, in Sweden, for instance, where Colonel Ardant was military attaché, then, in the sixties, in Monaco, where he was one of the advisers to Prince Rainier's personal guard. His daughter's education was in the pure aristocratic tradition, "à la Don Quixote," as Ardant would put it. Even though the family was not very wealthy, she lived in high style—private schools, good French lycées abroad, formal balls, and horse races. At twenty, she followed a three-year course of study in political science in Aix-en-Provence, where she wrote a paper on surrealism and anarchy. She then went to live in Paris after a short stay in London. But in the mid-seventies, she was lured away from the university by the theater. After taking an acting course at the Ecole Perimoni, she started to get her first parts. She played Pauline in Corneille's *Polyeucte*, produced as part of the 1974 Festival du Marais in Paris; then she was cast in Montherlant's *Le Maître de Santiago*, Racine's *Esther*, Giraudoux's *Electra*, Paul Claudel's *Tête d'or*. Finally, in 1978, she was noticed in a television drama based on Balzac, *Les Mémoires de deux jeunes mariées* (The Memoirs of Two Young Newlyweds). The following year, Mag Bodard and Nina Companeez gave her the lead role in *Les Dames de la côte*.[57]

On the evening of the César awards, January 31, 1981, Truffaut's first impression of the actress was reinforced. During the traditional supper at Fouquet's following the ceremony, Truffaut was surrounded by all the actors from *The Last Métro*: "Fanny Ardant came to join us, Gérard Depardieu and me, at our table. When I saw them together, it became plain to me that they were to be my lovers."[58] He was referring to the lovers in the script that he had started working on "clandestinely."[59] The desire to cast them together impelled him to speed up the preproduction work on this new film; he started drafting the dialogues daily and on weekends. Later, in talking about Fanny Ardant, Truffaut would admit that he had been seduced "by her large mouth, her deep voice and its unusual intonations, her big black eyes and her triangular face."[60] He liked the vitality of her acting, her enthusiasm and humor, her "penchant for secrecy, her distant, slightly unsociable side, and, above all, her vibrancy."[61]

The theme of *La Femme d'à côté* (*The Woman Next Door*) dated far back in Truffaut's work program, as was true for most of his films. "I could give royalties to Catherine Deneuve," he said in jest to Claude de Givray during their taped interviews in June 1984. For the screenplay of *The Woman Next Door* was inspired, in large part, by his amorous relationship with the actress. Truffaut had even written five pages at the end of 1972, a first synopsis entitled "*Sur les rails* (On the Rails)," the story of two former lovers who accidentally meet after an eight-year separation. The synopsis described this passionate but impossible reunion, the man's depression (changed to the woman's in *The Woman Next Door*), the "little multicolored pills" which more or less cure lovesickness, the emblematic song ("Without Love One Is Nothing"), and a less pessimistic ending than the later version. In 1972, Truffaut thought of bringing together Jeanne Moreau and Charles Denner as the couple whose passion can be summarized in this simple phrase, "neither with you nor without you."

Truffaut started working on this project again with Jean Aurel in the autumn of 1980. "We established an oral continuity, scene by scene, as we went along," Aurel recalls. "We had to have the meeting in the supermarket, the nervous breakdown for the dramatization, with the idea of intentional illness which came from my reading of Groddeck. The dramatic ending was planned. It could only end in death. . . . And then the idea, François's idea, which he told me bashfully, that they would die while making love."[62] Subsequently, Truffaut split his working time between Jean Aurel and Suzanne Schiffman. The first focused on the construction of the whole, finding ideas to fill out the twenty sequences in the synopsis; the latter shaped the continuity and deepened the psychology of the characters. Suzanne Schiffman developed the character of Madame Jouve, the manager of the tennis club the two couples belong to, a generous woman, haunted and traumatized by a former passion, who becomes the confidante of each of the lovers. By the end of February 1981, the last draft of the script for *The Woman Next Door* was finished—just over three months had gone by, from the first synopsis to the final version.

"Lovesickness is a disease. The doctor cannot cure it": Around this epigraph, taken from an old French song, the screenplay offers one of François Truffaut's most limpid and tragic stories. Bernard Coudray and Mathilde Bauchard had loved each other passionately and had gone through a painful separation. They meet again seven years later when Mathilde, recently married to Philippe, comes to live in the house next door to Bernard's, where he lives with his wife, Arlette, and their son, Thomas. Bernard has found happiness with Arlette, and they lead a calm and peaceful life in a small village about twelve miles from Grenoble. As for Mathilde, her marriage to Philippe, who is older than she, has given her a certain equilibrium.

Inevitably, the two couples establish neighborly relations; both Bernard and Mathilde are silent about their old relationship and try to stifle their feelings. In spite of their efforts, their passion is reignited. The lovers meet in a hotel room. But, during a party at Mathilde's, Bernard has a violent fit of rage on learning that Mathilde wants to break up. Mathilde undergoes a severe depression and is treated in a clinic. Her husband puts the house up for sale. One night, Bernard sees a light inside the house. It is Mathilde. The two lovers embrace. While they are making love, Mathilde shoots Bernard and then shoots herself.

Truffaut wanted to film *The Woman Next Door* quickly. His reasons were compelling: He wished to preserve the emotional power of its subject matter and dispel the new image of himself as an establishment director. Furthermore, Gérard Depardieu was in great demand and free for only six weeks, between March and April 1981. "Gérard Depardieu had been hired to act in Francis Veber's *The Goat*," recalls Jean-Louis Livi, who was then the actor's agent as well as Truffaut's agent. "François told me he wanted to shoot immediately. I asked him if he was ready and he answered, 'No, but after a success like *The Last Métro*, I can't wait.' I worked things out with Gaumont, which was producing *The Goat*, to put off the shoot so that Gérard would be free for *The Woman Next Door.*"[63]

Truffaut was therefore obliged to work swiftly, which didn't displease him. He had no difficulty choosing actors for the remainder of the small cast. Henri Garcin was cast in the part of Philippe, Mathilde's husband, and Michèle Baumgartner,[64] in that of Arlette, Bernard's wife. Véronique Silver was to play Madame Jouve, and Philippe Morier-Genoud, an actor from the Centre dramatique national des Alpes, the part of the psychiatrist who tries to cure Mathilde.

At the end of March 1981, Truffaut moved to Grenoble, where the shoot was to take place from April 1 to May 15. He found the two neighboring houses that serve as the basic set for the film in a village about ten miles from Grenoble. The only significant change in his technical team was the camera crew, now headed by William Lubtchansky, assisted by Caroline Champetier and Barcha Bauer. *The Woman Next Door* was a coproduction deal between Carrosse, Gaumont (which would also be its distributor), and TF1. The financial arrangements were the same as for *The Last Métro*, but the budget was one-third the size and the shoot only half as long. The film fits in the category of Truffaut's happy shoots, like *Jules and Jim* and *Mississippi Mermaid*, made when the director was in love with the actress he was filming. As was his habit, Truffaut was secretive about this new affair. "François was extremely discreet," says Gérard Depardieu. "One night, coming home to the Hôtel du Commerce at around midnight, I was talking to the porter, as usual, when the elevator door opened and I saw François, who lived in town. He shut the door and I looked away as though I hadn't seen him, because I sensed his discomfort. What was he doing there? At first, I told myself that he had probably come to 'coach' Fanny. It was only later that I understood their relationship."[65] This love and harmony was apparent in Truffaut's praise of his actress: "As soon as a scene is shot, her face lights up, she remains silent and breaks into a smile that seems to say: 'I am satiated, I am fulfilled, I am gratified.' "[66]

A first rough cut was ready in mid-June 1981, a mere two and a half months after the beginning of the shoot. But Truffaut wasn't fully satisfied with its structure. Suzanne Schiffman then suggested that they make Madame Jouve into the narrator. At the beginning of the film, she would recount a news event to the viewer: "It was still night when the police car left Grenoble. . . . My name is Odile Jouve. . . . The business started six months ago. . . ." Then she would narrate the story of the lovers throughout the entire film, summarizing their tragedy with the line "Neither with you nor without you." Truffaut liked the idea and shot an additional sequence with Véronique Silver, on June 13, in front of the Corenc Tennis Club, about six miles from Grenoble.

The first reactions, prior to the release of the film on September 30, 1981, were unanimously positive and several commentators hailed the emergence of a great actress. "Fanny Ardant's entire being blazes with a strange, romantic flame. She is a sort of disquieting Fate whose dark gaze and obsession recall both the Maria Casarès of *Orphée* and the Adjani of *Adèle H.,*"[67] Michel Pascal declared over the radio, on Europe 1, while *Le Film français* prophesied: "*A Star is born,* unquestionably, and François Truffaut is the supervisor of this flamboyant metamorphosis."[68] But the most acute analysis of the film was offered by Serge Daney in *Libération:*

> If *The Woman Next Door* is such an effective movie and so moving in the end, it is because Truffaut, the enemy of exhibitionism in passions and ideas, the man of the golden mean and compromise, has tried this time to film compromise itself, to make it the substance and form of his film. . . . Truffaut's gamble with *The Woman Next Door,* is to escape from *The Green Room,* to combine the Hyde scenario (morbid, private passion) and the Jekyll scenario (other people, public life). To combine them without letting one prevail over the other, without making the viewer choose between them. . . . For, through a paradox that is unique to him, his art of compromise plunges him into a riskier cinema, without any safety net. In *The Woman Next Door,* his art of directing has become broad and free enough to accommodate Hyde and Jekyll in the same breath.[69]

A SINGULAR COUPLE

François Truffaut's last great love reinstilled passion and intensity in his romantic life. After the editing of *The Woman Next Door*, he rented a large house not far from Paris, where, from the end of June to the end of August 1981, he hoped to spend what he called in a handwritten note "the FT/Fanny vacation in Fontainebleau."[70] But Fanny Ardant wasn't free, for she was working for most of the summer in the Bordeaux region, on a made-for-television movie, *Le Chef de famille* (The Head of the Family), directed by Nina Companeez. Feeling despondent and lonely, Truffaut preferred his Paris apartment to his summer rental, and he entertained Laura and her boyfriend, Steve Wong, who were vacationing in France. Though he had just undergone a serious dental operation from which he had not fully recovered, he submitted at the end of June and the beginning of July to lengthy interviews conducted by Jérôme Prieur and Jean Collet, for a film directed by José Maria Berzosa. In this *leçon de cinéma,* consisting of two one-hour interviews intercut with excerpts from his films, he discussed each film, often with a critical eye, as he sat in a screening room at I.N.A. (the Institut National de l'Audiovisuel), in Bry-sur-Marne, looking somewhat uncomfortable. In a letter to Jean Collet, he described himself at the time as "in very bad shape physically and mentally."[71]

Fortunately, in mid-September, he was reunited with Fanny and they took several trips together over the next two months, promoting *The Woman Next Door* in the provinces and abroad. At the beginning of October, Fanny Ardant and François Truffaut, joined by Helen Scott, presented *The Woman Next Door* at the New York Film Festival and stayed for a week at the Carlyle Hotel. They no sooner returned to Paris than they set off again for the United States, on November 4, 1981, for a longer stay—first in Chicago, where they attended a tribute to Truffaut, then in San Francisco and Los Angeles, where the couple stayed at the Beverly Hills Hotel. Truffaut introduced Fanny to his Californian friends, among them Dido Renoir, who was charmed by the young French actress.

François Truffaut and Fanny Ardant formed a singular couple. By mutual agreement, they had decided not to live together and to keep their independence, even though they were practically neighbors in the sixteenth arrondissement. "I adore large families," said Fanny in *Figaro Madame*, "but for me love must remain illicit, with no ring on the finger. I also love large houses, but not couples. The priest's benediction is like signing a contract to get trapped! One shouldn't live together. It's so wonderful to have assignations and be like a guest in each other's house."⁷² At thirty, Fanny Ardant had arranged to live on the fringes. "Unconventional people like me often come from very strict, repressive families . . . because such families give you a fanatical taste for freedom."⁷³ She lived alone with Lumir, her daughter born in 1975, named after the Claudel heroine in *Crusts.* She and Truffaut shared this "fanatical taste for freedom" and had the same sense of humor, a certain lightness, a pleasure in telling stories, a desire to work together, and a mutual admiration. They had in common a passionate love of reading. At Fanny's, there were books everywhere, a piano, and some prints adorning the white walls. They both loved Balzac, Proust, Miller, and James; and Fanny also liked Julien Gracq, Jane Austen, Elsa Morante, and F. Scott Fitzgerald. They saw each other several times a week, in a restaurant, at the movies, at each other's house. Their quasi-illicit love began to mean everything to them.

ON THE SIDELINES

In May 1981, France elected a socialist president, François Mitterrand. Passionately interested in politics but wary of political commitment, Truffaut had nonetheless supported the campaign publicly, and he joined the committee to elect Mitterrand in March, even allowing his picture to appear on one of the committee's posters, along with eighteen other personalities, among them Jean-Claude Casadesus, Vladimir Jankélévitch, Françoise Sagan, Alexandre Minkowski, Haroun Tazieff, Anna Prucnal, Catherine Lara, Gérard Depardieu, and Anny Duperey. Truffaut was disappointed by the picture they chose, which was taken from *The Green Room;* in it, he wore turn-of-the-century eyeglasses and looked pale and sweaty. At the committee's request, he delivered a speech at a UNESCO forum on March 19, at a meeting of about a thousand intellectuals from various countries. He also joined fifty film professionals—including René Allio, Gérard Blain, Claude Chabrol, Constantin Costa-Gavras, Gérard Depardieu, Jacques Demy, Michel Piccoli, Marie Dubois, and Brigitte Fossey—in signing an appeal to vote for Mitterrand "against fear, manipulation and the lies of the people in power." Finally, on April 26, on the eve of the first round in the presidential election, he joined a last-minute appeal to "defeat Giscard by casting a useful ballot in the first round."

Truffaut's real motive was to see a change in the political workforce, and other players active in public life. During his entire adult life, Truffaut had known only conservative governments. But he didn't commit himself to the point of personally going out to vote. In fact, Laura openly criticized him, for she was more than delighted to have acquired, thanks to Valérie Giscard d'Estaing, the right to vote at eighteen. "I told him this was not right—if you urge people to vote, you should vote yourself. He said the opposite, that he exerted a far greater influence by urging others to vote."[74] But Truffaut was as ever full of contradictions when it came to politics.

Truffaut supported Mitterrand but was only moderately fond of him, for he saw him as too political, a skillful strategist more than a moral authority. Yet the two men had made a determined effort to try to get to know each other and had lunched several times together at the Brasserie Lipp in the seventies.[75] As in 1974, Truffaut initially favored Michel Rocard, when the latter and Mitterrand were still the rival Left candidates in the presidential elections. On the day after a much-talked-about Rocard television appearance, Marcel Ophuls wrote to Truffaut to convince him to lend his support to the former head of the Socialist party: "Should it turn out to be necessary, I would try to convince you. I know that I have a certain prestige in your eyes as a 'political mind.' I would like to take advantage of it now because I think it's very important. . . ."[76] In mid-April 1980, Truffaut and Ophuls met Rocard, ready to lend their support to his candidacy. Several weeks later, when it became clear that a large majority in the Socialist party sided with Mitterrand, Rocard withdrew. Eleven months later, Truffaut joined the committee to elect Mitterrand, at the request of Jack Lang and Roger Hanin.

Undeniably, François Truffaut rejoiced at Mitterrand's victory on May 10, 1981. On May 21, the day of the inauguration, he was in the third row of the procession marching behind the new president to the ceremony at the Panthéon, and several days later, he was among the many personalities Mitterrand invited to the Intercontinental Hotel, where he thanked his supporters. The president had a long private conversation with him and thanked him warmly. Truffaut was delighted by two of the first measures taken by the new government—the television broadcast of *The Sorrow and the Pity* in May 1981 and the abolition of the death penalty, which was voted into law by the National Assembly on September 17. This latter measure had been proposed by Robert Badinter, the former lawyer of, among others, Roberto Rossellini, and now Minister of Justice in Prime Minister Pierre Mauroy's government.

But Truffaut's political commitment had no effect on the principles that guided his behavior. Hence, when Jack Lang, the new Minister of Culture, informed him that he was to receive the Légion d'honneur during the traditional presentation on Bastille Day, the national holiday, Truffaut declined to accept. He would still accept only "distinctions pertaining to his profession, the cinema."[77] Wary of any ruling power, whether on the Right or Left, Truffaut justified himself in an interview with Luce Vigo, published in the Communist weekly *Révolution*. "My first reaction was: 'Oh, that's good, the Left has won.' But we must not have a relationship with them because we must not 'suck up to them.' By definition, we must be against, or perhaps not necessarily against the government, but at any rate separate from it."[78]

In October of the same year, Jack Lang asked Truffaut to present himself for the presidency of the Cinémathèque française.[79] But the director wanted to "stay on the sidelines," as he bluntly told Jean Riboud, the head of Schlumberger, who had been a great friend of Langlois, Renoir, and Rossellini and who, as a board member of the Cinémathèque, wanted to give new prestige to the old institution. "Madame Jack Lang called me," Truffaut wrote to Riboud. "Having turned down medals, positions, receptions and official trips since the month of May, I didn't think I could get out of lunch at rue de Valois on Wednesday, November 3. I'll stay completely evasive concerning the Cinémathèque, since we decided to discuss it together later. It is my conviction that Jacques Rivette would be perfectly suited in this area, the ideal programming director in any case."[80] During this luncheon at the Ministry of Culture, Truffaut did indeed remain very evasive concerning the Cinémathèque française. It was also the occasion of a rather outspoken conversation between him and Jack Lang, the minister finding it difficult to understand Truffaut's attitude regarding the Socialist government. They discussed the "Yorktown affair," an episode where Truffaut had failed to obey protocol. Two weeks before this luncheon, François Mitterrand had made an official trip to Yorktown, the historic American city, for a meeting with Ronald Reagan. The French president had wanted to have a retinue of cultural personalities and, on the morning of October 12, Truffaut had been invited to join the delegation. But on that very day, he was in New York with Fanny Ardant, presenting *The Woman Next Door.* Jack Lang's office had been very insistent about his extending his stay in the United States and his going to Yorktown. A record of a series of rather curt exchanges can be found—recorded by Josiane Couëdel—on the register of telephone calls at Les Films du Carrosse: "I said you were returning tomorrow, because you had many appointments and that you had to leave for Germany on the 18th for the opening of *The Last Métro* there. Monsieur Lang answered that this was not about just anybody, but the president, Monsieur Mitterrand, and that consequently you would do well to change your attitude."

Six months later, another episode illustrates the reserve Truffaut intended to maintain with regard to the leftist government. In April 1982, he was in Tokyo for a week, for a retrospective devoted to his work. Mitterrand and a delegation of several ministers, including Jack Lang, were on an official visit to Tokyo at the same time. Earlier, in planning this trip with Koichi Yamada, Truffaut had informed him of his desire to avoid any political-diplomatic reception, preferring to "see two good recent Japanese films rather than play penguin with the ambassador."[81] Fearing he had made a faux pas, Truffaut eventually changed his schedule for April 16. "On Friday, we must absolutely change the schedule so that I can attend President Mitterrand's reception at the embassy," he wrote to Yamada, "for it would really be impolite not to attend. The conflict on the following day between the showing of *The Woman Next Door* and the Lang reception is less serious, but we might have to divide the book-signing session in two so I can spend fifteen minutes at the Jack Lang gathering."[82]

Truffaut was truly ill at ease with the Socialist protocol and eager to preserve his freedom of movement and opinion. Concrete action was what had always counted for him on issues that he felt personally concerned about. Hence, when he was contacted at the end of 1981 by the C.F.D.T. (French Democratic Confederation of Labor) because it intended to produce a film on troubled childhood, Truffaut immediately agreed to participate in a study group to define the guidelines of the project. In January and February 1982, he worked on the documents that the study group had assembled (the screenplay concerns a strike by women in a textile factory, with children joining the strikers in occupying the factory), but he eventually abandoned the project. He justified this to Edmond Maire, the secretary-general of the affiliated unions, as follows: "The esteem I have for you and your action at the C.F.D.T. made me want to try this experiment, but since I'm a director from before the advent of television, it intimidates me, and I prefer to continue working within the film industry for several more years."[83] Whatever happened, Truffaut, while curious and available, maintained a staunchly independent position in his relations with political power as with television.

CONFIDENTIALLY YOURS!

While screening the rushes of the last scene of *The Woman Next Door*— where Mathilde, wearing a beige trench coat, shoots Bernard, her lover and neighbor, and then shoots herself—it suddenly struck Truffaut that Fanny Ardant looked like a *film noir* heroine. This immediately made him want to find a crime thriller to adapt, so he could cast his lover in the lead. A short time later, Suzanne Schiffman suggested a Charles Williams novel, *The Long Saturday Night* (*Vivement dimanche!*), whose rights Truffaut had wanted to acquire in the sixties as a possible vehicle for Jeanne Moreau.[84] What Truffaut most liked about it was the possibility of making the woman conduct the police investigation, "not a killer or a woman detective, but an ordinary woman, a valiant secretary, determined to prove her boss's innocence."[85] This was an ideal part for Fanny Ardant, a part where she could "gallop headlong into a trotting universe."[86]

During the entire autumn of 1981, Truffaut was busy with the release of *The Woman Next Door*, traveling incessantly, in France and abroad. At the beginning of the following year, he could finally start adapting *Vivement dimanche!* (*Confidentially Yours!*) with help from Suzanne Schiffman and Jean Aurel. The trickiest part consisted in overhauling the structure of the novel to make the screen heroine portrayed by Fanny Ardant more active and decisive. "In the Charles Williams novel, not his best," says Suzanne Schiffman, "it was the man, after all, who conducted the investigation and the woman who stayed in the agency. . . . She wasn't active enough! But what if the man were confined to the agency and she were to take over the entire investigation? François approved."[87]

In fact, François Truffaut wasn't really pleased with his script, finding it lacked credibility. So much so that he even considered giving up the film shortly before the shoot was to start. But he gave the script to Fanny Ardant to read and she found it amusing. "I laughed a lot on reading it," she now recalls, "but it was Gérard Lebovici's opinion that clinched matters. 'You'd be crazy not to make it! And this is not my opinion as a businessman, but as a connoisseur friend.' "[88] Oddly enough, Truffaut resented Suzanne Schiffman for having pointed him in the direction of that particular novel. The tension between them cast a shadow over their collaboration that never let up in the course of the shoot. Yet the other coscenarist, Jean Aurel, defends the project to this day: "It's a crazy screenplay, there's no logic of space or time, it's conceived as an entertainment. The subject of the film isn't exactly the action that unfolds, it serves as support for the rest."[89] At the end of May 1982, Truffaut and his screenwriters isolated themselves in a rented house in Villedieu, in Provence, and set to work again. The trio returned three weeks later with scripted dialogue that was practically a final screenplay. Truffaut finally completed the script after another work session at the Hôtel de Rochegude, near Avignon, this time in the company of Fanny Ardant and Suzanne Schiffman, spinning out an improbable plot of nearly two hundred pages.

Julien Vercel, the owner of a real estate agency in a small town, is accused of a double murder—that of his wife, Marie-Christine, and her lover, Jacques Massoulier, both brutally shot in the head one morning while hunting. With the circumstantial evidence against him, Julien Vercel decides to conduct his own investigation. But very soon, he becomes the suspect in a third murder and is forced to hide from the police and let his secretary, Barbara Becker, pursue the investigation. An ironical brunette, a graduate of the Cours Pigier (a secretarial school), and a clever amateur detective, Barbara throws herself into situations that are alternately alarming and unexpected in her attempt to discover the identity of the true guilty party, who is none other than Vercel's own lawyer, Maître Clément. As a romantic backdrop to this comic thriller, the relationship between Julien and Barbara changes from one of irritation to complicity, culminating in their marriage at the end of the film.

FANNY IN BLACK AND WHITE

For Truffaut, it was obvious that *Confidentially Yours!* had to be made in black and white. His aesthetic gamble consisted in "restoring the mysterious and glossy nocturnal ambiance of the American detective comedies that used to delight us."[90] In fact, since he had doubts about his script, Truffaut knew that the best way to rescue his film was to find a rapid, spirited pace in the shooting. To conform to the *film noir* logic, black and white was essential, an idea that very much appealed to Nestor Almendros. He would try to re-create the stylized lighting of detective films by using a range of different black-and-white emulsions. During preproduction, Almendros even came upon some old Fresnel lamps from the fifties in a studio in the Paris suburbs; they produced a harsher lighting, illuminating clearly defined areas and projecting very distinct shadows. Truffaut and Almendros hired Hilton McConnico, an American production designer, who built entire sets painted in black and white. Similarly, Michèle Cerf's and Franckie Diago's costumes and props were conceived in the black, gray, and white spectrums.

But Carrosse's financial partners disapproved of this esthetic decision and considered it uncommercial. Television was particularly hostile, refusing to finance a film that wouldn't really fit into peak-hour programming. TF1's film subsidiary refused to coproduce *Confidentially Yours!* and Antenne 2 was interested but hesitant. Even Gérard Lebovici admitted he was reluctant. Truffaut did everything he could to convince him: "The Venice Film Festival just awarded the Golden Lion to *The State of Things*, which was made by Wim Wenders in black and white," he wrote him on September 9, 1982, in a rather vehement letter where he enumerated recent well-known black-and-white films—*The Last Picture Show, Manhattan, Raging Bull, Veronika Voss, The Elephant Man.* And his conclusion was marvelous: "Films are not cans of food. Like human beings, they must be thought about, scrutinized, and considered one by one."[91] In his plea, Truffaut stuck up for his film, of course, but also requested respect for his freedom as an auteur and independent producer. He felt slighted by the attitude of the television networks—slighted on principle, because their rejection of black and white stemmed from a desire to standardize film, which he objected to, and slighted on a personal level, because with *The Last Métro* and *The Woman Next Door,* he felt TF1 had concluded two excellent business deals, both financially and as a way of enhancing its reputation with television viewers. Lebovici finally came around to Truffaut's point of view.

And Antenne 2 agreed to coproduce *Confidentially Yours!* By the end of September 1982, after two months of anxiety and struggle, Truffaut finally balanced his 7-million-franc budget.

The ideal partner still had to be found for Fanny Ardant—a well-known actor who would still let her be the star. The Julien Vercel character is indeed full of contradictions: irritating but attractive, passive but conducting the investigation by proxy, a notable but slightly shady man, someone who likes only blond women but ends up marrying a brunette. His role in the story is not unlike that of a director who organizes everything on the set without appearing on-screen. Truffaut decided to cast Jean-Louis Trintignant in the part, an actor he had never previously directed. Trintignant had taken the first step, in 1979, by writing to Truffaut; he had found a casual way of saying he was available.

> I would love to be in your films. I am sure you would have been pleased with me as an actor and I'm sure I would have been very good. Perhaps there is something about me, or my acting style, you don't like. This letter isn't at all aggressive. Quite the opposite. We actors are often a bit dumb. We take a foolish pride in waiting to be selected. It's our slightly feminine side—feminine in the sense of our mothers, not our wives. There, I'm only writing you all this now because I've stopped thinking of myself as an actor really, or a director, or even less a car racer. I think of myself as a man who has the time to do all the things he likes to do. This might be a sign of aging, and I'm on the lookout for those very signs these days."[92]

Trintignant's frankness appealed to Truffaut, who later acknowledged that Trintignant was the only actor who could have played the parts he himself had played in his films—Dr. Itard in *The Wild Child,* Julien Davenne in *The Green Room,* Ferrand in *Day for Night.* Indeed, Truffaut and Trintignant were only two years apart in age and had the same physical appearance. Their voices were similar—original, almost colorless, neutral in tone and devoid of dramatic effect. "If you choose this part as you would choose a pair of shoes, your feet won't hurt, for we'll tread softly, as if we were wearing moccasins,"[93] Truffaut wrote to Trintignant when offering him the role of Julien Vercel.

The supporting cast in *Confidentially Yours!* was crucial to making the crime-thriller atmosphere convincing. For the part of the lawyer, Truffaut sought a reliable actor, but one who hadn't been seen too often in films or on television. He certainly didn't want a "bad guy" whom the public would instantly identify as a negative or suspicious character. This was why he tried to convince his friend Serge Rousseau to take the part. For Truffaut, Rousseau was kindness itself, and competent enough for the part, since he had begun his career as an actor before being an agent at Artmédia. But Rousseau turned him down. Two weeks before the filming, Truffaut still tried to convince him: "Time is pressing, for I've run out of options. You know that in casting, I'm never the least bit concerned with fashion or box-office appeal, but with appropriateness and plausibility. I need you for this part. Don't let me down, for as Raymond Devos says, the person who is let down goes down."[94] Serge Rousseau didn't change his mind, but it is he who recommended Philippe Laudenbach. For the part of Jacques Massoulier, an enigmatic priest who is conducting his own investigation and hindering Barbara's, Truffaut first considered the writer and *Nouvel Observateur* journalist Jean-François Josselin, then, strongly encouraged by his daughter Eva, he took Jean-Pierre Kalfon, the Rivette actor (*Out One*). He also cast Caroline Sihol in the part of Marie-Christine Vercel, and Philippe Morier-Genoud as the police superintendent. Lastly, he once again convinced Jean-Louis Richard to accept the part of the "bad guy," Louison, the shady owner of a Riviera nightclub.

Having shot one scene of *The Woman Next Door* in Hyères, in the Var—on Jean-Louis Richard's property, in fact—Truffaut very much wanted to shoot this new film on location in that region. Suzanne Schiffman, who was sent scouting for locations between Toulon and the Giens peninsula, found a huge abandoned clinic, Les Kermes, about six miles from Hyères. Hilton McConnico and his technicians would divide the space into several sets, offering nearly the same shooting conditions as a studio. The filming of *Confidentially Yours!* began on November 4, 1982, and lasted eight weeks. "It's a strange experience, as though everyone had been struck with color blindness,"[95] wrote a reporter for the *Matin de Paris* who visited the set and was surprised to find a dreamlike atmosphere where everything—set and actors' costumes—was black, gray, and white.

At the end of the shoot, François Truffaut and Fanny Ardant rested in Provence for about ten days before returning to Paris. Then the editing had to be done immediately and very fast to meet the release date, which had already been set for "around August 10 in the big cities, while the critics are in the country,"[96] he wrote to Georges Delerue, who had been living in Los Angeles for some time, and from whom he requested a score "recalling the Warner Brothers style, like the Max Steiner–Franz Waxman films, whose masterpiece was *The Big Sleep*."[97] The answer print of *Confidentially Yours!* was ready on May 20. Truffaut had succeeded in making his film in a mere six months, under the shooting conditions of a French B film, with the woman he loved as star.

THE LAST VACATION

It was a rather bold decision on the part of A.A.A., the distribution company founded by Gérard Lebovici, to release *Confidentially Yours!* in the middle of the summer, on Wednesday, August tenth, in a deserted Paris, overrun by tourists. In the meantime, François Truffaut contemplated taking a vacation. At the end of May, he gave himself a few days off in Rome, where Fanny Ardant was finishing the shoot of *Benvenuta*, directed by the Belgian filmmaker André Delvaux. On June 29, at the town hall of the sixteenth arrondissement, François Truffaut and Madeleine Morgenstern attended the marriage of their elder daughter, Laura, to Steve Wong, who worked at the Pacific Film Archive in Berkeley, California. Only a handful of close friends were present at the ceremony—Camille de Casablanca, a great childhood friend of Laura, and Nestor Almendros, whom she very much liked. Many more friends attended the dinner that evening, at the restaurant of L'Hôtel, on rue des Beaux-Arts, for it was also Eva's birthday celebration—among them Helen Scott, Claudine Bouché, and her daughter Tessa. By then, after a long period of estrangement, François had grown closer to his father, so Roland Truffaut was also present at the ceremony. He met Eva, whom he had never seen before, for she had always refused to acknowledge him as her grandfather. As for Laura, this was only the second time she had met Roland, whom she had first seen four years earlier, when her father's paternal grandmother died.[98]

On the following day, Truffaut and Fanny Ardant left for a vacation on the Norman coast. He had asked Marcel Berbert, who owned an apartment in Trouville, to find him a quiet house to rent, where he could rest, work on his forthcoming films, and entertain friends and collaborators. The choice of Normandy, not far from Paris, was to allow Truffaut to make a few round-trips in his convertible, to respond to journalists' queries and supervise the promotion of *Confidentially Yours!* Thanks to an auctioneer with whom he had maintained contact since the shoot of *The Green Room*, Berbert heard that the house owned by France Gall and Michel Berger, near Honfleur, was available for rent for two months in the summer. In June, Truffaut made a quick trip to see it and give his approval. Le Clos Saint-Nicolas was a pretty manor house in the hamlet of Vasouy. It was there that Truffaut and Fanny Ardant settled in the beginning of July.

By then, it was no longer a secret to anyone close to the couple that Fanny was expecting a child, due in September 1983. Having recently turned fifty-one, Truffaut felt no great eagerness to become a father again, yet he didn't feel he had to justify himself vis-à-vis his daughters, Laura and Eva, who were initially somewhat upset on hearing the news.

Thanks to this heralded birth, he seemed to believe in a new start. His optimism even led him to forsake his usual secrecy and to tell his friends the news: "I won't be coming to New York this year," he wrote to Annette Insdorf in June 1983, "mainly because I'm expecting a baby; Fanny Ardant won't be coming either and for the same reason! I preferred to tell you in writing before the rumors start spreading."[99] Fanny Ardant wanted a second child, "a quasi-visceral desire," she confided to *Figaro Madame* in the spring of 1981. In this early summer of 1983, she felt happy, fulfilled: "The child that will turn my life upside down,"[100] she said.

In accord with this new life, François Truffaut was poised to embark on a new cycle in his cinematic oeuvre. He was planning to use his two-month vacation in Honfleur to develop future scripts. "He no longer had any projects lined up," confirms Claude de Givray, "he who liked to have three or four scripts in process—one with Gruault, one with Jean-Louis Richard, one with Bernard Revon and me, and also one with Suzanne Schiffman. He had to get the storytelling machine going again."[101] Claude de Givray was invited to come stay in Honfleur. The two men soon had several projects in the works. Two were at a reasonably advanced stage, so much so that Truffaut expected to shoot them back-to-back in the same year, 1985. The first was a remake of *Nez-de-Cuir*, a new adaptation of La Varende's novel that he wanted to film with Fanny Ardant and Gérard Depardieu; the second was *La Petite Voleuse* (*The Little Thief*). "In La Varende's novel, there are two female characters, a twenty-year-old girl and a forty-year-old woman," says Givray. "François wanted them condensed into one, a thirty-year-old woman. He also said to me, 'No hunting scenes!' He felt that nothing could be more boring to film. However, the novel is filled with hunting scenes. . . ."[102]

With Jean Gruault, Truffaut considered adapting *Le Petit Ami,* the autobiographical novel by Paul Léautaud, a writer who fascinated him. Carrosse had acquired the rights to the novel in the spring of 1981 from Mercure de France and had also negotiated permission to use part of the writer's nineteen-volume *Journal littéraire.* Truffaut was also very interested by *Lettre à ma mère*, another autobiographical text by Léautaud. Taken together, these works would allow him to give a complete account of the writer's childhood, in the early part of the century, in the Lorettes neighborhood, and depict his complex relationship with his mother, who had abandoned him when he was very young and whom he saw periodically in his adult years. Of course, though derived from Léautaud, this narrative had an odd resemblance to Truffaut's own childhood, his personal development, his ambiguous relationship with his mother. However, he gave the project up when he learned that Pascal Thomas also intended to make a film based on Léautaud.

Truffaut then turned his attention to another ambitious idea, assigning the writing to Gruault: "oo-14" was the code name of a script about Paris during the *Belle Epoque*—a saga spanning the period between the world's fair at the beginning of the century and the declaration of war in August 1914. The script was to follow four characters and the events of their time and make them meet historical, political, and literary figures. These four characters were the industrialist Louis Renault—a part that would go to Gérard Depardieu; a young anarchist worker who gradually changed camps—Truffaut thought of Jean-Pierre Léaud; Alice, Louis Renault's mistress, played by Fanny Ardant; and Laure, Renault's young wife. Truffaut saw oo-14 as midway between Milos Forman's *Ragtime* and Ingmar Bergman's *Fanny and Alexander*, two works he particularly admired. Truffaut and Gruault gathered abundant research material on the *Belle Epoque* and read a great many biographies, memoirs, and journals; they became fascinated by the assassination of Gaston Calmette, the head of *Le Figaro*, in March 1914, by Henriette Caillaux, the wife of Finance Minister Joseph Caillaux, whom Calmette had slandered in the press. Truffaut and Gruault also acknowledged this project was partially inspired by Proust and they envisioned it as suitable for both film and television.[103] Following in the steps of Bergman's *Fanny and Alexander*, Truffaut wanted this script to be the basis for a three-hour film as well as a multiepisode television series. Indeed, Antenne 2 had virtually approved the project and was on the verge of signing a contract. After *Confidentially Yours!*, with a script he had regarded as weak, Truffaut was determined to take control over his stories again, to write them with pleasure and rigor, thanks to the collaboration of his different screenwriters. His projects were varied, far-ranging, and ambitious, combining a taste for history with an authentic autobiographical thread. Truffaut realized he had found an ideal alter ego in Gérard Depardieu; he wanted to conceive certain projects with him in mind, or as a partner again with Fanny Ardant. According to Depardieu, "Truffaut was done with his past"[104] and ready for a new cycle. He intended to inaugurate it in the coming months, resuming the rhythm of one film a year.

Other projects were in their early stages, like the story of a lady-killer, a Landru figure, a perfume-maker living in Grasse who was both a seducer and a criminal. A variation on the theme of *The Man Who Loved Women*, in which he would cast Guy Marchand, an actor whom he had enjoyed directing in *Such a Gorgeous Kid Like Me* and had liked in Pialat's *Loulou* and Diane Kurys's *Entre Nous*. Truffaut wrote him a little note: "One of these days, I'll bring you a script, but it will be the leading role or nothing. The idea is fomenting in my mind, I'll let it grow and, when the time comes, bingo, on paper, and then in the mail for you to read."[105]

Truffaut had also vowed to take time in Honfleur to update his book of interviews with Alfred Hitchcock, for he wished to establish a definitive edition that would include the director's last films. Between the publication of the book in 1966 and Hitchcock's death in 1980, the director had made *Topaz, Frenzy,* and *Family Plot.* Though Truffaut didn't consider these to be among Hitchcock's best films, he nevertheless wanted to discuss them in a final chapter and write a new preface for the book. His editor, Robert Laffont, had refused to consider the new, expanded edition, so Truffaut succeeded in recovering his rights to the book in March 1981. After several unsuccessful attempts at interesting Gallimard, Flammarion, and Daniel Filipacchi in a new edition, Truffaut followed the advice of René Bonnell, who was then working at Gaumont, which had just bought the Editions Ramsay. He signed a contract with Ramsay on June 30, 1983, just before leaving on vacation.

Truffaut therefore took his research material to Normandy so he could work on this expanded edition: "I wrote a sixteenth chapter 'covering' Hitchcock's last three films and describing the last three years of his life. For me, this version constitutes the definitive edition and I hope that some foreign publishers will use it when they reprint the book,"[106] he wrote to Koichi Yamada, his faithful Japanese friend and correspondent, on August 4. Truffaut had found it painful to write the chapter devoted to the films Hitchcock had made when he was ill. The definitive edition of the Hitchbook came out in November 1983 and sold extremely well.

Truffaut spent several days in Paris, as planned, in the beginning of August 1983 for the opening of *Confidentially Yours!* He attended the preview screening at the Cinémathèque française, where the picture was greeted with enthusiasm.[107] This was a great relief to him, for he had had little faith in it. On the evening of August 10, Laura, whose vacation in France was drawing to an end, accompanied her father to the offices of Gérard Lebovici on rue Keppler. "The results were coming in from each separate movie theater; Everyone was a bit euphoric because the film was doing well and holding its own against *Superman II,* which had opened on the same day,"[108] Laura recalled. Everyone was cheerful. Truffaut was delighted and relieved; Lebovici opened a bottle of champagne. A few hours later, Laura and her father parted; she set off for Berkeley to resume her university studies; he went to join Fanny Ardant again in Honfleur and serenely enjoy the last stretch of their summer vacation.

The following day, Truffaut made his way back to the Clos Saint-Nicolas in Vasouy, at the wheel of his black convertible. On the morning of August

12, Gérard Depardieu was passing through Normandy with his daughter Julie, who was the same age as Fanny Ardant's daughter, Lumir. The two men discussed common projects, *Nez-de-Cuir*, 00-14. On the same day, Truffaut worked until late in the afternoon with Claude de Givray. But at dinner, he suddenly felt faint, "as though a firecracker had exploded in his head,"[109] de Givray recalls. During the night, he threw up some blood. The next day, the physician in Honfleur diagnosed a case of acute sinusitis; his friends attributed this to the fact that Truffaut had driven between Paris and Honfleur with his head exposed to the wind. Three days went by, during which Truffaut talked with his friends, read, and rested. But the headache persisted. Alain Resnais and Florence Malraux made a short trip to Honfleur, for Resnais wanted to see Fanny Ardant, whom he was going to cast in his next film, *Love Unto Death*. In the train going to Trouville, Florence Malraux remembers Resnais saying, "François is such a fulfilled, happy man." Fanny Ardant came to welcome them at the station, alone. "François has been having very bad migraines," she said, "but he is expecting you." The four friends lunched together, but Florence Malraux says that "François was in a bad state"[110] and that a strange cloud hung over the otherwise-harmonious mood of the day, the pretty house, and the soon-to-be-born baby.

On the morning of August 16, still suffering from painful migraines, Truffaut went to the Honfleur medical center. The physician reassured him by prescribing an aggressive treatment against "ophthalmological-type migraine cephalitis."[111] Eight days later, Truffaut consulted an ophthalmologist in Deauville, Dr. Camille Malo. Alarmed by his examination of the back of Truffaut's eye, Dr. Malo immediately sent him to Professor Rozenbaum, at the Caen regional hospital center, specifying that "additional examinations would be advisable in order to establish etiologic certainty."[112] The following day, Dr. Rozenbaum detected "bell-shaped spots"[113] on the right temporal region, the sign of a persistent hematoma. There was the danger of a cerebral hemorrhage, a ruptured aneurysm, or a brain tumor.

While Fanny Ardant closed the vacation house in Honfleur, François Truffaut was transferred at once by ambulance to Paris; at his own request, he was checked into the American Hospital in Neuilly and examined by Professor Bernard Pertuisé, an internationally known neurosurgeon. He underwent an arteriograph under anesthetic. He then remained in the hospital for a week, where he was visited by his family and close friends. After a second scan, on September 3, he was given permission to leave the hospital— "demobilization," as he noted in the daily logbook he kept at the time.[114] He spent the weekend at home, at avenue Pierre 1er-de-Serbie, with his family at his side. On Monday, he was back at the American Hospital, in Professor Planchon's department of nuclear medicine. There, he underwent a "dynamic study by scintigraph camera,"[115] which allowed the brain to be scrutinized with extreme precision. The examination, according to Dr. Planchon's report, allowed the "hypothesis of an underlying aneurysm to be rejected," but it confirmed the presence "of a late diffuse fixation in the right temporal region,"[116] in other words, a brain tumor. Professor Pertuisé decided on an emergency operation. The physicians at the American Hospital tried to reassure Truffaut about his condition. In his letters, Truffaut described "an aneurysm from birth which provoked a cerebral hemorrhage," "an aneurysm that will be lessened by opening my head."[117] The word *tumor* was never mentioned in his presence. But Professor Pertuisé did explain to Madeleine Morgenstern that Truffaut had a malignant tumor, a glioma, in the right frontal region of the brain, which had bled on the evening of August 12 and caused his malaise. The condition was incurable and terminal. François Truffaut had only a few months to live, a year at most.

Before his operation, Truffaut wanted to legally recognize his unborn child, but French law doesn't allow a child to be recognized prior to birth. Truffaut then considered marriage, but time was short. The surgery was scheduled for September 12, and Truffaut had to enter the clinic on the 10th. On the eve of the 10th, in his apartment, he wrote a few letters to friends abroad—Dido Renoir, Leslie Caron, Koichi Yamada in Japan, Robert Fischer in Germany, Richard Roud and Annette Insdorf in the United States. Though these letters were often amusing and full of irony, behind their merry aloofness there lurked a gnawing anxiety. To his "old pal Richard" Roud, Truffaut announced that he was "entering the American Hospital to have my skull opened," and wanted to express to the director of the New York Festival his "gratitude for the almost annual celebration of which I was the beneficiary and you the conductor."[118] To Annette Insdorf, he confided that "he must be operated on for a brain aneurysm," and he added, "film critics were twenty years ahead of official medicine, for, as soon as my second film, *Shoot the Piano Player*, opened, they declared the film couldn't possibly have been made by someone whose brain was functioning normally."[119] He announced to Robert Fischer that he was to undergo "an operation following a vascular accident."[120] Finally to his friend Yamada, he said he was in "good spirits, but should things go wrong, I want to express to you my thanks, my friendship and my desire that you always be my representative-translator-friend-alter-ego—in a word, my Japanese brother. If all goes well, I'll be able to write you again in October, and by then I'll be the father of a small child, the one Fanny Ardant is expecting; goodbye, dear Yamada, see you soon, yes, see you soon, I very much hope so, love François."[121] Truffaut ended each one of his letters with a "soon, I hope" which was not quite his usual style, habitually lighter and less pessimistic.

The operation on September 12 lasted three hours but went exactly as planned. A great many get-well messages awaited him in his room, including those from President François Mitterrand, Dido Renoir, Lillian Gish, and Robert Bresson. Later, Isabelle Adjani wrote him, "I think you think I never think of you and I don't think you ever think of me, so I don't dare send you my thoughts, except to tell you that I've thought about you a great deal these last few days. I very much hope you feel better."[122] One week after his surgery, on September 20, Truffaut was back in his apartment. On the 24th, in a paparazzo photo published "exclusively"[123] in the *France-Soir* weekly supplement, he could be seen coming out of the hospital, looking tired and weak, his head completely shaved, supported by Madeleine Morgenstern and his servant Ahmed. Less than a week later, on September 28, Fanny Ardant gave birth to a baby girl named Joséphine, François Truffaut's third daughter.

OBSERVING SILENCE

After his operation, François Truffaut settled back into his apartment. He was very weak, but he had been told—in somewhat vague terms—that his convalescence would be brief, as is indicated in Dr. Pertuisé's first letter to him, on the very day of his release from the hospital: "Don't forget that in medicine prediction is uncertain. Make a great film for us very soon. . . ."[124] In fact, the true gravity of his condition was never alluded to in his presence.

In the eighties, in France, cancer was still poorly understood, the word itself was still taboo, and obituaries usually made use of a conventional phrase, "died after a long illness." Truffaut himself seemed not to want to know the truth. And most of his immediate entourage, even Fanny Ardant, were not aware of just how seriously ill he was. With this kind of tumor, radiation treatment can add a few months to a patient's life, but remission is impossible. Truffaut, who had made a good recovery from his operation, was in less pain than before. His tumor was in the frontal cortex; it affected neither his language function nor his memory; however, he tired easily and had difficulty concentrating. He seemed more relaxed, and he joked with his daughters and friends. His mood darkened only when he was alone.

In November, Madeleine decided to share her secret. The first person in whom she confided and told the physicians' diagnosis was Marcel Berbert. She also confided in Laura and Eva. Several weeks later, in January 1984, she was invited for dinner at the home of Lucette and Claude de Givray in Puteaux. De Givray had just been asked to direct a television film, with the actress Nicole Courcel; he hesitated to accept the offer, since he had previous scriptwriting commitments with Truffaut. Madeleine took him aside and told him the truth: "Claude, you shouldn't turn down any work. François has terminal cancer. . . ."[125]

The Carrosse family rallied around Truffaut during his illness, protected him from rumors, and had orders not to breathe a word outside their circle. Josiane Couëdel transmitted the same message to all the countless people who phoned the office to ask after the director's health: "François had a ruptured aneurysm, his operation went well; he is now convalescing. . . ." More than ever, the Carrosse family mobilized and maintained its protective role toward Truffaut, but not without pain. "François, my only remorse is that, for a year, I watched you slowly sink into suffering without having the courage to live up to my old threat from the days when you used to get too much on my nerves: to knock you over the head with your Oscar!"[126] Josiane Couëdel would say after Truffaut's death.

"Fanny didn't yet know the truth, nor Jean-Pierre Léaud, nor Helen Scott, since François himself didn't know!"[127] says Claude de Givray. His very close friends—Suzanne Schiffman, Jean Aurel, Jean Gruault, Jean-Louis Richard, and Janine Bazin—asked after him regularly. Some of them knew the truth; most did not.

In the meantime, Truffaut showed forethought and, on the advice of Georges Kiejman, consulted a lawyer, who urged him to prepare for any eventuality. Every morning, at around eleven, Marcel Berbert—who had retired in 1982—came by the apartment on avenue Pierre 1er-de-Serbie to take notes for the drafting of Truffaut's last will and testament, a task that kept the director busy until Christmas 1983. "The document is very specific in its instructions; everything had to be clear,"[128] Madeleine recalls. Truffaut requested that Les Films du Carrosse cease all production activities and put Madeleine Morgenstern in charge of the future distribution of his films.

In December, Truffaut was so weak that he was unable to work. "Given the state I'm in, I'd no sooner step off the night train than I'd melt in the snow and disappear before having time to utter the master's name: 'Alfredd . . .'"[129] he wrote the director of the Avoriaz festival, who had invited him to a Hitchcock tribute. The prognosis now stressed the long term: "Everyone tells me to expect a three-year convalescence, of which only the first year is really confining."[130] Truffaut had to cancel his plans, such as presenting *Confidentially Yours!* at the British Film Institute in London, and activities tied to the promotion of his Hitchcock interview book. Knowing it would be some time before he would get around to making a new film, he decided to restore the uncut version of *Two English Girls,* a project that had been on his mind since the spring of 1983. He assigned the task to Martine Barraqué, his editor, who spliced back the scenes that had been cut in 1971, at the time of the film's release. Now restored to its original 132 minutes, *Two English Girls* was ready for a new commercial release; it would be his film for 1984.

François Truffaut gradually started working again. Madeleine encouraged him, as did all his close friends—Claude de Givray, Gérard Depardieu, Jean-Louis Livi, and Serge Rousseau. The screenplay of *La Petite Voleuse* was unfinished, but Truffaut felt that the material, as it was, was completely satisfactory and ready to be filmed. He even asked Serge Rousseau to find a young actress for the lead. Truffaut wanted everything to be ready for a shoot sometime in 1985, as soon as he would be sufficiently recovered. In the meantime, he resumed work on the script of *Nez-de-Cuir* with Claude de Givray, though less intensively than the preceding summer in Honfleur. Gérard Depardieu, who had visited Truffaut repeatedly at the American Hospital in September 1983, did everything to encourage him: "I said to François, 'Nez-de-Cuir has a hole in his mug, you have a hole in your head, we're doing well!' "[131] Depardieu continued to think about *Nez-de-Cuir* even when he was far from Paris, on the set of Alain Courneau's *Fort Saganne* in the Mauritanian desert, acting in a part that Truffaut had strongly urged him to accept: "You should play the part of a military man, like Gabin in *Gueule d'amour!*"[132] The actor even devised an original way of conveying his feelings to Truffaut: He recorded his impressions of the shoot on a cassette, which he gave to Jean-Louis Livi, who had come to see him in Mauritania, to give to Truffaut. He wrote him concerning the film they planned to shoot together: "Thank you, François, for your support and for taking on this romantic gentleman who has me daydreaming. Seen from here, I'm deeply moved and I feel it will be so strong, simple, funny and dignified. . . . Excuse me, Fanny, you know I don't always have words at my command. I prefer to think about the two of you, the three of you now, and about us later. I love you, you make me feel good."[133]

In the weeks following his release from the hospital, it was easiest for Truffaut to return to his own apartment; he gave up the idea of moving into a large apartment near Passy with Fanny Ardant. Fanny came every day, so he could see his little girl. But that year, the actress had a great deal of work. Two months after Joséphine's birth, she replaced Isabelle Adjani on short notice in Strindberg's *Miss Julie,* opposite Niels Arestrup. In spite of fatigue from his radiation sessions, Truffaut attended a performance of the play, and he was happy and proud of Fanny's triumph. Immediately thereafter, in February 1984, she went to work in Uzès, in the Cévennes, on Alain Resnais's film *Love Unto Death,* followed by Nadine Trintignant's film, *L'Eté prochain.* Madeleine Morgenstern went to the apartment on avenue Pierre 1er-de-Serbie every day to see Truffaut and attended to all practical matters. Dusk was the most difficult hour for him, a time when he was gripped by intense angst. "I was there to help him get through the nightfall,"[134] says Madeleine, who got into the habit of staying until dinner. At around nine, after watching television, Truffaut would fall asleep, a refuge and escape from exhaustion and anguish. His daughters Laura and Eva were also by his side, Laura having returned from Berkeley to spend Christmas 1983 with her family. Her memory of first seeing her ailing father is still painful: "He wasn't the same man; he was smaller, gray; the physical change was enormous." Laura arranged to stay almost a month in Paris to be near her father for as long as possible. "I lived that period like an egoist, for he was there, available, because of the illness. We had long conversations; he was almost my hostage,"[135] she recalls.

LIFE REGARDLESS

At the beginning of 1984, Truffaut seemed to regain some strength. At the end of January, he spent a few days at the Colombe d'Or in Saint-Paul-de-Vence with Fanny Ardant. He regained some weight, got back some color; he could even drive his car and go to the movies and the theater with Fanny. He liked Fellini's *And the Ship Sails On*, Gérard Mordillat's *Vive la sociale*, and Woody Allen's *Zelig*. Filled with hope, he ordered a Mercedes convertible for the fine weather ahead. It was as if he wanted to ward off the rumor spreading in Paris.

On the occasion of the rerelease of five Hitchcock films in Paris and the simultaneous publication of the new edition of his interview book, Truffaut was the guest on February 12, 1984, of the RTL radio show, "Journal inattendu," and was interviewed at length by Philippe Labro. "I was very insistent that he come," Labro admits, "and no doubt François wanted to prove he could come to the broadcast."[136] After discussing Hitchcock at length, Truffaut signed off by giving news of his health. There again, the "official" version was far from the medical truth—to wit, the following dialogue between Labro and Truffaut at the very end of the broadcast:

I know you were somewhat ill; this is the first time you've spoken publicly in a long time.

I was actually very ill, since I underwent a brain operation. But in consolation I told myself that the film critics—you know, when you're in this business you often blame film critics—that the film critics were twenty years ahead of official medicine, since, when I released my second film, Shoot the Piano Player, *twenty years ago, some critics wondered whether my brain worked properly. Now that my brain's been operated on, maybe I'll be able to make films that will be more to their liking.*

RTL listeners hold you very dear and it's been ages since they've

*had any worries about the way your brain works. And I hope to see
you beating the path back to the studios.*

Truffaut spent time in his office at Les Films du Carrosse again. He wrote
to his friends and recovered his taste for cigars. "I narrowly missed the great
crossing: a brain hemorrhage," he wrote to Liliane Siegel in February 1984.
"I have questioned some people who have had the same experience. The first
year is difficult, very difficult, you think you'll never make it. The second
year, work resumes, you regain your strength. The third year, you're out of
danger (almost). So I'm waiting and I'm prudent, in bed at nine almost every
night, plenty of sleep and naps, not just half a work schedule but a quarter
schedule. That's my diminished life, the life I'm leading at present."[137]
François Truffaut continued to believe in his recovery, and in this he was
encouraged by the case of his Japanese friend, Koichi Yamada, who had
recovered from an operation on his cerebellum in 1969, following a ruptured
aneurysm. Indeed, this experience strengthened the bond between the two
men, regardless of the geographical distance that separated them. Truffaut
resolved that from now on, out of both friendship and superstition, he would
give his "Japanese alter ego" the gift of a plane ticket every year. Three
months after his visit to Paris in June 1983, having learned of Truffaut's brain
operation, Yamada wrote to the man he admired most in the world: "I imagine you must feel a world of emotions after your operation. Let my friendship
reassure you: we are brothers in this kind of trial, since, you might remember,
I underwent exactly the same operation fourteen years ago. And you'll agree
that no trace of it remains either physically or mentally!"[138] The two men saw
each other one last time in Paris, from June 20 to 27, 1984, when Truffaut
received Yamada at his home. "I was unbelievably moved to see you, if not in
perfect health, at least well on the way," his Japanese friend wrote him on his
return to Tokyo. "You looked rather tired, but, confident from my personal
experience, I can tell you that it will only be a passing state and that the only
important thing is to be as patient as possible."[139]

Truffaut wished to show such confidence in broad daylight. On March 4,
1984, he therefore decided to attend the César ceremony at the Théâtre de
l'Empire, after he had been talked into it by his friend Claude Berri, whose
film *Tchao Pantin* had a good chance of winning some prizes. Fanny Ardant
had received a best-actress nomination for her performance in *Confidentially Yours!* and Truffaut was by her side during the award ceremony. He
also handed Maurice Pialat the César for best film for *A Nos Amours*. The
two men, who had known each other for many years,[140] embraced, and it was
a truly moving moment. Truffaut seemed cheerful that evening and many
people believed he was on the road to recovery. He later dined at Fouquet's
with Fanny Ardant and Isabelle Adjani, who wrote him a warm note the fol-

lowing day: "I was moved to see you, you looked both tired and happy. Life is so wonderful when one has been really ill. You had such tender gazes yesterday evening. I love you and admire you always and forever."[141]

On the day after the Césars, the press felt entitled to announce the return of François Truffaut: HE IS ACTIVELY RESUMING WORK was the *France-Soir* headline. "Truffaut is directing again: a film recounting the adventures of a little girl right after the war," ventured the magazine *Première*. In March, Truffaut spent a few days again at the Colombe d'Or, this time with Madeleine and their friends Serge Rousseau and Marie Dubois. This was right after the murder of Gérard Lebovici, on March 3, 1984, in a Champs-Elysées parking area. Truffaut and Rousseau were very attached to Lebovici, each for his own reasons. Truffaut trusted the man completely, was impressed by his intelligence and culture, and was fascinated by his double life as a public man in film and a politically committed publisher of Guy Debord and the situationists. As for Rousseau, he had worked with Lebovici at Artmédia for about twenty years. March 13 was Serge Rousseau's birthday. At the Colombe d'Or, Marie Dubois asked Truffaut, "Should we do something for Serge's birthday?" And, she says, "François had this marvelous reply, 'But life goes on!' "

In mid-April, Truffaut inaugurated a movie theater bearing his name in Romilly-sur-Seine, in the Aube; Marcel Carné was also present, for another theater was dedicated in his name. Truffaut was surrounded by Marie Dubois, Brigitte Fossey, Macha Méril, Jean-Pierre Léaud, and André Dussollier. He participated in Bernard Pivot's literary talk show, *Apostrophes,* on a night when it was devoted to cinema, and talked about the new edition of his Hitchcock interview book. With him were Roman Polanski, who had just published his memoirs, Marcello Mastroianni, who talked about his friend Fellini, and the daughter of Suso Cecchi d'Amico, Visconti's screenwriter. Frequently called upon by Pivot, Truffaut told many anecdotes about Hitchcock, including the famous episode of their first meeting at the Joinville Studios, when Chabrol and he fell into a pool of freezing water. For all those who were seeing him for the first time in months, the man's intense effort to overcome his physical weakness and transmit the ardor and clarity of his ideas was deeply moving.

THE DIMINISHED LIFE

Truffaut's follow-up brain scan at the end of April 1984 was hardly cause for optimism. Stronger doses of cortisone would have to be administered, which meant he would have to rest over the summer and avoid travel. But he still wanted to believe in recovery. Nor did he give up the idea of making *Nez-de-*

Cuir. With this in mind, he arranged for a screening of the Yves Allégret version with Jean Marais, at the Cinémathèque française on May 25, 1984. Truffaut had invited cinematographer Nestor Almendros, Gérard Depardieu, Marcel Berbert, and Jean-Louis Livi, who had been assigned the task of negotiating the rights to the book. What he liked about the La Varende novel was the opportunity to rework the theme of *The Man Who Loved Women,* but in an entirely different context. A soldier returns from the Napoléonic wars completely disfigured, his face mauled. He assumes his life as a seducer is over; but the exact opposite happens: His leather nose becomes a fetishistic element that helps him seduce women. At the end of the screening, as they climbed up the stairs of the Cinémathèque, Gérard Depardieu had no real illusions: "François was already very weak. I remember everyone had already left; I was there, about to put on my motorcycle helmet. François was at the bottom of the Cinémathèque steps. He looked at me and pulled down his hat, but too far down, to just above his eyes, without realizing it. It was a dreadful sight! That's when I really saw the disease; I understood that he didn't really feel things anymore. That's actually the last image I have of him, because I didn't want to go see him at home; I preferred to phone him."[142]

In June, Truffaut spent his days in his room, in peace and quiet. He made some summer plans, including spending a holiday in Brittany with Fanny Ardant and little Joséphine. Ardant had asked Claude de Givray to accompany her to the region around Roscoff to find a house to rent. But Truffaut could no longer travel. It was then that Fanny learned the truth. "Me, whose life has always been organized around a schedule," he said to Serge Toubiana, "this is the first time I'm living in uncertainty, I'm no longer in command of my time," Truffaut confided at the time. Many of his friends were struck by his melancholy, as Jean-Claude Brialy put it: "François said to me: 'I'm getting used to the idea of death,' and the look in his eyes had become sad."[143] This state of mind did not dampen his determination to face up to the ordeal; and in his case, facing up meant keeping his sense of humor to the end: "The last time I saw him," said Jean-Louis Richard, "I asked him if I could do something for him. He was suffering at that moment and he said to me, 'Lend me your gun, I'll return it tomorrow.' And he burst into giggles. He laughed just like the two of us used to in the old days."[144]

He did have one last project, however: to summon whatever strength he still had to recount the story of his life and write his autobiography. This was a desire he had already confessed to his friend Annette Insdorf a few years earlier: "I'll open my files when the doctors forbid me to make films and I'll start writing my memoirs."[145] That day had now arrived, and this was an added reason why he wanted to see his oldest friends again, to refresh his memories of youth. He got back together with Robert Lachenay, his oldest friend and playmate. "Did we meet in '43 or '44?" Truffaut wrote him. "I'm opting for

October '43, when I was eleven. . . . These days my thoughts often turn to the past. Our common experience belongs to that period in life one never forgets, adolescence and the formative years. Everything related to that period is part of chemical memory, I think that's what biologists call it. In other words, should we become more or less senile, the only memories forever fresh and lively that will always stream before our eyes, like a film edited in a 'loop,' will be those that stretch from Barbès to Clichy, Abesses to Notre-Dame-de-Lorette, the Delta Ciné-club to the Champollion theater. . . ."[146]

Truffaut decided to put his archives in order, those numerous files that he had methodically kept since his youth. He reimmersed himself in his childhood and reread dozens of documents, letters, and intimate journals. In view of this projected autobiography—which he deeply cared about and which would primarily deal with the "critical years" in his life—he contacted a publisher. "In the life I now lead as a convalescent, my thoughts often turn to my childhood and youth, the thirties, forties, fifties," Truffaut wrote on July 6, 1984, to Charles Ronsac at Robert Laffont. "I don't know what cinema—or my health—have in store for me in the future, but I'm considering dusting off my portable typewriter and attempting an autobiography, entitled *Le Scénario de ma vie* (or *The Script of My Life*). What do you think of this idea, you who were just about the first person to have suggested it to me six or seven years ago?"[147] Charles Ronsac assured him he was interested in this manuscript, which would never see the light of day.

Truffaut had been unable to concentrate well enough to write. He had tried another approach—a series of taped interviews with Claude de Givray. The latter encouraged him, pointing to the example of *Fellini by Fellini*, which had just hit the bookstores. The interview sessions lasted for two afternoons, with pauses, for Truffaut had to recover from the fatigue provoked by the rush of memories. At the end of the last recording, made in June 1984, there is this exchange with Claude de Givray:

> *The excuse, at school after you played hooky, "My mother died,"*
> *which comes from Alphonse Daudet and which you put in* The 400
> Blows, *you didn't actually use that excuse in real life?*
> *Yes I did, I did use it. It was in 1943.*

Then the tape was interrupted, leaving *The Script of My Life* unfinished.

THE FAREWELL CEREMONY

On July 10, 1984, a new brain scan showed that the tumor had spread. The press even announced "François Truffaut's hospitalization," an erroneous news item picked up on the TF1 evening news on July 16 and on Europe 1 on the morning of the 17th. Get-well messages began to stream into Les Films du Carrosse from everywhere, from artists, actors, directors, and many ordinary filmgoers. Other letters, from family and close friends, were sent directly to Truffaut. "I'm thinking of you all the time," said Floriana Lebovici. "I'm writing you what Gérard would have said to you: don't give up the fight, struggle with all your might. There are many alternate treatments, don't neglect them. You must try everything, absolutely everything, to the end. But really, above all, don't be defeated. Life is so strong for you and you have so much to do."[148]

With the onset of summer, changes had to be made in organizing Truffaut's daily life. Ahmed, his majordomo, would be absent from Paris for five weeks, and Fanny Ardant was starting work on a film with Nadine Trintignant. Since he couldn't remain home alone, Truffaut moved in with Madeleine Morgenstern, at rue du Conseiller Collignon. There he had frequent, thoughtful visits from his doctor, Jacques Chassigneux, whose moral support and deep humanity were of great help. In the absence of Professor Pertuisé, he was referred, thanks to Catherine Deneuve, to Professor Aron for a consultation about his eyesight, which had considerably altered. Laura, who was in France at the time, kept her father company and spent many long hours by his side. "François slept a great deal," says Madeleine Morgenstern, "but when friends came to see him, he was very brilliant, he laughed, and was lively and funny; visits stimulated him."[149] Fanny Ardant came to see him whenever she could get away from her work on the set. During the entire summer, a procession of friends dropped by, day after day: Dido Renoir, Jean Aurel, Alain Vannier, Claude de Givray, Suzanne Schiffman, Serge Rousseau, as well as Claude Berri and Milos Forman, who was visiting Paris for the opening of *Amadeus*. The three men shared a long-standing friendship, and they discussed Forman's new film, of course. In his eagerness to please Truffaut, Berri was prepared to do anything to make it possible for him to attend a private screening of *Amadeus*. "François so wanted to see the film that I said to Madeleine, 'Let him come in pajamas; we'll drive the car into the courtyard and François will only have to walk a few steps!' "[150] But Truffaut had no strength left. On the following day, Jean-Pierre Léaud stopped by the apartment on rue du Conseiller Collignon. Liliane Siegel remembers meeting Léaud not far from her house, wandering distraught down the boulevard Raspail: "I said to him, 'You look upset!' and Jean-Pierre answered, 'François is dying! He is very sick and is dying. . . .' "[151] Roland Truffaut stopped by to see François; he was, as Madeleine Morgenstern put it, "unhappy and dismayed." The conversation between father and son was slightly awkward, even though, deep down, Truffaut never really had any resentment toward Roland. In the beginning of September, he had visits from Jeanne Moreau,

Catherine Deneuve, Claude Miller, Marcel Ophuls, and Leslie Caron, and, at a later date, from Jean-José Richer, as well as Pierre Hebey and Anne François, who were working on the release of *Two English Girls.*

But the afternoons were long in these final days of the Parisian summer. Truffaut had difficulty walking; his headaches sometimes made him gloomy and silent. He didn't complain, but his anguish was increasingly pronounced. "My present vegetable state is degrading," he wrote to Liliane Siegel. "There's an enormous fatigue that begins after breakfast and sends me back to bed or to the corner of a window. This is bearable only by setting small goals, important dates, the birthday of one of my daughters, the visit of a faraway friend, the publication of such and such a book. Autumn is the next goal. Such is the state of my slow brain, dear Liliane."[152] The creator of *The Green Room,* fascinated by this crossing, was preparing to die. Most of his interests, visions, and readings concerned death. He discussed Sartre's death at length with Liliane Siegel. Simone de Beauvoir's *La Cérémonie des adieux* (in English, the book is entitled *Adieux: A Farewell to Sartre*), which recounts Sartre's last years, became his bedside book. "It was by reading Sartre and Beauvoir that he tried to prepare for death, to find a meaning for the end of his life,"[153] said Claude de Givray. Truffaut also read Painter's biography of Proust. In the correspondence between Proust and Madame Strauss, which was being issued at that time, he noted the passage where the dead are referred to as "so much more numerous than the living." His few hours of concentration were divided among reading, visits from his closest friends, and the screening of films on videocassette—films by Chaplin, Lubitsch, Renoir, Bresson, and Becker.

During the summer, François Truffaut told Madeleine Morgenstern he wished to be buried in the Montmartre cemetery. He also asked to see Father Mambrino, the Jesuit priest and film enthusiast who had been André Bazin's friend. When Jean Mambrino went to see him at Madeleine's, he thought Truffaut wanted to make his final confession. In fact, Truffaut questioned him about the next life. Madeleine recalls hearing the two men laugh. After Mambrino's departure, François said to Madeleine, "He knows no more than anyone else!"[154]

Claude Berri and Robert Lachenay would be his last visitors, on September 19. "In his bed, François looked like Sacha Guitry, in the picture—one of the last—where you see him editing a film," says Lachenay. "We talked about literature, like in the good old days. . . . Even on his deathbed, François was the same, merry, still forever joking. . . . When it was time to leave, he got up to walk me to the door. On the landing, I realized I wouldn't see him again, that this was the last time. . . . And, for the first time in forty years of friendship, we embraced. . . ."[155]

On the afternoon of September 28, François Truffaut returned to the

American Hospital, for his condition had suddenly worsened. He remained in the hospital for the last three weeks of his life, and he suffered a painful death. Fanny and Madeleine were by his bedside, and they were soon joined by Laura and Eva. He died on October 21, 1984, at 2:30 p.m.

As he had requested, he was cremated at the Père-Lachaise crematorium on October 24 and his ashes buried in the Montmartre cemetery. Thousands of people—first and foremost, his family, the women he had loved, his friends, actors, and film lovers—attended his burial under a splendid autumn sun. As had been Truffaut's wish, Claude de Givray and Serge Rousseau spoke a few words by his graveside. De Givray had first thought of using Sartre's famous line, "Any man who feels he is indispensible is a bastard!"—a line often uttered by Truffaut, who was aware of his fame but feared being too self-important in the eyes of his friends. In the hearse, de Givray scribbled down some notes on a piece of paper, taking inspiration from the Frank Capra film that Truffaut very much liked, *It's a Wonderful Life*. James Stewart plays a generous man who is saved from suicide by a guardian angel named Clarence, who lets him briefly visit a world where he wouldn't have existed; he is shown what the lives of his dear ones would have been like if he had not been born. And so it was that the friend delivered a fittingly cinema-inspired oration to the crowd gathered around the director's grave: "If François had not been born, if he had not been a director . . ."

One month later, on November 21, 1984, a Mass was celebrated at the church of Saint-Roch by the priest of the Artists' parish and by Father Mambrino. This had been Truffaut's wish; the ceremony had doubtless been discussed during that last interview with the Jesuit father at rue du Conseiller Collignon. Though a nonbeliever, Truffaut wasn't opposed to the ritual of a church benediction. And the church of Saint-Roch was associated in his mind with the yearly anniversary Mass celebrated every October in memory of Jean Cocteau. As in the scene in *The Green Room* where Julien Davenne, played by François Truffaut, celebrates the cult of the dead, hundreds of candles burned in the nave of Saint-Roch, creating a veritable forest of light.

NOTES

1.
A CLANDESTINE CHILDHOOD:
1932–1946

1. Birth certificate, town hall of the seventeenth arrondissement, number BL/178.
2. *Livret de famille* (family record book of the Truffauts), archives of Les Films du Carrosse, file "Archives très privées [very private archives] 1."
3. Interview with the authors, 1995.
4. Letter from Suzanne de Saint-Martin to François Truffaut, July 11, 1968, archives of Les Films du Carrosse, file "Archives très privées 1."
5. Claude de Givray's interview of François Truffaut, June 1984, archives of Les Films du Carrosse, pp. 22–23. These were taped interviews made in June 1984, when Truffaut was already very ill. He never had the time or strength to reread these interviews, as opposed to all the other interviews he gave, which he always corrected and reworked with great care. Hence their extremely chatty tone.
6. Archives of Les Films du Carrosse, file "Ma Vie [My Life] 2."

7. Salary statements of the Truffauts, archives of Les Films du Carrosse, file "Archives très privées 1."
8. Letter from Denise Dehousse to François Truffaut, May 13 1959, archives of Les Films du Carrosse, file "Ma Vie 1."
9. Letter from Henry Moins to François Truffaut, undated, archives of Les Films du Carrosse, file "Ma Vie 1."
10. Archives of Les Films du Carrosse, file "Archives très privées 1."
11. Subsequently, after nearly drowning in a kayak, François Truffaut developed a permanent loathing for water.
12. Archives of Les Films du Carrosse, file "Ma Vie 1."
13. Archives of Les Films du Carrosse, file "Archives très privées 1."
14. Ibid.
15. Truffaut/de Givray interview, archives of Les Films du Carrosse, p. 23.
16. Ibid., p. 24.
17. Ibid., p. 16.
18. Note for the project "Le scénario de ma vie [The Script of My Life]," archives of Les Films du Carrosse, file "Ma Vie 1."

19. Truffaut/de Givray interview, archives of Les Films du Carrosse, pp. 18–19.

20. Robert Lachenay quoted in *Le Roman de François Truffaut*, special issue of *Cahiers du cinéma*, December 1984, p. 19.

21. Truffaut/de Givray interview, archives of Les Films du Carrosse, p. 17.

22. Ibid., p. 16.

23. Ibid.

24. Ibid., p. 13.

25. Roland Truffaud, *Du Kenya au Kilimanjaro:* Expédition française au Kenya, 1952 (Paris: Julliard, 1953), p. 243.

26. Truffaut/de Givray interview, archives of Les Films du Carrosse, pp. 37–38.

27. Letter from Janine Truffaut to her brother, Bernard, undated, archives of Les Films du Carrosse, file "Ma Vie 1."

28. Archives of Les Films du Carrosse, file "Archives très privées 1."

29. The reason he did not take the exam is given in a letter written by Truffaut, quoted on pages 300–301. Clearly, the young Truffaut maintained a tremendous grudge against his parents for this mistake, which he considered a major cause of his failure at school.

30. Truffaut/de Givray interview, archives of Les Films du Carrosse, pp. 8–9.

31. Ibid., p. 9.

32. Ibid., pp. 30–31.

33. Ibid., pp. 39, 65.

34. Ibid., pp. 9–10.

35. Robert Lachenay quoted in *Le Roman de François Truffaut*, p. 15.

36. Monsieur Lachenay paid dearly for this position and these material advantages at the time of the Liberation. He was found guilty of collaboration and black-marketeering and incarcerated. He died in a military prison in the immediate postwar period.

37. Letter included in *François Truffaut: Correspondance* (Paris: Hatier, 1988), p. 20; U.S. edition: François Truffaut, *Correspondence 1945–1984*, trans. Gilbert Adair (New York: Noonday Press, 1988).

38. Claude Vega quoted in *Le Roman de François Truffaut*, p. 21.

39. Truffaut/de Givray interview, archives of Les Films du Carrosse, pp. 10–11.

40. Ibid., p. 11.

41. Ibid., p. 56.

42. Ibid., p. 15.

43. Robert Lachenay quoted in *Le Roman de François Truffaut*, p. 15.

44. Truffaut, *Correspondance*, pp. 20–22.

45. Jean Gruault, *Ce que dit l'autre* (Paris: Julliard, 1992), pp. 276–277.

46. François Truffaut, *Les Films de ma vie* (Paris: Flammarion, 1975), p. 15; U.S. edition: *The Films in My Life*, trans. Leonard Mayhew (New York: Simon and Schuster, 1978). This expression is also used by Eric Rohmer to designate the "film enthusiast period" in his life; see *Le Roman de François Truffaut*, p. 17.

47. Truffaut/de Givray interview, archives of Les Films du Carrosse, p. 19.

48. Ibid., p. 20.

49. Ibid., p. 32.

50. Truffaut often used to refer to Jacques Siclier's book, *La France de Pétain et son cinéma* (Paris: Veyrier, 1981): "Thanks to Siclier's thick book, which is remarkable, it's very easy for me to know all the films I saw during the war. He's the only guy to have seen the 200 films of the period. Me, I didn't see 200, but I must have seen a third or half and they're all in the book." Truffaut/de Givray interview, archives of Les Films du Carrosse, p. 20.

51. Truffaut, *The Films in My Life*, pp. 3–4.

52. Truffaut/de Givray interview, archives of Les Films du Carrosse, p. 21.

53. Ibid., p. 43.

54. Ibid., p. 44.

55. Ibid., p. 45.

56. Ibid., p. 43.

57. Ibid., p. 53.

58. Ibid., pp. 53–54.

59. Ibid., pp. 54–55.

60. Ibid., p. 55.

61. Ibid., p. 7.

62. In *The Last Métro*, this is the scene where the character Bernard Granger witnesses the arrest of a Resistance fighter with whom he has an appointment.

63. Truffaut/de Givray interview, archives of Les Films du Carrosse, p. 23.

64. Ibid., p. 27.

65. Archives of Les Films du Carrosse, file "Archives très privées 1."

66. Archives of Les Films du Carrosse, file "Ma Vie 1."

2.
FOUR HUNDRED BLOWS:
1946–1952

1. This is according to Robert Lachenay, in *Le Roman de François Truffaut,* special issue of *Cahiers du cinéma,* December 1984, p. 16.

2. François Truffaut, "Sacha Guitry cinéaste," in Sacha Guitry, *Le Cinéma et moi* (Paris: Ramsay, 1977), pp. 19–20.

3. François Truffaut's journal from August 21, 1951 to May 31, 1952, archives of Les Films du Carrosse, file "Ma Vie 2," p. 56.

4. Truffaut/de Givray interview, archives of Les Films du Carrosse, p. 30.

5. Archives of Les Films du Carrosse, file "Ma Vie 1."

6. Robert Lachenay quoted in *Le Roman de François Truffaut,* p. 16.

7. Archives of Les Films du Carrosse, file "Ma Vie 1."

8. *François Truffaut. Correspondance* (Paris: Hatier, 1988), p. 25.

9. "André Bazin, l'Occupation et moi," in André Bazin, *Le Cinéma de l'Occupation et de la Résistance* (Paris: U.G.E., 1975), pp. 20–21. U.S. edition: *French Cinema of the Occupation and Resistance: The Birth of a Critical Esthetic;* trans. Stanley Hochman (New York: Ungar, 1981). Preface by François Truffaut.

10. Archives of Les Films du Carrosse, file "Ma Vie 1."

11. Ibid.

12. Truffaut/de Givray interview, archives of Les Films du Carrosse, p. 40.

13. Jean-Charles Tacchella quoted in *Le Roman de François Truffaut,* pp. 22–23.

14. *Libération,* December 30, 1948.

15. Truffaut/de Givray interview, archives of Les Films du Carrosse, p. 41.

16. A selection of articles from the *Revue du cinéma* can be found in the 1992 book *Anthologie* (introduction by Antoine de Baecque), published by Gallimard in its series "Tel": *La Revue du cinéma. Anthologie.* A facsimile edition of the *Revue du cinéma* was issued in 1979 by éditions Pierre Lherminier, edited by Odette and Alain Virmaux.

17. Truffaut/de Givray interview, archives of Les Films du Carrosse, p. 41.

18. Ibid.

19. Ibid., p. 42.

20. The discovery of American cinema by enraptured Parisian movie buffs in the postwar period was well described by two witnesses: Jean-Charles Tacchella and Roger Thérond, *Les Années éblouissantes. Le cinéma qu'on aime: 1945–1952* (Paris: Filipacchi, 1988).

21. *Bulletin du Ciné-Club du Quartier Latin,* April 1950.

22. "Citizen Kane: The Fragile Giant," in François Truffaut, *The Films in My Life,* trans. Leonard Mayhew (New York: Simon and Schuster, 1978), pp. 279–280.

23. André Bazin, "Pour en finir avec le profondeur de champ," *Cahiers du cinéma* no. 1 (April 1951).

24. Archives of Les Films du Carrosse, file "Archives très privées 1."

25. In Rouen, Jacques Enfer founded a small magazine in 1950 entitled *Les Cahiers du cinéma.* Since Jacques Doniol-Valcroze had come up with the same title for the magazine he wanted to start with André Bazin and Lo Duca, he had to negotiate with Jacques Enfer to buy the title before publishing the first issue of *Cahiers du cinéma* in April 1951.

26. Dudley Andrew, *André Bazin* (Paris: Editions de l'Etoile, 1983); preface by François Truffaut. U.S. edition: (New York: Oxford University Press, 1978).

27. Archives of Les Films du Carrosse, file "Archives très privées 1."

28. Robert Lachenay quoted in *Le Roman de François Truffaut,* p. 16.

29. Archives of Les Films du Carrosse, file "Archives très privées 1."

30. Ibid.

31. Ibid.

32. Ibid.

33. Ibid.

34. Archives of Les Films du Carrosse, file "Ma Vie 1."

35. Archives of Les Films du Carrosse, file "Archives très privées 1."

36. Ibid.

37. Ibid.

38. Ibid.

39. Ibid.

40. Ibid.

41. Minutes from the clerk's office of the justice of the peace in the ninth

arrondissement of Paris, file "Paul Martin, juge de Paix."

42. Archives of Les Films du Carrosse, file "Ma Vie 1."

43. Archives of Les Films du Carrosse, file "Archives très privées 1."

44. Ibid.

45. Louis Daquin, "Remarques déplacées," *L'Ecran français*, March 8, 1949.

46. Archives of Les Films du Carrosse, file "Ma Vie 1"; published in Truffaut, *Correspondance*, p. 32.

47. Ibid.

48. Antoine de Baecque, *Les Cahiers du cinéma: Histoire d'une revue,* vol. 1, (Paris: Editions de l'Etoile, 1991), pp. 221–222.

49. Charles Bitsch quoted in *Le Roman de François Truffaut,* p. 48.

50. Claude Chabrol, *Et pourtant je tourne* (Paris: Robert Laffont, 1976), p. 109.

51. Jean Douchet, *Artpress,* special issue on Jean-Luc Godard, January–February 1985, p. 70.

52. On the Parisian love of movies in the postwar period, see the published proceedings (eds. Antoine de Baecque and Thierry Frémaux) of the colloquium L'Invention d'une culture: Une histoire de la cinéphilie (1895–1995), Actes Sud/Institut Lumière, 1997.

53. Claude Chabrol quoted in *Le Roman de François Truffaut,* p. 38.

54. Jean Gruault, *Ce que dit l'autre* (Paris: Julliard, 1992), pp. 143–144.

55. Truffaut mentioned that his first critical essays were written in 1948 for *Cités,* the magazine edited by Jacques Enfer, but no trace of these can be found. On the other hand, in the file "Ma Vie 1" in the archives of Les Films du Carrosse, there is a fiction project entitled *Références,* which might well be François Truffaut's first piece of writing.

56. Archives of Les Films du Carrosse, file "Ma Vie 1."

57. Gruault, *Ce que dit l'autre,* pp. 147–151.

58. Truffaut's journal, p. 14.

59. Ibid., p. 15.

60. Archives of Les Films du Carrosse, file "Archives très privées 1."

61. Archives of Les Films du Carrosse, file "Ma Vie 2."

62. Ibid.

63. Archives of Les Films du Carrosse, file "Ma Vie 1."

64. Ibid.

65. Ibid.

66. Ibid.

67. Truffaut, *Correspondance,* p. 41.

68. Archives of Les Films du Carrosse, file "Ma Vie 1."

69. Ibid., letter published in *Correspondance,* pp. 42–44.

70. Ibid.

71. Ibid.

72. Ibid.

73. Ibid.

74. Archives of Les Films du Carrosse, file "Ma Vie 2."

75. Ibid.

76. Archives of Les Films du Carrosse, file "Ma Vie 1."

77. Ibid.

78. Ibid.

79. Ibid.

80. Ibid.

81. Ibid.

82. Excerpt from *The Thief's Journal (Journal d'un voleur)* recopied by hand by Truffaut, archives of Les Films du Carrosse, file "Archives très privées 1." Translation used is from Edmund White, *Genet: A Biography* (New York: Alfred A. Knopf, 1993), p. 8; the mistake ("My mother [*sic*] remains unknown") has been corrected here.

83. On this period in the life of Jean Genet, see White, *Genet,* pp. 372 ff.

84. Archives of Les Films du Carrosse, file "Ma Vie 1."

85. Archives of Les Films du Carrosse, file "Archives très privées 1."

86. Jean-Paul Sartre, foreword to *The Thief's Journal,* trans. Bernard Frechtman (New York: Grove Press, 1964).

87. Archives of Les Films du Carrosse, file "Ma Vie 1."

88. Archives of Les Films du Carrosse, file "Archives très privées 1"; photocopies of this correspondence were also kept in a file entitled "Ecrivains [Writers]."

89. Archives of Les Films du Carrosse, file "Ma Vie 1."

90. François Truffaut immediately sent Genet a letter of explanation and apology: "I returned from Stockholm last night; today I worked all day and took no calls because I'm leaving for the Midi again tomorrow morning. As soon as I heard you

were looking for me I called the Lutetia. I told you, I'll come at 7, we'll talk till 8. After your call, my wife phoned because my younger daughter was sick and there was medication to pick up at the pharmacy. Foreseeing a delay, I called my office so they would warn you: 8 o'clock instead of 7. I had to pick up the medications and bring them home, then go to the Lutetia, you know the rest. I'm not too mad at being called *petit emmerdeur* [damn little pain] because when I was a kid I was called a *petit merdeux* [little squirt]; this shows some progress. If your friend, who has nothing to do with our respective *emmerdements* [damned troubles], phones me Tuesday morning, I'll see him that same day or the next day, at the latest. In some sense, I dare say I was pleased to miss you and I thought of those days when I used to walk down the boulevard de Clichy hoping and fearing to meet you; when I think about it now, I tell myself you were very patient with me; my turn to say, greetings." "Archives très privées 1," and file entitled "Ecrivains."

91. Archives of Les Films du Carrosse, file "Ma Vie 1."

92. Ibid.

93. Archives of Les Films du Carrosse, file "Archives très privées 1."

94. Truffaut's journal, p. 1.

95. Ibid., p. 7.

96. Ibid., pp. 18–19.

97. Ibid., pp. 22–23.

98. Letter of July 27, 1951, from Lieutenant Le Masne de Chermont, archives of Les Films du Carrosse, file "Archives très privées 1."

99. Archives of Les Films du Carrosse, file "Archives très privées 1."

100. Ibid.

101. Ibid.

102. Ibid.

103. Ibid.

104. Truffaut's journal, pp. 174–175.

105. Ibid., pp. 177–178.

3.
LIFE WAS THE SCREEN:
1952–1958

1. Archives of Les Films du Carrosse, file "Archives très privées 1."

2. François Truffaut's journal, archives of Les Films du Carrosse, file "Ma Vie 2," pp. 233–234.

3. Archives of Les Films du Carrosse, file "Bazin."

4. Ibid.

5. Janine Bazin quoted in *Le Roman de François Truffaut,* special issue of *Cahiers du cinéma,* December 1984, pp. 24–25.

6. Archives of Les Films du Carrosse, file "Archives très privées 1."

7. *Cinémonde,* May 14, 1953.

8. Olivier Barrot, *L'Ecran français; 1943–1953* (Paris: Editeurs français réunis, 1979).

9. The manuscript of this first version of what would finally be titled "A Certain Tendency of the French Cinema" can be found in the archives of Les Films du Carrosse, file "Archives très privées 2."

10. Truffaut's journal, p. 172.

11. Ibid., pp. 100–101.

12. On the genesis, publication, and effects of this essay, see Antoine de Baecque, "Contre la Qualité français: Autour d'un article de François Truffaut," *Cinémathèque* 4 (Fall 1993): 44–66.

13. Wheeler Winston Dixon, *The Early Film Criticism of François Truffaut* (Bloomington: Indiana University Press, 1993).

14. In his answer to this letter, Pierre Bost shows himself to be magnanimous and a good loser: "Dear Sir, your article in *Cahiers du cinéma* contains some things that are intelligent, some that are unfair, and others that are inaccurate. But there is also something else—and this is the only matter I will bring up today. In my day one did not come to a person's house to borrow writings, make public use of them, and exploit them for acerbic criticism. Especially not confidential writings, since we are talking about a script that has not yet been filmed. I admit that your behavior surprised me, and that I will now feel a mistrust that is not in my nature—here's the proof. I do not hold any of your reproaches against you. I merely wish that none of the many details you give should come from me (after all, I may have spoken to you too and your piece sometimes takes on the tone of a police report). In any case, you have lacked elegance, I'm sorry to have to tell you so, but I'm entitled to say at least that." Letter in the archives

of Les Films du Carrosse, file "Archives très privées 2."

15. *Cahiers du cinéma* 33 (March 1954).

16. Archives of Les Films du Carrosse, file "Archives très privées 2."

17. *Cahiers du cinéma* 33 (March 1954).

18. *Cahiers du cinéma* 36 (June 1954).

19. On this episode in the history of *Cahiers du cinéma,* see Antoine de Baecque, *Les Cahiers du cinéma: Histoire d'une revue,* vol. 1, (Paris: Editions de l'Etoile, 1991), pp. 89–125.

20. Archives of Les Films du Carrosse, file "Archives très privées 1." This synopsis was published in *Cahiers du cinéma* in May 1994.

21. François Truffaut, *Correspondance,* (Paris: Hatier, 1988), pp. 107–108.

22. François Truffaut, "Un colossal enfant" (written in 1973), *Approches,* February 1974.

23. Archives of Les Films du Carrosse, file "Ecrivains." Audiberti's writings on cinema were published as *Le Mur du fond: Ecrits sur le cinéma,* ed. Michel Giroud, with an introduction by Jérôme Prieur (Paris: Editions des Cahiers du cinéma, 1996).

24. Truffaut, "Un colossal enfant."

25. *Ibid.* Truffaut also had the project of directing an Audiberti play for the stage. On August 19, 1960, he told him in a letter of his desire to direct *Pomme, Pomme, Pomme.* Audiberti answered, "In any case, I would be *delighted* that we operate in concert on a theater stage, you as director and me as the directed!" When they met, Audiberti suggested another play to Truffaut, on the myth of Joan of Arc, entitled *La Pucelle*—written and first produced in 1950, but which he was then rewriting. Several months later, Audiberti and Truffaut found producers for their theatrical venture: Robert Yag and Madeleine Declercq, two friends of the playwright. In July 1961, the news could be announced in the press: TRUFFAUT SWITCHES TO THEATER was the headline in *Paris-Presse.* Over the summer, with the premiere scheduled for November 1961, Truffaut's main work consisted in casting the play: Marie Dubois, Albert Rémy, Pierre Mondy, Marie-José Nat, Françoise Vatel, Serge Gainsbourg, and Yvette Etiévant, as well as Henri Virlojeux, Jean-Pierre Léaud, Claude Mansard, François Darbon, Rosy Varte, so many actors used by Truffaut in his films. The project took shape, as well as the main directing ideas. But Robert Yag, the producer, found the casting excessive, risky, and too burdensome financially. In August 1961, Truffaut therefore abandoned the project of directing *La Pucelle* for the stage.

26. See Antoine de Baecque, "Contre la Qualité française."

27. Letter from François Truffaut to Charles Bitsch, September 1956, archives of Les Films du Carrosse, file "CCH 1 (1953–1957)."

28. Truffaut *Correspondance,* p. 103.

29. Pierre Braunberger quoted in *Le Roman de François Truffaut,* p. 51.

30. François Truffaut, "Les Dessous du Niagara," *Cahiers du cinéma* 28 (November 1953).

31. François Truffaut, "Vous êtes tous témoins dans ce procès: le cinéma français crève sous de fausses légendes," *Arts,* May 15 1957.

32. *Arts,* February 14, 1955.

33. Archives of Les Films du Carrosse, file "CCH 1 (1953–1957)."

34. Ibid.

35. *Les Temps Modernes,* December 1952.

36. *L'Express,* November 14, 1954.

37. *Positif* 21.

38. Ibid.

39. François Truffaut, "Si Versailles m'était conté," *Cahiers du cinéma* 34 (April 1954).

40. Ibid.

41. Robert Belot, *Lucien Rebatet: Un itinéraire fasciste* (Paris: Editions du Seuil, 1994). Rebatet wrote about his meetings with Truffaut in the newspaper *Dimanche-Matin,* February 3, 1957. Also relevant is Eric Neuhoff, *Lettre ouverte à François Truffaut* (Paris: Albin Michel, 1987), pp. 70–73.

42. Letter from Lotte Eisner to François Truffaut, undated (1978), archives of Les Films du Carrosse, file "CCH 1978 (2)."

43. Archives of Les Films du Carrosse, file "CCH 1 (1953–1957)."

44. Ibid.

45. Ibid.

46. *Le Roman de François Truffaut,* p. 42.

47. *Cahiers du cinéma* 36 (June 1954).

48. Eric Rohmer quoted in *Le Roman de François Truffaut*, p. 28.

49. Letter from François Truffaut to Robert Lachenay, undated, archives of Les Films du Carrosse, file "Archives très privées 1."

50. Ibid.

51. Lydie Mahias quoted in *Le Roman de François Truffaut*, p. 47.

52. François Truffaut subsequently drew inspiration from Robert Mallet's radio interviews with Paul Léautaud for his book on Alfred Hitchcock.

53. *France-Observateur*, March 24, 1960.

54. Archives of Les Films du Carrosse, file "CCH 1 (1953–1957)."

55. Ibid.

56. Jean-Claude Brialy quoted in *Le Roman de François Truffaut*, pp. 49–50.

57. Letter from Julien Duvivier to François Truffaut, of August 13 1956, archives of Les Films du Carrosse, file "CCH 1 (1953–1957)."

58. Interview with Marcel Ophuls, filmed by Michel Pascal and Serge Toubiana, for the documentary *François Truffaut: Portraits volés* (*Stolen Portraits*), 1992.

59. Letter from Max Ophuls to François Truffaut, February 17, 1955, archives of Les Films du Carrosse, file "CCH 1 (1953–1957)."

60. François Truffaut, "La Bataille du Marignan," *Arts*, December 19, 1955.

61. Letter from Max Ophuls to François Truffaut, January 7, 1956, archives of Les Films du Carrosse, file "CCH 1 (1953–1957)."

62. Roberto Rossellini's writings and interviews in *Cahiers du cinéma* were collected in *Le Cinéma révélé*, (Paris: Editions de l'Etoile, 1984).

63. On *Viaggio in Italia*, see Jacques Rivette, "Lettre sur Rossellini," *Cahiers du cinéma* 46 (April 1955).

64. Interview with the authors, 1996.

65. François Truffaut, "Il préfère la vie," *L'Express*, September 10, 1959.

66. Ibid.

67. Ibid.

68. *La Peur de Paris*, thirty-seven-page synopsis, archives of Les Films du Carrosse, file "Archives très privées 2."

69. Letter from François Truffaut to Robert Lachenay, September 16, 1956, archives of Les Films du Carrosse, file "Archives très privées 2."

70. See de Baecque, *Les Cahiers du cinéma*, vol. 1, pp. 147–152.

71. *Cahiers du cinéma*, 34 (April 1954).

72. François Truffaut, "Voici les trente nouveaux noms du cinéma français," *Arts*, January 15, 1958.

73. *Cahiers du cinéma* 47 (May 1955).

74. Ibid.

75. André Bazin, "De la politique des auteurs," *Cahiers du cinéma* 70 (April 1957).

76. *Cahiers du cinéma* 86 (August 1958).

77. *Cahiers du cinéma* 44 (February 1955).

78. François Truffaut, "Hitchcock est le plus grand inventeur de forme," *Arts*, December 4, 1957.

79. François Truffaut, "L'admirable certitude," *Cahiers du cinéma* 46 (April 1955).

80. François Truffaut, "Journal du festival de Cannes: une histoire de fous," *Arts*, May 9, 1956.

81. Letter from Jean Delannoy to François Truffaut, November 13, 1955, archives of Les Films du Carrosse, file "CCH 1 (1953–1957)."

82. François Truffaut, "Cannes, un incontestable succès? Non, Monsieur le Ministre," *Arts*, May 16, 1956.

83. Truffaut, *Correspondance*, p. 120.

84. Interview with the authors, 1995.

85. Ibid.

86. François Truffaut, "Henri-Pierre Roché revisité," 1980 essay, a portion of which was published as a preface to the German edition of *Jules and Jim;* also as in François Truffaut, *Le Plaisir des Yeux* (Paris: Editions de l'Etoile, 1987); subsequently published as a foreword to Henri-Pierre Roché, *Carnets* (Marseille, Editions André Dimanche, 1990).

87. François Truffaut, "*Le Bandit* d'Edgar Ulmer," *Arts*, March 14, 1956.

88. Letter from Henri-Pierre Roché to François Truffaut, April 11, 1956, archives of Les Films du Carrosse, file "CCH 1 (1953–1957)."

89. Letter from Henri-Pierre Roché to François Truffaut, April 3, 1959, archives of Les Films du Carrosse, file "CCH 1 (1953–1957)."

90. Archives of Les Films du Carrosse, file "Archives très privées 1."

91. Ibid.

92. Ibid.

93. Ibid.

94. Maurice Pons, *Souvenirs littéraires* (Paris: Quai Voltaire, 1993).

95. "Les Mistons," in Maurice Pons, *Virginales* (Paris: Julliard, 1955), pp. 97–110.

96. Interview with the authors, 1995.

97. Letter from Bernadette Lafont to François Truffaut, July 8, 1957, archives of Les Films du Carrosse, file "CCH 1 (1953–1957)."

98. Interview with the authors, 1995.

99. Marcel Berbet quoted in *Le Roman de François Truffaut,* p. 68.

100. François Truffaut, "Vous êtes tous témoins dans ce procès: le cinéma français crève sous de fausses légendes," *Arts,* May 15, 1957.

101. Ibid. Quoted from François Truffaut, *The Films in My Life,* op. cit. p. 19.

102. François Truffaut, "Autant-Lara, faux martyr, est un cinéaste bourgeois," *Arts,* June 19, 1957.

103. François Truffaut, "Mefiez-vous fillettes: gangsters, filles, cinéastes, censeurs, dans le même panier," *Arts,* July 3, 1957.

104. François Truffaut, "Le Droit de répondre," *Arts,* June 12, 1957.

105. François Truffaut, "Le règne du cochon de payant est terminé," *Arts,* November 6, 1957.

106. François Truffaut, "Clouzot au travail ou le règne de la terreur," *Cahiers du cinéma* 77 (December 1957).

107. François Truffaut, "Si votre techniramage...," *Cahiers du cinéma* 84 (June 1958).

108. François Truffaut, "Sacha Guitry fut un grand cinéaste réaliste," *Arts,* July 31, 1957.

109. François Truffaut, "Les critiques de cinéma sont misogynes: B.B. est victime d'une cabale," *Arts,* December 12, 1956.

110. Ibid.

111. Letter from Brigitte Bardot to François Truffaut, December 13, 1956, archives of Les Films du Carrosse, file "CCH 1 (1953–1957)."

112. *Midi libre,* August 4, 1957.

113. Interview with the authors, 1995

114. Truffaut, *Correspondance,* p. 130.

115. Interview with the authors, 1995

116. Truffaut, *Correspondance,* p. 130.

117. Interview with the authors, 1995

118. Truffaut kept a radioscopic test dated October 7, 1957, archives of Les Films du Carrosse, file "Santé [Health]."

119. Truffaut, *Correspondance,* p. 141.

120. *France-Soir,* November 19, 1958.

121. *France-Soir,* February 14, 1959.

122. Madeleine Morgenstern's interview with the authors, 1995.

123. Ibid.

124. Ibid.

125. Ibid.

126. Archives of Les Films du Carrosse, file "Archives très privées 1."

127. Interview with the authors, 1995.

128. Ibid.

129. Ibid.

130. Archives of Les Films du Carrosse, file "Archives très privées 1."

131. *L'Express,* January 14, 1964.

132. Archives of Les Films du Carrosse, file "CCH 1 (1953–1957)."

133. Letter from André Parinaud to François Truffaut, September 19, 1957, archives of Les Films du Carrosse, file "CCH 1 (1953–1957)."

134. Letter from François Truffaut to André Parinauld, September 21, 1957, archives of Les Films du Carrosse, file "CCH 1 (1953–1957)."

135. Archives of Les Films du Carrosse, file "Archives très privées 1."

136. Archives of Les Films du Carrosse, file "CCH 1 (1953–1957)."

4.
NEW WAVE:
1958–1962

1. François Truffaut, *Correspondance* (Paris: Hatier, 1988), p. 139.

2. Ibid., pp. 138–139.

3. Letter from Pierre Braunberger to François Truffaut, February 15, 1958, archives of Les Films du Carrosse, file "CCH 1958."

4. Namely, in Nantes, at the end of March 1958, in Reims in mid-April, and then in the Brussels world festival of short films, where it received the prize for best direction.

5. *Arts,* May 14, 1958.

6. François Truffaut, "Si des modifications n'interviennent pas, le prochain festival est condamné," *Arts,* May 21, 1958.

7. Marcel Berbert's interview with the authors, 1995.

8. Interview with the authors, 1995.

9. François Truffaut's 1958 date book, archives of Les Films du Carrosse, file "Archives très privées 1."

10. Letter from François Truffaut to Robert Lachenay, April 30, 1958, archives of Les Films du Carrosse, file "Archives très privées 1." Other titles were considered for this film, including *Les petits copains* [*The Little Pals*]: "Because of my mother: 'Your little pals—always your little pals,'" Truffaut wrote to Lachenay on April 28, 1958.

11. Interview with the authors, 1991.

12. Truffaut, *Correspondance*, p. 144.

13. Ibid., p. 145.

14. Letter from Fernand Deligny to François Truffaut, February 4, 1959, archives of Les Films du Carrosse, file "Fernand Deligny."

15. Letter from Fernand Deligny to François Truffaut, August 20, 1958, archives of Les Films du Carrosse, file "Fernand Deligny."

16. Archives of Les Films du Carrosse, file "Fernand Deligny."

17. *Paris-Journal,* May 21, 1959.

18. Letter of January 27, 1958, archives of Les Films du Carrosse, file "Jean-Pierre Léaud."

19. Unpublished interview with Maurice Terrail, December 1979, archives of Les Films du Carrosse, file "CCH 1979 (2)."

20. François Truffaut, "Il faisait bon vivre," *Cahiers du cinéma* 90 (December 1958).

21. Ibid.

22. François Truffaut kept all the call sheets from his shoots, filed away by film. Thanks to the archives of Les Films du Carrosse, one can therefore follow the daily life on his sets.

23. Interview with the authors, 1995.

24. Ibid.

25. Ibid.

26. *Elle,* May 8, 1959.

27. Jacques Audiberti, "Avec ses '400 coups' d'essai, Truffaut a réussi un coup de maître." *Arts,* May 13, 1959.

28. Jacques Doniol-Valcroze, "Cannes 59," *Cahiers du cinéma* 96 (June 1959).

29. *Cinéma* 58, February 1958.

30. Jacques Siclier, *Nouvelle vague?* (Paris: Editions du Cerf, 1960); André S. Labarthe, *Essai sur le jeune cinéma français* (Paris: Editions Eric Losfeld, 1960); Raymond Borde, Freddy Buache, and Jean Curtelin, *Nouvelle Vague* (Lyon: Editions Serdoc, 1962).

31. *Cahiers du cinéma* 101 (November 1959).

32. See specifically *Positif* 46 (June 1962) and its special report, entitled "Feux sur le cinéma français."

33. *Lui,* September 1964.

34. *Santé Publique,* May 15, 1959.

35. *France-Soir,* June 6, 1959.

36. *Elle,* May 8, 1959.

37. *Cahiers des Saisons,* Fall 1959.

38. Philippe Labro's interview with the authors, 1996.

39. Interview with the authors, 1995.

40. Letter from Roland Truffaut to François Truffaut, April 17, 1959, archives of Les Films du Carrosse, file "Archives très privées 2."

41. Archives of Les Films du Carrosse, file "Archives très privées 2."

42. Letter from Roland Truffaut to François Truffaut, May 20, 1959, archives of Les Films Carrosse, file "Archives très privées 2."

43. Archives of Les Films du Carrosse, file "Archives très privées 2."

44. Ibid.

45. Letter from Madeleine Truffaut to Roland and Janine Truffaut, January 7, 1962, archives of Les Films Carrosse, file "Archives très privées 2."

46. Letter from Roland and Janine Truffaut to Madeleine Truffaut, January 11, 1962, archives of Les Films Carrosse, file "Archives très privées 2."

47. Interview with the authors, 1995.

48. Letter from François Truffaut to Roland Truffaut, May 28, 1962, archives of Les Films du Carrosse, file "Archives très privées 2."

49. Psychoanalysis always fascinated François Truffaut, and he read many books on child psychology, among other things. He considered undergoing analysis several times, but always changed his mind, probably because he felt that analysis would interfere with his work as a filmmaker. This is the opinion of his friend Liliane Siegel (interview with the authors, 1995): "When François mentioned psychoanalysis to me, I told him, 'If you start therapy, you'll never be the same and you won't make the same kinds of films.' He answered, 'I think

you're right, so I've been told.' I think he went to see a psychoanalyst two or three times, then decided not to undergo analysis. But he probably hesitated."

50. Letter from François Truffaut to Janine Truffaut, October 19, 1963, archives of Les Films du Carrosse, file "Archives très privées 2."

51. Interview with the authors, 1995.

52. Letter from Simone Jollivet to François Truffaut, June 12, 1961, archives of Les Films du Carrosse, file "CCH 61."

53. Interview with the authors, 1995.

54. Letter from François Truffaut to Helen Scott, December 27, 1960, archives of Les Films du Carrosse, file "Helen Scott."

55. Letter from François Truffaut to Helen Scott, March 1960, archives of Les Films du Carrosse, file "Helen Scott."

56. Interview with the authors, 1996.

57. Letter from François Truffaut to Helen Scott, March 29, 1960, archives of Les Films du Carrosse, file "Helen Scott."

58. Words used by François Truffaut in his letters to Helen Scott between 1960 and 1962.

59. Letter from François Truffaut to Helen Scott, March 14, 1963, archives of Les Films du Carrosse, file "Helen Scott."

60. Interview with the authors, 1995.

61. Letter of April 14, 1960, archives of Les Films du Carrosse, file "Jean-Pierre Léaud."

62. Liliane David's interview with the authors, 1995.

63. Madeleine Morgenstern's interview with the authors, 1995.

64. Marcel Berbert's interview with the authors, 1995.

65. Marcel Berbert quoted in *Le Roman de François Truffaut*, special issue of *Cahiers du cinéma*, December 1984, p. 44.

66. Article published in *Arts*, December 15, 1961; reprinted in François Truffaut, *The Films in My Life*, p. 321.

67. Undated letter from Jean-Luc Godard to François Truffaut, archives of Les Films du Carrosse, file "Jean-Luc Godard."

68. Letter from Georges de Beauregard to François Truffaut, July 20, 1959, archives of Les Films du Carrosse, file "Jean-Luc Godard."

69. Undated letter from Jean-Luc Godard to François Truffaut, archives of Les Films du Carrosse, file "Jean-Luc Godard."

70. Letter from Jean Cocteau to François Truffaut, May 20, 1959, archives of Les Films du Carrosse, file "Ecrivains."

71. Undated letter (June 1959) from Jean Cocteau to François Truffaut, archives of Les Films du Carrosse, file "Ecrivains."

72. Letter from François Truffaut to Roberto Rossellini, July 5, 1962, archives of Les Films du Carrosse, file "Roberto Rossellini." Several months later, Truffaut would give up the idea of coproducing this Rossellini project. For more information on this project, see Gianni Rondolino, *Roberto Rossellini* (Turin: Utet, 1989).

73. Archives of Les Films du Carrosse, file "CCH 60."

74. Truffaut and Les Films du Carrosse produced other short films during this period—by Claude Jutra (*Anna la bonne*), Jean Aurel (*Les Aventures extraordinaires*), Michel Varesano (*La Fin du voyage*), Fernand Deligny (*Le Moindre Geste*), Max Zelenka, Alain Jeannel, and Jean-Claude Roché (*Vie d'insecte*).

75. Letter from Marcel Ophuls to François Truffaut, dated "second day of shoot," archives of Les Films du Carrosse, file "Marcel Ophuls."

76. Interview with the authors, 1995.

77. Press kit, *Shoot the Piano Player*, 1960.

78. Liliane David's interview with the authors, 1996.

79. Claude de Givray's interview with the authors, 1996.

80. Letter from François Truffaut to Maurice Le Roux, May 11, 1960, archives of Les Films du Carrosse, file "CCH 60."

81. *Journal musical français*, September-October 1966.

82. François Truffaut, "Le chanteur sous-titré," in *Boby Lapointe* (Paris: Editions Encres, 1980); republished in François Truffaut, *Le Plaisir des yeux* (Paris: Editions de l'Etoile, 1987), pp. 184–185.

83. *Le Plaisir des yeux*, pp. 184–185.

84. *Le Film français*, May 23, 1964.

85. *Lui*, February 1964.

86. Suzanne Schiffman quoted in *Le Roman de François Truffaut*, p. 52.

87. Press kit for *Shoot the Piano Player*, 1960.

88. *New York Times*, November 17, 1959.

89. *New York Herald Tribune,* December 14, 1959.

90. *New York Post,* November 17, 1959.

91. Archives of Les Films du Carrosse, file "CCH 60."

92. Helen Scott quoted in *Le Roman de François Truffaut,* p. 113.

93. Henry Miller, then sixty-nine, was a cult figure for the young Truffaut, one of the writers he most admired, particularly his book *Sexus,* which Truffaut always listed among the books that truly "changed his life." And Miller held Truffaut in high regard. The two men met again in New York in April 1962 and Miller gave Truffaut his first play, *Just Wild About Harry,* written in 1942 (unpublished and untranslated in France), at a time when the young director was not averse to directing for the stage. Truffaut, who couldn't read English at the time, gave it to his wife, Madeleine, to read and to Marcel Moussy. Madeleine liked the play, finding it "amusing, sentimental, and unusual," while Moussy had his doubts: "An outmoded, risky play," he wrote Truffaut at the end of May 1962. Meanwhile, on the basis of Madeleine's positive opinion, François Truffaut, recontacted Henry Miller by telegram while the writer was vacationing in the Formentor Hotel in Majorca: "Dear Mr. Miller. Stop. Possibility of staging play this winter and would very much like to do business with you. Stop. Yours with admiration. Stop." Henry Miller was delighted and immediately answered Truffaut with a letter written in French: "I should tell you right away that this is my first play and it might very well be bad. I call it 'melo-melo,' which means a mixture of farce, burlesque, slapstick and sentimentality. I think it is amusing and that no one will fall asleep. There are about twenty characters and four leads. I think there is a lot of 'business,' as they say—perhaps too much. But the Germans and Norwegians accepted it and up to now didn't criticize me for it. But you'll see for yourself. I'm flattered that someone like you is interested; believe me, I was very touched by your gesture. So see you soon, for I'll be in Paris next week—for only a few days." The two men did indeed meet in Paris, at the end of May 1962, and then spent a weekend working together near Nîmes, at the home of Lawrence Durrell, a great friend of Henry Miller. Yet the project never saw the light of day because of lack of enthusiasm on the part of Jean-Louis Barrault, the director of the Théâtre de France, who disliked the play and refused to mobilize twenty-odd actors at the Odéon theater for a work he considered "a bit lowbrow" and "very risky." (Letter to François Truffaut from Jean-Louis Barrault, Archives of Les Films du Carrosse, file "Ecrivains.") Miller would always have regrets about this aborted project.

94. Letter from Helen Scott to François Truffaut, March 3, 1960, archives of Les Films du Carrosse, file "Helen Scott."

95. Letter from François Truffaut to Helen Scott, March 29, 1960, Archives of Les Films du Carrosse, file "Helen Scott."

96. Letter from François Truffaut to Helen Scott, April 14, 1962, archives of Les Films du Carrosse, file "Helen Scott."

97. Archives of Les Films du Carrosse, file "CCH 60."

98. Letter from François Truffaut to Helen Scott, February 27, 1960, archives of Les Films du Carrosse, file "Helen Scott."

99. Letter from Elie Wiesel to François Truffaut, December 10, 1960, archives of Les Films du Carrosse, file "CCH 60."

100. Letter from François Truffaut to Helen Scott, November 16, 1960, archives of Les Films du Carrosse, file "Helen Scott."

101. Letter from François Truffaut to Alexandre Chambon, June 15, 1962, archives of Les Films du Carrosse, file "CCH 62."

102. Those responding to this appeal were Raoul Lévy, Pierre Kast, Philippe de Broca, Chris Marker, Jacques Doniol-Valcroze, Claude Chabrol, Pierre Braunberger, Marcel Ophuls, Alain Resnais, François Reichenbach, Jean-Luc Godard, Daniel Boulanger, Jacques Demy, Françoise Giroud, Agnès Varda, Georges Franju, Simone Signoret, Jean-Pierre Melville, Alexandre Astruc, Marguerite Duras, Louis Malle, Jean Rouch, Roger Vadim, Edouard Molinaro, and Georges de Beauregard.

103. Guy Teisseire, who died in 1993, later

became a journalist and film critic, writing for *L'Aurore, Parisien libéré, Matin de Paris,* and so on. He was also a screenwriter (*Il faut tuer Birgit Haas*) and a novelist (*Un peu plus loin que l'Occident* and *La Main d'Abraham,* both published by Editions Jean-Claude Lattès).

104. *Clarté* 42 (March 1962).

105. Letter from François Truffaut to Helen Scott, October 24, 1961, archives of Les Films du Carrosse, file "Helen Scott."

106. Letter from Claude Gauteur to François Truffaut, August 28, 1960, archives of Les Films du Carrosse, file "CCH 60."

107. Letter from Dionys Mascolo to François Truffaut, September 13, 1960, archives of Les Films du Carrosse, file "CCH 60."

108. For more information on this subject, see Jean-Pierre Rioux and Jean-François Sirinelli, eds., *La guerre d'Algérie et les intellectuels français* (Paris: Institut d'Histoire du Temps Présent, 1988), and Jean-François Sirinelli, *Intellectuels et passions françaises: manifestes et pétitions au XXe siècle* (Paris: Fayard, 1990).

109. Undated letter (October 1960) from Robert Benayoun to François Truffaut, archives of Les Films du Carrosse, file "CCH 60."

110. *France nouvelle,* November 4, 1960.

111. Letter from François Truffaut to Helen Scott, October 1, 1960, archives of Les Films du Carrosse, file "Helen Scott."

112. Letter from François Truffaut to Helen Scott, October 18, 1962, archives of Les Films du Carrosse, file "Helen Scott."

113. Letter from François Truffaut to François Leterrier, July 4, 1963, archives of Les Films du Carrosse, file "CCH 63."

114. Interview with the authors, 1995.

115. Letter from Pierre Braunberger to François Truffaut, August 20, 1960, archives of Les Films du Carrosse, file "CCH 60."

116. Letter from Pierre Braunberger to François Truffaut, August 30, 1960, archives of Les Films du Carrosse, file "CCH 60."

117. Letter from Jean Cocteau to François Truffaut, September 9, 1960, archives of Les Films du Carrosse, file "Ecrivains."

118. François Truffaut, "Petit journal du cinéma," *Cahiers du cinéma* 69 (March 1957).

119. Jeanne Moreau quoted in *Le Roman de François Truffaut,* p. 94.

120. François Truffaut, "Louis Malle a filmé la première nuit d'amour du cinéma," *Arts,* September 10, 1958.

121. Florence Malraux's interview with the authors, 1995.

122. Jeanne Moreau's interview with the authors, 1995.

123. René-Jean Clot, in a memo to Truffaut written in February 1960, offers his own adaptation in a few sentences: "The subject concerns a schoolteacher's reintegration into a primary school after a mental breakdown, her arrival in a new job, the reactions among her students and colleagues, and finally her removal from the community. It opposes two people, Madame Langlois, the newly arrived schoolteacher, tolerated at first and then hated, and Monsieur Fraipoint, a schoolteacher who will reveal himself to be the school's 'ringleader.' This man is rigid, meticulous, dissatisfied, and jealous of other people's success. He considers this new teacher 'suspicious,' with her superior culture and intellect; since he is frightened, he becomes aggressive and petty toward her and his fear gradually changes to hatred. He influences his colleagues to share his fear and very soon Madame Langlois becomes a sort of 'secular witch' who is harmful to the students and must be sent back where she came from. In spite of the kindness and generosity of the school inspector, stupidity will triumph and Madame Langlois will be transferred, but not without having to conceal a deep, new wound."

124. Letter from François Truffaut to Helen Scott, September 26, 1960, archives of Les Films du Carrosse, file "Helen Scott."

125. Letter from François Truffaut to Helen Scott, December 27, 1960, archives of Les Films du Carrosse, file "Helen Scott."

126. *Arts,* November 14, 1959.

127. *L'Express,* February 25, 1960.

128. Undated letter (1960) from Jean-Luc Godard to François Truffaut, archives of Les Films du Carrosse, file "Jean-Luc Godard."

129. Undated letter from François Truffaut to Jean Domarchi, undated, archives of Les Films du Carrosse, file "CCH 60."

130. *Signes du temps,* December 1959.

131. Letter from François Truffaut to Helen Scott, December 27, 1960, archives of Les Films du Carrosse, file "Helen Scott."

132. *France-Observateur,* October 19 1961.

133. François Truffaut, written in 1963 (press kit for the film); republished in Truffaut, *The Films in My Life,* trans. Leonard Mayhew (New York: Simon and Schuster, 1978), pp. 324–325.

134. Letter from François Truffaut to Helen Scott, October 24, 1961, archives of Les Films du Carrosse, file "Helen Scott."

135. For example, with its special issue "Nouvelle Vague" in December 1962. See Antoine de Baecque, *Les Cahiers du cinéma: Histoire d'une revue,* vol. 2 (Paris: Editions de l'Etoile, 1991), pp. 18–26, 70–86.

136. Letter from François Truffaut to Helen Scott, March 11, 1961, archives of Les Films du Carrosse, file "Helen Scott." Another explanation for Truffaut's prudence was the fact *Jules and Jim* was to be coproduced by Carrosse and SEDIF, which was then headed by his mother-in-law.

137. Letter from François Truffaut to Helen Scott, September 26, 1960, archives of Les Films du Carrosse, file "Helen Scott."

138. Jean Gruault describes the writing of the *Jules and Jim* screenplay in *Ce que dit l'autre* (Paris: Julliard, 1992), pp. 193–195, 199–200, 207–208.

139. *L'Alsace,* March 17, 1961.

140. Jeanne Moreau's interview with the authors, 1995.

141. Ibid.

142. Florence Malraux's interview with the authors, 1995.

143. Jean-Louis Richard's interview with the authors, 1992.

144. Jeanne Moreau's interview with the authors, 1995.

145. Marcel Berbert's interview with the authors, 1995.

146. "Henri-Pierre Roché revisité," in *Le Plaisir des yeux,* pp. 146–155.

147. "Jeanne Moreau, rieuse et tendre," in *Le Plaisir des yeux,* p. 187.

148. Liliane David's interview with the authors, 1995.

149. Jeanne Moreau's interview with the authors, 1995.

150. Florence Malraux's interview with the authors, 1995.

151. Interview with the authors, 1995.

152. Letter from François Truffaut to Helen Scott, November 9, 1961, archives of Les Films du Carrosse, file "Helen Scott."

153. Claudine Bouché's interview with the authors, 1995.

154. Ibid.

155. Jean Aurel's interview with the authors, 1995.

156. *Journal de Fahrenheit 451*, published with the screenplay of *La Nuit américaine* (Paris: Seghers, 1974), p. 228.

157. Jean Aurel's interview with the authors, 1995.

158. "Henri-Pierre Roché revisité," pp. 146–155.

159. Truffaut, *Correspondance,* p. 188.

160. Letter from François Truffaut to Helen Scott, December 20, 1961, archives of Les Films du Carrosse, file "Helen Scott."

161. Letter from Jean Renoir to François Truffaut, February 8, 1962, archives of Les Films du Carrosse, file "Jean Renoir."

162. Letter from Jean Cocteau to François Truffaut, February 7, 1962, archives of Les Films du Carrosse, file "Ecrivains."

163. Letter from Denise Roché to François Truffaut, February 4, 1962, archives of Les Films du Carrosse, file "CCH 62."

164. Letter from Helen Hessel to François Truffaut, January 30, 1962, archives of Les Films du Carrosse, file "CCH 62." Truffaut answered several days later: "I was very happy to receive your letter and I read it with much emotion. I filmed *Jules and Jim* with profound respect, for I've never liked a book as much as this one and I'm very worried about how the spectators who knew Henri-Pierre Roché will react. This is why your letter increases my anxiety while it also gives me great joy. On learning of your letter, Mademoiselle Jeanne Moreau felt the same emotion as I

and joins me in sending you our most respectful thoughts."

165. *France-Observateur,* February 1, 1962.

166. Interview with the authors, 1996.

167. Letter from François Truffaut to Helen Scott, December 20, 1961, archives of Les Films du Carrosse, file "Helen Scott."

168. Marie-France Pisier quoted in *Le Roman de François Truffaut,* p. 96.

169. Ibid.

170. Interview with the authors, 1995.

171. Letter from François Truffaut to Helen Scott, December 24, 1961, archives of Les Films du Carrosse, file "Helen Scott."

172. Letter from François Truffaut to Helen Scott, January 4, 1962, archives of Les Films du Carrosse, file "Helen Scott."

173. Letter from François Truffaut to Helen Scott, January 18, 1962, archives of Les Films du Carrosse, file "Helen Scott."

174. Letter from François Truffaut to Helen Scott, October 18, 1962, archives of Les Films du Carrosse, file "Helen Scott."

175. Ibid.

176. Letter from François Truffaut to Helen Scott, January 14, 1963, archives of Les Films du Carrosse, file "Helen Scott."

177. Letter from François Truffaut to Roberto Rossellini, November 30, 1962, archives of Les Films du Carrosse, file "Roberto Rossellini."

178. Letter from Marcel Varesano to François Truffaut, November 13, 1961, archives of Les Films du Carrosse, file "CCH 61."

179. Undated letter (1962) from Robert Lachenay to François Truffaut, archives of Les Films du Carrosse, file "Archives très privées 1."

180. Undated letter (1961) from Jean-Luc Godard to François Truffaut, archives of Les Films du Carrosse, file "Jean-Luc Godard."

5.
THE SLOW YEARS:
1962–1968

1. *La Libre Belgique,* May 14, 1963.

2. Interview with the authors, 1995.

3. Jean-Dominique Bauby, *Raoul Lévy: un aventurier du cinéma* (Paris: Jean-Claude Lattès, 1995).

4. Interview with the authors, 1995.

5. Memo from Don Congdon to Helen Scott, April 24, 1962, archives of Les Films du Carrosse, file "Ecrivains."

6. Letter from François Truffaut to Ray Bradbury, April 27, 1962, archives of Les Films du Carrosse, file "Ecrivains."

7. Letter from Ray Bradbury to François Truffaut, May 3, 1962, archives of Les Films du Carrosse, file "Ecrivains."

8. From his experiences with Maurice Pons, René-Jean Clot, Jacques Audiberti, and Henry Miller, François Truffaut realized that it was very tricky for a film director to work directly with a writer. After a while, he preferred to collaborate with his screenwriter, who was rarely a professional writer.

9. Interview with the authors, 1995.

10. *La Cinématographie française,* May 7, 1964.

11. Letter from François Truffaut to Ray Bradbury, September 24, 1962, archives of Les Films du Carrosse, file "Ecrivains."

12. Letter from François Truffaut to Charles Aznavour, January 18, 1963, archives of Les Films du Carrosse, file "CCH 63."

13. Letter from François Truffaut to Helen Scott, March 20, 1963, archives of Les Films du Carrosse, file "Helen Scott."

14. Marcel Berbert quoted in *Le Roman de François Truffaut,* special issue of *Cahiers du cinéma,* December 1984, p. 46.

15. Letter from François Truffaut to André Pépin, July 16, 1963, archives of Les Films du Carrosse, file "CCH 63."

16. Letter from François Truffaut to Don Congdon, November 16, 1962, archives of Les Films du Carrosse, file "Congdon."

17. This is a point Truffaut makes at the end of an article on *Rear Window* written for *Arts,* April 6, 1955: "No, this devil of a man hasn't yet revealed all his secrets, but each new film allows us to better understand a very rich oeuvre that is one of the subtlest in contemporary cinema."

18. Introduction to François Truffaut, *Le Cinéma selon Alfred Hitchcock* (Paris: Robert Laffont, 1966). U.S. edition: *Hitchcock* (New York: Simon and Schuster, 1967), p. 8.

19. Letter from François Truffaut to

Alfred Hitchcock, June 2, 1962, archives of Les Films du Carrosse, file "Alfred Hitchcock." Excerpts from this letter are from François Truffaut, *Correspondance 1945–1984*, trans. Gilbert Adair (New York: Noonday Press, 1988), p. 177.

20. Ibid (Gilbert Adair's translation, p. 179).

21. *Archives* of Les Films du Carrosse, file "Alfred Hitchcock."

22. Letter from François Truffaut to Helen Scott, June 20, 1962, archives of Les Films du Carrosse, file "Helen Scott."

23. Letter from François Truffaut to Don Congdon, November 16, 1962, archives of Les Films du Carrosse, file "Congdon."

24. Letter from François Truffaut to Helen Scott, August 24, 1962, archives of Les Films du Carrosse, file "Helen Scott."

25. Letter of April 14, 1963, archives of Les Films du Carrosse, file "Simon and Schuster."

26. Letter from François Truffaut to Helen Scott July 5, 1962, archives of Les Films du Carrosse, file "Helen Scott."

27. Archives of Les Films du Carrosse, file "Alfred Hitchcock."

28. Helen Scott quoted in *Le Roman de François Truffaut*, p. 114.

29. Letter from François Truffaut to Helen Scott, August 24, 1962, archives of Les Films du Carrosse, file "Helen Scott."

30. Ibid.

31. Interview with the authors, 1995.

32. Letter from François Truffaut to Helen Scott, July 18, 1963, archives of Les Films du Carrosse, file "Helen Scott."

33. Letter from François Truffaut to Helen Scott, September 9, 1963, archives of Les Films du Carrosse, file "Helen Scott."

34. Letter from François Truffaut to Helen Scott, January 14, 1964, archives of Les Films du Carrosse, file "Helen Scott."

35. Press kit for *Les Deux Anglaises et le Continent*, 1971.

36. Marcel Berbert's interview with the authors, 1995.

37. Letter from François Truffaut to Helen Scott, September 27, 1963, archives of Les Films du Carrosse, file "Helen Scott."

38. Lucas Steiner is the name Truffaut gave to the character played by Heinz Bennent in *The Last Métro*—the Jewish director hidden in the basement of the theater.

39. Interview with the authors, 1995.

40. Ibid.

41. Archives of Les Films du Carrosse, file "CCH 63."

42. Letter from François Truffaut to Kashiko Kawakita, April 22, 1963, archives of Les Films du Carrosse, file "CCH 63."

43. Letter from François Truffaut to Helen Scott, August 20, 1963, archives of Les Films du Carrosse, file "Helen Scott."

44. Interview conducted by Michel Pascal and Serge Toubiana for the documentary *François Truffaut: Portraits volés* (*Stolen Portraits*), 1992.

45. Letter from François Truffaut to Helen Scott, January 1, 1964, archives of Les Films du Carrosse, file "Helen Scott."

46. Letter from François Truffaut to Helen Scott, September 9, 1963, archives of Les Films du Carrosse, file "Helen Scott."

47. Interview with the authors, 1995.

48. *Val d'or. Quotidien québecquois*, November 17, 1965.

49. Ibid.

50. Press kit for *La Peau douce*, 1964.

51. Truffaut shot so many sequences that he was able to edit the outtakes into a short ten-minute film, *Les Voix d'Orly* (*Voices of Orly*), which he himself defined as "a cinema poem structured around visual and sound relationships, a poem playing on the contrast between the noise of the jets on the runway and the idyllic three-note bell summoning passengers to waiting areas."

52. Letter from François Truffaut to Helen Scott, November 14, 1963, archives of Les Films du Carrosse, file "Helen Scott."

53. Letter from François Truffaut to Helen Scott, December 18, 1963, archives of Les Films du Carrosse, file "Helen Scott."

54. Ibid.

55. In one scene in the film, Jean-Louis Richard goes up to Franca in the street and offers to show her "dirty pictures." She publicly insults him.

56. Jean-Louis Richard's interview with the authors, 1995.

57. Claudine Bonché's interview with the authors, 1995.

58. Letter from François Truffaut to Helen Scott, January 1, 1964, archives of Les Films du Carrosse, file "Helen Scott."

59. Interview with the authors, 1995.

60. Letter from François Truffaut to Helen Scott, May 10–12, 1964, archives of Les Films du Carrosse, file "Helen Scott."

61. Claudine Bonché's interview with the authors, 1995.

62. Marcel Berbert's interview with the authors, 1995.

63. Archives of Les Films du Carrosse, file "Helen Scott."

64. Undated letter from Jean-Luc Godard to François Truffaut, archives of Les Films du Carrosse, file "Jean-Luc Godard."

65. Letter from François Truffaut to Helen Scott, May 28, 1964, archives of Les Films du Carrosse, file "Helen Scott."

66. Letter from Claude Jutra to François Truffaut, August 1, 1964, archives of Les Films du Carrosse, file "CCH 64."

67. Letter from François Truffaut to Helen Scott, February 22, 1964, archives of Les Films du Carrosse, file "Helen Scott."

68. Interview with the authors, 1995.

69. Letter from François Truffaut to Helen Scott, February 22, 1964, archives of Les Films du Carrosse, file "Helen Scott."

70. Interview with the authors, 1995.

71. Excerpt from the want ad in *Le Figaro,* May 19, 1965.

72. Interview with the authors, 1994.

73. Letter from François Truffaut to Helen Scott, November 27, 1964, archives of Les Films du Carrosse, file "Helen Scott."

74. Interview with the authors, 1995.

75. Ibid.

76. It was a tricky case for the defense, since Truffaut and Richard had indeed seen and read the Sainte-Colombe screenplay.

77. Letter from François Truffaut to Helen Scott, November 27, 1964, archives of Les Films du Carrosse, file "Helen Scott."

78. Ibid.

79. Letter from François Truffaut to Helen Scott, May 28, 1964, archives of Les Films du Carrosse, file "Helen Scott."

80. Letter from François Truffaut to Princess Soraya, July 17, 1964, archives of Les Films du Carrosse, file "CCH 64."

81. Letter from François Truffaut to Marcel Berbert, April 2, 1964, archives of Les Films du Carrosse, file "CCH 64."

82. Ibid.

83. Interview with the authors, 1995.

84. Ibid.

85. Letter from François Truffaut to Elinor Jones, September 7, 1964, archives of Les Films du Carrosse, file "CCH 64."

86. Archives of Les Films du Carrosse, file "Jean-Luc Godard."

87. Archives of Les Films du Carrosse, file "CCH 65."

88. Letter from François Truffaut to Elinor Jones, July 2, 1965, archives of Les Films du Carrosse, file "CCH 65."

89. Letter from Eugene Archer to François Truffaut, September 3, 1962, archives of Les Films du Carrosse, file "CCH 62."

90. Letter from François Truffaut to Helen Scott, August 20, 1963, archives of Les Films du Carrosse, file "Helen Scott."

91. Letter from François Truffaut to Lewis Allen July 3, 1963, archives of Les Films du Carrosse, file "CCH 63."

92. Letter from François Truffaut to Lewis Allen, June 5, 1963, archives of Les Films du Carrosse, file "CCH 63."

93. Letter from François Truffaut to Lewis Allen, July 3, 1963, archives of Les Films du Carrosse, file "CCH 63."

94. Letter from Lewis Allen to François Truffaut, November 7, 1963, archives of Les Films du Carrosse, file "CCH 63."

95. Letter from François Truffaut to Lewis Allen, September 13, 1963, archives of Les Films du Carrosse, file "CCH 63."

96. Letter from Lewis Allen to François Truffaut, November 7, 1963, archives of Les Films du Carrosse, file "CCH 63."

97. Letter from François Truffaut to Lewis Allen, October 18, 1963, archives of Les Films du Carrosse, file "CCH 63."

98. Letter from François Truffaut to Helen Scott, December 16, 1964, archives of Les Films du Carrosse, file "Helen Scott."

99. Telegram of October 29, 1964, archives of Les Films du Carrosse, file "CCH 64."

100. Interview with François Truffaut, *Elle,* September 28, 1966.

101. Letter from François Truffaut to Terence Stamp, December 21, 1965, archives of Les Films du Carrosse, file "CCH 65."

102. *Journal de Fahrenheit 451*, published with the screenplay of *La Nuit Américaine* (Paris: Seghers, 1974), p. 168.

103. Letter from François Truffaut to Jacques Doniol-Valcroze, January 17, 1966, archives of Les Films du Carrosse, file "CCH 66."

104. Suzanne Schiffman quoted in *Le Roman de François Truffaut*, p. 52.

105. For further information on this shoot, see the marvelous *Journal de Fahrenheit 451*, about which Peter Bogdanovich wrote to Truffaut in the fall of 1966: "I don't know which I prefer, your film *Fahrenheit* or your journal on the shoot. The latter will serve as inspiration to *all* directors and be a kind of guide." (Archives of Les Films du Carrosse, file "CCH 66.")

106. *Journal de Fahrenheit 451*, p. 168.

107. Ibid., p. 169.

108. Letter from François to Marcel Berbert, January 22, 1966, archives of Les Films du Carrosse, file "CCH 66."

109. Interview with the authors, 1996.

110. The issue of *Cahiers du cinéma* with Anna Karina on the cover was number 177, which had a special report on the censorship of Jacques Rivette's *La Religieuse* (*The Nun*). For more details about this matter, see Antoine de Baecque, *Les Cahiers du cinéma: Histoire d'une revue*, vol. 2 (Paris: Editions de l'Etoile, 1991), pp. 173–176.

111. *Journal de Fahrenheit 451*, p. 219.

112. Ibid., p. 177.

113. Ibid., p. 175.

114. Ibid., p. 186.

115. Ibid., p. 219.

116. Letter from François Truffaut to Thom Noble, October 10, 1966, archives of Les Films du Carrosse, file "CCH 66."

117. Telegram of August 31, 1966, archives of Les Films du Carrosse, file "Ecrivains."

118. Letter from François Truffaut to Ray Bradbury, January 1, 1967, archives of Les Films du Carrosse, file "Ecrivains."

119. Letter from François Truffaut to Helen Scott, May 3, 1965, archives of Les Films du Carrosse, file "Helen Scott."

120. Letter from Alfred Hitchcock to François Truffaut, October 22, 1965, archives of Les Films du Carrosse, file "Alfred Hitchcock."

121. Letter from Alfred Hitchcock to Odette Ferry, June 17, 1966, archives of Les Films du Carrosse, file "CCH 66."

122. Letter from Robert Laffont to François Truffaut, January 13, 1966, archives of Les Films du Carrosse, file "CCH 66."

123. Letter from François Truffaut to Helen Scott, November 27, 1964, archives of Les Films du Carrosse, file "Helen Scott."

124. *Les Nouvelles littéraires*, November 22, 1966.

125. Letter from Alfred Hitchcock to François Truffaut, December 9, 1966, archives of Les Films du Carrosse, file "Alfred Hitchcock."

126. Letter from François Truffaut to Helen Scott, August 13, 1964, archives of Les Films du Carrosse, file "Helen Scott."

127. Letter from François Truffaut to Helen Scott, August 19, 1964, archives of Les Films du Carrosse, file "Helen Scott."

128. Press kit for *The Bride Wore Black*, 1968.

129. Interview with the authors, 1995.

130. Letter from François Truffaut to Don Congdon, August 19, 1964, archives of Les Films du Carrosse, file "Congdon."

131. Letter from François Truffaut to Ray Bradbury, January 25, 1967, archives of Les Films du Carrosse, file "Ecrivains."

132. Letter from Ray Bradbury to François Truffaut, May 14, 1969, archives of Les Films du Carrosse, file "Ecrivains."

133. Letter from François Truffaut to Nicole Stéphane, August 31, 1964, archives of Les Films du Carrosse, file "CCH 64." Nicole Stéphane produced *Un amour de Swann* (*Swann in Love*) in 1983, directed by Volker Schlöndorff.

134. Madeleine Morgenstern's interview with the authors, 1995.

135. Claudine Bouché's interview with the authors, 1995.

136. *Le Nouvel Observateur*, March 8, 1967.

137. Interview conducted by Michel Pascal for the film *François Truffaut: Portraits volés*, 1992.

138. Memo to the collaborators, artists, and technicians of *The Bride Wore Black*,

undated, archives of Les Films du Carrosse, file "La Mariée. Feuilles de service."

139. Interview with the authors, 1995.

140. Jeanne Moreau quoted in Le Roman de François Truffaut, p. 94.

141. Ibid.

142. Letter from François Truffaut to Alfred Hitchcock, August 31, 1967, archives of Les Films du Carrosse, file "Alfred Hitchcock."

143. Letter from Alfred Hitchcock to François Truffaut, June 17, 1968, archives of Les Films du Carrosse, file "Alfred Hitchcock."

144. Handwritten note, undated, archives of Les Films du Carrosse, file "CCH 67."

145. Letter of May 11, 1967, archives of Les Films du Carrosse, file "CCH 67."

146. Cahiers du cinéma 190 (May 1967).

147. L'Express, October 28, 1966.

6.
PARALLEL LIVES:
1968–1971

1. Claude de Givray's interview with the authors, 1995.

2. Ibid.

3. The refrain from the song "Que reste-t-il de nos amours?": "Bonheur fané/ Cheveux au vent/Baisers volés/Rêves mouvants/Que reste-t-il de tout cela?"

4. Press kit for Stolen Kisses, 1968.

5. François Truffaut, in Le Plaisir des yeux (Paris: Editions de l'Etoile, 1967), p. 174.

6. Undated letter (January 1968) from Delphine Seyrig to François Truffaut archives of Les Films du Carrosse, file "CCH 68."

7. Press kit for Stolen Kisses, 1968.

8. Interview with the authors, 1991.

9. Ibid.

10. The writing and rewriting of the screenplay of Stolen Kisses is revealing of the "Truffaut method." Thanks to the different stages of the project, it is possible to shed light on his writing process. See the book by Carole Le Berre, François Truffaut, Ed. de l'Etoile, Paris, 1993. Truffaut revised the screenplay of Stolen Kisses in December 1967. This was the first time a fully researched and investigated story came to him virtually "ready to use." Though Truffaut kept all of his scriptwriters' research work for the film, he was very critical of their character portrayals, situations, and dialogue. His notes on the original screenplay are very revealing. Truffaut also rejected the name "Martine"—"People who call their daughter Martine or Caroline are morons who have been under the spell of Martine Carol between 1950 and 1955. Like Brigitte later and now Sylvie, etc. . . . Hence no Martine"—only the heroine herself from the Revon and de Givray script. Indeed, in the screen version of Stolen Kisses, "Christine Darbon" is no longer a slightly bitchy, very snobbish girl from the upper bourgeoisie of the sixteenth arrondissement, but the "serious daughter" of a couple from the petite bourgeoisie living in a house in the Paris suburbs. Similarly, Truffaut rejected the name "Cyprienne" for the "forty-year-old woman": "It's straight out of boulevard theater." Instead, he came up with the name "Fabienne Tabard." This elegant woman is no longer the wife of a military man stationed far away, but of a shoe store owner. He also changed his scriptwriters' suggested locations: the Opéra Comique would not be kept for the film, nor the fashionable restaurant, nor the social evenings in beautiful apartments, and opposite the tennis match at the Pierre-de-Coubertin stadium he noted, "I hate stadiums." Finally, Truffaut particularly objected to the dialogue in this original screenplay: "Very bad, 1937 dialogue for Renée Saint-Cyr"; "Terrible lack of invention. This is all banal"; "False, false. Not serious, not realistic. A cheat and too quick"; "All of this is hardly serious, really. I told you: do it as you would for yourself, not Chabrol"; "What film are we in? This smacks of Georges Conchon, i.e., Paris high society and boulevard satire which is to Edouard et Caroline what L'Eau à la bouche is to La Règle du jeu."

11. Undated letter (April 1968) from Delphine Seyrig to François Truffaut, archives of Les Films du Carrosse, file "CCH 68."

12. Ibid.

13. Press kit for Stolen Kisses, 1968.

14. G. P. Langlois and G. Myrent, Henri Langlois: Premier citoyen du cinéma (Paris: Denoël, 1986); republished by Ramsay (on the affair of February 1968, see pp. 319–357). Richard Roud, Henri Langlois: l'homme de la Cinémathèque

(Paris: Belfond, 1985). U.S. edition: *A Passion for Films: Henri Langlois and the Cinémathèque Française* (New York: Viking, 1983). Also, on the Langlois affair, see Antoine de Baecque, *Les Cahiers du cinéma: Histoire d'une revue,* vol. 2 (Paris: Editions de l'Etoile, 1991), pp. 177–183.

15. As of January 1969, François Truffaut wanted to stop working for the Cinémathèque Defense Committee. Indeed, he couldn't bear Langlois's "fumblings, constant improvisations, doubtful decisions concerning fundamental choices . . . particularly when they are institutionalized" (letter of September 5, 1969). Truffaut therefore wrote Langlois a "rather sad" letter in January 1969 to tell him of his resignation: "If the Defense Committee served any purpose in the course of 1968, it's not because it functioned *with* you, but *by your side* and definitively *for* you. If, as you say, the Prix Delluc for *Stolen Kisses* comes with a check, I'll give it to the Defense Committee and it will be the last check signed and endorsed François Truffaut, Treasurer. Naturally I'll withdraw without making a fuss or doing anything that could harm you; I'll simply transmit the files to Doniol-Valcroze, since he is the assistant treasurer, and that's all. . . ." (Letter of January 13, 1969, archives of Les Films du Carrosse, file "Henri Langlois").

16. Archives of Les Films du Carrosse, file "Henri Langlois."

17. *Combat,* February 12, 1968.

18. *France-Soir,* February 13, 1968.

19. Archives of Les Films du Carrosse, file "Henri Langlois."

20. Letter from François Truffaut to Jean-Louis Comolli, March 8, 1968, archives of Les Films du Carrosse, file "Henri Langlois."

21. Letter from François Truffaut to François Mitterrand, March 26, 1969, archives of Les Films du Carrosse, file "Henri Langlois."

22. Archives of Les Films du Carrosse, file "Henri Langlois."

23. Letter from François Truffaut to Louis Marcorelles, May 12, 1968, archives of Les Films du Carrosse, file "Henri Langlois."

24. Georges Kiejman quoted in *Le Roman de François Truffaut,* special issue of *Cahiers du cinéma,* December 1984, p. 133.

25. Interview with the authors, 1995.

26. *L'Intransigeant,* May 20, 1968; *Paris-Jour,* May 20, 1968.

27. *L'Express,* July 15, 1968.

28. *Le Cinéma s'insurge* 1 (May 1968), the brochure of the Etats généraux du cinéma, Eric Losfeld editor.

29. Ibid.

30. *L'Express,* July 15, 1968.

31. Ibid.

32. *Les Nouvelles littéraires,* July 25, 1968.

33. *L'Express,* July 15, 1968.

34. Ibid.

35. Ibid.

36. Letter from François Truffaut to Helen Scott, October 14, 1967, archives of Les Films du Carrosse, file "Helen Scott."

37. Archives of Les Films du Carrosse, file "Ma Vie 1." This report by Albert Duchenne should be read with some wariness. The details of the investigation are not given and his conclusions are subject to caution.

38. Truffaut/De Givray interview, June 1984, archives of Les Films du Carrosse, p. 34.

39. In an article on *La Femme d'à côté (The Woman Next Door), Libération,* September 30, 1981, Serge Daney referred to a "Jekyll Truffaut" and a "Hyde Truffaut."

40. Interview with the authors, 1995.

41. Ibid.

42. In a letter to Tanya Lopert, who had just lost her father, Truffaut expressed his feelings concerning "his" dead. It can be seen as the germ of what would later become *The Green Room:* "There are far too many dead around me whom I have loved, and since Françoise Dorléac's death, I have decided not to go to any funerals, which, as you can imagine, does not prevent the presence of sadness, darkening everything for a while and never really being completely obliterated, even as the years go by, for we don't just live with the living, but also with all those who have counted in our lives." Undated letter (February 1970), archives of Les Films du Carrosse, file "CCH 70 (1)."

43. It was then that he established the principal files of his intimate life: "Ma Vie 1," "Ma Vie 2," "Archives très privées 1," and "Archives très privées 2," which are presently kept at Les Films du Carrosse.

44. Letter from Suzanne de Saint-Martin

to François Truffaut August 24, 1969, archives of Les Films du Carrosse, file "Ma Vie 1."

45. The Monferrand family disagreed with this interpretation of the facts. Monique de Monferrand, for example, felt the breakup between Roland Lévy and Janine de Monferrand was the former's decision and that he had left his girlfriend of the time without even knowing that he had made her pregnant.

46. Archives of Les Films du Carrosse, file "Ma Vie 1."

47. Press kit for *Stolen Kisses*, 1968.

48. *Paris-Soir*, September 14, 1968.

49. *New York Times*, March 5, 1969.

50. Marcel Berbert's interview with the authors, 1995.

51. Archives of Les Films du Carrosse, file "Gérard Lebovici."

52. Letter from François Truffaut to Don Congdon, October 14, 1967, archives of Les Films du Carrosse, file "Don Congdon."

53. Letter from François Truffaut to Ilya Lopert, November 13, 1968, archives of Les Films du Carrosse, file "CCH 68."

54. Interview with François Truffaut, *Playboy*, January 1975.

55. Suzanne Schiffman's interview with the authors, 1995.

56. François Truffaut, "En travaillant avec Catherine Deneuve," *Unifrance Film Magazine*, 1969. Reprinted in *Le Plaisir des yeux*, pp. 175–177.

57. Letter from François Truffaut to Catherine Deneuve, September 2, 1968, archives of Les Films du Carrosse, file "CCH 68."

58. Ibid.

59. Laurence Benaïm, *Yves Saint-Laurent* (Paris: Grasset, 1993).

60. Interview with the authors, 1995.

61. Ibid.

62. Letter from François Truffaut to Jean Narboni, January 14, 1969, archives of Les Films du Carrosse, file "CCH 69."

63. Letter from François Truffaut to Helen Scott, November 29, 1968, archives of Les Films du Carrosse, file "Helen Scott."

64. Telegram of December 10, 1968, archives of Les Films du Carrosse, file "CCH 68."

65. François Truffaut, "En travaillant avec Catherine Deneuve," *Unifrance Film Magazine*, 1969.

66. Interview with the authors, 1995.

67. Ibid.

68. Letter from François Truffaut to Jean Narboni, January 14, 1969, archives of Les Films du Carrosse, file "CCH 69."

69. "I'm quite moved because I just saw my first mistress again," he wrote to Helen Scott in May 1965, "the first woman I ever lived with." (Archives of Les Films du Carrosse, file "Helen Scott.")

70. Mirieille G. also inspired the screenplay of *La Petite Voleuse*, written by François Truffaut and Claude de Givray, which was directed by Claude Miller in 1988, four years after Truffaut's death.

71. This sequence had been written for Françoise Dorléac in the script of *The Soft Skin*, then cut in the editing by Truffaut, who reshot it identically five years later with Catherine Deneuve.

72. Catherine Deneuve quoted in *Le Roman de François Truffaut*, p. 98.

73. Call sheets for *Mississippi Mermaid*, archives of Les Films du Carrosse, file "F. S. Sirène."

74. The island was baptized Réunion Island in 1793 following the events of August 10, 1792, the day of the taking of the Tuileries castle, the abolition of the monarchy, and the establishment of the French Republic, all events illustrated by Renoir in *La Marseillaise*.

75. Letter from Jean Renoir to François Truffaut, August 27, 1969, archives of Les Films du Carrosse, file "Jean Renoir."

76. Letter from François Truffaut to Helen Scott, May 14, 1969, archives of Les Films du Carrosse, file "Helen Scott."

77. *Le Nouvel Observateur*, June 30, 1969.

78. Undated letter (October 1969) from François Truffaut to François Weyergans, archives of Les Films du Carrosse, file "CCH 69."

79. Letter from François Truffaut to Helen Scott, June 6, 1969, archives of Les Films du Carrosse, file "Helen Scott."

80. Letter from François Truffaut to Aimée Alexandre, June 14, 1969, archives of Les Films du Carrosse, file "Aimée Alexandre."

81. Interview with Claude-Marie Tremois, *Télérama*, June 15, 1969.

82. *Paris-Match,* March 8, 1969.

83. "En travaillant avec Catherine Deneuve."

84. Interview with the authors, 1995.

85. Letter from François Truffaut to Helen Scott, June 6, 1969, archives of Les Films du Carrosse, file "Helen Scott."

86. Letter from François Truffaut to Aimée Alexandre, June 14, 1969, archives of Les Films du Carrosse, file "Aimée Alexandre."

87. *Le Roman de François Truffaut,* p. 58.

88. Lucien Malson, *Les Enfants sauvages: Mythe et réalité* (Paris: Union Générale d'Edition, 1964).

89. Jean Gruault, *Ce que dit l'autre* (Paris: Julliard, 1992), p. 238.

90. Letter from François Truffaut to Jean Gruault, November 29, 1965, archives of Les Films du Carrosse, file "CCH 65."

91. François Truffaut helped Fernand Deligny and Jean-Pierre Daniel to produce their film on autistic children, *Le Moindre geste* (1965). Then, between 1972 and 1974, he financed *Ce gamin-là,* a film made by Renaud Victor in Monoblet with Deligny.

92. Letter from François Truffaut to Fernand Deligny, November 15, 1968, archives of Les Films du Carrosse, file "Fernand Deligny."

93. Interview with François Truffaut, *Heures Claires,* December 1965.

94. Marcel Berbert's interview with the authors, 1995.

95. Jean-Louis Livi's interview with the authors, 1996.

96. Nestor Almendros, *A Man with a Camera,* trans. Rachel Phillips Belash (New York: Farrar, Straus and Giroux, 1984), p. 84.

97. Letter from François Truffaut, June 6, 1969, archives of Les Films du Carrosse, file "Helen Scott."

98. Ibid.

99. Interview with the authors, 1995.

100. Interview with François Truffaut, *Télérama,* February 28, 1970.

101. Letter from Jean Grualt to François Truffaut, August 2, 1969, archives of Les Films du Carrosse, file "CCH 69."

102. Letter from François Truffaut to Gilles Jacob, July 13, 1969, archives of Les Films du Carrosse, file "CCH 69."

103. *Télérama,* February 28, 1970.

104. Ibid.

105. Letter from Jean-Pierre Cargol to François Truffaut, May 22, 1970, archives of Les Films du Carrosse, file "CCH 70 (1)."

106. Letter from François Truffaut to Patrice Hovald, March 14, 1969, archives of Les Films du Carrosse, file "CCH 69."

107. Letter from François Truffaut to Jacques-Louis Roustant, September 20, 1971, archives of Les Films du Carrosse, file "CCH 71."

108. Letter from François Truffaut to Patrice Hovald, March 14, 1969, archives of Les Films du Carrosse, file "CCH 69."

109. Interview with François Truffaut, *Image et Son,* December 1970.

110. Press kit for *Bed and Board,* 1970.

111. Interview with François Truffaut, *Le Progrès,* October 20, 1970.

112. Interview with François Truffaut, *Le Journal du dimanche,* September 6, 1970.

113. Ibid.

114. Interview with François Truffaut, *Dernière heure lyonnaise,* October 22, 1970.

115. Interview with François Truffaut, *Le Journal du dimanche,* September 6, 1970.

116. *Les Aventures d'Antoine Doinel* (Paris: Mercure de France, 1970). U.S. edition: *The Adventures of Antoine Doinel: Four Autobiographical Screenplays,* trans. Helen Scott (New York: Simon and Schuster, 1971).

117. Nestor Almendros quoted in *Le Roman de François Truffaut,* p. 70.

118. Almendros, *A Man with a Camera,* p. 94.

119. Ibid., p. 93.

120. *Le Nouvel Observateur,* March 2, 1970.

121. Ibid.

122. "Lettre ouverte de François Truffaut à Annie Girardot," June 23, 1970, archives of Les Films du Carrosse, file "RTL 70."

123. Letter from François Truffaut to Jean Collet, June 26, 1970, archives of Les Films du Carrosse, file "CCH 70 (1)."

124. Letter of September 14, 1970, archives of Les Films du Carrosse, file "CCH 70 (2)."

125. Philippe Labro's interview with the authors, 1996.

126. Claude Chabrol's interview with the authors, 1996.

127. Alain Vannier's interview with the authors, 1996.

128. *New York Times,* January 18, 1971.

129. Archives of Les Films du Carrosse, file "Alfred Hitchcock."

130. Letter from François Truffaut to André Malraux, June 14, 1967, archives of Les Films du Carrosse, file "CCH 67."

131. *Le Nouvel Observateur,* March 2, 1970.

132. Interview with the authors, 1995.

133. *Image et Son,* December 1970.

134. *Cahiers du cinéma* 172 (November 1965).

135. *Le Roman de François Truffaut,* pp. 114–115.

136. Letter of May 7, 1968, archives of Les Films du Carrosse, file "CCH 68."

137. Letter from François Truffaut to Jacques Doniol-Valcroze, January 22, 1970, archives of Les Films du Carrosse, file "CCH 70 (1)."

138. Ibid.

139. *L'Express,* February 14, 1970.

140. Interview with the authors, 1995.

141. Interview conducted by Michel Pascal for the film *François Truffaut: portraits volés, (Stolen Portraits),* 1992.

142. Open letter from François Truffaut to the court, September 8, 1970, archives of Les Films du Carrosse, file "CCH 70 (2)."

143. Letter of October 21 1969, archives of Les Films du Carrosse, file *"Cahiers du cinéma."*

144. Letter from François Truffaut to Sylvie Pierre, November 20, 1970, archives of Les Films du Carrosse, file *"Cahiers du cinéma."*

145. Letter from François Truffaut to Helen Scott, April 23, 1970, archives of Les Films du Carrosse, file "Helen Scott."

146. Interview with the authors, 1995.

147. Anne Gillain, ed., *Le Cinéma selon François Truffaut* (Paris: Flammarion, 1998), p. 247.

148. Letter from François Truffaut to Aimée Alexandre, December 23, 1970, archives of Les Films du Carrosse, file "Aimée Alexandre."

149. Letter from Aimée Alexandre to François Truffaut, December 31, 1970, archives of Les Films du Carrosse, file "Aimée Alexandre."

150. Letter from François Truffaut to Liliane Siegel, December 6, 1971; letter loaned to the authors.

151. Letter from François Truffaut to Aimée Alexandre, March 10, 1971, archives of Les Films du Carrosse, file "Aimée Alexandre."

7.
CINEMA MAN:
1971–1979

1. Letter from François Truffaut to Jean-Loup Dabadie, February 14, 1971, archives of Les Films du Carrosse, file "CCH 71 (1)."

2. Letter from François Truffaut to Liliane Siegel, August 15, 1971, letter loaned to the authors.

3. Undated letter (July 1971) from François Truffaut to Marcel Berbert, archives of Les Films du Carrosse, file "CCH 71 (2)."

4. Ibid.

5. Interview with the authors, 1995.

6. Henri-Pierre Roché, *Les Deux Anglaises et le Continent* (Paris; Gallimard, 1955).

7. Undated letter (May 1971) from Jean-Claude Brialy to François Truffaut, archives of Les Films du Carrosse, file "CCH 71 (2)."

8. Henri-Pierre Roché, The *Carnets* (Marseille: Editions André Dimanche, 1990), with a preface by François Truffaut.

9. Letter from François Truffaut to Claude Gallimard, October 14, 1968, archives of Les Films du Carrosse, file "CCH 68."

10. Press kit for *Two English Girls,* 1971.

11. Interview with François Truffaut, *Le Nouveau Cinémonde,* July–August 1971.

12. *AFP,* November 24, 1971.

13. As told by Truffaut in *Télérama,* August 14, 1971.

14. Letter from François Truffaut to Oscar Lewenstein, February 12, 1971, archives of Les Films du Carrosse, file "CCH 71 (1)."

15. Nestor Almendros quoted in *Le Roman de François Truffaut,* special issue of *Cahiers du cinéma,* December 1984, *op cit.* p. 72.

16. Press kit for *Two English Girls,* 1971.

17. Letter from François Truffaut to Liliane Siegel, May 20, 1971, letter loaned to the authors.

18. Letter from François Truffaut to Liliane Dreyfus, May 16, 1971, letter loaned to the authors (when she married in 1963, Liliane David took the name Dreyfus).

19. Letter from François Truffaut to Liliane Siegel, August 15, 1971, letter loaned to the authors.

20. Interview with the authors, 1995.

21. Letter from François Truffaut to Nestor Almendros, September 9, 1971, archives of Les Films du Carrosse, file "CCH 71 (2)."

22. Letter from François Truffaut to Nestor Almendros, September 11, 1971, archives of Les Films du Carrosse, file "CCH 71 (2)."

23. Letter from Louis Marcorelles to François Truffaut, November 22, 1971, archives of Les Films du Carrosse, file "CCH 71 (2)."

24. Letter from Paul Vecchiali to François Truffaut, December 5, 1971, archives of Les Films du Carrosse, file "CCH 71 (2)."

25. Letter from Jean Eustache to François Truffaut, December 12, 1971, archives of Les Films du Carrosse, file "CCH 71 (2)."

26. Letter from Denise Roché to Franço is Truffaut, November 28, 1971, archives of Les Films du Carrosse, file "Ecrivains."

27. *France Soir,* December 4, 1971.

28. Letter from Hercule Mucchielli to François Truffaut, December 17, 1971, archives of Les Films du Carrosse, file "CCH 71 (2)."

29. *L'Avant-Scène,* issue on *Two English Girls,* December 14, 1971.

30. This interview was published in 1972 by Radio Canada and republished by Ramsay in 1987, with the title *Aline Desjardins s'entretient avec François Truffaut.*

31. Letter from François Truffaut to Liliane Stegel, December 30, 1971, letter loaned to the authors.

32. *Pour la Presse,* February 4, 1972; Reused in the press kit for *Such a Gorgeous Kid Like Me,* 1972.

33. *L'Humanité,* May 18, 1967.

34. *Pour la Presse,* February 4, 1972.

35. *Le Soir* (Marseille), March 29, 1972.

36. Letter from François Truffaut to Jean-Loup Dabadie, May 7, 1971, archives of Les Films du Carrosse, file "CCH 71 (1)."

37. Ibid.

38. Letter from François Truffaut to Liliane Siegel, August 21, 1971, letter loaned to the authors.

39. Truffaut's memorandum to Dabadie concerning the first draft of the screenplay of *Such a Gorgeous Kid Like Me,* undated (December 1971), archives of Les Films du Carrosse, file "Scénario/Une belle fille...."

40. Ibid.

41. Undated letter (September 1971), from François Truffaut to Jean-Loup Dabadie, archives of Les Films du Carrosse, file "CCH 71 (1)."

42. Interview with the authors, 1995.

43. Letter from François Truffaut to Liliane Siegel, March 3, 1971, letter loaned to the authors.

44. Bernadette Lafont's interview with the authors, 1995.

45. Ibid.

46. Liliane Dreyfus's interview with the authors, 1995.

47. Bernadette Lafont's interview with the authors, 1995.

48. François Truffaut, "Le Cinéma en action," written as an introduction to the screenplay of *La Nuit américaine* (Paris: Seghers, 1974). U.S. edition: *Day for Night,* trans. San Florès (New York: Grove Press, 1975).

49. Jean-Louis Richard quoted in *Le Roman de François Truffaut,* p. 63.

50. For Truffaut, the death of an actor is the only tragedy that can interfere with the completion of a shoot. This plot twist in *Day for Night* inevitably calls to mind the tragic death of Françoise Dorléac; her fatal car accident took place on the same stretch of road as the one that casts a pall on the cast and crew working at the Victorine studios.

51. Truffaut, "Le cinéma en action."

52. *La Nuit américaine,* p. 46.

53. Ibid., p. 76.

54. Truffaut had already used the expression "a train in the night" to describe a film shoot in the press kit for *The Soft Skin.* He uses it again here, spoken by the director Ferrand.

55. Press kit for *Day for Night,* 1973.

56. François Truffaut had initially wanted to cast Louis Jourdan in the part of Alexandre, but he was not available. He had also hoped to convince Simone Simon, who had retired in 1956, to make a movie

comeback and play the part of Séverine. Then he approached Madeleine Renaud, who had to turn the offer down because of a theatrical tour.

57. *Le Monde,* May 18, 1973.

58. See two articles about Jean-Pierre Léaud published at that time: *Le Monde,* February 14, 1972; *Elle,* May 21, 1973.

59. Archives of Les Films du Carrosse, file "CCH 72 (1)."

60. *La Nuit américaine,* p. 83.

61. Jacqueline Bisset's interview with the authors, 1995.

62. Nathalie Baye's interview with the authors, 1995.

63. Jacqueline Bisset's interview with the authors, 1995.

64. Alexandra Stewart's interview with the authors, 1995.

65. Letter from François Truffaut to Alexandra Stewart, December 23, 1972, letter loaned to the authors.

66. Letter from François Truffaut to Helen Scott, March 14, 1973, archives of Les Films du Carrosse, file "Helen Scott."

67. Letter from Jean-Pierre Aumont to François Truffaut, May 6, 1973, archives of Les Films du Carrosse, file "CCH 73 (1)."

68. Letter from Nathalie Baye to François Truffaut, June 11, 1973, archives of Les Films du Carrosse, file "CCH 73 (1)."

69. *Le Parisien,* May 16, 1973.

70. *Le Figaro,* May 17, 1973. But the fact that Jean Delannoy, Truffaut's inveterate enemy, was on the Cannes jury would certainly not have helped the film had it been entered in the competition.

71. Letter from François Truffaut to Gilles Jacob, May 27, 1973, archives of Les Films du Carrosse, file "CCH 73 (1)."

72. *Le Nouvel Observateur,* May 28, 1973.

73. *Le Monde,* May 16, 1973.

74. *Le Figaro,* May 15, 1973.

75. Letter from François Truffaut to Simon Benzakein, June 13, 1973, archives of Les Films du Carrosse, file "CCH 73 (1)."

76. Interview with the authors, 1996. Things are actually more complicated, since Godard included *The 400 Blows, Shoot the Piano Player, Jules and Jim,* and *The Soft Skin* in his "10 best films of the year" lists published by *Cahiers du cinéma* in the early sixties.

77. *Le Nouvel Observateur,* March 2, 1970.

78. Letter included in *François Truffaut: Correspondance* (Paris: Hatier, 1988), pp. 423–424.

79. Ibid., pp. 425–431.

80. Janine Bazin's television program *Vive le cinéma* was censored by the government (in June 1972), and Godard offered her no support whatsoever. Truffaut showed his solidarity with Bazin and André Labarthe by refusing to participate in *Dossiers de l'écran* on July 5, 1972, which had as its theme "freedom of thought," following the screening of *Fahrenheit 451.* "I'm willing to bet," he wrote to Armand Jammot, the producer of the program, "that the word 'censorship' won't even be mentioned in the discussion and that the true issues will be skirted over. From now on I wish to have nothing more to do, therefore, with the black *Dossiers de l'écran.*"

81. This is a reference to an expression coined by Truffaut to refer to his friendship with, and feelings of solidarity for, the young New Wave filmmakers, an expression which he reused as a part title in his book *The Films in My Life.*

82. Undated letter (June 1973) from Janine Bazin to François Truffaut, archives of Les Films du Carrosse, file "Bazin."

83. *Le Nouvel Observateur,* December 2, 1974.

84. Letter from François Truffaut to Jean-Louis Bory, December 11, 1974, archives of Les Films du Carrosse, file "CCH 74 (2)."

85. Ibid.

86. For example, Truffaut had a falling-out with the actor Oskar Werner. After the negative experience of *Fahrenheit 451,* the two men ignored each other. But at the beginning of January 1971, Truffaut, who was then in the midst of a depression—"in this port of shadows where I am, haunted by ghosts, shades and nightmares"—he recontacted him, hoping the actor would give him moral support. He sent him a copy of *Jules and Jim* as a gift. Werner was very touched by this show of friendship and expressed his "eternal affection" to Truffaut. But the relationship once again began to deteriorate when Werner asked Truffaut to cofinance his first film as a director, *So Love Returns,* with a New York company, newly created by Steve McQueen, Paul Newman, Sidney Poitier,

and Barbra Streisand, the First Artists Production Company. Truffaut turned him down on May 8, 1973, admitting to Werner that he had doubts about his ability to direct a film. "I was shocked by your letter," the actor replied on December 30, 1973. "It was written by a journalist, a gossip, not an artist. You allow yourself to pass judgment on me from evidence that you cannot possibly have. You are wrong, François, for you don't know me at all. Contrary to what you may think, I have no contempt for the world. I only hate megalomaniacs. I don't think that, in the one hundred and ten parts I have played on stage and twenty-five film parts, I have shown, as you say, 'a kind of arrogance and contempt for others.' However, I do believe this arrogance you accuse me of is very widespread among film directors, who are emblems of narcissism today. We are separated by about ten years, and that's enormous. You were 5 years old when I earned my first paycheck at 15 for a film. You were 6 years old when I saw the first Jews persecuted in the streets of Vienna, when I saw the SA use torches to burn the books of Freud, Werfel, Zweig, Heine, Friedell, Mann, Hesse, Adler (and, believe me, it was rather different from the way you showed it in *Fahrenheit 451*, and Cusack is like a choirboy compared to the SA and SS who burned synagogues). I also heard the cries from the crowd, vociferation from the masses, and how they were put in trances by this joyous spectacle. You were 8 years old when I was put in a Nazi labor camp and tried to commit suicide when my mother was arrested by the Gestapo. You were 12 years old when I was hiding as a deserter, to escape Hitler's army, with my 7-month daughter and my Jewish wife in the woods around Vienna. And this 'dance of death' which lasted four and a half months had nothing to do with Johann Strauss's Viennese waltzes. I am not telling you these stories to provoke pity. But when one survives such events— living hell—the rest is purgatory: one listens and sees the world more clearly. One can more confidently distinguish truth from hypocrisy, genius from phoniness, nobility from vulgarity, the sublime from the mediocre. You can see why I believe that though you were sometimes touched

by truth, genius, nobility and the sublime, with *Jules and Jim* and *The Wild Child*, your recent attitude and films seem to me hypocritical, false, vulgar and mediocre."

87. Letter from François Truffaut to Robert Laffont, March 8, 1974, archives of Les Films du Carrosse, file "CCH 74 (1)."

88. Interview with the authors, 1995.

89. *Pomme d'Api*, July 15, 1972.

90. Interview with the authors, 1995.

91. Jean Gruault, *Ce que dit l'autre* (Paris: Julliard, 1992), p. 282.

92. Interview with Eva Truffaut, *Cahiers du cinéma*, May 1994.

93. *Paris-Match*, May 14, 1974.

94. Interview with the authors, 1995.

95. Letter from François Truffaut to Liliane Siegel, April 20, 1971, letter loaned to the authors.

96. Letter from François Truffaut to Liliane Siegel, September 15, 1972, letter loaned to the authors.

97. Letter from François Truffaut to Liliane Siegel, December 6, 1971, letter loaned to the authors.

98. Interview with the authors, 1995.

99. Letter from François Truffaut to Isabelle Adjani, April 14, 1976, archives of Les Films du Carrosse, file "CCH 76 (1)."

100. Gruault, *Ce que dit l'autre*, p. 283.

101. Letter from François Truffaut to Jean-Claude Brialy, January 24, 1978, archives of Les Films du Carrosse, file "CCH 78 (1)."

102. Alexandra Stewart's interview with the authors, 1996.

103. Madeleine Morgenstern's interview with the authors, 1995.

104. Letter from François Truffaut to Liliane Siegel, August 14, 1973, letter loaned to the authors.

105. Letter from François Truffaut to Simon Benzakein, March 10, 1974, archives of Les Films du Carrosse, file "CCH 74 (1)."

106. Letter from François Truffaut to David Susskind (New York agent), May 16, 1975, archives of Les Films du Carrosse, file "CCH 75 (1)."

107. Letter from François Truffaut to Guy Teisseire about an interview for *Ciné Revue*, July 1973, archives of Les Films du Carrosse, file "CCH 73 (2)."

108. Interview with the authors, 1995.

109. Letter from François Truffaut to

Helen Scott, July 9, 1973, archives of Les Films du Carrosse, file "Helen Scott."

110. Ibid.

111. *Memo from David O. Selznick*, ed. Rudy Behlmer (New York: Viking Press, 1972).

112. Interview with the authors, 1996.

113. Todd McCarthy quoted in *Le Roman de François Truffaut*, pp. 157–158.

114. Letter from François Truffaut to Helen Scott, July 9, 1973, archives of Les Films du Carrosse, file "Helen Scott." (Helen Scott had introduced Truffaut to the actor-writer Buck Henry, who played in Milos Forman's *Taking Off* and wrote the screenplays for Mike Nichols's *The Graduate* and *The Day of the Dolphin*.)

115. Ibid.

116. François Truffaut, "Jean Renoir, 1273 Leona Drive," December 1975; published under the title "Jean Renoir: Quatre-vingts ans d'étonnements," *Le Nouvel Observateur*, March 4, 1978; reprinted in *Le Plaisir des yeux* (Paris: Éditions de l'Etoile, 1987), pp. 140–146.

117. Interview with the authors, 1995.

118. Ibid.

119. Truffaut, "Jean Renoir, 1273 Leona Drive."

120. Letter from François Truffaut to Madeleine Morgenstern July 13, 1973, letter loaned to the authors by Madeleine Morgenstern.

121. *Le Figaro*, April 4, 1974.

122. Letter from François Truffaut to Marcel Berbert, July 21, 1975, archives of Les Films du Carrosse, file "CCH 75 (2)."

123. Archives of Les Films du Carrosse, file "CCH 74 (2)."

124. Letter from François Truffaut to Liliane Siegel, August 14, 1973, letter loaned to the authors.

125. This series of unpublished articles is kept in the archives of Les Films du Carrosse, file "Politique."

126. Letter from François Truffaut to Liliane Siegel, August 15, 1971, letter loaned to the authors.

127. Interview with the authors, 1995.

128. Letter from François Truffaut to Liliane Siegel, January 4, 1975, letter loaned to the authors.

129. The project involved almost eighty people—political militants, historians, researchers, and academics.

130. Letter from François Truffaut to Frances Vernor Guille, April 13, 1973, archives of Les Films du Carrosse, file "CCH 73 (1)."

131. Letter from Jean Hugo to François Truffaut, January 31, 1971, archives of Les Films du Carrosse, file "CCH 71 (1)."

132. Letter from Jean Gruault to François Truffaut, July 6, 1974, archives of Les Films du Carrosse, file "CCH 74 (2)." See also Gruault, *Ce que dit l'autre*, pp. 298–299.

133. Catherine Deneuve's interview with the authors, 1995.

134. Undated letter (October 1974), from François Truffaut to Isabelle Adjani, archives of Les Films du Carrosse, file "CCH 74 (2)."

135. Interview with Isabelle Adjani, *Cinématographe*, December 1984.

136. Undated letter (October 1974), from François Truffaut to Isabelle Adjani, archives of Les Films du Carrosse, file "CCH 74 (2)."

137. *Cinématographe*, December 1984.

138. *France Soir*, September 30, 1975.

139. Letter from François Truffaut to Liliane Siegel, January 27, 1975, letter loaned to the authors.

140. *France Soir*, September 30, 1975.

141. Interview with the authors, 1995.

142. *L'Express*, March 3, 1975.

143. Interview with the authors, 1995.

144. Ibid.

145. Letter from François Truffaut to Helen Scott, February 9, 1975, archives of Les Films du Carrosse, file "Helen Scott."

146. Letter from François Truffaut to Liliane Siegel, February 14, 1975, letter loaned to the authors.

147. Letter from François Truffaut to Jean-Loup Dabadie, April 30, 1975, archives of Les Films du Carrosse, file "CCH 75 (1)."

148. Letter from Gilles Jacob to François Truffaut, November 15, 1975, archives of Les Films du Carrosse, file "CCH 75 (2)."

149. Letter from Marcel Ophuls to François Truffaut, November 6, 1975, archives of Les Film du Carrosse, file "CCH 75 (2)."

150. Letter from Jean Gruault to François Truffaut, of November 26, 1975, archives

of Les Films du Carrosse, file "CCH 75 (2)."

151. Letter from François Truffaut to Gilles Jacob, November 21, 1975, archives of Les Films du Carrosse, file "CCH 75 (2)."

152. Ibid.

153. Letter from Jean Hugo to François Truffaut, October 30, 1975, archives of Les Films du Carrosse, file "CCH 75 (2)."

154. *Projet pour un film sur les enfants* (Project for a film about children), 1972, memo for Suzanne Schiffman, archives of Les Films du Carrosse, file "Scénario/Argent de poche." One of the anecdotes is taken from a Sacha Guitry anthology, *Si j'ai bonne mémoire*. It's the story of a boy who is in love with the mother of a friend and gives her a bouquet of flowers. She responds by saying, "Please thank your father for me." Among other stories, which he didn't use, there is the autobiographical one: "A thirteen-year old boy is home alone and discovers his father's old date books while rummaging around. Curiosity leads him to look up what his father wrote on the day of his birth. He notices that there is no mention of his birth on that day or on any of the following days. This is how he discovers that his father is not his father. He finds definite confirmation of this fact by consulting the family record book."

155. Truffaut continued his militant activity for children throughout the seventies, supporting various associations, Perce Neige for example, created by Lino Ventura, and the Association for the Support of Deaf Children, as well as schools and experimental centers for "maladjusted" or mentally handicapped children. He gave generously to these various associations and was always ready to make public statements in the press in support of this cause.

156. This schoolteacher's speech was published in *Télérama*, March 8, 1976.

157. Steven Spielberg quoted in *Le Roman de François Truffaut*, p. 121.

158. Truffaut remembered Julia Phillips from the Academy Awards ceremony he had attended in April 1974, where she went onstage to collect her Oscar for *The Sting*. He decided that if he ever made a Hollywood film, it would be with her, and he told her so in a letter of March 19, 1976. Their relationship deteriorated considerably in the course of the shoot, as can be seen from the following excerpt from his letter to Madeleine Morgenstern on July 13, 1976: "Instead of a noisy, refrigerated trailer I asked to have an office in this warehouse, and again this was a big deal. I had to pretend to be angry and prepared to go on strike to get what I wanted; for example, I won't go drink champagne with the producer tonight so she'll understand that she's the one I resent. She was lucky enough to produce *The Sting* and *Taxi Driver*, but actually she's lazy; next year she herself will be directing a feminist erotic film, *Fear of Flying*, and she thinks that by being glued to the camera all day and staring at the actors, she'll learn something!. . . ." And on July 29, 1976, he wrote to Madeleine again: "The funny thing is, I'm now on bad terms with the producer, we don't greet each other, we pretend not to see each other, and what I gain in this is that she doesn't dare sit next to the camera, she remains slightly on the sidelines." Julia Phillips described her experience as a Hollywood producer in *You'll Never Eat Lunch in This Town Again* (New York: Signet, 1991).

159. Telegram of March 15, 1976, archives of Les Films du Carrosse, file "Close Encounters."

160. Letter from François Truffaut to Julia Phillips, March 19, 1976, archives of Les Films du Carrosse, file "Close Encounters."

161. Spielberg was quite clear about the fact that *Close Encounters* was a homage to Howard Hawks's 1951 film *The Thing*. It was initially going to be entitled *Watch the Sky*, the last line in *The Thing*.

162. Letter from François Truffaut to Jean-Loup Dabadie, August 18, 1976, archives of Les Films du Carrosse, file "CCH 76 (2)."

163. Letter from François Truffaut to Serge Rousseau, July 29, 1976, archives of Les Films du Carrosse, file "CCH 76 (2)."

164. Letter from François Truffaut to Nestor Almendros, archives of Les Films du Carrosse, file "CCH 76 (2)."

165. Letter from François Truffaut to Marcel Berbert, July 19, 1976, archives of

Les Films du Carrosse, file "Close Encounters."

166. Letter from François Truffaut to Madeleine Morgenstern, July 13, 1976, letter loaned to the authors by Madeleine Morgenstern.

167. Letter from François Truffaut to Marcel Berbert, July 19, 1976, archives of Les Films du Carrosse, file "Close Encounters."

168. Letter from François Truffaut to Madeleine Morgenstern, July 13, 1976, letter loaned to the authors by Madeleine Morgenstern.

169. Steven Spielberg quoted in *Le Roman de François Truffaut,* p. 121.

170. Letter from Steven Spielberg to François Truffaut, December 22, 1977, archives of Les Films du Carrosse, file "Close Encounters."

171. Steven Spielberg quoted in *Le Roman de François Truffaut,* p. 121.

172. Bruno Bettelheim, *The Empty Fortress: Infantile Autism and the Birth of Self* (New York: The Free Press, 1967), p. 241.

173. Liliane Dreyfus's interview with the authors, 1996.

174. Ibid.

175. Ibid.

176. Madeleine Morgenstern's interview with the authors, 1995.

177. Claude Chabrol's interview with the authors, 1996.

178. Phillippe Labro's interview with the authors, 1996.

179. Michel Fermaud's interviews with the authors, 1995 and 1996.

180. *France Soir,* April 22, 1977.

181. Letter from Michel Fermaud to François Truffaut, February 18, 1975, archives of Les Films du Carrosse, file "CCH 75 (1)."

182. Michel Fermaud's interview with the authors, 1995.

183. Comparison comes from an article in *Midi libre,* January 9, 1977.

184. *Elle,* May 2, 1977.

185. Marcel Berbert's interview with the authors, 1995.

186. Jean-Louis Livi's interview with the authors, 1996.

187. Leslie Caron's interview with the authors, 1995.

188. Press kit for *L'Homme qui aimait les femmes,* 1977.

189. Interview with the authors, 1995.

190. Ibid.

191. Henry Chapier in *Le Quotidien de Paris,* May 5, 1977.

192. *Pariscope,* June 22, 1977.

193. Letter from François Truffaut to Charles Denner, March 29, 1977, archives of Les Films du Carrosse, file "CCH 77 (1)."

194. Interview with François Truffaut, *Lumière du cinéma,* May 1977.

195. *Le Nouvel Observateur,* May 9, 1977.

196. This remake was a lucrative deal for Les Films du Carrosse, since they were paid $300,000 for the rights to the film.

197. Interview with the authors, 1996.

198. Ibid.

199. *L'Express,* March 13, 1978.

200. Ibid.

201. *Le Matin de Paris,* June 5, 1977.

202. *L'Express,* March 13, 1978.

203. *Humanité-Dimanche,* April 7, 1978.

204. Aimée Alexandre died in 1981, at the age of eighty-seven. She had become blind and was never able to see *The Green Room,* a film which owed so much to her.

205. Henry James, *L'Autel des morts,* trans. and with a preface by Diane de Margerie (Paris: Stock, 1974).

206. Letter from François Truffaut to Jean Gruault, of July 21, 1974, archives of Les Films du Carrosse, file "CCH 74 (2)."

207. Ibid.

208. Ibid.

209. Letter from François Truffaut to Jean Gruault of November 21, 1975, archives of Les Films du Carrosse file "CCH 75 (2)."

210. The name of Paul Massigny, Julien Davenne's worst enemy, even in death, comes from this rereading of Proust, as well as many details throughout the screenplay. Note that it is possible to recognize Serge Rousseau, one of Truffaut's best friends, in the supposed portrait of Massigny.

211. Telegram, February 23, 1977, archives of Les Films du Carrosse, file "CCH 77 (1)."

212. Interview with the authors, 1996.

213. *L'Aurore,* April 3, 1978.

214. Interview with the authors, 1996.

215. Press kit for *La Chambre verte,* 1978.

216. Nathalie Baye's interview with the authors, 1996.

217. Marie de Poncheville's interview with the authors, 1996.

218. Letter from Isabelle Adjani to François Truffaut, April 9, 1978, archives of Les Films du Carrosse, file "CCH 78 (1)."

219. Letter from Alain Delon to François Truffaut, October 2, 1979, archives of Les Films du Carrosse, file "CCH 79 (2)."

220. Letter from Eric Rohmer to François Truffaut, April 26, 1978, archives of Les Films du Carrosse, file "CCH 78 (1)."

221. Letter (dated Whitsunday 1978) from Antoine Vitez to François Truffaut, archives of Les Films du Carrosse, file "CCH 78 (1)."

222. *Le Nouvel Observateur,* April 3, 1978.

223. *L'Express,* March 13, 1978.

224. Letter from François Truffaut to Michel Drucker, April 3, 1978, archives of Les Films du Carrosse, file "CCH 78 (1)."

225. Letter from François Truffaut to François Porcile, May 8, 1978, archives of Les Films du Carrosse, file "CCH 78 (1)."

226. *Paris-Match,* May 4, 1978.

227. Letter from François Truffaut to Annette Insdorf, May 10, 1978, archives of Les Films du Carrosse, file "CCH 78 (1)."

228. Interview with the authors, 1996.

229. Letter from François Truffaut to Annette Insdorf, May 10, 1978, archives of Les Films du Carrosse, file "CCH 78 (1)."

230. *France Soir,* November 3, 1977.

231. Interview with the authors, 1996.

232. Letter from François Truffaut to Jean-Louis Bory, September 1, 1978, archives of Les Films du Carrosse, file "CCH 78 (2)."

233. Letter from François Truffaut to Jean Nachbaur, January 26, 1978, archives of Les Films du Carrosse, file "CCH 78 (1)."

234. For information concerning economic changes in the French film industry, see Jean-Michel Frodon, *L'Age moderne du cinéma français: De la Nouvelle Vague à nos jours* (Paris: Flammarion, 1995), pp. 533–537, chapter entitled "Artmédia en position dominante."

235. Interview with the authors, 1996.

236. Archives of Les Films du Carrosse, file "Agence Magic."

237. Interview with the authors, 1996.

238. Letter from François Truffaut to Henning and Else Carlsen, October 13, 1978, archives of Les Films du Carrosse, file "CCH 78 (2)." Truffaut added, "To a certain extent I owe *Love on the Run* to you, for it was because of the Dagmar Theater's [movie house run by the Carlsens in Copenhagen] initiative of showing all the Doinel films chronologically in one day that I had the idea of making a last Doinel, which would include flashbacks excerpted from the four preceding films."

239. Archives of Les Films du Carrosse, file "Scénario/L'Amour en fuite."

240. *France Soir,* January 27, 1979.

241. Ibid.

242. Letter from François Truffaut to Annette Insdorf, May 10, 1978, archives of Les Films du Carrosse, file "CCH 78 (1)."

243. Interview with the authors, 1992.

244. Letter from François Truffaut to Alain Souchon, July 10, 1978, archives of Les Films du Carrosse, file "CCH 78 (2)."

245. Suzanne Schiffman quoted in *Le Roman de François Truffaut,* p. 54.

246. Undated letter (beginning of January 1979), from François Truffaut to Alain Souchon, archives of Les Films du Carrosse, file "CCH 79 (1)."

247. Jean-Louis Richard quoted in *Le Roman de François Truffaut,* p. 65.

248. *Le Figaro,* January 20, 1979.

249. *Le Monde,* January 25, 1979.

250. Undated letter (end of January 1979), from François Truffaut to Jacques Siclier, archives of Les Films du Carrosse, file "CCH 79 (1)."

251. RTL, "Le journal inattendu," February 14, 1979.

8.
THE UNFINISHED FIGURE:
1979–1984

1. Letter from François Truffaut to Helen Scott, November 27, 1964, archives of Les Films du Carrosse, file "Helen Scott."

2. Letter from François Truffaut to Helen Scott October 14, 1965, archives of Les Films du Carrosse, file "Helen Scott."

3. Truffaut and Claude de Givray worked on the script of *La Petite Voleuse* again in 1983, in Honfleur. It was one of the films

Truffaut wanted to shoot after *Confidentially Yours!* After his death, Claude Berri wanted to direct the film and acquired the rights to the screenplay as well as to the screenplay of *L'Agence Magic.* In the end, the film was directed by Claude Miller in the summer of 1988; it starred Charlotte Gainsbourg. Claude Berri was the producer of the film.

4. Letter from François Truffaut to Pierre Kast, May 14, 1979, archives of Les Films du Carrosse, file "CCH 79 (1)."

5. Undated letter (May 79), from Pierre Kast to François Truffaut, archives of Les Films du Carrosse, file "CCH 79 (1)."

6. Letter from Pierre Kast to François Truffaut, July 9, 1979, archives of Les Films du Carrosse, file "CCH 79 (2)."

7. Letter from François Truffaut to Pierre Kast, May 30, 1979, archives of Les Films du Carrosse, file "CCH 79 (1)." In his letter, Truffaut wrote, "The story about Stendhal is terrific, but I can't seem to visualize it, or rather I can't see filming, for an hour and a half, an actor who has to be chosen for both his talent and his physical resemblance to the original. But if you feel that Philippe Noiret would make a possible Stendhal, why don't you give him *Henri et Clémentine* to read?"

8. Truffaut felt that the ideal actor for *Le Garde du corps* would be Patrick Dewaere. "But I don't think he wants to work with me," he wrote to Jacques Veber on May 28, 1979. "This wouldn't be the case with Jacques Dutronc, whom I very much admire, but I have the impression that, consciously or not, you wrote with Dewaere in mind."

9. Suzanne Schiffman quoted in *Le Roman de François Truffaut,* special issue of *Cahiers du cinéma,* December 1984, p. 54.

10. *France Soir,* March 4, 1970.

11. Truffaut was also active in getting *The Sorrow and the Pity,* which was censored by the ORTF, broadcast on television. The film wouldn't be shown on television until 1981.

12. Unpublished interview with Mireille Le Dantec, December 1977, archives of Les Films du Carrosse, file "Robert Bresson."

13. Letter from François Truffaut to Michael Korda, May 25, 1982, archives of

Les Films du Carrosse, file "CCH 82 (1)."

14. Letter from François Truffaut to Jean-Loup Dabadie, October 8, 1976, archives of Les Films du Carrosse, file "CCH 76 (2)."

15. Interview with the authors, 1995.

16. He also used Hervé Le Boterf's *La Vie parisienne sous l'Occupation.* He was a journalist Truffaut had met in the fifties at *Cinémonde.*

17. The character of Daxiat in *The Last Métro* is all the more believable in that he is modeled on the collaborationist critic Alain Laubreaux, who had written a play, *Les Pirates de Paris,* under the pseudonym Daxiat. He was a gifted and brilliant polemicist and famous for his insults at the time. He called Jean Marais "The man with the Cocteau [play on the word *couteau,* meaning "knife"] between his teeth." At the Liberation, Laubreaux fled to Spain, where he died in 1960.

18. Interview with the authors, 1995.

19. Truffaut coscripted *Mata-Hari,* a film with Jeanne Moreau, directed by Jean-Louis Richard and produced by Les Films du Carrosse.

20. Jean-Louis Richard's interview with the authors, 1992.

21. Gérard Depardieu's interview with the authors, 1992.

22. Jean-Louis Livi's interview with the authors, 1996.

23. Gérard Depardieu quoted in *Le Roman de François Truffaut,* p. 100.

24. Truffaut had written a very complimentary article in *Arts* about Jean Poiret's performance in Sacha Guitry's *Assassins et Voleurs.*

25. *Le Roman de François Truffaut,* p. 47.

26. Letter from François Truffaut to Jean-Claude Grumberg, January 15, 1980, archives of Les Films du Carrosse, file "CCH 80 (1)."

27. Undated letter (February 1980), from François Truffaut to Jean-Claude Grumberg, archives of Les Films du Carrosse, file "CCH 80 (1)."

28. This letter (January 21, 1980) was inspired by Spielberg's behavior during the filming of *Close Encounters.*

29. Letter from François Truffaut to Janine Bazin, February 28, 1980, archives of Les Films du Carrosse, file "Bazin."

30. Letter from François Truffaut to Jean

Aurel, April 23, 1980, archives of Les Films du Carrosse, file "CCH 80 (1)."

31. Interview with the authors, 1995.

32. Preface to the revised edition of François Truffaut, *Hitchcock* (New York: Simon and Schuster, 1984), p. 12.

33. Interview with the authors, 1991.

34. Letter from François Truffaut to Richard Roud, September 3, 1980, archives of Les Films du Carrosse, file "CCH 80 (2)."

35. Suzanne Schiffman quoted in *Le Roman de François Truffaut*, p. 54.

36. *Lire* 62 (October 1980).

37. Letter from François Truffaut to Richard Roud, September 3, 1980, archives of Les Films du Carrosse, file "CCH 80 (2)."

38. Interview with the authors, 1995.

39. Henri Amouroux's chronicles were appearing every week at that time and were very popular, "Les Années 40," "La grande histoire des Français sous l'Occupation," and "Les beaux jours des Collabos."

40. Letter from François Truffaut to Georges Cravenne, March 3, 1981, archives of Les Films du Carrosse, file "CCH 81 (1)."

41. Interview with François Truffaut, *Première*, August 1983.

42. Interview with the authors, 1995.

43. TF1 wanted to broadcast *The Last Métro* during the 1982 Christmas holidays and was legally entitled to do so. Truffaut did everything he could to get the broadcast legally postponed for a year. He finally succeeded, which allowed him to extend exhibition of the film in movie houses.

44. *Le Quotidien de Paris*, February 2, 1981.

45. *Les Nouvelles littéraires*, October 1, 1981.

46. Interview with the authors, 1996.

47. *Télérama*, July 14, 1978.

48. Letter from Jean-Luc Godard to François Truffaut et al., August 19, 1980, archives of Les Films du Carrosse, file "Jean-Luc Godard."

49. Undated letter (August 1980) from François Truffaut's to Jean-Luc Godard, archives of Les Films du Carrosse, file "Jean-Luc Godard."

50. *Cahiers du cinéma* 315 and 316 (September and October 1980).

51. Truffaut used this expression in an interview in *Les nouvelles littéraires*, September 17, 1980.

52. The only responsibility that Truffaut accepted at that time, out of film lover's loyalty, was presiding over the Fédération Internationale des Ciné-Clubs. Asked by Jean Roy, who was then a delegate to the FICC, he was elected during a general assembly in Marly-le-Roi in June 1979. Truffaut was reelected to the presidency of the FICC, in October 1981, somewhat against his will, and remained president until 1983.

53. Letter from François Truffaut to Claude Autant-Lara, of April 12, 1983, archives of Les Films du Carrosse, file "CCH 83 (1)."

54. *Cahiers du cinéma* 316 (October 1980).

55. Interview with the authors, 1995.

56. François Truffaut, "Introducing Fanny Ardant," press kit of *The Woman Next Door*, (October 1981, republished in *Le Plaisir des yeux* (Paris: Editions de l'Etoile, 1987), pp. 166–167.

57. Before being discovered by Truffaut, Fanny Ardant was given her first screen appearances by Alain Jessua (*Les Chiens*) and Claude Lelouch (*Les Uns et les Autres*).

58. *Le Matin de Paris*, October 2, 1981.

59. Letter from François Truffaut to Jean Collet, January 9, 1981, archives of Les Films du Carrosse, file "CCH 81 (1)."

60. Truffaut, "Introducing Fanny Ardant."

61. Ibid.

62. Jean Aurel quoted in *Le Roman de François Truffaut*, p. 67.

63. Interview with the authors, 1996. In 1981, Gérard Lebovici became a producer and left the management of Artmédia to Jean-Louis Livi, who then became Truffaut's agent.

64. Michèle Baumgartner, a young theater actress, died suddenly several months after the filming of *The Woman Next Door*.

65. Interview with the authors, 1992.

66. Truffaut, "Introducing Fanny Ardant."

67. Europe 1, September 29, 1981.

68. *Le Film Français*, October 2, 1981.

69. Serge Daney, *Libération*, September 30, 1981.

70. Archives of Les Films du Carrosse, file "CCH 81 (2)."

71. Letter from François Truffaut to Jean Collet, August 5, 1981, archives of Les Films du Carrosse, file "CCH 81 (2)."

72. *Le Figaro Madame,* September 26, 1981.

73. *Le Figaro,* September 3, 1981.

74. Interview with the authors, 1995.

75. According to Truffaut's date book Mitterrand and Truffaut had lunch together four times between 1975 and 1980.

76. Letter from Marcel Ophuls to François Truffaut, February 26, 1980, archives of Les Films du Carrosse, file "CCH 80 (1)."

77. Note of June 17, 1981, archives of Les Films du Carrosse, file "CCH 81 (1)."

78. *Révolution,* October 2, 1981.

79. It was also at that time that Professor Blin at the Collège de France suggested Truffaut apply for a position at that prestigious institution. Truffaut refused, even though, as Professor Blin put it, "he had every chance of being elected."

80. Letter from François Truffaut to Jean Riboud, November 2, 1981, archives of Les Films du Carrosse, file "CCH 81 (2)."

81. Letter from François Truffaut to Koichi Yamada, March 27, 1982, archives of Les Films du Carrosse, file "Yamada."

82. Letter from François Truffaut to Koichi Yamada, April 3, 1982, archives of Les Films du Carrosse, file "Yamada."

83. Letter from François Truffaut to Edmond Maire, February 3, 1982, archives of Les Films du Carrosse, file "CCH 82 (1)."

84. *The Long Saturday Night* was published by Gallimard, in their Série noire, in 1962, under the title *Vivement dimanche!*

85. Press kit for *Vivement dimanche!,* 1983.

86. *Le Matin de Paris,* August 10, 1983.

87. Suzanne Schiffman quoted in *Le Roman de François Truffaut,* p. 55.

88. Interview with the authors, 1996.

89. Jean Aurel quoted in *Le Roman de François Truffaut,* p. 57.

90. Letter from François Truffaut to Gérard Lebovici, September 9, 1982, archives of Les Films du Carrosse, file "CCH 82 (2)."

91. Ibid.

92. Undated letter (October 1979) from Jean-Louis Trintignant to François Truffaut, archives of Les Films du Carrosse, file "CCH 79 (2)."

93. Letter from François Truffaut to Jean-Louis Trintignant, July 9, 1982, archives of Les Films du Carrosse, file "CCH 82 (2)."

94. Letter from François Truffaut to Serge Rousseau, October 20, 1982, archives of Les Films du Carrosse, file "CCH 82 (2)."

95. *Le Matin de Paris,* January 14, 1983.

96. Letter from François Truffaut to Georges Delerue, September 30, 1982, archives of Les Films du Carrosse, file "CCH 82 (2)."

97. Ibid.

98. François Truffaut's grandmother died in June 1979 at the age of ninety-eight. He helped her a great deal in her final years.

99. Letter from François Truffaut to Annette Insdorf, August 3, 1983, archives of Les Films du Carrosse, file "CCH 83 (2)."

100. *Le Figaro Madame,* March 14, 1981.

101. Interview with the authors, 1996.

102. Ibid.

103. *Belle Epoque* was made for television in 1995 by Gavin Millar. Jean Gruault discusses the screenplay in *Le Roman de François Truffaut,* pp. 61–62, and in *Cahiers du cinéma* 447 (September 1991). Gruault published this screenplay as a novel with Gallimard.

104. Interview with the authors, 1992.

105. Letter from François Truffaut to Guy Marchard, April 28, 1983, archives of Les Films du Carrosse, file "CCH 83 (1)."

106. Letter from François Truffaut to Koichi Yamada, August 4, 1983, archives of Les Films du Carrosse, file "Yamada."

107. *Confidentially Yours!* inaugurated a cycle programmed by Truffaut and entitled "Série noire en noir et blanc." It included twelve black-and-white films adapted from Gallimard's Série Noire such as Melville's *Doulos the Finger Man,* Dassin's *Rififi,* Sautet's *The Big Risk,* Godard's *Band of Outsiders,* and Preminger's *Where the Sidewalk Ends.*

108. Laura Truffaut's interview with the authors, 1995.

109. Claude de Givray's interview with the authors, 1996.

110. Florence Malraux's interview with the authors, 1995.

111. Archives of Les Films du Carrosse, file "Santé."

112. Ibid.

113. Ibid.

114. Ibid.

115. Ibid.

116. Ibid.

117. Letter from François Truffaut to Koichi Yamada, September 9, 1983, archives of Les Films du Carrosse, file "Yamada."

118. Letter from François Truffaut to Richard Roud, September 9, 1983, archives of Les Films du Carrosse, file "CCH 83 (2)."

119. Letter from François Truffaut to Annette Insdorf, September 9, 1983, archives of Les Films du Carrosse, file "CCH 83 (2)."

120. Letter from François Truffaut to Robert Fischer, September 9, 1983, archives of Les Films du Carrosse, file "CCH 83 (2)."

121. Letter from François Truffaut to Koichi Yamada, September 9, 1983, archives of Les Films du Carrosse, file "Yamada."

122. Letter from Isabelle Adjani to François Truffaut, October 4, 1983, archives of Les Films du Carrosse, file "CCH 83 (2)."

123. *France-Soir,* September 24, 1983. There was also an article on the same page of *France-Soir:* "Two weeks ago, the American Hospital in Neuilly was taken by surprise by the emergency arrival of François Truffaut. His physician decided he should be hospitalized because of his violent and persistent headaches. Auscultation and X rays led to the discovery of a hematoma in the brain and the danger of a fatal cerebral hemorrhage. Dr. Pertuisé decided to operate on Monday, September 12. Three hours later, the operation was a success, the hematoma reduced and the patient back in his room. On the following day, almost completely well, he declared: 'I'm no longer suffering, it's wonderful.' Since he was healing well, he was able to leave the hospital last Monday for a month of convalescence at a slow pace."

124. Letter from Dr. Bertrand Pertuisé to François Truffaut, September 20, 1983, archives of Les Films du Carrosse, file "Santé."

125. Madeleine Morgenstern's interview with the authors, 1995.

126. Josiane Couëdel quoted in *Le Roman de François Truffaut,* p. 49.

127. Claude de Givray's interview with the authors, 1996.

128. Madeleine Morgenstern's interview with the authors, 1995.

129. Letter from François Truffaut to Lionel Chouchan, December 16, 1983, archives of Les Films du Carrosse, file "CCH 83 (2)."

130. Letter from François Truffaut to Robert Cortes, director of the Festival of Prades, February 17, 1984, archives of Les Films du Carrosse, file "CCH 84 (1)."

131. Gérard Depardieu quoted in *Le Roman de François Truffaut,* p. 101.

132. Ibid.

133. Letter from Gérard Depardieu to François Truffaut, October 10, 1983, archives of Les Films du Carrosse, file "CCH 83 (2)."

134. Madeleine Morgenstern's interview with the authors, 1995.

135. Laura Truffaut's interview with the authors, 1995.

136. Philippe Labro's interview with the authors, 1995.

137. Letter from François Truffaut to Liliane Siegel, February 17, 1984, letter loaned to the authors.

138. Letter from Koichi Yamada to François Truffaut, September 18, 1983, archives of Les Films du Carrosse, file "Yamada."

139. Letter from Koichi Yamada to François Truffaut, July 1, 1984, archives of Les Films du Carrosse, file "Yamada."

140. In 1968, Truffaut had indeed coproduced Maurice Pialat's *L'Enfance nue,* with Mag Bodard, Claude Berri, and Véra Belmont.

141. Letter from Isabelle Adjani to François Truffaut, March 5, 1984, archives of Les Films du Carrosse, file "CCH 84 (1)."

142. Interview with the authors, 1992.

143. Jean-Claude Brialy quoted in *Le Roman de François Truffaut,* p. 34.

144. Jean-Louis Richard quoted in *Le Roman de François Truffaut,* p. 65.

145. Letter from François Truffaut to Annette Insdorf, July 24, 1980, archives of Les Films du Carrosse, file "CCH 80 (2)."

146. Letter from François Truffaut to Robert Lachenay, December 22, 1983, archives of Les Films du Carrosse, file "CCH 83 (2)."

147. Letter from François Truffaut to Charles Ronsac, July 6, 1984, archives of Les Films du Carrosse, file "CCH 84 (2)."

148. Letter from Floriana Lebovici to François Truffaut, July 13, 1984, archives of Les Films du Carrosse, file "CCH 84 (2)."

149. Madeleine Morgenstern's interview with the authors, 1995.

150. Claude Berri's interview with the authors, 1995.

151. Liliane Siegel's interview with the authors, 1995.

152. Undated letter (June 1984) from François Truffaut to Liliane Siegel, letter loaned to the authors.

153. Claude de Givray quoted in *Le Roman de François Truffaut,* p. 58.

154. Interview with the authors, 1995.

155. Interview conducted by Michel Pascal and Serge Toubiana in 1992 for the film *François Truffaut: Portraits volés* (*Stolen Portraits*). Truffaut very much liked this photo of Sacha Guitry, made by Willy Rizzo. For him, it showed the courage and valor of a man who worked on his film to the very last.

BIBLIOGRAPHY

FRANÇOIS TRUFFAUT'S PRINCIPAL WORKS

Selected articles (listed chronologically)

"René Clair au Ciné-Club." *Bulletin du Ciné-Club du Quartier Latin,* 4 (February 1950).

"*La Règle du jeu* (Jean Renoir)." *Bulletin du Ciné-Club du Quartier Latin,* 5 (May 1950).

"Avenue de l'Opéra: Trois ladies de Paname." *Elle,* June 12, 1950.

"*Sudden Fear* (David Miller)." *Cahiers du cinéma* 21 (March 1953).

"*Les Neiges du Kilimandjaro* (Henry King)." *Cahiers du cinéma* 23 (May 1953).

"*Le Bistro du péché* (Bruce Humberstone)." *Cahiers du cinéma* 24 (June 1953).

"Le Cinémascope: en avoir plein la vue." *Cahiers du cinéma* 25 (July 1953).

"*Niagara* (Henry Hathaway)." *Cahiers du cinéma* 28 (November 1953).

"F comme Femme." *Cahiers du cinéma* 30 (Christmas 1953).

"Une certaine tendance du cinéma français." *Cahiers du cinéma* 31 (January 1954).

"*Règlement de comptes* (Fritz Lang)." *Cahiers du cinéma* 31 (January 1954).

"*La Red* (Emilio Fernandez)." *Cahiers du cinéma* 32 (February 1954).

"*Touchez pas au grisbi* (Jacques Becker)." *Cahiers du cinéma* 34 (April 1954).

"*Si Versailles m'était conté* (Sacha Guitry)." *Cahiers du cinéma* 34 (April 1954).

"*Une femme qui s'affiche* (George Cukor)." *Cahiers du cinéma* 35 (May 1954).

"Un homme seul, Roberto Rossellini." *Radio-Cinéma-Télévision,* July 4, 1954.

"*Rivière sans retour* (Otto Preminger)." *Cahiers du cinéma* 38 (August 1954).

"Howard Hawks, intellectuel." *Arts,* August 18, 1954.

"Sir Abel Gance." *Arts,* September 1, 1954.

"*Un jour de terreur* (Tay Garnett)." *Arts,* September 29, 1954.

"Un trousseau de fausses clés (sur Alfred Hitchcock)." *Cahiers du cinéma* 39 (October 1954).

"Georges Sadoul et la vérité historique." *La Parisienne,* October 1954.

"Silence! Jean Renoir tourne *French Cancan.*" *Arts,* October 27, 1954.

"*Le Démon des eaux troubles* (Samuel Fuller)." *Arts,* December 15, 1954.

"Rossellini 55." *Arts,* January 19, 1955.

"*Ali Baba* (Jacques Becker) et la politique des auteurs." *Cahiers du cinéma* 44 (February 1955).

"Crise d'ambition du cinéma français." *Arts,* March 30, 1955.

"*Johnny Guitare* (Nicholas Ray)." *Cahiers du cinéma* 46 (April 1955).

"Ingrid Bergman: 'J'ai échappé à Hollywood et à Sacha Guitry'." *Arts,* April 6, 1955.

"*Fenêtre sur cour* (Alfred Hitchcock)." *Arts,* April 6, 1955.

"*Voyage en Italie* (Roberto Rossellini)." *Arts,* April 20, 1955.

"Cannes: palmarès anticipé selon les règles du jeu." *Arts,* April 27, 1955.

"*La Tour de Nesle* (Abel Gance)." *Cahiers du cinéma* 47 (May 1955).

"Antoine et l'orpheline." *La Parisienne,* May 1955.

"Hulot parmi nous." *Arts,* May 11, 1955.

"*Battle Cry* (Raoul Walsh)." *Arts,* June 15, 1955.

"*Futures Vedettes* (Marc Allégret)." *Arts,* June 22, 1955.

"*La Comtesse aux pieds nus* (Joseph Mankiewicz)." *Cahiers du cinéma* 49 (July 1955).

"Les sept péchés capitaux de la critique." *Arts,* July 6, 1955.

"*En quatrième vitesse* (Robert Aldrich)." *Arts,* September 21, 1955.

"*Il Bidone* (Federico Fellini)." *Cahiers du cinéma* 51 (October 1955).

"*Les Mauvaises Rencontres* (Alexandre Astruc)." *Arts,* October 19, 1955.

"Portrait d'Humphrey Bogart." *Cahiers du cinéma* 52 (November 1955).

"*Chiens perdus sans collier* (Jean Delannoy)." *Arts,* November 9, 1955.

"*L'Homme de la plaine* (Anthony Mann)." *Arts,* December 7, 1955.

"Hitchcock aime l'invraisemblance." *Arts,* December 28, 1955.

"*Lola Montès* (Max Ophuls)." *Cahiers du cinéma* 55 (January 1956).

"*La Pointe courte* (Agnès Varda)." *Arts,* January 11, 1956.

"*Nuit et Brouillard* (Alain Resnais)." *Cahiers du cinéma* 56 (February 1956).

"*Entrée des artistes:* Joëlle Robin." *Arts,* February 22, 1956.

"*Les salauds vont en enfer* (Robert Hossein)." *Arts,* February 29, 1956.

"*Sept Ans de réflexion* (Billy Wilder)." *Cahiers du cinéma* 57 (March 1956).

"Comment peut-on être jeune turc?" *Cahiers du cinéma* 57 (March 1956).

"*Le Bandit* (Edgar Ulmer)." *Arts,* March 14, 1956.

"*La Fureur de vivre* (Nicholas Ray)." *Arts,* April 4, 1956.

"James Dean est mort." *Arts,* April 11, 1956.

"*Le Temps des assassins* (Julien Duvivier)." *Arts,* April 18, 1956.

"Cannes: un palmarès ridicule." *Arts,* May 16, 1956.

"*La Nuit du chasseur* (Charles Laughton)." *Arts,* May 23, 1956.

"*Monsieur Arkadin* (Orson Welles)." *Arts,* June 13, 1956.

"Les assassins du dimanche." *Arts,* June 27, 1956.

"Il y a dix ans, *Citizen Kane.*" *Cahiers du cinéma* 61 (July 1956).

"*La Prisonnière du désert* (John Ford)." *Arts,* August 15, 1956.

"Présence de Marilyn Monroe." *Arts,* August 19, 1956.

"Venise, festival courageux, exemple d'austérité." *Arts,* September 12, 1956.

"*La Traversée de Paris* (Claude Autant-Lara)." *Arts,* October 31, 1956.

"*Le Pays d'où je viens* (Marcel Carné), une consternante pochade." *Arts,* October 31, 1956.

"*Un condamné à mort s'est échappé* (Robert Bresson)." *Arts,* November 14, 1956.

"Boxeur, officier, acteur, peintre, écrivain, cinéaste, John Huston ne sera-t-il toujours qu'un amateur?" *Arts,* November 14, 1956.

"Renaissance du court métrage français." *Arts,* November 21, 1956.

"*Et Dieu créa la femme* (Roger Vadim)." *Arts,* December 5, 1956.

"Les critiques de cinéma sont misogynes: B.B. est victime d'une cabale." *Arts,* December 12, 1956.

"En 1956, cinq grands films, sept bons films. Un événement: Il est démontré que le cinéma peut se passer des scénaristes." *Arts,* December 19, 1956.

"*Bob le Flambeur* (Jean-Pierre Melville)." *Arts,* December 19, 1956.

"Qui est Elia Kazan?" *Arts,* January 2, 1957.

"*Derrière le miroir* (Nicholas Ray)." *Arts,* February 20, 1957.

"*Ecrit sur du vent* (Douglas Sirk)." *Arts,* February 20, 1957.

"*Courte Tête* (Norbert Carbonnaux)." *Arts,* March 6, 1957.

"*Assassins et Voleurs* (Sacha Guitry)." *Cahiers du cinéma* 70 (April 1957).

"Avec Max Ophuls, nous perdons un de nos meilleurs cinéastes." *Arts,* April 3, 1957.

"*Un vrai cinglé de cinéma* (Frank Tashlin)." *Arts,* April 24, 1957.

"Vous êtes tous témoins dans ce procès. Le cinéma français crève sous les fausses légendes." *Arts,* May 15, 1957.

"Cannes: Un échec dominé par les compromis, les combines et les faux pas." *Arts,* May 22, 1957.

"Asphyxie de la critique: Nous sommes tous des condamnés." *Arts,* May 29, 1957.

"Claude Autant-Lara, faux martyr, n'est qu'un cinéaste bourgeois." *Arts,* June 19, 1957.

"*Méfiez-vous fillettes* (Yves Allégret): Gangsters, filles, cinéastes, censeurs dans le même panier." *Arts,* July 10, 1957.

"Sacha Guitry fut un grand cinéaste réaliste." *Arts,* July 31, 1957.

"Avec *Oeil pour oeil,* Cayatte et Curd Jurgens font reculer les bornes du grotesque à l'écran." *Arts,* September 18, 1957.

"*Un roi à New York* (Charlie Chaplin) est un film génial." *Arts,* October 30, 1957.

"Clouzot au travail, ou le règne de la terreur." *Cahiers du cinéma* 77 (December 1957).

"Hitchcock est le plus grand inventeur de formes." *Arts,* December 4, 1957.

"*Positif,* copie 0." *Cahiers du cinéma* 79 (January 1958).

"Seule la crise sauvera le cinéma français." *Arts,* January 8, 1958.

"Voici les trente nouveaux noms du cinéma français." *Arts,* January 8, 1958.

"Les plus grands cinéastes du monde ont plus de 50 ans." *Arts,* January 15, 1958.

"*Bonjour tristesse* (Otto Preminger)." *Arts,* March 12, 1958.

"Redécouvrons Max Ophuls." *Arts,* March 26, 1958.

"*Charlotte et Véronique* (Jean-Luc Godard)." *Cahiers du cinéma* 83 (May 1958).

"Si jeunes et des Japonais (*Passion juvénile* de Kô Nakahira)." *Cahiers du cinéma* 83 (May 1958).

"*Le Beau Serge* (Claude Chabrol)." *Arts,* May 21, 1958.

"Si des modifications radicales n'interviennent pas, le prochain Festival est condamné." *Arts,* May 21, 1958.

"*Barrage contre le Pacifique* (René Clément)." *Cahiers du cinéma* 84 (June 1958).

"*La Soif du mal* (Orson Welles)." *Arts,* June 4, 1958.

"Le nouveau grand du cinéma mondial, Ingmar Bergman, a dédié son oeuvre aux femmes." *Arts,* June 11, 1958.

"*Jet Pilot* (Josef von Sternberg)." *Arts,* July 9, 1958.

"*En cas de malheur* (Claude Autant-Lara)." *Arts,* September 10, 1958.

"Louis Malle a filmé la première nuit d'amour du cinéma." *Arts,* September 10, 1958.

"Il faisait bon vivre." *Cahiers du cinéma* 91 (January 1959).

"Je n'ai pas écrit ma biographie en 400 coups." *Arts,* June 3, 1959.

"Aznavour donne le *la.*" *Cinémonde,* May 5, 1960.

"L'affaire Vadim." *France-Observateur,* December 22, 1960.

"L'agonie de la Nouvelle Vague n'est pas pour demain (*Paris nous appartient,* de Jacques Rivette)." *Arts,* December 20, 1961.

"*Adieu Philippine* (Jacques Rozier)." *Lui,* November 1963.

"*Muriel* (Alain Resnais)." *Lui,* January 1964.

"*Le Vieil Homme et l'enfant* (Claude Berri)." *Le Nouvel Observateur,* March 8, 1967.

"La savate et la finance, ou deux ou trois choses que je sais de lui (sur Jean-Luc Godard)." *Les Lettres françaises,* March 16, 1967.

"*La Marseillaise* (Jean Renoir)." *L'Express,* October 30, 1967.

"Jean Renoir le patron." *Le Monde,* January 18, 1968.
"Lubitsch était un prince." *Cahiers du cinéma* 198 (February 1968).
"L'antimémoire courte." *Combat,* February 12, 1968.
"À propos d'Audiberti." *Théâtre du Cothurne* (Lyon), December 1973.
"Les 80 ans de Jean Renoir." *Le Film français,* July 3, 1974.

François Truffaut's principal interviews for *Cahiers du cinéma* were published as *La Politique des auteurs* (Paris: Champ Libre, 1971; reprinted by Editions de l'Etoile in 1983 and by Ramsay in 1988).

BOOKS

Le Cinéma selon Hitchcock (avec la collaboration de Helen Scott). Paris: Robert Laffont, 1966. Republished under the title *Hitchcock-Truffaut.* Paris: Ramsay, 1984.
Hitchcock (with the collaboration of Helen G. Scott). New York: Simon and Schuster, 1967; revised, expanded edition, 1984.
Les Aventures d'Antoine Doinel. Paris: Mercure de France, 1970.
Les Films de ma vie. Paris: Flammarion, 1975.
The Films in My Life. Trans. Leonard Mayhew. New York: Simon and Schuster, 1978.
Le Plaisir des yeux. Paris: Editions de l'Etoile, 1987.
François Truffaut: Correspondance. Paris: Hatier, 1988.
Correspondence 1945–1984. Trans. Gilbert Adair. New York: The Noonday Press, Farrar, Straus and Giroux, 1989.

The scripts of *Les Mistons, Histoire d'eau, Tirez sur le pianiste, Jules et Jim, La Peau douce, L'Enfant sauvage, Les Deux Anglaises et le Continent, L'Histoire d'Adèle H., La Chambre verte, L'Amour en fuite, Le Dernier Métro, La Femme d'à côté,* and *Vivement dimanche!* were published by *L'Avant-Scène cinéma.*

PREFACES

Le Trou (script, Jacques Becker film). *L'Avant-Scène cinéma* 13 (1962).
Vivre sa vie (script, Jean-Luc Godard film).
L'Avant-Scène cinéma 19 (1962).
Casque d'or (script, Jacques Becker film). *L'Avant-Scène cinéma* 43 (1964).
Gheur, Bernard. *Le Testament d'un cancre.* Paris: Albin Michel, 1971.
Bazin, André. *Jean Renoir.* Paris: Champ Libre, 1971.
Bazin, André. *What Is Cinema?* Berkeley: University of California Press, 1971.
Bazin, André, and Eric Rohmer. *Charlie Chaplin.* Paris: Cerf, 1973.
Guarner, José-Luis. *Roberto Rossellini.* Madrid: Editorial Fundamentos, 1973.
La Grande Illusion (script and album of the Jean Renoir film). Paris: Balland, 1974.
Bazin, André. *Le Cinéma de la cruauté.* Paris: Flammarion, 1975.
Bazin, André. *Le Cinéma de l'Occupation et de la Résistance.* Paris: UGE, 1975.
Kostariski, Richard. *Hollywood Directors* (1914–1940). New York: Oxford University Press, 1976.
Aumont, Jean-Pierre. *Le Soleil et les Ombres.* Paris: J'ai lu, 1977.
Guitry, Sacha. *Le Cinéma et moi.* Paris: Ramsay, 1977.
Andrew, Dudley. *André Bazin.* New York: Oxford University Press, 1977 (French translation, Paris: Editions de l'Etoile, 1983).
Bazin, André. *Orson Welles.* New York: Harper & Row, 1978.
La Toile d'araignée (Nouvelles de William Irish) Paris: Pierre Belfond, 1980.
Almendros, Nestor. *Un homme à la caméra.* Paris: Hatier, 1980. (U.S. edition, *A Man with a Camera.* Trans. Rachel Phillips Belash. New York: Farrar, Straus and Giroux, 1984).
Oeuvres de cinéma (édition intégrale des scénarios et des écrits de Jean Vigo) Paris: Lherminier/Cinémathèque française, 1985.
Roché, Henri-Pierre. *Carnets.* Marseille: Editions André Dimanche, 1990.

INTERVIEWS WITH FRANÇOIS TRUFFAUT (LISTED CHRONOLOGICALLY)

Le Monde, April 21, 1959.
L'Express, April 23, 1959.
Arts, April 29, 1959.
Les Lettres françaises, May 28, 1959.
Cinéma 59, June 1959.
Télé-Ciné, June 1959.
Signes du temps, December 1959.
France-Observateur, December 3, 1959.
Le Monde, November 24, 1960.
Cinéma 61, January 1961.
France-Film, February 1961.
Télé-Ciné, March 1961.
France-Observateur, October 19, 1961.
Cinémonde, October 31, 1961.
Cinéma 62, January 1962.
Le Monde, January 24, 1962.
Les Lettres françaises, January 25, 1962.
Clarté, March 1962.
Script, April 1962.
New York Film Bulletin, Summer 1962.
Les Nouvelles littéraires, November 15, 1962.
Cahiers du cinéma 138 (December 1962).
L'Express, January 24, 1963.
Télérama, February 14, 1963.
Télérama, February 2, 1964.
Réalités, May 1964.
Cinéma 64, May 1964.
L'Express, May 14, 1964.
Les Nouvelles littéraires, May 21, 1964.
Le Monde, May 22, 1964.
Cinéma 64, June 1964.
Lui, September 1964.
Art et Essai, March 1966.
Télé-Ciné, May 1966.
Télérama, August 14, 1966.
Arts-Loisirs, September 14, 1966.
Les Lettres françaises, September 15, 1966.
Le Monde, September 18, 1966.
Télé-Cinéma, October 1966.
Paris-Match, October 1, 1966.
Télérama, October 2, 1966.
Lectures pour tous, December 1966.
Midi-Minuit fantastique, December 1966.
Cinéma 67, January 1967.
Les Lettres françaises, April 14, 1967.
Cahiers du cinéma 190 (May 1967).
Cinéma 67, December 1967.
Le Nouvel Adam, February 1968.
Les Lettres françaises, April 10, 1968.
Le Monde, April 18, 1968.

Télérama, April 28, 1968.
May 68: ce n'est qu'un début 2 (May 1968).
Jeune Cinéma, May 1968.
L'Express, May 20, 1968.
Télé-Cinéma, October 1968.
Cahiers du cinéma 200 (April 1969).
Le Monde, May 21, 1969.
Télérama, June 14, 1969.
New York Times, June 15, 1969.
Journal du show-business, June 27, 1969.
Télé-Ciné, March 1970.
Le Nouvel Observateur, March 2, 1970.
Cinémonde, September 1970.
Les Lettres françaises, September 9, 1970.
Les Nouvelles littéraires, September 10, 1970.
The National Observer, October 12, 1970.
Cinéma 70, November 1970.
Image et Son, December 1970.
Télérama, August 14, 1971.
Le Monde, November 25, 1971.
Les Nouvelles littéraires, December 3, 1971.
Ecran 72, January 1972.
Le Technicien du film, March 15, 1972.
Le Soir (Marseille), March 29, 1972.
Télérama, April 15, 1972.
Vingt Ans, January 3, 1973.
Le Monde, May 18, 1973.
Ecran 73, July 1973.
Cinématographe, Summer 1973.
Time Out, November 30, 1973.
Cinéma/Québec, December 1973.
Real Paper, January 2, 1974.
Village Voice, January 24, 1974.
Jeune Cinéma, March 1974.
Playboy (France), January 1975.
Télérama, April 27, 1975.
Cinématographe, October 1975.
Ecran 76, March 15, 1976.
Les Nouvelles littéraires, March 18, 1976.
Jeune Cinéma, May–June 1976.
Le Quotidien de Paris, April 26, 1977.
Lumière du cinéma, May 1977.
Cinématographe, May 1977.
L'Express, March 13, 1978.
Le Matin de Paris, March 29, 1978.
L'Humanité-dimanche, April 7, 1978.
Télérama, April 8, 1978.
Christian Science Monitor, November 27, 1978.

Sight and Sound 4 (Winter, 1979).
Le Matin de Paris, January 24, 1979.
Washington Post, February 22, 1979.
Les Nouvelles littéraires, February 22, 1979.
The Chronicle Review, March 19, 1979.
Le Quotidien de Paris, June 11, 1980.
Cahiers du cinéma 315 and 316 (September and October 1980).
Les Nouvelles littéraires, September 18, 1980.
Film-Bruxelles, October 1980.
New York Times, October 14, 1980.
Wide Angle 4, 4 (1981).
Le Journal de Montréal, February 17, 1981.

Le Devoir (Montréal), February 21, 1981.
La Presse (Montréal), February 21, 1981.
Télérama, September 30, 1981.
Première, October 1981.
Les Nouvelles littéraires, October 1, 1981.
Révolution, October 2, 1981.
L'Hebdo-Belge, November 1981.
Lire, April 1982.
Première, February 1983.
Pilote, August 1983.
Le Nouvel Observateur, August 5, 1983.
Télé 7 jours, August 6, 1983.
Le Matin de Paris, August 8, 1983.
Révolution, August 12, 1983.
Les Lettres françaises, October 24, 1983.
Cinématographe, December 1984.

BOOKS AND ARTICLES ON TRUFFAUT

Auzel, Dominique. *Truffaut: Les Mille et Une Nuits américaines.* Paris: Henri Veyrier, 1990. (Album of film posters.)
de Baecque, Antoine. "François Truffaut, spectateur cinéphile." *Vertigo* 10 (1991).
———. "Contre la 'Qualité française.' François Truffaut écrit 'Une certaine tendance du cinéma français'." *Cinémathèque* 4 (Autumn 1993).
Bastide, Bernard. *François Truffaut, Les Mistons,* Nîmes; Ciné-Sud, 1987.
Bonnafons, Elisabeth. *François Truffaut.* Lausanne: L'Âge d'homme, 1981.
Cahiers du cinéma. Le Roman de François Truffaut. Special issue, December 1984.
Cahoreau, Gilles. *François Truffaut.* Paris: Albin Michel, 1986.
Cinématographe. 105 (December 1984). "François Truffaut."
Collet, Jean. "L'oeuvre de François Truffaut, une tragédie de la connaissance." *Etudes,* December 1966.
———. *Le Cinéma de François Truffaut.* Paris: Lherminier, 1977.
———. *François Truffaut.* Paris: Lherminier, 1985.
Comolli, Jean-Louis. "Au coeur des paradoxes." *Cahiers du cinéma.* 190 (May 1967).
Dalmais, Hervé. *Truffaut.* Paris: Rivages/Cinéma, 1987.
Aline Desjardins s'entretient avec François Truffaut. Ottawa: Editions Léméac/Radio Canada, 1973; revised edition, Paris: Poche Cinéma, Ramsay, 1988.
Dixon, Wheeler Winston. *The Early Film Criticism of François Truffaut.* Bloomington: Indiana University Press, 1993.
Fanne, Dominique. *L'Univers de François Truffaut.* Paris: Le Cerf, 1972.
Gillain, Anne. *Le Cinéma selon François Truffaut.* Paris: Flammarion, 1988.
———. *François Truffaut: Le Secret perdu.* Paris: Hatier, 1991.
Insdorf, Annette. *François Truffaut.* Boston: Twayne Publishers, 1978, revised edition, New York: Simon and Schuster, 1989. (French translation entitled *François Truffaut: Le Cinéma est-il magique?* Paris: Ramsay, 1989.)
Le Berre, Carole. *François Truffaut.* Paris: Éditions de l'Etoile, 1993.
Moullet, Luc. "La balance et le Lien." *Cahiers du cinéma* 410 (July–August 1990).
Petrie, Graham. *The Cinema of François Truffaut.* New York: International Film Guide Series, A. S. Barnes, 1970.
Rabourdin, Dominique. *Truffaut par Truffaut,* Paris: éditions du Chêne, 1985. U.S. edition: trans. Robert Erich Wolf. New York: Harry N. Abrams, 1987.
Simondi, Mario, ed. *François Truffaut.* Florence: La Casa Usher, 1982.
Toubiana, Serge. "François Truffaut, domaine public." *Trafic* 5 (1992).
Waltz, Eugene P. *François Truffaut: A Guide to References and Resources.* Boston: G. K. Hall, 1982.

ACKNOWLEDGMENTS

This book could never have been written without the help of François Truffaut's many friends, relatives, and collaborators, who shared their recollections with us, offered their opinions, and gave us access to their personal archives. May we express our deepest thanks to them all, and particularly to: Fanny Ardant, the late Jean Aurel, Nathalie Baye, Janine Bazin, Marcel Berbert, Claude Berri, Jacqueline Bisset, Charles Bitsch, René Bonnell, Claudine Bouché, Jean-Claude Brialy, Leslie Caron, Jacqueline Caspar, Claude Chabrol, Don Congdon, Josiane Couëdel, Claude Davy, Gérard Depardieu, Jean Douchet, Liliane Dreyfus, Marie Dubois, Michel Fermaud, the late Odette Ferry, Claude Gauteur, Claude de Givray, Jean-Luc Godard, Jean Gruault, Pierre Hebey, Annette Insdorf, Claude Jade, Georges Kiejman, André S. Labarthe, Bertrand de Labbey, Philippe Labro, Robert Lachenay, Bernadette Lafont, Jean-Louis Livi, Monique Lucas (de Monferrand), Lydie Mahias, Florence Malraux, Claude Miller, François-Xavier Mollin, Jeanne Moreau, Luc Moullet, Jean Narboni, Marcel Ophuls, Marie-France Pisier, Marie de Poncheville, Jérôme Prieur, Jean-Louis Richard, Jean-José Richer, Eric Rohmer, Serge Rousseau, François-Marie Samuelson, Suzanne Schiffman, Jacques Siclier, Liliane Siegel, Alexandra Stewart, Bertrand Tavernier, Nadine Trintignant, Alain Vannier, Claude Véga. The authors are, of course, solely responsible for the interpretation given to their statements.

Thanks are also due to Colline Faure-Poirée, Patricia Guédot, Pierre Guislain, Hélène Quinquin, all of whom followed this project from the beginning and generously gave us the benefit of their attentive reading and remarks, as did Isabelle Gallimard, Emmanuèle Bernheim, Carole Le Berre, Sylvie de Baecque, Marc Grinsztajn, Manuel Carcassonne, and Laurence Giavarini.

Thank you to Michel Pascal, with whom the making of the film *François Truffaut: Portraits volés* (*Stolen Portraits*), in 1992, shed much light on François Truffaut's life and work.

Finally, Madeleine Morgenstern, Laura Truffaut, and Eva Truffaut gave us unrestricted access to the archives of Les Films du Carrosse. They also helped us on count-less occasions, with their opinions, advice, recollections, and friendship. We were very touched by their trust and are deeply grateful to them; without them, this book would not exist. Monique Holvëck at Les Films du Carrosse gave us invaluable help and always showed great kindness and patience.

INDEX

PHOTOGRAPH CREDITS

1. Coll. F. Truffaut family
2. "
3. "
4. "
5. "
6. "
7. "
8. "
9. "
10. Coll. Robert Lachenay
11. Ph. © André Dino/Films du Carrosse
12. Archives F. Truffaut
13. Coll. F. Truffaut family
14. Films du Carrosse D.R.
15. "
16. "
17. "
18. Coll. *Cahiers du Cinéma*
19. Coll. *Cahiers du Cinéma*
20. Ph. © Raymond Cachetier
21. Ph. © André Greffen/*Cahiers du Cinéma*
22. Coll. *Cahiers du Cinéma* D.R.
23. Coll. F. Truffaut family. D.R.
24. "
25. "
26. "
27. Ph. © Botti/Stills
28. Films du Carrosse D.R.
29. Coll. *Cahiers du Cinéma* D.R.
30. Ph. © André Dino/Films du Carrosse
31. Ph. © C. Werle/Films du Carrosse
32. Archives F. Truffaut
33. Films du Carrosse D.R.
34. Ph. © Robert Lachenay/Films du Carrosse
35. Coll. F. Truffaut family D.R.
36. "
37. Ph. © Philip Halsman/Magnum
38. "
39. "

INSERT 2

1. Ph. © Raymond Cauchetier/Films du Carrosse
2. Films du Carrosse/D.R.
3. Ph. © Raymond Cauchetier/Films du Carrosse
4. Ph. © Marilu Parolini/Films du Carrosse
5. Films du Carrosse D.R.
6. Ph. © Tourte/Stills
7. Ph. © Marilu Parolini/Films du Carrosse
8. Ph. © Léonard de Raemy/Coll. *Cahiers du Cinéma*
9. "
10. Ph. © Pierre Zucca/Films du Carrosse
11. Ph. © Léonard de Raemy/Coll. *Cahiers du Cinéma*
12. Ph. © Raymond Depardon/Magnum
13. Ph. © Raymond Cauchetier/Films du Carrosse
14. Ph. © Pierre Zucca/Films du Carrosse
15. Ph. © Marilu Parolini/Films du Carrosse
16. Coll. F. Truffaut family/D.R.
17. Ph. © Sheedy and Long USA
18. Coll. F. Truffaut family
19. "
20. Ph. © Hélène Jeanbrau/Films du Carrosse
21. Ph. © Bernard Prim/Films du Carrosse
22. Archives F. Truffaut
23. Ph. © Jean-Pierre Fizet/Coll. *Cahiers du Cinéma*
24. Ph. © William Karel/Sygma
25. "
26. "
27. Ph. © Dominique Le Rigoleur
28. "
29. "

A NOTE ABOUT THE AUTHORS

Antoine de Baecque is a historian whose special field of study is the French Revolution. He is editor-in-chief of Cahiers du Cinéma, *and has written a history of that journal, published in France in 1991. He is also the author of a forthcoming book on the New Wave.*

Serge Toubiana has headed the Cahiers du Cinéma *since 1981. In 1993, he co-directed a documentary titled* François Truffaut: Stolen Portraits.